A
CHECKLIST OF
AMERICAN IMPRINTS
for
1839

Items 53806-59415

compiled by

CAROL RINDERKNECHT

The Scarecrow Press, Inc.
Metuchen, N.J., & London
1988

Library of Congress Catalog No. 64-11784

ISBN 0-8108-2124-9

A

A Beckett, Gilbert Abbott, 1811-1856. The turned head. A farce, in one act.... New York: Samuel French and Son [1839] 16 p. OCl. 53806

Abbot Female Seminary, Andover, Massachusetts. Course of study in the teacher's department of the Abbot Female Seminary, Andover, Mass. With a catalogue for the spring and summer terms, 1839. Andover: printed by Gould, Newman and Saxton, 1839. 12 p. MAnA. 53807

Abbott, Benjamin, 1732-1796. Experience and gospel labors of the Rev. Benjamin Abbott; to which is annexed a narrative of his life and death, by John Ffirth...New York: T. Mason and G. Lane, 1839. 284 p. TxGR; ViPet. 53808

[Abbott, Jacob] 1803-1879. Caleb in the country. A story for children. By the author of the Rollo books. Boston: Crocker and Brewster, 1839. 180 p. DLC; MeB; RPB. 53809

----. ----. New York: T. Y. Crowell and Company [1839?] 180 [2] p. MB; MWinchn. 53810

----. Caleb in town. A story for children. By the author of the Rollo books. Boston: Crocker and Brewster, 1839. 180 p. MeB; NUt; OClWHi; RPB; ScCMu. 53811

----. ----. New York: Thomas Y. Crowell and Company, 1839. 180 p. MeBa; MH; OCl; WHi. 53812

----. Hoaryhead; or truth through fiction.... 2nd edition. Boston: Crocker and Brewster, 1839. 304 p. MBAt; MeB; NjPT; NNC; RPB. 53813

----. Jonas's stories; related to Rollo and Lucy. By Jacob Abbott, author of the Rollo books. Boston: Ticknor, Reed and Fields, 1839. 180 p. DLC; ICU; MH; NUt; PWc. 53814

----. McDonner; or truth through fiction.... Boston: Crocker and Brewster, 1839. 283 p. CtHT: MBAt; MCon; MeB; ScUn. 53815

----. The Mount Vernon reader; a course of reading lessons, selected with reference to their moral influence on the hearts and lives of the young. Designed for junior classes. By the Messrs. Abbott. Boston: Otis, Broaders and Company, 1839. 162 p. DLC; MH; NN. 53816

----. ----. New York: Collins, 1839. 252 p. IaU. 53817

----. Rollo at play; or safe amusements. By the author of "Rollo learning to talk".... 5th edition. Boston: Weeks, Jordan and Company, 1839. 191 p. MH; MHi; NNC; ScCLiTO. 53818

----. Rollo at school; by the author of "Rollo learning to talk," and "learning to read." New York: Samuel Colman, 1839. 197 p. MH; MHi; MiK; RKi; TxH. 53819

----. Rollo at work; or the way for a boy to learn to be industrious. By the author of "Rollo learing to talk." 2nd edition. Boston: Weeks, Jordan and Company, 1839. 191 p. TxU. 53820

----. ----. 5th edition. Boston: Weeks, Jordan and Company, 1839. MH; MHi; OCl. 53821

----. Rollo learning to read.... Boston: 1839. MH. 53822

----. Rollo learning to talk; by the author of "Rollo learning to read," "Rollo at work," etc. New edition. Boston: Weeks, Jordan and Company, 1839. DLC; MH; MHi; NBuG; ScCliTO. 53823

----. Rollo's experiments. By the author of "Rollo learning to talk" ... Boston: Weeks, Jordan and Company, 1839. 180 p. DLC; MB; MH; MHi; NNU; ScCliTO. 53824

----. Rollo's museum. By the author of "Rollo learning to talk," etc. Boston: Weeks, Jordan and Company, 1839., 187 p. DLC; MH; MHi; MTem; ViU. 53825

----. Rollo's vacation. By the author of "Rollo at school," etc., etc. Boston: William Crosby and Company, 1839. CtHWatk; DLC; MH. 53826

----. The teacher; or moral influences employed in the instruction and government of the young. New stereotype edition; with an additional chapter on "the first day in school."... Boston: Whipple and Damrell, 1839. 314 p. MB; MeB; NjP; NNUT. 53827

Abbott, John Stevens Cabot, 1805-1877. The mother at home; or the principles of maternal duty. Familiarly illustrated. 10th edition. Stereotyped. Boston: Crocker and Brewster, New York: Leavitt, Lord and Company, 1839. 177 p. ICBB. 53828

----. THe school-boy; or a guide for youth to truth and duty.... Boston: Crocker and Brewster, 1839. 180 p. CSmH; DLC; MeB; MH; OClW. 53829

Abel, Henry I. Traveller's and emigrant's guide to Wisconsin and Iowa. ...Accompanied with a new and improved map of those territories, with the addition of parts of Illinois, Indiana and Michigan. Philadephia: printed for the author, 1839. IaDaP; IaU; MWA. 53830

Abercrombie, John, 1780-1844. THe harmony of Christian faith and Christian character, and the culture and discipline of the mind. New York: Harper and Brothers, 1839. 145 p. ArCH; GDecCT; MoSpD; NBuDD; PPPrHi. 53831

----. ...Inquiries concerning the intellectual powers, and the investigation of truth.... From the 2nd Edinburgh edition. New York: Harper and Brothers, 1839. 376 p. CoD; IaGG; MDeeP; PPWa; WU. 53832

----. The philosophy of the moral feelings, an introductory chapter with additions and explanations, to adapt the work to the use of schools and academies...by Jacob Abbott. Boston: Otis and Company, 1839. 250 p. KWiU; MBC; NjP; PPM; ViU. 53833

----. ----. From the 2nd Edinburgh edition. New York: Harper and Brothers, 1839. 236 p. ICU; MH; NjP; PPM; ScDuE. 53834

Abert, John James, 1788-1863. Statement in reply to an order of the House...9th February, 1839. ...Relative to surveys made in...1838, for the route of the Maryland Canal [Annapolis: 1839] 39 p. MdBP; NH; NjPT. 53835

----. ----. [Baltimore? 1839?] 39 p. MH-BA. 53836

An abridgement of the Christian doctrine. With proofs of Scripture on points controverted, by way of questions and answers. Composed in 1649, by H. T., of the English College at Doway: now revised by the Rt. Rev. James Doyle, D.D. and prescribed by him to be used in the United Dioceses of Kildare and Leighlin. Philadelphia: Eugene Cummiskey [1839] 107 p. MdW. 53837

An account of some of the most celebrated battles, sieges and sea-fights, recorded in history; from the time of Alexander the Great to the present day. New York: Robinson, Pratt and Company, Collins, Keese and Company, Watertown: Knowlton and Rice, 1839. 252 p. MiD-B; NCaS; NRMA. 53838

An account of the special convention at Auburn, May 8 and 9, 1839. Connected with the consecration of William H. DeLancey, D.D., Utica: Hobart Press, 1839. 23 p. MBD; MdBD; NBuDD. 53839

Adam, Alexander, 1741-1809. Adam's Latin grammar, with some improvements, and...a metrical key to the Odes of Horace; a list of Latin authors.... Boston: Hilliard, 1839. 299 p. CtHWat-K; InLW; MH; MNBedf; NPV; PAnL. 53840

----. Rudiments of Latin and English grammar. With numerous expansion and addition. ...By James D. Johnson, A.M. New York: W. E. Dean, 1839. MoSU; OClJC. 53841

Adams, Daniel, 1773-1864. ...Arithmetic in which the principles of operating by numbers are analytically explained, and synthetically applied.... Keene, N.H.: J. and J. W. Premtiss, 1839. 180 p. OClWHi; OHi. 53842

----. Modern geography in three parts. Pt. 1. a grammar of geography concisely arranged; to be committed to memory; with practical questions on the maps.... Boston: Davis, 1839. 315 p. PPL; PPWi. 53843

----. The monitorial reader, designed for the use of academies and schools; and as a monitor to youth holding up to their view models whereby to form their own characters. Concord, N.H.: Boyd and White, 1839. 288 p. InU; MH; N; Nh-Hi; NjP. 53844

----. ----. Keene, N.H.: J. and J. W. Prentiss, 1839. 288 p. IaU. 53845

----. Adams's new arithmetic in which the principles of operating by numbers are analytically explained. Keene, N.H.: J. W. Prentiss, 1839. 255 p. MB; MFiHi; MH; NL; TxBrdD. 53846

----. ----. 262 p. Keene, N.H.: J. and J. W. Prentiss, 1839. MB; MH; MiU-C; Nh; NICLA. 53847

Adams, John Greenleaf. History of the apostles: a catechism for the use of sabbath schools. Boston: 1839. 52 p. MB; PHi. 53848

Adams, John Jay. The charter oak, and other poems. New York: S. Colman, 1839. 60 p. CtSoP; IaU; MH; PPM; RPB. 53849

Adams, John Quincy, 1767-1848. Discourse on the 50th anniversary. See his Jubilee of the Constitution.

----. The jubilee of the Constitution. A discourse delivered at the request of the New York Historical Society, in the city of New York, on Tuesday, the 30th of April, 1839.... New York: S. Colman, 1839. 136 p. CU; ICN; PHi; TxU; WaPS. 53850

----. Letter. To the inhabitants of the 12th congressional district of Massachusetts, and particularly to those of them who charged me with petitions to be presented to the house, at the 3rd session of the 25th congress. [Dated] Qunicy, June 4, 1839. [Quincy?: 1839] MH. 53851

----. Letter II. To the citizens of the United States, whose petitions, memorials and remonstrances, have been entrusted to me, to be presented to the house, at the 3rd session of the 25th congress. Quincy, May 21, 1839. B[oston: 1839] MH. 53852

----. The subile of the Constitution. See his jubilee of the Constitution.

----. Two lectures, on the bequest of James Smithson to the United States, for the increase and diffusion of knowledge among men. Lecture 1. Divered at Boston, before the Mechanics Apprentices Library Association, 14th Nov., 1839 [Boston: 1839] MH. 53853

Adams, Nehemiah, 1806-1878. My baptism. From the baptized child, by Nehemiah Adams, pastor of Essex Church, Boston. Revised by the committee of publication. Boston: Sabbath School Society, 1839. 32 p. DLC; MB; MBAt; MWA; NjPT. 53854

----. A sermon preached to the Essex street congregation, Boston, September 1, 1839, on occasion of the death of Lucy Pierce Tappan, and her mother Mrs. Sarah Tappan, wife of John Tappan, Boston: Perkins and Marvin, 1839. 23 p. CSansS; MBAt; MH; OCHP; RPB. 53855

Addison, Joseph, 1672-1719. Selections from the spectator: embracing the most interesting papers by Addison, Steele and others. In two volumes. New York: Harper and Brothers, 1839. 2 v. MdBC; PPGi; RKi; ViNo; WaU. 53856

Address of the carrier of the Churchman. 1839 [New York: 1839] Broadside. MH. 53857

Address of the Whig members of the legislature.... New York: Sackets Harbor, 1839. 143 p. NN. 53858

Address of the Whig members of the legislature, to the people of Virginia. Richmond, Va.: Bailie and Gallaher, printers, 1839. 16 p. NN; PPULC; Vi. 53859

An address on the centenary of Methodism. By a member of the Philadelphia conference.... Baltimore: Armstrong and Berry, 1839. 23 p. DLC. 53860

Addres on the propriety of legislation for the improvement of agriculture. Frankfort: 1839. PPL. 53861

An address to a portion of our southern brethren in the U.S. on the subject of slavery.... Philadelphia: J. Richards, 1839. 10 p. OClWHi. 53862

An address to plain people on the duty of family prayer [New York: published by the Protestant Episcopal Tract Society, 1839] 8 p. InID. 53863

Address to the abolitionists of Massachusetts. Boston: 1839. MWA. 53864

Address to the adverse occupants of lands in the state of Georgia, which are claimed by various companies and individuals of whom William

Primrose is the authorized agent [Savannah: 1839] 7 p. ScHi. 53865

An address, to the people of Bourbon, being an expose of the way in which grog-shop keepers evade the license laws, and of the abuses of the license system. Paris, Ky.: 1839. 8 p. MnU. 53866

An address to the planters and farmers of South Carolina, on the subject of agriculture. Charleston: printed by Burges and James, 1839. 30 p. DLC; MB. 53867

Adler, C. A. The last polka. Composed by C. A. Adler. Boston: 1839. 2 p. RHi. 53868

Advice to a young gentleman, on entering society. By the author of "the laws of etiquette." Philadelphia: Lea and Blanchard, 1839. 295 p. CtY; DLC; NCasti; PFal; VtMidSM. 53869

Aeschines. The orations of Aeschines and Demosthenes on the crown. With modern Green prolegomena, and English notes, by Alexander Negris. Stereotpye edition. Boston: Hilliard, Gray and Company, 1839. 304 p. CtMW; DLC; NcD; NjR; TJaU. 53870

Aeschylus. Translated by the Rev. R. Potter, M.A., President of Norwich. New York: Harper and Brothers, 1839 [75]-342 p. InLW; KWiU; NbU; OWoC; PMy. 53871

Aesopus. Aesop's fables, with upwards of one hundred and fifty emblematic devices. New York: N. and J. White, 1839. 228 p. ViU. 53872

----. ----. Philadelphia: Thomas, Cowperthwait and Company, 1839. 228 p. MdBG; NcAS; NPV; PU. 53873

The African. No. 1. [Boston: 1839] MB; MH. 53874

African Bible pictures; or Scripture scenes and customs in Africa. Philadelphia: 1839. 6, 69 p. CJ; IRA. 53875

African Methodist Episcopal Church. Minutes of the general and annual conferences of the African Methodist Episcopal Church, comprising four districts, from 1836 to 1839, inclusive. Brooklyn, N.Y.: 1839. 71 p. ICF; WHi. 53876

African Union Church. The African Union

hyumn book, designed as a companion for the pious, and freinds of all denominations; collected from different authors. 3rd edition, enlarged. Published by Peter Spencer, for the African Union Church in the United States. Wilmington: printed by Porter and Naff, 1839. DeWi; IEG. 53877

Agnew, Emily C. Geraldine: a tale of conscience. By E. C. A. 1st American, from the 2nd London edition.... Philadelphia: Eugene Cummisky, 1839. 3 v. CU; LN; LNB; MoFloSS; MoK. 53878

Agricultural almanac, for the year 1840, arranged after the system of German calendars.... Lancaster: printed by John Bear [1839] [32] p. NjR; WHi. 53879

----. Philadelphia: Prouty, Libby and Prouty.... J. Van Court, printer [1839] [16] 17-71 [1] p. MWA; PPM. 53880

Aikin, John, 1747-1822. Evenings at home; or the juvenile budget opened, by Dr. Aikin and Mrs. Barbauld. From the 15th London edition, illus. with engravings after Harvey and Chapman, by Adams. New York: Harper [1839] 382 p. NjP. 53881

----. The farmyard journal. For the amusement and instruction of children. Cooperstown: H. and E. Phinney, 1839. 31 p. N. 53882

----. The juvenile budget opened: being selections from the writings of Doctor John Aiken, with a sketch of his life. Boston: Marsh, Capen, Lyon and Webb, 1839. 288 p. MB; MH; MnSM. 53883

Ainsworth, Robert, 1660-1743. An abridgment of Ainsworth's Dictionary of English and Latin. Philadelphia: Hunt, 1839. GAuY. 53884

Ainsworth, William Harrison, 1805-1882. Jack Sheppard; a romance. Philadelphia: Lea and Blanchard, 1839. 2 v. KyCov; MH; NBuG; NNS; VvWeo. 53885

Akin, James. Facts connected with the life of James Carey, whose eccentric habits caused a post-mortem examination by gentlemen of the faculty; to determine whether he was Hermaphroditic. Philadelphia: 1839. DNLM; DSG; PHi. 53886

Alabama. Governor, 1837-1841 [Arthur P.

Bagby] Governor's message, to the legislature of Alabama. Delivered on the 3rd day of December, 1839. Executive department, Tuscaloosa, December 2, 1839. Gentlemen of the Senate and of the House of Representatives.... [Tuscaloosa? 1839] 15 p. TxU. 53887

----. Laws, Statutes, etc. Acts passed at the annual session of the General Assembly of the state of Alabama, begun and held at Tuscaloosa in November, 1838. Tuscaloosa: Hale and Eaton, state printers, 1838 [1839?] 216 p. DLC; In-S; Nj; PU; R. 53888

----. ----. Acts relating to the state bank and branches, passed at the session of 1838 and 1839, for the branch at Mobile. Printed at the Commercial Register office, 1839. 12 p. ABBS; ABS. 53889

----. University. Laws of the University of the state of Alabama.... Tuscaloosa: M. O. J. Slade, 1839. 27 p. A-Ar; AU; DLC; MH. 53890

Albany, New York. Chamberlain. The chamberlain's report...from May 1st, 1838, to May 1st, 1839. Albany: Hoffman and White, printers, 1839. 16 p. MBAt; NN; NNS. 53891

Albany Academy for Girls. Circular and catalogue. 1839. Albany: [1839-] 77. 24 v. in 4. MB. 53892

Albany and Schnectady Railroad Company. Report of the superintendent to the president and directors of the Mohawk and Hudson Railroad Company, for the year 1838. Printed for the use of the stockholders, by order of the board, May 24th, 1839. Albany: printed by Packard, Van Benthuysen and Company, 1839. 17 p. NN. 53893

Albany Medical College. Catalogue and circular of the Albany Medical College, Albany: printed by Packard, Van Benthuysen and Company, 1839-1891. ICU; MB; MiD-B; OC. 53894

Albany Society for the Relief of Destitute Children. Annual report of the directors, 9th February, 1839 [Albany: 1839] 16 p. MB. 53895

Alcott, William Alexander. See Alcott, William Andrus, 1798-1859.

Alcott, William Andrus, 1798-1859. Adventures of Lot, the nephew of Abraham. By William A. Alcott, author of the "first foreign mission," the

"second foreign mission,".... 2nd edition. Boston: Massachusetts Sabbath School Society, 1839. 108 p. ICMcHi. 53896

----. ...Breathing bad air, by Dr. William Alcott.... Boston and New York: G. W. Light, 1839. 56 p. CtMW; CtW; DSG; NN. 53897

----. Charles Hartland, the village missionary. Boston: Weeks, Jordan and Company, 1839. 191 p. DLC; IEG; MB; MBC; OO. 53898

----. City and country [Boston: 1839] 2 p. MH. 53899

----. Confessions of a school master. Andover, [Mass.] New York: Gould, Newman and Saxton, 1839. 316 p. ICU; InCW; MAnP; PAtM. 53900

----. Dosinig and drugging, or destroying by inches. Boston and New York: George W. Light, 1839. 48 p. DLC; MH-M; MWA. 53901

----. The house I live in; or the human body. For the use of families and schools. Boston: 1839. MdAS; MDeeP; MH-M; OMC. 53902

----. ----. 4th stereotyped edition. Boston, etc.: G. W. Light, 1839. MB; MH. 53903

----. ----. 5th stereotype edition. Boston and New York: George W. Light, 1839. 264 p. MBM; MWA; NbOM; TWcW; WBeloC. 53904

----. ----. 6th stereotype edition. Boston: George W. Light, 1839. 264 p. MBM; MH; MoSpD; NBMS. 53905

----. ----. 7th stereotype edition. Boston and New York: George W. Light, 1839. 264 p. CtY; NWattJHi; ViRu. 53906

----. How to prevent consumption. By Dr. William A. Alcott. Contents.... Boston: George W. Light, 1839. 24 p. MWA. 53907

----. Jesus at Nain; or the widows son raised. By the author of Mount Carmel. Written for the Massachusetts Sunday School Society and revised by the committee of publication. Boston: Sabbath School Society, 1839. 72 p. DLC; MB. 53908

----. The life of Peter the apostle. By William A. Alcott. Written for the Massachusetts Sabbath School Society, and revised by the committee of publication. Boston: Sabbath School Society, 1839. 188 p. DLC; MBC; MiOC. 53909

----. ----. 2nd edition. Boston: Massachusetts Sabbath School Society, 1839. 184 p. NNC. 53910

----. Religion at court; or Daniel in the Kings gate. Boston: 1839. MBC. 53911

----. Sketches of William Penn. Boston: D. S. King, 1839. 137 p. CtY; DLC; MBAt; RPB; ScU. 53912

----. Stories of Eliot and the Indians. 2nd edition. Boston: Massachusetts Sabbath School Society, 1839. 140 p. MeBa; OMC; PP; PPULC. 53913

----. Story of Ruth the Moabitess by the author of "first foreign mission," "second foreign mission," "happy family." 2nd edition. Boston: Massachusetts Sabbath School Society, 1839. 17-128 p. 53914

----. Tea and coffee. By William A. Alcott. Author of the young husband, young wife, young mother, young man's guide, etc. Boston: George W. Light, 1839. 174 p. CtY; ICJ; MiD; RBr; WU. 53915

----. Thoughts on bathing. Boston: etc., G. W. Light, 1839. 32 p. MH. 53916

----. The young housekeeper; or thoughts on food and cookery. 4th stereotype edition. Boston and New York: G. W. Light, 1839. 424 p. CtMW; CtY; MH. 53917

----. The young husband, or duties of man in the marriage relation. Boston: George W. Light, 1839. 388, 10 p. IEG; MB; MWA; NjR; PU. 53918

----. ----. 2nd edition. Boston: G. W. Light, 1839. 388 p. CBPSR; MiToC; OO; PU. 53919

----. ----. 3rd edition. Boston: 1839. 388 p. MB. 53920

----. The young man's guide. 13th edition. Boston: Perkins and Marvin, 1839. 360 p. IU; MB; NjMD; NUt; PPM. 53921

----. ----. 14th edition. Boston: Perkins and Marvin, 1839. 360 p. IaDaP; MBC; MeB; MH; PPM. 53922

----. The young mother; or management of children in regard to health. 7th stereotype edition. Boston: George W. Light, 1839. 342 p. DSG; IU; PPF; PPFr; VtMidSM. 53923

----. The young wife. 8th edition. Boston: 1839. MB; MBAt. 53924

Alden, Ebenezer. An account of the Massachusetts Medical Society with biographical notices of its founders, etc. [Boston: 1839] 14 p. MH-M. 53925

Alden, Timothy, 1771-1839. An historical sketch of the Pine Creek Church, with a biographical notice of the late Rev. Joseph Stockton, A.M.... Pittsburgh: printed by William B. Stewart, 1839. 15 p. CSansS; DLC; MA. 53926

Alexander, Charles A. The fall of Aztalan, and other poems. By A. Alexander, Esq. Washington: W. M. Morrison, 1839. 79 p. MH; NcD; NNUT; RPB. 53927

[Alexander, James Waddell] 1804-1859. The American mechanic. By Charles Quill. 3rd edition. Philadelphia: Henry Perkins, Boston: Perkins and Marvin, 1839. 285 p. DLC; MBox; PPDrop; ScCliTO. 53928

----. The working-man. By Charles Quill [pseud.].... Philadelphia: Perkins and Purves, 1839. 287 p. CtHT; ICJ; MB; MiU; ODaU. 53929

Alexander, Thomas Stockett, 1801-1871. A summary of the practice of the Court of Chancery, and County Courts, as Courts of Equity in Maryland, together with an appendix, containing the most usual forms, and the rules of the Court of Appeals, Court of Chancery, and Baltimore County Court, as a Court of Equity. Baltimore: Fielding Lucas, Jr., 1839. 422 p. DLC; MdBE; MdBJ; MdHi; MH-L. 53930

Alger, Israel. Alger's Perry. The orthoepical guide to the English tongue.... Boston: Simpkins and Burge, 1839. 166 p. MH; NNC. 53931

Aliquis Homo, pseud. The captive; or "the great western" dialogians, talking about private jails, factories, the slave trade and the "curiosities" of N. O. In dialogues between Henry and plain John. Cincinnati: S. A. Alley, 1839. 40 p. OClWHi. 53932

Allan, Chilton, 1786-1858. Letter to the people

of Kentucky [By Chilton Allan] Lexington, Ky.: Observer and Reporter, printer, 1839. 48 p. MH; NN. 53933

Allcine, Joseph. An alarm to unconverted sinners...By Joseph Allcine. New York: American Tract Society [1839] 168 p. NPalK. 53934

Allen, Hannah Bowen. Farmer Housten, and the speculator. A New England tale. Portland: O. L. Sanborn and Company, 1839. 69 p. MB; MH; MnU. 53935

Allen, Joseph, 1790-1873. Questions on the acts of the Apostles. Designed for the higher classes in Sunday schools.... 3rd edition. Boston: B. W. Greene, 1839. 143 p. MB-W; MH; MoSpD. 53936

Allen, Richard. Catechism of religious faith and practice. 3rd edition. Waterford [New York?] 1839. 40 p. PHC; PPULC. 53937

Allen, William, 1784-1868. A sermon preached in Attleborough, sabbath afternoon, January 13, 1839 [at the funeral of Mrs. Abigail S. Perry Woodcock] Pawtucket: Sherman and Kinnicutt, 1839. 17 p. MiD-B; MoSpD; OClWHi. 53938

Allgemeine deutsche schulzeitung. Hrsg. von H. Scheib und P. M. Wolsieffer. bdl; 15, Jun: 1839-30 Mai 1840. Baltimore [Gedruckt von L. B. Schwarz] 1839-40. 208 p. DLC; PPG. 53939

Das allgemeine traum-buck Alphabetisch Geordnet Harrisburg, Pa.: G. S. Peters, 1839. 128 p. PPeSchw; PPULC; PSt. 53940

Allston, Washington, 1779-1843. Exhibition of pictures, painted by Washington Allston, at Harding's Gallery. Boston: John H. Eastburn, printer, 1839. 8 p. MB; MH; MWHi; RPB; WHi. 53941

Alton [Illinois] Presbyterian Church. Church manual for the communicants of the Presbyterian Church...containing all their names with the names of all the church officers also, a sketch of the history of the church.... Alton: Parks, 1839. PPPrHi. 53942

Alton Marine and Fire Insurance Company, Alton, Illinois. Charter, Alton, Ill.: 1839. MBI. 53943

Alvord, Benjamin, 1813-1884. Address before the Dialectic Society of the Corps of Cadets, in commemoration of the gallant conduct of the nine graduates of the Military Academy.... Delivered at West point, N. Y., on the 29th of December, 1838.... New York: Wiley and Putnam, 1839. ICN; LNH; MB; PPAmP; WHi. 53944

Always do right; or the story of Shadrach, Meshach and Abednego. Boston: 1839. 64 p. MWA. 53945

The American almanac.... for the year 1840. Boston: David H. Williams [1839] 334 [2] p. IaB; IaHi; MWHi; RPaw. 53946

American Antiquarian Society, Worcester, Massachusetts. Catalogue of the officers and members of the American Antiquarian Society. May, 1839. Worcester: printed by T. W. and J. Butterfield, 1839. 15 p. DLC; MeHi; MHi; NIC; OO. 53947

----. Semi annual reports [May and Oct., 1839] with a catalgoue of officers and members, 1839 [Worcester: printed by T. W. and J. Butterfield, 1839] 16, 15 [1] 3 [1] p. CSt; DLC; KHi; NjP; PHi. 53948

The American Anti-slavery almanac for 1840.... New York and Boston: the American Anti-slavery Society, New York: J. A. Collins [1839] 48 p. CU; FNp; MWA; NeD; WHi. 53949

American Anti-slavery Society. American slavery as it is: testimony of a thousand witnesses.... New York: American Anti- slavery Society, 1839. 224 p. CtMW; KHi; MWA; PU; ScU. 53950

----. The chattel principle: the abhorrence of Jesus Christ and the apostles; or no refuge for American slavery in the New Testament. New York: 1839. 71 p. NN. 53951

American Art Union, New York. Transactions...for the year 1839- 1849. New York: 1839-1850. 11 v. DLC; IEN; MWA; PHi; TxU. 53952

American Atlantic Steam Navigation Company. An act to incorporate the American Atlantic Steam Navigation Company of the city of New York. Passed February 23rd, 1839. New York: E. B. Clayton, printer, 1839. 7 p. DLC. 53953

American Board of Commissioners for Foreign

Missions. Constitution, laws and regulations of the American Board of Commissioners for Foreign Missions. Boston: printed by Crocker and Brewster, 1839. 23 p. CtY; DLC; MA. 53954

American Chesterfield, or way to wealth, honour and distinction; being selections from the letters of Lord Chesterfield to his son; and extracts from other eminent authors, on the subject of politeness; with alterations and additions, suited to the youth of the United States. By a memeber of the Philadelphia bar. Philadelphia: Grigg and Elliot, 1839. WvBe. 53955

American comic almanack. Boston: S. N. Dickinson, 1839. MWA. 53956

American Dramatic Library. Comprising Athenia of Damascus, Bianca Visconti, Tortessa with Usurer. New York [1839?] CtHWatk; MH. 53957

The American farmer, and spirit of the agricultural journals of the day; containing original essays and communications on agriculture and horticulture...new series. Baltimore: John Sands, 1839-[1843] 5 v. MdBLC; NjR. 53958

American farmer's almanac, for 1840. Boston: Allen and Company [1839] MeBaHi; MHi; MWA. 53959

American Female Home Education Society. Circular and constitution. Nov., 1839. Boston: 1839. MB. 53960

American Health Convention. A report of the proceedings of the 2nd American Health Convention...New York...May 8, 1839. Boston [1839] 16 p. MHi. 53961

American Historical Society, Washington, D. C. Transactions of the American Historical Society: institutied at the city of Washington, October 12, 1835. Vol. 1. Washington: printed by Jacob Gideon, Jr., 1839. 522 p. CoCsC; DLC; MiU; OO; PHi. 53962

The American housewife: containing the most valuable and original receipts in all the various branches of cookery.... By an experienced lady. New York: Collier, 1839. 144 p. NNNAM. 53963

----. Collins, Keese and Compnay, 1839. 144 p. MCR; NN; NNT-C; NNNAM. 53964

American Institute of the city of New York. Charter of the American Institute of the city of New York, and the act incorporating the repository of the American Institute; with the by-laws of the American Institute.... New York: 1839. 16 p. NjP; NRoM. 53965

----. ...Circular of the 12th annual fair of the American Institute of the city of New York, to be held at Niblo's garden, October 7th, 1839.... New York: James Van Norden, printer, 1839. 8 p. MHi; MiU-C; MWA. 53966

The American Joe Miller: or the jester's own book. Being a choice collection of anecdotes and witticism. Philadelphia: Fischer and Brother, 1839. 219 p. MWA; NN. 53967

American journal of dental science, devoted to original articles, reviews of publications, the latest improvements in surgical and mechanical dentistry, and biographical sketches of distinguished dentists. New York: 1839-. V. 1-. CoDMS; ICJ; MHi; OClW. 53968

The American journal of homeopathy, V. 1. No. 1, 1-6; Aug., 1838- July, 1839. Volume first. Philadelphia: published by W. L. J. and Company, 1839-. NNNAM. 53969

American Life Insurance and Trust Company. Report of the committee of trustees appointed for the purpose of examining the books, vouchers and documents in the offices and of ascertaining the state of...affairs, previous to the declaration of a dividend.... New York: G. and C. Carvill, 1839. 14 p. CtY; ViU. 53970

American masonic register and literary companion. V. 1-August 31, 1839. Albany, N.Y. [L. G. Hoffman, 1839-1847] 8 v. C-S; DLC; N; NN. 53971

The American medical almanac, for 1839, designed for the daily use of practising physicians, surgeons, students and apothecaries...and general medical directory of the United States. By J. V. C. Smith, M.D.... Vol. I, to be continued annually. Boston: Marsh, Capen and Lyon, 1839 [-1841] MWA; NNNAM. 53972

American miniature almanac, 1840. Boston: Allen and Company, [1839] MWA. 53973

American Physiological Society. Tracts on health. No. 12. 1839. [Boston: the Society, 1839]

MH-M. 53974

American pocket almanac, for 1840. New York, N.Y.: Tanner and Disturnell [1839] MWA. 53975

American practical navigator. 11th edition. Washington: 1839. MB. 53976

The American Quarterly Register. A general index to the first ten volumes...from July, 1827, to May, 1838. Boston: printed by Perkins and Marvin, 1839. 16 p. CtY; IaGG; OC; PWaybu. 53977

American Reformed Covenanter. V. 1. New York: Oliver, 1839. PPPrHi. 53978

American Silk Society. Journal of the American Silk Society, and rural economist. By Gideon B. Smith, editor. V. 1-2, V. 3, No. 1/ 2-5, Jan., 1839-May, 1841. Baltimore: American Silk Society, 1839-1841. 3 v. DLC; MH-A; MiU-C; NjPAT; PPAmP. 53979

American Society of Civil Engineers. Constitution proposed for the American Society of Civil Engineers, with proceedings in reference to the same. April, 1839. Philadelphia: printed by J. C. Clark, 1839. 16 p. DLC; NRom; PHi. 53980

American Sunday School Union. The drowning boy. Philadelphia: By the American Sunday School Union, 1839. CMadC. 53981

----. Missionary manual: a sketch of the history and present state of Christian missions to the heathen. Revised by the committee of publication. Philadelphia: American Sunday School Union, 1839. 81 p. NIC. 53982

----. The new Sunday school hymn book. Prepared for the American Sunday School Union, and revised by the committee of publication. Philadelphia: American Sunday School Union, 1839. 160 p. MdBD. 53983

----. The pink slippers; or a cure of vanity. Written for the American Sunday School Union, and revised by the committee of publication. Philadelphia: American Sunday School Union [1839] 34 p. MScitHi; RPB. 53984

----. The teacher taught; an humble...See Packard, Frederick Adolphus, 1794-1867.

----. Union questions; or questions on select portions of Scripture, from the Old and New Testaments. Philadelphia: American Sunday School Union [1839] 11 v? AmSSchU; IEG; GMilvC; NcWfc. 53985

American Tract Society. Family hymns. New York: American Tract Society, 1839. 216 p. CtMW; ICBB; MBC. 53986

----. The temperance volume; embracing seventeen tracts. New York: the Society [1839] 1 v. MH; NN; ViU. 53987

Americanisher Stadt und Land Calender for 1840. Philadelphia: Conrad Zentler [1839] MWA. 53988

Americanisher Unabbangigkerts Kalender, 1840. Philadelphia: C. F. Stollmeyer [1839] MWA. 53989

The American's guide comprising the Declaration of Independence; the Articles of Confederation; the Constitution of the United States; and the constitutions of the several states composing the union. Philadelphia: Hagan and Thompson, 1839. 419 p. CoU; GAuY; KyLxT; LNMas; PPL. 53990

[Der] Amerikanisch-Deutsch Hausfreund und Baltimore Calendar for 1840. Baltimore: Johann T. Hanzsche [1839] MWA. 53991

Ames, Julius Reubens, 1801-1850. Liberty. The image and superscription on every coin issued by the United States of America.... The inscription on the bell in the old Philadelphia statehouse, which was rung July 4, 1776, at the signing of the Declaration of Independence. New York: American Anti-slavery Society, 1839. 120, 21 p. CtY; KyDC; MB; NjP; WHi. 53992

Amherst College. Catalogue of the officers and students of Amherst College, 1839-1840. Amherst [Mass] J. S. and C. Adams, printer, 1839. 24 p. CBPSR; IaGG; MeB; MH. 53993

----. Order of exercises...1839. MBC. 53994

Amussat, Jean Zulema, 1796-1856. Amussat's lessons on retention of urine, caused by strictures of the urethra, and on the diseases of the prostate. Edited by A. Petit.... Tr. from the French by James P. Jerney, M.D. With notes. Charleston, S.C.: D. J. Dowling, printer, 1839. 246 p. MdUM. 53995

Ancient Edom; and the fulfilment of prophecy in the present state of Arabia Petrea. Philadelphia: American Sunday School Union, 1839. 139 p. ICBB; KyBC; MBAt; MH-AH; WHi. 53996

Anderson, Rufus, 1796-1880. An address, delivered in South Hadley, Mass., July 24, 1839, at the 2nd anniversary of the Mount Holyoke Female Seminary.... Boston: printed by Perkins and Marvin, 1839. 24 p. CtY; ICP; MDeeP; MH; NjR. 53997

Andover and Haverhill Railroad Corporation. A brief statement of facts in relation to the Andover and Haverhill Railroad. [Andover? 1839?] 4 p. CSt; NN. 53998

Andover Theological Seminary. Bulletin. No. 1. 1839. Andover: 1839. PPAmP; PPULC. 53999

----. Catalogues of the officers and students for Jan., 1839. A.: 1839. 11 p. CtY; MB. 54000

----. The constitution and associate statutes of the theological seminary in Andover. Andover: Gould, Newman and Saxton, 1839. 38 p. CSmH; MAnP; MeB; NNUT; PU. 54001

----. Triennial catalogue of the theological seminary, Andover, Mass., 1839. Andover: printed by Gould, Newman and Saxton, 1839. 46 p. GDecCT; MAnP; MB; MeB; MeHi. 54002

----. Library. Catalogue of books belonging to the library of the Porter Rhetorical Society, Theological Seminary, Andover, Mass.: April, 1839. Andover: Gould, Newman and Saxton, 1839. 53 p. CSmH; MAnP; MBC; RPB. 54003

Andrews, Ethan Allen, 1787-1858. First lessons in Latin; or an introduction to Andrews and Stoddards' Latin grammar. By Prof. E. A. Andrews. 3rd edition. Boston: Crocker and Brewster, 1839. CtY; MH; NFred; TxU-T. 54004

----. The first part of Jacobs' and Doring's Latin reader: adapted to Andrews and Stoddard's Latin grammar. 4th edition. Boston: Crocker and Brewster, 1839. 266 p. KSteC; MB; MH; MStou-Hi; NNC. 54005

----. A grammar of the Latin language; for the use of schools and colleges. By E. A. Andrews and S. Stoddard. 6th edition. Boston: Crocker and Brewster, 1839. 323 p. KTW; MH; NjR; PPL-R;

TBriK. 54006

----. Latin exercises; adapted to Andrews and Stoddard's Latin grammar. By Prof. E. A. Andrews.... Boston: Crocker and Brewster, 1839. 336 p. IU; MNBedf; RPB; Sc. 54007

----. ----. 2nd edition. Boston: Crocker and Brewster, 1839. 336 p. GGaB; IaPeC; MH; OkU; WaPS. 54008

----. Questions upon Andrews and Stoddard's Latin grammar. Boston: Crocker and Brewster, etc., etc., 1839. 52 p. MH; NFred; PU. 54009

Andrews, John Whiting, 1811-1893. Speech of J. W. Andrews, of Franklin, on the engrossment of the bill relating to fugitives from labor or service from other states. Delivered in the House of Representatives of Ohio, Saturday, February 9, 1839. Columbus: 1839. CtY. 54010

Andrus Bernardus Smor [in German] Philadelphia: 1839. 106 p. PPFHi. 54011

Angell, Oliver, 1787-1858. The union, number five. Revised stereotype edition. Philadelphia: W. Marshall and Company, 1839. MH. 54012

Animal biography; or a visit to the menagerie. New Haven: S. Babcock, 1839. 24 p. CtY; MH; MSaP. 54013

Annapolis, Maryland. Ordinances, etc. The by-laws of the city...with amendments. Annapolis: J. Green, printer, 1839. 57 p. MdAN; NN. 54014

Annapolis, Washington and Baltimore Railroad Company. The first annual report of the directors of the Annapolis and Elkridge Railroad Company [Reports upon the surveys, location and progress of construction of the Annapolis and Elkridge Railroad by G. W. Hughes] Annapolis: William McNeir, 1839. CSmH; MdBP; NjR; NN; NNC. 54015

Anniversary ball. Your company is respectfully requested at an anniversary ball, to be given at the Wisconsin House, in the city of Burlington, on the 8th of January, instant. Managers...Jan. 1, 1839 [Burlington, Ia.: 1839?] Broadside. IaDaP. 54016

Anthon, Charles, 1797-1867. First Greek lessons, containing the most important parts of the grammar of the Greek language, together with appropriate exercies in the translating and writing of Greek for the use of beginners. By Charles Anthon, LL.D.... New York: Harper and Brothers, 1839. 238 p. IaDuU; ICU; MWi; NNC; OMC. 54017

----. First Latin lessons, containing the most important parts of the grammar of the Latin language, together with appropriate exercises in the translating and writing of Latin, for the use of beginners. New York: Harper and Brothers, 1839. 363 p. CoD; CtMW; MBAt; MeB; PPM. 54018

----. A grammar of the Greek language, for the use of schools and colleges.... New York: Harper and Brothers, 1839. 284 p. GMM; ICU; KBB; MeB; ScCliTO; TChU. 54019

----. A system of Greek prosody and metre...to which are appended remarks on Indo-Germanic analogies. By Charles Anthon, LL.D.... New York: Harper and Brothers, 1839. 270 p. CtMW; LNH; MiD; NjP; ViU. 54020

Anthony, Joseph Biles, 1795-1851. Report on liens of the commonwealth upon the lands of John Nicholson and Peter Baynton, made to the Governor, Joseph B. Anthony, esq. Commissioner.... Harrisburg: Boas and Coplan, printers, 1839. 56 p. DLC; MHi; PHi; PPi; PPM. 54021

Anti-bell Ringing Society, Boston, Massachusetts. Constitution of the Society, instituted Oct. 26, 1838. Boston: printed by Henry P. Lewis, 1839. 16 p. MB; MBAt; MH; MHi. 54022

Anti-slavery almanac for 1839. Boston: [1838] MWA. 54023

Anti-slavery Convention of American Women. 3rd, Philadelphia, 1839. An address from the convention of American women, to the Society of Friends, on the subject of slavery. Philadelphia: Merrihew and Thompson, 1839. 10 p. DLC; MH; NNC; PHC; PSC-Hi. 54024

----. ----. Proceedings of the 3rd Anti-slavery Convention of American Women, held in Philadelphia, May 1st, 2nd and 3rd, 1839. Philadelphia: printed by Merrihew and Thompson, 1839. 28 p. AB; DLC; MH; OClWHi; TNF. 54025

Anti-slavery Examiner. No. 13. The Anti-slavery Examiner on the condition of the free people of color in the United States. New York: American Anti-slavery Society, 1839. 23 p. A-Ar; MdBD; PPULC. 54026

----. The chattel principle, the abhorrence of Jesus Christ and the Apostles: or no refuge for American slavery in the New Testaments. New York: Anti-slavery Society, 1839. ICT; KyDC; MdHi; MeWaC; MNtCA; TxU. 54027

Anti-slavery lecturer. Utica: 1839. V. 1. NIC; OO. 54028

An apology for uniting with the Methodists designed to point out the misrepresentations contained in a late publication, entitled candid reasons for not uniting with the Methodists; By Bernard. By a Methodist preacher. Middlebury, Vt.: J. W. Copeland, 1839. VtMidbC. 54029

An Appeal on behalf of the Oberlin Institute, in aid of the abolition of slavery in the United States of America. n.p. [1839] 3 p. OO. 54030

An appeal to the citizens of Connecticut, in behalf of the Wesleyan University. Middletown: W. D. Starr, printer, 1839. 16 p. CtY; DLC; MH; N. 54031

An appeal to the citizens of New York, by a tax payer. March, 1839. New York: 1839. 16 p. InHi; LNH; MBC; MH. 54032

Appeal to the parishioners and pen-holders of St. Stephen's parish, Cecil County, Maryland [n.p.] 1839. 7 p. MdHi. 54033

Arabian nights. The Arabian nights entertainments, consisting of 1001 stories, told by the Sultaness of the Indies.... Containing a familiar account of the customs, manners and religion of the eastern nations.... 9th American from the 18th English edition. Tr. from the Arabian mss.... Exeter: J. and B. Williams, 1839. 2 v. DLC; MnSCC; OO. 54034

Arbon Land Company. Articles of association and by-laws of the Arbon Land Company. Associated April 27th, 1838. Printed by order of the board. Philadelphia: printed by John C. Clark, 1839. 21 p. NBu. 54035

Archibald, ? Speech of Mr. Archibald, of Arkansas, upon the resolution reported from the select committee on public lands; delivered in the House of Representatives, 20th and 26th February, 1839. Washington: Blair and Rives, printers, 1839. 15 p. TxU. 54036

Arkansas. Laws, Statutes, etc. Acts passed at the 2nd session of the General Assembly of the state of Arkansas: which was begun and held, at the capitol, in the city of Little Rock, on Monday, the 5th day of November, 1838, and ended on Monday, the 17th day of December, 1838. Published by authority. Little Rock: printed by Edward Cole, printer to the state, 1839. 116 p. ArCH; DLC; In-SC; NNLI; Or-SC; 54037

The Arkansas star [Weekly] Sept. 7, 1839, to Feb. 18, 1841. Little Rock: D. Lambert and S. Mc-Curdy, 1839-41. 2 v. DLC. 54038

Armstrong, John. A treatise on agriculture; comprising a concise history of its origin and progress; the present condition of the art abroad and at home, and the theory and practice of husbandry, to which is added, a dissertation on the kitchen and fruit garden. New York: Harper and Brothers, 1839. GMilvC; In; NICLA; NRU. 54039

Armstrong, John, 1758-1843. Lives of Anthony Wayne and Sir Henry Vane. Boston: Hilliard, Gray and Company, 1839. 403 p. CSfP; NcGA; PMA; RKi. 54040

Armstrong, John, 1784-1829. Lectures on the morbid anatomy, nature and treatment of acute and chronic diseases; delivered in the theatre of anatomy, edited by Joseph Rix. Philadelphia: Haswell, 1839. 687 p. MdBM. 54041

Arnault, Antoine Vincent, 1766-1834. Memoirs of the public and private life of Napoleon Bonaparte. See Reid, William Hamilton, d. 1826.

Arnold, Samuel George, 1806-1891. Memoir of Hannah More; with brief notices of her works, contemporaries, etc. New York: T. Mason and G. Lane, for the Methodist Episcopal Church, 1839. 184 p. CoU; DLC; GEU; NcD. 54042

The art of love, with a remedy for love. Translated from the French. To which are added, the court of love. And the history of love, etc.... Philadelphia: printed for the publisher, 1839. 131 p. DLC; RPB. 54043

Arthur Lee and Tom Palmer; or the sailor

reclaimed.... Boston: James Munroe and Company, 1839 [6] 78 p. MB; NNC. 54044

----. 2nd edition. Boston: J. Munroe and Company, 1839. TxU. 54045

----. 3rd edition. Boston: James Munroe and Company, 1839. 78 p. MB. 54046

Articles of faith and order for regular Baptist Churches. The reader of these articles is affectionately requested to turn to the various Scripture texts referred to, and examine them carefully, and with prayer, as he proceeds. Burlington: Powell and George, printers, 1839. 12 p. PCA. 54047

Aspin, Jehoshaphat. Picture of the world; or a description of the manners, customs and costumes of all nations. By J. Aspin. A new and enlarged edition. Illustrated by engravings. Hartford: Philemon Canfield, 1839. 256 p. KyLoSX; MWA. 54048

Associate Reformed Church of North America. Pennsylvania Presbytery. Narrative concerning the maintenance of the reformation testimony. Delcaration and testimony for the doctrine and order of the Church of Christ and against the errors of the present times. Acts and ordination vows [Philadelphia? 1839?] 250 p. ICU. 54049

Associate Reformed Synod of the West. Ohio. Extracts from the minutes of the proceedings of the Associate Reformed Synod of the West held at Chillicothe, October 16, 1839, and continued by adjournment. Hamilton, O.: I. M. Walters, printer, 1839 [2] 36p. NcMHi; OCHP; PPiXT. 54050

Associate Synod of North America. A display of the religious principles of the Associate Synod of North America. 6th edition. Philadelphia: William S. Young, 1839. 250 p. NcMHi; PAle; PPPr-Hi. 54051

Association of Friends for the Instruction of Poor Children. Origin and proceedings.... Philadelphia: 1839. PHi. 54052

Astronomy and general science [Please to read this bill attentively, and mention the appointment among your friends.... [Newport: 1839] Broadside. RNHi. 540533

At the sign of the glass ship.... Cambridge: 1839. MB. 54054

Atkinson, S. Solomon, d. 1805. An essay on marketable or doubtful titles to real estate. From the last London edition. Philadelphia: Littell, New York: Halstead and Voorhies, 1838. DLC; KyU; MiU-L; PPT-L; WaU-L. 54055

Attempts at rhyming, by an old field teacher. Raleigh: Lemay, 1839. 124 p. MiU-C; NcD; NcU. 54056

Atwater, Lyman Hotchkiss, 1813-1883. The completion of two centuries.... Bridgeport, Connecticut: Standard office, 1839. 15 p. CSmH; KWiU; MBC; MiD-B; PPAmP. 54057

Auburn Theological Seminary. Appeal in behalf of the Auburn Theological Seminary. Published by order of the prudential committee. Auburn: printed at the Recorder office [1839] 16 p. NAuT; NCH; NNUT. 54058

----. Catalogue of the officers and students of the Auburn Theological Seminary. 1838-1839 [Auburn: 1839] [8] p. MH; N; NAuHi. 54059

----. Catalogue of the officers and students of the Auburn Theological Seminary. 1838-1839 [Auburn: 1839] [8] p. MH; N; NAuHi. 54060

----. Triennial catalogue, of the Auburn Theological Seminary, 1839. Auburn: Oliphant and Skinner, printers [1839] 14 p. MH; N; NAuT. 54061

Audubon, John James, 1785-1851. The birds of America.... By John James Audubon.... New York: G. R. Lockwood, 1839. 8 v. CoU; ICJ; MMet; OCY; PPM. 54062

----. Ornithological biography; or an account of the habits of the birds of the United States of America; accompanied by descriptions of the objects represented in the work entitled the birds of America, and interspersed with delineations of American scenery and manners. Philadelphia: Carey, 1839. 5 v. CSt; DLC; LU; OrU; WU. 54063

Augsburg Confession. Die Augsburgische Confession, mit einer kurzgefassten nachricht vom tiefem verfalle der Catholischen kirche, und von der entstehung der protestantischen Confession nebenbei enthaltend interessante anekdoten

beruhmter manner aus genannter zeit, besonders von Luther und Philip Melanchton. Nazareth, Pa.: Senseman, 1839. 114 p. IU; PNazMHI; PPG; PPLT. 54064

Augusta College. Catalogue of the officers and students of Augusta College, for the year commencing October 1, 1838. July, 1839. Cincinnati: printed at the Methodist Book Room. R. P. Thompson, printer, 1839. 16 p. KyLx. 54065

Austin, Ivers James, 1808-1889. An oration delivered by request of the city authorities before the citizens of Boston, on the 63rd anniversary of American independence, July 4, 1839. Boston: J.H. Eastburn, city printer, 1839. 36 p. CtSoP; ICN; MB; PPL; RPB. 54066

----. ----. 2nd edition. Boston: John H. Eastburn, city printer, 1839. 36 p. CtY; MHi; MiD-B; MnU. 54067

Austin, James Trecothick, 1784-1870. An address delivered before the Massachusetts Charitable Mechanic Association, at the celebration of their 11th triennial festival, and 2nd exhibition and fair, October 3, 1839.... Boston: the Association, 1839. 36 p. DLC; MH; MWA; PHi; RP. 54068

----. Review of the Rev. Dr. Channing's letter to Jonathan Phillips, esq. on the slavery question. Boston: J. H. Eastburn, printer, 1839. 77 p. CSmH; LNX; NcD; RPB; WHi. 54069

Austin, John Mather. A voice to youth, addressed to young men and young ladies.... 2nd edition. Utica: Grosh and Hutchinson, 1839. 424 p. NdFM. 54070

----. ----. 3rd edition. Utica: Grosh and Hutchinson, 1839. 424 p. CtSoP; NNMer. 54071

Aycrigg, B[enjamin] Communication from B. Aycrigg...relative to the West Branch and Allegheny Canal, supplementary to the reports on the same subject, read Dec. 15, 1836, and March 1, 1837. Read in the House of Representatives, February 19, 1839. Harrisburg: Boas and Coplan, printers, 1839. 61 p. DLC; MnHi; PEaL; PHi. 54072

----. Communication made to the House of Representatives, February 19, 1839, relative to the West Branch and Allegheny Canal, supplementary to the reports on the same subject, read December 15, 1836, and March 1, 1837. By B. Aycrigg...Printed by order of the Senate, March 19, 1839. Harrisburg: printed by E. Guyer, 1839. 66 p. DLC; MH-BA; NNE; PHi; WHi. 54073

----. Reports of Benjamin Aycrigg, as principal engineer appointed to explore the country between the West Branch improvements and the town of Franklin, in Verango Co., read March 1, 1837. Harrisburg: Boas and Coplan, 1839. 12 p. MiU; PHi; PPULC. 54074

Aydelott, B. P. The intelligent mechanic, an introductory lecture, delivered...by request of an as-sociation of mechanics. Cincinnati: printed at the Cincinnati Gazette office, 1839. 8 p. DLC; MdBD; NjPT. 54075

Ayrault, Charles. Habits of mind, or character. A lecture, delivered before the Young Men's Association of Geneva, March 21, 1839. Geneva: J. Stow, Jr. and B. Frazee, 1839. 36 p. DLC; NGH; OClWHi; PPL. 54076

----. An oration...delivered at Geneva, July 4th, 1839. Published by request. Geneva, N. Y.: printed by J. Stow, Jr. and B. Frazee, 1839. 24 p. N; NGH. 54077

B

Babcock, Rufus, 1796-1875. Tales of truth, for the young: or waters from the living fountain, flowing at all seasons.... 2nd edition. Philadelphia: George W. Donahue, 1839. 180 p. DLC; ICBB. 54078

Babcock, Sidney, Bookseller and Stationer, New Haven. Circular to the friends of literature respecting the elementary books by Noah Webster [New Haven: 1839?] ICU; MH; NN. 54079

Baby sister. Boston: Massachusetts Sabbath School Society, 1839. 8 p. CtY; ICU. 54080

Bache, Alexander Dallas, 1806-1867. Reorganization of the Central High School of Philadelphia.... [Philadelphia: 1839] 12 p. MB; PPULC. 54081

----. Report on education in Europe, to the trustees of the Girard College for Orphans. Philadelphia: printed by Lydia R. Bailey, 1839. 666 p. CU; LNH; MdBP; OU; PPA. 54082

----. Report to the controllers of the public schools on the reorganization of the Central High School of Philadelphia [Philadelphia: 1839] 54 p. DLC; MB; PPAmP; PHi; PPL. 54083

Backus, Augustus. History, theory, and analysis of music: designed for the music department of the Troy Female Seminary.... Troy: Tuttle, Belcher and Burton, 1839. 108 p. DLC; MiGr; NT; OClWHi; WM. 54084

Backus, Charles, 1749-1803. Discourses of Rev. Charles Backus...on the Scripture doctrine of regeneration; abridged and put into the form of an essay. Boston: American Doctrinal Tract Society, 1839. 108 p. IaB; MH; MNtCA; NbCrD; RPB; VtU. 54085

Backus, Isaac, 1724-1806. Church history of New England from 1620 to 1804...with a memoir of the author. Philadelphia: Baptist Tract Depository, 1839. 250 p. ArCH; IaB; MBAt; PHi; RWe. 54086

Bacon, Delia Salter, 1811-1859. The bride of Fort Edward; [a dialogue] founded on an incident of the revolution. Boston: 1839. MBAt. 54087

----. ----. New York: Colman, 1839. 174 p. CtMW; GU; ICN; PU; RPB. 54088

Bacon, Francis, 1561-1626. Moral, economical, and political essays, by Francis Bacon, Baron of Verulam, Viscount of St. Albans, and Lord High Chancellor of England. A new edition. Boston: Otis, Broaders and Company, 1839. 216 p. NAda. 54089

Bacon, Leonard, 1802-1881. An address before the New England Society of the city of New York, on forefathers' day, December 22, 1838.... New York: E. Collier, 1839. 46 p. Ct; MBC; MH-AH; NNUT; PHi. 54090

----. Thirteen historical discources on the completion of two hundred years, from the beginning of the first church in New Haven, with an appendix.... New Haven: Durrie and Peck, New York: Gould, Newman and Saxton, 1839. 400 p. CtB; ICU; LU; MWiW; PPA. 54091

Bacon, William Thompson, 1814-1881. Poems. New Haven: Benjamin and William Noyes, Boston: C. C. Little and Company, 1839. 212 p. CtSoP; ICU; MB; MPeaI; NcD. 54092

The bad effects of speculative theology and false philosophy, on the religion and morals of mankind. 3rd edition. With the rise and progress of perfectionism in Western New York. Philadelphia [1839] 48 p. CtY; MBAt; MH; PPULC; PU. 54093

Badger, P. D. People's book of health. Boston: 1839. CtHT. 54094

Bagioli, Antonio, 1790-1870. New method of singing; with an accompaniment for the pianoforte or harp, and by him respectfully inscribed to the public. 2nd edition. New York: published by the author, 1839. CtY; DLC; GS;

MB; NN. 54095

Bailey, Ebenezer, 1795-1839. First lessons in algebra, being an easy introduction to that science.... Improved stereotype edition. Boston: G. W. Palmer, 1839. 252 p. CtY; MB; MiD; PU; RPB. 54096

----. Key to first lessons in algebra. Boston: G. W. Palmer and Company, 1839. 84 p. MH; RPB. 54097

----. The young ladies' class book; a selection of lessons for reading, in prose and verse. 19th stereotype edition. Boston: Kendall and Lincoln, New York: Sheldon and Company [etc., etc.] 1839. 408 p. DLC; P. 54098

----. ----. 21st edition. Boston: Gould, Kendall and Lincoln, 1838. 408 p. CtY; Nh. 54099

Bailey, Philip James, 1816-1902. Festus; a poem. 13th edition. New York: James Miller...1839. 391 p. OkMan. 54100

Bailey, Phinehas, 1787-1861. A pronouncing stenography, containing a complete system of short hand writing; governed by the analogy of sounds, and adapted to every language. 3rd edition. Burlington [Vt.] C. Goodrich, 1839. 32 p. DLC; MB; NN; OCHP; VtU. 54101

Bailey, Robert S. The church is the widerness. Narrative of a visit to the Right Rev. Philander Chase, bishop of Illinois.... Charleston [S. C.] printed by A. E. Miller...1839. 8 p. CSmH; MH; NN. 54102

Bain, William T. Letters and meditations of religious and other subjects. Raleigh: printed at the office of the Raleigh Register, 1839. 148 p. DLC; NcAS; NcG. 54103

Baird, Robert, 1798-1863. Memoir of Mrs. Eliza Astor Rumpff, and of the Duchess de Broglie, daughter of Madame de Stael.... New York: American Tract Society [1839] 80 p. ICU; LNH; MH; NjR; OO. 54104

----. Transplanted flowers, or memoirs of Mrs. Rumpff, daughter of John Astor, esq., and the Duchess de Broglie, daughter of Madame de Stael. With an appendix.... New York: J. S. Taylor, 1839. 159 p. DLC; MBC; MNe; NjN; TxU. 54105

Bakewell, Robert, 1768-1843. Introduction to geology, intended to convey a practical knowledge of the science.... First American from the fifth London edition. Edited and with an appendix by Professor B. Silliman, Yale College. New Haven: B. and W. Noyes, 1839. 632 p. IaDaM. 54106

----. ----. 596 p. CtHT; ICU; NCH; OCo; TNV. 54107

----. ----. 3rd American from the 5th London edition, with an appendix by Professor B. Silliman.... New Haven: B. and W. Noyes, 1839. 596 p. CU; KyBC; MSaP; PPM; ViU. 54108

Balch, William Stevens, 1806-1887. A grammar of the English language. Boston: B. B. Mussey, 1839. DLC; MH; NNC; VtReg; WM. 54109

----. Individual freedom, the foundation of a democratic government. An oration, delivered in Pawtucket, Rhode Island, July 4, 1839. Pawtucket: Sherman and Kinnicutt, printers, 1839. 34 p. MWA; RPaw; RPB. 54110

----. A manual for sunday schools.... Boston: 1839. RPB. 54111

Baldwin, Austin. A table book, and primary arithmetic, compiled and arranged for the introductory department of the New York high schools.... 10th edition. New York: R. Lockwood, 1839. 72 p. NjR. 54112

Baldwin, James Fowle, 1782-1862. Water. Report to the mayor of the city of Boston and chairman of the committee on the introduction of water [1839] 15 p. MCM; MH; MHi. 54113

Baldwin, Loammi, 1780-1838. His report; embracing his survey and estimates of the water power and manufacturing privileges owned by the Sewall's Falls Locks and Canal Corporation on the east side of the Merrimack River. Concord, N. H.: McFarland, 1839. 21 p. Nh; NhD; PHi. 54114

Ballou, Adin, 1803-1890. Non-resistance in relation to human governments. Boston: Non-resistance Society, 1839. 24 p. GU; MB; OO; PPL; RP. 54115

----. Practical Christianity and its non-resistance in relation to human governments [Boston: 1839?] 20 p. NN. 54116

----. Standard of practical Christianity. Boston:

1839. MB. 54117

Ballou, Hosea, 1771-1852. Sermon delivered in the Second Universalist meeting House, in Boston, March 3, 1839: occasioned by the recent decease of several of its members, published by request. Boston: J. N. Bang, printer, 1839. 16 p. DLC; ICN; MiD- B; MMeT; NCaS. 54118

----. A treatise on atonement; in which the finite nature of sin is argued, its cause and consequences as such; the necessity and nature of atonement, and its glorius consequences, in the final reconciliation of all men to holiness and happiness. 6th edition. Utica: Grosh and Hutchinson, 1839. 228 p. ICP; KyLoP; MB; MH. 54119

Ballou, Hosea, 1796-1861. Collection of Psalms and hymns. 5th edition. Boston: Benjamin B. Mussey, 1839. 540 p. MWHi. 54120

----. ----. 6th edition. Boston: Benjamin B. Mussey, 1839. 540 p. MBUGC. 54121

----. ----. 8th edition. Boston: Benjamin B. Mussey, 1839. 540 p. MBAU. 54122

----. ----. 9th edition. Boston: 1839. 494 p. MB; MWA; NNUT. 54123

----. ----. 9th edition: Boston: B. B. Mussey, 1839. 636 p. MBNMHi. 54124

----. The universalist hymn book.... 9th edition. Boston: Benjamin B. Mussey, 1839. 638 p. MMeT-Hi. 54125

Baltimore. Burn's Club. The constitution and by-laws of the Burn's Club of Baltimore, in the state of Maryland. Baltimore: printed by William Woody, 1839. 14 p. MdHi. 54126

----. City Council. First Branch. Journal of the proceedings of the city council of Baltimore. January session, 1839, and extra sessions, 1838. Baltimore: printed by Samuel Sands, 1839. 25, 28, 505 p. MdHi. 54127

----. ----. Second Branch. Journal of the proceedings of the second branch of the city council of Baltimore. January session, 1839, and extra sessions, 1838. Baltimore: printed by Samuel Sands, 1839. MdHi. 54128

----. Fourth Ward. List of names registered in the Fourth Ward, Baltimore, September 20, 1839. Baltimore: printed by Lucas and Deaver, 1839. 16 p. MdHi. 54129

----. General Dispensary. Charter, by-laws.... Baltimore: W. Woody, printer, 1839. 13 p. DLC; MdBLC; MdHi. 54130

----. Green Mount Cemetary. The dedication of Green Mount Cemetary. July 13, 1839. Baltimore: printed by Woods and Crane, 1839. 36, 4 p. CSmH; ICMe; MB; NGH; PHi. 54131

----. ----. Prospectus and terms of subscription of the Green Mount Cemetary. Incorporated by the legislature of Maryland. Baltimore: J. DS. Toy, 1839. 14 p. DLC; MdBP; MH; PHi. 54132

----. Mercantile Library Association. Constitution, rules, regulations, etc. Established November 14, 1839. Baltimore: Bull and Tuttle, 1839. 9 p. MdHi; MdU; OCHP; ScHi; ScC. 54133

Baltimore and Susquehanna Railroad Company. Report of a committee of the stockholders appointed May 9, 1839 [Baltimore? 1839] DLC. 54134

The Baltimore book, a christmas and New Year's present; edited by W. H. Carpenter and T. S. Arthur. Baltimore: Bayly and Burns [1839] 269 p. MB; NjP; WHi. 54135

Baltimore City College. Prospectus...1839-1840. Baltimore: 1839-. 10 p. PHi; PPULC. 54136

Baltimore Clipper [Daily] Baltimore: 1839-1863. DLC; MdBP. 54137

The Baltimore Literary Monument. Edited by J. N. McJilton and T. S. Arthur. V. 1-2; October, 1838-1839. Baltimore: T. S. Arthur, 1839. 2 v. ICN; MB; MdBP; NN; PPM. 54138

Banco; or the tenant of the spring. A legend of the White Sulphur. Printed by request for presentation. Philadelphia: C. Sherman and Company, 1839. 28 p. DLC; MB; NcD; RPB; Vi. 54139

Bancroft, Aaron, 1755-1839. The life of George Washington, commander in chief of the American Army.... Boston: E. Littlefield, 1839. 2 v. IEG; MWA; PHi; RNHi; VtWmt. 54140

Bancroft, George, 1800-1891. Fellow

citizens...[attack upon him in reference to his intention to deliver a democratic address. Boston: 1839?] 1 p. MH. 54141

----. History of the colonization of the United States. 5th edition. Boston: Charles C. Little and James Brown, 1839. 7 v. RNHS. 54142

----. ----. 6th edition. Boston: C. C. Little and J. Brown, 1839. 3 v. OClW; ViU. 54143

----. History of the United States from the discovery of the American continent. Boston: Charles C. Little and James Brown, 1839. 9 v. GAM-R. 54144

----. ----. [edition?] Boston: Little, Brown and company, 1839- 1844. 3 v. CtMW. 54145

----. ----. Boston: Little, Brown and Company, 1839-1860. 10 v. LNL. 54146

----. ----. ? edition. Boston: Charles C. Little and James Brown, 1839-1874. 10 v. MDed; RBr; WBeloC. 54147

----. ----. Boston: 1839-1875. 10 v. MNowd. 54148

----. ----. 5th edition. Boston: Charles C. Little and James Brown, 1839-[1840] 3 v. CtHT; IaCrM; KyHi; NN; PLFM. 54149

----. ----. 5th edition. Boston: Charles C. Little, and James Brown, 1839-1854. 6 v. MeWebr. 54150

Bangor, Maine. The charter and ordinaces of the city of Bangor, with certain acts of th legislature relating to the city. Bangor: Edwards and Smith, printers, 1839. 122 p. MeB; MeHi; MH-L. 54151

Bangor Theological Seminary. Bangor, Maine. Catalogue of the theological seminary, Bangor, Maine, 1838-1839. Bangor: printed by Samuel S. Smith, 1839. 12 p. CBPSR; MeB; MeHi. 54152

Bangs, Nathan, 1778-1862. Centenary sermon, in Vestry Street Church, New York City, October 25, 1839 on 100th year of Methodism. New York: T. Mason and G. Lane, 1839. 26 p. CtY; MBC; MBNMHi; PHI; RPB. 54153

----. A discourse on the occasion of the death of the Reverend Wilbur Fisk...delivered in the Greene Street Church, New York...March 29, 1839. New York: T. Mason and G. Lane for the Methodist Episcopal Church, 1839. 24 p. DLC; IEG; MH-AH; PHi; RPB. 54154

----. A history of the Methodist Episcopal Church...from the year 1793 to the yer 1816.... New York: T. Mason and G. Lane, 1839. 2 v. FOA; GDecCT; MiD-B; ODaB; TChU. 54155

----. ----. New York: T. Mason and G. Lane, 1839-[1840] 4 v. CoDI; IC; MnHi; MWA; OCl. 54156

----. ----. 3rd edition, revised and corrected. New York: T. Mason and G. Lane, 1839 464 p. CSmH; LNH; MBAt; NjMD; OBerB. 54157

----. ----. 3rd edition, revised and corrected.... New York: T. Mason and G. Lane, 1839-[1840] 3 v. IaU; MeLewB; Nh; NUt; TCollSJ. 54158

----. ----. 3rd edition. New York: Mason, 1839-1840. 4 v. InGrD; MDBMP; NNMHi; MSCliM. 54159

----. ----. 3rd edition, revised. New York: Mason and Lane, 1839- 1841. 4 v. DLC; IaLamG; IaMvC; ICT; NN. 54160

----. ----. 3rd edition. New York: 1839-1842. 4 v. MoS. 54161

----. ----. 3rd edition, revised and corrected. New York: T. Mason and G. Lane, 1839-[1845] 4 v. CSansS; PCC; PHi; PPM; PU. 54162

----. Life of the Reverend free born Garrettson, compiled from his printed and manuscript journals, and other authentic documents. 4th edition revised. New York: T. Mason and G. Lane, 1839. CtY-D; GEU; InGrD; ScSpW; TMeC. 54163

----. An original church of Christ; or a scriptural vindication of the orders and powers of the ministry of the Methodist Episcopal Church. New York: T. Mason and G. Lane for the Methodist Episcopal Church...1839. 388 p. MPiB. 54164

[Banim, John] 1798-1842. The croppy. A tale. By the O'Hara family.... Philadelphia: E. L. Carey and A. Hart, 1839. 2 v. CtHT; DLC; InNd; OClJC; WU. 54165

Bank of Commerce in New York. Articles of association of the Bank of Commerce in New York, with the general banking laws of the state of New York [New York: 1839] 28 p. CtY; DLC; MH;

MH-BA; NNC. 54166

Bank of South Carolina, Charleston. Proceedings of the stockholders...held at their banking
house on Monday, July 2, 1839. Charleston:
printed by A. E. Miller, 1839. 8 p. ScHi. 54167

Bank of Tennessee, Nashville. Report...to the
General Assembly of Tennessee, October 9, 1839.
Nashville: J. Geo. Harris, printer, 1839. 56 p. T;
TNV. 54168

Banner of the cross. 1839-1852, 1854-1861.
Philadelphia: 1839-1861. 22 v. IEG; PHi; PP; PPL.
54169

The Baptist advocate. New York: 1839-1845. 3 v.
in 2. DLC; NRAB; PPULC. 54170

Baptists. Alabama. Muscle Shoals Association.
Minutes of the 20th annual Muscle Shoal Associa-
tion of Baptists, convened at Russel Valley Meet-
ing House, Franklin County, Alabama, on Friday,
September 20, 1839. Tuscumbia: printed at the
North Alabamian office, 1839. 8 p. KyLoS. 54171

----. ----. State Convention. Minutes of the 16th
anniversary of the Baptist State Convention, of
Alabama; held at Oakmulgee Meeting House,
Perry County, commencing on Saturday, Novem-
ber 9, 1839 [Tuscaloosa: 1839] 16 p. KyLoS; NHC-
S. 54172

----. ----. Tuscaloosa Association. Minutes of the
7th session of the Tuscaloosa Baptist Association
held at Hopewell Meeting House, Tuscaloosa
County, from the 5th to the 8th October, 1839.
Tuscaloosa: printed at the Independent Monitor
office, 1839. 8 p. NHC-S. 54173

----. ----. Union Association. Minutes of the
Union Association held at Beauleauh Meeting
House, Pickens County, Alabama, from the 21st
to the 23rd of September, 1839. Pickensville,
Alabama: Wm. D. Lyles and Company, 1839. 8 p.
ICU. 54174

----. Arkansas. Arkansas Association. Minutes
of the Baptist Association of Arkansas, held at Little Rock, September 13th and 14th, 1839 [n. p.:
1839?] 4 p. MoSM. 54175

----. Connecticut. Fairfield County Association.
Minutes of the second session of the Fairfield
County Baptist Association, held with the First

Baptist Church in Stanford, August 26th and 27th,
1839. Bridgeport, Conn.: Standard office, 1839. 16
p. NHC-S. 54176

----. ----. New London Baptist Association.
Minutes of 22nd anniversary of the New London
Baptist Association, held with the Baptist Church
in Lebanon, September 25th and 26th, 1839....
New London: Ebenezer Williams [1839?] 16 p.
MNtCA; NHC-S; PCA. 54177

----. Georgia. Georgia Association. Minutes of
the Georgia Baptist Association, held at Double
Branches, Lincoln County, Georgia, on the 11th,
12th and 14th days of October, 1839. Washington,
Georgia: printed by M. J. Kappel, at the office of
the Christian Index, 1839. 13 [2] p. NHC-S; NcD.
54178

----. Illinois. Blue River Association. Minutes of
the 7th annual meeting of the Blue River Association, of United Baptists, held with Salem Church,
Pike County, Illinois, August 23rd and days following, 1839. Jacksonville: printed by C. and R.
Goudy, 1839. 6, 2 p. ISB; NRCR-S. 54179

----. ----. North District Association. Minutes of
the 11th annual meeting of the North District Baptist Association, Friends to humanity, held with
the Salem Church, Greene County, Illinois, September 6th and days following, 1839. Jacksonville:
printed at Goudy's Job office, 1839. 10 p. ISB;
NRCR-S. 54180

----. ----. South District Association. Minutes of
the annual meeting of the South District Baptist
Association, Friends to Humanity, held with
Upper Silver Creek Church, Madison County, Illinois, commencing October 4, 1839. Chester, Illinois: Smith and Abbott, printers, 1839. 8 p. IAlS;
ISB; NRCR-S. 54181

----. ----. Springfield Association. Minutes of the
second annual meeting...held with the Baptist
Church in Diamond Grove, Morgan County, Illinois, commencing the 2nd of October, 1839.
Springfield: printed at the Journal office, 1839. 8
p. ISB. 54182

----. Indiana. General Association. Minutes of
the 7th, 16th, 17th, 22nd anniversary of the Indiana
Baptist General Association.... Indianapolis:
1839-1854. 4 v. CSmH; OCIWHi. 54183

----. ----. ----. Proceedings of the 7th anniversary

of the General Association of Baptists in Indiana, held at the Baptist meeting house in Delphi, on the 3rd, 4th and 5th days of October, 1839. Indianapolis: Stacy and Williams, 1839. 20 p. CSmH; ICU; MHi; OClWHi; PCA. 54184

----. Kentucky. Bethel Association. Minutes of the 15th Bethel Baptist Association, held at Pleasant Grove, Logan County, Ky., on the 21st, 22nd, and 23rd days of September, 1839.... Russellville: printed at the Advertiser office, 1839. 8 p. LNB. 54185

----. ----. General Association. Minutes of the first annual meeting of the General Association of Baptists in Kentucky, held at Bowling Green, commencing Saturday, September 29, 1838. Louisville: Penn and Eliot, printers, 1839. 40 p. MHi; PCA; ViRU. 54186

----. Maine. Bowdoinham Association. Minutes of the fifty-third anniversary of the Bowdoinham Association, holden at Leeds, September 24, 25, and 26, 1839. Hollowell: Glazier, Masters and Smith, 1839. 16 p. PCA. 54187

----. ----. Convention. Minutes of the Maine Baptist Convention, holden as Sedgwick...1839. Fifteenth anniversary. Brunswick: press of J. Griffin, 1839. 24 p. MeBa; MoSM; PCA. 54188

----. ----. Cumberland Association. Minutes of the 28th anniversary of the Cumberland Baptist Association, held at the meeting house of the Free Street Baptist Church, Portland, Maine, on August 28, 29, 1839. Portland: printed by Charles Day...1839. 12 p. MeHi; PCA. 54189

----. ----. Hancock Association. Minutes of the 5th anniversary of the Hancock Baptist Association, held in the Baptist meeting house at Eden, on September 26 and 27, 1839. Portland: printed by Charles Day, 1839. 12 p. PCA. 54190

----. ----. Kennebec Association. Minutes of the 10th anniversary of the Kennebec Baptist Association, held at the Union Meeting House, in Cornville, September 4 and 5, 1839, with a summary view of the churches. Hallowell: Glazier, Masters and Smith, 1839. 16 p. PCA. 54191

----. ----. Lincoln Association. Minutes of the Lincoln Association, held with the First Baptist Church in Jefferson, September 18, and 19, 1839. Thomaston: H. P. Coombs, printer, 1839. 15 p.

PCA. 54192

----. ----. Oxford Association. Minutes of the Oxford Baptist Association, held at Paris, September 18 and 19, 1839. Paris, Maine: G. W. Millett, printer, 1839. 8 p. M; PCA. 54193

----. ----. Washington Association. Minutes of the fifth anniversary of the Washington Baptist Association, held in the Baptist meeting house, in East Machias, on September 4, and 5, 1839. Calais, Maine: George Washburn, printer, 1839. 16 p. PCA. 54194

----. Maryland. Union Association. Minutes of the fourth meeting of the Maryland Baptist meeting house, Nanjemay, Maryland, October 3 and 4, 1839. Baltimore: Woods and Crane, 1839. 11 p. MiD-B; PCA; ViRU. 54195

----. Massachusetts. Berkshire Association. Minutes of the 12th anniversary of the Berkshire Baptist Association, held in the meeting house of the Baptist church, Tyringham, Mass., October 9 and 10, 1839. Lenox, Massachusetts: Charles Montague, printer, 1839. 12 p. MB; MPiB; PCA. 54196

----. ----. Berkshire County Association. Minutes of the 10th anniversary of the Berkshire County Baptist Association, and the first anniversary of the Berkshire County Bible Society, held in the Baptist meeting house in Otis, on October 11 and 12, 1839. Troy, New York: printed at Budget office, 1839. 18 p. MPiB. 54197

----. ----. Boston Association. The 28th anniversary of the Boston Baptist Association, held in the meeting house of the First Baptist Church in Woburn, September 18 and 19, 1839..... Boston: Press of John Putnam, 1839. 24 p. MiD-B; MoSM. 54198

----. ----. Franklin Association. Minutes of the Franklin County Baptist Association, held at the Baptist meeting house in Ashfield, Massachusetts, September 11 and 12, 1839. Greenfield, Mass.: Phelps and Ingersoll, printers, 1839. 8 p. PCA. 54199

----. ----. Old Colony Association. Minutes of the Old Colony Baptist Association, held with the Baptist Church in Foxboro; September 2 and 3, 1839. Boston: Press of Putnam and Hewes, 1839. 16 p. MNtcA; NRAB; PCA. 54200

----. ----. Salem Association. Minutes of the 12th anniversary of the Salem Baptist Association and the 27th anniversary of the Salem Bible Translation and Foreign Mission Society; held in the Baptist meeting house in Lynn, September 25 and 26, 1839. Lowell: Leonard Huntress, printer, 1839. 23 p. TxFwSB. 54201

----. ----. State Convention. Annual report of the Massachusetts Baptist Convention, presented by the board of directors at the 37th anniversary in Boston, May 30, 1839. Boston: William D. Ticknor, 1839. 36 p. PCA. 54202

----. ----. Sturbridge Association. Minutes of the Sturbridge Association, held with the Baptist Church in Wilbraham and Monson, August 23 and 29, 1839. Southbridge: printed by Edwin B. Carter, 1839. 9 p. MNtCA; PCA. 54203

----. ----. Worcester Association. Minutes of the Sabbath School Teachers Convention of the Worcester Baptist Association, held with the Baptist Church in Princeton, October 8, 1839. Worcester: printed by Spooner and Howland, 1839. 16 p. MWA. 54204

----. Mississippi. Mississippi Association. The 32nd anniversary of the Mississippi Baptist Association, held with the New Providence Church, Amite County, Miss., October 5th, 6th and 7th, 1839. 15 p. ICU; LNB; MBC; Ms-Ar. 54205

----. ----. South-western Convention. Proceedings of the convention of South-western Baptists, held at Columbus, Mississippi, on the 16th, 17th and 18th of May, 1839. Aberdeen: 1839. 14 p. MoSM; Ms-Ar. 54206

----. ----. State Convention. Proceedings of the third annual meeting of the convention of the Baptist Denomination of the state of Mississippi, held at Middleton, Carroll County, on the 24th, 25th, 27th and 28th of May, 1839. Matchez: printed by Newcomb and Lee, 1839. 20 p. DLC; ICN; ICU; MoSM; NHC-S. 54207

----. ----. Union Association. Minutes of the Union Baptist Association, held at Antioch Church, Warren County, Miss., on the 12th, 13th and 14th of October, 1839. Raymond: King and North, printers, 1839. 14 p. ICU; MBC. 54208

----. Missouri. Blue River Association. Minutes of the Blue River Association of Baptists met at the Big Sniabar Meeting House, Lafayette County Missouri on the third Saturday in September, 1838 and continued by adjournment until the Monday following, inclusive. Liberty: printed by the Western Star office, 1839. 3 p. MoLiWJ. 54209

----. New Hampshire. Dublin Association. Minutes of the 13th anniversary of the Dublin Baptist Association, held with the Baptist Church in Sullivan, September 4 and 5, 1839.... [New Hampshire] printed by J. and J. W. Prentiss, 1839. 16 p. PCA. 54210

----. -----. Meredith Association. Minutes of the 50th anniversary of the Meredith Baptist Association, held at Campton, on Wednesday and Thursday, September 11 and 12, 1839. Concord: printed at the Baptist Register office, 1839. 16 p. PCA. 54211

----. ----. State Convention. Proceedings of the New Hampshire Baptist State Convention, together with the New Hampshire branch of the N. B. Educational Society...and the Baptist Antislavery Society, at their annual meetings held at Claremont, October 22 and 23, 1839. Concord: printed at the Baptist Register office, 1839. 44 p. PCA. 54212

----. New Jersey. State Convention. Minutes of the 10th annual meeting of the New Jersey Baptist State Convention for missionary purposes; held at the meeting house of the First Newark Baptist Church, November 6 and 7, 1839. Trenton: printed by Phillips and Boswell, 1839. 32 p. PCA. 54213

----. ----. West New Jersey Association. Minutes of the 28th Anniversary of the New Jersey Baptist Association, held at Haddonfield, September 24, 25 and 26, 1839. Burlington: printed by J. L. Powell, 1839. 16 p. C; MiD-B; MoSM; PCA. 54214

----. New York. Black River Association. Minutes of the 30th anniversary of the Black River Baptist Association, convened at Adams-Centre, Jefferson County, New York, June 12 and 13, 1839; together with the circular and corresponding letters. Lowville: printed by A. W. Clark, 1839. 16 p. NRC-R; PCA. 54215

----. ----. Cattaraugus Association. Minutes of the 4th anniversary of the Cattaraugus Baptist Association, held with the church in Cuba, July 3rd and 4th, 1839 [Buffalo: Thomas and Company,

1839] 12 p. NHC-S; PCA. 54216

----. ----. Cayuga Association. Minutes of the 39th anniversary of the Cayuga Baptist Association, convened at Venice, Cayuga County, New York, September 19 and 20, 1839. Auburn: printed by Miller and Stow, 1839. 16 p. NHC-S; NRCR. 54217

----. ----. Education Society. Twenty-Second annual meeting of the Baptist Education Society of the state of New York; held at Hamilton, August 20, 1839. With the reports of the board, treasurer.... Utica: Bennett and Bright, 1839. 28 p. DLC; MB; MWA; NRC-R; TxFwSB. 54218

----. ----. Franklin Association. Minutes of the 28th anniversary...held at West Meredith, Delaware County, New York, June 28 and 29, 1839. Delhi: A. M. Paine, printer, 1839. 16 p. NRCR; PCA. 54219

----. ----. Genesee Association. Minutes of the 21st anniversary of the Genesee Baptist Association, held with the West Church in Middlebury June 18 and 19, 1839.... Perry, New York: Mitchell and Warren, printers, 1839. 12 p. MNtCA. 54220

----. ----. Holland Purchase Association. Minutes of the 24th anniversary of the Holland Purchase Baptist Association, held with the Washington St. Baptist Church, in Buffalo on the 10th and 11th of July, 1839. Buffalo: printed by Thomas and Company, 1839. NBu; NHC; PCA. 54221

----. ----. Hudson River Association. The 24th anniversary of the Hudson River Baptist Association, statement of belief held in the meeting house of the First Baptist Church, Troy, New York, June 18, 19 and 20, 1839. New York: printed by John Gray, 1839. 28 p. MoSM; PCA. 54222

----. ----. Missionary Convention. Proceedings of the 18th anniversary of the Baptist Missionary Convention of the state of New York, held at Saratoga Springs, October 16 and 17, 1839; with the reports of the board.... Utica: printed by Bennett and Bright, 1839. 44 p. PCA. 54223

----. ----. Monroe Association. Minutes of the 12th anniversary of the Monroe Baptist Association, held at the Second Baptist Meeting House, Parma, October 2nd and 3rd, 1839. Rochester: printed by Shepard and Strong, 1839. 10 p. ICU; NRCR; PCA. 54224

----. ----. New York Association. Minutes of the 49th anniversary of the New York Baptist Association, held at the meeting house of the North Beriah Baptist Church, New York, on May 28, 29, and 30, 1839. New York: printed by John Gray, 1839. 28 p. PCA. 54225

----. ----. Niagra Association. Reprint of the minutes of the Niagra Baptist Association convened in the First Baptist Church, Albion, June 12, 13, 1839. Lockport, N. Y.: printed originally by J. C. Bacon, 1839. 14 p. PCA. 54226

----. ----. Oneida Association. Minutes of the 19th annual meeting of the Oneida Baptist Association, held at Whitesboro, Oneida County, New York, on September 3rd and 4th, 1839. Utica, Press of Bennett and Bright, 1839. 16 p. NRC-R. 54227

----. ----. Rensselaerville Association. Minutes of the 41st anniversary of the Rensselaerville Baptist Association, held with the Rensselaerville and Bern Church, at Rensselaerville, September 18 and 19, 1839. Lexington, New York: printed by the L. L. Hill, Christian Repository office, 1839. 12 p. PCA. 54228

----. ----. Saratoga Association. The 35th anniversary of the Saratoga Baptist Association, held in the meeting house of the Baptist Church, in Stillwater, June 25, 26 and 27, 1839. Saratoga Springs: G. M. Davison, printer, 1839. 24 p. MoSM. 54229

----. ----. Union Association. Minutes of the 29th anniversary of the Union Baptist Association, held with the Baptist Church in Fishkill, Shenandoah, New York, September 4th and 5th, 1839. Peekskill: printed by Samuel Huestis [1839] 16 p. PCA. 54230

----. ----. Worcester Association. Minutes of the 9th anniversary of the Worcester Baptist Association, held in the meeting house of the Baptist Church, Maryland, Otsego County, New York, July 3 and 4, 1839. Lexington, N. Y.: printed at the Christian Repository office, 1839. 16 p. NRCR; PCA. 54231

----. Ohio. Cleveland or Rocky River Association. Minutes of the 8th anniversary of the Rocky River Baptist Association, held at Strongville, Cuyahoga County, Ohio, June 19th and 20th, 1839: Together with their corresponding letter.

Cleveland: Penniman and Aikin, printers, 1839. 15 p. CSmH. 54232

----. ----. Huron Baptist Association. Minutes of the 18th anniversary of the Huron Baptist Association, held by appointment at Monroeville, Huron County, Ohio, October 2nd and 3rd, 1839. Norwalk, Ohio: S. and C. A. Preston, printers, 1839. 16 p. OClWHi. 54233

----. ----. Lorain Baptist Association. Minutes of the First anniversary of the Lorain Baptist Association, held at Elyria, Lorain County, Ohio, June 26 and 27, 1839. Together with their circular and corresponding letter. Elyria, Ohio: printed by A. Burrell, 1839. 12 p. OCl; WHi. 54234

----. ----. Maumee River Association. Minutes of the 5th anniversary of the Sandusky River Baptist Association, held with the Jackson and Liberty Church; September 13 and 14, 1839. Findlay, Ohio: J. Rosenberg, printer, 1839. 8 p. OClWHi. 54235

----. ----. Meigs Creek Association. Minutes of the 14th anniversary of the Meigs' Creek Baptist Association, held by appointment , with the Blue Rock Church, August, 1939. Zanesville, Ohio: printed by J. Glessner, 1839. 14 p. PCA. 54236

----. ----. Miami Association. Minutes of the Miami Association of Regular Baptists, held with the East Baptist Church, at Lebanon. September 4th and 5th, 1839. Middletown: printed by Gallagher and Company, 1839. 8 p. OClWHi; PCA. 54237

----. ----. Salem Association. Minutes of the Salem Baptist Association held by appointment with the Troy Church, Athens County, Ohio, September 21, 22, and 23, 1839. Gallipolis: Vance and Nash, printers, 1838. 7 p. OClWHi. 54238

----. ----. Scioto Association. Minutes of the Scioto Baptist Association, held by appointment with the Refugee Church, Fairfield County, Ohio, Lancaster: printed by C. H. Brough, 1839. 7 p. OClWHi. 54239

----. ----. Zoar Regular Association. Minutes of the 13th anniversary of the Regular Baptist Association held with the Stillwater Church, Flushing Township, Belmont County, Ohio, August 24, 25 and 26, 1839. St. Clairsville, Ohio: printed at the office of Gill, Heaton and Company, 1839. 16 p.

OClWHi. 54240

----. ----. Pennsylvania. Abington Association. Minutes of the 32nd anniversary of the Abington Baptist Association, held by appointment in the Baptist meeting house, in Damascus, Wayne County, Pa., September 4 and 5, 1839. Bethany, Pa.: Richard Nugent, printer, 1839. 12 p. PCA. 54241

----. ----. Bradford Association. Minutes of the 5th annual session of the Bradford Baptist Association, held by appointment with the Baptist Church in East Sullivan, on June 5th and 6th, 1839. Elmira, New York: Pratt and Bearsley, printers, 1839. 20 p. PCA. 54242

----. ----. Bridgewater Association. Minutes of the Bridgewater Baptist Association, at their 14th anniversary, held by appointment in the Baptist meeting house at Montrose, Susquehanna County, Pa., August 28 and 29, 1839. Montrose: printed by Post and Worden, 1839. 11 p. PCA. 54243

----. ----. Central Union Association. Minutes of the 7th annual session of the Central Union Association of Independent Baptist Churches, held in the meeting house of the Lower Dublin Church, Philadelphia County, Pa., May 26 and 29, 1839. Burlington, N. J.: printed by Powell and George, 1839. 15 p. PCA. 54244

----. ----. Clarion Association. Minutes of the second anniversary of the Clarion Baptist Association, held with the Zion Church, Clarion County, Pennsylvania, on the 18th and 19th days of October, 1839. Indiana, Pa.: printed at the Jefferson Democrat office, 1839. 8 p. NRAB; PCA. 54245

----. ----. French Creek Association. Minutes of the 16th anniversary of the French Creek Baptist Association, held with the Church in Conneautville, Crawford County, Pa., September 18 and 19, 1839. Conneaut, Pa.: printed at the office of the Gazette [1839] 12 p. PCA. 54246

----. ----. Phildelphia Association. Minutes of the 132nd anniversary of the Philadelphia Baptist Association, held by appointment in the meeting house of the Second Baptist Church, Philadelphia, October 2, 1839. Philadelphia: J. Sharp, 1839. 28 p. MiD-B; PCA. 54247

----. ----. Pittsburgh Association. Pittsburgh Baptist Association. Annual report. Pittsburgh [1839-] V. 1-. PPC; PPi. 54248

----. ----. State Annual. Minutes of the second anniversary of the Pennsylvania Baptist Convention, held in the meeting house of the First Baptist Church, April 25 and 26, 1839. with the annual report of the board. Philadelphia: printed by William F. Rackcliff, 1839. 17 p. PCA. 54249

----. Rhode Island. Warren Association. Minutes of the Warren Baptist Association, held with the Baptist Church in Westerly, R. I., September 11 and 12, 1839. Providence: H. H. Brown, printer, 1839. 16 p. MNtCA; PCA; RHi; RPB. 54250

----. South Carolina. Reedy River Association. Minutes...Greenville, S. C.: Enterprise Book and Job Press, Hoyt and Keys [etc.] 1839-1939. 10 v. ScU. 54251

----. Tennessee. Big Hatchie Association. Minutes of the Big Hatchie Baptist Association, held with Philadelphia Church, Fayette County, Tennessee, commencing on Saturday before the fourth Lord's day in October, 1839. Bolivar, Tennessee: printed at the Sentinel office, 1839. 5 p. MoSM. 54252

----. ----. Concord Association. Minutes of the 29th annual meeting of the Concord Association of United Baptists, held at Union Meeting House, Wilson County, Tennessee, and protracted from August 31-September 5, 1839. Nashville: B. R. M'Kennie, printer, Whig and Steam Press, 1839. 8 p. T. 54253

----. ----. Duck River Association. Minutes of the Duck River Association of Baptists, met and convened at Big Flat Creek Church, Bedford County, Tennessee, on Saturday, before the first sunday in September, 1839 and following days.... Shelbyville, Tennessee: printed at the Advocate office, 1839. 6 p. MsCliBHi. 54254

----. ----. Nolachucky Association. Minutes of the Nolachucky Association of Baptists, convened at Concord Meeting House, Greene County, East Tennessee, September 4, 1839, and following days. Rogersville: East Tennesseean office, S. C. Murphey, printer, 1839 4 p. NHC-S. 54255

----. ----. State Convention. Proceedings of the 6th annual session of the Baptist Church in Nashville. October 12-16, 1839. Nashville: B. R.

M'Kennie, printer, 1839. 30 p. ICU; NHC-S; T. 54256

----. Vermont. Addison County Association. Minutes of the 6th anniversary of the Addison County Baptist Association, held with the Baptist Church in Middlebury, September 25 and 26, 1839. Brandon, Vt.: Vermont Telegraph office, 1839. 8. PCA; VtMidSM. 54257

----. Virginia. Albemorle Assoication. Minutes of the Albemarle Baptist Associaton, held at Mount Shiloh M. H., Nelson County, Va., on the 17, 18 and 19 of August, 1839. Richmond: printed by Wm. Sands, at the office of the Religious Herald, 1839. 7 p. ViRu. 54258

----. ----. Concord Associaton. Minutes of the Concord Baptist Association, held at Reedy Creek M. H., Brunswick County , Va., on the 17, 18, and 19 of August, 1839. Richmond: printed by Wm. Sands, at the office of the Religious Herald, 1839. 19 p. ViRu. 54259

----. ----. Dover Association. Minutes of the Dover Baptist Association: convened at Bethel M. H., Elizabeth City County, Va., on October 12-14, 1839. Richmond: printed by Wm. Sands, 1839. 14 p. ViRu. 54260

----. ----. Roanoke District Association. Minutes of the Roanoke District Association, held at Arbor Meeting House, Halifax County, August 3, 4, and 5, 1839. Danville, Va.: printed at the Reporter office, 1839. 8 p. ViRu. 54261

----. ----. Shiloh Association. Minutes of the Shiloh Baptist Association, held at Beth-Car M. H. Madison County, Va., on the 29th and 30th of August, 1839. Richmond: printed by Wm. Sands at the office of the Religious Herald, 1839. 12 p. ViRu. 54262

----. Wisconsin [territory] Central Association. Minutes of the first anniversary of the First Baptist Association of Central Wisconsin, held with the Baptist Church at Prairie Village, October 23, 1839. Milwaukee: Harrison Reed, printer, 1839. 8 p. WHi. 54263

Bar meeting to the memory of James H. Perkins. Cincinnati: Clarke, 1839. 20 p. OCIWHi. 54264

Barang hikajet deri dalam kitab Allah. Tjaritera akan kadjadian langit dan boemi. Tertara di

Batavia, kampong parapattan, 1839 [51] p. MWA.
54265

Barbaroux, Charles Oge, 1792-1867. L'histoire
des etots unis D'Amerique. Par C. O. Barbaroux,
avocat, etc.... Philadelphia: Hogan and
Thompson, 1839. 304 p. Ct; LNB; MeBa; MLy;
RLa. 54266

Barbauld, Anna Letitia [Aiken] 1743-1825.
Hymns in prose for children. Worcester: C. A.
Mirick, 1839. 63 p. MWA. 54267

----. Lessons for children. Boston: W. D. Ticknor, 1839. MH. 54268

Barber, Edward Downing, 1806-1855. An oration, delivered before the Democrats of
Washington County, at Montpelier, on the 4th of
July, 1839 [Montpelier] printed at the Patriot office, 1839. 18 p. CSmH; DLC; MBC; PHi; VtHi.
54269

Barber, John Warner, 1798-1885. Historical col-
lections, being a general collection of interesting
facts, traditions, biographical sketches, anecdotes, etc., relating to the history and antiquities
of every town in Massachusetts, with geographical
descriptions.... Worcester: Dorr, Howland and
Company, 1839. 624 p. CoD; DLC; MeBa; MWA;
RPB. 54270

Barefoot, Isaac. Collection of psalms and hymns
in the Mohawk language, for the use of the six nation Indians. Hamilton: 1839? 80 p. DLC; MBC.
54271

Barker, J. The gospel triumphant or a defence of
Christianity against system of R. Owen. Newcastle: 1839. MB. 54272

Barker, J. Jr. A poem pronounced before the
Ciceronean Club and other citizens of Tus-
caloosa, on July 4, 1839. Tuscaloosa: printed by M.
D. J. Slade, 1839. 33 p. A-Ar; N; NcD. 54273

[Barker, Matthew Henry] 1790-1846. Hamilton
King; or the smuggler and the dwarf, by the old
sailor, author of "Tough yarns".... Philadelphia:
Lea and Blanchard, 1839. 2 v. FTU; MH; MoWg;
NN; RPB. 54274

----. Naval foundling. Philadelphia: Lea and
Blanchard, 1839. 2 v. IaWel; NBuG. 54275

Barlow, William. Character and reward of the
just man. A funeral discourse, commemorative of
the life and virtues of the late Hon. Stephen Van
Rensselaer. Delivered at Ogdensburgh, February
17, 1839. Albany: printed by Packard, Van Benthuysen and Company, 1839. 47 p. ICU; MB; NjR;
PHi; WHi. 54276

Barnard, Daniel Dewey, 1797-1861. An address
delivered at Amherst, before the literary societies
of Amherst College, August 27, 1839. Albany:
printed by Hoffman and White, 1839. 63 p.
CoCsC; DLC; MH; NjR; PPL. 54277

----. An address delivered at Rochester, before
the Rochester Athenaeum and Young Men's Associaton, July 18, 1839. Albany: printed by Hoffman and White, 1839. 63 p. MB; NIC; NRHi.
54278

----. A discourse of the life, services and character of Stephen Van Rensselaer; delivered before
the Albany Institute, April 15, 1839.... Albany:
printed by Hoffman and White, 1839. 144 p.
CSmH; DLC; MH-AH; PPA; RPB. 54279

----. ----. 70 p. CSmH; DLC; MiD; OU; PHi.
54280

----. Speech of Mr. Barnard, of New York; in
relation to the contest for seats from the state of
New Jersey: delivered before the representatives
of the 26th congress, December 4, 1839.
Washington: printed by Gales and Seaton, 1839.
11 p. MB; MH; MiD- B; MWA. 54281

----. Speech...on the proposition to refuse the
oath to five members returned from New Jersey:
delivered before the representatives of the 26th
congress, December 18, 1839. Washington:
printed by Gales and Seaton, 1839. 15 p. Ct; CtY;
CtHWatk; MB; MWA. 54282

Barnes, Albert, 1798-1870. A manual of prayer:
designed to assist Christians in learning the subjects and modes of devotion.... 3rd edition.
Philadelphia and Boston: 1839. 306 p. CtY; CU;
MDeeP; MWA; PLT. 54283

----. The nature of the Gospel: a sermon
preached...1839, at installation of the Rev. S. M.
Sparks.... Pittsburgh, Jaynes, 1839. 24 p. MBC;
OClWHi; PPPrHi. 54284

----. Questions on the historical books of the New

Testament, designed for Bible classes and sunday schools. New York: Robinson and Franklin, 1839. 128 p. MB; MH; ScCoT; VtMidSM. 54285

Barnes, William. Modern geography; Being entirely a new plan, on the classification system.... Adopted to the use of classes and private learners. Troy: J. L. Stevenson, 1839. DLC; MH. 54286

Barnett, John, 1802-1890. The spot where I was born. A ballad...arranged for the guitar by F. Blanchor. Philadelphia: Willig, 1839. 2 p. MB. 54287

Barnett's country almanac for 1840. Charleston, S. C.: W. N. Barnett [1839] MWA. 54288

Barr, John. Barr's complete index and concise dictionary of the Holy Bible...revised from the 3rd Glasgow edition, by the editors. New York: published by T. Mason and G. Lane, 1839. 210 p. NNMHi. 54289

Barr, John T. The recollections of a minister; or sketches drawn from life and character.... New York: T. Mason and G. Lane, 1839. 92 p. N. 54290

Barrow, John, 1764-1848. Description of Pitcairns Island and its inhabitants, with an authentic account of the meeting of the ship Bounty. New York: Harper and Brother, 1839. 303 p. MeB; MiD; PPL; TxGR. 54291

----. A memoir of the life of Peter the Great. New York: Harper and Brothers, 1839. 320 p. NNUT; NRU; PPF; ScDuE; TxGR. 54292

Barry, John A. The Barry case. A review of, and strictures on the opinion of his Honor the Chancellor of the state of New York, delivered August 26, 1839, in the late case of the people, ex-relatione John A. Barry versus Thomas R. Mercein.... New York: Appleton and Company, 1839. 64 p. Ct; DLC; MdHi; PPULC; RWe. 54293

Bartlett, John Stephen, d. 1840. Report of the evidence in the case of John Stephen Bartlett...versus the Massachusetts Medical Society, as given before a committee of the legislature at the session of 1839.... Boston: Dutton and Wentworth, state printers, 1839. 55 p. DSG; MBC; MiD-B; Nh; RPB. 54294

Bartlett [John Stephen] and Peirson. Memorial and remonstrance relating to Massachusetts Medical Society, 1839. 15 p. DNLM; DSG; MBC; MH-L. 54295

Bartlett, Josiah. A memoir of the Hon. Josiah Bartlett, of Stratham, N. H., who died April 16, 1838, aged seventy years. Gilmanton, New Hampshire: Alfred Prescott, 1839. 7 p. DLC; MH; Nh-Hi; OCGHM. 54296

Bartlett, Montgomery Robert. The juvenile orator; or every scholar's book. Being a series of simple rules in the art of reading, showing the proper application of the principal modulations of the voice to the enunciation of every species of sentence, with appropriate exercises in prose and verse. Philadelphia: R. W. Desilver, 1839. 216 p. DLC; MH; PU; PWW. 54297

Bartlett, William Holms Chambers, 1804-1893. An elementary treatise on optics, designed for the use of the cadets of the United States Military Academy.... New York: Wiley and Putnam, 1839. 231 p. KyLo; MoSU; PU; RPB; ViU. 54298

Bartol, Cyrus Augustus, 1813-1900. A discourse delivered in the West Church in Boston, March 3, 1839. Boston: Freeman and Bolles, printers, 1839. 14 p. CtY; ICMe; MWA; NNUT; PPL. 54299

----. [Sermons] Boston: 1839-1882. CBPac; MB. 54300

Barton, Charles Crillon, d. 1851. Manifest of the charges preferred to the navy department...against J. D. Elliott...for unlawful conduct while commodore of the late Mediterranean squadron; and a refutation of the recrimination raised by that officer [Philadelphia?] 1839. 46 p. DLC; MB; MWA; PHi; PP. 54301

Bassett, George W. A thanksgiving sermon, delivered at the Brick Church in West Bloomfield, on November 28, 1839. Rochester: Masrshall and Wells, printers, 1839. 19 p. ICP; IU; ICMcC. 54302

Battles, sieges and sea fights recorded in history from the time of Alexander the Great to the present day. Watertown: Knowlton and Rice, 1839. NRMA. 54303

Baxley, Henry Willis, 1803-1876. Introductory lecture, delivered by H. Willis Baxley, before the medical class of the University of Pennsylvania. Baltimore: John D. Toy, printer, 1839. 29 p. DLC; DNLM; MdBM; MdHi. 54304

Baxter, Richard, 1615-1691. Duties and responsibilities of the pastoral office being an abridgement of the reformed pastor. Philadelphia: William S. Martien, 1839. 233 p. ABBS; NjPT; PAtM; TxBrdD; ViRut. 54305

----. Die ewige ruhe der heligen. New York: Amerikanischen Tractat Gesellschaft, 1839. 480 p. ODaB. 54306

----. The life of Rev. Richard Baxter. Chiefly compiled from his own writings. New York: American Tract Society [1839?] 144 p. NNUT. 54307

----. The reformed pastor; showing the nature of the pastoral work. Abridged by Thomas Rutherford. New York: J. Collord, printer, 1839. 298 p. IaFayU; GEU-T; ODW; TNT; WWdeps. 54308

----. The saints everlasting rest. Abridged by Benjamin Fawcett. Boston: Gould, Kendall and Lincoln, 1839. 320 p. CtY; KyLoS; MH; NoRSh; ScCliP. 54309

Bay State Democrat. Established August 31, 1839. Boston: 1839. CtY; NN. 54310

Bayard, James. Brief exposition of the Constitution of the United States; with an appendix, containing the Declaration of Independence, and the Articles of Confederation, and a copious index.... Philadelphia: Hogan and Thompson, 1839. 178 p. CtMW; ILM; IU; ScOrC; WHi. 54311

Bayly, Mrs. Thomas Haynes. I cannot dance tonight. Cincinnati: Peters, 1839. 2 p. MB. 54312

Baynes, J. W. Alfred Montrose: or the way I should go. Boston: 1839. 153 p. DLC; MWA. 54313

The Beacon. Rhode Island temperance tale. By a gentleman of Providence. Founded on fact. Providence: B. T. Albro, printer, 1839. 35 p. DLC; NN; RPB. 54314

Beaconsfield, Benjamin Disraeli, 1804-1881. The works of Disraeli the younger.... Philadelphia: E. L. Carey and A. Hart, 1839. 838 p. DLC; MB; NjP; NNF; ScCMu. 54315

Beardsley, Eben Edwards. A historical sermon, delivered in St. Peter's Church, Cheshire...1839; it being the last sunday on which devine service was performed in the old church.... Hartford: Case, Tiffany and Company, 1839. 16 p. CtSoP; MWA; Nh; NjR; RPB. 54316

Beattie, W. D. Treatise on arithmetic, for common schools and academies. 2nd edition. New York: A. M. Common School Union, 1839. 229 p. IaHi. 54317

Beauleauh, Alabama. Union Association. See Baptists. Alabama. Union Association.
Beaumont, Joseph, 1764-1837. Memoirs of Mrs. Mary Tatham late of Nottingham. New York: T. Mason and G. Lane, 1839. 322 p. CtMW; IaFayU; IEG; RPB; TxGR. 54318

Beaver Meadow Railroad and Coal Company. Report of the board of directors to the stockholders at a special meeting, August 15, 1839, together with proceedings of the meeting, and bylaws enacted. Philadelphia: 1839. MH-BA; PHi; PPL. 54319

Beck, John Brodhead, 1794-1851. Valedictory address, to the students in medicine of the college of physicians and surgeons of the University of the state of New York, delivered, February 28, 1839. 24 p. DLC; MB; MdBM; NNC; PPL. 54320

Beck, Theodoric Romeyn, 1791-1855. Statistics of the medical colleges of the United States. From the transactions of the Medical Society of the state of New York. Albany: 1839. 64 p. MBM; MH-AH; NN; NNN; OC. 54321

----. ----. Albany: J. Munsell, 1839. 12 p. CtY; DLC; MHi; NN; NNC. 54322

Beck, William. Money and banking, or their nature and effects considered...by a citizen of Ohio. Cincinnati: W. Beck, 1839. 212 p. IU; LU; MB; PHi; WU. 54323

Bedel, Gregory Townsend, 1793-1834. It is well; or faith's estimate of afflictions. altered from original work of Rev. John Hill. Rector of St. Andrew's Church, Philadelphia. Philadelphia: Henry Perkins, 1839. 109 p. NSchU. 54324

----. "Pay thy vows," a pastoral address subsequent to confirmation. By the late G. T. Thomas Latimer, Bedell.... Philadelphia: 1839. NNG. 54325

Bedford, Gunning Samuel, 1806-1870. Introductory lecture before the Albany Medical College, delivered October 1, 1839.... Albany: printed by J. Munsell, 1839. CtY; DLC; MH-M; NjR; PPL-R. 54326

Beethoven, Ludwig Van, 1770-1827. Fidelio; or cnstancy rewarded. An opera, in three acts. As performed at the Park theatre. The music by L. Van Beethoven. New York: H. Kimber, and Company, 1839. 30 p. MB; MH; MWA; PU; TxU. 54327

----. Songs, duetts, chorusses, etc., of Fidelio; an opera in three acts as performed at the Park theatre. Music by L. Van Beethoven. New York: J. C. House, 1839. 24 p. MH. 54328

Belcher, Joseph. Interesting narratives from sacred volumes,
illustrated and improved from the 2nd London edition. New York: Robert Carter, 1839. 284 p. GDecCT; ICP; NjPT; NR. 54329

Bell, ? Dr. Bell's lessons on the human frame, designed for schools, families.... Philadelphia: 1839. 158 p. CtHWatk; IaU; MBC; MBM; MDBS. 54330

[Bell, Charles Henry] 1823-1893. Life of William M. Richardson, Late Chief Justice of the Supreme Court in New Hampshire. Concord: Israel S. Boyd and William White, 1839. 90 p. DLC; MWA; Nh-Hi; OClWHi; WHi. 54331

Bell, Henry Glassford. Life of Mary, Queen of Scots. Harper's stereotype edition. New York: Harper and Brothers, 1839. 2 v. InCW; MiD; MPeaI; TxGR. 54332

Bell, John. Electric journal of medicine. v. 3. Haswell, Barrington and Haswell. New Orleans: John J. Haswell and Company, 1839. 468 p. MWHi. 54333

Bellows, Henry Whitney, 1814-1882. Respectability, or holiness. Sermon delivered...in Boston, Sunday evening, December 9, 1838. Boston: Weeks, Jordan and Company, 1839. 21 p. ICMe; MHi; MiD-B; MWA; RPB. 54334

Belmont County Agricultural Society. First report...to the chairman of the committee on agriculture of the House of Representatives. n. p.: 1839. 2 p. OClWHi. 54335

Beman, Nathan Sydney Smith. The intellectual position of our country, an introductory lecture delivered before the Young Men's Association for Mutual Improvement, in the city of Troy, December 10, 1839. Troy: N. Tuttle, 1839. 23 p. CtY; MBC; MnHi; NjR; NN. 54336

Benjamin, Asher, 1773-1845. Architect, or practical house carpenter...a...development of the Grecian order of architecture. 6th edition. Boston: 1839. 119 p. IaB; MnM; NcD. 54337

----. The builder's guide, illustrated by sixty-six engravings, which exhibit the orders of architecture and other elements of the art. Designed for the use of builders, particularly of carpenters and joiners. Boston: Perkins and Marvin, 1839. 83 p. DLC; ICRL; KEmT; MiU. 54338

----. Practice of architecture.... 4th edition. Boston: published by the author...1839. 116 p. DAIA; ICA-B; InAnd; PPULC. 54339

Bennett, James Arlington. The American system of practical book-keeping...exemplified in one set of books kept by double entry, embracing five different methods of keeping a journal. 19th edition. New York: Collins, Keese and Company, 1839. 104 p. InCW; MH; NjP; ODW. 54340

Bent, N. T. The signs of the times...a sermon, preached in St. Paul's Church, Philadelphia on November 17, 1839. Published by request. Philadelphia: printed by William Stavely and Company [1839] 22 p. ICMe; MB; MWA; NCH; PHi. 54341

Bentley, Rensselaer. Pictorial spelling book. New York: Sheldon and Company [1839] MB; NbU. 54342

Benton, Calvin. A discourse on Christian baptism; preached in the Baptist meeting house, Waldoborough, August 11, 1839. By Calvin Benton, professor of Hebrew and Biblical theology in the Thomaston Theological Institution. Published by request. Waldoboro': G. W. and F. W. Nichols, 1839. 47 p. CBPSR. 54343

Benton, Thomas Hart, 1782-1858. Remarks of Mr. Benton, of Missouri, on his motion for leave to introduce a bill for the repeal of the salt duties and fishing bounties; and in reply [to] Mr. Davis of Massachusetts. Delivered in the Senate of the United States, January, 1839. Washington: Blair and Rives, 1839. 22 p. DLC; MB; MH; NNC; OClWHi. 54344

----. Speech on the graduation bill and in reply to Mr. Clay's attack upon General Jackson; delivered in the Senate, January 4, 1839. Washington: Blair and Rives, 1839. 8 p. ICN; NcU; OCHP; PHi; TxU. 54345

Berg, Joseph Frederick, 1812-1871. The saint's harp: a collection of hymns and spiritual songs, adapted to prayer and social meetings, and arranged by J. F. Berg. Philadelphia: Lippincott, 1839. 266 p. PPPrHi; PPULC. 54346

Bernays, Adolphus. Compendious German grammar with a dictionary of prefexes and affixes.... Philadelphia: 1839. MB. 54347

Berry, Lucien W. Correspondences on baptism [Indianapolis?] W. Emmons, 1839. 36 p. RPB. 54348

. The deformer deformed; or corruption exposed. Being an address to the people of Noblesville; to which is prefixed a correct copy of the letter published by F. W. Emmons. Indianapolis: Stacy and Williams, 1839. 40 p. In. 54349

Bethune, George Washington, 1805-1862. The fruit of the spirit. Philadelphia: Harrison Hall, 1839. 210 p. InCW; MH-AH; NNUT; OO; PPA. 54350

----. ----. 2nd edition. Philadelphia: J. Whetham, 1839. 210 p. CtMW; MoSpD; NbCrD; PU; TWcW. 54351

----. True glory. A sermon preached before the Third Reformed Dutch Church of Philadelphia, February 3, 1839. on the occasion of the death of Stephen Van Rensselaer. Philadelphia: printed by John C. Clark, 1839. 24 p. CtY; MBC; MH; NIC; PPA. 54352

Bethune, Joanna [Graham] 1770-1860. The life of Mrs. Isabella Graham. New York: Taylor, 1839. DLC; MWiW; Nh-Hi; OCl; WHi. 54353

Betts, Samuel Rossiter, 1786-1868. A summary of practice in instance, revenue and prize causes in the admiralty courts of the United States for the southern district of New York, and also on appeal to the Supreme Court. New York: Halstead and Voorhies, 1839. 214 p. DLC; IU; MH; PPULC; WaU-L. 54354

Beveridge, William, 1637-1708. The advantage of frequent communion.... New York: 1839. 18 p. MB. 54355

----. The great necessity and advantage of public prayer.... New York: 1839. 7 p. MB. 54356

----. Private thoughts upon religion, and a christian life. In two parts. New York: Robert Carter, 1839. 325 p. MdBD; MLow; NjPT. 54357

Beverly, Robert Mackenzie, 1798-1868. Heresy of a human priesthood, traced in letters on the present state of the visible church of Christ. New York: 1839. MdBP. 54358

Beyle, Marie Henri, 1783-1842. The life of Haydn, in a series of letters written at Vienna.... Boston: J. H. Wilkins and R. B. Carter, Philadelphia: Thomas, Cowperthwait and Company, 1839. 389 p. CtMW; DeWi; MBBC; PU; TxU. 54359

Bianchi and Son, Paris. Catalogue.... New York. G. F. Nesbitt, 1839. 23 p. DLC. 54360

Bible. The Acts of the Apostles. Translated into the Chocktaw language. Chisus Kilaist. Boston: printed for the American Board of Commissioners for Foreign Missions, Crocker and Brewster, 1839. 165 p. MBAt; MH. 54361

----. Die Bibel. 5th edition. New York: A. B. S., 1839. PPeSchw. 54362

----. Die Bibel ober die ganze Heilige Schrift, Alten und Neuen Testaments.... New York: Amerikanischen Bibel Gesellschaft, 1839. 1050 p. PReaAT. 54363

----. ----. mit zugabe des dritten buchs der Maccabaer.... Philadelphia: George W. Mentz und Sohn, 1839. 2 pts. in 1. PPCS. 54364

----. ----. 828, 288 p. MH; PHi. 54365

----. ----. 827, 272 p. PReaHi. 54366

----. ----. nach Dr. Martin Luther's Uebersetzung. 12th edition. New York: Amerikanische Bebelgesellschaft, 1839. 828, 272 p. MBU- A; MdW; OCH. 54367

----. ----. 12. Aufl. Philadelphia: George W.

Mentz und Sohn, 1839. 972, 320 p. PLatS. 54368

----. The Bible reader; being a new selection of reading lessons from the Holy Scriptures, for the use of schools and families. Boston: the author, 1839. 283 p. MB; MBAt; MH; NN. 54369

----. The book of Psalms, translated out of the original Hebrew and with the former translations diligently compared and revised. New York: American Bible Society, 1839. 112 p. KWiU; MB. 54370

----. Comprehensive Bible. 3rd edition, corrected. New York: Robinson and Franklin, 1839. ViW. 54371

----. The comprehensive comentary of the Holy Bible; containing the text according to the authorized version; with marginal references; Matthew Henry's connentary, condensed but retaining the most useful thoughts; the practical observations of Rev. Thomas scott.... Brattleboro: 1839. 5 v. NcD. 54372

----. The comprehensive commentary of the Holy Bible. Edited by Rev. William Jenks.... Brattleboro, Vt.: Brattleboro Typographic Company, 1839. 924 p. ICP; NcRSh; TxShA. 54373

----. The Cottage Bible, and family expositor; containing the Old and New Testaments, with practical expositions and explanatory notes, by Thomas Williams; to which are added, the references and marginal readings of the Polyglott Bible...complete in 2 volumes. New York: Robinson, Pratt and Company, 1839. 2 v. WM. 54374

----. English Bible. Philadelphia: 1839. 681, 186 p. IaDuCM. 54375

----. The English version of the Polyglott Bible, containing the Old and New Testaments, with the marginal readings; together with a copious and original selection of references to parallel and illustrative passages exhibited in a manner hitherto unattempted. Concord, N. H.: Roby, Kimball and Merrill, 1839. 587, 189 p. DLC; MB; NBu-T; NNC. 54376

----. ----. Philadelphia: R. P. Desilver, 1839. 981 p. NRU. 54377

----. ----. Philadelphia: Thomas, Cowperthwait and Company, 1839. 597, 190 p. KyLoP; MB; NjP;

OMC. 54378

----. Explanatory notes upon the New Testament. By John Wesley. New York: T. Mason and G. Lane, 1839. 734 p. CBPSR; KWS; NcD; NcGC; NjMD. 54379

----. Extracts from Genesis and the Psalms, with the third chapter of Proverbs and the third chapter of Daniel, in the Dacota language. Translated from the French Bible, by Joseph Renville, Sr. Compared with other translations by Thomas S. Williamson. Cincinnati: 1839. 72 p. InIH; MdBD; MHi; NN; WBeloC. 54380

----. Extracts from the Gospels of Matthew, Luke and John, from the Acts of the Apostles, and from the First Epistle of John, in the language of the Dacota or Sioux Indians. Translated from the French, as published by the American Bible Society. By Joseph Renville, Sr., Thomas S. Williamson. Cincinnati: Kendall and Henry, printers, 1839. 47 p. MnHi; IaDuMtC; MHi. 54381

----. The four Gospels; with notes, chiefly explanatory; designed for teachers in sabbath schools and Bible classes, and as an aid to family instruction. By Henry J. Ripley.... 4th edition. Boston: Gould, Kendall and Lincoln, Utica: Bennett and Bright, 1839. 2 v. FJC; TNT. 54382

----. ----. 5th edition. Boston; Gould, Kendall and Lincoln, etc., etc., 1839. 2v. in 1. ICU. 54383

----. The gospels according to Mark, and extracts from some other books of the New Testament, in the language of the Dakotas, translated from th French by Joseph Renville, Sr. Written and prepared for the press by Thomas S. Williamson, M. D. Published for the American Board of Commissioners for Foreign Missions. Cincinnati: Kendall and Henry, printers, 1839. 96 p. MnHi; WHi. 54384

----. A harmony of the four gospels. Founded on the arrangement of the Harmonia evangelica, by the Rev. E. Greswell, with the practical reflections of Dr. Doddridge. Designed for the use of families and schools and for private edification. By the Rev. E. Bickersteth. Philadelphia: Hooker and Claxton, 1839. 420 p. IEG; NbOP; NjPT; PU; Tx-GeoS. 54385

----. A harmony of the Gospels in Greek, in the general order of Le Clerc and Newcome, with

Newcome's notes. Printed from the text and with various readings of Knapp. The whole revised and the Greek text newly arranged, by Edward Robinson, D. D. Andover: Gould, Newman and Company, 1839. 328 p. CSansS. 54386

----. Hebrew Bible [Old and New Testaments] Philadelphia: Bagster Jewish Era 5599 [1839] 178 p. OO. 54387

----. The Holy Bible.... 1st edition. New York...For the American and Foreign Bible Society, 1839. NHC-S. 54388

----. ----. New York: American Bible Society, 1839. 824, 251 p. NN. 54389

----. ----. 832, 254 p. NN; NNAB. 54390

----. ----. 839, 252 p. NN. 54391

----. ----. 984 p. NN. 54392

----. ----. New York, printed by D. Fanshaw for the American Bible Society, 1839. 669 p. CSansS. 54393

----. ----. New York: Stereotype for the American Bible Society, by A. Chandler, 1839 [1213 p.] 4 v. NN; NNAB; NNUT. 54394

----. ----. With notes by J. Benson. New York: G. Lane, etc., 1839-1843. 5 v. MB. 54395

----. ----. Philadelphia: Hogan and Thompson, 1839. 576, 96, 3, 1, 579-754 p. NN. 54396

----. ----. 2 v. in 1. PWbO. 54397

----. ----. 576, 96, 579-768 p. NN. 54398

----. ----. Philadelphia: M'Carty and Davis, 1839. 2, 676, 836- 1076 p. NN. 54399

----. ----. Portland: O. L. Sanborn, 1839. 852, 259 p. MH. 54400

----. The Holy Bible containing the Old and New Testaments.... Middletown, Conn.: E. Hunt and Company, 1839. 824, 251 p. NN. 54401

----. ----. New York: printed by D. Fanshaw, for the American Bible Society, 1839. 1214 p. CSansS. 54402

----. The Holy Bible, containing the Old and New Testaments, according to the authorized version. With explanatory notes, practical observations, and copious marginal references, by Thomas Scott. Stereotype edition. Boston: Samuel T. Armstrong, 1839. 6 v. NN; Or; WM. 54403

----. ----. From the latest London edition...by the Rev. John Brown, of Thaddington. New York: Samuel Hannay, 1839. 3 v. InThE; LNL; MoSC; NBOP; ViRu. 54404

----. ----. With the references and marginal readings of the Polyglott Bible, with numerous additions from Bagster's Comprehensive Bible. Philadelphia: Robert P. Desilver, 1839. 982 p. MeB; NbOM; PP. 54405

----. The Holy Bible, containing the Old and New Testaments, according to the present authorized version with critical, explanatory and practical notes. New York: Mason, 1839. 953 p. MCE. 54406

----. ----. A copious collection of parallel texts; summaries of each book and chapter; and the date of every transaction and event recorded in the sacred oracles...by Rev. Joseph Benson. New York: T. Mason and G. Lane, 1839-1841. 5 v. IEG; NjPT; ODW; ScCoA; TxGR. 54407

----. The Holy Bible, containing the Old and New Testaments: Translated out of the original tongues: and with the former translations diligently compared and revised. Baltimore: Armstrong and Berry, 1839. 1018, 328 p. CoP; LNHT; MdBD; MdW; NN. 54408

----. ----. New York: American Bible Society, 1839. InU. 54409

----. ----. New York: D. Fanshaw for the American Bible Society, 1839. 852 p. C-S. 54410

----. ----. New York: stereotype by J. S. Redfield, for the American Bible Society...printed by D. Fanshaw, 1839. 939, 192 p. NNUT. 54411

----. ----. New York: New York Bible and Common Prayer Book Society, 1839. 1044 p. NHem. 54412

----. ----. New York: Robinson and Franklin, 1839. 2 v. in 1. DLC. 54413

----. ----. New York: Smith and Valentine, printer, D. Fanshaw, 1839. 979 p. FTU. 54414

----. ----. Philadelphia: Hogan and Thompson, printed by Jesper Harding, 1839. 768 p. OkMu; OWervO. 54415

----. ----. Sandbornton: 1839. 684 p. MWA. 54416

----. ----. 5th edition. New York: stereotype by A. Chandler, printed by D. Fanshaw, for the American Bible Society, 1839. 984 p. CtY-D; NN. 54417

----. ----. 7th edition. New York: American Bible Society, 1839. 1213 p. PPLT. 54418

----. ----. 22nd edition. New York: American Bible Society, 1839. 824, 251 p. IU; NN. 54419

----. ----. The references and marginal readings of the Polyglott Bible, with numerous additions from Bagster's Comprehensive Bible. New York: Robinson, Pratt and Company, 1839. 40, 773 p. TCollSJ. 54420

----. ----. With Canne's marginal notes and references. Cincinnati: 1839. In. 54421

----. ----. With Canne's marginal references. Together with the apocrypha and concordance.... An account of the lives and martyrdom of the Apostles and evangelists.... New York: Robinson and Franklin, 1839. 1 v. NICLA: NN; P; USI; ViU. 54422

----. ----. Philadelphia: Hogan and Thompson, 1839. 2v in 1. 726 [36, 28] p. PWbO. 54423

----. ----. With Canne's marginal notes and references to which are added an index, an alphabetical table of all the names in the Old and New Testaments.... Concord, N. H.: Roby, Kimball and Merrill, 1839. 768, 31 p. IEG; MB; Nh-Hi; OAk. 54424

----. ----. Philadelphia: C. Alexander, 1839. 2 v. in 1 [829 p.] ICP; MdBAHi; NIC; P; PHi. 54425

----. The Holy Bible containing the Old Testament and the New; according to the commonly received version.... London, 1611; imprinted by Robert Barker. Hartford: Andrus, Judd and Franklin, 1839. 222 p. MBD. 54426

----. ----. New York, for the American and Foreign Bible Society, 1839. 839, 252 p. NN. 54427

The Holy Bible, translated from the Latin Vulgate; diligently compared with the Hebrew, Greek, and other editions, in diverse languages.... First stereotype, from the 5th Dublin Edition. Newly revised and corrected according to the Clementin edition of the Scriptures. Philadelphia: Eugene Cuminskey, 1839. 691 p. KySoP; ScCliTO. 54428

----. Illustrations of the Holy scriptures, derived principally from the manners, customs, rites, traditions, forms of speech, antiquities, climate, and works of art and literature, of the eastern nations; embodying all that is valuable in the works of Harmer, Burder, Paxton and Roberts.... Edited by Rev. George Bush.... Brattleboro', Vt.: Brattleboro' Typographic Company, 1839. 656 p. GDecCT; MCET; MH; NN; TBriK. 54429

----. Minuajimauinau St. Matthiu. The Gospel according to Matthew in the Ojibwa language. Boston: ABC, 1839. 112 p. MH-AH. 54430

----. Ne kaghyadonghsera ne royadadokenghay ne Isaiah. New York: printed for the American Bible Society, D. Fanshaw, printer, 1839. 243 p. CU; ICP; MB; OCHP; PU. 54431

----. Das Neue Testament unsers herrn und heilandes Jesu Christi. Nach der Deutchen uebersetzung von Martin Luther. Philadelphia: G. W. Mentz und Sohn, 1839. MB; MBC; P; PPeSchw. 54432

----. ----. Mit kurzem Inhalt eines jeden Capitols, vollstandiger anweisung gleicher schriftstellen und aller sonn-und festtaglichen evangelien und cpistelm. 10 aufl. Harrisburg, Pa.: gedruckt und zu haben bey C. S. Peters, 1839. MH. 54433

----. ----. Nebst einer vollstandigen anweisung der episteln und evangelien aller sonn-und festtage durche ganze jahr. Philadelphia: Kimber und Sharpless, 1839. 420 p. ANA; ICP; MB; NN; OO. 54434

----. A new hieroglyphical Bible; for the amusement and instruction of youth. Being a selection of the most useful lessons and interesting narratives, from Genesis to John.... Cooperstown, N. Y.: Phinney, 1839. 30 p. MB; N. 54435

----. New Testament. Stereotype by J. A. James. Philadelphia: 1839. 469 p. PHi. 54436

----. ----. Portland: O. L. Sanborn, 1839. 226 p. IaHi. 54437

----. New Testament in Bengali and English. New York: W. M'Dowall, 1839. 603 p. IaPeC. 54438

----. The New Testament in the common version. With amendments of the language, by Noah Webster. New Haven: S. Babcock, 1839. 267 p. CtY; ICN; MB; NN; WNaE. 54439

----. The New Testament of our Lord and Saviour Jesus Christ...by Rev. Joseph Benson. New York: T. Mason and G. Lane, for the Methodist Episcopal Church, at the Conference office, 1839. 2 v. ArPb; CoAlT; MoS; NCaS; Tx-DatS. 54440

----. ----. Stereotyped by James Conner, New York: Robinson and Franklin, successors to Leavitt, Lord and Company, 1839. 312 p. NNAB. 54441

----. ----. Translated out of the original Greek; and with the former translations diligently compared and revised. Concord, N. H.: Roby, Kimball and Merrill, 1839. 254 p. MB; NN; Nh-Hi; PMA. 54442

----. ----. Hartford: Andrus, Judd and Franklin, 1839. 156 p. LNH. 54443

----. ----. New York: American Bible Society, 1839. 371 p. ICU; MWA; NNAB. 54444

----. ----. New York: Benjamin Olds, 1839. 288 p. MWA; NjP; WHi. 54445

----. ----. New York; Mason, 1839. 284 p. OO. 54446

----. ----. Philadelphia: Bible Society of Philadelphia, 1839. 416 p. NNAB. 54447

----. ----. Philadelphia: Bible Society of Philadelphia, Stereotype by L. Johnson, 1839. 415 p. MH-AH. 54448

----. ----. 4th edition. New York: stereotyped by Redfield and Lindsay, for the American Bible Society, instituted in New York, 1816. Printed by D. Fanshaw, 1839. 431 p. KWiU; MB. 54449

----. ----. 16th edition. New York: stereotyped by Smith and Valentine, for the American Bible Soceity, printed by D. Fanshaw, 1839. 344 p. Ky-HoHi; NN; WHi. 54450

----. New Testament of our Lord and Saviour Jesus Christ. With critical, explanatory, and practical notes; marginal readings of most approved printed copies of New Testament. Others countenanced by the original Greek.... New York: J. Collard, 1839. 808 p. MBNMHI. 54451

----. New Testament of our Lord and Saviour Jesus Christ with the marginal readings. Keene: J. and J. W. Prentiss, 1839. 422 p. Nh- Hi; NN. 54452

----. ----. Illustrated by original references, both parallel and explanatory, and a copius, selective, carefully chosen and newly arranged. Philadelphia: Thomas, Cowperthwait and Company, 1839. 184 p. WyHi. 54453

----. New Testament of our Lord and Saviour Jesus Christ with the references and marginal readings of the Polyglott Bible. New York; Taylor and Dodd, 1839. RPAt. 54454

----. Notes, critical and practical, on the book of Genesis.... Andover: Gould, Newman and Saxton, 1839-1840. 2 v. NbOM. 54455

----. ----. designed as a general help to biblical reading and instruction. By George Bush, prof. of Hebrew and Oriental Literature at New York City University. 2nd edition. New York: E. French, 1839. 25-364 p. CoFcS; MH; TWcW. 54456

----. ----. 3rd edition. Andover, New York: Gould, Newman and Szxton, 1839. 2 v. CtY; MH. 54457

----. Notes, explanatory and critical on the New Testament. New York: Harper, 1839-1867. 11 v. MoK. 54458

----. Notes, explanatory and practical on the epistle to the Romans. 8th edition. New York: 1839. MNan. 54459

----. Notes, explanatory and practical on the first epistle of Paul to the Corinthians. 2nd edition. New York: 1839. MNan. 54460

---. ----. 2nd edition. New York: Robinson and Franklin [etc.] 1839. 357 p. NbCrD. 54461

----. Notes on second Corinthians and Galatians. New York: Harper and Brothers, 1839. InUpT. 54462

----. Notes on the Acts of the Apostles. 9th edition. New York: 1839. 356 p. PHi. 54463

Notes of the epistle to the Romans. 8th edition. New York: 1839. 329 p. MWA. 54464

----. A Novo Testamento...traduzido en Protuguez segundo a Vulgata. Pelo Padre Antonio Pereira. Nova York: American Bible Society, stereotyped by J. S. Redfield, printed by D. Fanshaw, 1839. 282 p. CtMW; CU; LNH; PU; RNR. 54465

----. Novum Testamentum ad exemplar Millianum, cum emendationibus et lectionibus Griesbachii, praecipuis vocibus elipticis, thematibus omnium vocum difficiliorum, atque locis scripturae parallelis. Studio et labore Gulielmi Greenfield. Hanc editionem priman Americanam, summa cura recensuit...Philadelphia: Sumptibus H. Perkins, Bostoniae: Perkins et Marvin, 1839. 510 p. CtHT; GOgU; MBC; MiU; PPAmP. 54466

----. The Old Testament, arranged in historical and chronological order...by Rev. George Townsend. Boston: Perkins and Marvin, 1839. 1188, 24 p. GAU; MdBP; OrPD; PPWe; TBriK. 54467

----. Otokahe Ekta Wahantanka Taku Owasin kage cin qa IX Genesis eciyapi qa, Odawan wakan qa is psam eciyapi, wowapi wakan waxicu tawa hetanhan psincinca Ie ska dena oyaka qa. Pejihuta wicaxta owa kin ee. Maza on Kagapi. Cincinnati: 1839. 72 p. MBAt. 54468

----. The Polyglott Bible, containing the Old and New Testaments.... New York: Robinson, Pratt and Company, 1839. NbKT. 54469

----. ----. Philadelphia: Thomas, Cowperthwait and Company, 1839. 3-587, 190 p. MB; NN. 54470

----. ----. 2 v. in 1. MB. 54471

----. Polymicrian Greek lexicon to the New Testament. Phialdephia: 1839. MBC. 54472

----. Psalms, in metre, selected from the Psalms of David.... Philadelphia: E. L. Carey and A. Hart, 1839. 62 p. IEG; NNG. 54473

----. ----. with hymns, suited to the feasts and fasts of the church, and other occasions of public worship. Philadelphia: Protestant Episcopal Female Prayer Book Society, 1839. 248 p. MnHi; WNaE. 54474

----. ----. Philadelphia: Thomas, Cowperthwait and Company, 1839. 248 p. AMob; CtMMHi; NN; ViU. 54475

----. The Psalms of David imitated in the language of the New Testament and applied to the Christian state and worship. By Isaac Watts. Sandborton, N. H.: 1839. 310 p. IEG. 54476

----. ----. 254 p. NcMHi. 54477

----. ----. 272, 192 p. MWA. 54478

----. The Psalms of David in Metre [Philadelphia: 1839?] 28 p. NNAB. 54479

----. ----. Allowed by the authority of the General Assembly of the Kirk of Scotland. Philadelphia: Hogan and Thompson, 1839. 424 p. NNUT; PPL-R. 54480

----. ----. Philadelphia: William S. Young, 1839. 386 p. DLC-P4; NcmHi; NNUT. 54481

----. Psalter des Konige a propheten David.... Philadelphia: Mentz, 1839. PPG. 54482

----. The sacred writings of the apostles and evangelists of Jesus Christ, commmonly styled the New Testament. Translated from the original Greek, by Dr. George Campbell.... 6th edition. Pittsburgh: Forrester and Campbell, 1839. CBB; IaDmD; KBB; PWW; TxDaM. 54483

----. La Sainte Bible, qui contient le vieux et le Nouveau Testament; revue sur les originaux, par David Martin. New York: Stereotype par Henry W. Rees, pour la Societe Biblique Americaine. D. Fanshaw, imprimeur, 1839. 819, 216 p. CtHT; GEU; LNH; NBuG; PPL. 54484

----. ----. 2nd edition. New York: Societe Biblique Americaine, 1839. 819, 261 p. MtU; NcA; RPB; WBeloC. 54485

----. Wotanin waxte Markus owa kin dee. Maza on Kagopi. Cincinnati: Ixtawayazan wi Omaka, 1839. 96 p. MBAt. 54486

Bible biography, in the form of questions: with reference to scripture for answers. For the use of schools and private families.... Boston [J. H. Francis] 1839. 98 p. ICMe; MH; MHi; MWA; NjPT. 54487

Bickersteth, Edward, 1786-1850. A harmony of the four gospels.... With practical reflections of Dr. Doddridge.... Philadelphia: Hooker and Claxton, 1839. 420 p. MMeT. 54488

----. A help to the study of the scriptures: abridged. Edited with additional matter, by Chauncey Colton. Columbus: I. N. Whiting, 1839. 139 p. OSW. 54489

Bigland, John, 1759-1832. A natural history of birds, fishes, reptiles and insects. Illustrated by twelve coloured plates, engraved mostly from the original drawings. Philadelphia: J. Grigg, 1839. 179 p. InCW; LNH; MWA; OSW; OrP. 54490

Billard, Charles Michel, 1800-1832. A treatise on the diseases of infants...with notes by Dr. Ollibier.... Translated from the 3rd French Edition, with an appendix by James Stewart. New York: G. Adlard [etc., etc.] 1839. 620 p. CSt-L; ICJ; NNC; PPCP; TNV. 54491

Billerica, Massachusetts. A statement of the expenses of the town of Billerica, April 1, 1838, to April 1, 1839. n. p.: 1839. Broadside. MBilHi. 54492

Bingham, Caleb, 1757-1817. The columbian orator, containing a variety of the original and selected pieces. Stereotype edition. Boston: J. H. A. Frost, etc., etc., 1839. 303 p. AAP; MH. 54493

Binney, Amos, 1802-1878. The theological compend, containing a system of divinity. Cincinnati: Hitchcock and Walden, 1839. 128 p. IaScM; ILM. 54494

Binns, John, 1772-1860. An exposition of the law accompanied by remarks on rights and duties of master and apprentice, etc. 2nd edition. Philadelphia: Nicklin and Johnson, 1839. 33 p. MH-L; MiU-L; PHi; PPB. 54495

Binny, John. Specimen of printing type.... Philadelphia: 1839. 34 l. NN. 54496

Biographical notices of Daniel Schlesinger, the pianist [New York? 1839?] MB; NN. 54497

Biographical notices of Mr. Charles Hayward, Jr. See Wheeler, Charles Stearn, 1816-1843.

Bird, Charles Smith, 1795-1862. The popes claim to supremacy examined and confuted.... Reading: Richard Welch, 1839. 45 p. MBAt. 54498

----. Transubtantiation tried by scripture and reason.... 2nd edition. Reading: 1839. 42 p. CtY. 54499

Bird Robert Montgomery, 1806-1854. The adventures of Robin Day. By the author of Calavar.... Philadelphia: Lea and Blanchard, 1839. 2 v. in 1. ICN; MWA: PU; TKL; WaU. 54500

Birney, James Gillespie, 1792-1857. A letter on the political obligations of abolitionists, with a reply by William Lloyd Garrison. Boston: Dow and Jackson, printers, 1839. 36 p. DLC; MB; NcD; TNF. 54501

Birthday gifts for little heads and little hearts; selected from London books. New York; S. Colman, 1839. 148 p. MNBedfHi, MWA. 54502

Bishop, Charles. Catechism on singing. New York: 1839. NjMD. 54503

Bishop Francis G. Brief history of the Churchi of Jesus Christ, of Latter Day Saints, from their rise until the present time...and likewise a summary view of their religious faiths. Salem: printed by Blum and Son, 1839. DLC; NcD. 54504

Bishop, Robert Hamilton, 1777-1855. Elements of the science of government being an outline of a portion of the studies of the senior class in Miami University...Oxford, Ohio: R. H. Bishop, jr., 1839. 166 p. Ct; DLC; ICP; KEmC; ODaB. 54505

----. The God of Israel the protector...A sermon occasioned by the death of James R. Hughs.... Oxford, Ohio: printed by W. W. Bishop, 1839. 12 p. ICP; PPPrHi; PPULC. 54506

Black, John, 1768-1849. Slavery contrary to the Bible: an address delivered to the students at the Theological Hall, Cannosburg. Pittsburgh: printed by W. Allinder, 1839. 28 p. NNUT; PPPrHI; ViRVU. 54507

Blackaller, Henry. A liturgy: or manual of sunday school devotion and instruction, adapted to the capacities of children. Boston: James B. Dow,

1839. 34 p. MBD; MdBD. 54508

Blainville, Henri Marie Ducrotay de, 1777-1850. Osteographie, ou description incongraphique comparee du squelette et du systeme dentaire des mammiferes recents et fossiles pour servir de base a la zoologie et a la geologie.... New York: Bailliere Brothers, 1839-1864. 4 v. CU; DLC; PPWI; NjP; ScU. 54509

Blair, Hugh, 1718-1800. Lectures on rhetoric and belles lettres. With a life of the author. Stereotype library edition. Philadelphia: James Kay, jr. and Brother, Pittsburgh: C. H. Kay and Company, 1839. 557 p. IaMvC; KKcBT; NbU; TxU; WBeloC. 54510

Blake, John Lauris, 1788-1857. Conversations on natural philosophy see Marcet, Jane [Haldimand] 1769-1857.

----. First book in Astronomy...for the use of common schools.... Boston: Gould, Kendall and Lincoln, 1839. 120 p. KBB; MB; MDeeP; MoS; RPB. 54511

----. A general biographical dictionary comprising a summary account of the most distinguished person of all ages, nations and professions. New York: E. French and A. V. Blake, 1839. 1096 p. DLC; KyLoS; NjR; OMC; ScU. 54512

----. ----. 2nd edition. New York: E. French and A. V. Blake, 1839. 1096 p. LU; MdBJ; MiU; TJoV; WaPS. 54513

----. The juvenile companion and fireside reader, consisting of historical and biographical anecdotes, and selections in poetry. New York: Harper and Brothers, 1839. 252 p. RLA, RPB. 54514

----. Letters to an only daughter on confirmation: being a manual for the youth of the Protestant Episcopal Church.... Philadelphia: J. Whetham, 1839. 216 p. CtY; DLC; MdBD; NbCrD; PWaybu. 54515

----. Young orator; and New York class book; especially designed to prevent dullness and monotony in the reading and declamation of schools. 2nd edition. New York: 1839. 252 p. NTaHi; OO. 54516

Blanchard, Amos of Cincinnati. American military biography, containing the lives and characters of the officers of the revolution.... Cincinnati: E. Walters, 1839. 615 p. GFtv. 54517

Blanchard, Jonathan, 1811-1892. A perfect state of soceity. Address before the "Society of inquiry," in Oberlin Collegiate Institute. Delivered at Oberlin Lorain County, Ohio, at the annual commencement, September 3, 1839. Cincinnati: Oberlin, Steele, 1839. 16 p. CSmH; ICP; KyLx; OClWHi; PPPrHi. 54518

Blanchor, F. Maid of Judah, or "no more shall the children of Judah sing." Arranged for the Spanish quitar by F. Blanchor. Philadelphia: Willig, 1839. 2 p. MB. 54519

Blenon, Peter Anthony, 1759ca-1836. Copy of the auditor's report on the account of the executors of the last will and testament of Peter Anthony Blenon, deceased. Philadelphia: printed by T. B. Town, 1839. 40 p. MiD-B; NNC. 54520

Blessington, Marguerite [Power] Farmer Gardiner, 1789-1849. Desultory thoughts and reflections. By the Countess of Blessington. New York: Wiley and Putman, 1839. 101 p. CtY; LNP; MoS; NBu; NjP. 54521

----. Gems of beauty displayed in a series of twelve highly finished engravings of Spanish subjects, from designs by the first artists. With fanciful illustrations, in verse.... New York: Appleton, 1839. MeB; MB; NjP; ViU. 54522

----. The governess. By the Countess of Blessington.... Philadelphia: Lea and Blanchard, 1839. 2 v. CtY; MBAt; MWA; NjP; ViU. 54523

----. The idler in Italy. By the Countess of Blessington.... Philadelphia: Carey and Hart, 1839. 2 v. MiD; PPA; ScU; TNP; ViU. 54524

Bliss, Leonard, 1811-1842. A comprehensive grammar of the English language: Introductory lessons. Louisville, Ky.: Morton and Griswold, 1839. 73 [3] p. DLC; NNC. 54525

Bliss Lansingburgh almanac for 1849. Luther Bliss. Troy, N. Y.: printed by N. Tuttle [1839] MWA. 54526

Blois, John T. Gazetteer of the state of Michigan...with statistical tables, and a directory for emigrants. Detroit: S. L. Rood and Company, New York: Robinson, Pratt and Company, 1839.

418 p. DLC; ICJ; MWA; PU; UPB. 54527

The Bloomington Post. Job printing. Deal and Brown, proprietors of the Bloomington Post, would respectively inform their friends and the public generally, that they have just received a large assortment of book.... Bloomington, Ia.: 1839. Broadside. In. 54528

Blue Beard. The popular story of Blue Beard. Embellished with neat engravings. Cooperstown: printed by H. and E. Phinney, 1839. 31 p. MB; MH; NPV; NUt. 54529

Blunt, Henry, 1794-1843. Discourses on some of the doctrinal articles of the Church of England. Also, lectures on the history of Saint Peter.... First American from the last London edition. Philadelphia: Hooker and Claxton, 1839. CtY; GDecCT; MB; NNUT; PP. 54530

----. Lectures on the history of Abraham and Jacob.... First American edition, from the 12th London edition. Philadelphia: Hooker and Claxton, 1839. 348 p. CtY; FHe; IaFayU; GDecCT; MiU. 54531

----. Lectures on the history of Elisha.... Philadelphia: H. Hooker, 1839. 256 p. CtY; LNX; MH; NNUT; PPWe. 54532

----. Lectures upon the history of our Lord and Saviour Jesus Christ. 1st American edition. Philadelphia: Hooker and Claxton, 1839. 2 v. GDecCT; KyLoP; NjMD; OrPD; PLT. 54533

----. Lectures upon the history of St. Paul, delivered during Lent, at the Church of the Holy Trinity, Upper Chelsea.... 1st American from the 7th London edition. Philadelphia: Hooker and Claxton, 1839. 382 p. CtY; InCW; MdBD; NjMD; ViAl. 54534

----. Practical exposition of the epistles to the seven churches of Asia.... Philadelphia: Hooker and Claxton, 1839. CtHT; ICBB; MdBD; MiU; PP. 54535

Boardman, Henry Augustus, 1808-1880. The scriptural doctrine of original sin; explained and enforced in two discourses by H. A. Boardman. Philadelphia: Wm. S. Martien, 1839. 124 p. DLC; ICP; MiU; PPM; ViRut. 54536

----. A treatise on the scripture doctrine of original sin; with explanatory notes. Philadelphia: Presbyterian Board of Publication, William S. Martien, publishing agent, 1839. 130 p. CSansS; DLC; NjP; PPPrHi; ViRut. 54537

----. ----. 3rd edition. Philadelphia: Presbyterian Board of Publication, 1839. 122 p. IEG; NbOP; NCH; PPWe; ViRut. 545438

----. The vanity of a life of fashionable pleasure. Sermon preached...1839. Philadelphia: Martien, 1839. 41 p. PPPrHi; PPM; PPULC. 54539

Bogardus, James W., and others. To the heirs of Anneke Jantz, claiming recovery of real estate and account of proceeds of real estate, against the Trinity Church of the city of New York [New York: 1839] Broadside. NN. 54540

Bolles, John Augustus, 1809-1878. Essay on a congress of nations, for the spacific adjustment of international disputes.... Boston: Whipple and Damrell, 1839. 84 p. Ct; DLC; NN. 54541

----. An oration delivered July 4, 1839, at Medfield, Massachusetts at a temperance celebration, in which the citizens of Medfield and eight of the surrounding towns united without distinction of party. Boston: Whipple and Damrell, 1839. 30 p. MB; MBAt; MBC; MMeT; NN. 54542

Bolmar, Antoine. A collection of colloquial phrases, on every topic necessary to maintain conversation.... A new edition, revised and corrected. Philadelphia: Lea and Blanchard, successors to Carey and Company, 1839. 208 p. CtHT-W; MB; NN; NNC; PPULC. 54543

----. A theoretical and practical grammar of the French language; in which the present usage is displayed agreeably to the decisions of the French Academy.... Philadelphia: E. L. Carey and A. Hart, 1839. 468 p. MoKiT; MoJa; NPV. 54544

----. ----. 5th edition. Philadelphia: E. L. Carey and A. Hart, 1839. 294, 173 p. MMal; NRSB; PHi; ScCCit. 54545

----. A theoretical grammar of the French language...with the addition of a complete treatise on the gender of French nouns and also with the addition of all French verbs.... 5th edition. Philadelphia: E. L. Carey and A. Hart, 1839. 249, 173 p. MsWJ. 54546

Bonar, Andrew Alexander, 1810-1892. Narrative of a mission of inquiry to the Jews from the Church of Scotland in 1839.... Philadelphia: Presbyterian Board of Publication, 1839. 555 p. CSans-S; KyLxT; MeU; NbOP; ViRut. 54547

----. ----. 3rd edition. Philadelphia: Presbyterian Board of Publication, 1839. 555 p. PP. 54548

Bonaventura, Saint Cardinal, 1221-1274. Saint Bonaventura's life of our Lord and Saviour Jesus Christ. Translated from the original Latin. To which are added, the devotion to the three hours agony of our Lord on the cross; and the life of the glorious Saint Joseph.... New York: John Doyle, 1839. 308, 52 p. DGU; InNd; LNB; MiD-M; MoSU. 54549

Bond, Thomas Emerson, 1782-1856. Methodism, not a human contrivance: but a providential arrangement. Substance of a sermon preached at the celebration of the centenary of Methodism, in Exeter Street Church, North Baltimore Station, on October 25, 1839. Baltimore: Isaac P. Cook, 1839. 28 p. ICP; DLC; MBC; PPM. 54550

Bonnycastle, Charles, 1792-1840. A lecture introductory to the course of mathematics, of the University of Virginia, delivered at the commencement of the session of 1839. Charlottesville, printed by James Alexander, 1839. 16 p. DLC; ICU; TxU; Vi; ViU. 54551

Bonnycastle, John, 1750?-1821. An introduction to mensuration and practical geometry.... To which are added, a treatise on guaging [!] and also the most important problems in mechanics. Philadelphia: Kimber and Sharpless, 1839. 288 p. CSt; DLC; InCW; NjP; PWcT. 54552

----. ----. Key to the American edition. containing solutions to all the questions left unsolved in that work; by Benjamin +Hallowell; adapted to the revised edition of the Mensuration by James Ryan. 3rd edition. Philadelphia: Kimber, 1839. 288 p. OO; OOxM; PPULC; PU. 54553

Bonsall, J. The war exterminated [Cincinnati: 1839] 8 p. DLC; IEN-M; OClWHi. 54554

A book of good manners, for girls and boys.... Providence: Geo. P. Daniels, 1839. 16 p. MH; RHi. 54555

Book of pleasures; pleasures of hope by Thomas Campbell; pleasures of memory by Samuel Rogers; pleasures of the imagination by Mark Akenside. Philadelphia: F. W. Greenough, 1839. 187 p. CtHT; FTa; MH; PP; RPB. 54556

The book of the months, a gift for the young. New York: Leavitt, Lord and Company, 1839. 196 p. DLC; MH; NBuG; NNC; RPB. 54557

Boone, Suzanna [Waring] The revocation of the Edict of Nantes, and its consequence to the Protestant Churches of France and Italy; containing memoirs of some of the sufferers in the persecution attending that event. Philadelphia: Presbyterian Board of Publication, 1839. 215 p. GDecCT; LNB; MoS; OAU; ViRut. 54558

Booth, Abraham, 1734-1806. The reign of grace from its rise to it consummation. Philadelphia: Baptist Tract Depository, 1839. 291 p. CtY; LNB; KyLoS; PCA; ScCoB. 54559

Booth, Jas. C. Report of the geological survey to Charles Marem, esq., secretary of the state of Delaware: 1839 [3] 25 p. MoS. 54560

Boston, Thomas, 1677-1732. The crook in the lot; or a display of the sovereignty and wisdom of God in the afflictions of men, and the Christian's deportment under them. Philadelphia: William S. Martien, 1839. 162 p. GHi; MsSpD; NjR; PPPrHi; WM. 54561

Boston, Massachusetts. Act of supplying the city with pure water. Boston: 1839. 11 p. MBC. 54562

----. Report on debt and resources of Boston. Boston: 1839. MB. 54563

----. Report on the reduction of the city debt, March 7, 1839 [Boston: 1839] 11 p. MHi. 54564

----. Boylston Street Baptist Church. The articles of faith, with the church covenant and list of members of the Boyleston Street Baptist Church, Boston. Constituted March 27, 1839. Boston: Gould, Kendall and Lincoln, 1839. 12 p. NBLiHi; PCA. 54565

----. City Council. Committee on Finance. Report on the debt and resources of the city of Boston. Boston: J. H. Eastburn, city printer, 1839. 24 p. DLC; IU; MH; MH-AH; PPULC. 54566

----. Common Council. Rules and orders of the common council of the city of Boston. Boston: John H. Eastburn, city printer, 1939. 72 p. MoS. 54567

----. Fire Department. Letters to the Board of Aldermen; 1839. Boston: 1839. MB. 54568

----. ----. List of officers and members, etc. September 17, 1839. Engineer's office, city hall, September 17, 1839.... Boston: 1839. 43 p. DLC; MB; MBB. 54569

----. First Baptist Church. A brief history of the First Baptist Church in Boston; with a list of its members. Boston: 1839. 36 p. M; MHi. 54570

----. Hollis Street Church. Adjourned meeting, September 30, 1839 [Boston: Clapp and Son's Press, 1839] 4 p. CtY; MBAt; NNP; NNUT. 54571

----. ----. Adjourned meeting, October 14, 1839 [Boston: Clapp and Son's Press] 4 p. DLC; ICN; MH; MWA; NNP. 54572

----. ----. Annual meeting of the proprietors of the Hollis Street Church. Boston: Clapp and Son's, 1839 8 p. CtY; MBAt; MWA; NNP; NNUT. 54573

----. ----. Proceedings in the controversy between a part of the proprietors and the pastor of Hollis Street Church, Boston, 1838 and 1839. Boston: S. N. Dickinson [1839] 60 p. CtY; IU; MB; MHi; NNUT. 54574

----. ----. Report. The committee of the proprietors of the meeting house in Hollis Street, who were instructed to consider what order the society shall take upon the result of the late mutual ecclesiastical council, have considerd the subject and submit the following report [Boston: Clapp and Son, 1839] 21 p. DLC. 54575

----. ----. Report of the committee of the proprietors of the meeting house in Hollis Street, upon the result of the late mutual ecclesiastical council.... [Boston: Clapp and Son, 1839] 23 p. DLC; MBAt; MiD-B; NNUT; OO. 54576

----. Joint Standing Committee on Water. Soft water [Report with the resolve accompanying. Boston? 1839] 20 p. DLC; MH; MH-BA; PPULC. 54577

----. Maverick Church. The articles of faith and covenamt of the Maverick Church. With rules and names of members. Boston: 1839. 12 p. MHi. 54578

----. Mayor [Samuel Atkins Eliot] Address...to the city council... January 7, 1839. Boston: 1839. 12 p. MHi. 54579

----. ----. Address to the school committee [Boston: 1839] 18 p. WHi. 54580

----. Mercantile Library Association. Constitution and by-laws of the Mercantile Library Association; together with a catalogue of books, and names of members. Instituted 1820. Boston: 1839. 77 p. CtY; DLC; MB; NN. 54581

----. School Committee. [Report of sub-committee appointed to inquire into the origin of the primary school, and of the primary school committee. Boston: 1839. 10 p. NN. 54582

----. ----. Rules of the school committee and regulation of the public schools for 1839-1860. Boston: 1839- [1860] CtY; ICU; MHi. 54583

----. Suffolk Street Church. Order of performances on the occasion of laying the corner stone, May 23, 1839 [Boston: 1839] MBAt. 54584

----. Union Church. Confession of faith and covenant. Also a brief history of Union Church, Essex Street, Boston. Boston: printed for the use of the members, 1839. 55 p. MBLiHi; MHi; MiD-B. 54585

Boston Academy of Music. Boston Academy's collection of choruses. Boston: J. H. Wilkins, R. B. Carter and Palmer, 1839. MBNEC; MH; PPULC; ViU. 54586

----. The Boston Academy's collection of church music: consisting of the most popular psalm and hymn tunes.... Including also original compositions by German, English and American authors.... 7th edition. Boston: J. H. Wilkins and R. B. Carter, 1839. 357 p. ICU; MH; NjP; OCl; ViU. 54587

Boston almanac and business directory. Boston: Dickinson, 1839. MS. 54588

The Boston almanac for the year 1839. By S. N. Dickinson. Boston: Thomas Groom, 1839. 95 p.

CoCsC; MeB; MPeaHi; NhPet. 54589

The Boston almanac for the year 1840. By S. N. Dickinson. Boston: Thomas Groom [1839] 132 p. IaHi; MWA; RP; WHi. 54590

Boston Athenaeum. Catalogue of the first exhibition of sculpture in the athenaeum gallery, 1839. Boston: John H. Eastburn, printer [1839] 9 p. MB; MH; MWA; WHi. 54591

----. Catalogue of the 13th exhibition of paintings in the athenaeum gallery. Boston: 1839. 15 p. CtY; MdBJ; MHi; WHi. 54592

Boston Children's Friend Society. Report, 1st. Boston: 1839-1906. 1st-. MB. 54593

Boston comic almanack for 1840. Boston: James Fisher [1839] MWA. 54594

The Bsoton directory, containing the names of the inhabitants...and the city register.... Boston: Charles Stimpson, Jr., 1839. 449 p. IaHi; MiD-B; WHi. 54595

Boston notion. By G. Roberts [Boston: 1839-1843] DLC; MB; MWA. 54596

Both sides of religious ceremonies; a monthly periodical, devoted to the investigation of every variety of rituals in religion. Edited by Robert Smith. Cincinnati: Looker and Graham, printers, 1839-1840. 284 p. DLC; OClWHi; TNDL; TU. 54597

Botta, Carlo Giuseppi Guglielmo, 1766-1837. History of the war of independence of the United States of America. Translated from the Italian, by George Alexander Otis, esq. 9th edition, revised and corrected. New Haven: T. Brainard, 1839. 2 v. ABBS; KyHi; NcD; ODa; ScU. 54598

Botts, John Minor, 1802-1869. Speech...on the election of United States Senator. Delivered in the House of Delegates of Virginia, February 16, 1839. Richmond: Bailie and Gallaher, printers, 1839. CSmH. 54599

Bourdon, Louis Pierre Marie, 1779-1854. Elements of algebra: Translated from the French of M. Bourdon. Revised and adapted to the course of mathematical instruction it the United States. Hartford: A. S. Barnes and Company, 1839. 355 p. IaDaM; MoU; WWaupu. 54600

Bouton, Nathaniel, 1799-1878. Memoir of Mrs. Elizabeth McFarland; or full assurance of hope. The reward of diligence in the Christian life. Concord, N. H.: Marsh, Capen and Lyon, 1839. 319 p. ArCH; CtY; DLC; MWA; NjMD. 54601

----. ----. 2nd edition. Concord: Asa McFarland, 1839. 313 p. LNH; NbCrD; Nh; NLM. 54602

----. ----. 3rd edition. Boston: Crocker and Brewster, 1839. 313 p. CSmH; MH-AH; NhD; UPB. 54603

Bouvier, John, 1787-1851. A law dictionary, adapted to the constitution and laws of the United States of America, and of the several states of the American union.... Philadelphia: T. and J. W. Johnson, 1839. 2 v. Ct; MoS; NcD; OrHi; PPA. 54604

Bowditch, Nathaniel, 1773-1838. The new American practical navigator: being an epitome of navigation; containing all the tables necesary to be used with the nautical almanac in determining the latitude, and the logitude by lunar observations, and keeping a complete reckoning at sea.... 11th new stereotyped edition. New York: Blunt, 1839. 447 p. CoGr; MSaP; NCH; RNR. 54605

Bowditch, Nathaniel Ingersoll, 1805-1861. De la Place marquis, Mecanique Celeste...with a memoir of the translator by his son, Nataniel Ingersoll Bowditch.... Boston: C. Little and James Brown, 1839. 168 p. MNF; MNtCA. 54606

----. Memoir of Nathaniel Bowditch by his son Nathaniel Ingersoll Bowditch.... Boston: C. C. Little and J. Brown, 1839. 172 p. CU; LNH; MH-AH; PU; RPAt. 54607

Bowdoin Port-folio. Conducted by the undergraduates of Bowdoin College. Brunswick: Joseph Griffin, printer [1839] 248 p. MB; MBC; MeB; MeBa; MeHi. 54608

Bowen, Daniel, b. 1759 or 1760. A history of Philadelphia, with a notice of villages, in the vicinity...containing a correct account of the city improvements, up to the year, 1839; also.... Philadelphia: D. Bowen, 1839. 200 p. ICN; MB; MdBJ; PPA; WHi. 54609

Bowen, Francis. Kant and his philosophy. Cambridge: Folsom, Wells, and Thurston, 1839. 27 p. MH. 54610

Bowen, J. T. Map of a part of Maine showing the disputed territory. Philadelphia: 1839. 1 p. PHi. 54611

----. The United States drawing book; comprising elements of the art of drawing with the lead pencil, chalk, or crayon, or with water colours; and a series of exercises, among which are views of the most intersting scenery in the United States.... Philadelphia: I. Wardle, 1839. 24 p. CtY; PHi; PPULC. 54612

Bowen, William W. Calumny refuted: an answer to the exposition of Thomas H. Lewis. New Orleans; printed by J. Gibson, 1839. 27 p. CSmH; LU; MoSM; RPB; TxU. 54613

Bowling Green, Kentucky. Presbyterian Church. An exposition of the views of the Presbyterian Church...relative to the late dismemberment of the Presbyterian Church in the United States. Cincinnati: Kendall, 1839. IEG; NNUT; PPPrHi. 54614

Boyer, Abel, 1667-1729. Boyer's French dictionary; with useful words and phrases from the dictionaries of Boiste, Waulby, Catineau, and others. Boston: Hilliard, Gray and Company, 1839. KyU; LNOP; MB-FA; MiD; NBuDD. 54615

Boyle, Isaac. A historical view of the council of Nice with a translation of documents. New York: T. Mason and G. Lane, 1839. 480, 59 p. CtHT; OO; PU; TNS; WaTC. 54616

Boy's own book of amusement and instruction. Embellished with cuts. Providence: Geo. P. Daniels, 1839. 23 p. CtY. 54617

The boy's scrap book. 1839. Philadelphia: American Sunday School Union [1839?] 255 p. CtY; DLC; MnU; MWA; RPB. 54618

Brace, Joab, jr. The principles of English grammar. With copious exercises in parsing and syntax. Arranged on the basis of Lennie's grammar. Philadelphia: H. Perkins, Boston: Perkins and Marvin, 1839. 144 p. MB; MiU; NNC; NcWsM; RPB. 54619

Brackenridge, Henry Marie, 1786-1871. History of the late war, between the United States and Great Britain comprising a minute account of the various military and naval operations. Philadelphia: J. Kay, jun., and Brother, Pittsburgh: C. H.

Kay and Company, 1839. 298 p. ABBS; DeWi; ICU; PCC; TxDaM. 54620

Bradford, James. Review of the past; a sermon at Sheffield, January 1839, the 25th anniversary of [his] settlement in that place. Piitsfield [Mass.] Phinehas Allen and Son [1839] 47 p. ICN; MBC; NjR; OClWHi; RPB. 54621

Bradford, Vincent L. Report on imprisonment for debt. Lancing, Michigan: 1839. PPL; PPULC. 54622

Bradford Academy, Bradford, Massachusetts. Catalogue of the officers and students of Bradford Academy, Bradford, Massachusetts, October, 1839. Haverhill: G. H. Safford, 1839. 14 p. MHa. 54623

Brady, James T. In memoriam.... New York: Baker, 1839. 52 p. PU. 54624

Brainerd, Thomas. the duty of immediate repentance. A sermon preached in...Philadelphia, January 13, 1839. Philadelphia: Geddes, 1839. PPPrHi. 54625

[Branagan, Thomas] b. 1774. The beauties of philanthropy. By a philanthropist. Illustrated with engravings. New York: the author, 1839. 2v. in 1. ICBB; MBC; MdBE; NIC; OClWHi. 54626

----. The guardian genius of the federal union or patriotic admonitions on the signs of the times...Human slavery...By a philanthropist.... New York: the author, 1839. 104 p. CtMW; ICN; MBBC; NjR; OClWHi. 54627

Bray, Anna Eliza [Kemp] Stothard. Trials of the heart. Philadelphia: Lea and Blanchard, 1839. 2 v. ICBB; MB; MH. 54628

Brayton, Isaac. Sermons on the death of Mrs. Maria Lansing, wife of Robert Lansing, preached...March 31, 1839. New York: James Van Norden, 1839. 14 p. MBuG; PPPrHi; PPULC. 54629

Breckinridge, John, 1797-1841. A memoir of Mrs. Margaret Breckinridge. In two parts. Part 1. Memoir and funeral sermon. Part 2. Letters to her surviving children. Philadelphia: William S. Martien, 1839. GDecCT; KyLoP; NNUT; PHi; ViRut. 54630

Breckinridge, Robert Jefferson, 1800-1871. Memoranda of foreign travel. Containing notices of France, Germany, Switzerland and Italy.... Philadelphia: Joseph Whetham, 1839. GDecCT; ICP; MBAt; NcD; PPA. 54631

----. A plea for the restoration of the scriptures to the schools, being the substance of an address delivered at the 23rd anniversary of the American Bible Society, in the city of New York, on the 8th day of May, 1839. Baltimore: Matchett and Neilson, 1839. 15 p. CtHT-W; GDecCT; MdHi; NjPT; PWW. 54632

----. Review of the correspondence between the archbishop and mayor of Baltimore [Baltimore: 1839] MdBP; MdHi; PPL. 54633

----. Tracks to vindicate religion and liberty. No. 1. Containing the review of the case of Olevia Neal, the Earmelite nun, and the review of the correspondence between the archbishop and mayor of Baltimore. Baltimore: Matchett and Neilson, 1839. 35 p. MdBE; MdHi; MnU; PPPrHi; ViU. 54634

Brewerton, John. Report of Captain Brewerton, connected with the improvement of the Hudson river Navigation. December 26, 1838. Albany: printed by H. D. Stone and Company, 1839. 24 p. InHi; MBAt; MWA; N; NjR. 54635

Brewster, David, 1781-1868. Letters on natural magic; address to Sir Walter Scott. New York: Harper and Brothers, 1839. 314 p. LN; OAU; PPM; RNR; TxGR. 54636

----. The life of Sir Isaac Newton. New York: Harper and Brothers, 1839. 323 p. GMW; MWA; PHi; ScC; TxGR. 54637

----. A treatise on optics. A new edition, with an appendix, containing an elementary view of the application of analysis to reflexion and refraction.... Philadelphia: Lea and Blanchard, 1839. 323-95 p. ICU; LNOP; MH; MoSW; NjR. 54638

Brice, James F. Castle Crosier, a romance. By an American. Annapolis: William M. Neir, printer, 1839. 118 p. CoU; MdBD. 54639

Brice, James R. Secrets of the Mount Pleasant State Prison...an account of the unjust proceedings against James R. Brice, esq...affidavits to prove his innocency; also an account of the in-human treatment of prisoners by some of the keepers.... Albany: printed for the author, 1839. 64 p. MB; NjR; NN. 54640

A bridal gift. From the 4th London edition. Hartford: 1839. 204 p. DLC; MiU; MWA; RPB. 54641

Bridge, B. The new American reader, No. 3. Comprising selections in prose and verse, for the use of schools. Cincinnati: E. Morgan and Company, 1839. 251 p. DLC. 54642

Bridge, Bewick, 1767-1833. A treatise on the construction, properties, and analogies of the conic sections. From the 2nd London edition, with additions and alterations by the American edition. New Haven: Durrie and Peck, New York: Collins, Keese and Company, 1839. 136 p. CtHT; MH; NjP; NbU; OClW. 54643

----. A treatise on the elements of algebra. 2nd American, revised and corrected from the 7th London edition. Philadelphia: F. W. Greeough, 1839. ICBB; MH; PHi; PP. 54644

A brief memoir of Mother Mary Charles Malony, who died in the Ursuline Convent, in this city, on July 28, 1839, aged 54 years. Charleston: printed by Burges and James, 1839. 10 p. MBtS. 54645

A brief statement...by a layman. New York: printed by James Van Norden.., 1839. 10 p. NNS. 54646

Brief statement touching the Rev. Dr. Schroeder's late publication, entitled "Documents concerning recent measures of the vestry of Trinity Church." New York: J. van Norden, 1839. 10 p. CtY; MBC; NdBD; NBLiHi. 54647

The Brigantine; or Admiral Lowe. A tale of the 17th Century, by an American. New York: Crowen and Decker, 1839. 201 p. DLC; IU; MH; NjP; ViU. 54648

[Briggs, Charles Frederick] 1804-1877. The adventures of Harry Franco; a tale of the great panic.... New York: F. Sanders, 1839. 2 v. CSmH; DLC; ICU; MBAt; MWA. 54649

Briggs, George Nixon. Remarks on the motion to re-commit th report of the committee of ways and means of the finances... Delivered in the

House of Representatives...the 2nd and 5th of February, 1839. Washington: printed by Gales and Seaton, 1839. 8 p. MB; MdHi; MLow; MHi; NcD. 54650

Briggs, James A. Carrier's new year's address to the readers of the Cleveland Daily Herald and Gazette, January 1, 1839. Broadside. OClWHi. 54651

Brigham, David. Report of the trial of the Rev. David Brigham, before referees, charged by the trustees of Framingham Academy with falsehood and duplicity. Lowell: 1839. 32 p. MBC; MBNEH; MBS; MH; MLow. 54652

Brighton, Massachusetts. School Committee. Map. Report 1-35 of the school committee. Cambridge: 1839-1873. 2 v. MB; MH. 54653

Bristol Academy, Taunton, Massachusetts. A catalogue of the officers and students from 1838\1839-1851\1852. Taunton: 1839- 1852. 2 v. MDAt. 54654

Broad grins, or Joe Miller in America; collected by a real Kentuckian. Manchester: W. Willis, 1839. 64 p. MH. 54655

Brooke, H. The fool of qulaity; the history of Henry, Earl of Moreland, abridged by John Wesley. Cincinnati: U. P. James, 1839. 2 v. MB; MdBD; NjMD; OClW. 54656

Brooke, John Thomson. Scriptural comfort in death: illustrated by an example. A sermon, By Rev. John T. Brooke, rector of Christ Church, Cincinnati, July, 1839. Cincinnati: Hefley, Hubbell and Company, printers, 1839. 10 p. OC; OCHP; OClWHi. 54657

----. Sorrow improved. Abstract of a sermon. Cincinnati: 1839. 10 p. MdBD. 54658

Brookes, Richard. A new universal gazetteer...originally compiled by R. Brookes. The whole re-modelled and the historical and statistical department brought down to the present period, by John Marshall.... Philadelphia: J. Marshall and Company, 1839. 816 p. CU; IaHA; NjPT; PP; ScAb. 54659

Brooklyn. First Baptist Church. Names and residences of the members of the First Baptist Church in Brooklyn, New York. Connected with the Hudson River Association. Silas Ilsey, pastor. Brooklyn: printed by R. Sears, 1839. 16 p. PCA. 54660

Brooklyn directory. Brooklyn: 1839-[1912] 41 v. MH; NN; NNA; WHi. 54661

Brooklyn Horticultural Soceity. Constitution and by-laws. Brooklyn: 1839. NBLiHi. 54662

Brooks, Thomas. The mute Christian under the smarting rod, with sovereign antidotes for every case. Philadelphia: Presbyterian Board of Education, William S. Martien, publishing agent, 1839. 301 p. MdBD; NjPT; OSW; ScCoT; TWcW. 54663

Brougham and Vaux, Henry Peter Brougham, 1778-1868. A dissertation of the eloquence of the ancients. Philadelphia: E. L. Carey and A. Hart, 1839. 252 p. MA. 54664

----. Historical sketches of statesman who flourished in the time of George III, to which is added remarks on party, and an appendix. 1st series. Philadelphia: Lea and Blanchard, 1839. AU; DLC; MWA; PPA; RPB. 54665

----. ----. 2nd series. Philadelphia: Lea and Blanchard, 1839. 2 v. ArVb; FTU; MiD-B; PPA; WGr. 54666

----. Lord Brougham on education, edited by J. Orville Taylor. New York: Taylor and Cleament, 1839. 91 p. KyLxT; MH; NjR; PU; ViU. 54667

----. Opinions of Lord Brougham, on politics, theology, law, science, education, literature....Philadelphia: Lea and Blanchard, 1839. 2 v. ArCH; KyLoP; Me; OClW; Pu. 54668

----. Sketches of public characters, discourses and essays...to which is added a dissertation on the eloquence of the ancients.... Philadelphia: E. L. Carey and A. Hart, 1839. 2 v. IGK; LNH; NjP; PPA; SCU. 54669

Brown, Bedford, 1795-1870. An address delivered before the two literary societies, of the University of North Carolina: in Gerard Hall; on the day preceding the annual commencement, in June, 1839. Under the appointment of the Dialectic Society. Raleigh, N. C.: printed by T. Loring, 1839. 39 p. A-Ar; MBAt; MH; NcU; PPL. 54670

----. Remarks on presenting the North Carolina

resolutions, in the Senate, January 14, 1839. Washington: Blair, 1839. 8 p. DLC; NcU. 54671

Brown, David Paul, 1795-1872. Oration on the centennial anniversary of the organization of the Fire Department of Philadelphia: December 31, 1838. Philadelphia: J. Van Court, printer, 1839. 16 p. DLC; MiD-B; NN; PHi; PPL. 54672

Brown, Deidamia [Covell] Memoir of the late Rev. Lemuel Covell, missionary to the Tuscarara Indians and the Provines of Upper Canada, also a memoir of Rev. Alanson L. Covall....Brandon: Telegraph office, 1839. 2 v. in 1. DLC; ICN; MWA; NhD; WHi. 54673

[Brown, Erastus] The trial of Cain, the first murderer, in poetry, by rule of court, in which a Presbyterian, a universalian and an Armenian argue as attorneys at the bar; by a moral agent, free [sic] a Methodist.... Brooklyn: Samuel Barnes, 1839. 45 p. NNMHi; RPB. 54674

Brown, Francis H. New York light guard's quick step [for pf.] New York: 1839. CtY. 54675

Brown, James, 1815-1841. An English syntascope, developing the constructive principles of the English phrenod, or language. Philadelphia: James Kay, Jun. and Brother, Pittsburgh: C. H. Kay and Company, 1839. 236, 12, 12 p. CtY; MB; NNC; OO; PU. 54676

Brown, James Robert. Essay on infant cultivation; with a compendium of the analytical method of instruction...adopted at Spitalfields to infants' school.... Philadelphia: Clark, 1839. 56 p. PPPrHi. 54677

Brown, John, 1722-1787. A brief concordance to the Holy Scriptures of the Old and New Testaments; by which all or most, of the principal texts of scriptures may be easily found out...revised and corrected. Concord, N. H.: Roby, Kimball and Merrill, 1839. 31 p. CSmH; MMhHi. 54678

----. A concordance to the Holy Scriptures of the Old and New Testaments. Concord, N. H.: Roby, Kimball and Merrill, 1839. 264 p. IaAt; IJI; MBoy; Nh-Hi; NNUT. 54679

----. A dictionary of the Holy Bible. From the 12th and latest Edinburgh edition. New York: Harper and Brothers, 1839. 272 p. GMM; KyLo. 54680

Brown, John Ball, 1784-1862. Remarks on the operation for the cure of club feet, with cases. Also, letters to John C. Warren, on curvature of the spine. Boston: D. Clapp, Jr., 1839. 27 p. MB; MeB; MWA; NNN; RPB. 54681

Brown, John Newton, 1803-1868. Encyclopedia of religious knowledge; or dictionary of the Bible, theology, religious biography, all religions, ecclesiastical history and missions...to which is added a missionary gazeteer.... Brattleboro', Vt.: Brattleboro' Typographic Company, 1839. 1275 p. MWA: OCalN. 54682

Brown, Jonathan. The history and present condition of St. Domingo. 2nd edition. Boston: Weeks, Jordan and Company, 1839. 2 v. IaB; MMal; MNan; MW; WBeloC. 54683

Brown, Mary Ann B. An address on moral reform; delivered before the Worcester Female Moral Reform Society, October 22, 1839 [Worcester: 1839?] 23 p. IU; MB; MH. 54684

Brown, Matthew, 1776-1853. Address delivered in the chapel of Jefferson College, Canonsburgh, Pa., on July 4, 1839, by M. Brown, President.... Pittsburgh: printed by A. Jaynes, 1839. 20 p. CSmH; ICN; MnSM; PWW; WHi. 54685

----. Address to the graduates of Jefferson College, delivered on the day of commencement, September 27, 1838. Washington: printed by U. W. Wise, 1839. 10 p. CSmH; DLC; ICP; PPPrHi. 54686

Brown, Silas C. The warning voice. A sermon delivered at the funeral of Mr. S., January 9, 1839. Perry: Mitchell, 1839. 15 p. OO. 54687

Brown, Solyman. An infallible method of preventing diseases of the teeth, mouth and gums, by Solyman Brown, dentist.... New York: Kelly and Fraetas, printers, 1839 16 p. NNNAM. 54688

Brown, Thomas. Lectures on the philosophy of the human mind. Corrected from the last London edition. Hallowell: Glazier, Masters and Smith, 1839. 538 p. GEU-T; MBM; NcD; PWW; ViRA. 54689

Brown, William of Illinois. Addresses delivered in the hall of the House of Representatives...for the purpose...of exhibiting the importance of education...including a knowledge of the principles of government.... Vandalia, Ill.: William Hodge, printer, 1839. 22 p. ICHi; MWA; OO; WHi. 54690

Brown University. Catalogue of the officers and students of Brown University, for the academic year, 1839-1840. Providence: Knowles, Vose and Company, 1839. 24 p. MeB. 54691

----. Library. Catalogue of the library and members of the United Brothers' Society, of Brown University. Founded 1806. Providence: Knowles and Vose, printers, 1839. 51 p. MeB; MNBedf; PCA. 54692

----. Phi Beta Kappa. Catalogue of the fraternity of Phi Beta Kappa Alpha of Rhode Isalnd, Brown University...1839. Providence: 1839. 15 p. MeHi; MH; NNC; RHi; RPB. 54693

Browne, Lewis Crebasa. Review of the life and writings of N. Hale Smith; with a vindication of the moral tendency of Universalism, and the moral character of Universalism. Boston: 1839. 360 p. Nh- Hi. 54694

Browne, Thomas, 1605-1682. Religio medici. Hydriotaphia, and the letter to a friend. with an introduction and notes by J. W. Willis Bund. Scribner, N. Y.: 1839. 192 p. OClM. 54695

Brownles, William Craig, 1784-1860. Christian youth's book, and manual for young communicants. New York: Carter [1839] 480 p. DLC; MeBat; NjPT; OC; OO. 54696

----. Popery, an enemy to civil and religious liberty; and dangerous to our republic.... 4th edition.... New York: 1839. 216 p. CtY; GAU; ICP; NbOP; NN; PPL. 54697

Brown's almanack for 1840. Boston: Otis, Broaders and Company [1839] MB; MWA. 54698

----. Concord, N. H.: John F. Brown [1839] MWA. 54699

----. 3rd edition. Concord: J. F. Brown [1839] MWA. 54700

Brown's improved almanack, pocket memorandum, and account book, for...1839...published annually. No. II. Concord, N. H.: John F. Brown...1839. 70 p. MWA; NhHi. 54701

----. 3rd edition. Concord, N. H.: John F. Brown...1839. 70 p. MWA. 54702

Brownson, Orestes Augustus, 1803-1876. An oration delivered before the United Brothers Society of Brown University, at Providence, R. I. September 3, 1839.... Cambridge: Metcalf, Torrey and Ballou, 1839. 24 p. CtY; MiD-B; RPB. 54703

Brunswick and Florida Railroad Company. Charter.... Brunswick: Charles Davis, 1839.DBRE; NN. 54704

Brunswick Land Company [Ga.] To the stockholders of the Brunswick Land Company [Circular concerning Brunswich new stock] Boston: 1839. [2] p. MHi. 54705

Bryant, Samuel. An oration delivered at Mount Aaron, in West Dedham, July 4, 1839. 2nd edition [with a song by Thomas Paine. For the 4th of July] Dedham: 1839. 12 p. HCL; MH. 54706

Bryant, William Cullen, 1794-1878. Poems by William Cullen Bryant. 5th edition. New York: Harper and Brothers, 1839. 276 p. CSmH; DLC; MeB; NN; PHC. 54707

----. Selections from American poets.... New York: Harper and Brothers, 1839. 316 p. C; NBuCC; ODa; RPAt; WvFT. 54708

Buchan, William. Domestic medicine. A treatise on the prevention and cure of diseases. Revised and enlarged and adapted to the diseases of the United States. Cincinnati: U. P. James, 1839. InU-M. 54709

----. ----. To which is annexed a dispensatory for the use of private practitioners...from the 22nd English edition, with considerable additions, and notes. Exeter: J. and B. Williams, 1839. 495 p. MdBJ-W; PPCP. 54710

Buchanan, James, 1791-1868. Speech of Mr. Buchanan, of Pennsylvania. In Senate, February, 1839. On the bill to prevent interference of certain federal officers with elections [n. p.: 1839] 15 p. CtY; MiD-B; MiU-C; P. 54711

Buck Mountain Coal Company. An act incorporating the Buck Mountain Coal Company, and the supplements thereto. Philadelphia: printed by John C. Clark, 1839. 32 p. NNE; PHi. 54712

Buckingham, James Silk, 1786-1855. Public address in defence of his lectures on Palestine, against the criticisms of Eli Smith, published anonymously in the New York Observer, 1839. New York: Molineux, 1839. 36 p. CtHT-W; MB; MH; PHi; PPL. 54713

Buckminster, Joseph Stevens, 1784-1812. The works of Joseph Stevens Buckminster with memoirs of his life.... Boston: James Munroe and Company, 1839. 2 v. CtY; ICU; MBAt; MWA; PU. 54714

Buckner, Richard Aylett, 1763-1847. Speech in the House of Representatives in the legislature of Kentucky, upon the bill to confer banking privileges on the stock-holders in the Charleston, Louisville, and Cincinnati Railroad Company, Frankfort, Ky.: 1839. 27 p. MHi; NN; PPAmP; PPULC; ViU. 54715

The bud of promise; or the memoir of Eliza Darrow. New York: Scofield and Voorhies, Boston: Whipple and Damrell, 1839. 88 p. MH; NcWsS. 54716

Buel, Jesse, 1778-1839. Address of the Hon. Judge Buel, delivered before the Agricultural and Horicultural Societies of New Haven County.... New Haven: printed by B. L. Hamlen, 1839. 35 p. Ct; CtY; DLC; MBHo; MHi. 54717

----. The farmer's companion; or essays on the principles and practice of American husbandry.... Boston: Marsh, Capen, Lyon and Webb, 1839. 303 p. MBAt; MH; PU; RPAt; VtU. 54718

----. The farmer's instructor; consisting of essays, practical directions, and hint for the management of the farm and the garden. New York: Harper and Brothers, 1839. 2 v. in 1. GMilvC; MiD; NRU. 54719

Buffalo, New York. Charter. Charter of the city of Buffalo: with the several amendments; to which are added the laws and ordinances of the city of Buffalo. Revised, January, 1830. Buffalo: press of Thomas and Company, 1839. 93 p. MH-L; NIC; WHi. 54720

----. Ordinances. Laws and ordinances of the city of Buffalo. Revised January, 1839. Buffalo: Thomas and Company, 1839. 105 p. MH-L; NIC. 54721

----. Washington Street Baptist Church. A summary declaration of the birth and practice of the Church of Christ. Buffalo: 1839. MH. 54722

The Buffalo city directory; containing a list of the names, residence and occupation of the heads of families, householders, etc. on the first of May, 1839. Buffalo: Faxon and Graves and A. W. Wilgus, 1839. 144 p. CSmH; MH; MWA; NBuG; WHi. 54723

Buffalo Nursery and Horticultural Garden, Buffalo, New York. Catalogue of fruit and ornamental trees and shrubs, herbaceous and green house plants; cultivated and for sale at the nursery by Benjamin Hodge. Buffalo: press of Day and Steele, 1839. 20 p. CSmH. 54724

----. ----. Buffalo: Press of Day and Steele, 1839-1840. 20 p. CSmH. 54725

Bugard, Mons. Bertrand Francois. French practical teacher. A complete grammar of the French language on the progressive system...comprising 244 exercises, mostly written in the style of conversation and a vocabulary.... Boston: Joseph H. Francis, New York: C. S. Francis [etc., etc.] 1839. CtY; ICU; MB; TxU-T. ViU. 54726

----. French practical translator; or easy method of learning to translate French to English....3rd edition. Boston: Munroe and Francis, New York: C. S. Francis, 1839. DLC; KyLxT; MB; MMal; TxU-T. 54727

Buist, Robert, 1805-1880. The American flower garden directory: containing practicl directions for the culture of plants in the flower garden, hot house , green house, rooms or parlour windows, for every month in the year. 2nd edition. Philadelphia: Carey and Hart, 1839. 379 p. CtHT; GU; IaDaM; PPA; RNR. 54728

Bunyan, John, 1628-1688. The pilgrim's progress. Most carefully collated with the edition containing the author's last additions and corrections. With explanatory notes, by William Mason and a life of the author, by Josiah Conder.... Boston: D. H. Williams, 1839. 447 p. ICP; ICU; IU; MB. 54729

----. ----. In two parts. Middletown, N. Y.: Hunt and Noyes, 1839. 385 p. PWaybu. 54730

Burder, George. Village sermons; or one

hundred and one plain and short discourses, on the principal doctrines of the Gospel; intended for the use of families, sunday schools, or companies assembled for religious instruction in country villages. Philadelphia: Griggs and Elliot, 1839. 476 p. ICU; ScSp; TxSaU-W; ViRu; WaPS. 54731

Burder, Henry Forster. The pleasures of religion. Philadelphia: Presbyterian Board of Publication, William S. Martien, publishing agent, 1839. 302 p. InFtwC; NbOP; NcG; PPPrHi; ViU. 54732

Burditt, Benjamin A. the Dennis quick step as performed by the Boston Brigade band...dedicated to Major Louis Dennis officers...of the Hancock Light Infantry. Boston: Reed, 1839. 3 p. MB. 54733

Burford, Robert, 1791-1861. Description of a view of the city of Lima and the surrounding country, now exhibiting at the Panorama, Broadway, New York. Painted by Robert Burford, from drawwings taken in 1834 by W. Smyth. New York: W. Osborn, 1839. 12 p. DLC; MH; NBuG; NjR. 54734

----. Description of a view of the falls of Niagara now exhibiting at the Panorama. Boston: 1839. MH. 54735

----. Description of a view of the great temple of Karnak, and the surrounding city of Thebes, now exhibiting at the Panorama, broadway, New York. Painted by Robert Burford, from the drawings taken in 1834, by F. Catherwood. New York: printed by W. Osborn, 1839. 16 p. CSmH; DLC; MWA; PHi; ScU. 54736

Burges, Tristam, 1770-1853. Battle of Lake Erie with notices of Commodore Elliot's conduct in that engagement. Boston: B. B. Mussey, 1839. 132 p. CLU; MBL; MWA; OClWHi; PHi. 54737

----. ----. Philadelphia: W. Marshall and Company, 1839. CtY; MdBP; OO; PPA; RPE. 54738

----. ----, Providence: Brown and Cady, 1839. 132 p. CU; DLC; MH; PPA; RP. 54739

----. Correspodence with Thomas W. Dorr [n. p.] 1839. PPL; PPULC. 54740

Burke, Edmund, 1729?-1797. The works of Edmund Burke. Boston: Charles L. Little and James

Brown, Freeman and Bolles, printers, 1839. 9 v. CoD; FOA; KyDC; OCX; RPAt. 54741

Burke, Edmund, 1809-1882. An address delivered before the Democratic Republican citizens of Lempster, N. H., on the 8th of January, 1839. Newport, N. H.: H. E. and S. C. Baldwin, printers, 1839. 23 p. DLC; MWA; Nh; NhD. 54742

Burlington, New Jersey. St. James' Hall. Statement of the plan of education and other arrangements of St. James' Hall, near Bristol. With catalogue. Burlington: 1839. 23 p. PHi. 54743

----. St. Mary's Hall. Annual catalogue. Burlington: 1839-. PHi; PPL. 54744

Burnet, Jacob] 1770-1853. Speech...in the Whig National convention, giving a brief history of the life of Genral William Henry Harrison. Washington: printed at the Madisonian office, 1839. 8 p. CSmH; MBC; MWA; NCH; VtBrt. 54745

Burns, John. The principles of midwifery...From the 8th London edition revised and greatly enlarged with improvements and notes by T. C. James.... New York: Charles S. Francis, 1839. 806 p. Ia; IEN-M; MdBM; NbU-M; TxDaBM. 54746

Burns, Robert, 1759-1796. The works of Robert Burns; containing his life by John Lockhart, Esq. The poetry and correspondence of Dr. Currier's edition.... Hartford: Judd Loomis Publishing Company, 1839. 425 p. NcRA. 54747

----. ----. New York: Robinson and Franklin, 1839. AMob; DLC; MoSM; OHi; ViAl. 54748

----. ----. Philadelphia: J. Cressy, 1839. 258 p. FLwo; IAIS. 54749

Burr, David H., 1803-1875. The American atlas exhibiting the post offices, post roads, railroads, canals and the physical and political divisions of the United States. Boston? 1839. NIC.
----. An atlas of the state of New York, designed for the use of engineers.... Ithaca, New York: Stone and Clark, 1839. IaHA; NIC; NNE; NRU. 54750

----. [Map] City of New York: J. H. Colton and Company, 1839. MH. 54751

----. Map of Florida, exhibiting the post offices,

post roads, canals and railroads...engraved by John Arrowsmith, 1839. DLC; MiU-T; NN. 54752

----. Map of Georgia and Alabama, exhibiting the post offices, post roads, canals, railroads, etc. [Washington: the author] 1839. DLC; WM. 54753

----. Map of Illinois and Missouri, exhibiting the post offices, post roads, canals, railroads, etc. Washington: the author, 1839. DLC; WM. 54754

----. Map of Kentucky and Tennessee, exhibiting the post offices, post roads, canals, railroads, etc. [Washington? 1839] DLC; MiU; NN. 54755

----. Map of Maine, New Hampshire, Vermont, Massachusetts, Rhode Island and Connecticut, exhibiting the post offices, post roads, canals, railroads, etc. [Engraved by John Arrowsmith, 1839] CtY; DLC; MB; MiU; Nh. 54756

----. Map of Michigan and part of Wisconsin Territory. Exhibiting post offices, post roads, canals, railroads, etc. [Engraved by John Arrowsmith, 1839] DLC; MiU; NN. 54757

----. Map of Mississippi, Louisiana, and Arkansas. Exhibiting post offfices, post roads, canals, railroads, etc. [Engraved by John Arrowsmith, 1839] DLC; MiU; NN. 54758

----. Map of New York. Exhibiting post offices, post roads, canals, railroads, etc. [Engraved by John Arrowsmith, 1839] DLC; MiU; MWA; NN. 54759

----. Map of North and South Carolina; exhibiting the post offices, post roads, canals, railroads, etc. Washington: author, 1839. CtY; MiU; NcU; NN; WM. 54760

----. Map of Ohio and Indiana, exhibiting the post offices, post roads, canals, railroads, etc. [Washington: author] 1839. DLC; MiU; MiU; NN. 54761

----. Map of the county of St. Lawrence [N. Y.] Published by the surveyor general pursuant to an act of the legislature. Ithaca, N. Y.: Stone and Clark, republishers, 1839. NIC. 54762

----. Map of the state of New York and the surrounding country, designating county, towns, canals, railroads, senatorial and congressional divisions also principle mail routes. Ithaca, N. Y.:

Stone and Clark, 1839. NIC. 54763

----. Map of the state of Ohio. New York: Colton and Company, 1839. OOxM; PPAmP; PPULC. 54764

----. Map of the United States of North America, with parts of the adjacent countries. 13 pts. [Washington, D. C.] 1839. ICN; MC; WM. 54765

----. Map of the West Indies, with part of Guatemala. New York: 1839. 1 p. PHi; PPULC. 54766

----. Map of Virginia, Maryland and Delaware, exhibiting the post offices, post roads, canals, railroads, etc. [Engraved by John Arrowsmith, 1839] DBRE; DLC; MiU-T; NN. 54767

----. Report on joint improvement of the Wabash River [Indianapolis: 1839] MH-BA. 54768

Burritt, Elijah Hinsdale, 1794-1838. The geography of the heavens, and class book of astronomy; accompanied by a celestial atlas. 5th edition. New York: F. J. Huntington and Company, 1839. 305 p. KyHi; MnSM; NNC; OClWHi; RPAt. 54769

Burroughs, Charles, 1787-1868. Eulogy delivered in St. John's Church, Portsmouth [!] N. H. at the interment of James Hervey Pierpont, M. D. January 27, 1839, by request of the medical faculty. Portsmouth, N. H.: J. W. Foster. 1839. 58 p. DLC; MB; MWA; Nh-Hi; PPPrHi. 54770

Burton, Edward, 1794-1836. History of the Christian church, from the ascension of Jesus Christ, to the conversion of Constantine.... 1st American edition, with a memoir of the author.... New York: Wiley and Putnam, 1839. 407 p. GDecCT; MB; NNUT; TChU. 54771

Burton, Walter Henry, d. 1828. An elementary compendium of the law of real property...From the last London edition. Philadelphia: John S. Littell, New York: Halstead and Voorhies, 1839. 277 p. Ct; NcD; OO; PP; TxHYM-L. 54772

[Burton, Warren] 1800-1866. White slavery: a new emancipation cause, presented to the people of the United States. Worcester: M. D. Phillips, Boston: C. C. Little and Company, 199 p. ICN; MdBP; MWA; NjP; PPL. 54773

Burton, William Evans. Burton's comic songster.

Being entirely a new collection of original and popular songs. Edited by W. E. Burton. Philadelphia: Kay, 1839. 320 p. MB; MWA; RPB. 54774

[Bury, Charlotte (Campbell)] 1775-1861. Continuation of the diary illustrative of the times of George IV, interspersed with original letters from the late Queen Caroline, and from various other distinguished persons, edited by John Galt.... Phialdelphia: Lea and Blanchard, 1839. 2 v. DeWi; LU; MWiW; NcD; NN. 54775

[----?] Flirtation: answer to Fanny Grey [Voice and pf.] Philadelphia: 1839. CtY. 54776

Bush, George, 1796-1859. A grammar of the Hebrew language....2nd edition, corrected and enlarged. New York: Gould, Newman and Saxton, 1839. 276 p. CtHT; MH-AH; NbOM; PU; ViU. 54777

----. Illustrations of the Holy Scripture derived principally from the manners, customs, rites, tradltlons, forms of speech, antiquities.... Brattleboro': Brattleboro' Typographic Company. 1839. 656 p. CtY; MH; NjPT; PRosC; PV. 54778

----. The life of Mahommed, founder of the religion of Islam, and of the empire of th Saracens. New York: Harper and Brothers, 1839. 112 p. CStoC; MPeaI; NGlc; OAU; PPM. 54779

Bushnell, Horace, 1802-1876. A discourse on the slave question, delivered in the North Church, Hartford, January 10, 1839. Hartford: printed by case, Tiffany and Company, 1839. 32 p. CU; DLC; MH-AH; NcD; RP. 54780

----. ----. 2nd edition. Hartford: printed by Case, Tiffany and Company, 1839. 32 p. CtHt; IEG; MBAt; MWA; NCH. 54781

----. ----. 3rd edition. Hartford: printed by Case, Tiffany and Company, 1839. 32 p. MiD-B; NjR. 54782

Butler, Benjamin Franklin, 1795-1858. Address before Dialectic Society of the corps of cadets of the military academy, West Point, June 19, 1839. New York: Samuel Colman, 1839. 45 p. OClWHi. 54783

----. Military profession in the United States and the means of promoting its usefulness and honour;

an address delivered at West Point, June 19, 1839. New York: S. Colman, 1839. 46 p. CtY; MH; MWA; NjR; PPi. 54784

Butler, Charles. The American lady. Philadelphia: Hogan and Thompson, 1839. 288 p. CtY; MiD; NjP; PPi; TxU. 54785

Butler, Clement Moore. The year of the church: hymns and devotional verse for sunday and holy days of the ecclesiastical year; with brief explanations of their origin and design. Utica: press of Eli Maynard, 1839. 166 p. DLC; IEG; NNUT; RPB; TWoW. 54786

Butler, J. H. The evil of partiality. Northampton: John Metcalf, 1839. ICBB. 54787

----. The peach orchard. Northampton: John Metcalf, 1839. ICBB. 64788

Butler, Joseph, 1692-1752. The analogy of religion, natural and revealed, to the constitution and course of nature. New York: Robinson and Franklin, Boston: Crocker and Brewster, 1839. 348 p. CSt; GAU; MeBa; MH; NbOP. 54789

Butler, Mann, 1784-1852. An historical sketch of the Natchez, or district of Natchez, in the state of Mississippi, from 1763 to 1798 [New York: 1839] ICN. 54790

Butler, Samuel, 1612-1680. Hudibras; in three parts: written in the time of the late wars. With a life of the author, annotations, and an index. New York: Robinson and Franklin, 1839. 312 p. CSmH; LNH; MH; PBa; TNT. 54791

Butler, Samuel, 1774-1840. An atlas of ancient geography. Stereotyped by J. Howe. Philadelphia: Lea and Blanchard, 1839. CtMW; MiD; NjP; OWoC; RPB. 54792

Buttmann, Philipp Karl, 1764-1829. A Greek grammar for the use of high schools and universities. Translated from the German by Edward Robinson. 2nd edition. Andover: Gould, Newman and Saxton, 1839. 494 p. C-S; KyLoS; MB; NjP. 54793

Buxton, Thomas Fowell, 1786-1845. The African slave trade. 1st American from the 2nd London edition. Philadelphia: Merrihew and Thompson, 1839. 188 p. CtY; KyBC; MBBC; PCC; ViU. 54794

Bynum, Jesse A. Speech of Mr. Bynum, of North Carolina, on the motion of Mr. Wagener to be excused from serving on the investigating committee to examine into the defalcation of Samuel Swartwout, in the House of Representatives, January, 1839. Washington: Blair and Rives, printers, 1839. 13 p. MdHi; TxU. 54795

Byron, George Gordon Noel Byron, 6th Baron, 1788-1824. Letters and journals...with notices of his life. New York: Harper, 1839. 2 v. PP; PPULC; PU. 54796

----. Poetical works. Philadelphia: R. W.

Pomeroy, 1839. IaWel; MH; PP; TxU. 54797

----. The works of Lord Byron in verse and prose; including his letters, journals, etc. With a sketch of his life. New York: Alexander V. Blake, etc., etc., etc., 1839. 627 p. CtY; DLC; MdW; PU; PPULC. 54798

----. ----. Philadelphia: E. L. Carey and A. Hart, 1839. 8 v. GCu; MoSU; OCl; PSC; OTif. 54799

----. ----. including the sppressed poems. Also a sketch of his life, by J. W. Lake.... Philadelphia: Grigg and Elliot, 1839. 764 p. CSmH; KyDC; NcAS; PPA; ViSwc. 54800

C

Cabinet of curiosities, or wonders of the world displayed: forming a repository of whatever is remarkable, in the regions of nature and art...from the 13th London edition.... New York: J. C. Riker, 1839? 2 v. in 1. MB; MiU; NN; TxU. 54801

Casear, C. Julius. Commentaries on the Gallic war; and the first book of the Greek paraphrase; with English notes, critical and explanatory, plans of battles, sieges, etc., and historical, geographical and archaeological indexes. By Charles Anthon, LL. D.... New York: Harper and Brothers, 1839. 493 p. MdW; MeBaT; NPV; PMy; VtPifi. 54802

----. Commentarii de bello gallico ad codices parisinos recensiti A.N.L. Achaintre et N.E. Lemaire.... Curavit F. P. Leverett. Bostoniae: Hilliard, Gray et soc., 1839. 220 p. MH; NjR. 54803

----. Quae Extant, interpretatione et motis illustravit Johannes Godvinus, Professor Regious, in usum delphini. The notes and interpretations translated and improved by Thomas Clark. New edition, carefully corrected by comparison with a standard London edition and containing various amendations in the notes, by William Mann, A.M. Philadelphia: Thomas, Cowperthwaite and Company, 1839. KyMad. 54804

----. ----. 5th edition. Philadelphia: published by Desiboer, 1839 [9] 410-[6] p. OrPU. 54805

Cairo City and Canal Company. An act to incorporate the Cairo City and Canal Company, in the state of Illinois. New York: printed by Narine and Company, 1839. 16 p. MiD-B. 54806

----. Prospectus and engineers' report relating to the city of Cairo, incorporated by the state of Illinois. St. Louis: T. Watson and Son, 1839. 35 p. DBRE. 54807

Caldwell, Charles, 1772-1853. Thoughts on the true connexion of phrenology and religion, in a letter to the editor of the American Phrenological Journal and Miscellany in Philadelphia. Louisville: J. Maxwell, Jr., City Gazette, printer, 1839.

24 p. ICU; KyBgW; MHi. 54808

Caldwell, William B. Address delivered before the graduates of the Erodelphian Society, of the Miami University...August 7, 1839.... Oxford, Ohio: printed by W. W. Bishop, 1839. 22 p. MWA; NN; OHi; OUr; PPiXT. 54809

Calhoun, John Caldwell, 1782-1852. Remarks...on the bill to prevent the interference of certain federal officers in elections; delivered in the Senate of the United States, February 22, 1839. Washington: Blair and Rives, printers, 1839. 14 p. CSmH; DLC; TxU; ViU. 54810

----. Remarks on the graduation bill. In Senate, Jan. 15, 1839. Washington: printed by Blair and Rives, 1839. 7 p. CtSoP; DLC; NjR; PHi; TxDaM. 54811

Calhoun, Philo. A lecture on the study of mathematics, delivered in Washington College, September 5, 1839.... Richmond: P. D. Bernard, printer, 1839. 1 vol. A-Ar; CSmH. 54812

Callender, F. B., and Company. Catalogue of theological and classical works, sold Aug. 1. Boston: 1839. MBAt. 54813

Cambridge, Massachusetts. List of voters. Nov. 11, 1839. [Cambridge: 1839] MH. 54814

----. Town and county taxes assessed in the town of Cambridge for the year 1839. Cambridge: 1839. M; MB; MBAt; MHi. 54815

----. School Committee. Regulations for the public schools in Cambridge, adopted by the school committee, 1839 [Cambridge] Cambridge press, Metcalf, Torry and Ballou, 1839. 22 p. CSmH. 54816

Cammlung von Geiftlechen Liedern, our firchlichen und hauslechen Gottesdienft.... Cincinnati: Berlegt von J. F. Wright and L. Swormstedt, fur die bifchdf-liche methodistenfirche, 1839. 480 p. ScCoT. 54817

Campbell, Alexander, 1788-1866. An address on the amelioration of the social state delivered at the request of a literary association as introductory to a course of popular lectures in Louisville. Louisville: Prentice and Weissinger, 1839. 31 p. DLC; MHi; NcMHi; NN; OCHP. 54818

----. The Christian system in reference to the union of Christians and a restoration of primitive Christianity as plead in the current reformation. 2nd edition. Bethany, Va.: Forrester and Campbell, 1839. 368 p. GMM; ICP; IEG; NBuDD; PCC. 54819

----. ----. 2nd edition. Cincinnati: Bosworth, Chase and Hall [1839] 358 p. IU; MB; OCl; PPC; TU. 54820

----. ----. [2nd editon] Cincinnati: Standard Publishing Company [1839] 358 p. IaDmD; MB; NbOP; OCl; PCC.54821

----. ----. [2nd edition] Pittsburg: Forrester and Campbell, 1839. 368 p. DLC; LNB; OClWHi; TxDaM; ViU. 54822

----. Supernatural facts: an address, delivered to the Maysville lyceum...March 25th, 1839.... Bethany, Va.: printed by A. Campbell, 1839. CSmH; MiU; WvBeC. 54823

Campbell, Samuel D. Infant baptism by Samuel D. Campbell, of Brandon, Mississippi. Lexington, Va.: Letcher and Gillock, printers, 1839. 9 p. MWA; NjPT; PPPrHi. 54824

Campbell, Thomas, 1777-1844. The poetical works of Thomas Campbell including Theodric and many other pieces not contained in any former edition. Philadelphia: J. Crissy, and J. Grigg, 1839. 182, 38 p. CSansS; GEU; IGK; LNDil; MH. 54825

Campbell, William W., 1806-1861. Lecture on the life and military services of General James Clinton. read before the New York Historical Society, Feb., 1839. New York: printed by William Osborn, 1839. 23 p. CSmH; LNH; MB; MWA; PHi. 54826

Canandaigua Academy. Catalogue and circular of the Ontario Female Seminary, Canandaigua: for the year ending June, 1839. Printed by C. Morse, 1839. 8 p. NCanHi; NGH. 54827

Canby, William. Album. New York: J. C. Riker, 1839. PHC; PPULC. 54828

A candid statement respecting the Philadelphia County ticket [Philadelphia: 1839?] 63 p. DLC; MH; PPL. 54829

----. Philadelphia: January, 1839. 32 p. DLC; OClWHi; PHi. 54830

Candour, Timothy. The fifteen gallon keg. A sermon occasioned by the passing of an act to regulate the sale of spiritous liquors in the commonwealth of Massachusetts. Boston: 1839. 28 p. MAbD; MH. 54831

Canfield, Russel. Atheism abjured, and the libels of infidels self-refuted. Philadelphia: 1839. 24 p. ICMe; KyDC; PHi; PPULC. 54832

The canons of good breading; or the hand book of the men of fashion. By the author of "the laws of etiquette.".... Philadelphia: Lea and Blanchard, 1839. 234 p. ICU; LU; MB; MFi; PU. 54833

Canterbury, New Hampshire. Congregational Church. Articles of faith and covenant, to which are added articles of government and practice, and a list of members. Concord: 1839. 16 p. Nh-Hi. 54834

Carbondale journal. 1839-1840 [Pennsylvania Newspaper] PHi; PPULC. 54835

Carden, Allen D. The Missouri harmony; or a collection of psalm and hymn tunes, and anthems, from eminent authors, with an introduction to the grounds and rudiments of music by Allen D. Carden; to which is added a supplement.... by an amateur, Cincinnati: Morgan, 1839. 200, 36 p. MiU; MoHi; NcU; NNUT; OClWHi. 54836

Carey, John L. Some thoughts concerning domestic slavery, in a letter to...Esq. of Baltimore, by John L. Carey. 2nd edition. Baltimore: D. Brunner, 1839. 115 p. DLC; MdBD; MdBP; NcD; RP. 54837

Carey, Mathew, 1760-1839. The querist. An humble imitation of a work under a similar title, published by the celebrated Berkley, Bishop of Cloyne. Addressed to citizens of all parties and of no particular party, by whatever name they are designated.... By an octagenarian citizen of Philadelphia. Philadelphia [n. pub. or pr.] 1839. 10

p. MdBP; PPM; PU. 54838

----. To whom it may concern, report on case of industrious females. M. C. President, Philadelphia: 1839. 8 p. PHi; PPULC. 54839

----. Vindiciae hibernicae; or Ireland vindicated. By M. Carey.... 3rd edition, enlarged and improved. Philadelphia: R. P. Desilver, 1839. 474 [4] p. CtY; NNAIHi. 54840

Carey and Hart, publishers. Carey and Hart's catalogue of choice, rare and valuable books.... Philadelphia: Carey and Hart, 1839. [2]-30 p. LNT. 54841

Carleton, William, 1794-1869. Father Butler and the Lough Dearg Pilgrim.... To which is added national tales. By Thomas Hood.... Philadelphia: T. K. and P. G. Collins, 1839. 2 v. MH. 54842

----. Neal Malone, and other tales of Ireland. Philadelphia: E. L. Carey and A. Hart, 1839. 2 v. OCh; OMC; PFal. 54843

Carlisle, Pennsylvania. Regulations, studies, and systems of the common schools of Carlisle, Pennsylvania. Established 15th of August 1836.... Carlisle: Sanderson and Corman, printers, 1839. 16 p. MH; P. 54844

Carlow, John. Journal of adventures at sea, before and during the late war between Great Britain and the United States of America. Portland [Me] C. W. Pennell, printer, 1839. 102 p. CtY; MeHi; MiU-C. 54845

Carlyle, Thomas, 1795-1881. The French revolution; a history. 2nd edition. Boston: C. C. Little and James Brown, London: James Fraser, 1839. 3 v. CtMW; MdBP; MH; PU; WyU. 54846

----. Wilhelm Meisters apprenticeship and travels complete in one vol. New York: A. L. Burt, 1839. 387 p. NNopo; NR; WvWel. 54847

----. ----. New York: P. F. Collier and Son, 1839. 435 p. NbOC. 54848

----. ----. From the German. New York: Thomas Y. Crowell and Company, 1839. 2 v. NcDurN. 54849

----. The works of Thomas Carlyle.... Critical and miscellaneous essays. In 16 volumes. New York: Peter Fenelon Collier, 1839-69. 16 v. OkPer. 54850

Caroline almanack, and American freeman's chronicle, for 1840. Rochester, N.Y.: Mackenzie's Gazette office [1839] MB; MWA. 54851

Carpenter, Benjamin Owen. Adventures of a copy of Swedenborg's treatise, concerning heaven and hell, "by itself." ...Arranged for the press by Benjamin Owen Carpenter. Chillicothe: for the author, 1839. 41 p. OClWHi; OUrC; PBa; PPULC; R; ViU. 54852

Carpenter, Thomas. Scholar's spelling assistant. 1st American edition. New York: 1839. CTHWatk. 54853

Carter, William B. Circular of the Hon. William B. Carter, to the freemen of the 1st congressional district of Tennessee [Elizabethtown, Tenn.: 1839] 12 p. PPL-R. 54854

Cash, Merit H. Address on education, delivered on the occasion of the examinaton of the students of West-Town Academy, October 1, 1839.... Goshen, O.: printed by V. M. Drake, 1839. 16 p. NN. 54855

Cass, Lewis, 1782-1866. An historical, geographical and statistical account of the Island of Candia; or ancient Crete. By the American minister at Paris.... Richmond: Thomas W. White, 1839 [2]-12 p. DLC; MH; PPL-R; RP. 54856

----. Remarks on Stephen's "incidents of travel in Egypt, Arabia Petraea, and the Holy Land." First published in the "North American Review." Cambridge: Folsom, Wells and Thurston, 1839. MB; ViU. 54857

Castle, Thomas, 1804?-1840? A manual of surgery founded upon the principles and practice lately taught by Sir Astley Cooper, bart., F. R. S. and Joseph Henry Green, Esq., F. R. S.... 4th edition. Edited by Thomas Castle, F. L. S. Boston: Munroe and Francis, New York: Charles Francis, 1839 [13]-467 p. CtY; LNX; MiDW-M; PPCP; ViU. 54858

Castleton Medical College, Castleton, Vermonmt. Announcements and catalogues of the students and graduates...1840-. Albany: 1839-. PPCP. 54859

----. Circular of the Vermont academy of

medicine, for the session of 1840. Castleton, Vermont, Dec., 1839. Albany: printed by Henry D. Stone and Company, 1839. 14 p. NNNAM. 54860

A catechism of American law, adapted to popular use. Phildelphia: Atkinson, 1839. 256 p. MdBLC; PLFM. 54861

Catholic Church. Liturgy and ritual. Ursuline manual; revised by J. Power. New York: 1839. MoS. 54862

----. ----. Officia propria. Baltimore. Officia propria Archidioecesis et Seminarii S. Mariae, Baltimorensis.... Baltimore: Murphy, 1839. 128 p. MdBS. 54863

Catholic Tract Society of Baltimore. Addres of the editorial committee of the...society...to the public. Baltimore: John Murphy, printer, 1839. 24 p. MdCatS; MdHi; OCX; PLatS. 54864

Cazenovia Junior College for Women. Catalogue of the officers and students of the Oneida Conference Seminary. Cazenovia, New York, 1838-9. Cazenovia: printed at the Union Herald office, 1839. DLC. 54865

Cecil, Catharine. Memoirs of Mrs. Hawkes, late of Islington; including remarks in conversation and extracts from sermons and letters of the late Rev. Richard Cecil. 2nd American edition. Philadelphia: J. Whetham, 1839. 468 p. GDecCT; IEG; MdBe; MWA; ViAl. 54866

Ceres; Eine Zeitschrift fur den Landwirth. Redigirt von Dr. Adolf Bauer. Hrsg. von Samuel Miller. Labenon, Pa.: 1839. PPG; PPULC. 54867

Cervantes Saavedra, Miguel de, 1547-1616. The life and exploits of Don Quixote De La Mancha. Trans. from the original Spanish of Miguel De Cervante Saavedra. By Charles Jarvis.... Exeter: J. and B. Williams, 1839. 4 v. 244 p. MBBC; MH; ViU. 54868

Chadwick, Jabez. Scripture proofs of the perpetual obligation of the 7th day sabbath. Medina: 1839. MBAt. 54869

Challoner, Richard. Memoirs of missionary priests, and other Catholics of both sexes, that have suffered death in England on religious accounts, from the year 1577, to 1684.... Philadelphia: John J. Green, 1839. 2 v. in 1. IaDuCl;

MdBLC; MoSU; MWA; PPM. 54870

Chalmers, Thomas, 1780-1847. The works of Thomas Chalmers, D.D., minister of the Tron church, Glasgow.... Philadelphia: Haswell, Barrington and Haswell, New Orleans: Alexander Towar, 1839. 469 p. IaB; LNB; MeLewB; NcU; OWoC. 54871

Chamier, Frederick, 1796-1870. Jack Adams, the mutineer. By Captain Chamier.... Philadelphia: E. G. Dorsey, printer, 1839. 2 v. CtY; RPB. 54872

Chandler, Amariah. Approved pastor; a sermon at the installation of Andrew Govan over the Evangelical Congregational Church and Society in Rowe, Sept. 5, 1838. Greenfield: 1839. 23 p. MBC; MiU; MWA; RPB. 54873

Chandler, Joseph Ripley, 1792-1880. An address, delivered before the Goethean and Diagnothian societies of Marshall College, at their annual celebration September 24, 1839.... Philadelphia: J. Crissy, printer, 1839. 44, 30 p. CSmH; MiD-B; NCH; OClWHi; PPM. 54874

----. Orations delivered before the Northern Lyceum...at their anniversaries in 1837-8. By Joseph R. Chandler and Morton M'Michael, Esqs. Philadelphia: J. Perry, printer, 1839. 40 p. DLC; MiD-B; NcD. 54875

Channing, William, 1800?-1855. The reformation of medical science, demanded by inductive philosophy; a discourse delivered before the New York Physician's Society, on their anniversary, November 21, 1838. New York: Wiley and Putnam, 1839. 58 p. CSt; MBAt; NBMS; PPM; PU. 54876

----. ----. 2nd edition. New York: Wiley and Putnam, 1839. 58 p. CtY; CU; ICU; MBM; RPB. 54877

Channing, William Ellery, 1780-1842. Lecture on war. Boston: Dutton and Wentworth, 1839. 50 p. ICMe; MB; MWA; PPL; ScU. 54878

----. Remarks on the slavery question, in a letter to Jonathan Phillips, Esq. Boston: J. Munroe and Company, 1839. 91 p. ArU; MBBC; NcD; RPB; WaSp. 54879

----. Self-culture. An address introductory to the Franklin lectures, delivered at Boston, September, 1838. Boston: J. Munroe and Company, 1839. 57 p. CSt; MeAu; MWA; PU; RHi. 54880

The chapel hymn book. 3rd edition. Boston: Simpkins, 1839. ICMe; MB; MHi; NN. 54881

Chapin, Alonzo B. A sermon, delivered in Christ church, West Haven...1836, the hundredth anniversary of laying the foundation of the church, by...A. B. Chapin.... New Haven: Hitchcock and Stafford, 1839. 28 p. CtY; LNH; MBC; NjR; RPB. 54882

Chapin, Stephen, 1778-1845. A sermon, delivered at Long Branch Church, Fauquier County, Va., at the ordination of Traverse D. Herndon and Charles S. Adams, December 24, 1838. Published by request. Washington: printed by Peter Force, 1839. NCH-S; ViRU. 54883

Chapin, William, 1802-1888. A complete reference gazetteer of the U. S. of North America; containing a general view of the United States, and of each state and territory, and a notice of the various canals, railroads and internal improvement.... together with all the post offices in the United States.... New York: W. Chapin and J. B. Taylor, 1839. 347 p. CU; LU; MBC; NjP; WaPS. 54884

----. Ornamental map of the United States. New York: 1839. OO. 54885

Chaplin, J. E. Captain Ball's experience. Philadelphia: 1839. MB. 54886

----. The rose-bushes. Boston: 1839. MB. 54887

Chapman, Jonathan, 1775-1847. An oration delivered before the Whigs of Bristol County, at Taunton, July 4, 1839. Taunton: I. Amsbury, Jr., printer, 1839. 34 p. CSmH; MB; MBAt; MNBedf; MWA. 54888

Chapman, Maria [Weston] 1806-1885. Right and wrong in Massachusetts. By Maria Weston Chapman.... Boston: Dow and Jackson's Anti-slavery press, 1839. 177 p. IaU; MWA; NjN; OClWHi; ViU. 54889

Chaptal de Chanteloup, Jean Antoine Claude, 1756-1832. Chymistry applied to agriculture...translated from the 2nd French edition. Boston: Hilliard, 1839. 365 p. CU; MiD; MPiB; OMC; WU-A. 54890

Charleston, South Carolina. Rules for the government of the poor house, and of the poor. Charleston: 1839. MBAt. 54891

----. Fire Department. A report from the board of fire masters, and, also, a report by the mayor, in relation to the ordinance to reorganize the fire department. Ratified Feb. 11, 1839.... Charleston: 1839. 24 p. DLC. 54892

----. ----. Rules of the board of fire masters, together with the late ordinance of council, for the organization of the fire department. Charleston [S.C.] 1839. 12 p. DLC. 54893

----. Mayor, 1839 [H. L. Pinckney] A report containing a review of the proceedings of the city authorities from 1st Sept., 1838, to 1st Aug., 1839. Charaleston: 1839. 94 p. MH; NcD; ScHi; ScU. 54894

----. ----. Report, respecting the general condition of city affairs; with suggestions for the improvement of the different branches of the public service. Printed by order of council, Charleston: 1839. 11 p. ScU. 54895

Charleston Orphan House, Charleston, South Carolina. Rules.... Charleston: 1839. PPL. 54896

Charleston Port Society for Promoting the Gospel among Seamen, Charleston, S.C. Proceedings and address of the Charleston Port Society in behalf of the establishment of a sailor's home, in this city.... Charleston: S.S. Miller, 1839. 8 p. DLC. 54897

Charlestown, Massachusetts. Boylston Chapel Sunday School. A service book for sunday schools. Added, a collection of hymns. 4th edition. Boston: Green, 1839. 95 p. MB. 54898

----. School Committee. Rreport, 1838-1873. Charlestown: 1839-74. 35 v. DLC; MB; MH. 54899

Charlestown Debating Society, Charlestown, Mass. Constitution and by-laws of the Charlestown Debating Society adopted November, 1838 [Charlestown] Bunker Hill Aurora office, 1839. 12 p. M; NN. 54900

Charlestown Wharf Company. Report of the committee appointed by the stockholders. Boston: Sleeper, Dix and Rogers, 1839. 16 p. MH; MH-BA. 54901

Charlton, Robert Milledge, 1807-1854. Eulogy on the late Doctor John Cumming, delivered before the Hibernian Society, on the festival of St. Patrick. Savannah: Purse, 1839. 15 p. GHi; GU-De; NcD. 54902

----. Poems, by Robert M. Charlton, and Thomas J. Charlton.... Boston: C. C.Little and J. Brown, 1839. 174 p. GMW; IU; NcD; TxU; ViL. 54903

Chase, Philander. Address and other services, at the laying of the cornerstone of the chapel and school house of Jubilee College, Illinois, on the 3rd day of April, 1839. Peoria: S. H. Davis, 1839. 12 p. CtHT; MdBD; NNG; OCHp; RPB. 54904

----. An address, delivered at Saint James' Church, Chicago, to the 5th annual convention, of the Protestant Episcopal Church, of the Diocese of Illinois, June 3, 1839. Printed at the office of the Chicago American, 1839. 11 p. MBD; MBDil; MWA. 54905

Chauncey, Henry, defendant. The life of Eliza Sowers, together with a full account of the trial of Dr. H. Chauncey, Dr. William Armstrong and W. Nixon, for the murder of that unfortunate victim of illicit love; containing the examination of witnesses.... Philadelphia: Sage, printer, 1839. 37 p. MdHi; NHi; PP; PPB. 54906

Cheever, George Barrell, 1807-1890. The American common-place book of poetry, with occasional notes. Philadelphia: Herman Hooker, 1839. 404 p. CLSU; FTU; NcD. 54907

----. The American common-place book of prose; a collecton of eloquent and interesting extracts from the writings of American authors. Philadelphia: Thomas, Cowperthwait and Company, 1839. 468 p. MH; NCH; NIC; OPosm. 54908

Chesapeake and Ohio Canal Company. Communication from G. C. W., President of the Chesapeake and Ohio Canal Company, in answer to the report made to the House of Delegates by the chairman of the committee on internal improvements in relation to the said company. Annapolis: 1839. MdHi. 54909

----. ----. [Washington?: 1839] 23, 3 p. CtY; DLC. 54910

----. Report of the general committee of the stockholders of the Chesapeake and Ohio Canal Company.... Washington: printed by Gales and Seaton, 1839. 36 p. MdHi; NNE. 54911

Chevalier, Michel, 1806-1879. Probable fall in the value of gold: the commercial and social consequences that may ensue, and the measures which it invites. New York: D. Appleton, 1839. MiD. 54912

----. Society, manners and politics in the United States: being a series of letters on North America. Tr. from the 3rd Paris edition. Boston: Weeks, Jordan and Company, 1839. 467 p. ArU; CU; MB; TxHR; WBeloC. 54913

Chicago. Ordinances. The law and ordinances of the city of Chicago passed in common council. Chicago: printed by Edward H. Rudd, 1839. 46 [6] p. ICHi. 54914

Chickering, John White. Christian morality: a series of discourses on the Decalogue.... Boston: Crocker and Brewster, 1839. 257 p. InCW; MBC; MeB; OT; ViRut. 54915

Child, Lydia Maria [Franics] 1802-1880. Anti-slavery catechism. By Mrs. Child.... 2nd edition. Newburyport: C. Whipple, 1839. 36 p. DLC; IaHi; MWA; PPL; RPB. 54916

----. The evils of slavery and the cure of slavery. The first proved by the opinion of southerners themselves, the last shown by historical evidence.... 2nd edition. Newburyport: Charles Whipple, 1839. 24 p. CtSoP; DLC; MBAt; NcD; ViHaI. 54917

----. Philothea. A romance...By Mrs. Child...2nd edition. Boston: Otis, Broaders and Company, 1839. 284 p. DLC; MB; MBev; MWA; NcD. 54918

The child's commandment and the child's promise. Philadelphia: 1839. 3 v. DLC. 54919

The child's favorite.... Hartford: L. Stebbins, 1839. CtY. 54920

The child's first book, comprising exercises in the alphabet on an improved plan, adapted to the capacity of small children according to Webster's orthography. 5th edition. Hartford: R. White, 1839. MH. 54921

The child's first book of thought. Boston: S. G. Simpkins, 1839. 72 p. MH; NNC; NUt. 54922

The child's gem, by a lady. New York: S. Coleman [1839] MH. 54923

China mission advocate.... [Boston] 1839. 383 [1] p. NjP; ViRU. 54924

----. Louisville, Ky.: 1839. 1 v. KyBgW; NN; NRAB; PPULC. 54925

Chipman, Richard Manning, 1806-1893. A discourse on free discussion, delivered in Harwinton, Ct., February 17th, 1839; by Richard M. Chipman. Hartford: L. Skinner, printer, 1839. CtY; DHU. 54926

----. A discourse on the nature and means of ecclesiastical prosperity: delivered at the dedication of the house of worship in Terryville, Ct., August 8th, 1838. By...pastor of the church in Harwinton.... Hartford: L. Skiner, 1839. 22 p. Ct; MBC; MWA; NjPT; RPB. 54927

Chitty, Joseph, 1776-1841. A practical treatise on bills of exchange, checks on bankers, promissory notes, bankers' cash notes and bank notes.... 9th American from the 8th London edition.... Springfield: G. and C. Merriam, 1839. 986 p. Ct; ICLaw; MoS; NNLI; WaU. 54928

----. A practical treatise on the law of contracts, not under seal; and upon the usual defences to actions thereon. By Joseph Chitty...4th American edition from the 2nd London edition, corrected and greatly enlarged, by the author. With notes of former editions, to which are now added, copious notes of American decisions to the present time, by J. C. Perkins, esq. Springfield [Mass] G. and C. Merriam, 1839. 757 p. CU-Law; Ia; MiDU-L; ViU; WU-L. 54929

----. Precedents in pleading...By Joseph Chitty, Jun.... 1st American from the 1st London edition.... Springfield: G. and C. Merriam, 1839. 2 v. CU; Ia; MH-L; PU-L; Vi-L. 54930

Christ refected; the quaker, and other poems. Philadelphia: 1839. 191 p. PHi. 54931

The Christian almanac. New York: American Tract Society, 1839. 47 p. FStPHi. 54932

The Christian almanac for New England...1840...Boston: published for the American Tract Society, and for Gould, Kendall and Lincoln [1839] 46 p. RNHi; WHi. 54933

The Christian almanac for New York, Connecticut and New Jersey, for the year of our Lord and Saviour, Jesus Christ, 1840; being the bissextile, or leap year, and until July 4th, the 64th of the independence of the U. S.... New York [1839] 46 [2] p. MWA; NCH; NjMo; PCA. 54934

Christian almanac for Pennsylvania and Delaware for 1840. Philadelphia, Pa.: Pennsylvania Branch of the American Tract Society [1839] MWA. 54935

Christian almanac for Pennsylvania and the middle states for 1840. Philadelphia, Pa.: Philadelphia Tract Society [1839] MWA. 54936

The Christian almanac for western Pennsylvania, for the year of our Lord and Saviour, Jesus Christ, 1840: being bissextile, or leap year, and, until July 4, the 64th of the independence of the United States.... Pittsburgh: Patterson and Ingram [1839] 46 [2] p. OClWHi. 54937

Christian almanack for 1840. Boston, Mass.. published for the American Tract Society, and for Gould, Kendall and Lincoln [1839] MWA. 54938

The Christian economy: translated from the original Greek of an old manuscript, found in the island of Patmos, where St. John wrote his book of Revelations. Lowell [Mass.] E. A. Rice and Company, 1839 [23]-92 p. CSmH. 54939

The Christian magistrate, a memoir of the Hon. Ezra Butler, late governor of Vermont, by a lady. Philadelphia: Baptist General Tract Society, 1839 [2] 16, 3, 4 p. MiU-C; NjPT. 54940

The Christian offering, and churchman's annual; edited by Rev. John W. Brown. New York: Sherman and Trevett, 1839. 204 p. CtY; IaB; NjR; RNR. 54941

Christison, Robert, 1797-1882.... On granular degeneration of the kidneys, and its connection with dropsy, inflammations and other diseases.... Philadelphia: A. Waldie, 1839. CtY; MdBJ; Nh; PPA; ViU. 54942

The Christmas school primer; designed for schools and families carefully compiled for the instruction and improvement of the infant mind and heart.... New York: George F. Cooledge, 1839. 48 p. NjR; NN; RPB. 54943

Church, Benjamin, 1639-1718. The history of Philip's War, commonly called the Great Indian War of 1675 and 1676.... 2nd edition with plates. Exeter, N.H.: J. and B. Williams, 1839. 360 p. KSteC; MdHi; NN; OClWHi. 54944

Church, Pharcellus, 1801-1886. An address delivered at the dedication of Mount Hope Cemetary, Rochester, Oct. 2, 1838.... Rochester: David Hoyt, 1839. 21 p. CtY; MH; MiD-B; MWelC; NRHi. 54945

Churchill, Fleetwood, 1808-1878. Outlines of the principal diseases of females, chiefly for the use of students. By Fleetwood Churchill, M.D. Philadelphia: A. Waldie, 1839. 302 p. CoCsC; ICU-R; MeB; PPA; TU-M. 54946

The churchman armed against error. New York: 1839. 68 p. MiAlbC; MWA. 54947

The churchman's almanac for the year of our Lord, 1840.... New York: John R. M'Gown, 1839. 36 p. IEG; MWA; NBuDD; NCH; OrPD. 54948

Cicero, Marcus Tullius. Ad qunitum fratem dialogi tres de oratore; cum exerplis ex notis variorum. Edited by Jac. L. Kinglsey. New York: Alexander V. Blake, 1839. 252 p. NElmC. 54949

----. ----. New York: Clark and Austin [1839] 252 p. LShD. 54950

----. ----. Novi-Portus: Sumtibus B. Et Gul. Noyes, 1839. 239 p. CtHT-W; DeWI; GAU; NN; PU; ViSwC. 54951

----. Cicero the oration, translated by Duncan, the offices by Cockman, and the Cato and Laelius by Melmoth.... New York: Harper and Brothers, 1839. 3 v. CSansS; MWeA; ScNC. 54952

----. Ciceronis selectae qua edam epistolae; 2nd edition. Cura M. L. Hurlbut. Philadelphia: H. Perkins, 1839. 316 p. MB; MH; NjMD; WaU. 54953

----. Orationes quaedam selectae, notis illustratae; in usum academiae Exoniensio [Edited by Charles Folsom] Bostoniae, sumptibus Hilliarld, Gray et soc., 1839. 278 p. CSt; MB; MH; NjP; OCl. 54954

----. Select orations of Cicero, with English notes, critical and explanatory, and historical, geographical and legal indexes. By Charles Anthon, LL.D.... New York: Harper and Brothers, 1839. 518 p. CoGr; MH-AH; NNC; RPB; WBeloC. 54955

----. De senectute et De amicitia. Ex editionibus Oliveti et Ernesti. Accedunt notae Anglicae. Cura C. K. Dillawway. 2nd edition. Bostoniae: Perkins et Marvin, Philadelphiae: H. Perkins, 1839. 156 p. IaOskJF; IEG; MB; NN; RNR. 54956

----. The Tusculan questions of Marcus Tullius Cicero. Translated by George Alexander Otis, Esq. Boston: James Dow, 1839. 316 p. InCW; MBL; PU; RPAt; WBeloC. 54957

----. [Works] the Orations translated by Duncan, the offices by Cockman and The Cato and Laelius by Melmoth. New York: 1839. 3 v. MH-Ah; NbU. 54958

Cincinnati. Controversy in relation to the medical schools of Cincinnati and Commercial Hospital and Lunatic Asylum of Ohio. Cincinnati: 1839. OCHP. 54959

----. Academy of Fine Arts. Academy of Fine Arts catalogue of the first exhibition of paintings and statuary. 1839. Cincinnati: 1839. OCHP. 54960

----. General Board of Underwriters. Report of the committee, and standard tariff of premiums in the fire and marine department, adopted by the General Board of Underwriters of Cincinnati, October, 1839 [Cincinnati] Printed at the Cincinnati Gazette office [1839] 47 p. OCHP. 54961

----. Minister at large. Semi-annual report of the minister at large in Cincinnati [Cincinnati: 1839?] 15 p. O. WHi. 54962

The Cincinnati almanac, for...1839, being a complete picture of Cincinnati and its environs.... Cincinnati: Glazer and Shepard, 1839. MWA; OC; OCHP; OClWHi. 54963

----. Cincinnati: Robinson and Jones, 1839. ICU. 54964

Cincinnati College. A catalogue of officers and students in the medical and law departments of Cincinnati College...session, 1839-40.... Published under the direction of the board. Cincinnati, Ohio: G. W. Bradbury and Company, printers,

1839. 8 p. NNNAM; OCGHM; PPCP. 54965

Cincinnati directory. The Cincinnati, Covington, Newport and Fulton directory, for 1840.... Cincinnati: printed by J. B. and R. P. Donogh, 1839. 520 p. CSmH; KyCov; OC; OSW; PHi. 54966

Cincinnati Fire Association. The constitution and by-laws...with a list of officers and members of the association, and of the different fire companies attached to the fire department. Also a list of the cisterns and fireplugs.... Cincinnati: 1839. 34 p. MH; OC; OCHP. 54967

Cincinnati Historical Society. Transactions of the Historical and Philosophical Society of Ohio. Part second. Vol. I. Published by order of the society. Cincinnati: George W. Bradbury and Company, printers, 1838-1839. 334 p. CU; DLC; GU; MWA; ViU. 54968

Cinderella; or the fairy and little glass slipper: an opera in 3 acts. Music by Rossini.... New York: S. French, 1839. 35 p. C. 54969

Circular to the congregation of St. Bartholomew's Church, New York: New York: E. B. Clayton, 1839. 7 p. MdBD. 54970

The circulating library...Part 1. 1839. Philadelphia: Adam Waldie, 1839. 250 p. LNT. 54971

Citizen's and farmer's almanac for 1840. Original calculations by Charles F. Egelmann. Baltimore: John T. Hanzsche [1839] MWA. 54972

Citizen's Bank of Louisiana, New Orleans. Report of the committee of investigation [selected from the stockholders] appointed by the direction of the Citizens' Bank of Louisiana in conformity with the resolution of the board of 18th October, 1838. New Orleans: printed by E. Johns and Company, Stationers' Hall, 1839. 62 p. MH-BA; LNHT; LU. 54973

Claggett, Rufus. The American expositor, or intellectual definer. Designed for the use of schools.... Boston: 1839. 190 p. CtHWatk; RHi. 54974

Claggett, William, 1790-1870. An address, delivered before the Portsmouth Anti-slavery Society, on the 4th, A.D. 1839, being the 63rd anniversary of the independence of the United States of America. Portsmouth, N.H.: printed by

C. W. Brewster, 1839. 20 p. CtSoP; ICN; MWA; Nh; PHi. 54975

The claims of Japan and Malaysia upon Christendom, exhibited in notes of voyages made in 1837, from Canton, in the ship Morrison and brig. Himmaleh.... New York: E. French, 1839. 2 v. MH; OMC; PPL-R; RNR; Vi. 54976

Clark, John. Synopsis of a valuable collection of old Italian paintings, and other rare articles of fine arts in the possession of Mr. John Clark, now exhibiting at 261 Broadway opposite the Washington Hotel.... New York: 1839. 24 p. NBuG; PPPM; PPULC. 54977

Clark, John Alonzo, 1801-1843. Letters on the church, by Rev. John A. Clark...with an introduction, by Stephen H. Tyng, D.D.... Philadelphia: William Stavely and Company, 1839. 44 p. MBC; MCET; NNG; PHi; RHi. 54978

Clark, John C. Speech of John C. Clark, of New York, on motions pending to refer the president's message. Delivered in the House of Representatives, Jan. 30, 1839. In committee of the whole. Washington: printed at the Madisonian office, 1839. 15 p. MBAt; MdHi; NCH; NUtHi; T. 54979

Clark, Ransom. Narrative of Ransom Clark, the only survivor of Major Dade's command in Florida; containing brief descriptions of what befell him from his enlistments in 1833, till his discharge, by the Indians and Negroes of Major Dade's detachment. Binghamton: printed by Johnson and Marble, 1839. 16 p. MBC; NN. 54980

Clarke, Adam, 1760?-1832. An account of the infancy, religious and literary life of Adam Clarke, written by one who was intimately acquainted with him from his boyhood to the 16th year of his age. Edited by the Rev. J. B. B. Clarke. New York: J. Collard, printer, 1839. v.p. GAGTh. 54981

----. An account of the religious and literary life of Adam Clarke...written by one who was intimately acquainted with him from his boyhood to the 60th year of age edited by the Rev. J. B. B. Clarke.... New York: T. Mason and G. Lane for the Methodist Episcopal Church, J. Collord, printer, 1839. 821 p. GEU; MnSH; NcD; PReaAT; TxHuT. 54982

----. Christian theology: By Adam Clarke, LL.D. Selected from his published and unpublished writings, and systematically arranged. With a life of the author: By Samuel Dunn. New York: T. Mason and G. Lane, 1839. 438 p. MoFayC; ODaB; OSW; TBriK. 54983

----. A concise view of the succession of sacred literature, in a chronological arrangement of authors and their works, from the invention of alphabetical characters, to the year of our Lord, 1445.... New York: T. Mason and G. Lane, J. Collard, printer, 1839. 2-420 p. CoDI; KBB; MeLew-B; NjMD; MoS. 54984

----. Memoirs of Mrs. Mary Cooper, of London, who departed this life June 22, 1812, in the 26th year of her age: extracted from her diary and epistolary correspondence. New York: J. Collord, printer, 1839. 240 p. CtY-D; MBNMHi; Nh; NNMHi. 54985

Clarke, Dorus. A sermon, delivered at Chicopee Falls, March 24, 1839, on occasion of the death of William L. Wyman, of Brookline, Vt., who was drowned in the Chicopee river. By Dorus Clarke.... Springfield [Mass] printed by Merriam, Wood and Company, 1839. CSmH; CtY; MBC; MH-AH. 54986

Clarke, James Freeman. The Unitarian reform. 1st series. No. 138. By Rev. James F. Clarke. Boston: James Munroe and Company, 1839. 15 p. IEG; MBAU; MDeeP; MeB; MH. 54987

Clarke, John, of Philadelphia. A treatise on the mulberry tree and silkworm. And on the production and manufacture of silk...By John Clarke.... Philadelphia: Thomas, Cowperthwait and Company, 1839. 363 p. GHi; ICJ; KyLx; NbOM; PPAmP. 54988

----. ----. 2nd edition. Philadelphia: Thomas, Cowperthwait and Company, 1839. 363 p. DLC; LNH; OCY; PU; RPAt. 54989

Clarksville, Tennessee, Trinity Church. Articles of association, of the rector, wardens and vestrymen of Trinity Church, Clarksville, Tennessee. Nashville: S. Nye and Company, printers, 1839. 6 p. T. 54990

Class book, No. 6; Pennsylvania biography. Philadelphia: 1839. 268 p. PHi. 54991

The class book of nature; comprising lessons on the universe, the three kingdoms of nature, and the form and structure of the human body.... Edited by J. Frost. 4th edition. Hartford: Belknap and Hamersley, 1839. 278 p. CtY; ICBB; NNT-C; OMC; PPCP. 54992

Claxton, Timothy, b. 1790. Memoir of a mechanic. Being a sketch of the life of Timothy Claxton, written by himself. Together with miscellaneous papers. Boston and New York: G. W. Light, 1839. 179 p. CtY; ICMe; MWA; OCo; RPAt. 54993

Clay, Henry, 1777-1852. The beauties of the Hon. Henry Clay, to which is added a biographical and critical essay. New York: E. Walker, 1839. 235 p. ArL; KyBC; MB; MWA; OMC. 54994

----. Speech of the Hon. Henry Clay, in the Senate of the United States, on the subject of abolition petitions, February 7, 1839. Boston: James Munroe and Company, 1839. 42 p. ICMe; MHi; MWA; Nh; RPB. 54995

----. ----. New Orleans: printed by John Gibson, 1839 [3] 14 p. MsJMC. 54996

----. ----. Washington: Gales and Seaton, 1839. 16 p. A-Ar; CtY; MoS; NUtHi; OClWHi. 54997

Claybaugh, Joseph, 1803-1855. Introductory address to the students of the theological seminary, of the second Associate Reformed Synod of the West. At the opening of its first session, Dec. 2nd, 1839. S.T.P. Oxford, Ohio: printed by John Christy, 1839. OOxM; PPPrHi; PPULC. 54998

Cleland, Thomas, 1778-1858. A manifesto containing a plain statement of facts, relative to the acts and doings of the General Assembly...[Signed by Thomas Cleland, Jon. C. Stiles, Dennis M. Winston and Samuel MacCoun] n.p. [1839?] 22 p. ICU. 54999

Clemens, James W. An address pronounced before the Jefferson and Philosophic Societies of Franklin College, on the 24th of September, 1839. St. Clairsville, Ohio: printed at the office of Gill, Heaton and Company, 1839. 37 p. CSmH; OClWHi. 55000

Clendinning, John. Experiments and observations relating to the pathology and pathological relations of the heart. Philadelphia: 1839. GU-M;IEN-M; MBM; OClM; PPHa. 55001

----. Medical and surgical monographs. By Dr. J. Clendinning, Sir A. Cooper, Mr. W. Coulson, Dr. Robley Dunglison, Dr. J. Osborne, Dr. R. Rowland and Mr. J. Syme. Philadelphia: A. Waldie, 1839. 310 p. CU-M; ICU-R; MdBJ; PPA; ViRA. 55002

Clifton, William. Fair beauteous queen: song and trio [with pf.] New York: 1839. CtY. 55003

----. She loved him dearly [Voice and pf.] New York: 1839. CtY. 55004

Clinton Bank, New York [City] Laws of the Clinton Bank in the city of New York, established under the general banking law. New York: M. P. O'Hern, 1839. 80 p. DLC; PHi; PPULC; TxU; WHi. 55005

Clissold, Augustus, 1797?-1882. The practical nature of the doctrines and alleged revelations contained in the writings of Emanuel Swedenborg...in a letter to his grace the Lord Archbishop of Dublin.... Boston: Otis Clapp, 1839 [13]-245 p. CSansS; GMM; MWA; OUrC; RPB. 55006

The closet companion, or help to self examination. Hartford: E. Geer, 1839. 40 p. MH. 55007

Clowes, John, 1743-1831. Dialogues on the nature, design and evidence of the theological writings of Emanuel Swedenborg.... Boston: Otis Clapp, 1839 70-[2] p. ICMe; MCNC; OUrC; PBa; PU. 55008

----. The only real road to wealth; cr a genuine definition of the term property.... Troy, N.Y.: Tuttle, Belcher and Burton, printers, 1839. 14 p. N; NjR. 55009

The cluster; or memoirs of six deceased members of a single Sabbath school in Waterville, Maine. By the superintendent. Published by the New England Sabbath School Union, Boston: printed by John Putnam, 1839. 216 p. MeBa; RLa. 55010

Clutterbuck, Henry, 1767-1856. Lectures on blood-letting; delivered at the general dispensary, Aldersgate Street. Philadelphia: Haswell, Barriington and Haswell, 1839. 120 p. CSt- L; LNOP; NjP; PPA; RPM. 55011

Coahuila and Texas [State] Laws, statutes, etc. Laws and decrees of the state of Coahuila and Texas, in Spanish and English. To which is added the constitution of said state.... By order of the secretary of state. Translated by J. P. Kimball, M.D. Houston: Telegraph Power press, 1839 [3] 4-353, 4-353, 6 [2] 2-4 [3] p. CSmH; Mh; NcD; OCHP; PHi; Tx. 55012

Coates, Reynell. An address introductory to a popular course of lectures on the history of organic development, and the mental and physical faculties, delivered October 30th, 1839. Philadelphia: T. K. and P. G. Collins, 1839. 22 p. MiD-B; PaHosp; PHi; PPL; PPM. 55013

Cobb, Jonathan Holmes, 1799-1882. A manual containing information respecting the growth of the mulberry tree.... 4th edition, enlarged. Boston: Weeks, Jordan and Company, 1839. 162 p. CtY; MB; MWA; OCl; PPAmP. 55014

Cobb, Lyman, 1800-1864. Cobb's explanatory arithmetic, no. 2. By Lyman Cobb. Stereotyped by Rees, Redfield and Ripley. New York: Harper and Brothers, 1839. 216 p. KyStjM. 55015

----. Cobb's juvenile reader, no. 2. Ithaca, N.Y.: Mack, Andrus and Woodruff, 1839. DLC; MH. 55016

----. Cobb's juvenile reader, no. 3, containing interesting historical, moral and instructive reading lessons, composed of words of a greater number of syllables than the lessons in nos. 1 and 2. Designed for the use of larger children in families and schools. Ithaca, N.Y.: 1839 [216 p.] MiGr. 55017

----. The reticule and pocket companion; or miniature lexicon of the English language. Stereotype edition. Ne York: Harper and Brothers, 1839. 818 p. MH. 55018

----. Cobb's spelling book. Being a just standard for pronouncing the English language. Revised edition. Erie, Pa.: Sparford and Sterrett, 1839. 168 p. MiHi; NBuG;NN; OkDurT. 55019

----. ----. Designed to teach the orthography and orthoepy of J. Walker. Revised edition. Ithaca, N.Y.: Mack, Andrus and Woodruff, 1839. 168 p. DLC; MWA; NIC; NIDHi. 55020

----. ----. St. Clairsville, Ohio: printed and published by Horton J. Howard, 1839. 168 p. PWCHi. 55021

Cocke, Richard Ivanhoe. An oration deliverd before the Franklinian society, of William and Mary College, on the 11th of Jan., 1839. By Richard Ivanhoe Cocke, of Powhatan County, Va. Richmond [Va.] Bailie and Gallaher, 1839. 21 p. CSmH; NcD. 55022

Cogswell, William. The Christian philanthropist; or harbinger of the millennium.... Introductory essay by James Matheson.... 2nd edition. Boston: Perkins and Marvin, Philadelphia: H. Perkins, 1839. 394 p. MAnP; MHi; MWA; MWiW; PPM. 55023

Coit, J. C. A sermon preached before the Presbyterian church at Cheraw, S.C., Jan. 20, 1839, Philadelphia: William S. Martien, 1839. 46 p. CSansS; MH-AH; NcMHi; PPPrHi. 55024

Colburn, Warren, 1793-1833. Arithmetic upon the inductive method of instruction. Being a sequel to intellectual arithmetic.... Boston: Hilliard, Gray and Company, 1839. 245 p. MB; MPeHi; MPiB; OMC; PPM. 55025

----. ...Intellectual arithmetic, upon the inductive method of instruction. Stereotyped at the Boston Type and Stereotype Foundry. Boston: Hilliard, Gray and Company, 1839. MH; TxU-T. 55026

----. An introduction to algebra, upon the inductive method of instruction. By the author of intellectual arithmetic and sequel to ditto. Boston: Hilliard, Gray and Company, 1839. 276 p. MH; NdFM; ViU. 55027

----. A key containing the answers to the examples in the introduction to algebra upon the inductive method of instruction. By Warren Colburn, A.M. Stereotyped at the Boston Type and Stereotype Foundry. Boston: Hilliard, Gray and Company, 1839. 50 p. MeB; NTRPI; RPB. 55028

Colby College. Waterville, Maine. Order of exercises for the 17th annual commencement of Waterville College, August 14, 1839. Augusta: printed by Severence and Dorr, 1839. 4 p. MNtCA. 55029

Cole, George F. The Maryland cadets' glee. Written, arranged and respectfully dedicated to the officers and privates of that corps [male quartet with pianoforte accompaniment. Baltimore: Willig] 1839 6 p. KU; MB. 55030

Cole, Isaac P. Cole's pocket edition of psalms and hymn tunes, containing most of the standard music used in the different churches throughout the country. To which is prefixed a brief introduction to vocal music. 10th edition. Albany: William G. Boardman, 1839. 300 p. NNUT. 55031

Coleridge, Samuel Taylor, 1772-1834. Aids to reflection.... London: W. Pickering, New York: Swords, Stanford and Company, 1839. 324 p. AU; LNB; MdBD; MH; OkU. 55032

----. The poetical works of Coleridge, Shelly and Keats.... Philadelphia: Thomas, Cowperthwait and Company, 1839. CSmH; CtY; MBBC; NcWfC; PPLT. 55033

Coleridge, Sara [Coleridge] 1802-1852. Phantasmion: prince of Palmland.... New York: S. Colman, 1839. 2 v. CtHT; GHi; KyBC; MeB; RPAt. 55034

Coles, George. History and character of Methodism; a centennary sermon preached in the Duane Street church, New York, Oct. 25, 1839.... [New York? 1839?] 40 p. CBPSR; MBC; NjPT. 55035

Colesworthy, Daniel Clement, 1810-1893. Opening buds.... Portland: C. W. Pennell, 1839. DLC; MH; RPB. 55036

----. The scholar's aid designed to instruct him in the way of usefulness.... By Timothy Goodwise.... Portland: S. H. Colesworthy, 1839. 134 p. MeHi. 55037

Colgate University, Hamilton, New York [Catalogue of the corporation, officers and students of Hamilton literary and theological institution, 1839-1840] Utica: printed by Bennett and Bright [1839?] 20 p. N. 55038

Collection of songs for pianoforte.... Baltimore: 1839-1860. 4 v. in 1. MB. 55039

Collyer, John, 1801-1870. A practical treatise on the law of partnership.... 2nd American from the last London edition.... Springfield [Mass.] G. and C. Merriam, 1839. 728 p. NcD; OCl; PU; TMeB; ViU. 55040

Collyer, Robert Hanham. Manual of phrenology, or the physicology of the human brain. Embracing a full description of the phrenological

...r exact location and the peculiarities ...acter produced by their various degree of ...velopment and combination.... 4th edition. Revised, enlarged and improved by superior wood cuts and drawings. Cincinnati: N. G. Burgess and Company, 1839. 156 p. DNLM; OC. 55041

Colman, Henry, 1785-1849. An address to the Middlesex Society of Husbandmen and Manufacturers, at their annual cattle show.... Boston: Weeks, Jordan and Company, 1839. 22 p. CtY; ICMe; MiD-B; MWA; RPB. 55042

----. On labor; address at the annual cattle shows of Worcester and the Hampshire, Hampden and Franklin agricultural societies...Oct., 1838. Boston: Otis, Broaders and Company, 1839. 23 p. CtY; MH; MH-AH; MPiB; RPB. 55043

Colonization Society of the County of Oneida. At a meeting of the Colonization Society of the County of Oneida, held at the Reformed Dutch Church in Utica, on the 20th day of November, 1838, It was resolved that the address to the inhabitants of this county, reported to this meeting by the committee appointed for that purpose, be published under the direction of the executive board. To the inhabitants of Oneida County. Fellow citizens.... [Utica: 1839] 8 p. NN. 55044

Colquhoun, Janet [Sinclair] 1781-1846. The world's religion, as contrasted with genuine Christianity. New York: John S. Taylor, 1839. 207 p. CtY; GMM; InCW; KyLoP; NdU. 55045

Colt, John Caldwell, 1810-1842? The science of double entry bookkeeping.... Cincinnati: N. G. Burgess and Company, 1839. 208 p. LNH. 55046

----. ----. 4th edition. Philadelphia: Thomas, Cowperthwait and Company, 1839. 105 p. 3 p. NNC; RPB. 55047

[Colton, Calvin] 1789-1839. Abolition a sedition. By a northern man. Philadelphia: G. W. Donohue, 1839. 187 p. CSmH; InCW; MBAt; RP; TxU. 55048

----. Colonization and abolition contrasted. Philadelphia: Herman Hooker [1839?] 16 p. IU; MH; PHi; TNF; WHi. 55049

Colton [J. H.] and Company, New York.

Description of the cities, townships and principal villages and settlements within thirty miles of the city of New York. New York: 1839. NB. 55050

----. General atlas containing maps, plans, etc. New York: 1839. PPL. 55051

Colton, John Hutchins, 1800-1893. Guide for the territory of Iowa with a correct map, showing the township surveys. Map. New York: 1839. 6 p. DLC; IaCrM. 55052

----. The western tourist and emigrant's guide, with a compendious gazeteer of the states of Ohio, Michigan, Indiana, Illinois and Missouri, and the territories of Wisconsin and Iowa.... Accompanied with a correct map...By J. Calvin Smith. New York: J. H. Colton, 1839. 180 p. CSmH; IaU; ICn; MiD; PHi. 55053

Colton, John Owen, 1810-1840. A Greek reader, consisting of new selections and notes.... New Haven: Durrie and Peck, New York: Collins, Keese and Company, 1839. 328 p. ICU; KyBC; MII, OMC, RPB. 55054

Colton, Simeon. Documents connected with the trial of Rev. Simeon Colton. Printed by order of Fayetteville Presbytery, for the use of the Synod of North Carolina, at their ensuing sessions. Fayetteville [North Carolina] Edward J. Hale, printer, 1839. 107 p. GDecCT; NcU; NjPT; PPPrHi. 55055

Columbia Insurance Company. Philadelphia. An act incorporating the Columbia Insurance Company of Philadelphia. Passed June 14, 1839. Philadelphia: John C. Clark, printer, 1839. 8 p. DLC; MiD- B; PHi; PPPI. 55056

Columbian almanac for 1840. Philadelphia, Pa.: Joseph M'Dowell [1839] MWA. 55057

Combe, Andrew, 1797-1847. The principles of physiology applied to the preservation of health, and to the improvement of physical and mental education.... New York: Harper and Brothers, 1839. 291 p. KyWA; MPeaI; NGlc; PRea; TxGR. 55058

Combe, George, 1788-1858. The constitution of man considered in relation to external objects...from the 3rd enlarged Edinburgh edition. New York: Collins, Keese and Company, 1839. 382 p. AU; IU; MB; PPL; ViU. 55059

----. ----. 5th American edition, materially

revised and enlarged. Boston: Bazin and Ellsworth, 1839. 392 p. PScrHi. 55060

----. ----. 8th edition, materially revised and enlarged. Boston: Marsh, Capen, Lyon and Webb, 1839. 436 p. GHi; MB; MtH. 55061

----. ----. 9th American from the latest English edition, corrected and enlarged. Boston: Ticknor, 1839, 412 p. DSG; IGK; OrU; PU; Vi. 55062

----. ----. 10th American edition, materially revised and enlarged. Boston: Marsh, Capen, Lyon and Webb, 1839 [1]-436 [24] p. MH; MStow; NcGC; OClWHi; WaSpG. 55063

----. Lectures on phrenology; by George Combe, esq. Including its application to the present and prospective condition of the United States. With notes, an introductory essay and an historical sketch: by Andrew Boardman.... New York: Samuel Coleman, 1839. 389 p. MBC; MiD; Nh; PPM; RJa. 55064

----. Lectures on popular education delivered to the Edinburgh Philosophical Association, in April and Nov., 1833, and published by request of the directors of the association.... 2nd American edition corrected and enlarged. Boston: Marsh, Capen, Lyon and Webb, 1839. 141 p. ICJ; MBAt; MoU; PP; TxU. 55065

----. A system of phrenology. 6th American from the 3rd Edinburgh edition. Revised and enlarged by the author. Boston: Marsh, Capen, Lyon and Webb, 1839. 664 p. CoU; IaGG; LNL; PP; ScU. 55066

Comly, John, 1773?-1850. English grammar, made easy to the teacher and pupil. Originally compiled for the use of Westtown Boarding School, Pennsylvania. 15th edition, corrected and enlarged. Philadelpha: Kimber and Conrad, 1839. 216 p. OCl; PPULC; PSC-Hi. 55067

Commercial Bank of Albany vs. Corning and Porter. Albany: 1839. PPL; PPULC. 55068

Commercial Bank of Rochester. Articles of association of the Commercial Bank of Rochester: also, the general banking law, passed by the legislature of the state of New York, under which the company was organized. Rochester: printed by David Hoyt, 1839. 18 p. NRHi. 55069

Commercial Bank of Troy, New York. Artick of association of the Commercial Bank of Troy, and the general banking law of the state of New York. Troy, N.Y.: Tuttle, Belcher and Burton, pritners, 1839. 15 p. CSmH; IU; NT. 55070

Commercial Convention of the States of Virginia and North Carolina, Norfolk, 1838. Proceedings of the commercial convention of the states of Virginia and North Carolina, held in Norfolk, Va., on the 14th, 15th, 16th and 17th of November, 1838. Norfolk: printed by T. G. Broughton and Son, 1839. 32 p. CSmH; NN; ViW. 55071

The commercial form, for the practical merchant, as well as those just commencing the mercantile business. Philadelphia: King and Baird, 1839. KyDC. 55072

Common almanac for 1839.... Watertown: Rice, 1839. 12 p. NNHist. 55073

Common almanac for the year of our Lord 1840: bissextile or leap year, and, till July 4th, the 63rd of American independence.... Watertown: Knowlton and Rice, 1839. WGrNM. 55074

The common school almanac.... Published by the American Common School Society. Depository: New York: 1839. 24 p. CtY; IU; MWA; NNT-C; RNRi. 55075

The common school journal. V. 1-10, Nov., 1838-Dec., 1848; V. 11- [new ser. V. 1-] Jan., 1849. Boston: Marsh, Capen, Lyon and Webb, [etc.] 1839-. IU; MB; NbU; OrU; PU. 55076

The complete practical farmer and gardener, comprising the rearing, breeding and management of every description of live stock.... 2nd edition. New York: Samuel Colman, 1839. 508 p. DLC; KHi; MiD-B; N; RPAt. 55077

The complete practical farmer including the culture of the orchard, the garden and the rearing and management of live stock, by an American. New York: Samuel Colman, Philadelphia: William Marshall and Company, 1839. 508 p. IaDu-MtC; ScCMu; WWauHi. 55078

A complete ready reckoner, in dollars and cents, to which are added, forms of notes, bills, receipts, petitions, etc.... Philadelphia: Michael Kelly, 1839. 178 p. MnS; ScCMu. 55079

Comstock, Franklin G. A practical treatise on the culture of silk, adapted to the soil and climate of the United States.... 2nd edition.... Hartford: P. B. Gleason and Company, 1839. CtSoP; CtY; IaHi; MnU; OO. 55080

Comstock, John Lee, 1789-1858. Comstock's common school philosophy.... Hartford: Reed and Barber, 1839. 258 p. IaDaP; ICU; Mh; MiD-U. 55081

----. Elements of chemistry.... 3rd edition[?] New York: Robinson, Pratt and Company, 1839. 420 [10] p. MFiHi. 55082

----. ----. 4th edition[?] New York: Robinson, Pratt and Company, 1839. 420 [12] p. NTRPI. 55083

----. ----. 22nd edition. New York: Robinson, Pratt and Company, 1839. 356 p. RPB. 55084

----. ----. 29th edition. New York: Robinson, Pratt and Company, 1839. 420 p. CtHT; FDef; MCM; MiD-T; NbOM. 55085

----. ----. 30th edition. New York: Robinson, Pratt and Company, 1839. 420 p. MH; NjP; NjPT. 55086

----. ----. 40th edition. New York: Robinson, Pratt and Company, 1839. 420 p. CSt; MH; NjP; NN; VtMidSM. 55087

----. An introduction to mineralogy; adapted to the use of schools, and private students. 3rd edition, improved. New York: Robinson, Pratt and Company, 1839. 369 p. ICLoy; KyBC; McBa; NNF; OWoC. 55088

----. An introduction to the study of botany, including a treatise on vegetable physiology, and descriptions of the most common plants in the middle and northern states.... 5th edition. New York: Robinson, Pratt and Company, 1839. 480 [5] p. ArBaA; KyU; MBBC; NbOM; PPWa. 55089

----. Outlines of geology: intended as a popular treatise on the most interesting parts of the science. Together with an examination of the question, whether the days of creation were indefinite periods. Designed for the use of schools and general readers.... 3rd edition. New York: Robinson, Pratt and Company, 1839. 384 p. A-Ar; LN; MoU; NNN. 55090

----. Outlines of physiology, both comparative and human.... 2nd edition.... New York: Robinson, Pratt and Company, 1839. 310 p. CtMW; GHi; NbU-M; NNN; PPFrankI. 55091

----. Youth's book of astronomy. Hartford: Reed and Barber, 1839. 253 p. NN; OOxM; OU. 55092

Conant, Thomas Jefferson, 1802-1891. Exercises in Hebrew grammar, and a Hebrew chrestomathy, prepared with reference to the translation of Gesenius' Hebrew grammar.... Boston: Gould, Kendall and Lincoln, 1839 [5]-10 p. DLC; MB; MH-Ah; PBa; WaWW. 55093

Concealment: a novel.... Philadelphia: Lea and Blanchard, successors to Carey and Company [J. S. and C. Adams, book and job printers, Amherst, Mass.] 1839. 2 v. CSmH; DLC. 55094

Concord Female Moral Reform Society. Constitution. Concord: 1839. 12 p. Nh-Hi. 55095

Concord Literary Institution and Teachers' Seminary, Concord, N. H. Catalogue of the officers, instructors and students, 1839. Concord: 1839. D. MBAt. 55096

Confessions, trials, and biographical sketches of the most cold blooded murderers, who have been executed in this country.... Embellished with numerous engravings.... Boston: George N. Thomson [Marden and Kimball, printers] 1839. CSmH; MH. 55097

Congregational Churches in Connecticut. Lutheran. Connecticut. General Association. Minutes of the General Association of Connecticut, at their meeting in Danbury, June, 1839; with the report on the state of religion, etc. Hartford: E. Gleason, printer, 1839. 30 p. IEG; MoWgT. 55098

Congregational Churches in Illinois. The constitution and regulations of the Illinois Congregational Association...1839, n.p.: Bartlett and Sullivan, printers, 1839. 7 p. MBC. 55099

Congregational Churches in Maine. Minutes of the General Conference of Maine, at their annual meeting in Brunswick, June 25, 1839. Portland: Alfred Merrill, printer, 1839. 31 p. ICU; IEG; MeBat; MeLewB. 55100

Congregational Churches in Massachusetts.

Massachusetts General Association. Minutes of the General Association. of Mass. at their meeting at Plymouth, June, 1839. With the narrative of the state of religion, and the pastoral letter. Boston: printed by Crocker and Brewster, 1839. 51 p. VtMidSM. 55101

Congregational Churches in New Hampshire. General Association. An appeal to the Presbyterian and Congregational churches of New Hampshire, in behalf of the widows and oprhan children of ministers. Portsmouth [N.H.] C. W. Brewster, printer, 1839. 8 p. CSmH; Nh; Nh-Hi. 55102

Congregational Churches in New York. General Association. Minutes of the General Association of New York...1839. Whitesboro, N.Y.: press of the Oneida Institute, 1839. 1 v. CSmH; NN. 55103

Congregational Churches in Ohio. "Confession of faith." April, 1839. Michigan City, Indiana: 1839. In. 55104

Congregational Churches in Rhode Island. Evangelical Consociation. Evangelical Consociation and Home Missinary Society of Congregational churches in Rhode Island. Proceedings June, 1839. Providence: 1839. 21 p. IEG; MHi; Vt-MidbC. 55105

Congregational Churches in Vermont. Extracts from the minutes of the General Convention of Congregational and Presbyterian ministers in Vermont, at their session in Montpelier, 1839. Windsor: printed at the Chronicle press, 24 p. IEG; MiD-B; NjR; VtMidSM. 55106

Congregational Publishing Society. A gift for scholars. Boston: Massachusetts Sabbath School Society, 1839. MB. 55107

Conkling, Alfred, 1789-1874. Young citizen's manual; being a digest of the laws of the state of New York and of th U. S., relating to crimes and their punishments.... Rochester: Dean, 1839. MNS. 55108

----. ----. 2nd edition. New York: W. E. Dean, 1839. 279 p. DLC; MBC; MNS. 55109

Conklin, Gabriel. Examination of a pamphlet titled "truth as it is, published anonymously in Pa. Alexandria, D.C.: 1839. 16 p. MH. 55110

Connecticut. Bank Commissioners. Report of the Bank Commissioners, to the General Assembly, May session, 1839. Printed by order of the Senate. Hartford: Patriot Office Press, 1839. 22 p. Ct; CtHWatk. 55111

----. Board of Commissioners of Common Schools. First- [fourth]...annual report of the Board of Commissioners of Common Schools, together with the first-[fourth] annual report of the secretary of the Board...1838/39, 1841/42. Hartford: 1839-42. 4 v. in 1. Ct; CtY; DLC; MB; RP. 55112

----. Commission on the Culture of Hemp. Report of the commission. 2nd edition. Hartford: 1839. O. CtHT. 55113

----. Constitution. The constitution of the state of Connecticut, together with the amendments.... Hartford: C. Babcock, 1839. 17 p. Ct. 55114

----. County court. Fairfield County. Report of a committee, appointed by the County court for Fairfield County, at its January term, A.D. 1839, to inquire into the state of the prisons, in the county, and ascertain what changes ought to be made in their structure and regulations. Bridgeport: Stiles Nichols and Company, 1839. Ct. 55115

----. General Assembly. Committee on Petitions, of Sundry Persons in Relation to License Laws. Report of the joint select committee to whom was referred sundry petitions relative to the subject of slavery. Hartford: 1839. 8 p. CtHWatk; CtY; MB. 55116

----. ----. House of Representatives. Journal of the House of Representatives of the state of Connecticut, May session, 1839. Published by order of a resolution of the House. Hartford: printed at the Courant office, 1839 [3]-136 p. MiD-B. 55117

----. ----. ----. Report of the directors of the Connecticut State Prison, to the General Assembly, May session, 1839. House. Document no. 3. Hartford: Courant Office Press, 1839. 20 p. Ct. 55118

----. ----. Joint Committee on the Petition of Caleb Stockbridge and Others. Copy of the report of the Joint Committee...on the petition of Caleb Stockbridge and others...May session, 1836, [and copy of the report of the Joint Committee on the petition of the Hartford Bridge Company, May session, 1838. Hartford? 1839?] 7 p. CtY. 55119

----. ----. Joint Select Committee on Judiciary Expenses. Report of the committee appointed by the General Assembly, May session, 1838, on judicial expenses, to the General Assembly, May session, 1839. Hartford: Courant office, 1839. 48 p. Ct; CtSoP; CtY. 55120

----. Governor [William W. Ellsworth] Speech of His Excellency, William W. Ellsworth, governor of Connecticut, to the legislature of the state, May, 1839.... Hartford: Courant office press, 1839. 16 p. O. Ct. 55121

----. Laws, Statutes, etc. Public acts of the state of Connecticut, passed May session, 1839. Published agreeably, under the superintendence of the secretary of said state. State of Connecticut, SS: Office of the secretary of said state, June, 1839. Hartford: printed at the Courant office, 1839. 62, 136 p. Ar-SC; IaU-L; Nv; T; Wa-L. 55122

----. ----. The public statute laws of the state of Connecticut...to which is added the Declaration of Independence, Constitution of the U.S. and Constitution of the state of Connecticut.... Hartford: J. L. Boswell, 1839. 717 p. CtB; Ia; MiGr; NNLI; PU; WaU. 55123

----. ----. Resolves and private acts of the state of Connecticut, passed May session, 1839. Published agreeably to a resolve of the General Assembly, and prepared by and under the superintendence of the secretary of state. State of Connecticut, SS: office of the secretary of said state, June, 1839. Hartford: printed at the Courant office, 1839. 136 p. Ar-SC; IaU-L; Nj; T; Wa-L. 55124

----. Secretary of State. Report of the Secretary of the State relative to certain branches of industry. May session, 1839.... Hartford: 1839. 38 p. Ct; CtY; MH-BA. 55125

Connecticut almanac for 1840. Astronomical calculations by J. H. Gallup. Norwich City, Conn.: M. B. Young [1839] CtNwchA; DLC; MWA. 55126

The Connecticut annual register, and United States calendar, for 1839, to which is prefixed an almanack...No. 49. Published by Samuel Green, Durrie and Peck, and Canfield and Robins, 1839. 174 p. Ct. 55127

Connecticut College. Academical institution at New London. Catalogue, 1838-1840. D. Concord: 1838-1840. Nh-Hi. 55128

Connecticut Historical Society. The charter of incorporation and by-laws of the Connecticut Historical Society, together with a list of the officers, and an address to the public. Hartford: n. pub., Case, Tiffany and Company, printers, 1839. 11 p. CtSoP; MH; MWA; PHi; RPB. 55129

The Connecticut register: being a state calendar of public officers and institutions for 1839 [Hartford: S. Green, etc., 1839-[1868] 4 v. MnU. 55130

Consecrated life and guide to holiness? V. 1-75. July, 1839-Dec., 1901. Boston and New York, Philadelphia: 1839-1901. DLC; IEG; OCl. 55131

Considerations in regard to the application of the Shakers, for certain special privileges [Albany: 1839] 8 p. NN; OClWHi; WHi. 55132

Convention, dritte, der deutschen Burger der Vereinigten Staaten; gehalten zu Philippsburg im Bibergau, Pa. vom. 1. bis 8. Aug. 1839. Philadelphia: J. G. Wesselhoeft, 1839. pamph. PPG. 55133

Convention of American Women. Address from the Convention of American Women, to the Society of Friends, on the subject of slavery. Philadelphia: 1839. 10 p. MB; PHi. 55134

Convention of Civil Engineers, Baltimore, 1839. Address of the committee appointed at the Convention of Civil Engineers, which met in Baltimore, Maryland, February 11, 1839. Philadelphia: printed by Merrihew and Thompson, 1839. 8 p. CSmH; MB; PHi. 55135

Convention of Merchants and others, Charleston, 1839. Proceedings of the 4th Convention of Merchants, and others, held in Charleston, S.C., April 15, 1839, for the promotion of the direct trade. Charleston: A. E. Miller, printer, 1839. 64 p. DLC; GU; MH; PHi; ScU. 55136

Convention of Reformed Churches. Proceedings of the Convention of Reformed Churches, Session II. Philadelphia, September, 1839. Extracted from the minutes. New York: Craighead and Allen, printers, 1839. 15 p. NcMHi. 55137

Conversations on nature and art.... Philadelphia:

Lea and Blanchard, 1839. 333 p. CtY; GAuY; MiU; RJa; WGr. 55138

Cook, T. D. The kingdom shut. Two sermons, respectfully addressed to all who shut up the kingdom of Heaven against men. By T. D. Cook and A. B. Grosh. Utica: printed by Grosh and Hutchinson, 1839. 4-33 p. MMeT; MWA; NUt. 55139

Cook, William, 1807-1876. Monition for parents. A sermon, for the promotion of piety. By Rev. William Cook, A.B. Salem, the Gazette office, 1839. 14 p. CtHt-W; MBAt; MPiB; NjR; RPB. 55140

Cooke, Parsons, 1800-1864. Moral machinery simplified. A discourse, delivered at Andover, Massachusetts, July 4, 1839.... Andover: E. Pierce, 1839. 40 p. CU; DLC; MAnP; PHi; RPB. 55141

Cooley, Timothy Mather. Sketches of the life and character of the Rev. Lemuel Haynes, A.M., with some introductory remarks by William B. Sprague, D.D. New York:John S. Taylor, Brick Church Chapel, 1839. 348 p. ICu; LNH; MBC; MWA; RNR. 55142

Coolidge and Haskell. Conditions of sale of house lots in the vicinity of Bunker Hill Monument [Charlestown? 1839] MB. 55143

Cooper, Astley Paston, 1768-1841. The lectures of Sir Astley Cooper, bart., F.R.S...on the principles and practice of surgery, with additional notes and cases. By Frederick Tyrrell, Esq.... 5th American, from the last London edition. Complete in one volume. Philadelphia: Haswell, Barrington and Haswell, New Orleans: Alexander Towar, 1839. 580 p. CSt-L; ICU; MdBJ; OrUM; PPCP; TxDaBM. 55144

Cooper, James Fenimore, 1789-1851. The bravo; a tale. Philadelphia: Lea and Blanchard, 1839. 2 v. CtY; MeWebr. 55145

----. The headsman, or the Abbaye des Vignerons. A tale. Philadelphia: Lea and Blanchard, 1839. 2 v. GCu; MB; MeWebr; MWA; NGeno. 55146

----. The Heidenmauer; or the benedictines. A legend of the Rhine...[anon.] Philadelphia: Lea and Blanchard, 1839. 2 v. MeWebr; MiD; MWA; PPPrHi. 55147

----. The history of the Navy of the United States of America. By J. Fenimore Cooper. Philadelphia: Lea and Blanchard, 1839. 2 v. KyHe; MdBS; ODaU; PHi; TxDaM. 55148

----. The last of the Mohicans; a narrative of 1757. In two volumes, a new edition. Philadelphia: Lea and Blanchard, 1839. 2 v. MsCliM. 55149

----. Lionel Lincoln, or the leaguer of Boston.. A new edition. Philadelphia: Lea and Blanchard, 1839. 2 v. MsCliM. 55150

----. Notions of the Americans. Picked up by a travelling bachelor. A new edition. Philadelphia: Lea and Blanchard, 1839. 2 v. MB; MeB; MSCliM; MWH; Vi. 55151

----. The pathfinder...llustrated by Donald S. Humphreys. Philadelphia: Macraw Smith Company, 1839. 516 p. CoD; IaAlb; KGrb; MoSp; NjPaT. 55152

----. The pilot: a tale of the sea...[anon.]. Philadelphia: Lea and Blanchard, 1839. 2 v. CtY; KyU; IaCorn; LNH; ScLau. 55153

----. The pioneers on the sources of the Susquehanna; a descriptive tale. A new edition. Philadelphia: Lea and Blanchard, successors to Carey and Company, 1839. 2 v. CtY; MsCliM; MsJMC. 55154

----. Precaution.... Philadelphia: Lea and Blanchard, successors to Carey and Company, 1839. 2 v. in 1. MB; MnU; NcDaD; OU; PU. 55155

----. The red-rover.... By the author of "the pilot." ...A new edition. Philadelphia: Lea and Blanchard, 1839. 2 v. in 1. FSaFDB; MeWebr; MsJMC. 55156

----. The water-wtich, or the skimmer of the seas.... In two volumes. A new edition. Philadelphia: Lea and Blanchard, 1839. 2 v. MeWebr; MsCliM. 55157

----. The wept of wish-ton-wish. A tale.. Philadelphia: Lea and Blanchard, 1839. 2 v. CtHt; MAm; MB; MdW; TxU. 55158

----. The wing-and-wing, or le feu-follet. A tale. By J. Fenimore Cooper. New York and London: D. Appleton and Company, 1839. 494 p. MTop. 55159

----. ----. New York and London: G. P. Putnam's sons, the Knickerbocker Press, 1839. 470 p. MTop. 55160

Cooper, Samuel. A dictionary of practical surgery.... From the 6th London edition...notes...By David Meredith Reese, M.D.... New York: Harper and Brothers, 1839. 2 v. MdUM; NjP; NNN; ScCMu; WMAM. 55161

Cooper, Samuel M. The evidences of Christianity; designed for sabbath schools and Bible classes. Pittsburgh: Alexander Jaynes, printer [1839] 130 p. PPi. 55162

Cooper, Thomas, 1759-1840. Catalogues of his library.... Columbia: 1839. 37 p. PPAmP. 55163

Corbet, John. Self employment in secret.... By the Rev. John Corbet, with a preface of the late Rev. John Howe; and.... Philadelphia: Presbyterian Board, 1839. 90 p. GDecCT; OWoC; PPPrHi; RPB; ViRut. 55164

Corder, Susanna, 1788-1864. Memorials of deceased members of the Society of Friends. Compiled from various authentic sources. 2nd edition. Lindfield: Longman and Company, 1839. 379 p. IaU; MH; PHC; PSC-Hi. 55165

Cornell, Silas. Map of the city of Rochester. New York: C. B. Graham, Lithy, 1839. NR. 55166

The Corsair. A gazette of literature, art, dramatic criticism, fashion and novelty. V. 1; Mar. 15, 1839-Mar. 7, 1840. New York: 1839-40. 831 p. CSt; CtY; GU; MH; RPAt; ViU. 55167

Cortland Academy. Catalogue of the trustees, instructors and students...Homer Village, Cortland County, N. Y. December, 1830. Homer Village: printed at the Republican and Eagle offices, 1839. 16 p. N. NN. 55168

Cottom's Virginia and North Carolina almanack for 1840. Richmond, Va. [1839] MWA; Vi. 55169

Coulson, William, 1802-1877. On diseases of the bladder. Philadelphia: 1839. MBM; OClM; PPHa. 55170

Council of Trent. The catechism of the council of Trent published by command of Pope Pius the 5th. Translated into English by the Rev. J. Donovan.... New York: Christian Press Association Publishing Company [1839] 400 p. KyLoS. 55171

The court and camp of Bonaparte. Harper's stereotype edition. New York: Harper and Brothers, 1839. 389 p. InRch; LNH; MdBJ; Me; TxGr. 55172

Cove Academy, Covesville, Virginia. Announcement...1839/40? Richmond, Va.: Whittet and Shepperson, 1839? Vi. 55173

Covel, James. A concise dictionary of the Holy Bible, by Rev. James Covel, Jun., designed for the use of Sunday school teachers and families, with maps and numerous fine engravings. New York: Carlton and Porter [1839] 536 p. ArCh; CSansS; IaScM; KyPr; WWooU. 55174

----. Questions on the Acts of the Apostles by James Covel. New York: 1839. T. IEG. 55175

Coventry, Thomas. On conveyancers' evidence. By Thomas Coventry, Esq., of Lincol's Inn, barrister at law. Philadelphia: John S. Littell, New York: Halsted and Voorhies, 1839. 158 p. Ct; MdBb; NbCrD; PP; RPL. 55176

Coventry, Connecticut. First Congregational Church. Catalogue of the surviving members of the First Congregational Church in Coventry, Conn. Hartford: John L. Boswell, printer, 1839. 12 p. CtY; MiD-B; NBLIHI; NjPT; PPPrHi. 55177

Cowan, William Bowie. A description of Grand Tower on the Mississippi, by Col. William Bowie Cowan, with letters from distinguished individuals, containing a description of the country. New York: Alexander S. Gould, printer, 1839. 40 p. IC; MB; MH; MoS; OMC. 55178

Cowper, William, 1731-1800. Poems, by William Cowper, Esq.... and a sketch of his life by John Johnson, L.L. D.... New edition. Boston: Weeks, Jordan and Company, 1839. 3 v. MBC; MMen; MsJPED; OClWHi; PLor. 55179

----. Works of Cowper and Thomson, including many letters and poems never before published in this country; with a new and interesting memoir of the life of Thomson. Philadelphia: Grigg, 1839. 2 v. in 1. IU; KyLxT; OClW; TNP; WA. 55180

Cox, Melville Babbage, 1799-1833. Remains of Melville B. Cox, late missionary to Liberia, with a memoir by the Rev. Gershom F. Cox. New York: T. Mason and G. Lane, 1839. 250 p. DLC; GDecCT; IEG; NjMD; NNMr. 55181

Coxe, Margaret, b. 1800. The young lady's companion: in a series of letters, by Margaret Coxe.... Columbus: L. N. Whiting, 1839. 342 p. MoS; OClWHi; OHi; OMC; PAtM. 55182

Crabb, George, 1778-1851. A dictionary of general knowledge; or an explanation of words and things.... By G. Crabb.... 3rd edition. New York: J. C. Riker, 1839. 368 p. IaHa; MChiA; MNF; NcU; RJa. 55183

----.... Englisn synonymes, with copious illustrations and explanations. Drawn from the best writers. By George Crabb.... A new edition, enlarged. New York: Harper and Brothers, 1839 [65]- 535 p. CtY; GDecCT; MWA; NNF; PAtM. 55184

Crabbe, George, 1754-1832. Poetical works of Crabbe, Heber and Pollok. Philadelphia: Grigg, 1839. 396, 43, 79 p. InCW; MiD; OC; OWoC; PU; WGr. 55185

The cradle of liberty. Vol. I. March 23, 1839-July 18, 1840. Boston: 1839-1840. 1 v. MAtt; MB; NIC. 55186

Craik, George Lillie, 1798-1866. Pursuit of knowledge under difficulties.... New York: Harper and Brothers, 1839. 2 v. GAuY; MeB; OrP; PPGi; ScCC. 55187

Cramp, John Mockett, 1796-1881. The council of Trent. New York: American Tract Society, 1839. 190 p. IaPeC. 55188

Crandall, Daniel. The Columbian spelling book, containing the elements of the English language.... Stereotype edition. Cooperstown: H. and E. Phinney, 1839. 168 p. CLCM; MH; NN; NNC; OClWHi. 55189

Crane, William Carey, 1816-1885. A collection of arguments and opinions upon the subject of baptism. By William Carey Crane, A.M., pastor of the Baptist church, Montgomery, Ala. Montgomery: printed at the office of the Advertiser, 1839. 15 p. KyLOS; PCC; PPAmS. 55190

Crary, Isaac Edwin. Speech of Mr. Crary of Michigan, on the motions to refer the...President's annual message to the appropriate committees. In the House...January, 1839. Washington: Blair and Rives, printers, 1839. 8 p. DLC; MiU-C. 55191

Cresy, Edward, 1792-1858. A practical treatise on bridge building, and on the equilibrium of vaults and arches.... New York: Appleton and Company, 1839. 24 p. DLC; MB; MiU; NWM; PU. 55192

Crichton, Andrew, 1790-1855. The history of Arabia. Ancient and modern...With a map and engravings.... New York: Harper and Brothers, 1839. 2 v. IaPe; IC; MnHi; NUt; PU. 55193

----. Scandinavia, ancient and modern.... By A. Crichton and Henry Wheaton.... New York: 1839. 2 v. FTa. 55194

The cries of London. Cooperstown: Stereotyped, printed by H. and E. Phinney, 1839. 31 p. DLC; NN. 55195

Crockett, David, 1786-1836. An account of Col. Crockett's tour to the north and down east, in the year of our lord, 1834.... Cincinnati: U. P. James, 1839. 234 p. TxU. 55196

----. Col Crockett's exploits and adventures in Texas. See Smith, Richard Penn, 1799-1854.

----. Life of Martin Van Buren, heir-apparent to the "government" and the appointed successor of General Andrew Jackson...with concise history of the events that have occasioned his unparalleled elevation; together with a review of his policy as a statesman. Cincinnati: James, 1839. 209 p. ICN; InU; KyHi; MnDu; MnHi. 55197

----. A narrative of the life of David Crockett...Written by himself. Philadelphia: E. L. Carey and A. Hart, Cincinnati: U. P. James, 1839. 211 p. MiD-B. 55198

The Crockett almanac; 1839.... Nashville, Tennessee: Ben Harding, 1839. 35 p. MWH. 55199

Crockett almanac for 1840. Nashville, Tennessee: Ben Harding, [1839] DLC; MWA; RJa; WHi. 55200

Crockett's comic almanac for 1840. Albany, N.Y.: A. Skinflint, [1839] MWA. 55201

Crockett's free-and-easy song book: Comic, sentimental, amatory, sporting, African, Scotch, Irish, western and Texian, national, military, naval and anacreontic: A new collection of the most popular stage songs, as given by the best vocalists of the present day; and also of favorite dinner and parlour songs. Philadelphia: C. K. Kay and Company, 1839. 128 p. T. 55202

----. Together with glees, duets, recitations and medleys. With 40 engravigns. Philadelphia: James Kay, Jun. and Brother, Pittsburgh: C. H. Kay and Company, 1839. 320 p. NTi; T; TxU. 55203

Croes, Robert B. An essay; "be not righteous overmuch." New York: 1839. 52 p. MB. 55204

Croly, George, 1780-1860. Apocalypse of St. John, or prophecy of the rise, progress and fall of Church of Rome with Inquisition. Revolution of France, Universal War, and final triumph of Christianity. Philadelphia: Littell, 1839. 319 p. OO. 55205

----. Life and times of his late Majesty George the Fourth with anecdotes of distinguished persons of the last 50 years. New and improved edition. New York: Harper and Brothers, 1839. 414 p. MB- HP; NRU; RNR; ScDuE; TxGR. 55206

Cross, James Conquest. An address on American literature; delivered before the Philomathean Society of Indiana University, at its annual commencement, September 25th, 1839. Bloomington: printed at the Equator office, 1839. 86 p. InU; KyLxT; NjPT. 55207

Cross, Joseph, 1813-1893. The claims of missions on the liberality of Christians; a sermon, preached in behalf of the Female Missionary Society of the Methodist Episcopal Church in Ithaca, Aug. 4, 1839. Ithaca: Barnaby, 1839. 24 p. CSansS; KSalW; MoS; NCH. 55208

----. A plea for Sabbath schools, delivered at the Methodist Chapel in Binghamton, N.Y. October 6, 1839. Published by special request. Binghamton: Cooke and Davis, printers, 1839. 19 p. KSalW; KyLx; MH-Ah; N; NCH. 55209

----. The providence of God in the history of America. An oration, delivered before the citizens of Ithaca, July 4th, 1839. [Ithaca] A. E. Barnaby and Company, 1839. 20 p. CSmH; N; PHi. 55210

Cross, Marcus E. The museum of religious

knowledge, designed to illustrate religious truth.... Philadelphia: J. Whetham, 1839. 264 p. CSfCW; ICP; MoSpD; OMC; PPM. 55211

Cruden, Alexander, 1701-1770. Cruden's concordance to the Old and New Testament: or a dictionary and alphabetical index to the Bible. In two parts. To which is added, a concordance to the Apocrypha. With a compendium of the Bible, and a brief account of its history and excellency. With a sketch of the life and character of the author, by William Youngman. New York: D. Appleton and Company, Boston: Munroe and Francis, 1839. NICLA. 55212

Cruikshank, George, 1792-1878. Everyday life and everyday people. Philadelphia: Lea and Blanchard Publishing Company, 1839. TNL. 55213

Cruikshank, William. No intermediate place. A sermon, preached in the Reformed Dutch Church of Hyde Park, September 9th, 1838. Published by request. Poughkeepsie: printed by Platt and Ranney, 1839. 22 p. MBAt; MWA; NjR; NPV. 55214

Cuffee, Paul, b. 1796? Narrative of the life and adventures of Paul Cuffee, a Pequot Indian: during thirty years spent at sea, and in travelling in foreign lands. Vernon, [N.Y.]: printed by Horace N. Bill, 1839. 21 p. ICN; MiU; MSaP; MWA; NhD. 55215

Cumberland almanac for 1840. Nashville, Tenn.: S. Nye and Company [1839] MWA; T; THi. 55216

Cumberland Presbyterian Church. Constitution of the Cumberland Presbyterian Church in the United States of America; containing the confession of faith, the catechism and a directory for the worship of God.... Pittsburgh: Forrester and Campbell, 1839. OMC; NcMHi; PPi; PWaybu. 55217

Cumberland Road Convention. Proceedings of the Cumberland Road Convention, composed of delegates from the states of Ohio, Indiana and Illinois, held at Terre Haute, Indiana, July 8 and 9, 1839. Terre Haute: printed by J. and T. Dowling, 1839. 6 p. IU; MoSM. 55218

Cumings, Samuel. The western pilot...revised and corrected by Eppts. Charles Ross and Hugh McClain. Cincinnati: George Conclin, 1839. 144 p. ICu; InHi; MdBJ; MWA; NN. 55219

Cummings, Asa, 1791-1856. Blessedness of the faithful servant. A sermon preached in Pownal, January 31, 1839, at the interment of the Rev. Perez Chaplin.... Portland: Alfred Merrill, 1839. 32 p. CSmH; MeBa; MWA; NjPt; OClWHi. 55220

----. A memoir of the Rev. Edward Payson. By Rev. Asa Cummings. New York: American Tract Society, 1839. 486 p. MB; NcCJ. 55221

Cunningham, Allan, 1784-1845.... The lives of the most eminent British painters and sculptors, by Allan Cunningham. In 5 volumes. New York: Harper and Brothers, 1839. 3 v. DLC; InRch; Me; NCaS; OAU; TxH. 55222

Cunningham, Joseph L. Catalogue of old English books sold Nov. 21, 1839. Boston: 1839. MBAt. 55223

Cunningham, Robert, 1799-1883. Address on the advantages to be derived from the study of the ancient classics, delivered before the students of LaFayette College, Easton, Pa., at the opening of the summer session on 11th May, 1839. Easton [Pa.] printed on the college press by C. Priest, 1839. 24 p. CtY; MBAt; NNU; OClWHi; PEaL. 55224

Curie, Paul Francis, 1799-1853. Domestic homoeopathy. With additions and improvements, by Gideon Humphrey. Philadelphia: J. Harding, 1839. 250 p. GDecCT; MB; MBM; PPC; WaPS. 55225

Curtis, George Ticknor, 1812-1894. The American conveyancer; containing a large variety of legal forms.... Boston: Charles C. Little and James Brown, 1839. 281 p. Ct; MB; MBS; MH-AII; PU-L. 55226

Curtis, John Harrison, b. 1778. Observations on the preservation of sight, and on the choice, use and abuse of spectacles, reading glasses, etc. From the 3rd London edition. Oculist and aurist. Worcester: Spooner and Howland, 1839. 80 p. CtY-M; MWA. 55227

Curtis, Silas. The miracles of Salem; discourse at the minister's conference of the Bowdoin Q. M., Lewiston, Me., June 25, 1839. Dover [N.H.] 1839. 22 p. MBNMHi; MeLewB; RPB. 55228

Curtiss, Wilbur. Map of the seat of war, showing the disputed territory, and the boundry lines claimed by Maine and Great Britain and that proposed by the king of the Netherlands. Boston: T. Moore, 1839. MB; MH. 55229

Cushing, Abel. Historical letters on the first charter of Massachusetts government. Boston: J. N. Bang, printer, 1839. 204 p. CtSoP; IU; MWA; NjN; PPAmP. 55230

Cushing, Caleb, 1800-1879. A discourse on the social influence of Christianity, delivered...Sept., 1838, ...Brown University. Andover: printed by Gould and Newman, 1839. 28 p. DLC; KyBC; MB; NNC; RHi. 55231

----. An oration, on the material growth and territorial progress of the United States, delivered at Springfield, Mass., on the 4th of July, 1839. Springfield: Merriam, Wood and Company, 1839. 32 p. CtSoP; MH; MWA; Nh-Hi; RPB. 55232

----. Speeches of Mr. Cushing, of Massachusetts, on the Maine boundary question. Newburyport: Morse and Brewster, 1839. 14 p. DLC; MHi; MLow. 55233

Cushman, David Qimby, 1806-1889. Speech of Mr. Cushman, of New Hampshire. House of Representatives, January 2, 1839 [Washington: 1839] 8 p. ICU; ICN; MdHi. 55234

Cushman, Samuel, 1783-1851. Speech in House of Representatives, January 2, 1839. Washington: 1839. 8 p. DLC. 55235

Custead, William W. Catalogue of fruit and ornamental trees, flowering shrubs and creepers, herbaceous and green house plants, bulbous and tuberous rooted flowers; cultivated and for sale at the Cleveland nursery. Cleveland: press of the Advertiser, 1839. 23 p. OClWHi. 55236

Cuthbert, Alfred. Speech of Mr. Cuthbert, of Georgia, on the bill to prevent the interference of certain federal officers in elections. Delivered in the Senate of the United States, February 20, 1839. Washington: printed at the Globe office, 1839. 8 p. DLC; GU. 55237

Cuyler, Cornelius C. The signs of the times; a series of discourses deliverd in the Second Presbyterian Church, Philadelphia. Philadelphia: William L. Martien, 1839. 22 p. CSansS; ICMe; KyLoP; OWoC; PPL. 55238

D

Daboll, Nathan, 1750-1815. Complete schoolmaster's assistant:being a plain comprehensive system of practical arithmetic, adapted to the use of schools in the United States.... New London: W. and J. Bolles, 1839. MH. 55239

----. A key to Daboll's arithmetic, containing correct solutions to all the examples and questions, at full length, ...By John D. Williams, private teacher of mathematics and natural philosophy, and author of a key to Hutton's mathematics, key to Willett's arithmetic, an elementary treatise on arithmetic, and an elementary treatise on algebra. New York: H. and S. Raynor, 1839, 180 p, DAU, 55240

----. Daboll's schoolmaster's assistant...being a plain practical system of arithmatick.... by Nathan Daboll with the addition of the farmer's and mechanick's best method of bookkeeping, designed as a companion to Daboll's arithmatick, by Samuel Green, 1839. Ithaca, N.Y.: Mack, Andrus and Woodruff, 1839. 228 p. DLC; MeHi; MH; MiHi. 55241

----. ----. Utica: printed by Gardiner Tracy, 1839. ICU; MeHi; MHad; NIC; NNC; NUt. 55242

Dagg, John Leadley, 1794-1884. An interpretation of John III:5. By John L. Dagg, principal of the Alabama Female Athenaeum, Tuscaloosa. Philadelphia: published for the author, by I. M. Allen, 1839. 36 p. ICU; MWA; NHC-S; NjPT. 55243

Dale, James Wilkinson, 1812-1881. Essay upon the question, is medical science favourable to scepticism? By James W.... Philadelphia: Haswell, Barrington and Haswell, Barrington and Haswell, 1839. 22 p. CSt-L; LNT-M; NjR; PPA; ViU. 55244

Dalzel, Andreas, 1742-1806. Collectanea Graeco Majora, ad usum academicae Juventutis accommodata cum notis philologicis, quas partin collegit partim Scripsit, Andreas Dalzel, A.M.... Tounes 11. Complecteus excerpta exvarus poetis.

Editio quarta Americana ex autoribus correcta.... Boston: Hilliard, Gray and Company, Philadelphia: Kimber and Sharpless, 1839. 2 v. ICP; MdBD; NbOC; OUrC; WU. 55245

Dana, Daniel, 1771-1859. Letters to the Rev. Professor Stuart, comprising remarks on his essay on sin, published in the American Biblical repository for April and July, 1839.... Boston: printed by Crocker and Brewster, 1839. 46 p. CSmH; MH; MWA; NjR; PPPrHi. 55246

----. Sermon at installation John Brown in Pine Street Church, Boston. Boston: 1839. OCHP. 55247

Dante, Alighieri, 1265-1321. The vision; or hell, purgatory and paradise of Alighieri Dante. New York: D. Appleton, 1839. 587 p. KyDC; PPL. 55248

Danvers, Massachusetts. School Committee. Report of the School Committee of the town of Danvers. 1839. Printed by vote of the town. Salem: William Ives and Company, printers, 1839 [-1869] 3 v. MH; MPeaI. 55249

Danville and Pottsville Railroad Company. Report of the president and manager of the Danville and Pottsville Railroad Company to the stockholders. Philadelphia: printed by Joseph and William Kite, 1839. DLC; NN; PPM; WU. 55250

Darley, William Henry Westray, 1801-1872. Music of Christ Church and St. Stephens, being a collection of psalms and hymn tunes original and selected as sung in these churches, harmonized for four voices and provided with an organ or pianoforte accompaniment by M. H. W. Darley...and J. C. B. Standbridge.... Philadelphia: J. Kay and Brothers, 1839. 160 p. MB; NN; Vi. 55251

Darlington, William, 1782-1863. An essay on the development and modifications of the external organs of plants. Compiled chiefly from the writings of J. Wolfgang von Goethe, for a public lecture to the class of the Chester County cabinet of natural science. March 1, 1839. West Chester, Pennsylvania: 1839. 38 p. CtY; DLC; MH; NNC; PHi. 55252

Dartmouth College. A catalogue of the officers and students of Dartmouth College, September, 1839. Windsor, Vt.: printed by Tracy and Severance, 1839. 26 p. CBPSR; DLC; MBAt; McB; PPM. 55253

----. Phi Beta Kappa. Catalogue of the fraternity of Phi Beta Kappa, Alpha of New Hampshire, Dartmouth College, Hanover. July, 1839. Concord: printed by Asa McFarland, for the society, 1839. 23 p. KHi; MeLewB; NhD. 55254

----. Social Friends. Catalogue of the officers and members of the society of Social Friends...1839. Concord: printed by A. McFarland, 1839. 56 p. M; MiD-B. 55255

Daunt, William Joseph O'Neill, 1807-1894. The husband hunter, or "Das Schiksal." By Denis Ignatius Moriarty [pseud.] Philadelphia: Lea and Blanchard, 1839. 2 v. DLC; MBAt; MH; NN; PPL-R. 55256

Davenport, Bishop. A new gazetteer, or geographical dictionary of North America and the West Indies...new edition with abr. and additions. Philadelphia: B. Davenport and Company, 1839. 536 p. Ct; MnHi; PWmpDS. 55257

Davneport, J. O. A chapter in the history of abolitionism at Syracuse. 1839. 8 p. ArU. 55258

Davenport, Richard Alfred. A dictionary of biogroaphy; comprising the most eminent characters of all ages, nations and professions. 1st American edition, with numerous additions, corrections and improvements.... Exeter: J. and B. Williams, 1839. 527 p. IaCrM; MiU; NhD; ODaW; T. 55259

[Davenport, Rufus] The right aim. First aim to get first principles of right; then trust prevailing with progressive light; while freedom, art, trade, debt take first the ground all things for general good, the right aim found. Boston [Dow and Niles] 1839. 32 p. MH; MH-BA. 55260

Davidson, Robert. Address on the 11th anniversary of the city school of Lexington, August 1, 1839. Lexington, Ky.: 1839. 16 p. MH-AH. 55261

Davies, Charles, 1798-1876. Elements of algebra: tr. from the French of M. Bourdon. Revised and adapted to the course of mathematical instruction in the United States.... Revised edition. Hartford: A. S. Barnes and Company, New York: Wiley and Putnam [etc., etc.] 1839. 355 p. CEu; NHem; NjMD; NWM; TxU-T. 55262

----. Elements of analytical geometry; embracing the equations of the point, the straight line, the conic sections, and surfaces of the first and second order.... 2nd edition. Revised and corrected. Hartford: A. S. Barnes and Company, New York: Wiley and Putnam [etc. etc.] 1839. 352 p. DLC; MdBS; OO; PSC; ViU. 55263

----. Elements of descriptive geometry, with their application to spherical trigonometry, spherical projections and warped surfaces.... 2nd edition. New York: A. S. Barnes and Company, etc., etc., etc., etc., 1839. 174 p. MdBE; NbOC; OClWHi; OMC; TJaU. 55264

----. Elements of geometry and trigonometry. Translated from the French of A. M. Legendre, by David Brewster...Revised and adapted to the course of mathematical instruction in the U.S.... Hartford: A. S. Barnes and Company, New York: Wiley and Putnam; [etc.] 1839. 297, 62 p. ICMcHi; InI; OClWHi. 55265

----. Elements of surveying, with a descriptiono of the instruments and the necessary tables, including a table of natural sines?... 4th edition. Hartford: A. S. Barnes and Company, 1839. 170, 91 p. C; ILM; MWM; ScCliP; ViRU. 55266

----. Elements of the differential and integral calculus.... 2nd edition, edited, revised and corrected. Hartford: A. S. Barnes and Company, 1839. 283 p. CtHT; ICu; NjMD; PU; ScCC. 55267

----. First lessons in algebra, by Charles Davies. Hartford: A. S. Barnes and Company, New York: Wiley and Putnam, Collins, Keese and Company, Boston: Perkins and Marvin, Philadelphia: Thomas, Cowperthwait and Company, Baltimore: Cushing and Sons, 1839. 252 p. CU; IaHol; MeU; NNC; OMC. 55268

----. First lessons in geometry, with practical applications in mensuration, and artificers' work and mechanics. Hartford: A. S. Barnes and Company, etc., etc., 1839. GMM; InCW; LNP; MoU; TNP. 55269

----. Mental and practical arithmetic. Designed for the use of academies and schools. By Charles Davies. Hartford: A. S. Barnes and Company, 1839. 332 p. CTHWatk; ICBB; MS; ScCMu; TNP. 55270

----. ----. With a key. Chicago: S. F. Gales, 1839. 334 p. ICHi. 55271

----. Practical geometry with selected applications in mensuration in artificers work and mechanics by Charles Davies.... Philadelphia: A. S. Barnes and Company [1839] 252 p. MdBLC; MdBS; MWHi; NPotN; PP. 55272

----. A treatise on shades and shadows, and linear perspective. By Charles Davies.... 2nd edition. Hartford: A. S. Barnes and Company, New York: Wiley and Putnam [etc., etc.] 1839. [9]-159 p. COCA; DLC; MWA; RPB; ViU. 55273

Davies, John, 1796-1872.... Selections in pathology and surgery; or an exposition of the nature and treatment of local diseases; exhibiting new pathological views, and pointing out an important practical improvement...By John Davies...Philadelphia: A. Waldie, 1839. 119 p. KyLxT; NhD; OO; PPA; RNR. 55274

Davies, Thomas Frederick. A sermon delivered March 29, 1839...published by request of the Congregational Society in Green's Farms. New Haven: printed by B. L. Hamlen, 1839. 31 p. CSmH; DLC; MHi; NjR; PPAmP. 55275

Davis, Asahel, b. 1791. A lecture on the discovery of America by the Northmen 500 years before Columbus.... Rochester: D. Hoyt, printer, 1839. 22 p. ICn; NBu; NRU. 55276

----. ----. 2nd edition. Rochester: David Hoyt, printer, 1839. 22 p. N; NN. 55277

----. ----. 3rd edition. New York: S. Coleman, 1839. 23 p. CtY; DLC; NNUT; OClWHi; RHi. 55278

----. ----. 4th edition with additions. New York: S. Colman, 1839. 23 p. ICN; MWA; Nh-Hi; PPL; RPB. 55279

Davis, Emerson. The teacher taught; or the principles and modes of teaching. By Emerson Davis.... Boston: Marsh, Capen, Lyon and Webb, 1839. 138 p. CtY; ICU; MWA; PU: RKi. 55280

Davis, Jacob S. Treatise on the evolution of powers, simple and mixed. Cincinnati: R. P. Brooks, 1839. 55 p. MBAt; OCHP; RPB. 55281

Davis, John, 1787-1854. An address delivered before the American Institute, at their 11th anniversary in New York, Oct. 18, 1838. Springfield: A. G. Tannatt, 1839. 31 p. CtMW; MBC; MH: MWA; PPM. 55282

Davis, John Francis, 1795-1890. The Chinese: a general description of the empire of China and its inhabitants. By John Francis Davis, Esq., F.R.S., etc. In two volumes. New York: Harper and Brothers, 1839. 2 v. IEG; NCH; Nh-Hi; P; ScDuE. 55283

Davis, Mary Elizabeth [Moragne] 1815-1903. The British partizan: a tale of the times of old.... Augusta, Ga.: William T. Thompson, 1839. 150 p. CSmH; GU; NHU; ScC. 55284

Davy, Humphrey, hart., 1778-1829. Elements of agricultural chemistry, in a course of lectures for the Board of Agriculture: delivered between 1802-1812.... 2nd American from the 5th London edition. Petersburg: E. Ruffin, 1839. CtY. 55285

Dawes, Rufus, 1803-1859. Athenia of Damascus. A tragedy. By Rufus Dawes. New York: Samuel Coleman, 1839. 118 p. CSmH; MWA; NcU; PU; RPB. 55286

----. Geraldine, Athenia of Damascus, and miscellaneous poems. By Rufus Dawes. New York: Samuel Coleman, 1839. 343 p. ICN; NBuG; OCo; PP; RKi. 55287

----. Nix's mate: an historical romance of America, by the author of "Athenia of Damascus".... New York: S. Coleman, 1839. 2 v. in 1. CSt; MH; MWA; OCY; PU. 55288

----. Poems. New York: S. Coleman, 1839. 343 p. NjN; NjR; PPM. 55289

Day, Hartley W. The vocal school; or Pestalozzian method of instruction in the elements of vocal music: embracing a practical and philosophical demonstration of the philosophy of the scale.... Boston: Otis, Broaders and Company, 1839. 279 p. MB; MoSM; OO; PU-Penn. 55290

Day, Jeremiah, 1773-1867. A course of mathematics: containing the principles of plane trigonometry, mensuration, navigation and surveying.... New Haven: Durrie and Peck, New York: Collins, Keese and Company, 1839. GEU; ICU; NbHi; OO; ViU. 55291

----. Introduction to algebra, being the first part of a course of mathematics.... 34th edition. New Haven: Durrie and Peck, New York: Collins, Keese and Company, 1839. 332 p. CTHWatk; CU. 55292

----. ----. 35th edition. New Haven: Durrie and Peck, New York: Collins, Keese and Company, 1839. 332 p. CU; DLC; NTRPI; OU. 55293

----. ----. 36th edition. New Haven: Durrie and Peck, 1839. 332 p. CtY; MdBJ; NN; ScCC; WSeeT. 55294

----. ----. 37th edition. New Haven: Durrie and Peck, New York: Collins, Keese and Company, 1839. 322 p. MH; NRMA. 55295

----. The mathematical principles of navigation and surveying, with the mensuration of heights and distances, being the fourth part of a course of mathematics.... New Haven [Durrie and Peck, New York: Collins, Keese and Company] 1839. 119 p. CtHT; OO; ViU; WHi. 55296

----. A practical application of the principles of geometry to the mensuration of superficies and solids, being the third part of a course of mathematics, adapted to the method of instruction in the American colleges.... New Haven: Durrie and Peck [etc., etc.] 1839. 96 p. CtY; OO; ViU. 55297

----. A treatise on plane trigonometry, to which is prefixed a summary view of the nature and use of logarithms.... A course of mathematics.... New Haven: Durrie and Peck, 1839. 155 p. GEU; NjR; OO; ViU. 55298

Day's city and country almanac, for 1840. New York, N.Y.: Mahlon Day and Company [1839] MWA. 55299

Dayton, Aaron Ogden, d. 1858. Address delivered before the American Whig and Cliosophic societies of the College of New Jersey. September 24, 1839. By Aaron Ogden Dayton, esq. Princeton: printed by R. E. Hornor, 1839. 48 p. DLC; IEG; MWA; NcD; PPL. 55300

Dean, Amos. Introductory lecture before the

Young Men's Association for mutual improvement in the city of Albany. Delivered Dec. 17, 1839. Albany: printed by J. Munsell, 1839. 33 p. CtY; DLC; MB; MWA; NjR. 55301

----. The philosophy of human life. Being an investigation of the great elements of life...together with reflections adapted to the physical, political, popular moral and religious natures of man. Boston: Marsh, Capen, Lyon and Webb, 1839. 300 p. IC; MBAt; MoS; MWiW; RPAt. 55302

Dean, Christopher C. Memoir of Samuel Davies. 2nd edition. Boston: Massachusetts Sabbath School Society, 1839. 138 p. MB. 55303

Dearborn, Henry Alexander Scrammell, 1783-1851. Letters on the internal improvements and commerce of the west. Boston: printed by Dutton and Wentworth, 1839. 119 p. InI; LNH; MiD-B; RPAt; WHi. 55304

----. ----. Boston: H. P. Lewis, 1839. 75 p. DLC; IaU; MHi; NjP; OClWHi. 55305

Deerfield Association. Address to the churches connected with the Deerfield Association. Concord: 1839. 16 p. MHi; Nh-Hi; NN. 55306

Defoe, Daniel, 1661-1731. The adventures of Robin Hood.... In two volumes. Philadelphia: Lea and Blanchard, successors to Carey and Company, 1839. 2 v. MsNF. 55307

----. The life and advnetures of Robinson Crusoe, embellished with engravings, by William Robertson. Ithaca, N.Y.: Mack, Andrus and Woodruff [1839] 159 p. MiU; MWA; NIC; NIDHi; PU. 55308

----. ----. New York: Robinson and Franklin, 1839. 2 v. DLC; MIU; NIC. 55309

----. ----. Portland: Colesworthy, 1839. 134 p. NNC. 55310

----. New Robinson Crusoe, designed for youth. Ornamented with plates. Cooperstown: 1839. 27 p. MWA. 55311

----. Religious courtship: being historical discourses on the necessity of marrying religious husbands and wives only: as also, of husbands and wives being of the same opinions in religion with one another. Philadelphia: James Kay, Jr., and

Brother, 1839. KyLoP. 55312

DeGrasse, Isaiah G. A sermon on education....
New York: J. Van Norden, 1839. 19 p. CtY; DLC;
NBLiHi; NN. 55313

Degrees of bliss in Heaven. New York: Protestant Episcopal Tract Society, 1839. 16 p. DLC;
InID. 55314

Delafield, John, 1786-1853. An inquiry into the
origin of the antiquities of America. By John
Delafield, Jr. With an appendix, containing
notes.... Cincinnati: N. G. Burgess and Company,
1839. 142 p. CSmH; KyLo; Nj; OCoC; WHi. 55315

----. ----. New York: Colt, Burges and Company
[etc., etc.] 1839. 142 p. CtY; IHi; MWA; OkHi; P.
55316

DeLancey, William Heathcote, 1797-1865. Episcopal address to the 2nd annual convention of the
diocese of western New York, October 3, 1839. By
the Rt. Rev. William Heathcote DeLancey, D.D.,
bishop of the diocese. Utica: press of Griffith and
Bush [1839] 20 p. NBuDD. 55317

----. Farewell letter of the Rev. William H. De-
Lancey, D.D., to the vestry and congregation of St.
Peter's Church. May 2nd, 1839. Philadelphia:
Jesper Harding, printer, 1839. 11 p. MiD-B;
NBuDD; NjR; PHi; PPL. 55318

----. A pastoral letter, to the clergy and churches
in the diocese of western New York, on the regulation of the convention enjoining monthly collec-
tions for church objects. Genvea, N.Y.: Stow and
Frazee, 1839. 15 p. MB; MBD; N; NBuDD;
TScwU. 55319

----. Personal Holiness in the ministry. A sermon,
delivered in St. Peter's Church, Auburn, before
the special convention of the diocese of western
New York, festival of the ascension, Thursday,
May 9, 1839. Utica: Hobart Press, 1839. 13 p.
MBD; MiD-B; NUt; PPiXT; RPB. 55320

Delaware. General Assembly. House of
Representataives. Report exhibiting the reasons
of the House of Representataives of the state of
Delaware, for insisting on the election of a senator
in Congress by separate ballot; made in reply to a
report of the Senate, refusing to elect a senator by
that mode. Dover, Delaware: S. Kimmey, printer,
1839. 13 p. DLC; P. 55321

----. Geological and Mineralogical Survey. First
and second annual reports of the progress of the
geological and mineralogical survey of the state of
Delaware. Dover, Del.: Kimmey, 1839. 25 p. CU;
MA; PPF. 55322

Democratic almanac for Baltimore, 1840. Baltimore, Md.: William Wooddy [1839] DLC;
MWA. 55323

The democratic medley, or sayings and doings,
with the history of one day, to which is added the
Whig's lighthouse, and a trip through the custom-
house and post office. Calculated for the
meredian of Philadelphia, by a member of the
Democratic party. Philadelphia: printed for the
author [1839] 34 p. DLC; ICN; MnHi; P; PHi.
55324

Democratic Party. Alabama. Convention. 1839.
The journal and address of the democratic state
convention, held in the city of Tuscaloosa, on the
16th, 17th and 18th of December, 1839. Tuscaloosa: Hale and Eaton, printers, 1839. 29 p.
CSmH; MdHi; NcD; TxU; WHi. 55325

----. Illinois. Convention. 1839. Illinois
democratic state convention. Springfield, December 9th, 1839 [Springfield: 1839] 16 p. ICHi. 55326

----. ----. Jo Davies County. Proceedings and address of the democratic county convention...1839
[Galena, Ill.: 1839] 8 p. DLC; ICHi; M; 55327

----. Indiana. Congressional Convention. New
Albany Argus-Extra. Address of the democratic
congresional convention, 3rd district, held at Lexington, Scott County, Ia. on the 8th of January,
1839 [New Albany, 1839?] 16 p. In. 55328

----. Massachusetts. Convention, 1839. Proceedings of the Massachusetts democratic state convention held at the temple, Boston, October 2,
1839. 15 p. MBAt; MHi; WHi. 55329

----. North Carolina. State Rights Convention.
Address of the Democratic State Rights Conven-
tion assembled at Britton's Cross Roads. Britton's
Cross Roads, N.C.: 1839. NcU. 55330

----. Virginia. Convention. 1839. Proceedings of
the Republican convention. Monday, March 18
[20], 1839 [Richmond? Va.: 1839] CSmH; PPL; Vi.
55331

Democratic Whig Association of the city and county of Philadelphia. Address of the Democratic Whig Association of the city and county of Philadelphia, to the people of Pennsylvania. April, 1839. Philadelphia: printed for the Association, 1839. 26, 16 p. DLC; OClWHi; OO; PPL; PPM. 55332

Democrat's almanac, and political register for 1839. Containing the Delcaration of Independence, and the Constitution of the United States.... New York: published at the office of the Evening Post, 1839. DLC; MB; NjR; WaSp; WHi. 55333

Democrat's almanac and political register for 1840. New York, N.Y.: office of the Evening Post [1839] Last pages vary. MB; MHa; MWA. 55334

----. 2nd edition. New York: 1839. MH; MWA. 55335

Dempster, William Richardson, 1809-1871. A man's a man for a' that, a song, the poetry by Robert Burns. Arranged with an accompaniment for the pianoforte by W. R. Dempster. B[oston] 1839. 5 p. MH; MNF. 55336

Dennis, Jonathan, jr. Dennis' silk manual; containing complete directions for cultivating the different kinds of mulberry trees, feeding silkworms and manufacturing silk to profit.... New York: M. Day and Company, 1839. 107 p. CtY; DLC; MH; RPB. 55337

Denny, William. Oration delivered July 4th, 1839, at Ellicott's Mills, Anne Arundel County, Maryland.... Baltimore: printed by Samuel Sands, 1839. 20 p. Md; MdBLC; MdHi; PHl. 55338

Depositions of members of the New Jersey legislature.... Jersey City? 1839. 20 p. DLC. 55339

A descendant of Cape Cod. Song written for the second centennial celebration at Barnstable, Sept. 3, 1839. Boston: Eastburn Press, [1839] Broadside. MB. 55340

Description, modes of capturing and anecdotes of the elephant. New Haven: S. Babcock, 1839. 24 p. CtY. 55341

A description of the cities, townships and principle villages and settlements, within thirty miles of the city of New York. New York: Colton and Disturnall, Sackett and Sargent, 1839. 78 p. ICarb-S; NNA; NNC; NNQ; RNR. 55342

Description of the island of Trinidad, and of the advantages to be derived from emigration to that colony. Philadelphia: Merrihew and Thompson, 1839. 8 p. DHU; MiD-B; PHi. 55343

Deslandes, Leopold. A treatise on the diseases produced by onanism, masturbation, self-pollution and other excesses.... Translated from the French, with many additions. 2nd edition. Boston: Otis, Broaders and Company, 1839. 252, 6 [2] p. MBM; MH- M; NNN; RPM. 55344

The destroyer, a thrilling tale; from passages from the diary of a late London physician. The last chapter. Middlebury [Vt.] R. E. Huntington, printer, 1839. 132 p. VtMidSM. 55345

Deutsche Gesellschaft von Pennsylvania. Philadelphia. Catalogue of the library of the German Society contributing for the relief of distressed Germans in the state of Pennsylvania. Prepared by the librarian. Philadelphia: printed by Conrad Zentler, 1839. 218 p. NNN; PHi; PPL-R; PPP. 55346

De Veaux, Samuel, 1789-1852. The falls of Niagara, or tourist's guide to this wonder of nature, including notices of the whirlpool, islands, etc. and a complete guide through the Canadas.... Buffalo: W.B. Hayden, 1839. 168 p. DLC; ICN; MnHi; NBu; PLFM. 55347

----. The travellers' own book, to Saratoga Springs, Niagara Falls and Canada, containing...a complete guide, for the valetudinarian and for the tourist, seeking for pleasure and amusement.... Buffalo: 1839. DSG; NGH. 55348

Dewees, William Potts. Compendious system of midwifery, chiefly designed to facilitate the inquiries of those who may be pursuing this branch of study.... 9th edition. Philadelphia: Lea, 1839. 660 p. IEN-M; MdUM; MH-M; NNN; PPCP. 55349

Dewey, Orville, 1794-1882. A discourse, delivered at the dedication of the Church of the Messiah, in Broadway, New York.... New York: Stationers' Hall Press, 1839. 26 p. CSmH; DLC; ICMe; MNe; RPB. 55350

----. On reading. A lecture delivered before the

Mechanic's Library Association in New York. New York: David Felt and Company, 1839. 20 p. DLC; MH; MMeT-Hi; NUtHi; RPaw. 55351

----. Remarks on the sacred scriptures, and on belief and unbelief. Boston: James Munroe and Company, 1839. 28 p. ICMe; MBC; MeBat; MH-AH; MMeT-Hi. 55352

----. Sermon, dedication Church of the Messiah, New York. New York: 1839. MB; MDeeP. 55353

DeWitt, Simeon, 1756-1834. An atlas of the state of New York, designed for the use of engineers, containing a map of the state, and of the several counties, projected and drawn by a uniform scale from documents deposited in the public offices of the state.... Ithaca, N.Y.: Stone and Clark, 1839. CSmH; NRom. 55354

DeWitt, Thomas, 1791-1874. Christ the resurrection and the life. A sermon, preached on the occasion of the death of the Rev. David S. Bogart, on the evening of Aug. 4, 1839, in the Middle Dutch church. By Thomas DeWitt.... New York: printed by G. P. Scott, 1839. 22 p. DLC; MA; MH; NNNG; PPPrHi. 55355

Dexter, Andrew Alfred. Report to the president and directors of the Selma and Tennessee Railrand [sic] Company. By A. A. Dexter, civil engineer. 2nd edition, abridged. Published by order of the board. Selma: printed at the Free Press office, 1839. 16 p. DBRE; DLC; MBAt; NN; ViW. 55356

A dialogue between Telemachus and Mentor on the rights of conscience and military requisitions. Philadelphia: printed by John Richards, 1839. 18 p. PReaHi. 55357

The diary for 1839, being an easy mode of registering incidents. New York: 1839-1845. DLC. 55358

The diary for 1840, containing almanac for 1840; New York: E. S. Mesier [1839] DLC. 55359

Diaz del Castillo, Bernal, 1492-1584. Full and true history of the conquest of Mexico by Cortez...Translated from the Spanish...by A. Prynne. Albany [1839] 32 p. CtY; MWA. 55360

Dibble, Sheldon, 1809-1845. History and general views of the Sandwich Islands' mission. By Rev. Sheldon Dibble.... New York: Taylor and Dodd, 1839 [13]-268 p. CU-B; KyBC; OrU; PPA; RPAt. 55361

Dick, John. Lectures on theology, by the late Rev. John Dick, D.D. Minister of the United Associate Congregation.... Philadelphia: F. W. Greenough, 1839. 2 v. ArCH; GDecCT; GAuP; MB; OTifH. 55362

Dick, Thomas. Celestial scenery; or the wonders of the planetary system displayed. New York: Harper and Brothers, 1839. 422 p. MB- HP; MPeal; NN; P. 55363

----. ----. Philadelphia: Edward C. Biddle, 1839. 387 p. AMaJ; MoS; ViLxW. 55364

----. The Christian philosophy, or the connection of science and philosophy with religion. Abridged by Rev. H. D. Gossking. New York: T. Mason and G. Lane, 1839. 265 p. IaScW. 55365

----. ----. Philadelphia: Edward C. Biddle, 1839. 350 p. LNB; MoS; RNR. 55366

----. ----. 2nd American edition. Hartf[ord] 1839. MH. 55367

----. An essay on the sin and the evils of covetousness; and the happy effects which would flow from a spirit of Christian beneficence...uniform edition.... Philadelphia: Edward C. Biddle, 1839. 304 p. MoS; OWoC; ViLxW. 55368

----. On the improvements of society. By the diffusion of knowledge: an illustration. Illustrated with engravings, the connexion of science and philosophy with religion. Hartford: H. F. Sumner and Company, 1839. 4 v. in 1. FOA; ScDuE; TxDaM; ViRut. 55369

----. ----. New York: Harper and Brothers, 1839. 442 p. FTa; ICu; MeBa; MPeal; TxGR. 55370

----. ----. New York: Robinson, Pratt and Company, 1839. 162 p. LNB. 55371

----. ----. Philadelphia: Edward C. Biddle, 1839. 386 p. OWoC. 55372

----. The philosophy of a future state.... Philadelphia: Edward C. Biddle, 1839. CoDI; MoS; PHi; ViRVal. 55373

----. The Philosphy of religion or an illustration of the moral laws of the universe. Philadelphia: Edward C. Biddle, 1839. 391 p. ICn; LNB; MoS; OWoC; RNR. 55374

----. The works of Thomas Dick, LL.D. Four volumes in one, viz. An essay on the improvement of society; the philosophy of a future state; the philosophy of religion; the Christian philosopher.... Hartford: H. F. Sumner and Company, 1839. 4 v. in 1. CtMW; IU; NbCrD; PPWe; WGr. 55375

Dickens, Charles, 1812-1870. The life and adventures of Nicholas Nickleby. Containing a faithful account of the fortunes, misfortunes, uprisings, downfallings and complete career of the Nickleby family.... With illustrations. New York: William H. Coyler, 1839. 2 v. in 1. IaHi; MH; MWA; OMC; PU. 55376

----. ----. New York: J. Turney, 1839. 624 p. MH; NN; PU. 55377

----. ----. Fiction. New York: A. L. Burt, 1839. 430 p. IaFc. 55378

----. ----. New York: Harper [1839] MQ. 55379

----. The life and adventures of Nicholas Nickleby. [Boz-]...With numerous illustrations by Phiz [pseud.] Philadelphia: Lea and Blanchard, 1839. 403 p. GMar; MH; OCl; PU; RBr. 55380

----. ----. Philadelphia: T. B. Peterson [1839?] DeWI; MB; NN; PPL. 55381

----. Oliver Twist, or the parish boy's progress. In two volumes.... Cincinnati: U. P. James, 1839. 2 v. CtY; OC. 55382

----. ----. With illustrations. Complete in one volume. New York: William H. Colyer, 1839. 296 p. MB; MWA; NjP; OClStM. 55383

----. ----. [Boz] Phialdelphia: Lea and Blanchard, 1839. 212 p. DLC; ICU; NIC; OU; PU. 55384

----. ----. 2 v. CSmH; GAuY; MWA; PP; RBr. 55385

----. Posthumous papers of the Pickwick Club. Philadelphia: 1839. PPL-R. 55386

----. Sketches by Boz [pseud.] illustrative of everyday life and everyday people. With 20 illustrations by George Cruikshank. New edition, complete. Philadelphia: Lea and Blanchard, 1839. 268 p. 10 numbers. CSmH; MB; MH; NjR; PU. 55387

----. ----. Philadelphia: T. B. Peterson [1839?] NcU; NIC; PU; ViU. 55388

Dickinson, Erastus. A sermon delivered in Chaplin, Conn., on the day of public thanksgiving, November 29, 1838. By Erastus Dickinson.... Norwich [Conn.] printed by M. B. Young, 1839. 16 p. CSmH; MBC. 55389

Dickinson College, Carlisle, Pennsylvania. Catalogue of the officers and students...Carlisle: 1839 [-1862] MHi. 55390

Dickson, Samuel Henry, 1798-1872. Manual of pathology and practice, being the outline of the course of lecture delivered by...in the Medical College of the state of South Carolina. Charleston: Observer Ofice Press, 1839. 204 p. CSt-L; MiDW-M; NBMS. 55391

----. On dengue: its history, pathology and treatment. By S. Henry Dickson...Philadelphia: Haswell, Barrington and Haswell, 1839. 23 p. DLC; IEN-M; MB; NjR; PPA. 55392

Digest of county laws containing the acts of assembly relating to counties and townships throughout the state and local laws relating to the county of Philadelphia [Philadelphia] 1839. MH-L; PU-L. 55393

Dillingham, William S. United States historical and statistical index, by William S. Dillingham. New York: William H. Hadley, printer [1839] Broadside. RNR. 55394

Dimitry, Alexander, 1805-1883. Address by Mr. Alexander Dimitry, before the Union Literary Society of Washington city, July 4, 1839. Washington: Blair and Rives, printers, 1839. 24 p. DLC; ICN; MdHi; NCH; OCHP. 55395

----. Lecture on the study of history, applied to the progress of civilization: delivered by appointment, before the Union Literary Society, May 2, 1839. Washington: Blair and Rives, printers, 1839. 23 p. DLC; PHi. 55396

Directory of the city of Mobile. Mobile directory, or strangers' guide for 1839: embracing names of firms, the individuals composing them, and citizens generally; together with their professions, residence and number, alphabetically arranged, with a cross index, by T. C. Fay. Copyright secured according to law. Mobile: printed by R. R. Dade [1839] 104, 96 p. DLC. 55397

Disasters by steam, fire and water. With elegant engravings. Worcester? 1839? 24 p. MWA. 55398

Discurso politico sobre lo importante y necesario de que el hombre este instruido en sus deberes. Noticia de obritas impresas que se benden: y oferta que se hace de la imprenta por el intere publico. Taos de Nueva Mexico: 1839. 20 p. DLC; NmHi. 55399

Disobedience. Boston: Massachusetts Sabbath School Society, 1839. 8 p. MH. 55400

Disosway, Gabriel Poillon, 1799-1868. Brief memoir of Achsah Wilkins Disosway. By her father. New York: T. Mason, 1839. 48 p. NN. 55401

Disraeli, Isaac, 1766-1848. Curiosities of literatures. 14th edition. New York: Armstrong, 1839. 21 v. in 3. IaFairP. 55402

Disturnell, John, 1801-1877. Hudson River guide, and the tour to the springs containing a description of all the landings and principal places on the river...tables of distance stage, canal and railroad routes, accompanied by a map. New York: Colton and Disturnell, 1839. 15 I p. MH; NPV; NWM; PHi; WHi. 55403

Dix, John Adams. Address delivered before the Alpha Phi Delta and Euglossian societies of Geneva College.... Albany: n. pub., printed by Packard, Van Benthuysen and Company, 1839. 68 p. CtY; DLC; MH; NjPT; PU. 55404

Doane, George Washington, 1799-1859. The beauty and the blessedness of early piety: an address to the persons confirmed in St. Mary's church, Burlington, on the 14th Sunday after Trinity, 13 of whom were pupils of St. Mary's hall.... Burlington [N.J.] Powell and George, printers, 1839. 15 [1] p. CSmH; DLC; NNG; PHi. 55405

----. Episcopal address to the annual convention of the diocese of New Jersey, May 29, 1839. Bur-

lington: 1839. 36 p. CSmH; MdBD; MH-AH; MWA; NBuDD. 55406

----. The inherited depravity of man. A sermon, delivered in St. Peter's church, Auburn, before a special convention of the diocese of western New York...Bishop of the diocese of New Jersey. Utica: Hobart press, 1839. 14 p. DLC; MBC; MBuDD; PPiXT; RPB. 55407

----. The introductory address, at the opening of the hall erected by the Burlington Lyceum...December 18, 1838.... Burlington [1839] 20 p. MH. 55408

----. Looking unto Jesus: a sermon...in St. Mary's church, Burlington...after the decease of the Rev. Benjamin Davis Winslow. Burlington: J. L. Powell, printer, 1839. 55 p. MB; MHi; NGH; PHi; RPB. 55409

----. The pastoral office: the 3rd charge to the clergy of the diocese of New Jersey.... Burlington: Powell and George, 1839. 32 p. MdBD; MH; MWA; PHi; PPL. 55410

----. The word of God to be studied with his works; the introductory address at the opening of the hall erected by the Burlington, N.J. lyceum...Dec. 18, 1838.... Burlington, N.J.: J. L. Powell, at the Missionary press, 1839. 20 p. MCET; MH; NjR; PHC. 55411

Documents referred to in the message of the governor, at the opening of the session of the General Assembly. Transmitted to the House, December 13, 1839. Springfield: William Walters, 1839. 28 p. IU; MB; MH; NjP; NN. 55412

Doctrinal discourse. Various subjects and authors. New York: 1839-1846. MBNMHi. 55413

Dodd, Stephen, 1777-1856. A family record of Daniel Dod, who settled with the colony of Branford, 1644, where he died in 1665, and also of his descendants in New Jersey. Comp. by Stephen Dodd. Printed for the author [New Haven] 1839. 24 p. CSmH; MBAt; MnHi; MWA; PPPrHi. 55414

Doddridge, Philip, 1702-1751. The family expositor or a paraphrase and version of the New Testament; with critical notes and a practical improvement to each section. Amercian edition with a memoir of the author by N. W. Fiske and an introductory essay by Moses Stuart. 13th edition. Amherst, Mass.: Charles McFarland, 1839. 998 p. ArCh; GMM; MB; NBuDD; NCH. 55415

Doggett, Simeon, 1765-1852. National union. A sermon, delivered in Raynham, on the day of annual fast, March 28, 1839. By Simeon Doggett, pastor of the 2nd Congregational Church in Raynham. Boston: printed by I. R. Butts, 1839. 16 p. DLC; ICMe; MBAt; MNBedf; MWA. 55416

The doings of a spirit shop; or the story of James and Mary Duffil. A tale of real life.... Boston: printed by David H. Ela, 1839. 12 p. MB; MBNMHi; NN. 55417

Donaldson, Peter. The life of Sir William Wallace, the Governor General of Scotland, and hero of the Scottish chiefs.... New York: Robinson and Franklin, 1839. 138 p. IP; PPP; PPPD. 55418

Donizetti, Gaetano, 1797-1848. Anna Bolena, tragedia licrica.... Philadelphia: 1839. PPL; PPM; PU. 55419

Donnegan, James, fl. 1841. A new Greek and English lexicon; principally on the plan of the Greek and German lexicon of Schneider.... 1st American, from the 2nd London edition, revised and enlarged by R. B. Patton. Boston: Hilliard, Gray and Company, 1839. 1413 p. MH; MoSU; NNC; RP; WNaE. 55420

Doolitte, Giles. The importance of being at peace with God: a sermon, preached at Hudson...at the funeral of Mrs. Ann S. Hall.... Ravenna: Ohio Star, 1839. 12 p. NNG. 55421

Dorchester, Massachusetts. Printed report of the receipts and expenditures...[1st-31st] Boston: 1839-1869. 2 v. MB; MH; MHi. 55422

----. School Committee. 1st annual report of the School Committee of the town of Dorchester, April 18, 1839. Boston: printed by D. Clapp, Jr., 1839 [Var. pag.] 356 p. CoGrS; MB; MH; MHi. 55423

----. Village Church. Confession of faith and covenant. Boston: 1839. 10 p. MBC. 55424

[Dorr, Benjamin] 1796-1869. The history of a pocket prayer book. Written by itself.... Philadelphia: G. W. Donohue; New York: Scofield and Voorhies, 1839. 192 p. DLC; MB; MWA; PHi; RLa. 55425

----. The recognition of friends in another world. By the Rev. Benjamin Dorr, D.D., rector of Christ Church, Philadelphia. 2nd edition. Philadelphia: G. W. Donohue, 1839. 96 p. GDecCT; ICMe; MH; MP; NNUT. 55426

Douglass, David Bates, 1780-1849. Catalogue of architectural, embellished...and historical books.... New York: Bangs, Richards and Platt, 1839. MH; NN. 55427

Douglass, Jacob M. Religious thoughts; or observations on subjects of practical religion. Philadelphia: Perkins, 1839. 162 p. PP; PPM. 55428

Dover, George James Welbore Agar-Ellis, 1797-1833. The life of Frederic the 2nd, king of Prussia. By Lord Dover.... New York: Harper and Brothers, 1839. 2 v. CtY; InRch; MB-HP; OAU; TxU. 55429

Dover Young Men's Lyceum. Constitution and by-laws. Dover: 1839. 11 p. Nh-Hi. 55430

Dow, Joseph, 1807-1889. An historical address, delivered at Hampton, New Hampshire, on the 25th of December, 1838, in commemoration of the settlement of that town: 200 years having elapsed since that event. By Joseph Dow.... Concord: printed by A. McFarland, 1839. 44 p. CtSoP; IU; MB; NhD; PPM. 55431

Dowdney, John. The treasure in earthen vessels. A discourse, delivered in St. John's church, Kingston, Ulster Co., N.Y., on Septugesima Sunday, 1839. By John Dowdney, Jr...Published by request. Hudson: printed by Ashbel Stoddard, 1839. 16 p. MWA; NGH; NjR; NNG. 55432

Dowling, John, 1807-1878. A vindication of the Baptists, from the charge of bigotry, and of embarassing operations, by translating and refusing to transfer in all their versions of the scriptures among the heathen, the words relating to baptism. 3rd edition. New York: P. L. Platt, 1839. 24 p. KyLoS; NcD; NHC-H. 55433

Drake, Benjamin, 1794-1841. The life and adventures of Black Hawk: with sketches of Keokuk, the Sac and Fox Indians, and the late Black Hawk war. Cincinnati: G. Conclin, 1839. 264 p. CSf; LNH; OClWHi; TxU; WHi. 55434

----. ----. Cincinnati: G. Conclin, 1839. 288 p. DLC; MB; MBAt; OC; ViU. 55435

Drake, Samuel Gardner, 1798-1875. Indian captivities; or life in the wigwam; being true narratives of captives who have been carried away by the Indians...from the earliest period to the present time.... Boston: Antiquarian Bookstore and Institute, 1839. 260 p. CtSoP; GEU; InHi; MBl; OFM. 55436

Draper, Alexander C. Observations on abortion. Philadelphia: 1839. DNLM; DSB. 55437

Dubois, Jean. Marriage physiologically discussed. Trans. from the French by William Greenfield. 2nd edition. New York: 1839. 4 pts. in 1 v. MB; MB-B; PPCP. 55438

DuCouret, Louis, 1812-1867. Travels in Arabia Petraea. New York: 1839. MBAt. 55439

Duffield, George, 1794-1868. Thanksgiving sermon: the religious character of a people, the true element of their prosperity. Detroit: 1839. 20 p. CSmH; ICn; MBC; MH; NBuG. 55440

Dumas, Alexandre, 1802-1870. Impressions of travel, in Egypt and Arabia Petraea. Tr. from the French by a lady of New York. New York: J. S. Taylor, 1839. 318 p. CtY; MB; NjMD; PPA; ScSoh. 55441

----. Paul Jones; a drama in five acts, tr. from the French of Alexander Dumas, by William Berger.... Philadelphia: printed by T. K. and P. G. Collins, 1839. 89 p. CtY; DLC; ICU; LNH; MH. 55442

Dumas, Mathieu, 1753-1837. Memoirs of his own time, including the revolution, the empire and the restoration. Philadelphia: Lea and Blanchard, 1839. 2 v. CU; GAuY; PHi; ViU; Wv. 55443

Dunbar, John W. An address on the parties and politics of the times delivered before Philomathean Society of Indiana University at its annual exhibition, March 26, 1839, by John W. Dunbar. Bloomington, Ia.: printed at the Franklin office, 1839. InU. 55444

Duncan, Alexander. Speech of Mr. Duncan, of Ohio [In the House of Representatives, Jan. 17, 1839, on a resolution providing for the appointment of a committee to inquire into the defalcations of S. Swartwout. Washington: 1839] 16 p.

CtY; IU; MH; MWA; OClWHi. 55445

Duncan, Henry, 1774-1846. Sacred philosophy of the seasons; illustrating the perfections of God in the phenomena of the year. By the Rev. Henry Duncan...With important additions and some modifications to adapt it to American readers, by F. W. P. Greenwood.... Boston: Marsh, Capen, Lyon and Webb, 1839. 4 v. CBPac; IU; MeB; RNR; ScU. 55446

Dunglison, Robley, 1798-1869. Introductory lecture to the course of institutes of medicine, and materia medica, in Jefferson Medical College, of Philadelphia. For the session of 1839-40, by Professor Dunglison.... Philadelphia: Members of the class, 1839. 20 p. DLC; MB; MHi; NNNAM; PPM. 55447

----. Medical lexicon. A new dictionary of medical science, containing a concise account of the various subjects and terms; with a vocabulary of synonymes in different languages, and formule for various officinal and empirical preparations, etc. 2nd edition, with numerous modifications and additions. Philadelphia: Lea and Blanchard, 1839. 821 p. CtMW; ICU; OCU-M; PPA; ViU. 55448

----. New remedies: the method of preparing and administering them; their effects on the healthy and diseased anatomy, etc. Philadelphia: Adam Waldie, 1839. 429 p. CSt-L; IA; NcU; PPA; WU-M. 55449

----. ----. Philadelphia: Lea and Blanchard, 1839. 503 p. CU; ICU; LU; OSW; PPAmP. 55450

Dunlap, William, 1766-1839. A history of New York, for schools. A new edition.... New York: Harper and Brothers, 1839. 2 v. NGlc; NNia; OClWHi; ScDuE. 55451

----. History of the New Netherlands, province of New York, to the adoption of the Federal constitution. In two volumes.... New York: printed for the author by Carter and Thorp, 1839 [-1840] 2 v. CtB; ICN; NhD; PPi; ScU. 55452

Dunn, Henry, 1800-1878. The school teacher's manual; containing practical suggestions on teaching and popular education. By Henry Dunn.... Prepared for publication in this country, with a preface, by T. H. Gallaudet. Hartford: Reed and Barber, 1839. 223 p. InCW; MiHi; OO; PU; RKi. 55453

[Dunn, Nathan] "Ten thousand Chinese things." A descriptive catalogue of the Chinese collection, in Philadelphia. With miscellaneous remarks upon the manners, customs, trade and government of the Celestial empire. Philadelphia: printed for the proprietor [1839] 120 p. CtHT: MiGr; MWA; OCY; PPA. 55454

Dupin, Andre Marie Jean Jacques, 1783-1865. The trial of Jesus before Caiaphas and Pilate. Being a refutation of Mr. Salvador's chapter entitled "the trial and condemnation of Jesus." By M. Dupin.... Translated from the French, by a member of the American bar. Boston: C.C. Little and J. Brown, 1839. 88 p. IaPeC; MeB; NNUT; PP; ViRut. 55455

Dufee, Calvin. A sermon delivered before the Auxiliary Education Society of Norfolk County, at their annual meeting in the First Parish of Dedham, June 12, 1839. Boston: printed by Perkins and Marvin, 1839. 36 p. MBC; NhD; OO; RPB. 55456

Dwight, Theodore, 1764-1846. The character of Thomas Jefferson, as exhibited in his own writings. Boston: Weeks, Jordan and Company, 1839. 371 p. InU; MBBC; NcD; PPA; RNR. 55457

Dwight, Timothy, 1752-1817. Theology: explained and defended, in a series of sermons; by Timothy Dwight...with a memoir of the life of the author.... 10th edition. New Haven: T. Dwight and Son, 1839. 4 v. GAU; MiU; NbOM; PWW; ScDuE. 55458

Dwight, William Theodore, 1795-1865. The church, the pillar and ground of truth. A sermon, deliverd in Brunswick, June 26, 1839, before the Maine Missionary Society, at its 32nd anniversary. Portland: Alfred Merrill, 1839. 48 p. IaGG; MeB; MiU-C; MWA; NjPT. 55459

Dyer, Hiram. Feed the flock of God. A sermon preached at Preston, and afterwards at Norwich, Chenango County, N.Y., by Rev. H. Dyer. Utica: R. Northway, Jr., printer, 1839. 21 p. CSansS. 55460

Dymond, Jonathan, 1796-1828. Essays on the principles of morality, and on the private and political rights and obligations of mankind.... New York: Harper and Brothers, 1839. 432 p. DLC; InRchE; NNUT; RPAt; ViAl. 55461

Dyott, Thomas W., 1771-1861. The highly interesting and important trial of Dr. T. W. Dyott, the banker, for fraudulent insolvency, with the speeches of council, etc. Commonwealth vs. T. W. Dyott [Philadelphia: 1839] 28 p. MH-BA; MH-L; PPL; PHi. 55462

E

Earle, Pliny, 1809-1892. A visit to 13 asylums for the insane in Eurpoe, with statistic. Philadelphia: T. K. and P. G. Collins, 1839. 38 p. DLC; MBAt; MWA; OC; PPM. 55463

An earnest persuasive to the frequent receiving of Holy Communion. 1839. See Seabury, Samuel, 1729-1796.

East, John. My saviour: or devotional meditations in prose and verse, on the names and titles of the Lord Jesus Christ. By John East, rector of Croscombe, Somerset, England. 2nd edition. Boston: James B. Dow, 1839. 251 p. NcSalL. 55464

East, Timothy. The evangelical spectator, by the author of the "Evangelical rambler." Revised by the editors, New York: T. Mason and G. Lane, 1839. 125 p. IEG; GEU; PHi; PP; ScCliTO. 55465

East Boston. Maverick Congregational Church. Articles of faith and covenant of the Maverick Church, with the standing rules and names of members. Boston: B. True, 1839. 12 p. MBC; NN. 55466

East Boston Company. Act of incorporation and by-laws.... Boston: Centinel and Gazette Press, 1839. 16 p. MB; MH-BA. 55467

East Tennessee College, Knoxville, Tennessee. Catalogue of the officers and students of East Tennessee College, Knoxville, Tennessee, January, 1839. Knoxville, T.: printed by Ramsey and Craighead, 1839. 12 p. MBC; MH; OCHP; TKL-Mc. 55468

Eastern Railroad Company. Statement of facts in relation to the Eastern Railroad Company. [Boston?: 1839.] 4 p. CSt; CtY; NN. 55469

Eastern Railroad Company in New Hampshire. Acts of incorporation. By-laws and officers of the Eastern Railroad Company in New Hampshire.... Salem: William Ives and Company, printers 1839. 36 p. CSt; ICJ; MeHi; MWA; NN. 55470

Easy lessons, or leading strings to knowledge. Boston: Francis, 1839. NN. 55471

Eaton, John Henry, 1790-1856. Memoirs of Andrew Jackson, late major general and commander in chief of the southern division of the army of the United States. Compiled by a citizen of Massachusetts. Philadelphia: 1839. DLC. 55472

Eberle, John, 1787-1838. A treatise on the diseases and physical education of children.... 3rd edition. Philadelphia: Grigg and Elliot, 1839. 7, 555 p. CSt-L; ICU-R; LNOP; NBMS; OrU. 55473

Economical cookery.... Newark, N.J.: Benjamin Olds, 1839. 144 p. NNT-C. 55474

Edwards, Bela Bates, 1802-1852. Selections from German literature. By B. B. Edwards and E. A. Park, professors, Theological Seminary, Andover: Gould, Newman and Saxton [etc.] 1839. 472 p. CtMW; InCW; MAnP; PP; RPB. 55475

Edwards, Charles, 1797-1868. On receivers in chancery; with precidents.... New York: printed for the author, 1839. 603 p. NIC-L; NjP; PU-L; RPL; WaU. 55476

Edwards, Jonathan, 1703-1758. A history of the work of redemption: comprising an outline of church history. New York: American Tract Socicty [1839?] DLC; ICN; MWA; NNUT; RPB. 55477

Eells, Samuel, 1810-1842. Law and means of social advancement. Oration delivered before biennial convention of Alpha Delta Phi. Society at New Haven, Connecticut, Aug. 15th, 1839. Cincinnati, Ohio: Kendall and Henry, 1839. 69 p. KyLx; MiD-B; NcU; OOxM; TxU. 55478

Eggleston, Benjamin. An American field of Mars: or a universal history of all the important tragic events that have occurred in the United States of North America.... Cleveland: Penniman and Bemis, 1839. 3 v. DLC; OClWHi; OO; PMA. 55479

----. The wars of America; or a general history of all the important tragic events that have occurred in the United States of North America since the discovery of the western continent by Christopher Columbus. By a revolutionary soldier. Baltimore: Hazard and Bloomer, 1839. 404 p. DLC. 55480

Ehrenfried, Joseph. Colloquial phrases and dialogues in German and English, on every topic necessary to maintain conversation, with direction for pronunciation. By Joseph Ehrenfried. Philadelphia: Hogan and Thompson, 1839. 228 p. LN; MdW. 55481

Ein paar worte uber die Methodisten. Bath: Samuel Siegfried, 1839. PPeSchw. 55482

Eine Geschichte von der KocstlichenPerle. New Berlin, Pa.: Carl Hammer, 1839. 13 p. PReaAT. 55483

Eider, Alexi. A comprehensive grammar of the Latin language for the use of St. Mary's College, Baltimore. Baltimore: printed by J. Robinson, 1839. 375 p. InStmaS. 55484

Elder, William, 1806-1885. Address delivered before the Penn Institute at the first meeting after its organization, February 28, 1839, by Dr. William Elder. Published by order of the institute. Pittsburgh: printed by Alexander Jaynes, 1839. 22 p. PMA; PPiU; PU. 55485

Elizabethtown and Somerville Railroad Company. Acts relative to the Elizabethtown and Somerville Railroad Company.... Elizabethtown: printed by H. H. Hassey, 1839. 20 p. DLC; NN; NNE. 55486

----. To the president and directors...n. p. [1839] 32 p. NN. 55487

Ellen asking about prayer. Boston: Massachusetts Sabbath School Society, 1839. 8 p. MH. 55488

Ellen Hart; or the little servant girl. Written for the American Sunday School Union, and revised by the committee of publication. Philadelphia: American Sunday School Union [1839] 106 p. DLC; ScCliTO. 55489

Ellet, Charles, 1810-1862. An essay on the laws of trade, in reference to the works of internal improvement in the United States.... Richmond: P.

D. Bernard, 1839. 284 p. CSmH; ICU; PHi; OClWHi; ViU. 55490

----. Map of the county of Philadelphia, from survey under Charles Ellet, Jr. Philadelphia: 1839. 4 p. PHi. 55491

----. A popular exposition of the incorrectness of the tariffs of toll in use on the public improvements of the United States.... Philadelphia: C. Sherman and Company, 1839. 33 p. MdBP; MH-BA; NNE; PHi; Vi. 55492

----. A popular notice of wire suspension bridges. By Charles Ellet, Jr., civil engineer. Richmond: P. D. Bernard, printer, 1839. 12 p. DLC; MWA; OCHP. 55493

----. Report in relation to the water power on the line of the James River and Kanawha canal. By Charles Ellet, Jr.... Richmond: P. D. Bernard, 1839. 21 p. CtY; NcU; PPM; Vi; ViU. 55494

Ellet, Elizabeth Fries [Lummis] 1818-1877. The characters of Schiller. By Mrs. Ellet.... Boston: Otis, Broaders and Company, 1839. 296 p. LNP; MBBC; MWH; PPA; TxU. 55495

Ellicott, Thomas. Bank of Maryland conspiracy, as developed in the report to the creditors by Thomas Ellicott, trustee of said bank. Philadelphia: 1839. 134 p. IU; MB; MiD-B; NIC; PPM. 55496

Elliott, Charles Borleau, 1803-1875. Travels in three great empires of Austria, Russia and Turkey. Philadelphia: Lea and Blanchard, 1839. 2 v. CtY; MB; NjMD; PPA; RPAt. 55497

Elliott, Lynde. Address at the celebraton of the anniversary of St. John the evangelist, before the Grand Lodge of Indiana, on December 27, 1838, at the town of Indianapolis. Richmond, [Indiana?] Jeffersonian office, 1839. 20 p. NNFM; OCM; PPL. 55498

Ellis, Ferdinand. Discourse publicly to discuss the question: Is the doctrine of endless punishment taught in the Bible? Brunswick: 1839. 16 p. MBC. 55499

----. Substance of a discourse, delivered at the Universalist Meeting House in North Livermore, in compliance with a request from Mr. G. W. Quinby.... Brunswick: printed by T. W. Newman,

1839. 16 p. MeBa; MW. 55500

Ellis, Sarah Stickney, 1812-1872. The ministers family, by a country minister.... New York: Carter, 1839. 6, 258 p. NjP. 55501

----. The women of England.... New York: D. Appleton, 1839. 291 p. CtB; IU; MnHi; NBu; PPM. 55502

----. ----. Philadelphia: E. L. Carey and A. Hart, 1839. 2 v. CtY; MH; NcD; OrU; ViU. 55503

Ellms, Charles. Shipwrecks and disasters at sea, or historical narratives of the most noted calamities, and providential deliverances from fire and famine, on the ocean. With a sketch of the various expedients for preserving the lives of mariners, by the aid of life-boats, life preservers, etc. Compiled by Charles Ellms. Philadelphia: Thomas, Cowperthwait and Company, 1839. 13-122 p. CtHT; NcWilA. 55504

Ellsworth, William Wolcott, 1791-1868. Speech from his excellency, William W. Ellsworth, governor of Connecticut, to the legislature of the state, May, 1839.... Hartford: Patriot Office Press, 1839. 16 p. O. Ct; NIC. 55505

Elmer, Lucius Quintius Cincinnatus, 1793-1883. Practical forms of proceedings, under the laws of New Jersey. Bridgetown: James M. Newell, 1839. 479 p. MH-L; MnU; Nj; NjR; TJoT. 55506

Elmira, New York. Trinity Church. At a meeting of the corporation of Trinity Church, on the 11th March, 1839: The special committee on the memorial of various pew-holders and worshippers in St. Paul's Chapel, praying that the congregation of that chapel may be set off as a separate parish, made a report on the memorial... [New York: 1839] 9 p. CU; NN. 55507

Elmore, Franklin Harper, 1799-1850. Speech of Mr. Elmore, of South Carolina, on the resolutions offered by Mr. Prentiss, of Mississippi, and Mr. Thompson, of South Carolina, relative to a communication published in the Globe by Alexander Duncan, member of the House. Delivered in the House of Representatives, February 23, 1839. Washington: Blair and Rives, printers, 1839. 8 p. DLC. 55508

Elton's comic all-my-nack, 1840. New York [1839] CtY; ICU; MWA. 55509

Ely, Lebulon. Discourse in Lebanon at funeral of Jonathan Trumbull. Hartford: 1839. 16 p. PHi. 55510

Emancipation, a poem. Boston: 1839. 35 p. MBC. 55511

Embury, Emma Catherine [Manley] 1806-1863. Pictures of early life; or sketches of youth. By Mrs. Emma C. Embury.... Boston: Marsh, Capen, Lyon and Webb, 1839. 310 p. InCW; MB; MDeeP; MWH; NBLIHI. 55512

Emerson, Benjamin Dudley, 1781-1872. The first class reader; a selection for exercises in reading from standard British and American authors, in prose and verse.... Philadelphia: Hogan and Thompson, 1839. 276 p. OC; OrCA; PSt; ViU. 55513

----. Introduction to the national spelling books, with easy and progressive reading lessons; for the use of primary schools. New edition, revised and enlarged. Boston: G. W. Palmer and Company, 1839. MH. 55514

----. National spelling book...70th edition. Boston: 1839. CtHWatk. 55515

----. The national spelling book and pronouncing tutor. 100th edition. Boston: G. W. Palmer and Company, 1839. 168 p. MH; Nh. 55516

----. The second class reader: designed for the use of the middle class of schools in the United States. By B. D. Emerson.... Claremont, N.H.: Claremont Manufacturing Company, 1839 [9]-168 p. ICN; MWbro; OO; PPeSchw. 55517

Emerson, Fredrick, 1788-1857. Key to North American arithmetic, part second and third. By Fredrick Emerson. Boston: Jenks and Palmer, 1839. 70 p. MH; MWHi; ScNC. 55518

----. The North American arithmetic, part first, for young learners. Claremont [N.H.] Claremont Manufacturing Company, 1839. 48 p. MH; MiU. 55519

----. The North American arithemtic. Part second, uniting oral and written exercises, in corresponding chapters. By Frederick Emerson.... Boston: G. W. Palmer and Company, 1839. 190 [2] p. MH; NNC. 55520

----. The North American arithemtic. Part third, for advanced scholars. By Fredrick Emerson.... Boston: Jenks and Palmer, 1839. CSt; MH; MiU; NAnge; OO. 55521

Emerson, Joseph, 1777-1833. Questions and supplement to Goodrich's history of the United States. By Joseph Emerson, ...A new edition, revised, and adapted to the enlarged edition of the history. Claremont, N.H.: Claremont Manufacturing Company, 1839. 188 p. CtY; MH; MiD-B; NNC; OO. 55522

Emerson, Ralph Waldo, 1803-1882. The letters of Ralph Waldo Emerson.... New York: Columbia University Press, 1839. 6 v. DLC; MH; OrP; TxU; WaWW. 55523

Emerson, Thomas. Business letters to Waller and Emerson from Windsor, Vt., etc., April 3, 1838-April 25, 1839 [Windsor, Vt.? 1839?] 70 p. MB; MH-BA; MHi; PBL. 55524

Emery, Moses. Oration delivered in Saco, Maine, July 4, 1839.... Saco: printed by S. and C. Webster, 1839. 10 p. DLC; Me; MH. 55525

Emlen, Samuel, 1766-1837. An extract from the will of S. Emlen of Burlington, N.J., who died...1837, creating a trust for the benefit of persons of Indian and African descent. Philadelphia: 1839. 12 p. CtY; MH; PHC; PHi. 55526

Emma and her nurse or the broken promise. Sidney's press. New Haven: S. Babcock, 1839. 23 p. MH. 55527

Emmons, Richard, b. 1788. The battle of Bunker Hill, or the temple of liberty; an historic poem in four cantos.... 1st edition. New York: 1839. 144 p. MH; NNC; PU; TxU. 55528

----. ----. 2nd edition. New York [Sackett and Sargent, printers] 1839. 144 p. DLC; MB; RPB. 55529

Emmon's Single Rail Railroad. Patented under the new patent law, 17th April, 1837. New York: Narine and Company, printer, 1839. 8 p. NNE. 55530

Emory, John, 1789-1835. The Episcopal controversy reviewed. By John Emory, D.D.... Edited by his son, from an unfinished manuscript. New York: T. Mason and G. Lane, for the Methodist Episcopal Church, at the conference office, 1839. 183 p. PReaAT; TNMPH. 55531

Emory University, Atlanta, Georgia. Catalogue of the officers and students, in Emory College, Ga., and the report of the board of trustees to the Georgia conference. Oxford, Ga.: 1839. 8 p. CtY. 55532

Encyclopaedia Americana; a popular dictionary of arts, sciences, literature, history, politics and biography, brought down to the present time...edited by Francis Lieber, assisted by E. Wigglesworth. Philadelphia: Thomas, 1839. 13 v. CtHT; ICE; NP; PLFM; ScDuE. 55533

English Evangelical Lutheran Synod of Ohio and adjacent states. Annual reports; proceedings of 4th session of the synod and ministerium of the English Evangelical Lutheran Church in Ohio and adjacent parts. Convened at Millersburgh, Nov. 3, 1839. Canton: J. Saxton, 1839. 16 p. 55534

Entertaining anecdotes of Washington; exhibiting his patriotism and courage, benevolence and piety; with other excellent traits of character. With engravings. Boston: Weeks, Jordan and Company, New York: Samuel Colman, 1839. 138 p. CSmH; ICN; IU; PHi; WaU. 55535

Entick, John, 1703?-1773. Tyronis Thesaurus; or Entick's Latin- English dictionary, with a classical index of the preter-perfects and supines of verbs, designed for the use of schools, by William Crakelt, A.M., carefully revised and augmented throughout, by the Rev. M. G. Sarjant. From the latest London edition with numerous additions and improvements. Baltimore: William and Joseph Neal, 1839. 619 p. MiD; WU. 55536

Episcopal Institute, Troy, New York. Annual catalogue. Troy: 1839. MBAt. 55537

Erie and Kalamazoo Railroad Company. Acts incorporating the Erie and Kalamazoo Railroad Company and Bank.... Toledo: printed at the Blade office, by A. W. Fairbanks, 1839. 15 p. DLC; MiD-B. 55538

Die Ernsthafte Christenpflicht, darinnen schoene, Geistreiche Gebaeter, darmit sich fromme Christen-Harzen zu allen Zeiten und in allen Nothen trosten koennen. Canton, O.: Gedruckt bey Pet. Kaufmann und Company, 1839. 224 p. InGo. 55539

The errand boy; or new church messenger, April, 1839. Chillicothe, Ohio: 1839. V. 1, no. 1. OClWHi; PBa; PPAN. 55540

Eschenburg, Johann Joachim, 1743-1820. Manual of classical literature: from the German...with additions. By N. W. Fiske. 3rd edition. Philadelphia: Greenough, 1839. 753 p. CtY; LNL; MdBJ; OClW; PCC. 55541

Esling, Catharine Harbeson [Waterman] b. 1812. Flora's lexicon: an interpretation of the language and sentiment of flowers: with an outline of botany, and a poetical introduction. By Catharine H. Waterman. Philadelphia: Hooker and Claxton, 1839. 252 p. CtY; MiGr; PP; RBa; TxU. 55542

An essay on the credibility of Swedenborg in which his claims as the announcer of the dispensation mentioned in prophecy under the figure of the New Jerusalem are briefly considered and defended. From the 2nd London edition. Boston: Otis Clapp, 1839. 45 p. DLC; MCNC; NNG; OUrC. 55543

Etiquette for ladies; with hints on the preservation, improvement, and display of female beauty. Philadelphia: Lea and Blanchard, successors to Carey and Company, 1839. 224 p. ICMcHi; MHi. 55544

The Eton Latin grammar, or an introduction to the Latin tongue...as in praesenti, syntax and prosody, given in English, together with rules for construing, and a short system of rhetoric. 1st American edition, arranged and edited by the Rev. James Coghlan, A.B.... New York: Sherman and Trevett, 1839. 122 p. DeWi; NjPT; NNC; P. 55545

Euclides. Elements of geometry.... From the last London edition, enlarged. Philadelphia: A. Walker, agent, 1839 [17]-333 p. CtY. 55546

Euler, Leonard, 1707-1783. Letters of Euler on different subjects in natural philosophy addressed to a German princess, with notes and a life of Euler, by David Brewster, containing a glossary of scientific terms with additional notes of John Griscom. New York: Harper and Brothers, 1839. 2 v. AMaJ; NGlc; P; ScDuE; TxGR. 55547

Eusebius Pamphili. The ecclesiastical history of Eusebius Pamphilus, bishop of Cesarea, in Palestine. Trans. from the original by Rev. C. F. Cruse,

A.M.... and a historical view of the council of Nice; with a trans. of documents by the Rev. Isaac Boyle, D.D. New York: T. Mason and G. Lane, 1839. 480, 59 p. InRchE; KyLoP; NNUT; OCo; PU. 55548

An evangelical and familiar catechism. Petersburg [Va.] printed at the Intelligencer Job office, 1839. 8 p. Vi. 55549

Evangelical Association of North America. Die Geistliche Voile oder Eine kleine Sammlung alter und Neuer Geistreicher Lieder Siebente auflage New-Berlin, Pa.: C. Hammer, 1839. 236 p. PReaAT. 55550

Evangelical Lutheran Ministerium of Pennsylvania and Adjacent States. Verhandlungen der Deutschen Evangelisch-Lutherischen Synode von Pennsylvanien Gehalten zu Allentown in der Trinitatis Woche 1839. Easton [Pa.] LaFayette Collegiums, 1839. 34 p. MnMNL. 55551

Evangelical Lutheran Synod and Ministerium of North Carolina. Minutes.... Salisbury, N.C.: 1839. ICartC; WHi. 55552

Evangelical Lutheran Synod and Ministerium of South Carolina. 16th meeting. Extracts from the minutes...convened at Sandy Run Church, Lexington District, S.C. On Saturday the 9th of November, 1839, and continued its sessions on the 11th, 12th and 13th. Columbia, S.C.: printed by Isaac C. Morgan, 1839. 17 p. ScCoT. 55553

Evangelical Lutheran Synod of East Pennsylvania. Proceedings of the annual session of the Evangelical Lutheran Synod of East Pennsylvania convened at Philadelphia, Pa., Sept. 28, to Oct. 7, 1839. Gettysburg, Pa.: printed by H. C. Neinstedt...1839. 96 p. MdBLC; MoWgT; NcMHi; PLT. 55554

Evangelical Lutheran Synod of Maryland. Proceedings of the 20th annual session of the Evangelical Lutheran Synod of Maryland, convened at Waynesborough, Franklin Co., Pa., October 16th, 1839. Baltimore: printed by John Murphy, 1839. 36 p. ICartC; MdBLC. 55555

Evangelical Lutheran Synod of Tennessee. Report of the proceedings of the 19th session of the Evangelical Lutheran Synod of Tennessee, held in Emanuel's Church, Sullivan County, Tennessee, from the 7th to the 12th of September, 1839. Salem: printed by Blum and Son, 1839. 16 p.

ScCoT. 55556

Evangelical Lutheran Synod of the West. Journal of the 5th annual session of the Evangelical Luthern Synod of the West, convened at Hillsboro, Illinois, October 2nd-8th, 1839. Louisville: printed by Penn and Eliot, 1839. 35 p. ICHi; PPLT. 55557

Evangelical Lutheran Synod of Virginia. Proceedings of the Evangelical Lutheran Synod of Virginia, convened at Zion's Church, Roanoke County, Va., May 20th, 21st and 22nd, 1839. Winchester: printed at the Virginian office, 1839. 16 p. ScCoT; TU. 55558

Evangelical Lutheran Synod of West Pennsylvania. Proceedings of the annual session of the Evangelical Lutheran Synod of West Pennsylvania, convened at Chambersburg, Pa., June, 1839. Gettysburg, Pa.: printed by H. C. Neinstedt, 1839. 52 p. ICartC. 55559

Evangelical Union Anti-slavery Society of the city of New York. Address to the churches of Jesus Christ, by the Evangelical Union Anti-slavery Society, of the city of New York, auxiliary to the American Anti-slavery Society. With...April, 1839. New York: printed by S. W. Benedict, 1839. 51, 2 p. DLC; ICN; MB; OClWHi; PHC. 55560

Evans, Charles, 1802-1879. Account of the asylum for the relief of persons deprived of the use of their reason, near Frankford, Pennsylvania, with the statistics of the institution from its foundation to the 31st day, 12th month, 1838.... Philadelphia: T. K. and P. G. Collins, 1839. 15 p. DLC; MB; MHi; PHC; PHi. 55561

Evans, Hugh Davey, 1792-1868. Maryland common law practice. A treatise on the course of proceeding in the common law courts of the state of Maryland. Baltimore: J. Robinson, 1839. 622 p. C; Md; MdBE; MdHi. 55562

Evans, Thomas. Examples of youthful piety; principally intended for the instruction of young persons. By Thomas Evans.... 3rd edition. With additions. Philadelphia: printed for the author by J. Rakestraw, 1839. 256 p. InRchE; MH; NcD; PHC; PPF. 55563

[Eveleth, Ephraim] 1801-1829. History of the Sandwich Islands, with an account of the American mission established there in 1820. With a supplement, embracing the history of the wonderful displays of God's power in these islands in 1837-1839. Revised by the committee of publication of the American Sunday School Union. Philadelphia: American Sunday School Union [1839?] 231 p. CSt; CU-B; ICN; OHi; TNF. 55564

----. ----. 3rd edition. Philadelphia: American Sunday School Union [1839?] 231 p. CU-B. 55565

Everett, Alexander Hill, 1790-1847. An address to the literary societies of Dartmouth College, on the character and influence of German literature, delivered at Hanover, N.H., July 24, 1839. Boston: Henry L. Devereux, 1839. 60 p. MB; MeB; OClWHi; PHi; RNR. 55566

----. An oration delivered at Holliston, Mass., on the 4th of July, 1839, at the request of the Democratic citizens of the 9th congressional district.... Boston: Henry L. Devereux, printer, 1839. 48 p. ICN; MHi; MWA; NjR; PPL. 55567

Everett, Edward, 1794-1865. Life of John Stark. Boston, Mass.: Hilliard, 1839. 356 p. InCW; KyLx; NICLA. 55568

----. Lives of John Stark, Charles Brockden Brown, Richard Montgomery and Ethan Allen. New York: Harper and Brothers, 1839. 356 p. CSfP; MBNEH; NNC; PMA; RKi. 55569

----. Recommendations of Joseph Dixon's transfer process, signed by Edward Everett and 9 others; with a facsimile of page 524 of Schaaf's Syriac Lexicon Leyden, 1717, made by that process. Boston?: 1839? Broadside. MH. 55570

----. Selections from the works of Edward Everett, with a sketch of his life. Boston: J. Burns [1839?] 180 p. ICT; MB; MeLew; MH; MWA; WGr. 55571

Everett, Horace, 1780-1851. Speech of Horace Everett, in the House of Representatives of the United States. May 31, 1838, on the Cherokee treaty. Washington: printed by Gales and Seaton, 1839. 47 p. MBC; MdHi; MH; NCaS; PHi. 55572

Everett, James, 1784-1872. The village blacksmith; or piety and usefullness exemplified, in a memoir of the life of Samuel Hick, late of Micklefield, Yorkshire. From the 7th London edition. New York: T. Mason and G. Lane, 1839. 352 p. ABBS; InPerM; KHi; LShC; WHi. 55573

Everett, Oliver Capen. Hymns and prayers for children. Boston: Greene, 1839. MB. 55574

Evers, P. The students compendium of comparative anatomy. By P. Evers.... Philadelphia: A. Waldie, 1839. 389 p. CSt; KyLxT; MeB; PPA; TU-M. 55575

The every day book. New York: Charles S. Francis, Boston: Joseph H. Francis, 1839 [5] 334 p. ICBB; MBox; MeB; NjR. 55576

Ewing, James. A treatise on the office and duty of a justice of peace, sheriff, coroner, constable and of executors, administrators and guardians.... 3rd edition. Trenton, N.J.: D. Fenton, 1839. 591 p. C; Nj; NjPaT; NIC. 55577

Exchange Bank in Providence. Charter....

Providence: Knowles and Vose, 1839. 28 p. MH-BA. 55578

Exposition of some of the frauds practiced upon the Indians, during the treaty with them 1837-1839. Buffalo: 1839. 48 p. PHi. 55579

Extracts from writings of friends on the subject of slavery. Published by direction of the "Association of Friends for Advocating the Cause of the Slave and Improving the Condition of the Free People of Color." Philadelphia: Merrihew and Thompson, 1839. 24 p. IHi; MB; OClWHi; PHi. 55580

Eyre, John. The European stranger in America.... New York: 1839. 84 p. CU; ICU; MnHi; OClWHi; PPL-R; 55581

F

Fables for the nursery; original and select. Boston: Monroe and Francis, 1839. 224 p. MBAt; NcWsS. 55582

The Factory boy, or the child of providence. By a lady. Boston: New England Sabbath School Union, 1839. 141 p. MnOw; MH; MTop. 55583

Facts for the people, devoted to temperance, morality and law. Boston: 1839. MH. 55584

Fairfield, Connecticut. First Congregational Church. Confession of faith, covenant, and rules of discipline...with a catalogue of the officers and members. New Haven: Hamlen, 1839. 16 p. CtSoP; CtY; MBC; MiD-B; PPPrHi. 55585

Fairfield County, Connecticut. Committee Appointed to Inquire into the State of Prisons. Report...appointed by the county court...and ascertain what changes ought to be made in their structure and regulations. Bridgeport: 1839. 8 p. CSmH; NN; PPAmP. 55586

Fairfield, New York. College of Physicians and Surgeons of the Western District. Circular and catalogue...Albany: printed by Hoffman, White and Company, 1839. 22 p. OC. 55587

----. ----. ----. Albany: printed by J. Munsell, 1839. 22 p. CtY; DLC; NN; OC. 55588

----. ----. Circular and catalogue of the faculty and students...Fairfield, Herkimer County.... Albany: printed by J. Munsell, 1839. 16 p. NNN; NUtHi. 55589

Fairholt, Frederick William, 1814-1866. Home of Shakespeare, illustrated and described.... New York: W. Taylor and Company [1839] 64 p. WHi. 55590

Falconer, William, 1732-1769. The Shipwreck and other poems, with a sketch of his life. Philadelphia: M. Kelly, 1839. MDeeP; MH. 55591

A familiar conversational history of the Evan-

gelical churches of New York: Robert Carter, 1839. 222 p. ICU; MnHi; MWA; OClWHi; PPPrHi. 55592

The family magazine almanac for 1840. Calculations by John Armstrong. Pittsburgh [1839] MWA. 55593

Farley, Frederick A. A sermon, preached in Westminster Church, on November 10, 1839. Providence: B. Cranston and Company, 1839. 12 p. ICN; MB; MBAU; MWA; RPE. 55594

Farmer, John. Map of the surveyed part of Michigan. New York: 1839. IU. 55595

Farmer's almanac. By David Young. New York: O. Longworth, 1839. MWA. 55596

The farmer's almanac, calulated for the meridian of Hartford, for the year 1839.... Hartford: Reed and Barber, 1839. 22 p. CtHWatk; NGH; NjR. 55597

The farmer's almanac, calulated on a new and improved plan for the year of Our Lord, 1839.... By Robert B. Thomas.... Boston: G. W. Palmer and Company, 1839. 56 p. MoU. 55598

The farmer's almanac for the year 1839.... New York: Turner and Fisher, 1839. 35 p. MWA. 55599

----. being the 3d after bixsestile, or leap year, and after July 4th, the 64th of American independence.... Pittsburgh: G. W. Holdship, Luke Loomis, and Patterson Ingraham and Company [1839] 30 p. MtU. 55600

The farmer's almanac for 1840. By David Young. New York: Collins, Keese and Company [1839] MWA. 55601

----. New York: M. Day and Company [1839] MWA. 55602

----. Calculations by John Ward. Philadelphia: M'Carty and Davis [1839] MWA; NCH. 55603

Farmer's almanac, for the year 1840. By David Young.... New York: H. and S. Raynor [1839] MWA; NjR; NNMuCN. 55604

Farmer's almanac, for the year of our Lord 1840...by David Young, Philom. New York: Poinier and Snell [1839] WHi. 55605

The farmer's almanack, calculated on a new and improved plan, for the year of our Lord 1839...No. 47.... Established in 1793, by Robert B. Thomas... Boston: Carter, Hendee and Company [1839] CU; MNBedf. 55606

The farmer's almanack [No. 48] calculated on a new and improved plan for the year 1840.... Boston: Carter, Hendee and Company [etc.] 1839. CU. 55607

----. By Robert Thomas.... Boston: Jenks and Palmer [1839] 44 p. ICMe; MdHi; MeHi; MWA; NjR. 55608

Farmer's almanack for 1840. Calculations by Zadock Thompson. Burlington, Vt.: Vilas, Loomis and Company [1839] MWA; NCH. 55609

----. By Thomas Spofford. New York: Charles Small [1839] MWA. 55610

----. By Thomas Spofford. New York: D. Felt and Company [1839] MWA; NGos; WHi. 55611

----. By Robert B. Thomas. Portland, Maine: H. J. Little [1839] MeHi; MWA. 55612

The farmer's almanack for the year 1839. By Robert B. Thomas. Boston: G. W. Palmer and Company, 1839. 46 p. RNHi. 55613

The farmer's almanack...for the year of our Lord 1840...by Robert B. Thomas.... Portland, Maine: William Hyde [1839] 46 p. MeHi; MHaHi. 55614

Farmer's and mechanic's almanac for 1840. Pittsburgh: Alexander Ingram, Jr. [1839] 36 p. MWA. 55615

Farmer's and mechanics almanack, for the year of our Lord, 1840...by Charles Frederick Egelmann.... Philadelphia: George Mentz and Son [1839] 34 p. MWA; MWHi; WHi. 55616

Farmer's Bank of Geneva. Articles of association, also the general banking law, passed by the legislature of the state of New York, under which the bank is organized. Geneva: printed by Ira Merrell. 1839. 16 p. NGH. 55617

Farmer's calendar for 1840. Calculations by Charles F. Egelmann. Baltimore: Cushing and Sons [1839] MWA; NCH. 55618

The Farmer's mechanics and gentlemen's almanack, for the year...by Nathan Wild.... Amherst, Massachusetts: Adams, 1839. MNS. 55619

The farmer's, mechanic's and gentlemen's almanack, for 1840...by Nathan R. Wild. Keene, N. H.: J. and J. W. Prentiss [1839] 24 l. MWA. 55620

Farmer's monthly visitor; intended to promote the interest of the farmer, etc... Concord [N. H.] 1839-1846. 6 v. in 8 v. IaAS; MBAt; MMaL; Nh-Hi; TxU. 55621

Farmer's or Green County almanack. Cozsackie, New York: T. B. Carroll, 1839. MWA. 55622

Farmington, Connecticut. First Congregational Church. Confession of faith and covenant...with a catalogue of the members, from April 19, 1796, to July 1, 1839. 22 p. Ct; CtSoP; CtY; MiD-B. 55623

Farmington Academy. Maine. Catalogue of officers and students of Farmington, Maine, year ending May, 1839. Hallowell, Maine: Glazier, Masters and Smith, 1839. 12 p. MH; OKentU. 55624

Farrar, Eliza Ware [Rotch] 1791-1870. The Young lady's friend. New York: Samuel S. and William Wood, 1839. 432 p. GMars; NcGu; NT. 55625

Farrar, John, 1779-1853. Elements of electricity, magnetism, and electrodynamics, embracing the late discoveries and improvements, digested into the form of a treatise; being the second part of a course of natural philosophy compiled for the use of the students of the University at Cambridge, New England. Boston: Hilliard, Gray and Company, 1839. 376 p. InCW; MBAt; MH; MoS; PPFrankI. 55626

The fashionable American letter writer: or the art of polite correspondence. Containing a variety of plain and elegant letters on business, love, courtship, marriage.... Hartford: E. Strong [1839?] 127 p. CtY. 55627

The fashionable American Writer; or the art of polite correspondence, containing a variety of plain and elegant letters on business, love, courtship, marriage, relationship, friendship, etc., with forms of complimentary cards, to the whole is prefixed, directions for letter writing and rules for composition. Newark, N. J.: Benjamin Olds, 1839. 175 p. CSmH; DLC; NjR; OCl; PPL-R. 55628

Fay, Cyrus H. Address on the changes of the century, delivered before the members of Norwich University, at their annual commencement, August 21, 1839. Newport [N. H.] 1839. 31 p. OC. 55629

Fay, Samuel Al Tribute to the memory of a departed friend [Mrs. Harding P. Woods] Brookfield [1839] 97 p. MiD-B; MoSHi; MWA. 55630

Fay, Theodore Sedgwick. Sydney Clifton; or vicissitudes in both hemispheres. A tale of the 19th century.... New York: Harper and Brothers, 1839. 2 v. CU; MB; OCY; RPB; WU. 55631

Featherstonhaugh, George William, 1780-1866. Map of the disputed territory, reduced from the original of Mess. Featherstonhaugh, and Mudge. Washington: 1839. PPL. 55632

Felch, Walton. A phrenological chart. Brookfield: 1839. WHi. 55633

Felt, Joseph Barlow, 1789-1869. An historical account of Massachusetts currency.... Boston: printed by Perkins and Marvin, 1839. 259 p. CU; IaGG; MWA; PPA; TxU. 55634

Fenelon, Francois de Salinac de la Lothe, 1651-1715. Les aventures de Telemaque, fils d'Ulysse. Par ne Fenelon. Nouvelle edition, a laquelle on a ajoute, un petit dictionnaire; d'apres l'editonde Mr. Charles Le Brun. Philadelphia: Haswell, Barrington and Haswell, New Orleans, Alexander Towar, 1839. 420 p. AzTP; DLC; KBB; MWH; OCU. 55635

----. Les adventures de Telemaque, fils d'Ulysse. Par Fenelon. Nouvelle edition. soigneusement rev. et cor. sur l'edition de Didot, a paris. Par A. Bolmar.... Philadelphia: Lea and Blanchard, 1839. 323 p. CtMW; InHuP; LNT; PHi; WHi. 55636

----. A guide to true peace: or the excellency of inward and spiritual prayer. Compiled chiefly from the writings of Fenelon.... Philadelphia: T. Ellwood Chapman, 1839. 103, 8 p. ICBB; PSC; PSC-Hi. 55637

----. Key to the first eight books of the adventures of Telemachus, the son of Ulysses. With the help of which any person can learn how to translate French into English....Philadelphia: Lea and Blanchard, 1839. 222 p. CoPu; NBuG. 55638

Ferguson, Adam, 1723-1816. History of the progress and termination of the Roman Rep. Philadelphia: Wardle, 1839. 493 p. LNL; ODaB; PWW; ViRut; WvW. 55639

Fernald, Woodbury M. A discourse delivered in the First Universalist Church at Cabotville, Massachusetts, January 14, 1838. Repeated November 18, 1838.... Portsmouth: Abner Greenleaf, Jr. Printer, 1839. 32 p. MiD-B; MMeT-Hi. 55640

----. Valedictory discourse. A sermon delivered in the First Universalist Church, at Cabotville, Massachusetts, February 24, 1839. Springfield, Mass.: D. F. Ashley and Company, 1839. 16 p. MiD-B; MMeT-Hi. 55641

Ferris, Isaac. Address delivered April 27, 1839, at the opening of the Rutger's Female Institute. New York: William Osborne, 1839. 24 p. MBC; MWA; NjPT; PPL. 55642

Fessenden, Thomas Green, 1771-1837. The American gardener, containing practical directions on the culture of fruit and vegetables; including landscape and ornamental gardening, grape vines, silk.... 13th edition. Boston: Otis, Broaders and Company, 1839. 307 p. KMK. 55643

----. The complete farmer and ruaral economist; containing a compendious epitome of the most important branches of agriculture and rural economy. 4th edition, revised, improved, and enlarged. Boston: Otis, Broaders and Company, Philadelphia: Thomas, Cowperthwaite and Company, 1839. 345 p. CtMW; MoS; NNNBG; PU-V; TNL. 55644

----. The new American gardener, containing practical directions on the culture of fruits and vegetables; including landscape and ornamental gardening, grape vines, silk, strawberries.... 13th edition. Boston: Otis, Broaders and Company, Philadelphia: Thomas, Cowperthwaite and Company, 1839. 306 p. Ct; MH; MoS; OCY; OU. 55645

Feuchere, Leon, 1804-1857. L'art industriel, recueil de dispositions et de decorations interieures, comprendant des modeles pour toutes les industries dameublement et de luxe.... Paris and New York: Goupil and Compie [1839-1848] 72 pl.CtY; DLC; ICJ; MU: NjP. 55646

Feuchtwanger, Lewis, 1805-1876. A popular treatise on gems, in reference to their scientific value.... New York: 1839. PPAN. 55647

Few particulars concerning Eng and Chang Bunker, the united Siamese brothers, published under their own direction. New York: 1839. 16 p. MWA. 55648

Field, Barnum. The American school geography. 9th edition. Boston: 1839. 156 p. MHi. 55649

Field, Jacob T. Christian moderation; a sermon preached in the Presbyterian Church at Stroudsburg, January, 1839. n. p.: 1839. 16 p. PHi. 55650

Fielding, Henry, 1707-1754. Select works of Henry Fielding. With a memoir of the life of the author, by Sir Walter Scott, and an essay on his life and genius, by Arthur Murphy, esq.... A new edition. Philadelphia: Lea and Blanchard, 1839. 2 v. KyDC; KyLxT; ILM; ViR. 55651

Fire Association of Cincinnati. Constitution and by- laws...together with a list of officers and members...Also a list of the cisterns and fire plugs. Cincinnati: 1839. 34 p. OCHP. 55652

First lessons in chemistry. By Uncle Davy.... New York: American Common School Union, 1839. 94 p. DLC; ICU; Nh; OClWHi. 55653

Fisher, Samuel, 1777-1857. Divine sovereignty and human accountability: a sermon...at the opening of the...General Assembly of the Presbyterian Church in the U. S. in Philadelphia, May 16, 1839. Philadelphia: Ashmead, printer, 1839. 28 p. ICP; MBAt; MWA; NCH; PHi. 55654

Fisher, William Logan, 1781-1862. An account of the Fisher and Logan families.Wakefield: 1839. 24 p. DLC; PHi; PPL. 55655

----. Genealogical and other memoranda regarding the Logan and Fisher families of Philadelphia: 1839. PPL. 55656

----. The subjoined account of the family connexions of my father, Thomas Fisher, and of my mother, Sarah Fisher, has been collected with considerable care, and is believed to be authentic. Wakefield: 1839. 24 p. PHi; PPL. 55657

Fisher's celestial songster.... New York: Turner and Fisher, 1839 [40] p. MB; RPB. 55658

Fisk, Benjamin Franklin, d. 1832. A grammar of the Greek language. Stereotyped edition. Boston: Hilliard, Gray and Company, 1839. 263 p. ICU; ILM; MH; MoFloSS. 55659

----. Greek exercises; containing the substance of the Greek syntax, illustrated by passages from the best Greek authors.... stereotyped edition. Boston: Hilliard, Gray and Company, 1839. 171 p. MoFloSS; MsU; PPWa. 55660

Fisk, Wilbur, 1792-1839. Travels in Europe, viz., in England, Ireland, Scotland, France, Italy, Switzerland, Germany and the Netherlands. 5th edition. New York: Harper and Brothers, 1839. 688 p. CtMW; Nh-Hi; PP; RPB; ScDuE. 55661

Fitch, Charles. Views of sanctification. Newark, N. J.... Newark: Aaron Guest, printer, 1839. 24 p. MBAt; MeLewB; NCH; NjPT; OClWHi. 55662

Fitz, Asa, b. 1810. The scholars first lessons in music. by a teacher of music. Boston: Kidder and Wright, 1839. 36 p. MB. 55663

Fitz, Henry. The layman's legacy, or twenty-five sermons on important subjects. New York: P. Price, 1838 [-1840] 2 v. CtHT; IaMp; MH; NCaS; MMeT. 55664

Fitzgerald, W. P. N. A scriptural view of slavery and abolition.... A member of the New Haven Bar. New Haven: 1839. 24 p. CtHT; CtSoP; MWA; OClWHi; PPPrHI. 55665

----. ----. 2nd edition. New Haven: 1839. IC; MH-AH; NNG; TxU. 55666

Five letters to my neighbor Smith, See Goodrich, Samuel Griswold, 1793-1860 Five score and ten! A true narrative. Richmond: 1839. PPL. 55667

Flagg, Azariah Cutting, 1790-1873. Circular. Albany, October 1, 1839 [Letter of the corresponding committee of Albany County on fraud at elections; Followed by the laws of the state of New

York to preserve the purity of elections. Albany: 1839] 2 p. NN. 55668

Flagg, Edmund, 1815-1890. The far west, or a tour beyond the mountains [New York: 1839. MH. 55669

Fletcher, Alexander, 1787-1860. The fovorite son: or history of Joseph. 2nd edition. Boston: 1839. 72 p. MWA. 55670

Fletcher, James. The history of Poland: from the earliest period to the present time. With a narrative of the recent events obtained from a Polish patriot noblemen. New York: Harper and Brother, 1839. 339 p. DeWi; MPeaI; MsSC; ScCli-P; TxGR. 55671

Fletcher, John, phrenologist. The mirror of nature.... Boston: Casady and March, 1839. 2 v. in 1. DCU; In; NN. 55672

The fletcher family. Written for the Massachusetts Sabbath School Society, and revised by the committee of publication. Boston: Massachusetts Sabbath School Sciety, 1839. 64 p. IaDaP. 55673

Flint, Abel, 1765-1825. A system of geometry and trigonometry, with a treatise on surveying; in which the principles of rectangular surveying, without plotting, are explained. Stereotype edition, enlarged, with additional tables. By George Gillet.... Hartford: Belknap and Hammersley, 1839. 160, 62, 112 p. CtY; IaGG; ILM; VtBrt. 55674

Flint, Timothy, 1780-1840. Biographical memoir of Daniel Boone, the first settler of Kentucky: interspersed with incidents in the early annals of the country. Cincinnati: G. Conclin, 1839. 252 p. ICU; MHi; MWA. 55675

Flint, William, 1777?-1863. Shipwreck of the Tamarac; a poem. New York: printed for the author, 1839. 16 p. DLC; NSmb; RPB. 55676

Florida [territory] Laws, Statutes, etc. Acts of the Legislative Council of the territory of Florida, passed at its seventeeth session, commencing January 6, and ending March 4. 1839, also the resolutions of a public or general character adopted by the Legislative Council by authority. Tallahassee: S. S. Sibley, printer, 1839. 67 p. FU-L; In-SC; MdBB; NN; WaU. 55677

----. ----. Compilations of the public acts of the Legislative Council of the territory of Florida, passed prior to 1840. By John P. Duval, esq. Tallahassee: Samuel S. Sibley, printer, 1839. 476 p. IU; MH; RPL; TxU, Wa-L. 55678

Flow gently sweet aften. Arranged for the Spanish guitar. Philadelphia: Willig, 1839. 2 p. MB. 55679

Floyd, Thomas. New collection of instrumental music. In three parts. Arranged for the violin, clarionett, bass-vial. Boston: Musical Gazette press, Kidder and Wright, 1839. CtHWatk; NN. 55680

Flushing, New York. Charter, by-laws and ordinances of the village of Flushing. Jamaica, New York: I. F. Jones, 1839. 36 p. NN; NNQ; NSmb. 55681

Follen, Charles Theodore Christian, 1796-1840. A practical grammar of the German language. Stereotype edition. Boston: Hilliard, Gray and Company, 1839. 283 p. ICN; LNT: MH; OCHP; PU. 55682

----. ----. 3rd edition. Boston: 1839. 283 p. RPB. 55683

Follen, Eliza Lee [Cabot] 1787-1860. Hymns and exercises for the federal Street Sunday School.... Boston: 1839. 105 p. MHi. 55684

----. Nursery songs; by the author of "Married Life". New York: S. Coleman, 1839. MH. 55685

----. Poems. Boston: William Crosby, 1839. 192 p. CoCsC; MB; NIC; TxU; WHi. 55686

----. Sacred songs for sunday schools, original and selected. Boston: Green, 1839. 54 p. MB; MHi; RPB. 55687

----. ----. Boston: 1839. 105 p. RPB. 55688

----. Sketches of married life...Revised edition. Boston: Hilliard, Gray and Company, 1839. 291 p. CtY; ICU; MWA; NNU-W; ViW. 55689

Folsom, Nathaniel Smith, 1806-1890. Discourse before the Rhode Island State Temperance Society. Providence: 1839. 35 p. MH; NjPT. 55690

Fontaine, James. A tale of the Huguenots, or

memoirs of a French refugee family; translated and compiled from the original manuscripts by one of his descendants; with an introduction by F. L. Hawks. New York: J. S. Taylor, 1839. 266 p. MBC; NGlc; OCHP; ScC; TKL-Mc. 55691

Foot, Samuel Alfred, 1790-1878. An argument in favor of the constitutionality of the general banking law of this state, delivered before the Supreme Court, at the July term, 1839.... Geneva [N. Y.] I. Merrell, 1839. 101 p. CtY; ICU; MBC; MH; NBu. 55692

Forbes, E. C. Easy lessons on scripture history, designed for schools and families. Prepared for the New york Sunday School Union. New York: Scofield and Voorhies, 1839. 160 p. NNUT. 55693

Forrester, R. H. Address delivered before the Wirt Institute, on the seventh of January, 1839, the first anniversary. Pittsburgh: printed by A. Jaynes, 1839. 22 p. DLC; OClWHi; PHi. 55694

Foster, Benjamin Franklin. A concise treatise on commercial book keeping. 3rd edition. Boston: Perkins and Marvin, 1839. 192 p. ICU; InCW; MB; MH; MNBedf. 55695

Foster, Ephrain Hubbard, 1795?-1854. Speech on the bill to amend an act, entitled "an act authorizing the state of Tennessee to issue grants and perfect titles to certain lands therein described, and to sttle the claims to vacant and unappropriated lands within the same" Passed April 18, 1806, delivered in the Senate, January 23, 1839. Washington: 1839. 15 p. DLC; MdHi; MoS; MWA; TU. 55696

Foster, John, 1770-1843. Essays in a series of letters, on the following subjects: on a man's writing memoirs of himself, on decision of character...causes by which evangelical religion has been rendered less acceptable to persons of cultivated taste. 367 p. IaPeC; MWA; NNUT; RPAt; ViU. 55697

Foster Home Association. Annual report. 1-. Philadelphia: 1839-. PHi; PP. 55698

Fowle, William Bentley, 1795-1865. The French first class book: Being a new selection of reading lessons. 3rd edition. Boston: Crocker and Brewster, Jonathan Leavitt, 1839. 288 p. MH; NNC; WM. 55699

----. The practical French accidence; being a comprehensive grammar of the French language; with practical exercises for writing, and very complete and simple rules for pronouncing the language. Boston: Hilliard, Gray and Company, 1839. MB; MH; NbCrD; OMC; TxU-T. 55700

Fowler, Andrew, 1760-1850. An exposition of the articles of religion of the Protestant Episcopal Church, in the United States of America, to which are added some useful extracts.... Charleston, S. C.: 1839. ICN; IES; MdBD; ScCMu; WNaE. 55701

----. Lessons of the Protestant Episcopal Church of the U. S. A. 2nd edition. Charleston, S. C.: W. Estill, 1839. DLC. 55702

Fowler, Orson Squire, 1809-1887. Phrenology proved, illustrated, and applied, accompanied by a chart; embracing an analysis of the primary, mental powers in their various degrees of development. By O. Fowler, assistedby Samuel Kirkham. 4th edition. Philadelphia: Fowler and Brevoort, etc., etc., 1839. 420 p. MBAt; MH; MTop; NCH; PPCP. 55703

Fox, George, 1624-1691. A journal or historical account of the life, travels, sufferings, Christian experiences, and lobour of love, in the work of the ministry, of that ancient, eminent, and faithful servant of Jesus Christ, George Fox. Philadelphia: Kimber and Sharpless, 1839. DeWi; InRchE; MWA; NjMD; PHC. 55704

France and Mexico. Examination of the difficulties between those powers. By a citizen of the United States. N. p.: 1839. CU; DLC; MB; MdHi; NNC. 55705

Francis, Convers, 1795-1863. Life of John Eliot, the Apostle to the Indians. New York: Harper and Brothers, 1839. 357 p. NOg; ViRVU. 55706

----. Memoir of Gamaliel Bradford [Boston: 1839?] 7 p. DNLM; WHi. 55707

Franckean Evangelical Lutheran Synod. Constitution and standing ordinances...together with a discipline, recommended on a guide for the government of churches. Cooperstown, N. Y.: H. E. Phinney, 1839. 64 p. CSmH. 55708

Francoeur, Louis Benjamin, 1773-1849. Introduction to linear drawing, translated from French of M. Francoeur, with alterations.... Boston: Hilliard, Gray and Company, 1839. 94 p. MH; PU. 55709

Frankfort, Maine. First Congregational Church. Confession of faith and covenant, with ecclesiatical principles and rules.... Frankfort: 1839. 24 p. CBPSR; CtY. 55710

Franklin, Benjamin, 1706-1790. Memoirs written by himself. With his most interesting essays, letters, and miscellaneous writings. New York: Harper, 1839. 2 v. GU; MB; MHi; NBuCC; OrP. 55711

----. The works of Dr. Benjamin Franklin, consisting of essays, humorous, moral, and literary: With his life written by himself. Exeter: J. and B. Williams, 1839. 224 p. CtY; InG; MH; MiToC; OClWHi. 55712

----. ----. New York: Malon Day and Company, 1839. CtY; MVh; OClWHi; RBr. 55713

Franklin, Walter E. The liturgy of the Episcopal Church. A sermon.... Bethany, Pa.: printed by R. Nugent, 1839. 11 p. NjR; PPL. 55714

Franklin, New Hampshire. Village Congregational Church. Articles of faith and covenant. Concord: 1839. 14 p. MBC. 55715

Franklin almanac for 1840. Calculated by Charles F. Egelmann. Baltimore: Joseph N. Lewis [1839] MWA. 55716

----. Calculations by John Ward. Philadelphia: McCarty and Davis [1839] MWA. 55717

----. Calculations by John Armstrong. Pittsburgh: Johnston and Stockton [1939] MWA; OCHP. 55718

Franklin College, New Athens, Ohio. Catalogue of the officers and students of Franklin College, New Athen, Ohio, August, 1839. Cadiz, Ohio: printed by McGonagle and Dimock, 1839. 12 p. CSmH. 55719

Franklin County Benevolent Societies. Condensed report...made by the secretaries of the several societies...Colerain, October 10, 1838. Greenfield: printed by Phelps and Ingersoll, 1839. 11 p. MWA. 55720

Fraser, James Baillie. Historical and descriptive

account of Peria, from the earliest ages to the present time.... New York: Harper and Brothers, 1839. 345 p. Me; MPeaI; NcWfC; NjR; TxGR. 55721

Freckleton, George. Outlines of general pathology. Philadelphia: Haswell, Barington and Haswell, 1839. 151, 13020 p. ICJ; MdBJ; NjR; OClM; PPL. 55722

Fredonia Academy, Fredonia, New York. Catalogue of the officers and students of the Fredonia Academy for the year 1839. Fredonia: Winchester's Press, 1839. 16 p. NFred. 55723

Free American. Massachusetts abolitionist; August 8, 1839. Boston: 1839-1840. 3 v. MBAt; MiGr; MTaHi; NIC. 55724

Free and friendly remarks on a speech lately delivered to the Senate of the United States, by Henry Clay of Kentucky on the subject of abolition of North American Slavery. New York: M. Day and Company, 1839. 24 p. MWA; NcD; PHi; RP; WHi. 55725

Free Will Baptists. Hymns for Christian melody, selected from various authors. Dover: Trustees of the Free Will Baptist Connection, 1839. 608 p. MiHi. 55726

----. Sacred melodies for conference and prayer meetings.... 2nd edition, with additions. Dover: Trustees of the Free Will Baptist Connection, 1839. 192 p. MeLewB; Nh-Hi. 55727

----. A treatise on the faith of Freewill Baptists with an appendix containing a summary of their suages in church government, written under the direction of their general conference. Dover: Trustees of the Freewill Baptist Connection, 1839. 156 p. ViRU. 55728

----. ----. 2nd edition. Dover: Freewill Baptist Connection, 1839. 156 p. OO. 55729

----. Connection. Minutes of the 10th general conference of the Freewill Baptis Connection in North America, Conneaut, Ohio, October 2-7, 1839. Dover, N. H.: 1839. CtHWatk. 55730

Freeman, John D. An oration delivered on July 4, 1839, before the Fencibles, guards, Hussars, Light guards, Light Artiller, Mechanics Association, and citizens of the city of Natchez. Natchez:

Besancon and Haliday, printers, 1839. 35 p. Ms-Ar; NN. 55731

Freemasons. Alabama. Proceedings of the grand council of the state of Alabama, in convention, held at Tuscaloosa, December 13, 1838.... Tuscaloosa: Baldwin, 1839. NNFM. 55732

----. ----. Proceedings of the grand lodge of the state of Alabama.... Tuscaloosa: M. D. J. Slade, printer, 1839. 23 p. OCM. 55733

----. ----. Proceedings of the grand royal arch chapter of the state of Alabama.... Tuscaloosa: Hale and Eaton, printers, 1839. 16 p. LNMas; MBFM; NcD; OCM. 55734

----. Arkansas. Constitution and by-laws of the grand lodge of the state of Arkansas. Little Rock: printed by Edward Cole, 1839. 19 p. ArLFM. 55735

----. Georgia. Proceedings of the grand lodge of the state of Georgia at its annual communication, held in Milledgeville, November 5, 5839.... Milledgeville: printed at the Georgia Journal office, 1839. 26 p. NNFM. 55736

----. ----. Proceedings of the grand lodge of the state of Georgia, held in Milledgeville, 5838. Milledgeville: printed at the Federal Union office, by Park and Rogers, 1839. 21 p. NNFM. 55737

----. Indiana. Abstract of proceedings of the grand lodge of...at its annual communication held at Indianapolis on November 28, 5839. Indianapolis: printed by Douglass and Noel, 1839. 12 p. IaCrM; MBFM; NNFM. 55738

----. ----. Proceedings of the grand lodge of the state of Indiana, held in the town of Indianapolis, December 24, 5838. Indianapolis: Stacy and Williams, printer, 1839. 30 p. Ia CrM; NNFM. 55739

----. Kentucky. Proceedings at a called meeting of the grand lodge of Kentucky, begun and held at Mason's Hall, in the city of Lexington, on December 3, 1839, A. L. 5839. Frankfort, Ky.: A. G. Hodges, state printer, 1839. 7 p. NNFM. 55740

----. ----. Proceedings of the grand lodge of Kentucky; at a grand annual communication in the city of Lexington, commencing August 26, 5839. Frankfort: A. G. Hodges, state printer, 1839. 64 p. NNFM. 55741

----. Maine. The act of incorporation, and by-laws for the government and management of the masters, wardens and members of the Grand Lodge of Maine incorporated June 16, 1820, adopted January 11, 1821. Augusta, Maine: Smith and Robinson, printers, 1839. 23 p. IaCrM. 55742

----. ----. Grand lodge of the most ancient and honorable fraternity of free and accepted masons of the state of Maine.... Augusta: William Hastings, printer, 1839. 12 p. NNFM. 55743

----. Maryland. Proceedings of the G.R. A. chapter of the state of Maryland, at the special communications, held at the Masonic Hall, in the city of Baltimore, on August 21, 1838, April 23, 1839, and May 6, 1839 and at the annual communication, in May, 1839. Baltimore: printed by Jos. Robinson, 1839. 23 p. MdHi; NNFM. 55744

----. Massachusetts. Grand lodge...of free and accepted masons of Massachusetts.... Boston: press of the Bunker Hill Aurora and Boston Mirror, 1839. 14 p. NNFM. 55745

----. Mississippi. Extracts from the proceedings of the grand lodge of the state of Mississippi, at a grand annual communication, held at the Massonic Hall in the city of Natchez, commencing on January 7, 1839. Natchez: printed at the "Free trader" office, 1839. 71 p. MBFM; MSFM; MssLi-M; MsMFM; NNFM. 55746

----. New York. Abstract of the proceedings of the grand lodges of the United States, on the formation of a clandestine Association, in the city of New York, called St. John's Grand Lodge, by expelled Masons. New York: printed by Joseph M. Marsh, 1839. 8 p. PPFM; WHi. 55747

----. ----. Abstract of proceedings of St. John's Grand Lodge...from November 1,5817, to the present date inclusive. Containing the preamble and resolutions passed at the quarterly communication, March 6, 5838, relative to the futile attempts of the grand lodge of the state of New York to denounce and stigmatize the lodge as a "clandestine" Grand Lodge.... New York: printed by Theodore C. Baldwin, 1839. 33 p. NNFM; OCM. 55748

----. ----. Constitution und neben gesetze der Germania Loge No. 13, des unabhaengigen ordens der sonderbaren Brueder des staats New York, welce ihren sitz in der stadt hat und im

Februar 1834 von der gross loge des staats New York verbrieft wurde. Buffalo: Gedruckt von Georg Zahm, 1839. 32 p. IaDuW. 55749

----. ----. Proceedings of the grand lodge of Masonic lodge, in New York state; meeting held in 1839. New York: J. M. Marsh, 1839. 32 p. IaCrM. 55750

----. ----. Transactions of the right worshipful grand lodge of the ancient and honorable fraternity of free and accepted Masons in the state of New York, at the annual communication, on the 5th, 6th and 7th of June, 5839. 32 p. MH; NNFM; OCM. 55751

----. North Carolina. Proceedings of the grand lodge of ancient York Masons of North Carolina. A. L. 5838. Raleigh: printed by Thomas J. Lemay, 1839. 39 p. NNFM; OCM. 55752

----. Ohio. Journal of the proceedings of the crand council of royal and select masters of the state of Ohio, at the annual grand communication, held at Lancaster.... Circleville: Jason Case and Company, 1839. 7 p. LNMas; NNFM. 55753

----. ----. Proceedings of the grand lodge of...at the annual grand communication, A. L. 5839. Most worshipful William J. Reese, Grand Master. Circleville: printed by Brothers Jason Case and Company, 1839. 16 p. MBFM; NNFM. 55754

----. ----. Proceedings of the grand royal arch chapter of the state of Ohio.... Lancaster, October, 1839. Circleville: printed by Jason Case and Company, 1839 7 p. NNFM. 55755

----. Pennsylvania. By-laws of the New Jerusalem lodge no. 1. Philadelphia: 1839. 12 p. PHi. 55756

----. Tennessee. Proceeding of the grand royal arch chapterl, of the state of Tennessee, October, 1839. Nashville: S. Nye and Company, 1839. 20 p. T. 55757

----. ----. Proceedings of the grand lodge of the state of Tennessee, grand annual communication, held at the masonic Hall, in the city of Nashville, 1839. Nashville: S. Nye and Company, printers, 1839. 38 p. Ia CrM; MBFM; NNFM; T. 55758

----. Texas. Circular...to the masonic fraternity, dispersed over the superfices of the globe. Send greetins...February 25, 1839. Anno Lucis, 1839. 3 p. PPFM. 55759

----. Freemasons. Virginia. Proceedings of a grand annual communication of the grand lodge of Virginia, begun and held in the mason's hall, in the city of Richmond, January 14, 1839. Richmond: printed by John Warrock...1839. 32 p. IaCrM; NNFM; OCM. 55760

Freewill Baptist quarterly magazine. V. 1-2. June, 1839-March, 1841.Dover, New Hampshire [1839-1841] ICU; Nh; PCA. 55761

French, B. History of the Evangelical Churches of New York city. New York: Carter, 1839. 122 p. PPL-R. 55762

Friedheim, John. Governor Morton's grand march. Composed and arranged for the pianoforte by J. Friedheim. Respectfully dedicated to His Excellency Marcus Morton. Boston: Henry Prentiss, 1839? 3 p. M. 55763

The friendly reformer. V. 1, No. 1-3, 1839. Worcester: 1839. MB. 55764

Friendly Society. Bedford. Rules of the friendly society held at the Angel Inn, Bedford. Established May 29, 1826. Bedford: Hill and Son, 1839. 14 p. MH-BA. 55765

Friends, Society of. Testimony of the Society of Friends on the continent of America. New York: 1839. NcD. 55766

----. Baltimore Yearly Meeting. Meeting for Sufferings. On the Christian doctrine of the teaching of the Holy Spirit, as held by the Society of Friends. Baltimore: printed by J. D. Toy, 1839. 15 p. MdHi; MH; NjR; PHC. 55767

----. [Hicksite] Baltimore Yearly Meeting. A defence of the religious Society of Friends, who constitute the yearly meeting of Baltimore, angainst certain charges circulated by Joseph John Gurney. Baltimore: printed by W. Woody, 1839. 18 p. DLC; MdU; MH; OO; PPL. 55768

----. ----. New York Yearly Meeting. Narrative of recent proceedings of the committee appointed by the yearly meeting of friends of New York, in relation to the Indians in that state. New York: Mercein and Post's Press, 1839. 25 p. CSmH; DeWi; PHC; PHi; WHi. 55769

----. ----. Philadelphia Yearly Meeting. Rules of discipline. Philadelphia: Rakestraw, 1839. 191 p. PU. 55770

----. Indiana Yearly Meeting. At Indiana Yearly Meeting of Friends, held at White Water, in Wayne County, Indiana, on the 3d day of the 10th month, 1839 [Richmond? 1839?] ICU; In; InRE; WHi. 55771

----. ----. The discipline...revised bvy the meeting held at White Water in 1838, and printed by direction of the same. Cincinnati: A. Pugh, 1839. 97 p. CtY-D; IaHi; MH; OClWHi; PHC. 55772

----. ----. Meeting for Sufferings. To the quarterly and monthly meeting of Friends of Indiana yearly meeting [White Water, Ind.: 1839] PHC. 55773

----. New York Yearly Meeting. Discipline of the yearly meeting of Friends held in New York. For the state of New York and parts adjacent, revised, in the 6th month, 1839. New York: Mercein and Post's Press, 1839. 96 p. DLC; InRchE; MH; NjR; PSC-Hi. 55774

----. ----. Memorials concerning Anna M. Thorne and Sarah M. Upton, deceased; of the religious Society of Friends, within the limits of the yearly meeting of New York, with some of their last expressions. New York: M. Day and Company, 1839. 21 p. DLC; MH; NHi; PHC. 55775

----. North CArolina Yearly Meeting. The discipline of Friends. Revised and approved by the yearly meeting held at New Garden, in Guilford County, North Carolina, in the 11th month, 1838. Greensborough: printed at the Patriot office, 1839. 36 p. MH; PHC. 55776

----. Ohio Yearly Meeting. The discipline...printed by the direction of the meeting held at Mountpleasand, Ohio, in the year, 1819 [?] Mountpleasant, Ohio: printed by Enoch Harris, Jr., 1839. 116 p. InRchE; NcGu; OClWHi; OHi; PPF. 55777

----. Philadelphia Yearly Meeting. An address to a portion of our southern brethren in the United States on the subject of slavery.... Philadelphia: J. Richards, 1839. 10 p. CtY; ICU; NIC; OClWHi. 55778

----. ----. An address to the quarterly, monthly and preparative meetings, and the members

thereof...held in Philadelphia by the committee appointed at the late yearly meeting to have charge of the subject of slavery. New York: 1839. 12 p. DLC. 55779

----. ----. ----. Philadelphia: J. Richards, 1839. 12 p. CtSoP; ICN; MB; MiU-C; OClWHi. 55780

----. ----. Extracts and observations on the foreign slave trade. Published by the committee appointed by the yearly meting of Friends held in Philadelphia in 1839, on the subject of slavery. Philadelphia: printed for the committee, 1839. 12 p. CtSoP; IHi; MB; MiD-B; OO. 55781

----. ----. Minutes on slavery [Philadelphia: 1839] DLC; InU; PHC. 55782

----. ----. Junior Anti-slavery Society. Preamble and constitution...1836. Philadelphia: Merrihew and Thompson, 1839. PPFYR. 55783

Friend's Academy. New Bedford, Massachusetts. Catalogue of the officers and students of Friends Academy, New Bedford, Massachusetts. For the winter term, 1838-1839. New Bedford: printed by Benjamin Lindsey, 1839. 12 p. MHi; MNBedf. 55784

Friend's almanac for 1840. By Joseph Foulke. Philadelphia: Elijah Weaver [1839] MWA. 55785

Froeligh, Solmon. The precious and the vile, or a minister is God's mouth. A sermon.... New York: printed by G. A. C. Van Beuren, 1839. 16 p. IaDuU; PPPrHi. 55786

Frost, Henry Rutledge, 1790-1866. Syllabus of a course of lectures on the materia medica, delivered in the medical college of the state of South Carolina. 3rd edition. Charleston: Burgess and James, 1839. 107 p. DLC. 55787

Frost, John, 1800-1859. The American speaker. Philadelphia: Frederick W. Greenough and Thomas Cowperthwiat and Company, 1839. 448 p. MeHi; MH; MWHi. 55788

----. Easy exercises in composition: designed for the use of beginners. Philadelphia: W. Marshall and Company, 1839. CtHWatk; DLC; IU; NcU. 55789

----. ----. 2nd edition. Philadelphia: 1839. 120 p. PHi. 55790

----. ----. 3rd edition. Philadelphia: W. Marshall and Company, 1839. 120 p. ICBB. 55791

----. ----. 4th edition. Philadelphia: W. Marshall and Company, 1839. MH. 55792

----. A history of the United States; for the use of schools and academies.... New edition, with additions and corrections. Philadelphia: Greenough, 1839. 432 p. NjP; NNC; PHi; PWW. 55793

----. The life of William Penn, with a sketch of the early history of Pennsylvania. Philadelphia: Orrin Rogers, 1839. 239 p. DLC; ICMe; MnHi; PHC; PPi. 55794

----. Robert Ramble's stories selected from the history of England: from the conquest to the revolution. Phialdelphia: R. W. Pomeroy, 1839. 128 p. DLC; ICBB; N; NNU-W; PHi. 55795

----. The young merchant.... Philadelphia: R. W. Pomeroy, 1839. 288 p. GGaB; ICU; MLow; OMC; PU. 55796

Furman, J. C. Christian missions entitled to support; a discourse preached before the Welsh-Neck Baptist Association at their 7th anniversary, held with the Mispeh Church, Darlington District, South Carolina. Raleigh: Recorder office, 1839. 20 p. LNB; NcD; NcU. 55797

Furness, William Henry, 1802-1896. Our benevolent institutions. A discourse occasioned by the death of Julius R. Friedlander, principal of the Pennsylvania Institution for the Blind.... Philadelphia: C. Sherman and Company, printers, 1839. 24 p. CtY; MB; MWA; PPAmP; RPB. 55798

The future life of the good. Boston: Joseph Dowe, 1839. 108 p. MB; MBC; MH. 55799

G

Gadsden, Christopeher Edwards, 1785-1852. The sermon on the occasion of St. Philip's Church in Charleston, South Carolina. Charleston: Miller, 1839. 21 p. PPPrHi. 55800

Gaines, Edmund Pendleton, 1777-1849. General Gaines' letter to the Chamber of Commerce.... [New Orleans? 1839?] 6 p. DLC. 55801

Gaines, Major General. Communication from Major-General Gaines, United States Army, relative to a system of railroads. Annapolis: William M'Neir, printer, 1839. 9 p. MdHi. 55802

Gale, Leonard Dunnell, 1800-1883. Elements of natural philosophy; embracing the general principles of mechanics, Hydrostatics, hydraulics.... New York: Collins, Keese and Company, 1839. 276 p. OCHP; OCX; PBa. 55803

Gales, Weston R. An address delivered before the Philomathesian and Euzelian Societies of Wake Forest College.... Raleigh, North Carolina: printed at the office of the Raleigh Register, 1839. NcWfC. 55804

Gallaudet, Peter Wallace. Monuments of Washington's patriotism. An appeal to the public [Washington: 1839] 4 p. DLC; MB; MBAt. 55805

Gallaudet, Thomas Hopkins, 1787-1851. Child's book on the soul, with questions; two parts in one. 5th edition. Hartford: Belknap and Hamersley, 1839. 70, 78 p. InCW; MBr; MH; MH-AH. 55806

----. The child's picture defining and reading book. 4th edition, enlarged and improved with particular reference to infant schools. New York: F. J. Huntington and Company, 1839. MH. 55807

----. Hoike uhane: he kamaiilio e moakaka ai ka uhane o kanaka. T. H. Gallaudet, i unuhiia Buke II Honolulu: Mea pai palapala a na misionari, 1839. 65 p. CtY; DLC. 55808

----. The judges. Published by the American Tract Society, D. Fanshaw, printer, 1839. 161 p.

RNR. 55809

----. Scripture biography for the young; with critical illustrations and practical remarks.... New York: American Tract Society, 1839. 2 v. GDecCT; IaHA; MH; NcD; RLa. 55810

Gallup, Joseph Adams, 1769-1849. Outlines of the institutes of medicine, founded on the philosophy of the human economy, in health, and in disease. In three parts.... Boston: Otis, Broaders and Company, 1839. 2 v. CSt-L; ICJ; MeB; MWA; PMA. 55811

Galt, John, 1779-1839. The life of Lord Byron, New York: Harper and Brothers, 1839. 334 p. GCu; InRch; MB; MPeaI; ScDuE. 55812

Ganilh, Anthony. Odes, and fugitive poetry. Boston: Gould, Kendall and Lincoln, 1839. 36 p. RPB. 55813

Gannett, Ezra Stiles, 1801-1871. Atonement. 1st eries, No. 149. Boston: James Munroe and Company, 1839. 30 p. CBPac; ICMe; MeB; NjPT; OO. 55814

----. ----. 2nd edition. Boston: James Munroe and Company, 1839. 31 p. DLC; MeB; MH-AH; MHi; MWA. 55815

Garbett, Richard. Hymn of the seasons: performed by the Boston Musical Institute [Poetry from Thomson's the seasons] Composed by R. Garbett. Boston: Crocker and Brewster, 1839. 36 p. MB; NN. 55816

Gardiner Lyceum. Gardiner, Maine. Catalogue of the officers and students of the Gardiner Lyceum, Cardiner, Maine. Gardiner: William Palmer, printer, 1839. 12 p. MeHi. 55817

Gardner, Daniel. A new system of Indian doctoring. October, 1839. Windsor, Vt.: Stateman office, 1839. 12 p. MWA. 55818

Gardner, Edward M. Oration read before the

young men of Nantucket, in the First Congregational Church, July 4, 1839 [Nantucket] printed for Weeks, Jordan and Company, by Marden and Kimball, 1839. 24 p. MH; MiD-B. 55819

Gardner, John Lane, 1793-1869. Military control, or command and government of the Army. By an officer of the line. Washington: printed by A. B. Claxton and Company, 1839. 82 p. DLC; MBAt. 55820

[Garland, Hugh A.] 1805-1854. The second war of revolution; or the great principles involved in the present controversy between parties...by a Virginian.... Washington: office of the Democratic Review, 1839. 20 p. MiGr; MiU-C. NcD; Nh-Hi; WHi. 55821

Garland, James. Speech against the financial policy of the administration and in vindication of the conservative republicans; in the House of Representatives, February 23, 1839. Washington: 1839. MBAt; OCHP; OClWHi. 55822

Garland, Landon C. An adrress on the utility of astronomy; delivered before the Young Men's Society of Lynchburg, September 26, 1837. Richmond: White, 1839. 28 p. MWA; NcWfC. 55823

The garland for 1839; a Christmas, New Year, and birthday present. Boston: 1839. 331 p. MB; MBAt; MWA; Nh-Hi; TxD-W. 55824

Garretson, Garret J. An address...before the association of alumni of Rutgers College.... New Brunswick: John Terhune's Press, 1839. 14 p. N; NjR; PHi. 55825

Garrett, L. Church polity briefly examined and its practical operation exemplified. Nashville: J. Geo. Harris, printer, 1839. 43 p. KyLx; OCHP. 55826

Garrison, William Lloyd, 1805-1879. An address delivered before the Old Colony Anti-slavery Society, at South Scituate, Mass.... Boston: Dow and Jackson, 1839. 40 p. MBC; MH; MWA; NNG; PPM. 55827

Gauntt, Charles. Private record of Charles Gauntt. Commander in the navy of the United States, written by himself for the use of his sons, Charles Stockton Gauntt and Ireton Gauntt. Philadlephia: 1839. 88 p. PPFM. 55828

The gazetteer; containing descriptions of all the states, counties and towns in New England.... 7th edition. Concord, N. H.: Israel S. Boyd and William White, Boston: John Hayward, 1839. 220 p. MPly. 55829

Geauga County, Ohio. Agricultural Society. Report of the Geauga County Agricultural Society [for the year 1838] In house, presented by Mr. Ford [Columbus: 1839] 6 p. WHi. 55830

The gem; a Christmas and new year's present, for 1840. Philadelphia: Henry F. Anners, 1839-1841. 2 v. ICU; PU; RPAt; TxU; WU. 55831

Das gemeinschaftliche gesangbuch zum gottes dienstlichen Gebrauch der Lutherischen und reformirten gemeinden in Nord Amerika.... Philadelphia: Herausgegeben von Geort W. Mentz und Sohn...1839. 374 p. PPLT; PPT; PRea-Hi; PSt. 55832

Genealogy of the Redfield family in the United States [New York] J. S. Redfield, 1839 [10] p. MB; NhD. 55833

Genesee Wesleyan Seminary, Lima, New York. Catalogue of the officers and students of the Genesee Wesleyan Seminary, Lima, New York. For the year ending October 3, 1839. Rochester, New York: printed by William Alling, 1839. 24 p. NLG. 55834

Geneva, New York. Farmer's Bank. Articles of association of the Farmer's Bank of Geneva; also the general banking law, passed by the Legislature of the state of New York. Geneva: printed by Ira Merrell, 1839. 16 p. NGH. 55835

Geneva College. Address to the public by the trustees of Geneva College. Geneva: James Bogert, 1839. 15 p. NGH. 55836

----. A catalogue of the officers and students of Geneva College for the academical year, 1838-1839. Geneva: printed by Ira Merrell, 1839. 23 p. CtY; DSG; MiU; N; NGH. 55837

Geneva Female Seminary, Geneva, New York. Annual circular, report and catalogue of the Geneva Female Seminary, under the care of Mrs. Ricord. April, 1839 [Geneva?] Ira Merrell, printer [1839?] MH. 55838

George's Creek Coal and Iron Company

[Report] 1st. 1839 [Baltimore? 1839] 1st-. MdBE. 55839

Georgetown, D. C. Western Star Fire Company. Constitution...to which are added, by-laws and rules of order, and "an act of congress, to organize the several fire companies in the District of Columbia." Georgetown: W. A. Rind, 1839. 24 p. DLC. 55840

Georgia. Commission on State Finances. Report of the commissioners appointed by authority of the legislature, on the subject of the state finances. Milledgeville: Grieve and Orme, printers, 1839. 64 p. DLC; GEU; GU; NN. 55841

----. General Assembly, 1838. Acts of the General Assembly of the state of Georgia, passed in Milledgeville, at an annual session in November and December, 1838. Published by authority. Milledgeville: P. L. Robinson, state printer, 1839. 258 p. Ar-SC; GHi; IaU-L; MdBB; Mi-L. 55842

----. ----. Senate, 1839. Journal of the Senate of the state of Georgia, at an annual session of the General Assembly, begun and held in Milledgeville, November and December, 1839. 392 p. G-Ar; GMilvC; NcU. 55843

----. Laws, Statutes, etc. Journal of the convention of the General Assembly of the state of Georgia, assembled in Milledgeville, on May 6, 1839. Published by authority. Milledgeville: Robinson, state printer, 1839. 74 p. CtY; ICU; MdBB; TxU; WaU. 55844

Georgia Historical Society. Constitution. By-laws. Officers of the society. Elected June, 1839. Savannah: 1839 [2] p. MH. 55845

Georgia Railroad and Banking Company. Report of the engineer-in- chief of the Georgia Railroad and Banking Company to the convention of stockholders; together with the cashier's statement on the condition of the finances, on April 1, 1839. Athens, Georgia: printed at the Southern Banner office, 1839. 23 p. WU. 55846

[Gerstner, Franz Anton, Ritter von] Railroads in the kingdom of Belgium compared with those in the United States [Cincinnati: 1839] 4 p. OClWHi; PPAmP; PPL. 55847

Gesenius, Friedrich Heinrich Wilhelm, 1786-1842. Gesenius' Hebrew grammmar, translated from the 11th German edition, by T. J. Conant...with a course of exercises in Hebrew Grammar, and A Hebrew Chrestomathy, prepared by the translator. Boston: Gould, Kendall and Lincoln, 1839. 325 p. CtHT; LU; PCC; RPB; TNP. 55848

----. ----. 2nd edition. Boston: Gould, Kendall and Lincoln, 1839. 325 p. MdBP; NNC; TxU-T; WSte. 55849

Gettysburg Beneficial Association. The constitution and by-laws of the Gettysburg Beneficial Association. Instituted February 1, 1830. Gettysburg, Pa.: printed by R. G. Harper, 1839. 18 p. DLC. 55850

Gettysburg College. Catalogue of the officers and students of Pennsylvania College. Gettysburg, Pa.: 1839. 16 p. DLC; IaHA; PPLT. 55851

----. Regulations of Pennsylvania College. Published by order of the Faculty. Gettysburg, Pa.: printed by R. G. Harper, 1839. 7 p. DLC; MH; PAtM. 55852

Gettysburg College. Medical Department. Annual announcement. Philadelphia: 1839-1861. MdBM; PPCP. 55853

Gettysburg Railroad Company. Report of the committee relative to the Gettysburg Railroad. Harrisburg: 1839. 80 p. DLC; PHi. 55854

Gibbon, Edward, 1737-1794. History of the decline and fall of the Roman Empire. New York: Harper and Brothers, 1839. 4 v. GAuW; LNB; PWaybu. 55855

----. ----. 5th American from the last London edition.... New York: Harper and Brothers, 1839. 4 v. GAuW; IU; KyLoS; LU. 55856

Gibbons, Charles. Address delivered before the northern lyceum of the city and county of Philadelphia, at their anniversary meeting, November, 1839. Philadelphia [1839] 26 p. P; PHi; PPL-R; PPPrHi; WHi. 55857

Gibbs, Josiah William, 1790-1861. A Gissi or kissi vocabulary. A vai or vey vocabulary, and mendi vocabulary [New York: 1839] CtY. 55858

Gibson, John. Trial for libel. State of Louisiana vs. John Gibson. Before the Hon. Criminal Court of the First Judicial District of the state of Louisiana; faithfully reported by T. W. Collens, Esq., and W. G. Snethen.... New Orleans: John Gibson, editor of the True American, 1839. 70 p. LU; MH; MoSM. 55859

Gibson, Robert. The theory and practice of surveying; containing all the instructions requisite for the skillful practice of this art. With a new set of accurate mathematical tables. Hartford: Alfred S. Barnes and Company, 1839 [339 p.] LNH; MH. 55860

Gibson, William. 1788-1868. Sketches of prominent surgeons of London and Paris, introductory to a course of surgical lectures. Philadelphia: office of the Medical Examiner, 1839. 17 p. NjR; NNN; OClW; PHi; PPL. 55861

The gift: a Christmas and New Year's present for 1839. Philadelphia: Carey and Hart, 1839. 328 p. AzPh; KU; TxU. 55862

The gift: a Christmas and New Year's present for 1840, By Miss Leslie. Philadelphia: Carey and Hart, 1839. 328 p. CoCsSF; KyOw; MdBP; NcCJ; NSmB. 55863

A gift for good children. Northampton: John Metcalf, printer, 1839. 24 p. ICBB; MBridT; RPB. 55864

The gift; or true and false charity distinguished. Written for the American Sunday School Union, and revised by the Committee of Publication, 1839. 90 p. ScCliTO; ViU. 55865

Giles, Charles. The convention of drunkards: a satirical essay on intemperance. To which are added, three speeches on the same subject; an oration on the anniversary of the American independence; and an ode on the completion of the Erie Canal. New York: Published by request, 1839. 126 p. CtY; KSalW; MB; Mi; MWA. 55866

Gillett, Timothy Phelps. Death the Christian's gain; a sermon delivered at the funeral of Rev. Matthew Noyes, former pastor of the church in Northford; he died in Northford, September 25, 1839... by pastor of the church in Branford. Published by request. New Haven: printed by W. Storer, 1839. 20 p. Ct; CtY; MBC. 55867

Gillette, Francis, 1807-1879. A review of the Rev. Horace Bushnell's discourse on the slavery ques-

tion, delivered in the North Church, Hartford.... Hartford: S. S. Cowles, 1839. 44 p. CtMW; MnHi; NcD; PHi; RP. 55868

Gilliland, James. Schism. A sermon delivered at the opening of Ripley Presbytery, at its first meeting November 13, 1838.... Georgetown, Ohio: printed by P. W. Sellers, 1839. 20 p. NAuT; OClWHi; PPPrHi. 55869

Gillis, James Dunlap. 1798-1835. Sailing directions for pepper ports on west coast of Sumatra. Salem: 1839. 27 p. MB. 55870

Gilly, William Stephen, 1789-1855. The cause of missions, the cause of God. A sermon, preached in the parish church of Crossgate, Durham, England, on the second sunday after Epiphany, January 20, 1839.... New York: Swords, Stanford and Company, 1839. 16 p. CtHT; MWA; NGH; PPL; OClWHi. 55871

----. A memoir of Felix Neff, pastor of the high Alps. Boston: 1839. 318 p. IRA. 55872

Gilman, Caroline Howard, 1794-1888. Recollections of a southern matron.... New York: Harper and Brothers, 1839. 272 p. DLC; MB; MWA; OkU; TKL-Mc; ViU. 55873

----. Tales and ballads. New York: Samuel Coleman, 1839. 190 p. CtY; ICU; MB; ScU; ViU. 55874

Gilman, E. The economical builder; a treatise on tapia and pise walls. Washington: J. Gideon, Jr., printer, 1839. 23 p. DLC; DNW; ViFTBE. 55875

Gilman, Samuel, 1791-1858. A discourse on the life and character of the Hon. Thomas Lee.... Charleston: printed by Burges and James, 1839. 31 p. ICMe; MBAU; MWA; PHi; ScCC. 55876

----. Funeral address at the interment of Thomas W. Dickman, Charleston, S. C. December 20, 1838. Springfield: 1839. 8 p. MHi. 55877

Gilmanton Academy, Gilmanton, New Hampshire. Catalogue of the officers, instructors, and students...for the year ending May, 1839. Gilmanton, New Hampshire: 1839. 12 p. MiD-B. 55878

Gilmanton Theological Seminary. Catalogue of books in the library. Gilmanton: 1839. 36 p. Nh-

Hi. 55879

----. Constitution and by-laws. Gilmanton: 1839. 22 p. Nh-Hi. 55880

Gilmour, Andrew. The necessity of scriptural education in connection with the condition and character of females in pagan and Mohommedan countries. Greenock: Laing, 1839. 52 p. NN; PPPr-Hi. 55881

Gilpin, Henry D. Review of th report on the defalcations of Samuel Swartwout and others. Washington: 1839. PPL. 55882

Girard, Stephen, 1750-1831. The will of the late Stephen Girard, esq., procured from the office for the probate of wills, with a short biography of his life.... Philadelphia: printed by L. R. Bailey, 1839. 11, 44 p. MB; MBC; NNNG; PPL; OCIWHi. 55883

Girard almanac. Philadelphia: Thomas L. Bonsal [1839] MWA. 55884

Girard almanac for 1840. Philadelphia: Thomas L. Bonsal [1839] MWA. 55885

Girard College, Philadelphia. Account of receipts and payments of the mayor, alderman and citizens of Philadelphia, in trust for the Girard funds, from January 1, 1838 to January 1, 1839.... Philadelphia: 1839] 26 p. MH-BA. 55886

----. Reports of committees...relative to the organization of the Girard College for Orphans.... Philadelphia: Bailey, 1839. 55 p. DLC; PPFrankI; PHi; PP. 55887

Girault, Arsene Napoleon. The French guide; or an introduction to the study of the French language. Philadelphia: H. Perkins, Boston: Perkins and Marvin, 1839. 324 p. ViU. 55888

----. Recreations instructives et amusantes: ou chaix d'historiettes morales prises de bouilly, mde de choiseul, etc. Avec une liste alphabetique des idiotismes qui s'ytrauvent: A L'usage des etudeans de la longue Francaise.... Philadelphia: Henry Perkins, Boston: Perkins and Marvin, 1839. 323 p. IU; MH; NRivHi; WMNDC. 55889

Gird, Henry H. Introductory address, delivered before the Louisiana Institute for the promotion of education, December 16, 1839. New Orleans:

Published by the institute, 1839. 21 p. CtY; LU; MB; MHi. 55890

Girls own book of amusing and instructive stories. Providence: G. P. Daniels, 1839. CtY; MB. 55891

The girls scrap book. 1839 [Philadelphia] American Sunday School Union, 1839. 238 p. IaU; NjN; NjR; NUt; WU. 55892

Gleig, George Robert, 1796-1888. The history of the Bible.... New York: Harper and Brothers, 1839. 2 v. CSfMA; DLC; InRch; MiD; MPeaI. 55893

Glenn, Samuel F. Criticism: its use and abuse. Washington City: William Fischer, 1839. 11 p. IEG; MBAt; MH; PPM; ScU. 55894

----. Gravities and gaities. Washington: R. Farnham, 1839. 116 p. DLC; MB; NcD; RPB; PU. 55895

----. A reply to the critics. Washington: 1839. 8 p. MdHi. 55896

Glentworth, James B. A statement of the frauds on the elective franchise in the city of New York, in the fall of the year 1838 and spring of 1839.... New York: 1839. 79 p. NjR; PPB; PPL; WHi. 55897

Glynn, James. Cape Fear River, North Carolina surveyed in conformity to an act of congress, July 1839. Washington: 1839. NcU; RPAt. 55898

Go ahead!! No. 2. The Crockett almanac 1840. Containing adventures, exploits, sprees and scrapes in the West, and life and manners in the backwoods. Nashville: Ben Harding [1839] 33 p. MWA; RJa T; TN; WHi. 55899

Goddard, Paul Beck, 1811-1866. Plates of the arteries, with reference for the use of medical students. Philadelphia: J. G. Auner, 1839. 49 p. CSt-L; ICJ; MBM; PU; WvU. 55900

Goddard [William Giles] 1794-1846. Memoir of the Rev. James Manning, D. D., first president of Brown University; with biographical notices of some of his pupils.... Boston: Perkins and Marvin, 1839. 24 p. MBC; NCH; NjP; PHi; RPB. 55901

Goethe, Johann Wolfgang von, 1749-1864. Conversations with Goethe in the last years of his life; translated from the German of Eckermann. By S. M. Fuller. Boston: Hilliard, Gray and Company, 1839. CSansS; MH; NCH; PPA; RNR. 55902

----. Select minor poems, translated from the German with notes by J. S. Dwight. Boston: Hilliard, Gray and company, 1839. 439 p. CBPac; KyLo; MnU; PPA; WU. 55903

----. The sorrows of Werter; from the German of Baron Goethe. A new translation, revised and compared with all the former editions. Hartford: Andrus, Judd and Franklin, 1839. 135 p. CtY; KyHi; PBa; ViR. 55904

----. Wilhelm Meister's apprenticeship and travels, from the German of Goeth by Thomas Carlyle.... A new edition revised. Boston: Houghton Mifflin and Company [1839] 2 v. LNH; Nj; NOy; TxDaM. 55905

----. ----. New York: H. M. Caldwell, 1839. 2 v. NBellp. 55906

----. ----. New York: Dutton, 1839. KyWA. 55907

----. ----. Philadelphia: Coates [1839] GS; IEG; PU. 55908

Going, Jonathan. The inaugural address, at the anniversary of the Granville Literary and Theological Institution, August 8, 1838.... Columbus: Cutler and Pilsbury, 1839. 18 p. MB; MWA; NCH- S; OClWHi; WHi. 55909

The golden rule; a dialogue between littel grace and her mother.... Written for the Massachusetts Sabbath School Society, and revised by the Committee of Publication. 3rd edition. Boston: Massachusetts Sabbath School Society, 1839. OCl. 55910

Goldsmith, Oliver, 1728-1774. The Grecian history, from the earliest state to the death of Alexander the Great.... New York: Robinson and Franklin, 1839. 2 v. in 1. 316 p. CLU; NRU; OCin. 55911

----. ----. Revised and corrected. Philadelphia: John Grigg, 1839. 322 p. MiGR; NSherb. 55912

----. ----. Sandbornton: Charles Lane, 1839. 272 p. IaMpI; IU; MH; NjMD; ViU. 55913

----. History of Rome from the earliest state of the commonwealth, to the dissolution of the empire. Boston: 1839. OCMtSM. 55914

----. ----. New York: Harper and Brothers, 1839. 340 p. CSfMA. 55915

----. ----. Sandbornton, N. H.: Charles Lane, 1839. 2 v. CtY; IU; MH; NPlaK; NPV. 55916

----. A history of the earth and animated nature.... Philadelphia: Grigg and Elliot, 1839. 4 v. KAs; MoWgW; NBuG; NHuntL; TSewU. 55917

----. The miscellaneous works of Oliver Goldsmith, with an account of his life and writings, edited   by Washington Irving. Philadelphia: J. Crissy and Thomas, Cowperthwait and Company, 1839. 527 p. CtMW; TxFwTCU. 55918

----. Roman history for the use of schools. By William Grimshaw. Improved edition. Philadelphia: John Grigg, 1839. 232 p. GEU; MH; NSherb; PReaAT. 55919

----. The vicar of Wakefield, a tale, to which is annexed the deserted village. Exeter [N. H.] T. and B. Williams, 1839. 288 p. IaLyYMA; ViU. 55920

----. ----. Washington City: 1839. CTHWatk; DLC; MWA. 55921

Good, John Mason, 1764-1827. The book of nature. From the last London edition. To which is now prefixed a sketch of th author's life.... Hartford: Belknap, 1839. 467 p. KMK; MiU; NcD; OMC; WBeloc. 55922

A good old man. Boston: 1839. MB. 55923

Goode, Thomas, 1789-1858. The invalid's guide to Virginia Hot Springs: containing an account of the medical properties of these waters, with cases illustrative of their effects. Collected and published by Thomas Goode, M. D., the present proprietor. Richmond: printed by P. D. Bernard, 1839. 44 p. MBAt; MWA; PPL. 55924

Goodenow, Smith Bartlett. A systematic text book of English Grammar, on a new plan, with copious questions and exercises. Portland: William Hyde, 1839. 144 p. CU; MH; NNC; WU. 55925

Goodhue, John N. A sermon on probation: being

the labor of the Rev. John N. Goodhue, late pastor of the Union Church and Society, Marlborough, Mass.... Boston: Whipple and Damrell, 1839. 32 p. Ct; MB; MeBat; OMC. 55926

Goodman, John R. Pennsylvania biography; or memoirs of eminent Pennsylvanians: with occasional extracts, in prose and verse.... Philadelphia: J. Crissy, 1839. 268 p. MiD; PHC; VtStjAc. 55927

Goodrich, Charles Augustus, 1790-1862. The child's history of the United States. Designed as a first book of history for schools. Improved stereotype edition. Philadelphia: Thomas, Cowperthwait and Company, 1839. MH. 55928

----. The ecclesiastical class book; or history of the church from the birth of Christ to the present time. Adapted to the use of academies and schools. Brookfield: E. and L. Merriam, 1839. 255 p. RPB. 55929

----. ----. New York; F, T, Huntington, 1839. 255 p. GDecCT; NjMD; OSW; PPiW; ScNC. 55930

----. The family tourist: or a visit to the principal cities of the western continent; embracing an account of their situation, origin, plan extent...etc. Hartford: P. Canfield, 1839. 552 p. CtY; InThE; MPiB; Nh; OMC. 55931

----. A history of the church, from the birth of Christ to the present time...with a history of the several Protestant denominations...including biographical notices of the principal martyrs and promoters of Christianity.... Brattleboro', Vt.: Brattleboro' Typographic Company, 1839. 504 p. CtHC; FOA; MH; PLT; TxH. 55932

----. History of the United States. Philadelphia: 1839. 119 p. MWA. 55933

----. History of the United States of America from the discovery of the continent by Christopher Columbus, to the present time.... Boston: Crocker and Brewster, 1839. MH; MWbor. 55934

----. ----. Hartford: H. F. Sumner and Company, 1839. 592 p. CSfA; IaDmD; ScDuE; TxU; ViU. 55935

----. A history of the United States of America, on a plan adapted to the capacity of youths.... A new stereotype edition, revised and enlarged from the 64th edition. Claremont, N. H.: Claremont Manufacturing Company, 1839. 352 p. NhD. 55936

----. The lives of the signers of the Declaration of Independence. By N. Dwight, Esq. A new edition. New York: Harper and Brothers, 1839. 373 p. GAuY; NGlc; NRU; ViRVU. 55937

----. ----. 8th edition. New York: Thomas Mather, 1839. 460 p. GAuY; RNHi; MBAt; PP; PPi. 55938

----. The universal traveller; designed to introduce readers at home to an aquaintance with the arts, customs, and manners of the principle modern nations of the globe.... Hartford: Philemon Canfield, 1839. 504 p. MH; MH-P; NjP; NRHi; PPPCPh. 55939

----. ----. New York: Luther James, 1839. 502 p. MiHi. 55940

Goodrich, Chauncey Allen, 1790-1860. Elements of Greek grammar, used in Yale College, heretofore published as the grammar of Caspar Frederic Hachenberg. Stereotyped edition. Hartford: Belknap and Hamersley, 1839. 236 p. ILM; MH; MMonsA; OOxM. 55941

----. Lessons in Greek parsing; or outlines of the Greek grammar.... 2nd edition. New Haven: Durrie and Peck, 1839. 138 p. CtY; MeHi; NSyHi; OOxM; Pu. 55942

----. Lessons in Latin parsing; containing the outlines of the Latin grammar, divided into short portions, and exemplified by appropriate exercises in parsing. 3rd edition. New Haven: Durrie and Peck, etc., etc., 1839. MH. 55943

Goodrich, Samuel Griswold, 1793-1860. The first book of history, for children and youth. By the author of Peter Parley's tales. With sixty engravings and sixteen maps. Boston: G. W. Palmer and Company, 1839. 183 p. Ct; PPM; RNHi. 55944

----. The first reader for schools. Boston: Otis, Broaders and Company, 1839. 96 p. DLC; ICU. 55945

----. Five letters to my neighbor Smith, touching the fifteen gallon jug.... 5th edition. Tow which is added a sixth letter. Boston: Weeks, Jordan and Company, 1839. 35 p. CSmH; DLC; OClWHi;

OO. 55946

----. The fourth reader for the use of schools. Boston: Otis, Broaders and Company, 1839. 312 p. CtHWatk; CtY; MB; MH. 55947

----. ----. Louisville [Ky.] Morton and Griswold [1839] CU; MH; NPtw; OC; OOxM. 55948

----. Illustrated natural history of the animal kingdom.... New York: 1839. 2 v. PPAN. 55949

----. Peter Parley's book of anecdotes. Illustrated by engravings. Philadelphia: Thomas, Cowperthwait and Company, 1839. 14-144 p. 55950

----. Peter Parley's common school history. 6th edition. Philadelphia: Marshall, 1839. 407 p. PU. 55951

----. Peter Parley's first book of history for children and youth. Revised edition. Boston: C. J. Hendee, etc., 1839. CTHWatk; MH; MsU. 55952

----. Peter Palrley's method of telling about geography to children, with nine maps and seventy-five engravings; principally for the use of schools. New York: F. J. Huntington and Company, 1839. 120 p. CtY; MAbD; MH; NN. 55953

----. ----. New York: Harper and Brothers, 1839. 120 p. RPB. 55954

----. ----. Philadelphia: Thomas, Cowperthwait and Company, 1839. 120 p. PU; TNV. 55955

----. Peter Parley's rambles in England, Wales, Scotland and Ireland. New York: S. Coleman, 1839. 266 p. CtY; MB; MH; NjR; NUt. 55956

----. Peter Parley's tales about the sun, moon and stars. With numerous engravings. Philadelphia: Thomas, Cowperthwait and Company, 1839. 116 p. ViW. 55957

----. Peter Parley's tales of animals...revised edition, with questions, and other improvements. Louisville: Morton and Griswold, 1839. 360 p. MSaP. 55958

----. Peter Parley's universal history on the basis of geography. For the use of families. New York: S. Coleman, 1839. CtHC-W; CtY; MH; OU. 55959

----. A present from Peter Parley to all his little

friends. Philadelphia: R. W. Pomroy, 1839. 168 p. ICBB; MeB; MH; NcD. 55960

----. The second book of history, including the modern history of Europe, Africa, and Asia; illustrated by engravings and 16 maps, and designed as a sequel to the "First book of history...35th edition. Boston: Hendee, Jenks and Palmer, 1839. 180 p. MH; MiGr; NjR; PHi; WHi. 55961

----. The second reader for school. Louisville, Ky.: Morton and Griswold, 1839. 44 p. DLC; MH; NN; OrU. 55962

----. System of school geography; chiefly from Malte-Brun. 20th edition. New York: 1839. DLC; MBAt; MH; OO. 55963

----. ----. and arranged accordingly to the inductive plan of instruction. 27th edition. New York: F. J. Huntington and Company, 1839. 288 p. MB; MH; NcD; TxHuT. 55964

----. The tales of Peter Parley about America. With engravings. Revised Edition. Philadelphia: Thomas, Cowperthwait and Company, 1839. 144 p. MnU; RPE; ViU. 55965

----. The third book of history, containing ancient history in connection with ancient geography. Designed as a sequal to the first and second books of history.... 14th edition. Boston: C. J. Hendee, 1839. 189 p. MH; NNC. 55966

----. ----. Philadelphia: Thomas, Cowperthwait and Company, 1839. 189 p. ViW. 55967

----. The third reader for the use of schools. Louisville, Ky.: Morton [1839] 180 p. CtHWatk; MB; MH. 55968

Goodsell, Dana. The immorality and ruinous tendency of the dancing school and ball room; a discourse delivered in the First Congregational Church in Plainfield, Massachusetts, February 10, 1839. Concord, N. H.: D. Kimball, 1839. 20 p. CtY; MB; MH; MiU; MWA. 55969

Goodwin, Ezra Shaw. Alice Bradford, or experimental religion. Boston: S. G. Simpkins, 1839. 76 p. ICMe. 55970

----. ----. 2nd edition. Boston: S. G. Simpkins, 1839. 76 p. MH; PMA. 55971

Goodwin, Frederick D. A sermon on parental unbelief: preached by the Rev. F. D. Goodwin.... Staunton: K. Harper [839] 17 p. NNG. 55972

Goodwin, William. Goodwin's next of kin and heir at law inquirer: comprising valuable information, and advertisements, which have appeared in the London journals, for twenty years back.... New Haven: Hitchcock and Stafford, printers, 1839. 40 p. CtY; MBAt; MBNEH; NNNG; PHi. 55973

Goody Two Shoes. The history of Goody Two Shoes.... Cooperstown [N. Y.] H. and E. Phinney, 1839. 31 p. CU; N; NN. 55974

Gordon, David. Catechetical exercises upon the testimony of the Associate Church.... Philadelphia: William S. Young, 1839. 108 p. CtY; ICP; PWCHi. 55975

Gore, Catherine Grace Francis [Moody] 1799-1861. The cabinet minister. New York: Harper, 1839. 2 v. CtY; MBL; NNS; RPE; TNV. 55976

----. ----. Philadelphia: E. L. Carey and A. Hart, 1839. 2 v. CtY; MH. 55977

----. ----. The courtier of the days of Charles II, with other tales.... New York: Harper and Brothers, 1839. 2 v. MB; MH; MPiB; PNt. 55978

----. A good night's rest; a farce in one act. New York: Samuel French [1839?] 12 p. OCl. 55979

----. Prince and pedler. New York: 1839. 2 v. MBAt. 55980

Gorham Academy and Teacher's Seminary. Catalogue...August, 1839. Portland: A. Shirley, printer, 1839. 27 p. MeHi. 55981

Gott, Joseph Wadsworth. Oration occasioned by the death of David Humphreys, delivered before the Theta and Delta chapters of the Psi-Upsilon Society, Union College, July 24, 1839. Schenectady: James Riggs, 1839. 15 p. N; NN. 55982

Gould, Hannah Flagg, 1789-1865. Poems.... Boston: Hilliard, Gray and Company, 1839-1841. 3 v. CtHT; ICU; MWA; PP; WHi. 55983

----. Verses.... Boston: Hilliard, 1839 [-1841] 3 v. NPV. 55984

Gould, John W., 1814-1838. Private journal of a voyage from New York to Rio De Janeiro, together with a brief sketch and his occasional writings.... New York: Scatcherd and Adams, printer, 1839. 207 p. CSt; MB; MWA; NNA; WHi. 55985

Gould, Nathaniel Duren, 1781-1864. National church harmony, designed for public and private devotion with a supplement...stereotype edition enlarged. Boston: 1839. 339 p. MH; OO. 55986

----. The sabbath school harmony; containing appropriate hymns and music.... Boston: Gould, Kendall and Lincoln, 1839. 48 p. MPeHi. 55987

----. The sacred minstrel, a collection of psalm tunes, chants, anthems, sentences and select pieces. Original and selected from approved authors, ancient and modern. Boston: Gould, Kendall and Lincoln, 1839. 352 p. MB; MMe; NRU. 55988

Gould, William. Memoirs of Lusanna T. Pierce, who died in Freetown, Massachusetts, September 24, 1836, aged seven years and ten months.... Written for the Massachusetts Sabbath School Society.... 2nd edition. Boston: Massachusetts Sabbath School Society, 1839. 87 p. MiD-B. 55989

Gourlie, John Hamilton. An address, delivered before the Mercantile Library Association, January 8, 1839. History of the Association. New York: printed by James Van Norden, 1839. 20 p. ICU; MB: MWA; PPM; RPB. 55990

Gove, Mary Sargent Gove, 1810-1884. Solitary vice. An address to parents and those who have the care of children. Portland: 1839. 18 p. MB; MBM. 55991

Graglia, C. Italian pocket dictionary: in two parts...preceded by an Italian grammar. 1st American from the 14th London edition with corrections and additions. Boston: Hilliard, Gray and Company, 1839. 484 p. DLC; NGH; NN; ViU. 55992

Graham, David, 1808-1852. Speech of David Graham, jr., esq., in the board of assistant alderman, April 15, 1839, in favor of a law to preserve the purity of elections, by a registration of voters [New York: 1839] 23 p. DLC; NNC. 55993

----. A treatise on the organization and jurisdiction of the courts of law and equity, in the state of

New York.... New York: Holsted and Voorhies [1839] 659 p. MBS; NNU; NRAL; OCoSc; W. 55994

Graham [Isabella?] 1742-1814] Histories from scriptures, for children, exemplified by appropriate domestic tales by Miss Graham, embellished with elegant engravings by J. A. Adams. New York: John S. Taylor, 1839. 207 p. ICRL; MH-AH; NjN; NN. 55995

----. The life of Mrs Isabella Graham. By her daughter Mrs. Joanna Bethune. New York: J. S. Taylor, 1839. 144 p. DLC; INS; OCl; OrU. 55996

Graham, Sylvester, 1794-1851. A lecture to young men on chastity, intended also for the serious consideration of parents and guardians. 5th edition. Boston: Light, 1839. 246 p. MNF. 55997

----. ----. 6th stereotyped edition. Boston: G. W. Light, 1839. 246 p. NIC; WHi. 55998

----. Lectures on the science of human life.... Boston: Marsh, Capen, Lyon and Webb, 1839. 2v. CtMW; MWA; NbOM; PPiAM; TJoV. 55999

Granger, Arthur, 1813-1845. Ultra-universalism and its natural affinities by Paul. Hartford: Skinner, 1839. 51 p. CtMW; CtY; MMeT-Hi; PHi. 56000

Grant, James, 1802-1879. The bench and bar.... Philadelphia: E. L. Carey and A. Hart, 1839. 2 v. CtMW; InGrD; LU; MH-L; PU. 56001

----. Every day life in London. Philadelphia: Lea and Blanchard, 1839. 2 v. CtHT; MH; NjP; OMC; WBeloC. 56002

----. The metropolitan pulpit; or sketches of the most popular preachers in London.... New York: D. Appleton and Company, 1839. 416 p. CtHC; ICP; NBuG; OClW; PPM. 56003

----. Sketches of London.... Philadelphia: Carey and Hart, 1839. 2 v. DeWi; MBBC; OClW; PPL-R; WBeloC. 56004

Granville, Augustus Bozzi, 1783-1872. Extracts from the work on counter-irritation, its principles and practice, illustrated by 100 cases of the most painful and important diseases effectually cured by external applications.... Philadelphia: J. Hard-

ing, printer, 1839. 93 p. ICU; NjR; PPCP; PPL; RP. 56005

Graupner, Gottlieb. A new preceptor for the German flute; with a collection of airs, duets, marches, waltzes, etc. 8th edition. Compiled by John Patterson. Albany: Oliver Steele, 1839. 51 p. CtHWatk; ViU. 56006

Graves, Josiah M. A phrenological chart presenting a synopsis of the doctrine of phrenology. Harford: Hurlbut and Williams, 1839. 31 p. DNLM; MBAt; NN. 56007

Gray, Frederick Turell, 1804-1855. An address delivered before the [Boston] Society for the Prevention of Pauperism, January 14, 1839. Boston: printed by Weeks, Jordan and Company, 1839. 23 p. ICMe; MBC; MHi; MiD-B; NCH. 56008

----. Letter to the church and scoiety worshipping at the Pitts Street Chapel, December 31, 1839. 18 p. CBPac; CtY; ICMe; MB; WHi. 56009

Gray, John. The soldier, giving an affecting narrative of facts regarding his unparalleled wickedness and subsequent extraordinary conversion in the West Indies. Kinderhook, N. Y.: F. Van Schaak, 1839. 16 p. N. 56010

Great Britain. Court for the Consideration of Crown Cases Reserved. Crown cases reserved for consideration; and decided by the 12 judges of England, from the year 1799 to year 1824, by William Oldall Russell and Edward Ryan and others. Philadelphia: T. and J. W. Johnson, 1839. 600 p. In-SC; MnU; NcD; PWWL; WaU. 56011

----. ----. ----. Philadelphia: T. and J. W. Johnson, 1839-1853. 6 v. CLSU; IaDaGL; Mi-L; N. 56012

----. ----. ----. By William Moody...with references to the common law reports.... Philadelphia: T. and J. W. Johnson, 1839 [-1853] 2 v. C; MiD-B; OClW; PU-L; WaU. 56013

----. Court of Chancery. Reports of cases argued and determined in the High Court of Chancery, from 1757-1766, from the original manuscripts of Lord Chancellor Northington. Collected, arranged with notes and references to former an subsequent determinations and to the register's books. By the Hon. Robert Henley Eden.... First American from the last London edition. Philadelphia: R. H. Small, 1839. 2 v. in 1. CSt; ICLaw; MdBB; NcD; PU-L. 56014

Great western almanac for 1840. Calculations by C. F. Egelmann. Philadelphia: Jos. McDowell [1839] MWA. 56015

Great Western Iron Company. Charter and by-laws of the Great Western Iron Company; also an act to encourage the manufacture of iron in the state of Pennsylvania. n. p. [1839?] 16 p. ICJ. 56016

Green, Ashbel, 1762-1848. The case of the General Assembly of the Presbyterian Church before the Supreme Court of Pennsylvania. Philadelphia: A. M'Elroy, 1839. 628 p. CSansS; KyDC; MiD; NbOP; RPL. 56017

----. Report of the Presbyterian Church case: The commonwealth of Pennsylvania; at the suggestion of James Todd and others, vs. Asbel Green and others. By Samuel Miller Jr., Philadelphia: W. S. Martien, 1839. 596 p. CSansS; ICP; MiU; PPM; WaU. 56018

Green, Beriah, 1795-1874. The chattel principle, the abhorrence of Jesus Christ and the apostles; or no refuge for American Slavery in the New Testament.... New York: American Anti-slavery Society, 1839. 67 p. CU; MH; NBuG; PHC; TNF. 56019

----. The education of the apostles. A valedictory address, to the senior class of the Oneida Institute; delivered September 10, 1839. Published by request of the class. Whitesboro [N. Y.] Press of the Oneida Institute, 1839. 32 p. CtHC; MH; NCH; OClWHi. 56020

Green, Jacob, 1790-1841. Inferior surface of the trilobite discovered. Philadelphia: Dobson, 1839. 33 p. NjP; PPAN. 56021

Green, Jonathan, 1788?-1864. A practical compendium of the diseases of the skin. From the second London edition. Boston: Stimpson and Clapp, 1839. 252 p. CSt-L; ICU-R; MH-M; OCGHM; PPCP. 56022

Green, Richard W. Gradations in Algebra in which the first principles of analysis are inductively explained and made suitable for primary schools.... Philadelphia: E. H. Butler and Company, 1839. CtY; DLC; PPF; PPFrankI. 56023

Green Bay, Wisconsin. Presbyterian Church. Summary confession of faith and covenant with proof of texts and references, adopted by the Presbyterian Church of Green Bay, Wisconsin, January, 1839 [?] 12 p. OO. 56024

Green Mountain Junior College, Poultney, Vermont. Troy Conference Academy, West Poultney, Vt. Catalogue of the corporation, faculty and students.... 1838-1839. Lansingburgh, 1839. 19 p. N. 56025

Greene, Hugh Wentworth, 1811-1888. Letters addressed to Francis O. J. Smith, being a defence of the writer against the attacks made by him to that individual and a sketch of Mr. Smith's political life [Concord, N. H.?] 1839. 22 p. DLC; MH; MiU-C; NN; NjR. 56026

Greene, John P. Facts relative to the expulsion of the Mormans from the state of Missouri, under the "exterminating order". Cincinnati: printed by R. P. Brooks, 1839. 43 p. ICN; MiD-B; NHi; PU; WHi. 56027

Greene, Roscoe Goddard. A practical grammar of the English language, in which the principles established by Lindley Murray are inculcated and the theory of the modes clearly illustrated by diagrams.... Portland, Maine: William Hyde, 1839. 132 p. MH; WU. 56028

Greenfield, William. The polymicrian Greek lexicon to the New Testament in which the various senses of the words are distinctly explained in English and authorized by references to passages of scripture. Philadelphia: H. Perkins, etc., etc., 1839. ICU; MH- AH; MS; PPP. 56029

Greenfield, Massachusetts. Congregational Church. The articles of faith and covenamt of the Congregational Church, together with a list of the members. Greenfield: printed by S. S. Eastman, 1839. 11 p. MBC. 56030

Greenleaf, Benjamin, 1786-1864. A key to the national arithmetic, exhibiting the operation of the more difficult questions in that work, for the use of teachers only. Boston: Robert S. Davis and Gould, Kendall and Lincoln, 1839. 110, 12 p. MeB; MHa; MPeHi. 56031

----. The national arithmetic, on the inductive system. Improved stereotype edition. Boston: Robert S. Davis and Gould, Kendall and Lincoln,

1839. 314 p. MAm; NN; NRU-W; PHi; PPL. 56032

Greenleaf, Jeremiah, 1791-1864. Grammar simplified. New York: 1839. CtHWatk. 56033

----. Multum in parvo; or a brief and comprehensive system of English grammar. Upon a new plan: from which a knowledge of the subject can be obtained much quicker, and much easier.... Designed for the use of schools, and for private learners. 2nd edition. Boston: 1839. MH. 56034

[Greenleaf, Simon] 1783-1853. On the exclusion of witnesses for unbelief [Boston: 1839] 10 p. MH; MH-L. 56035

----. Remarks on the exclusion of atheists as witnesses. Boston: Weeks, Jordan and Company, 1839. 10 p. LU; MBAt; MiD-B; NN; RPB. 56036

Greenough, B. F. Report on his chemical oil. Boston: 1839. PPL. 56037

Green's New England almanack, farmer's friend, and mariners' guide for 1840. The astronomical calculations performed by Nathan Bowdich. New London [Conn.] Samuel H. Green [1839] MWA. 56038

Greenwood, Francis William Pitt, 1797-1843. The classical reader; By F. W. P. Greenwood, and G. B. Emerson, of Boston. Improved Stereotype edition. Boston: Robert S. Davis, 1839. 408, 4 p. MH; NNC; OMC. 56039

----. A collection of psalms and hymns for Christian worship.... 26th edition. Boston: Charles J. Hendee and G. W. Palmer and Company, 1839. 600 p. DLC; MH-AH; MiU; MNan. 56040

----. ----. 27th edition. Boston: 1839. MHi. 56041

----. ----. 29th edition. Boston: Charles J. Hendee, 1839. 609 p. IEG; MB; MBAU; MeB. 56042

----. A description of the principal fruit of Cuba [Boston: 1839] 41 p. MB; MBH; MH. 56043

----. The inheritance which a good man leaves to his children, a discourse occasioned by the death of James Freeman Curtis; and preached April 21, 1839. Boston: J. Munroe and Company, 1839. 20 p. CtY; MHi; MWA; NNC. 56044

----. Sermon preached at the ordination of the Rev. John T. Sargent...October 29, 1837 [with the charge by Joseph Tuckerman and right hand of fellowship by F. T. Gray] New York: 1839. 32 p. NNC. 56045

Greenwood Cemetery, Brooklyn, New York. Exposition of the palan and object of the Greenwood Cemetery, an incorporated trust, chartered by the legislature of the state of New York. New York: 1839. 28 p. CtY; MB; MH; NSmb; WHi. 56046

----. Report of the board of trustees, 1839-1886. New York and Brooklyn: 1839-1887. 48 v. MB: NBLiHi. 56047

Gregory, George, 1754-1808. A concise history of the Christian Church, from the first establishment to the present time...compiled from the works of Dr. Gregory, with numerous additions and improvements. By Martin Ruter, D. D. New York: T. Mason and G. Lane, for the Methodist Episcopal Church, 1839. 446 p. GDecCT; InGrD; MB; OSW; PCC. 56048

Grier, William. The mechanic's calculator, comprehending principles, rules, and tables in the various departments of mathematics and mechanics; useful to millwrights.... From the 5th Glasgow edition. Philadelphia: Thomas Wardle, 1839. 308 p. CtSoP; NTRPI; RPB; WM. 56049

Griffen, Joseph. Elements of modern Geography; or easy and systematic steps to the acquistion of geographical knowledge, in familiar lectures and exercises.... Trenton: D. D. Clark, 1839. 286 p. CTHWatk; NjR; NjT. 56050

Griffin, Edward Dorr, 1770-1837. Sermons by the late Rev. Edward D. Griffin, D. D. to which is prefixed a memoir of his life by William B. Sprague.... New York: Taylor, 1839. 2 v. CtMW; ICP; MBC; NjP; PPPrHi. 56051

Griffin's scientific miscellany [n. p.] Richard Griffin, 1839. 2 v. DLC; PPWa. 56052

Grigg, John, 1792-1864. Grigg's southern and western songster: being a choice collection of the most fashionable songs, many of which are original. New edition greatly enlarged. Philadelphia: Grigg and Elliot, 1839. 324 p. CLU; Ia; MH; MoHi; PHi. 56053

Grimes, James Stanley, 1807-1903. A new system

of phrenology. By J. Stanley Grimes.... Buffalo: O. G. Steel, New York: Wiley and Putnam, 1839. 320 p. CtY; ICMe; IU; MiU; NBu. 56054

Grimshaw, William, 1782-1852. History of England, from the first invasion by Julius Caesar, to the accession of William the Fourth, in 1830.... Philadelphia: Grigg and Elliot, 1839. 318 p. ICU; NN; PPeSchw; ScNC; TKC. 56055

----. History of the United States from their first settlement as colonies to the period of the fifth census in 1830.... Philadelphia: Grigg and Elliott, 1839. 326 p. DLC; DNW; GAGTh; ViSwc. 56056

Grimshawe, Thomas Shuttleworth, 1778-1850. A memoir of the Rev. Legh Richmond.... New York: Leavitt, 1839. 364 p. CtMW; OO. 56057

Griscom, John Hoskins, 1809-1874. Animal mechanism and physiology; being a plain and familiar exposition of the structure and functions of the human system...Illustrated by numerous woodcuts by Butler. New York: Harper and Brothers, 1839. 357 p. FTa; GU; NjR; PPWa; RPB. 56058

Griswold, William H. Address delivered at the public exercises of the Philotimian Society, August 7, 1839. Utica: Grosh, 1839. 12 p. MiD-B; RPB; TxU. 56059

Grosh, Aaron Burt. An inquiry into the teachings of the Holy Scriptures, in two lectures.I. Partialism not taught in the Bible. II. Scripture proofs of Universalism. Utica: Grosh and Hutchinson, 1839. 48 p. MMeT; MMeT-Hi; NUt. 56060

Gross, Samuel David, 1805-1884. Elements of pathological anatomy, illustrated by numerous engravings.... Boston: Marsh, Capen, Lyon and Webb, and J. B. Don, 1839. 2 v. GEU-M; MB; PPCP; TNV; WMAM. 56061

----. 3rd edition modified and thoroughly revised.... Boston: MArsh, 1839. 2 v. PPPH. 56062

Groves, John. A Greek and English dictionary, comprising all the words in the writings of the most popular Greek authors...with corrections and additional matter by the American editor.... Boston: Hilliard, Gray and Company, 1839. 616, 102 p. IU; MH; OAlM; WMMU; WNaE. 56063

The guide to Christian perfection; Rev. T. Merritt, editor. Boston: T. Merritt and D. S. King, 1839-. V. 1-. DLC; MB; Nh; RPB; Wv. 56064

Gummere, John, 1784-1845. A treatise on surveying, containing the theory and practice: to which is prefixed a perspicuous system of plane trigonometry.... 14th edition carefully revised and enlarged by the addition of articles on the theodolite, levelling and topography. Philadelphia: Kimber and Sharpless, 1839. 266 p. ICBB; MiD; NjP; OOxM; ViU. 56065

Gunn, John C. Domestic medicine, or poor man's friend in the hours of affliction, pain and sickness...It also contains description of the medicinal roots and herbs of the United States.... 1st revised edition. Philadelphia: 1839. 893 p. MBM; NNNAM; WU-M. 56066

----. ----. 8th edition. Pumkintown, Tennessee: S. M. Johnston, 1839. 635 p. IEN-M; MoS; MoSM; T; TKL-Mc. 56067

----. ----. 13th edition. Pittsburgh: J. Edwards and J. J. Newman, 1839. 726 p. DNLM; ICU; IRA. 56068

Gurley, Ralph Randolph, 1797-1872. Address at the annual meeting of the Pennsylvania Colonization Society, November 11, 1839. Philadelphia: H. Hooker, 1839. 40 p. CtSoP; ICU; MH-AH; PHi; TxU. 56069

----. Life of Jehudi Ashmun, late colonial agent in Liberia. With an appendix containing extracts from his journal and other writings; with a brief sketch of the life of the Rev. Lott Cary. 2nd edition. New York: Robinson and Franklin, 1839. 160 p. DLC; MdBE; OClWHi; PWW; RPB. 56070

Gurney, Joseph John, 1788-1847. Brief remarks on impartiality in the interpretation of the scripture. Also, a letter to the followers of Elias Hicks. With a defence of the Society of Friends. Baltimore [1839-1840] MdBP; MH; PSC-Hi. 56071

----. A letter to a friend on the authority, purpose and effects of Christianity, and especially on the doctrine of redemption. London: printed 1835, New York: reprinted by Mahlon Day and Company, 1839. 32 p. CtY; MH. 56072

----. Letter to Friends of the monthly meeting of Adrian, Michigan. New York: Mahlon Day, 1839.

15 p. DLC; MBBC; MH; MiGr; PSC-Hi. 56073

----. A letter to the followers of Elias Hicks, in the city of Baltimore, and its vicinity. Baltimore: Woods and Crane, printers, 1839. 26 p. DLC; ICU; MdBE; MnHi; PHC. 56074

Guthrie, George James, 1785-1856. Clinical lectures on compound fractures of the extremities, on excision of the head of the thighbone, the armbone and the elbow joint.... Delivered at the Westminister Hospital.... Philadelphia: A. Wal-

die, 1839. 90 p. ICU; MdBJ; OO; PP; ViU. 56075

Guy, Joseph, 1784-1867. Guy's elements of astronomy, and an abridgment of Keith's new treatise on the use of the globes. New American edition. with additions and improvemnts, and an explanation of the astornomical part of the American almanac. 19th edition. Philadelphia: F. W. Greenough, and Thomas, Cowperthwait and Company, 1839. 136, 173 p. CLCM; MH; MoU; OO; ViU. 56076

H

Habermann, Johann, 1516-1590. The Christian's companion. Harrisburg: G. S. Peters, 1839. PPeSchw. 56077

----. Das kleine Gebetbuch. Doylestown, Pa.: Jung, 1839. 128 p. CtY; PHi; PPeSchw; PPG. 56078

Haddock, Charles Brickett, 1796-1861. Wisdom in clergymen. Princeton [N.J.?] Princeton press, Bernard Connolly, printer, 1839. 22 p. IaGG. 56079

Hagerstown town and country almanack for 1840. By John F. Egelmann. Hagerstown, Md.: J. Gruber [1839] MWA. 56080

Hague, William, 1808-1887. An historical discourse delivered at the celebration of the 2nd centennial anniversary of the First Baptist Church in Providence, November 7, 1839. ...Providence: B. Cranston and Company, Boston: Gould, Kendall and Lincoln, 1839. 192 p. ICU; LNH; MWA; NjMD; PCC. 56081

Haight, Benjamin Issacs, 1809-1879. The Holy Child Jesus. New York: General Protestant Sunday School Union, 1839. MB. 56082

Haines, Isaac S. Catechism on chemistry, adapted to the course of lectures delivered in the Univesity of Pennsylvania. 2nd edition. Philadelphia: J. G. Auner, 1839 [9]-144 p. DLC; DGS; MH; PPCP. 56083

Haiti. Laws, Statutes, etc. The rural code of Haiti, literally translated from a publication by the government press, together with letter from that country, concerning its present condition. 3rd edition. New York: 1839. 48 p. CSmH; DLC; MH-L; NN. 56084

Hale, Benjamin, 1797-1863. Baccalaureate address; delivered at the annual commencement of Geneva College, August 7, 1839. Geneva, N.Y.: printed by Stow and Frazee, 1839. 32 p. MeB; MH; NjR; OCHP; PPL. 56085

----. The present state of the question in regard to the division of the dicoese of New York [Geneva] 1839. 27 p. MBD; NBuDD; NNC; PPM. 56086

Hale, Enoch, 1790-1848. Observations on the typhoid fever of New England. Read at the annual meeting of the Massachusetts Medical Society, May 29, 1839. Boston: Whipple and Damrell, 1839. 77 p. CSt-L; ICU; MeB; NNN; PU. 56087

Hale, Salma, 1787-1866. History of the United States, from their first settlement as colonies to the close of the war with Great Britain in 1815...to which are added questions adapted to the use of schools. Cooperstown, N.Y.: H. and E. Phinney, 1839. 298 p. CU; NPot; NRMA; RAp. 56088

----. ----. Keene, N.H.: J. and J. W. Prentiss, 1839. 254 p. IaDuU-Sem. 56089

----. ----. New York: Collins, Keese and Company, 1839. 298, 26 p. MH; RPB. 56090

Hale, Sarah Josepha [Buell] 1788-1879. Flora's interpreter, or the American book of flowers and sentiments. 7th edition, improved. Boston: Marsh, Capen, Lyon and Webb, 1839. CtHWatk; MH; WHi. 56091

----. ----. 8th edition. Boston: Marsh, Capen, Lyon and Webb, 1839. TxU. 56092

----. The good housekeeper, or the way to live well and to be well while we live. Boston: Weeks, Jordan and Company, 1839. 132 p. MB; MBev; MWA; NIC. 56093

----. ----. 2nd edition. Boston: Weeks, Jordan and Company, 1839. 144 p. CtY; MBevHi; MH; MWA. 56094

----. The ladies' wreath; a selection from the female poetic writers of England and America. With original notices and notes: prepared especially for young ladies. A gift-book for all seasons. 2nd edition. Boston: Marsh, Capen, Lyon and

Webb, 1839. 436 p. Ct; IEG; MH: MoS; RPB. 56095

----. My cousin Mary, or the inebriate. By a lady of Boston.... Boston: Whipple and Damrell, 1839. 64 p. CU; DLC. 56096

----. Sketches of American character.... 7th edition. Philadelphia: Henry Perkins, Boston: Perkins and Marvin, 1839. 287 p. ODW; ViL. 56097

[Haliburton, Thomas Chandler] 1796-1865. The bubbles of Canada. By the author of "Sam Slick".... Philadelphia: Lea and Blanchard, 1839. 262 p. LU; MH; MiGr; PU; RNR. 56098

----. The clockmaker; or the sayings and doings of Samuel Slick, of Slicksville. Concord: Boyd and White, 1839. 254 p. MB; MWA. 56099

----. ----. Philadelphia: Lea and Blanchard, 1839. 11-179 p. DLC; KyU; OClW; PU; ViW. 56100

----. ----. 2nd series. Philadelphia: Lea and Blanchard, 1839. 192 p. CtY; ICHi; MnHi; OClWHi; PU. 56101

----. ----. 3rd edition. Concord: Israel S. Boyd, 1839. 262 p. WaT. 56102

----. ----. 3rd series. Philadelphia: Lea and Blanchard, 1839. 179 p. DLC; NcU. 56103

[Hall, Allen A.] The counterfeit detector, or the leaders of the party exposed [Nashville, Tenn.: Republican Banner office, 1839] [1]-48 p. MH; NcU; T; TKL-Mc; WHi. 56104

Hall, Baynard Rush, 1798-1863. An address delivered to the young ladies of the Spring-villa seminary, at Bordentwon, N.J., at the distribution of the annual medal and premiums: on the evening of the 29th of August, 1839. Burlington: Powell and George, printers, 1839. 15 p. MH; PPL. 56105

Hall, Edward Brooks, 1800-1866. On the atonement. Printed for the American Unitarian Association. Boston: James Munroe and Company, 1839. 3-56 p. DLC; ICMe; MBC; MH; MWA. 56106

----. ----. 2nd edition. printed for the American Unitarian Association. Boston: James Munroe and Company, 1839. 56 p. MH; MH-AH; RHi.
56107.

Hall, Fanny W. Rambles in Europe, or a tour through France, Italy, Switzerland, Great Britain and Ireland, in 1836. New York: E. French, 1839. 2 v. MChiA; MeBaT; NjP; NNebg; ScSch. 56108

Hall, James, 1793-1868. Legends of the west. Philadelphia: 1839. PPL. 56109

----. The western reader; a series of useful lessons, designed to succeed the elementary reader. Revised and corrected by an expert teacher. Cincinnati: George Conclin, 1839. 192 p. WHi. 56110

Hall, John, 1783-1847. The reader's guide containing a notice of the elementary sounds in the English language; instructions for reading both prose and verse, with numerous examples and illustrations. Hartford: Canfield and Robins, 1839. 333 p. NTEW. 56111

----. The readers manual; designed for the use of common schools in the United States. Hartford: 1839. CtHWatk; MH; MoS. 56112

Hall, Louisa Jane [Park] 1802-1892. Hannah, the mother of Samuel the prophet and judge of Israel. A sacred drama. Boston: J. Munroe and Company, 1839. 94 p. CtHC; DLC; ICU; MBAt; MWH. 56113

Hall, Marshall, 1790-1857. The principles of diagnosis.... 2nd American edition, with notes by John A. Swett.... New York: D. Appleton and Company, 1839. 458 p. CU; KyU; MnU; RPM; ViU. 56114

----. Principles of the theory and practice of medicine. First American edition. Boston: Charles C. Little and James Brown, 1839. 724 p. A-Ar; ICJ; MB; PU; TNV. 56115

Hall, Robert, 1764-1831. Beauties of Robert Hall.... New York: John S. Taylor, 1839. 108 p. IEG; InCW; MWA; NbCrD; Nh. 56116

----. The works of the Rev. Robert Hall. With a brief memoir of his life, by Dr. Gregory, and observations on his character as a preacher, by the Rev. John Foster.... New York: Harper and Brothers, 1839. 3 v. GDecCT; IaB; MoSpD; OO; TNP. 56117

Hall, Samuel Read, 1795-1877. Lectures on

School-keeping. Boston: Richardson, Lord and Holbrook, 1839. 135 p. MBevHi. 56118.

----. School history of the United States, containing maps, a chronological chart, and an outline of topics for a more extensive course of study. Andover [Mass.] W. Peirce, 1839. 368 p. InCW; DLC; MB; MH-AH; MLy. 56119

Hall, Thomas H. To the people of the third congressional district of North Carolina.... Thomas H. Hall, June, 1839. 7 p. NcHiC. 56120

Hall, Willard. Lecture on our civil institutions before the Elkton Lyceum. Elkton: 1839. 16 p. MBAt. 56121

Hallam, Henry, 1777-1859. Introduction to the literature of Europe in the 15th, 16th and 17th centuries. New York: Harper, 1839. 4 v. InRch; MCR. 56122

----. Views of the state of Europe during the middle ages.... From the 6th London edition.... New York: Harper and Brothers, 1839. 568 p. KyLoS; MH; MOSU; ScDuE; WvC. 56123

[Halleck, Fitz-Greene] 1790-1867. Fanny, with other poems.... New York: Harper and Brothers, 1839. 130 p. CtMW; GEU; MBAt; OHi; PP. 56124

Hallet, Benjamin Franklin, 1797-1862. Oration before the Democratic citizens of Worcester County, Massachusetts, at Millbury, July 4, 1839. Worcester: E. W. Bartlett, 1839. 48 p. CtSoP; DLC; MH; MiD-B; MSo. 56125

Halliard, Jack. Voyages and adventures of Jack Halliard, in the Artic Ocean. Boston: William D. Ticknor, 1839. 130 p. MH; MHi. 56126

Halyburton, Thomas, 1674-1712. The great concern of salvation. Philadelphia: Presbyterian board of publication, 1839. 180 p. ICBB; NjR; PPPrHi; TxAuPT; ViRut. 56127

Hamilton, Alexander, 1757-1804. The opinion of Alexander Hamilton, on the expediency of incorporating the United States Bank. Dutches and Ulster Counties. New York: Samuel S. Freer, 1839. 24 p. ICN; FTaSU; InU; N; PHi. 56128

Hamilton, Alexander, 1786-1875. Late bank of Maryland. Baltimore: 1839. 1 p. PHi. 56129

----. Letter on the subject of banks and currency, proposing the creation of a state bank of issues, and the restriction of private banks to circulation discount and deposits. New York: 1839. 25 p. CtY; MH-BA; NNC; PU; WHi. 56130

Hamilton, Frank Hastings, 1813-1886. Introductory lecture before the surgical class of the College of Physicians and Surgeons, Fairfield, New York, delivered December 3, 1839.... Albany: printed by Hoffman, White and Company, 1839. CSmH; MHi; NBuU-M; NjR; OC. 56131

Hamilton, James Alexander, 1785-1845. A new theoretical and practical musical grammar, adapted to the present state of the science.... New York: Hewitt and Jaques, 1839. CtY. 56132

----. Practical catechism on singing; extracted from the best authorities, Italian, French and English, illustrated with numerous example.... New York: Hewitt and Jaques, 1839. 76, 52 p. MdBS; NNUT; PPM. 56133

Hamilton, William. A funeral discourse, delivered in the Government Street Church, Mobile, on Sabbath, August 18, 1839, in mmemory of Judge Henry Hitchcock, who died...of yellow fever. Mobile: printed at the Advertiser and Chronicle office, 1839. 33 p. A-Ar; InHi; MWA; PPL; RPB. 56134

Hamilton College. Catalogue of the corporation, officers, and students, of Hamilton College. Clinton, 1839-1840 [Utica: 1839] 20 p. MWA; NCH. 56135

----. Phoenix Society. Triennial catalogue of the Phoenix Society...October, 1839. Studia et artes colimus. Utica: printed for the society, by Bennett, Backus and Hawley [1839] 27 p. MWA; N; NCH. 56136

Hammond, Jabez Delano, 1778-1855. An address delivered by the Hon. J. D. Hammond, before the Otsego County Education Society, October 10, 1838. Cooperstown: H. and E. Phinney, 1839. 16 p. N; NjR; NN. 56137

Hammond, Wells Stoddard. Oration, delivered at Cherry Valley, on July 4, 1839. Published by and at the request of the committee of arrangements, for celebrating at Cherry Valley the 63d anniversary of American independence. Albany: printed by J. Munsell, 1839. 16 p. CtY; MB; MiU-C;

MWA; PPL. 56138

[Hamon, Andre Jean Marie] 1795-1874. Life of the Cardinal de Cheverus, archbishop of Bordeaux. By the Rev. J. Huen Doubourg [pseud.] Translated from the French by Robert M. Walsh. Philadelphia: Hooker and Claxton, 1839. 280 p. CtY; MBBC; MWA; NNUT; PPA. 56139

Hampden County, Massachusetts. Annual reports of benevolent societies in the County of Hampden...1839. Springfield: Merriam, Wood and Company, 1839. MB. 56140

Handel and Hayden Society, Boston. The Boston Handel and Haydn Society collection of church music being a selection of the most improved psalm and hymn tunes, anthems, sentences, chants, etc.... Boston: J. H. Wilkens and R. B.Carter, 1839. 357 p. CtHWatk; ICN; NIC; NRiv-Hi. 56141

Handy, William W., Speech...delivered in the House of Delegates of Maryland, April 4, 1839, in the debate on the proposition to release the private stockholders from paying up their stock to the Eastern Shore Railroad Company, 1839. MB; MdBP; PPL. 56142

Hannaford, Greley. The Herald of the glorious morning of Emanuel, and genius of Universal emancipation. Boston: published by the author, 1839. 80 p. MB; MeHi; Nh; OClWHi; PHi. 56143

Hannah, John, 1792-1867. A letter to a junior Methodist preacher.... New York: T. Mason and G. Lane, 1839. 116 p. DLC; NcD; NcRSh; NjMD. 56144

Hannah Swanton, the Casco Captive: or the Catholic religion in Canada, and its influence on the indians in Maine...[Taken chiefly from...C. Mather's Magnolia] 2nd edition. Boston: 1839. ICN; NN. 56145

Hannah, the mother of Samuel the prophet...See Hall, Louisa Jane [Park] 1802-1892.

Hanover College, Hanover, Indiana. Catalogue of the officers and students.... South Hanover: printed by James Morrow, 1839. CSmH; DLC; In; InHC; PPPrHi. 56146

The happy merchant: or the power of truth, illustrated in the last days of a young man.... 2nd edition. Boston: Massachusetts Sabbath School Society, 1839. 85 p. MNowdHi. 56147

Hard, William J. A sermon commemorative of Dr. Milton Anthony. Augusta, Ga.: Browne, Cushney and McCafferty, 1839. 19 p. PCA. 56148

Hardie, Robert. Hoyle made familiar: or a companion to the card table...with the rules and practice as admitted by the most fashionable establishments in the United Kingdom. New York: W. Mather, 1839. 119 p. NN. 56149

Harding's gallery, Boston. Exhibition of pictures, painted by Washington Allston...See Allston, Washington.

Hare, Augustus William, 1792-1834. Sermons to a country Congregation. 1st American from the 3rd London edition. New York: Appleton, 1839. 497 p. IEG; MPiB; PPP; TChU; ViRut. 56150

Hare, Edward, 1774-1818. A treatise of the scriptural doctrine of justification. New York: Carlton and Lanahan, 1839. 253 p. ICP; PReaAT. 56151

The harmonist; being a collection of tunes from the most approved authors; adapted to every variety of meter in the Methodist hymn book. And for particular occasions, a selection of anthems, pieces, and sentences. New York: T. Mason and G. Lane, for the Methodist Episcopal Church, 1839. 384 p. IEG; NFri; NRU; RPB. 56152

Harris, Chapin Aaron. The dental art, a practical treatise on dental surgery. Baltimore: Armstrong and Berry, 1839. 384 p. CSt- L; InU-M; MdHi; PPiU-D; TU-M. 56153

Harris, James D. Communication from the president of the Union Canal Company, accompanied with a report of James D. Harris, principal engineer, relative to enlarging the Union Canal. Read in the House of Representatives, February 9, 1839. Harrisburg: printed by Boas and Coplan, 1839. 24 p. DLC; MH-BA; MnHi; OSW. 56154

----. Report of a survey of a route for a railroad from Tunkhannsch to Binghamton. Harrisburg: 1839. 10 p. PHi. 56155

----. Report relative to enlarging the Union Canal. Read in the House, February 9, 1839. Harrisburg: 1839. 24 p. PHi. 56156

Harris, John, 1802-1856. The great teacher: characteristics of our Lord's ministry. With an introductory essay, by Humphrey Heman. Boston: Gould, Kendall and Lincoln, 1839. 430, 12 p. GAGTh; KyBC; MB; Nh; TChU. 56157

----. ----. 2nd edition. Amherst: 1839. MNtCA. 56158

----. House of prayer. 1st American edition. Boston: Gould, Kendall and Lincoln, 1839. 55 p. MBNMHI. 56159

----. Mammon; or covetousmess the sin of the Christian Church. New York: T. Mason and G. Lane, for the Methodist Episcopal Church, 1839. 249 p. CSt; IEG; MoS; NcD; OBerB. 56160

----. The witnessing church. 1st American edition. Boston: Gould, Kendall and Lincoln, 1839. 90 p. CtY; GDecCT; MH; OkEnS; PU. 56161

Harris, Robert William. A sermon occasioned by the death of Rev. Alexander H. Crosby.... New York: W. H. Vermilye, 1839. 29 p. MBAt; MdBD; NNG; PPL; TChU. 56162

Harris, Thaddeus William, 1795-1856. Descriptive catalogue of the North American insects belonging to the Linnaean genus sphinx in the cabinet of Thaddeus William Harris.... [Cambridge, Mass.: 1839] 40 p. ICJ. 56163

----. ----. [New Haven: 1839] 40 p. MH-Z; PPAmE. 56164

----. Remarks upon the North American insects belonging to the genus Cychrus of Fabricius, with descriptions of some newly detected species. Cambridge [Boston printed] 1839. 16 p. ICJ; OO; PPAmP; PPAN. 56165

Harris' Pittsburg and Allegheny directory, with the environs, etc., including the boroughs of Lawrenceship and Birmingham...with a variety of interesting statistical notices.... Pittsburgh: printed by A. A. Anderson, 1839. 212 p. NjR; PPi. 56166

Harrison, Albert Galliton, d. 1839. Speech...in the House of Representatives, February 15, 1839 [n. p.: 1839?] 15 p. DLC; MiU- C. 56167

Harrison, Gessner, 1807-1862. An exposition of some of the doctrines of the Latin grammar....

Charlottesville [Va.] J. Alexander, 1839. 2 v. PPAmP; Vi; ViU. 56168

Harrison, Thomas. Music simplified: or a new system of music, founded on natural principles; designed either for separate use, or as an introduction to the old system and intended chiefly for educational and religious purposes: to which is added a collection of Christian melodies. Springfield, Ohio: printed at the office of the Republic, 1839. 56 p. DLC; OSMH. 56169

Harrison, William Henry, 1795-1878. The tourist in Portugal...illustrated from paintings by James Holland.... New York: D. Appleton, 1839. 290 p. CtY; ICN; IU; LNH; MnS. 56170

Harry Barnes and his holiday. Northampton: J. Metcalf, 1839. 24 p. CtY; ICBB. 56171

Hart, Cyrus Wadsworth. Imaginary debate on the question, "Can one fall violently in love with a damsel rationally at first sight?" with other piesces in verse, chiefly in honor of women. Boston: F. A. G. Nicholson, printer, 1839. 24 p. CSmH; MH; MWA; NcD. 56172

Hartford, Connecticut. First School Society. Report of the school visitors of the...for 1838-1839. Together with the report of the school association and the proceedings of the annual meeting, held October 7 and November 5, 1839. Hartford: printed by Case, Tiffany and Company, 1839. 16 p. Ct; CtHWatk; ICN. 56173

----. North Church. Catalogue of the North Church, Hartford. Together with its history, articles of faith, and by-laws. Hartford: printed by P. B. Gleason and Company, 1839. 28 p. MBC; PPPr-Hi. 56174

----. Park Church. Catalogue...with its history, articles of faith and by-laws. Hartford: 1839. MBC. 56175

----. Public Library. Catalogue of books in the library of the young men's institute. Hartford: 1839. 64 p. CtSoP; CtY; ICN; CtHWatk. 56176

----. South Baptist Church. Articles of faith and covenant of the South Baptist Church. Hartford [1839?] 17 p. Ct. 56177

Hartford and Springfield Railroad Corporation. An act to incorporate the Hartford and

Springfield Railroad Corporation [Boston: 1839] CtY. 56178

----. Report of the engineer to the committee of surveys of the Hartford and Springfield Railroad. New Haven: Hitchcock and Stafford, printers, 1839. 24 p. CtY; CU; DBRE; NN; NNE. 56179

Hartford Young Men's Institute. First annual report of the executive committee...Hartford, June 4, 1839, together with the charter, bylaws.... Hartford: printed by Case, Tiffany and Burnham, 1839. 14 p. WU. 56180

Harvard University. Arrangemment of lectures and recitations in Harvard University.... Cambridge: Folson, Wells and Thurston, printers, 1839-1840. 3 pamphlets. M. 56181

----. A catalogue of the officers and students of Harvard University, for the academical year 1839-1840. Cambridge: Folsom, Wells and Thurston, printers to the University, 1839. 36 p. KHi; MoSU; MS. 56182

----. Catalogus eorum qui alicujus gradus laurea donati sunt. Cambridge: 1839. MWA. 56183

----. Catalogus senatus academici, et eorum qui munera et officia gesserunt, quique alicujus gadus laurea donati sunt in Universitate Harvardiana, Cantabrigiae, in Republica Massachusettensi. Cantabrigiae: Typis Folsom, Wells, et Thurston, academiae typographorum [1839] 81, 31 p. MiD-B; MNDedf. 56184

----. Order of exercises for commencement, August 28, 1839 [Cantabrigiae: Typis Folsom, Wells et Thurston, 1839] MdBJ; Nh. 56185

----. Order of performances for exhibition, May 7, 1839. Cambridge: Folsom, Wells and Thurston, printers to the University, 1839. 3 p. MdBJ. 56186

----. Order of performances for exhibition, July 17, 1839. Cambridge: Folsom, Wells and Thurston, printers to the University, 1839. 3 p. MdBJ. 56187

----. Law School. A catalogue of the students of law at Harvard University, from the establishment of the law school to the end of the spring term in the year 1839. Cambridge: 1839. 37 p. MHi. 56188

----. Phi Beta Kappa Alpha. Catalogue of the

fraternity. Cambridge: 1839-1861. MiU; NBLIHI; OCHP. 56189

----. Pierian Sodality. Catalogue of the honorary and immediate members of the Pierian sodality...instituted 1808. Cambridge: Metcalf, Torry and Ballou, 1839. 15 p. M; MBAt; MH. 56190

----. Porcellian Club. Cataloge of the honorary and immediate members and of the library of the Porcelliam club of Harvard University. Instituted 1791. Boston: J. H. Eastburn, printer, 1839. 95 p. DLC; OClWHi. 56191

Haskins, Roswell Wilson, 1796-1870. History and progress of phrenology [Read before the Western Phrenological Society, at Buffalo]...Buffalo: Steete and Peck, New York: Wiley and Putnam, 1839. 217 p. DLC; ICN; MWA; PPCP; VtU. 56192

Hastings, Thomas, 1784-1872. The Christian psalmist; or Watt's psalms and hymns, with copious selections from other sources. The whole carefully revised and arranged, with directions for musical expression. New York: D. Fanshaw, 1839. 626 p. IaCrM; MWA; NBuG; OO; PPL. 56193

----. Elements of vocal music arranged as a brief text book for classes. New York: Ezra Collier and Company, 1839. 36 p. ICN; LNH; NN; NNUT; RPB. 56194

----. The Manhattan collection of psalm and hymn tunes and anthems, compiled and composed under the special patronage of the New York Academy of Sacred Music.... New York: E. Collier, 1839. 352 p. DLC; MH; MH-AH. 56195

----. ----. New York: Fanshaw, 1839. 352 p. CtMW; ICN; MH; MH-AH; OMC. 56196

----. The mother's hymn book, compiled from various authors...for the use of maternal associations.... New York: Ezra Collier, 1839. 192 p. N; RPB. 56197

----. Spiritual songs for social worship. Thomas Hastings and Lowell Mason arrangers. 6th edition. Utica: printed by Gardiner Tracy, etc., etc., etc., 1839. 328 p. MBC; NNUT; NUtHi; RPB. 56198

Haven, John. A discourse delivered at the reopening and dedication of the meeting house of the First Congregational Parish in York, Maine. Portsmouth: printed by C. W. Brewster, 1839. 16 p. ICN; MB; MBC; MeBa. 56199

Haven, Kittridge. The world reprieved; being a critical examination of William Millers theory that the second coming of Christ and the destruction of the world will take place about 1843 A. D. Woodstock, Vermont: 1839. 48 p. CtHT; DLC. 56200.

Haverford College. Report of the managers of Haverford School Association. Read at the annual meeting, fifth month 8th, 1839. Philadelphia: Brown, Bicking and Guilbert, printer, 1839. 36 p. MB; PPM. 56201

Hauff, Wilhelm, 1802- 1827. Die Bettlerin vom pont des arts. Erzaehlung von Wilhelm Hauff. New York: Verlag der Buchhandlung von W. Radde, 1839. 191 p. MoS; PU; TNJU. 56202

Hawes, Joel, 1789-1867. Lectures to young men...addressed to the young men of Hartford and New Haven.... With additional lecture on reading.... 13th edition. Hartford: 1839. CtY; InCW; MWHi. 56203

----. Memoir of Normand Smith; or the Christian serving God in his business. New York: The American Tract Society, 1839? 72 p. CtHT; ICBB; MiU; NNC; Wa. 56204

----. ----. Hartford: Spalding and Storrs, 1839. 77 p. CtY; DLC; MiU; NjNbT; OO. 56205

[Hawks, Francis Lister] 1798-1866. The American forest; or Uncle Philip's conversations with the children about the trees of America. New York: Harper and Brothers, 1839. 250 p. AMaJ; MPiB; NGlc; TxU-T. 56206

----. Contributions to the ecclesiastical history of the United States. New York: John S. Taylor, 1839. 2 v. DLC; MdBD; NBuDD; TSewU; WHi. 56207

----. The early history of the southern states: Virginia, North and South Carolina and Georgia. Illustrated by tales, sketches and anecdotes, with numerous engravings. By Lambert Lily, schoolmaster [pseud.] Boston: Ticknor, 1839. 192 p. CtMW; MoK; NbU; NN; Vi. 56208

----. The history of New England... By Lambert Lilly, schoolmaster. Boston: William D. Ticknor, 1839. 184 p. MBB; MiD- B; RPB. 56209

----. The history of the middle states; illustrated by tales, sketches and anecdotes...by lambert Lilly, Schoolmaster [pseud.] Boston: W. D. Ticknor, 1839. 156 p. IC; NN; PHi. 56210

----. History of the United States: No. 1. or Uncle Philip's conversations with the children about Virginia. New York: Harper and Brothers, 1839. 232 p. NcAs; OClWHi; OO; ScDuE; Vi. 56211

----. [A narrative of events connected with the rise and progress of the Protestant Episcopal Church in Maryland] New York: J. Taylor, 1839. 523 p. MdBS; MWA; NcAs; NN; OMC. 56212

----. The story of the American revolution, illustrated by tales, sketches and anecdotes. By Lambert Lilly, schoolmaster [pseud.] Boston: Ticknor, 1839. 204 p. NcU; ViRU. 56213

----. Uncle Philip's conversations with the children about the whale fishery and polar seas.... New York: Harper and Brothers, 1839. 2 v. CtY; MH; NcA-S; RWoH; ScDuE. 56214

Hawley, Silas. A declaration of sentiments...to the Christian Union Convention, held in Syracuse, August 21, 1838.... Cazenovia: printed at the Union Herald office, 1839. 16 p. MWA; N; NIC. 56215

----. ----. 2nd edition. Cazenovia: 1839. 16 p. MHi. 56216

Hawthorne, Nathaniel, 1804-1864. The gentle boy: a thrice told tale; with an original illustration. Boston: Weeks, Jordan and Company, New York and London: Wiley and Putnam, 1839. 20 p. CSmH; DLC; IU; MBAt; NN. 56217

----. The sister years, being the carrier's address to the patrons of the Salem Gazette, for the January 1, 1839. Salem: 1839. 8 p. CSmH; MH; MoSW; NBuU; WHi. 56218

Hayden, Lucian. A vindication of the doctrine of election, in a sermon, delivered in the Franklin Street Baptist Meeting House, Dover: printed at the Gazette office, 1839. 23 p. MBNEH; MNtCA; NHC-S. 56219

Haydn, Joseph, 1732-1809. Seasons [from the German copy] Boston: Wilkins and Carter, and Jenks and Palmer, 1839. 48 p. DLC; IdU; MiD; MiU. 56220

----. ----. Philadelphia: 1839. 16 p. CtY. 56221

----. Words of the Seasons, a sacred oratorio, as performed by the Musical Fund Society of Philadelphia. Printed for the Musical Fund Society, 1839. 16 p. CtY; PHi; WHi. 56222

Hayward, George, 1791-1863. Remarks on some of the medical springs of Virginia, before the Society of Medical Improvement, September 23, 1839. Boston: D. Clapp, Jr., 1839. 11 p. DSG; MBAt; NN; NNNAM; RPB. 56223

Hayward, John, 1781-1862. The New England gazetteer, containing descriptions of all the states, counties and towns in New England: also descriptions of the principal mountains, rivers, lakes.... Boston: J. Hayward, Concord, N. H.: Boyd and White, 1839. 508 p. DLC; KyU; MH; NcD; PPGi. 56224

----. ----. 2nd edition. Concord, N. H.: Israel S. Boyd and William White, Boston: John Hayward, 1839. 508 p. CoCsC; MWA; NhRo; RWe; WHi. 56225

----. ----. 3rd edition. Concord, N. H.: Israel S. Boyd and William White, Boston: John Hayward, 1839. 504 p. MnSM; NIC; OClW; PPGi; RNR. 56226

----. ----. 4th edition. Concord, N. H.: printed by Israel S. Boyd and William White, Boston: John Hayward, 1839. 500 p. ICN; KCha; MBC; MeLew-B; Nh. 56227

----. ----. 5th edition. Concord, N. H.: Israel S. Boyd and William White, 1839. DLC; IEG; MnSM; MSo, VtMidSM. 56228

----. ----. 6th edition. Concord, N. H.: Israel S. Boyd and William White, Boston: John Hayward, 1839 [512] p. CtY; MeHi; Nh; OClWHi; PU. 56229

----. ----. 7th edition. Concord, N. H.: Israel S. Boyd and William White, Boston: John Hayward, 1839. Ct; MiU; PU; RBA; TN. 56230

----. ----. 8th edition. Concord, N. H.: Israel S. Boyd and William White, Boston: John Hayward,

1839. KTW; MHi; MWA; OClWHi; PHi. 56231

----. ----. 9th edition. Concord, N. H.: Israel S. Boyd and William White, 1839. 326 p. DLC; IaDaM; MeBa; M. 56232

----. ----. 10th edition. Concord, N. H.: Israel S. Boyd and William White, Boston: John Hayward, 1839. 56233

----. ----. 11th edition. Concord, N. H.: Israel S. Boyd and William White, Boston: John Hayward, 1839. 56234

----. ----. 13th edition. Concord, N. H.: I. S. Boyd and William White, Boston: J. Hayward, 1839 [512] p. KHi; MH; MiD; MSha; NbCrD. 56235

Hazen, Edward. The panorama of professions and trades; or every mans book. Philadelphia: Uriah Hunt, 1839. 320 p. MdBE; NjR; MPStA; ODaU; PP. 56236

----. The speller and definer; or class book, No. 2. designed to answer the purpose of a spelling book, and to supercede the necessity of the use of a dictionary as a class book. Philadelphia: Uriah Hunt, 1839. CtY; In; MB; NHem. 56237

----. The symbolical spelling book: in two parts.... Philadelphia: W. W. Walker, 1839. 2 v. DLC; MdBE; NbU. 56238

Heacock, Reuben B. An exposition of some of the frauds practiced upon the indians during the treaties with them in 1837, 38, 39.... Buffalo: printed by Day and Steele. 48 p. PHi. 56239

Hearley, J. F. The Adirondacks; or life in the woods. New York: 1839. NIC. 56240

Hearn, John. Guide to Salisbury and its vicinity. Salisbury: 1839. MBAt. 56241

[Heath, James Ewell] Whigs and Democrats; or love of no politics. A comedy in three acts.... Richmond: T. W. White, 1839. 80 p. MB; PPL; RPB; TxU; Vi. 56242

Heath, James P. 1777-1854. Reply...to a pamphlet...by H. May...relative to an intended duel between J. A. Young and J. H. Sothoron [Baltimore? 1839] DLC. 56243

Hedge, Frederic Henry, 1805-1890. Owe no man

anymore." A sermon preached at the Union Street Church, November 8th, 1839.... Bangor: printed by Edwards and Smith, 1839. 12 p. DLC; MBC; MeBat. 56244

Hedge, Levi, 1766-1844. Elements of logick; or a summary of the general principles and different modes of reasoning.... Boston: Hilliard, Gray and Company, 1839. 178 p. CtHC; ICU; MB. 56245

Heidelberg Catechism. The Heidelburg catechism: or method of instruction in the christian religion. New York: Scofield, 1839. 90 p. PPPrHi. 56246

----. ----. Philadelphia: Mentz and Son, 1839. 71 p. NIC. 56247

Helffenstein, Johann Conrad Albertus, 1748-1790. Eine Sammlung auserlesener predigten des ehrw. J. C. Albert Helffenstein, ehemaligen predigers zu Germantown, Pa., Harrisburg: Gedruckt und zu haben bei I. Weinbrenner,...1839, 290 p. PRHi; PPLT; PPeSchw; PReaHi. 56248

Heinarich, Anton Philipp, 1781-1861. L'esprit et la boute.... New York: David and Horn, 1839. MB. 56249

Hemans, Felicia Dorothea [Browne] 1793-1835. The political works of Mrs. Felicia Hemans; complete in one volume. New edition with a critical preface, and a biographical memoir. Philadelphia: Grigg and Elliott, 1839. 479 p. ArBaA; LNB; OCM; TMeT; ViU. 56250

----. ----. Philadelphia: H. F. Anners, 1839. 2 v. in 1. CtY; KHi; MnU; OCl; WU. 56251

Henley, Robert Henley Eden, 1789-1841. A treatise on the law of injunctions. 2nd American edition from the last London edition: to which is added copious notes and references to all the decisions of the courts of the United States.... New York: Gould, Banks and Company, Albany: W. and A. Gould and Company, 1839. 503 p. CU; LNB; MdBB; NcD; PP. 56252

Henry, Caleb Sprague, 1804-1884. Compendium of Christian antiquities. Philadelphia: Whetham, 1839. OMC. 56253

----. The importance of exalting the intellectual spirit of the nation: and need of a learned class. A discourse pronounced before the Phi Sigma Nu

Society of the University of Vermont, August 3, 1836. 2nd edition. New York: George W. Holley, 1839. 44 p. P. 56254

----. Moral and philosophical essays. Andover: Gould, Newman and Saxton, 1839. 135 p. NNG; OCIJC; OO; OSW. 56255

----. ----. New York: E. French, 1839. 135 p. CBCDS; GDecCT; MWiW; PPiW. 56256

Henry Joseph. A statement of facts respecting the condition and treatment of slaves, in the city of Vicksburgh and its vicinity, in the state of Mississippi, in 1838 and 1839. Medina, Ohio: 1839. 24 p. DLC; OFH. 56257

Henry, Joseph, 1797-1878. Contributions to electricity and magnetism.... Philadelphia: printed by James Kay, Jun. and Brother, 1839 [13]-51 p. MdAN; NIC; NjP; NN; NNe. 56258

Henshaw, David, 1791-1852. Letters from David Henshaw to the Boston Morning Post, on the Western Railroad, and the greatly beneficial effects of internal improvement. Boston: Beals and Greene, 1839. 16 p. CSt; M; MHi; MMeT; MNBedf. 56259

----. Letters on the internal improvements and commerce of the West.... Boston: Dutton and Wentworth, printers, 1839. 29 p. ICJ; MWA; PPAmP; RPB; VtU. 56260

Hentz Nicholas Marcellus, 1797-1856. A classical French reader...preceded by an introduction...and attended with notes.... Compiled for the use of the Round Hill School, etc. Philadelphia: 1839. MB. 56261

Hero of Tippecanoe. v. 1. [No. 1-9] Elizabethtown: 1839-1840. MB. 56262

Herodotus. Herodotus. By Rev. William Beloe. New York: Harper and Brothers, 1839. 3 v. CU; MeBaT; NNF; OCY; PAtM. 56263

----. Herodotus, translated from the Greek, with notes and life of the author. By the Rev. William Beloe. A new edition, corrected and revised. Philadelphia: 489 p. CtHC; GAuY; NNF; PCC; ViU. 56264

Herron, Francis, 1774-1860. An address delivered in the First Presbyterian Church, on the sabbath evening of January 27, 1839. to the young men of the city of Pittsburgh.... Pittsburgh: E. B. Fisher and Company, printers, 1839. 10 p. CSmH; NjR; OClWHi. 56265

Herschel, John Frederick William, 1792-1871. A preliminary discourse on the study of natural philosophy. New edition. Philadelphia: Lea and Blanchard, 1839. 279 p. ICU; MH; NcWfc; PV. 56266

----. Treatise on astronomy. By Sir F. W. Herschel...new edition, with a preface, and a series of questions for the examination of students, by S. C. Walker. Philadelphia: Lea and Blanchard, 1839. 417 p. IEN; LNP; MB; PAtM; NjP; ViU. 56267

Hersey, John, 1786-1862. Advice to Christian parents. Baltimore: Armstrong and Berry, 1839. 124 p. ICBB; MdHi; PU. 56268

----. The importance of small things; or a plain course of self- examination to which is added, signs of the times. Baltimore: Armstrong and Berry, 1839. 299 p. ICBB; MdHi. 56269

----. Inquiry into the character and condition of our children, and their claim to a participation in the privileges and blessings of the Redeemer's kingdom on earth, examined and established; also, some remarks on the mode of administering the ordinace of Baptism. Raleigh: Lemay, 1839. 36 p. ICBB; MdHi. 56270

----. Works. By John Hersey. Baltimore: 1839-1840. 4 v. in 1. NjPT. 56271

Herttell, Thomas, 1771-1849. Remarks comprising in substance Judge Herttells argument in the House of Assembly of the state of New York, in the session of 1837, in support of the bill to restore to married women, the right of property. By the constitution of this state. New York: Henry Durell, 1839. 83 p. IU; MH; NjR; OMC; PPi. 56272

Hetherington, William Maxwell, 1803-1865. The minister's family, by a country minister. New York: Robert Carter, 1839. ICBB; MWiW; NcCJ; PPiW; RLa. 56273

Hewit, Nathaniel, 1788-1867. The moral law; the essential element of American liberty. The substance of a lecture, to the Bridgeport lyceum, read

April 1839, 1839.... Bridgeport: 1839. CtHC; CtY; MBAt; NIC; NjPT. 56274

----. The wine question.... [Bridgeport, Conn.: 1839] 16 p. CtY; MBAt. 56275

Hewson, John, b. 1768? Doctrine of the new birth, exemplified in the life and religious experience of Onesimus, 1779-1793. Philadelphia: William F. Rackliff, 1839. 164 p. DLC; PHi; PPL; PPPrHi. 56276

Hickman, Nathaniel. The citizen soldiers at North Point and Fort M'Henry, September 12, and 13, 1814. Baltimore: 1839. 96 p. MHi. 56277

Hickok, J. H. Evangelical musick: or the sacred minstrel and sacred harp united.... Philadelphia: J. Whetham, New York: D. Appleton and Company, 1839. 312 p. NNUT. 56278

Higgins, William Mullinger. The earth; its physical condition and most remarkable phenomena. New York: Harper and Brothers, 1839. 408 p. AMaJ; LNL; OUrC; NcU; TxGR. 56279

Hildreth, Hosea, 1782-1835. A book for New Hampshire children in familiar letters from a father. 4th edition, revised and enlarged. Exeter: F. Grant, 1839. DLC; Nh; NhM; NN. 56280

----. ----. 5th edition, revised and enlarged. Exeter: F. Grant, 1839. 116 p. MH; NhD; RPB. 56281

[Hildreth, Richard] 1807-1865. Memoirs of Archy Moore. See his "The slave..."
----. My connection with the atlas newspapers; including a sketch of the history of the Armory Hall Party of 1838.... Boston: Whipple and Damrell, 1839. 24 p. MB; MBAt; MHi; NPV. 56282

----. The people's presidential candidate; or the life of William Henry Harrison, of Ohio. Boston: Weeks, Jordan and Company, 1839. 211 p. MB; MWA: Nh-Hi; OCHP; PPA. 56283

----. The slave; or memoirs of Archy Moore...[anon.] 2nd edition. Boston: Munroe and Company, 1839. 2 v. in 1. MB; OCHP. 56284

Hildreth, Samuel Prescott. Address of S. P. Hildreth, president of the third medical convention of Ohio, delivered at Cleveland, May 14, 1839. Cleveland: Penniman and Bemis, 1839. 33 p. DSG; KyLxT; MB; MH; OClWHi. 56285

Hill, Alnozo, 1800-1871. Life and charachter of the Rev. Aaron Bancroft. By Alonzo Hill, pastor of the Second Congregational Church in Worcester. Printed for the American Unitarian Association. Boston: James Munroe and Company, 1839. 30 p. IaK; MBC; MWA; PPAmP; RPB. 56286

----. ----. Worcester: Butterfield, 1839. 40 p. CtHC; ICU; MdBJ; MWA; PHI. 56287

Hill, Benjamin M. The moral responsibility of civil rulers: a sermon.... 2nd edition. New Haven: printed by Baldwin and Treadway, 1839. DLC. 56288

Hill, George, 1796-1871. The ruins of Athens; Titania's banquet, a mask; and other poems. Boston: Otis, Broaders and Company, 1839. 160 p. CSmH; MH; PP; RPB; TxU. 56289

Hill, J. B. Tennessee, Alabama, Mississippi and Arkansas almanac and state register, for the year of our Lord, 1840.... Fayetteville, Ten... E. Hill, Hernando, Mississippi: J. B. Hill, 1839 [30] p. MH; T. 56290

Hill, William, 1769-1852. A history of the rise, progress, genius and character of American Presbyterianism.... Washington City: J. Gideon, Jr., 1839. 224 p. CSf; ICT; NbO; PPM; ViRU. 56291

Hillhouse, James Abraham, 1789-1841. Dramas, discourses and other pieces.... Boston: C. C. Little and J. Brown, 1839. 2 v. CU; IaGG; MB; PPA; TxU. 56292

Hilliard, Henry Washington, 1808-1892. Remarks...on the sub- treasury resolutions. Introduced by Mr. Smith of Madison, in the House of Representatives of Alabama, at its session, December, 1838. Tuscaloosa: printed by M. D. J. Slade, 1839. 40 p. 56293

Hillyer, Giles M. Address delivered at the third anniversary celebration of the Alpha Delta Phi Soceity of Miami University, on the triumphs of mind. Cincinnati: L'Hommedieu and Company, printers, 1839. 30 p. ICU; MWA; NN; OCHP; OHi. 56294

Das himmlishe veryneugen in Gott. Allentown, Pa.: Brobst and Blumer, 1839. PPeSchw. 56295

Hinds, John. Veterinary surgeon; or farriery taught on a new and easy plan with additions.... By J. M. Smith. Philadelphia: 1839. RPAt. 56296

Hints and sketches by an American mother. New York: John S. Taylor, 1839. 151 p. ICN; MB; MPeaI; NjR; NNUT. 56297

Historical account of the circumnavigation of the globe, and of the progress of discovery in the Pacific Ocean, from the voyage of Magellan to the death of Cook. New York: Harper, 1839. 366 p. DLC; OO; ScDuE; TxGR; WHi. 56298

An historical...account of the Island of Candia.... Richmond: press of Thomas W. White, 1839. 12 p. RP. 56299

Historical and Philosophical Society of Ohio. Journal. See Cincinnati Historical Society. Transactions.

The historical register of the United States. From the declaration of war in 1812 to January 1, 1814. Edited by T. H. Palmer. 2nd edition. Philadelphia: G. Palmer, 1839. 351 p. MsJPED. 56300

The history of Jesus. New York: T. Mason and G. Lane, 1839. 80 p. ScCliTO. 56301

History of Joseph, in Sioux. See Pond, Samuel William.

History of Madagascar; embracing the progress of the Christian Mission and an account of the persecution of the native Christians...Prepared for the American Sunday School Union and revised by the committee of publication. Philadelphia: American Sunday School Union [1839] 342 p. CtMW; IaPeC; MoS; PU; WaS. 56302

A history of my father's dog Towzer. Providence: George P. Daniels, 1839. OCl. 56303

History of Robert Fowle. A story for the young. Boston: D. H. Ela, printer, 1839. 36 p. MB. 56304

History of the Bible. Cooperstown: printed by H. and E. Phinney, 1839. 192 p. MB; MH; MWA; OClWHi; WHi. 56305

History of the Federal and Democratic parties in the United States from their origin to the present time. Terre Houte: G. A. and J. P. Chapman, 1839. InU. 56306

A history of the New York Kappa Lambda Conspiracy.... New York: W. Stuart, 1839. 32 p. DLC; MH; MiD-B; NjR; NNC. 56307

The history of the pilgrims, or a grandfather's story of the first settlers of Massachusetts. 3rd edition. Boston: Sabbath School Union, 1839. 151 p. MHi; RPB. 56308

History of the Pirates. Hartford: Strong, 1839. OMC. 56309

A history of the "striped pig".... 4th edition. Boston: Whipple and Damrell, 1839. 72 p. M; OCHP; OrU; ViU. 56310

History of Tom Truant. Hamilton: N. and T. King, 1839. 8 p. NUt. 56311

Hitchcock, Edward, 1793-1864. Introductory essay and sermon on lessons taught by sickness in a wreath for the tomb. Amherst: 1839. MDeeP. 56312

----. A wreath for the tomb, or extracts from eminent writers on death and eternity.... Amherst: J. S. And C. Adams, 1839. 250 p. DLC; IEG; MBC; MeLew; MNan. 56313

Hobart, Aaron, 1787-1858. An historical sketch of Abington, Plymouth County, Massachusetts.... Boston: printed by Samuel N. Dickinson, 1839. 176 p. CoD; MWA; NNUT; PHi; RPB. 56314

Hobart, John Henry, 1775-1830. Christian's manual; or faith and devotion, containing dialogues and prayers suited to the various exercises of the christian life.... 5th edition. New York: Swords, Stanford and Company, 1839. 442 p. PPM. 56315

Hobart College, Geneva, New York. A catalogue of the officers and students of Geneva College for the academical year, 1838-1839. 23 p. MBC; MH; NGH; NIDHi. 56316

Der hoch-Deutsche Amerikansiche calender auf das jahr 1840. Philadelphia: Gedruckt und zu haben bey William W. Walker, 1839. 34 p. PReaHi. 56317

Hoch-Deutsche Germantaun calender for 1840. By Carl F. Egelmann. Philadelphia: Wm. W. Walker [1839] MWA; PPG. 56318

Hoch Deutschen Reformirten Kirche. Verhandlungen einer allgemeinen wie auch einer speciellen synode der Hochdeutschen Reformirten Kirche in den Vereinigten Staaten. Gehalten zu Philadelphia, vom 28sten September, bis zum 7ten October, 1839. Gettysburg, Pa.: H. C. Neinstedt, Drucker, 1839. 92 p. MdBSHG, MoWgT; PLERC-Hi. 56319

Hodge, Charles, 1797-1878. The constitutional history of the Presbyterian Church in the United States of America. Philadelphia: W. S. Martien, 1839 -[1840] 2 v. ArCH; CU; IaB; MWA; TxU. 56320

Hodge, Hugh Lenox, 1796-1873. An introductory lecture to the course on obstetrics, and diseases of women and children, delivered in the University of Pennsylvania, November 6, 1839. Philadelphia: printed by Lydia R. Bailey, 1839. 20 p. DSG; KyDC; NBuU-M; NNNAM; PHi. 56321

----. Foeticide, or criminal abortion; a lecture. Philadelphia: Lindsay and Blakinton, 1839. 44 p. DSG. 56322

Hodgson, Francis, 1805-1877. An examination of the system of new divinity, or new school of theology.... New York: T. Mason and G. Lane, 1839. 416 p. CSansS; MBC; OO; PPPrHi; TxDaM. 56323

Hoffman, David, 1784-1854. A peep into my note book. By the author of A. Grumbler's miscellaneous thoughts, etc. New York [Baltimore: John D. Toy, printer] 1839. 355 p. MdBP; MdHi; NN. 56324

Hoffmann, Ernst Theodor Amadeus, 1776-1822. Spieler Glueck. Erzachlung von E. T. A. Hoffmann. New York: Verlag der Buchhandlung von W. Radde, 1839. 32 p. CtMW; NN; PPeSchW; TNJU. 56325

Hofland, Barbara Wreaks Hoole, 1770-1844. The history of a merchants widow, and her young family. New York: W. E. Dean, 1839. 179 p. NN. 56326

----. The son of a genius.... New York: Harper and Brothers, 1839. 213 p. DLC; NNU-W; ScDuE. 56327

Holden, Horace, b. 1810. A narrative of the shipwreck, captivity, and sufferings of H. Holden and B. H. Nute, who were cast away in the

American ship Mentor on the Pelew Islands, 1832; and for two years afterwards were subjected to unheard of sufferings among the inhabitants of Lord North's Island. 4th edition. Boston: 1839. 133 p. CtHWatk; MSap; Nh-Hi. 56328

Holdich, Joseph, 1804-1893. Questions on the historical parts of the Old Testament for the use of Bible classes. New York: T. Mason and G. Lane, 1839. GEU; KyBgW; MoSpD. 56329

----. True greatness; a discourse on the character of Rev. Wilbur Fisk...delivered April 3, 1839. Middletown, Conn.: E. Hunt and Company, 1839. CtY; DLC; IEG; MiU; NjP. 56330

----. The Wesleyan student; or memoirs of Aaron Haynes Hurd.... Middletown: E. Hunt and Company, 1839. 281 p. DLC; IEG; MeB; NjMD; OClW. 56331

Holiday stories. Juvenile. Boston: 1839. 178 p. DLC; MWA. 56332

----. New York: S. Colman, 1839. 178 p. N. 56333

Holland, Henry, 1788-1873. Medical notes and reflections.... Philadelphia: Haswell, Barrington, and Haswell, New Orleans: John J. Haswell, and Company, 1839. 383 [36] p. ArU-M; CU-M; KyLxT; MB; PPA. 56334

Holley, George W. An oration, delivered on July 4, at Chicago [Chicago] printed at the Chicago American office, 1839. 12 p. MBC. 56335

Holloway, John. Bigelow's quick step...arranged for the piano forte by John Halloway. Boston: Henry Prentiss, 1839. 3 p. MB; MNF. 56336

Holmes, Ezekiel, 1801-1865. Report of an explaoration and survey of the territory on the Aroostock River, during the spring and autumn of 1838. Augusta: Smith and Robinson, 1839. 78 p. MB; NhD; OCHP; PPI; Vi. 56337

Holt, E. An appeal to the Presbyterian and Congregational Churches of New Hampshire, in behalf of the widows and orphan children of ministers. Portsmouth: C. W. Brewster, printer, 1839. 8 p. MBC; MWA. 56338

Homergue, John D. The sild culturist's manual: or a popular treatise on the planting and cultivation of mulberry trees, the rearing and propaga-
tion of silk worms, and the preparation of the raw material for exploration: addressed to the farmers and planters of the United States. Philadelphia: Hogan and Thompson, 1839. 406 p. IU; GHi; MiD; KMK; PPA. 56339

Homerous. The Illiad of Homer, from the text of Wolf. With English notes. By C. C. Felton. Stereotype edition. Bosotn: Hilliard, Gray and Company, 1839. 476 p. CoGr; ICU; OO; ViU; WU. 56340

----. ----. With notes for use of schools and colleges. By John J. Owens. New York: Leavitt and Allen, 1839. 740 p. IaHA. 56341

----. ----. Translated by Alexander Pope.... Philadelphia: R. W. Pomeroy, 1839. 2 v. InStmaS; MB; NSsA; ViRVal. 56342

Honest John, the sunday scholar. Northampton: John Metcalf, 1839. 24 p. CtY; ICBB; NNC. 56343

Honour, John H. Questions and answers, explanatory of the government of the Methodist Episcopal Church; interspersed with questions and answers explanatory of the government of the Methodist Protestand Church. Baltimore: Methodist Episcopal Church, 1839. 32 p. MdBS. 56344

Hood, Thomas, 1799-1845. Dream of Eugene Aram. Philadelphia: 1839. MB. 56345

----. National tales. Philadelphia: T. K. and P. G. Collins, 1839. 208 p. MH; NNS. 56346

----. Up the Rhine. Philadelphia: Porter and Coates [1839?] 339 p. ArAD; IaPeC; KyBC; PEdf; WyC. 56347

Hook, Theodore Edward, 1788-1841. Births, deaths, and marriages. By the author of "Sayings and doings", Philadelphia: Lea and Blanchard, 1839. 2 v. CtY; DLC; MiD-B; NNS; RP. 56348

----. Gurney married; a sequel to Gilbert Gurney. Philadelphia: Lea and Blanchard, 1839. 56349

----. Pascal Bruno; Sicilian story, to which is appended the atonement, a story by Theodore Hook. Philadlephia: Lea and Blanchard, 1839. 223 p. GAuY; MeB; NjHo. 56350

Hook, Walter Farquhar, 1798-1875. A book of

family prayer: compiled by...Walter Farquhar Hook.... Philadlephia: Hooker and Claxton, 1839. 106 p. MB; MH; NNG. 56351

----. A call to union on the principles of the English reformation; a sermon preached at the primary visitation of Charles Thomas, Lord Bishop of Ripan.... 4th edition. New York: R. Dawes, 1839. InU; MB; PPL; NBuDD; WNaE. 56352

----. "Who are the Catholics?' Answered in an account of the Protestant Episcopal Church in England.Extracted from a sermon preached before the Queen. New York: Protestant Episcopal Tract Society, 1839. 8 p. DLC; IEG; InID; KyLoF. 56353

Hooker, Edward William, 1794-1875. Divine discipline of the ministry; an address, delivered before the Society of Inquiry, in the Theological Institute East Windsor Hill, Connecticut, August 5, 1839. Hartford: E. Geer, 1839. 20 p. CtY; IaGG; MBC; NbCrD; NjR. 56354

----. Memoir of Mrs. Sarah Lanman Smith, late of the mission in Syria.... Boston; Perkins and Marvin, 1839. 407 p. CtMW; IaB; MWA; PWW; TxH. 56355

----. Sacred music in religious worship; an address delivered before the society of sacred music in the Theological Seminary of East Windsor, August 6, 1839. New York: Trow, 1839. 23 p. CtHC; MBC; NIC; OC; TxU. 56356

Hooker, Harace. The farmer's own book of intellectual and moral improvement. New York: Gould, Newman and Saxton, 1839. 180 p. CtHWatk, KMK; MB; NICLA; PMA. 56357

Hooper, Edward James, 1803-1892. The practical farmer, gardener and housewife; or dictionary of agriculture, horticulture, and domestic economy: including descriptions of the most improved kinds of live stock, their proper treatment, diseases.... Cincinnati: Geo. Conclin, 1839. 544 p. ICU; LU; OCHP; OClWHi. 56358

Hooper, Robert, 1792-1876. Lexicon medicum; or medical dictionary; containing an explanation of the terms in anatomy, botany, chemistry, etc., etc., 13th American edition. New York: Harper and Brothers, 1839. 2 v. ICU-R; MNF; NbOM; PU; VtU. 56359

Hopkins, Albet, 1807-1872. A sermon delivered at Williamstown, Massachusetts, on the annual state fast.... Troy, N. Y.: Stevenson and M'Call, printers, 1839. 21 p. ICMe; MB; NjR; OCl; PPPr-Hi. 56360

Hopkins, John Henry, 1792-1868. Twelve conquets; written, composed and arranged by John Hopkins for the use of the Vermont Episcopal Institute. New York: Firth and Hall, 1839. 31 p. NN. 56361

Hopkins, Mark, 1802-1887. A sermon delivered before his excellency Edward Everett, Governor...and the legislature of Massachusetts on election, January 2, 1839.... Boston: Dutton and Wentworth, printers, 1839. 40 p. CtHC; InID; MWA; NjR; PPL. 56362

Hopkins, Samuel. The curse upon the ground, a blessing. A sermon preached upon the day of public thanksgiving, November 29, 1838.... Saco, Maine: S. L. Goodale, 1839. 15 p. ICN; MBC; MiD-B; NjPT; RPB. 56363

----. "Fret not thyself because of evil doers." A sermon preached on Fast Day, April 18, 1839. By the pastor of the First Congregational Church in Saco, Maine. Saco: S. L. Goodale, 1839. 14 p. CBPSR; MBC; MiD-B; RPB. 56364

Horace Vernon: or fashionable life.... Philadelphia: Lea and Blanchard, 1839. 2 v. DLC; MH; NPV. 56365

Horatius Flaccus, Quintus. Opera. Accedunt calvis metrica et notae Anglicae, Juventuti accommodatae, Cuba B. A. Gould. Bostoniae: Sumptibus Hilliard, Gray et Societe, 1839. CBPSR; IaU; NbU; PHi. 56366

----. Opera; interpretatione et notis illustravit L. Desprez. Editio 5 in America stereotypis impresia, cum novissima parisiensi diligenter collata, caeterisque hactenus editis longe emendatior. Huic editioni acceserunt vila Horatii cum Daceui notis. Philadelphia: J. Allen, 1839. 559 p. DLC; InU; MdU. PSC; PHi. 56367

----. The works of Horace, with English notes, critical and explanatory. By Charles Anthon. A new edition with corrections and improvements. New York: Harper and Brothers, 1839. 681 p. CSto; CoDR; LNP; MMel; ViL. 56368

Horn, Charles Edward, 1786-1849. God is everywhere. A sacred song. The words by Campbell. The music newly arranged for the piano forte. New York: Davis and Horn, 1839. 5 p. NN. 56369

----. Six popular songs [With accompaniment for piano forte] New York: Davis and Horn, 1839. MB. 56370

Horne, Thomas Hartwell. An introduction to the critical study and knowledge of the Holy Scriptures. New edition from the 7th London edition, corrected and enlarged. Philadelphia: Thomas, 1839. 2 v. GMM; NNC; OkU; ScCC; VtU. 56371

Horner, Gustavus R. B. Medical and topographical observations upon the Mediterranean; and upon Portugal, Spain and other countries.... Philadelphia: Haswell, Barrington, and Haswell, 1839. 212 p. CSt-L; MB; NjR; PPA; ViU. 56372

Horner, William Edmonds, 1793-1853. A treatise on pathological anatomy. Philadelphia: Lea and Carey, 1839. MBCo; PPiAM. 56373.

----. A treatise on special and general anatomy. 5th edition, revised. Philadelphia: Lea and Blanchard, 1839. 2 v. KyLoJM; MdBM; PPC; WaSK. 56374

Hornyhold, John Joseph, 1706-1778. The commandments and sacraments explained. In 52 discourses. By the Rt. Rev. Dr. Hornyhold, author of the real principles of Catholics. Baltimore: Lucas Brothers, 1839. 560 p. LNL. 56375

Horton, James P. A narrative of the early life, remarkable conversion and spiritual labours of James P. Horton, who has been a member of the Methodist Episcopal Church upward of 40 years [New York] printed for the author, 1839. DLC; NSmB; TxHuT. 56376.

Horton, Robert John Wilmot. Letter to Dr. Birkbeck, the president and the members of the London Mechanics Institution on the subject of corn laws. Richmond: Wall, 1839. 24 p. PU. 56377

Hours for heaven, a small but choice selection of prayers [no author] Boston: Hilliard, Gray and Company, 1839. 109 p. ScCliTO. 56378

Housekeeper's almanac, or young wife's oracle

for 1840. New York: Elton [1839] DLC; MWA; NPalK. 56379

Houseworth, Henry. Federurbian, or United States lessons; intended to promote learning and a knowledge of republican principles, in the minds of our youth.... Philomath, Ind.: the author, 1839. 144 p. DLC; IaDmD; In. 56380

Houston, Samuel, 1793-1863. Report of Major-General Sam Houston, to his excellency, Henry Smith, Governor, January 30, 1836. Houston [Telegraph Power Press] 1839. 13 p. TxWFM. 56381

Hove, George M. Case of Lieutenant Hove, Court martial. Washington: 1839. PPL. 56382

How, Uriah Tracy. An oration delivered at Chester, Ohio, July 4, 1839. Gallipolis: 1839. 15 p. OCHP; OHi. 56383

How shall I read the Bible? Boston: 1839. MB. 56384

Howard, H. R. The history of Virgil A. Stewart, and his adventure in capturing the great western hand pirate and his gang; in commission with the evidence, also of the trials, confessions, and execution of...compiled by H. R. Howard. New York: Harper Brothers, 1839. 273, 13 p. Ct; KyLoF; MsSM; NcDaD; Tx. 56385

Howe, Samuel Gridley. Reader of extracts in prose and verse from English and American authors. Boston: printed for the blind, 1839. PPAmP. 56386

Howell, Robert Boyte Crawford. An address delivered before the University of Nashville, at the annual commencement, October 2, 1839, in the Presbyterian Church. Nashville, Tenn.: printed by B. R. McKennie, 1839. 27 p. DLC; KyLoS. MHi; THi; TxU. 56387

Howitt, Mary [Botham] 1799-1888. Birds and flowers and other country things. Boston: Weeks, Jordan and Company, 1839. 208 p. CtHC; MBC; MBev; PP; RKi. 56388

----. Sketches of natural history. Boston: Weeks, Jordan and Company, 1839. 198 p. ICBB; MPiB; WHi. 56389

----. Tales in prose; for the young. Boston:

printed by Tuttle, Dennett and Chishom, 1839. 183 p. CtY; CU; MH; MHi; MWA. 56390

----. Tales in verse. Boston: Weeks, Jordan and Company, 1839. CtY; MBev; MSa; PHC; WHi. 56391

Howland, Avis C. Rhode Island tales and tales of old times. By a friend to youth. New York: M. Day, 1839. 171 p. [Page 127-172 has spearate title] CtY; ICU; MWA; RNHi; RPB. 56392

Howland, Mary W., The infant school manual, or teacher's assistant. Containing a view of the system of infant schools. Also a variety of useful lessons; for the use of teachers. 9th edition. Worcester: Dorr, Howland and Company, 1839. 274 p. MH; MWHi; NIC; PU. 56393

Hubbard, Robert. Historical sketches of Roswell Franklin and his family. Drawn up at the request of Stephen Franklin. Danville, New York: A. Stevens, 1839. 103 p. DLC; ICN; MWA; OClWHi; WHi. 56394

Hubner, Johann, 1668-1731. Biblische Historien aus dem alten und Neuen Testament. Fur die jugend und volksschulen nach der anforderung unserer zeit aufs Neue Bearbeitet. Philadelphia: G. W. Mentz und Son, 1839. MH. 56395

The Hudson Mirror, and Columbia country farmer. Devoted to a polite literature, agriculture, the fine arts, etc., etc. Hudson: P. Dean Carrique, 1839-. v. 1-. DLC; N; NN. 56396

Hudson Rivber Bank. Articles of association and by-laws together with the banking law. New York: 1839. 22 p. PHI. 56397

The Hudson River chronicle [October 1, 1839] Sing sing, New York: M. L. Cobb [1839] NN. 56398

Hughes, George Wurtz, 1806-1870. Reports upon the surveys, location and progress of construction, of the Annapolis and Elk- ridge Railroad, by George W. Hughes, Chief engineer. Annapolis: William M'Neir, printer, 1839. 47 p. CSmH; DLC; IU; MdHi; NN. 56399

Hughs, Mary [Robinson] The ornaments discovered: A story founded on facts.... New York: Harper and Brothers, 1839. 194 p. ScDuE. 56400

Hugo, Victor Marie. The Rhine; a tour from Paris to Mayence by the way of Aix-la-chapelle. Boston: Estes and Lauriat [1839] 275 p. MDanv. 56401

Hull, Amos G., b. 1775. A plain account of the application and uses of Dr. A. G. Hull's Utero-abdominal supporter.... New York: W. Plows [1839] 16 p. DLC; DNLM; NNN; NNNAM; PPCP. 56402

----. Report of the proceedings in several suits, instituted by Dr. Amos G. Hull, against James Knight, M. D. for an alleged infringement upon a patent right. New York: 1839. 36 p. MBC; NNNAM; OC. 56403

Humboldt, Alexander Freiherr Von, 1769-1859. The travels and researches of Alexander Von Humboldt: being a condensed narrative of his journeys in the equinoctial regions of America, and in Asiatic Russia.... New York: Harper and Brothers, 1839. 367 p. Me; MPeaI; NGlc; OWor; TxGR. 56404

Hume, David, 1711-1776. Hume and Smollets celebrated history of England, from its first settlement to the year 1760. Accurately and impartially abridged, and a continuation from that period to the coronation of George IV. July 19, 1821.... New York: Robinson, Pratt and Company, 1839. 496 p. CoCra; PLatS. 56405

----. The history of England, from the invasion of Julius Caesar, to the revolution in 1688. With notes and references, exhibiting the most important differences between this author and Dr. Lingard. In two volumes. Philadelphia: M'Carty and Davis, 1839. 2 v. GMilvC; NcGvE; NNF; PPeSchw; ViAl. 56406

Humphrey, Heman, 1779-1861. A discourse delivered before the Connecticut Alpha of I. B. K., at New Haven, August 14, 1838.... New Haven, L. H. Young, Hitchcock and Stafford, printers, 1839. 23 p. CtHT; MAnP; MiU-C; RPB; TNP. 56407

----. The question, will the christian religion be recognized at the basis of the system of public instruction of Massachusetts? Discussed in four letters. Boston: Whipple and Damrell, 1839. 25 p. IaB; MB; MPiB; PHi; WHi. 56408

Humphreys, David, 1752-1818. Memoirs of the life, adventures and military exploits of Israel Putnam, Senior Major General in the Revolutionary army of the United States and next in rank to General Washington. Ithaca: Mack, Andrus and Woodruff, 1839. 119 p. CSmH; MB; MiD-B; MWA; OMC. 56409

Hun, Thomas. Introductory lecture before Albany Medical College; delivered November 12, 1839. Published by request of the class. Albany: printed by H. D. Stone and Company, 1839. 30 p. CLSR; MH- M; NjR; NNG; OMC. 56410

The hundred years almanac: for the present century, after the birth of Christ from 1799 to 1899.... First American edition [Winchester] Philip H. Spangler, 1839. 60 p. ViWin. 56411

Hunt, Benjamin Faneuil, 1792-1857. An oration delivered by their appointment before the Washington Society in Charlestown, S. C., on July 4, 1839. Charlestown: Miller, 1839. 45 p. DLC; MBAt; MH; MiD-B; ScC. 56412

Hunt, Richard S., Guide to the Republic of Texas: Consisting of a brief outline of the history of its settlement.... By Richard S. Hunt and Jesse F. Randel, 1839. 63 p. MH; MWA; PPPrHi; TxU; WHi. 56413

Hunt, Theodore G. Oration in the Rev. Theodore Clapp's Church, July 4, 1839. New Orleans: B. Levy, 1839. 20 p. DLC. 56414

Hunter, Henry. Sacred biography; or the history of the patriarchs. To which is added, the history of Deborah, Ruth, and Hannah, and also the history of Jesus Christ. Being a course of lectures delivered at the Scotch Church, London-Wall. Philadelphia: Marcus E. Cross, 1839. 596 p. ICU; KTW; NbOP; TWeW. 56415

Hunter, John, 1728-1793. Lectures on the principles of surgery.... With notes by James F. Palmer.... Philadelphia: Haswell, Barrington and Haswell, 1839. 400 p. CSt-L; GU-M; LNOP; PPA; RPM. 56416

----. The natural history of the human teeth. Explaining their structure, use, formation, growth, and diseases.... With notes by Eleazer Parmly. New York: 1839. 2 v. CtY; DLC; MdUD; MiU; NNN. 56417

----. A practical treatise on the diseases of the teeth, intended as a supplement to the natural history of those parts.... By John Hunter. New York:

1839. MWA. 56418

----. Treatise on the natural history and diseases of the human teeth; explaining their structure, use formation, growth and diseases. With notes by Thomas Bell.... Philadelphia: Haswell, Barrington, and Haswell, 1839. 127 p. CSt-L; KyU; NcD; PPA; ViU. 56419

----. A treatise on the venereal diseases. With notes by Geo. G. Babington.... Philadelphia: Haswell, Barrington and Haswell, 1839. 347 p. CSt-L; ICU; NhD; PPA; ViU. 56420

----. Works. Philadelphia: Haswell, Barrington and Haswell, 1839- 1840. 4 v. CSt-L; ICU; MdAS; MdBM; P. 56421

Hunter, Robert Mercer Taliaferro, 1809-1887. An address delivered before the society of alumni of the University of Virginia, at its second annual meeting, held in the Rotunda, on the 4th of July, 1839. Published by order of the Society. Charlottesville: printed by Tompkins and Noel, 1839. 31 p. MH-AH; NcD; TxU; ViU. 56422

Huntt, Henry, 1792-1838. A visit to the Red Sulphur Springs of Virginia, during the summer of 1837: with observations on the waters by Henry Huntt, M. D., with an introduction, containing notices of routes, etc., by an annual visitor. Boston: Dutton and Wentworth, printers, 1839. 40 p. CtY; ICU; MBC; MWA; PPAN. 56423

----. ----. Philadelphia: T. Cowperthwait, etc., 1839. 44 p. DGU. 56424

Hurka, Friedrich Franz, 1762-1805. Die glocke, ein gedicht von Friedrich V. Schiller.... New York: 1839. 24 p. CSt; MH; MNe; TNJU. 56425

Hurlbut, Elisha P. Civil office and politcal ethics...by E. P. Hurlbut. 3rd edition. New York [1839] 216 p. NNNAM. 56426

Hutchings improved almanac for 1840. By David Young. New York: A. and S. Raynor [1839] MWA; NjR. 56427

Hutchings improved farmers and mechanics almanac. New York: Turner and Fisher, 1839. MWA. 56428

Hutchins, Stephen. A solemn appeal to the Christian public, on the right and expediency of capital punishment; by the Rev. Stephen Hutchins, pastor of Baptist Church, Bennington, Vt. Published by request. Brandon: Telegraph office, 1839. 24 p. ICP. 56429

Hutchins improved almanac, for the year of our Lord, 1839, being the 3rd after bissextile and until the 4th of July.... New York: Robinson, Pratt, printers [1839] 36 p. NjMoW. 56430

----. By David Young, Philom. Newark, N. J.: Benjamin Olds [1839] 36 p. MWA; NjR. 56431

----. calculated for the horizon and meridian of New Jersey in equal or clock time. By David Young.... Somerville, N. J.: Thomas S. Allison [1839] NjR. 56432

Hutchison, William. An address delivered in the Baptist Meeting house, in Oswego, December 25, 1838, on the claims of foreign powers to hold territory and impose laws on this side of the Atlantic.... Oswego: printed by Richard Oliphant, 1839. 31 p. WHi. 56433

I

Illinois. Auditor of Public Accounts. Report...transmitted to both houses of the General Assembly, December 14, 1839. Springfield: William Walters, public printer, 1839. 31 p. A-SC; IaU-L; NN; TxU-L; WHi. 56434

----. Board of Commissioners of Public Works. Letter from the president ... relative to northern end of the Central Railroad, submitted to the House of Representatives, January 30, 1839. Vandalia: 1839. 24 p. WHi. 56435

----. ----. Report from the Commissioners of Public Works, in reply to resolutions of the Senate and House...transmitting abstracts of disbursements in each circuit. Vandalia: 1839. 111 p. WHi. 56436

----. ----. Report...relative to the survey of a route from Charleston, through the seat of justice of Clark County, to the Wabash River, January 11, 1839 [Vandalia: 1839] 8 p. WHi. 56437

----. ----. Statement from the Board of Public Works of the real estate purchased for the state...December 20, 1839. Springfield: Wm. Walters, public printer, 1839. 15 p. Nb; NN; WHi. 56438

----. Board of Fund Commissioners. Letter from...concerning the four million loan [Springfield: Wm. Walters, 1839?] 3 p. IHi; Nb. 56439

----. ----. Report...December 26, 1838, on amount of bond issued, money expended, etc. [Vandalia: 1839] 8 p. NN; WHi. 56440

----. Commissioners on the State House. Report...relative to the erection of the State House at Springfield, December 26, 1838 [Vandalia: 1839] 3 p. WHi. 56441

----. General Assembly. Reports made to the Senate and House of the state of Illinois, at their seeion begun and held in Vandalia, December 4, 1838. Accompanying the journals. Vandalia: Wil-

liam Walters, public printer, 1839. ICLaw; ILM; IRA; NN. 56442

----. ----. To the honorable, the General Assembly of the state of Illinois. The petition of the undersigned citizens of the counties of Cook, Will and McHenry...[praying] that an act may be passed...creating a new circuit to be set off from the 7th circuit [1839?] 1 p. 56443

----. ----. House. Journal of the House of the 11th General Assembly of the state of Illinois at their first session, begun and held in the town of vandalia, December 3, 1838. Vandalia, Ill.: William Walters, public printer, 1838 [1839] 607 p. IHi. 56444

----. ----. ----. Journal of the House of the 11th General Assembly, begun and held at Springfield, December 9, 1839. Springfield: Wm. Walters, public printer, 1839. 340 p. CU; DLC; IGK; IRA; NN. 56445

----. ----. ----. Committee on Cairo City and Bank. Report of the select committee on the city and bank of Cairo, submitted to the House...January 21, 1839. Vandalia: 1839. 8 p. MH-BA; WHi. 56446

----. ----. ----. Committee on Finance. Public lands in Illinois: report submitted by Mr. Lincoln from the Committee on Finance, January 17, 1839 [relative to the purchase of unsold lands within the state from the national government. Vandalia: 1839] 3 p. InU; WHi. 56447

----. ----. ----. Committee on Internal Improvements. Report...submitted to the House, February 16, 1839. Vandalia: H. Walters, 1839. 29 p. MiU; WHi. 56448

----. ----. ----. Committee on Judiciary. Divorces: report of the Committee on the Judiciary, February 28, 1839 [Vandalia: 1839] 2 p. WHi. 56449

----. ----. ----. ----. Fugitive slaves: report [relative

to a correspondence between the governor of Georgia and the Governor of Maine upon the refusal of Maine to deliver up citizens of Maine charged with abducting a negro slave named Atticus. Vandalia: 1839] 2 p. WHi. 56450

----. ----. ----. ----. Report...relative to the repeal of all laws authorizing the retailing of intoxicating liquors, submitted to the House, January 26, 1839. Vandalia: 1839. 13 p. WHi. 56451

----. ----. ----. Committee on Penitentiary. Report...submitted to the House...January 15, 1839. Vandalia: 1839. 22 p. WHi. 56452

----. ----. ----. Select Committee on Central Railroad. Report of the select committee on the proposed change of the southern termination of the Central railroad, submitted to the House...January 28, 1839. Vandalia: 1839. 13 p. WHi. 56453

----. ----. ----. Select Committee on Salaries. Report...relative to increasing salary of governor and judicial officers...submitted to the House, December 22, 1838. Vandalia: 1839. 7 p. WHi. 56454

----. ----. Joint Committee on Fund Commissioners and Board of Public Works. Report of the joint select committee of investigation appointed to examine the offices of the fund commisssioners and board of public works.... Vandalia: 1839. 131 p. IHi; WHi. 56455

----. ----. Senate. Journal of the Senate of the eleventh General Assembly of the state of Illinois, at their called session, begun and held at Springfield, December 9, 1839. Springfield: Wm. Walters, public printer, 1839. 235 p. CSmH; DLC; ICJ; IHi; NN. 56456

----. Governor, 1838-1842 [Thomas Carlin] Communication from the Governor of Illinois, transmitting the reports and documents in relation to canal claims [Springfield, Illinois: 1839] IAi. 56457

----. ----. Documents referred to in the message of the governor at the...General Assembly, transmitted to the House, December 13, 1839. Springfield: William Walters, public printer, 1839. 28, 3 p. Nb; WHi. 56458

----. ----. Message of the governor...transmitted to the General Assembly, December 11, 1839.

Springfield: Wm. Walters, public printer, 1839. 13 p. IHi; Nb; NN; WHi. 56459

----. ----. Message of the governor transmitting the report of the board of commissioners... to the legislature of Illinois, December 31, 1838. Vandalia: W. Walters, public printer, 1839. 90 p. ICHi; ICJ; IHi; ILM. 56460

----. Laws, Statutes, etc. Amendments to the Internal Improvement Laws: passed by the General Assembly of Illinois.... Vandalia: William Walters, printer, 1839. MH. 56461

----. ----. Incorporation laws of the state of Illinois, passed by the eleventh General Assembly, at their session begun and held at vandalia, the third day of December, 1838. Published by authority. Vandalia: William Walters, 1839. 249 p. DLC; ICN; MH- L; Mi-L; NNLI. 56462

----. ----. Laws of the state of Illinois, passed by the eleventh General Assembly at their session begun and held at Vandalia, on December 3, 1838. Published in pursuance of law. Vandalia: William Walters, public printer, 1839. 317 p. A-SC; IHi; MdBB; RPL; Wa-L. 56463

----. ----. Laws of the state of Illinois relative to justices of the peace. Published in pursuance of law. Vandalia: 1839. 91 p. DLC; ICLaw ILM; MH-L; WHi. 56464

----. ----. The public and general statutes, laws of the state of Illinois...first session, commencing December 1, 1834 and ending February 1835; and at their second session, commencing December 7, 1835 and ending January 18, 1836; and those passed...and at their special session commencing July 10, and ending July 22, 1837; which are not repealed: and also the militia law.... Chicago: Stephen F. Gale, 1839. 743 p. CSt; In-SC; MH; NcD; WaU. 56465

----. State Lottery. Drawing of the Illinois State Lottery authorized by the legislature to raise funds, for the purpose of drawing the ponds and lakes in the American Bottom and of improving the health thereof. Alton: 1839. IU. 56466

----. Supreme Court. Cases adjudged in the Supreme Court of the state of Illinois, from December term, 1832, to the close of June term, 1838, being a continuation from Breese's reports, with marginal notes and references. Vandalia:

William Walters, printer, 1839. 319 p. ICHi; DLC; MWA; NNB; WaU. 56467

Illinois College, Jacksonville, Illinois. Catalogue of officers and students, 1838-1839. Jacksonville: 1839. 14 p. IHi; In. 56468

----. To the judges and lawyers of Illinois...Illinois College, May 29, 1839 [Jacksonville? 1839] IHi. 56469

The Illinois farmer's almanac and repository of useful knowledge, for the year 1840...By R. Goudy, Jr. Jacksonville: C. and R. Goudy [1839] 24 p. MWA. 56470

The Illinois farmer's almanac for 1840. By R. Goudy, Jr. Jacksonville: C. and R. Goudy [1839] MWA. 56471

Illinois Land Company. Proceedings of the Illinois Land Company, 1839. New York: H. Ludwig, printer, 1839. 64 p. DLC; ICJ; MiU; PHi. 56472

Illinois Mutual Fire Insurance Company. Act of incorporation and by-laws with names of the officers. Alton, Illinois: 1839. MH; MH-BA; WHi. 56473

The illustrated annual of phrenology, and health almanac...1840. New York: O. S. and L. N. Fowler, etc., etc., 1839. DLC; ICU; MiU; NNUT; OO. 56474

Improved New England almanack... See the illustrated annual of phrenology and health almanac.

Incidents in the life of William Henry Harrison, the people's candidate for the presidency. Albany: printed at the Sun office, 1839. 24 p. MH-AH; MWA; WHi. 56475

Independent Presbyterian Church in the United States of America. The constitution and form of government...as adopted by the churches in convention, held at Salem Church, in Union District, South Carolina, 1833: together with Mr. Davis's solemn appeal to an impartial public. Columbia: 1839. 281 p. NcMHi; ScU; TMeSC. 56476

Index to Dental Literature in the English Language. Index of the periodical dental literature in the English language; a classified subject index, an alphabetical author index of dental books. Buffalo: Dental Index Bureau, 1839-. CU; ICU; MiU; OU; ViU. 56477

An index to the Holy Bible; or an account of the most remarkable passages in the books of the Old and New Testaments.... Philadelphia: 1839. NN. 56478

Indiana. General Assembly. House. Documents of the House...23rd session of the General Assembly of the state of Indiana.... Indianapolis: Osborn and Willets, printers, 1839. 677 p. InSbNHi. 56479

----. ----. ----. Journal of the House...23rd session of the General Assembly of the state of Indiana, commenced at Indianapolis on December 3, 1838. Indianapolis: Osborn and Willets, printers, 1839. 690 p. LU; IN-LB; MdBP; NcD; WHi. 56480

----. Governor [David Wallace] Messages and documents of David Wallace, December 3 and 4th, 1839. Indianapolis: 1839. InU. 56481

----. Laws, Statutes, etc. Laws of a general nature passed and published at the 23rd session of the General Assembly of the state of Indiana. Held at Indianapolis, on the first Monday in December, 1838. By authority. Indianapolis: Douglass and Noel, state printers, 1839. 103 p. Az; IaU-L; Nc-S; R; Wa-L. 56482

----. ----. Laws of a local nature passed and published at the 23rd session of the General Assembly of the state of Indiana. Held at Indainapolis, on the first Monday in December, 1838. By authority. Indianapolis: Douglass and Noel, state printers, 1839. 379 p. Ar-SC; IaHi; MdBB; Nj; Wa-L. 56483

----. State Geologist. Report of a geological reconnoissance and survey of the state of Indiana, made in the years 1837 and 1838. By David Dale Owen, M. D., geologist of the state, 1839. 34, 54 p. DSG; MH-Z; MnU; OCHP; OCN. 56484

----. ----. Second report of a geological survey of the state of Indiana, made in the year 1838, in conformity to an order of the legislature, by David Dale Owen, M. D., geologist of the state. Indianapolis: printed by Douglass and Noel, 1839. 46 p. DLC. 56485

----. ----. Indianapolis: printed by Osborn and

Willets, 1839. 54 p. DGS; ICP; InU; MCM; MoS. 56486

----. University. Catalogue of the officers and students of Indiana University, Bloomington, 1839. Bloomington: J. Dale, printer [1839?] 8 p. InU. 56487

The Indiana almanac for the year of our Lord 1839.... Indianapolis: Stacy and Williams, 1839. 48 p. In; InHi. 56488

The Indiana almanac for the year of our Lord, 1840: Being a Biseesxtile, and until July 4th, the 64th year of the Independence of the United States. Containing all of the customary calculations.... By David Young, Philom. Indianapolis: Stacy and Williams [1839?] 46 p. In; NWattJHi. 56489

Ingalls, William, 1769-1851. A lecture on the subject of phrenology not opposed to the principles of religion; nor the precepts of Christianity. Boston: Dutton and Wentworth, printers, 1839. 50 p. DLC; ICMe; MBAt; MHi; MWA. 56490

----. On Scarlatina, in a letter addressed to his son. 2nd edition, with an appendix. Boston: B. H. Greene, 1839. 40 p. MB; MBNEH; NNNAM. 56491

Ingersoll, Charles Jared, 1782-1862. Speech of Charles J. Ingersoll, on the right to repeal bank charters. Delivered in the convention of Pennsylvania. New York: L. Scott, 1839. 48 p. A-Ar; MdHi; NjR; PPM; ScU. 56492

Ingraham, Joseph Holt, 1809-1860. The American lounger or tales, sketches and legends, gathered in sundry journeyings.... Philadelphia: Lea and Blanchard, 1839. 273 p. DLC; MH; PU; RPB; TMeC. 56493

----. Captain Kid; or the wizard of the sea. A romance, by "The author of the southwest".... New York: Harper and Brothers, 1839. 2 v. DLC; LNH; MWA; RPB; ScU. 56494

An inquiry into the condition and prsospects of the African race in the United states: and the means of bettering its fortunes.... By an American. Philadlephia: Haswell, Barrington and Haswell, 1839. 214 p. ICU; MB; OO; PPA; WHi. 56495

Instruction in the principles and duties of the Christian religion for children and youth. Philadelphia: printed for the Tract and Book Scoiety of the Evangelical Lutheran Church of St. John, 1839. 108 p. MH-AH; PAtM. 56496

Interesting biographical sketches of distinguished men. Part 1 and 2. Hartford: L. Stebbins, 1839. 2 v. CtY; MB; NN; WHi. 56497

Internal improvement proceedings of meetings of the citizens of Rochester, Buffalo, Lockport and Palmyra. Expressive of the views of the people of Western New York. With references to the improvement of the Erie Canal. Rochester: printed by Shepard, Strong and Dawson, 1839. 8 p. CSt; NRU; NUtHi. 56498

Investigation into the fifteen gallon law... See Massachusetts. General Court. Joint Committee on Investigation...

Iowa [Territory] Governor, 1838-1841 [Robert Lucas] Message and etc. Executive Department, December 16, 1839. To the honorable, the House of Representatives of the Legislative Assembly [Burlington: J. H. McKenny? 1839] 3 p. DNA. 56499

----. Laws, Statutes, etc. Session laws, 1838-1937. Dubuque, 1839-. 62 v. IaHA; IU; RPL; WaU. 56500

----. Legislative Assembly. The statute laws of the Territory of Iowa, enacted at the first session of the Legislative Asembly of said territory, held at Burlington, 1838-1839. Dubuque: Russell and Reeves, printers, 1839. 597 p. CSmH; IaU; MiU; RPL; WaU. 56501

----. ----. Council. Journal. 1838-1845 [Iowa City] 1839-1846. Ia; IaHA; NIC. 56502

----. ----. House. Correspondence between his excellency, Governor Lucas and the Hon. Wm. B. Conway, Secretary of the Territory of Iowa [Burlington: 1839] DNA. 56503

----. ----. ----. Report of the committee on vetos, in the House, January 7, 1839 [Burlington: 1839] DNA. 56504

----. Library. Catalogue of the Iowa Territory. Library, 1839. Burlington: James E. Edwards, 1839. 18 p. IaCrM; MH. 56505

----. Supreme Court. Rules of practice, in the Supreme and District Courts for the Territory of Iowa, adopted at the July term, 1839 [Iowa City?] Clarke and M'Kenny [1839?] 7 p. DLC. 56506

Ipswich, Massachusetts. Seminary for Female Teachers. Catalogue of the officers and members of the Seminary for Female Teachers, at Ipswich, Massachusetts, for the year ending April, 1839. Salem: printed at the Register Press, 1839. 35 p. ICU; NRivHi. 56507

Iredell, James, 1788-1853. A digest of all the reported cases determined in the courts of North Carolina, from the year 1778 to the year [1845]...inclusive...Prepared by James Iredell.... Raleigh: Turner and Hughes, 1839-1846. 3 v. DLC; MB; NcD; PPB; ViU. 56508

Ireland. Court of Chancery. Reports of cases argued and determined in the High Court of Chancery in Ireland during the time of Lord Chancellor Manners [1807-1814] By Thomas Ball and Francis Beatty.... 1st American from the last London edition. Philadelphia: R. H. Small, 1839. 2 v. in 1. Ct; LNB; MiD-B; NhD; OU. 56509

The iris of prose, poetry, and art, for 1840. Illustrated with engravings by W. and E. Finden, from paintings by J. Browne. Edited by Mary Russell Mitford.... London: Charles Tilt, Philadelphia: Carey and Hart [1839] MiU; OCA. 56510

Irving, Christopher, d. 1856. A catechism of mythology; being a compendious history of the heathen gods, goddesses and heroes. Designed chiefly as an introduction to the study of the ancient classics.... 5th American edition. New York: Collins, Keese and Company, 1839. 84 p. NN. 56511

Irving, Washington, 1783-1859. The alhambra: a series of tales and sketches of the moors and Spaniards. By the author of the Sketch Book. A new edition. Philadelphia: Lea and Blanchard, 1839. 2 v. CtY; MoSU. 56512

----. The beauties of Washington Irving.... Philadelphia: Lea and Blanchard, 1839. 270 p. CtY. 56513

----.----. Philadelphia: Lea and Blanchard, for G. W. Gorton, 1839. 349 p. CtMW; LN; OSW; ViU. 56514

----. Bracebridge Hall; or the humourists. A medley, by Geoffrey Crayon, Gent. [pseud.].... Philadelphia: Lea and Blanchard, 1839. 2 v. CtY; MCli; MH; NT. 56515

----. A chronicle of the conquest of Granada. By Fray Antonio Agapida [pseud.].... Philadelphia: Carey, Lea and Carey, 1839. 2 v. CSmH; DLC; MWA; NN; PU. 56516

----. A history of New York, from the beginning of the world to the end of the Dutch Dynasty.... By Diedrich Knickerbocker [pseud.].... Philadelphia: Lea and Blanchard, 1839. 2 v. Ct; MB; MdU; NN; NNebg. 56517

----. History of the life and voyages of Christopher Columbus. A new edition, revised and corrected by the author.... Philadelphia: Lea and Blanchard, 1839. 2 v. GMM; LNT; MBAt; MoSU; PUnt. 56518

----. The life and voyages of Christopher Columbus. Including the author's visit to Palos.... Boston: Marsh, Capen, Lyon and Webb, 1839. 325 p. KyLoP; MWA; NBuCC; PHC; RWe. 56519

----.----. New York: Harper [1839] 325 p. NcU. 56520

----.----. Philadelphia: Lea and Blanchard, for Gorton, 1839. 2 v. MH. 56521

----. The sketch book of Geoffrey Crayon, gent. [pseud.] A new edition. Philadelphia: Lea and Blanchard, 1839. 2 v. CtY; KyDC; OMC; PHi; TJoT. 56522

Ithaca Academy. Annual catalogue. Ithaca: 1839. NIC. 56523

Ives, Elam, 1802-1864. American psalmody. A collection of sacred music...arranged with a figured base for the organ or piano forte; to which is prefixed elements of musical elocution.... Hartford: Huntington, 1839. 36 [33]-365 p. NjP. 56524

J

Jack Downing's song book, containing a selection of upwards of two hundred of the most popular songs, many of which are new. By Jack Downing. Providence: B. Cranston and Company, 1839. 256 p. NP. 56525

----. 4th edition. Providence: B. Cranston and Company, 1839. CtHWatk; NHi; RP; RPSh. 56526

----. 5th edition. Providence: B. Cranston and Company, 1839. 256 p. CSfCP. 56527

Jackson, Andrew, 1767-1845. Messages of General Andrew Jackson, with a short sketch of his life. Concord, N.H.: John F. Brown and William White, Boston: Otis Broaders and Company, 1839. 425 p. LNP; MLow. 56528

Jackson, Daniel, b. 1790. Alonzo and Melissa, or the unfeeling father. An American tale.... Boston: E. Littlefield, 1839. 256 p. CtY; MBAt. 56529

----. ----. Sandbornton, N.H.: C. Lane, 1839. 258 p. Ct; ICU; PPM; PU. 56530

----. The asylum; or Alonzo and Melissa. An American tale, founded on fact.... Boston: E. Littlefield, 1839. 256 p. CtY. 56531

Jackson, Francis, 1789-1861. Address to the abolitionists of Masaschusetts [Boston] 1839. MWA. 56532

----. Genealogy of the family of Edward Jackson, Senior of Newton [Boston: 1839] Broadside. M. 56533

Jackson, Henry. Arithmetical foundation.... 2nd edition. Portland: S. H. Colesworthy, 1839. CtHWatk; DLC; MeHi. 56534

Jackson, Isaac Rand, d. 1843. A sketch of the life and public services of William Henry Harrison. Commander in Chief of the north western army. During the war of 1812, etc. New York: printed at the office of the New York Express, 1839. 32 p. IHi; MWA; PP; TxDaM; WHi. 56535

Jackson, James. Brief view of the origin and progress of the fine arts. Viz of painting, engraving and sculpture. To which is added an appeal to the public, in favor of the Maryland Academy of the fine arts, and a prospectus for an academy of design, drawing and painting. Baltimore: 1839. 40 p. DLC; MB; NNC; PPL; ScU. 56536

Jackson, Samuel, 1787-1872. Introductory lecture to the course of the Institute of Medicine.... Philadelphia: 1839. PPL. 56537

Jackson, Samuel Cram, 1802-1878. The license law vindicated; discourse at Thanksgiving, Nov. 28, 1839. Andover: William Peirce, 1839. 32 p. RPB. 56538

----. The life and death of a faithful minister: discourse at the interment of Rev. Sylvester G. Pierce. Methuen: S. Jameson Varney, printer, 1839. 24 p. CSmH; ICN; KWiU; MBC; RPB. 56539

Jackson, Thomas, 1783-1873. The centenary of Wesleyan Methodism.... New York: T. Mason and G. Lane, 1839. 240 p. KyLoP; MiD; MWA; OU; PPM. 56540

----. ----. 279 p. ArAT; GMilvC; ICU; NNUT; OBerB; Wv. 56541

----. Wesleyan Methodism a revival of Apostolical Christianity. A sermon preached...before the Wesleyan conference, ...August 5, 1839, on occasion of the celebration of the centenary of Wesleyan Methodism.... New York: T. Mason and G. Lane, 1839. 38 p. IEG; MH; MWA; RPB; Vi. 56542

Jacobs, Friedrich, 1764-1847. The Greek reader, with...notes and corrections by D. Patterson. 10th New York from the 9th German edition, corrected and improved by P. S. Casserly. New York: W. E. Dean, 1839. 214, 97 p. MBC; NbCrD; WS; WU. 56543

----. ----. From the 12th German edition. Boston:

Hilliard, Gray and Company, 1839. 516 p. IGK; MH; RPB; TxU-T; WU. 56544

----. Jacob's Latin reader, first part. With a vocabulary, and English notes. For the use of schools, academies, etc. Boston: Hilliard, Gray and Company, 1839. 264 p. IaHi; ICU; MH; NcBe; ScCMu. 56545

Jacob's dream. New York: T. Mason and G. Lane, 1839. 8 p. NjR. 56546

Jahn, Johann, 1750-1816. Jahn's Biblical archaeology, translated from the Latin, with additions and corrections, by Thomas C. Upham, professor of moral and intellectual philosophy, and of the Hebrew language in Bowdoin College. 4th edition. Andover, N.Y.: Gould, Newman and Saxton, 1839. 1-573 p. CtHC; ICU; MAnP; OO; PU. 56547

----. ----.5th edition. Stereotyped.... New York: Mark H. Newman, 1839. 573 p. CtY; ScOiC; TxAbC. 56548

James, George Payne Rainsford, 1799-1860. Attila; a romance. New York: Harper and Brothers, 1839. 2 v. in 1. MB; MNF; OClWHi; RPA; RPB. 56549

----. Blanche of Navarre. A play.... New York: Harper and Brothers, 1839. 74 p. CtHT; MB; MiU; PP; RPB. 56550

----. A book of the passions. Illustrated.... under the superintendence of Mr. Charles Heath. Philadelphia: Lea and Blanchard, successors to Carey and Company, 1839. 363 p. CtY; FDeS; KyLxT; LNH; MLow. 56551

----. Charles Tyrrell; or the bitter blood. New York: Harper and Brothers, 1839. 2 v. ICN; MH; NcU; RPA; ViAl. 56552

----. De L'Orme. By the author of "Richelieu," and "Darnley." In two volumes. 2nd edition. New York: Harper and Brothers, 1839. 2 v. CtMW; KyU; MeB; MH. 56553

----. The gentleman of the old school. A tale.... New York: Harper and Brothers, 1839. 2 v. CLU; IaPeC; MH; NPtw; PHi. 56554

----. The gypsy. A tale by G. P. R. James, Esq. New York: Harper and Brothers, 1839. 231 p.

IaPeC. 56555

----. Henry Masterton; or the adventures of a young cavalier. By the author of "Richelieu," Darnley," etc.... New York: 1839. 2 v. CtMW; MLow. 56556

----. Henry of Guise; or states of Blois. New York: Harper and Brothers, 1839. 2 v. CtY; KyHi; MBL; NjHo; WHi. 56557

----. History of Charlemagne. By G. Payne Rainsford James. New York: Harper and Brothers, 1839. 408 p. InRch; LNH; MPeaI; OAU; PP. 56558

----. The history of chivalry.... New York: Harper and Brothers, 1839. 342 p. Ia; LN; OMC; ScDuE; TxGR. 56559

----. The Hugenot, a tale of the French Protestants by the author of "Richelieu".... New York: Harper and Brothers, 1839. CtHT; MH; NBuU; PLFM; ScU. 56560

----. Memoirs of celebrated women. Edited by G. P. R. James.... Philadelphia: 1839. 2 v. in 1. MWA; OCY; PPL-R; RPA; ViU. 56561

----. The robber. A tale. By the author of "Richelieu," "the gypsy," "Attila," etc., etc. New York: Harper and Brothers, 1839. 2 v. MeLew; MH. 56562

----. Tales illustrating the passions.... Philadelphia: Lea and Blanchard, 1839. 269 p. CtY; MBAt; MH; NN. 56563

James, John Angell, 1785-1859. The church member's guide with an introductory essay by Hubbard Winslow. Boston: Gould, Kendall and Lincoln, 1839. 240 p. MB. 56564

----. The young man from home N[ew] Y[ork] American Tract Society [1839] MH; NN. 56565

James, John Henry, 1800-1881. Address before Springfield, O., High School, Sept. 1, 1839. Cincinnati: 1839. 8 p. OCHP. 56566

James, Maria, 1793-1868. Wales, and other poems, by Maria James, with an introduction by A. Potter, D.D. New York: John S. Taylor, 1839. 174 p. CtMW; MeBaT; NBuG; PPWa; TxU. 56567

James Haswell, the ferryman, by the author of "little Flora." New York: Protestant Episcopal Sunday School Union, 1839. 43 p. DLC. 56568

Jameson, Anna Brownell [Murphy] 1794-1860. Memoirs of celebrated female sovereigns. New York: Harper and Brothers, 1839. 2 v. InCW; MPeaI; MTa; NGlo; ScDuE. 56569

----. Winter studies and summer rambles in Canada. By Mrs. Jameson.... New York: Wiley and Putnam, 1839. 2 v. CtMW; DeWi; IaU; NjR; PPA. 56570

Jameson, Robert, 1774-1854. Narrative of discovery and adventure in Africa, from the earliest ages to the present time: with illustrations of the geology, mineralogy and zoology.... New York: Harper and Brothers, 1839. [11]-359 p. MiD; OAU; PEaL; ScDuE; TxGR. 56571

Jamieson, Alexander. A grammar of logic and intellectual philosophy, on didactic principles; for the use of colleges, schools and private instruction.... 8th edition, stereotyped. New Haven [Conn.] A. H. Maltby, 1839. 304 p. CoDR; IaDUTM; MBBC; ODW; OO. 56572

----. A grammar of rhetoric and polite literature; comprehending the principles of language and style, the elements of taste and criticism.... 19th edition. New Haven: A. H. Maltby, 1839. CtHWatk; MH; MiD; P. 56573

Janney, Samuel Macpherson, 1801-1880. The last of the Lenape, and other poems. Philadelphia: H. Perkins, Boston: Perkins and Marvin, 1839. 180 p. DeWi; MH; OkHi; PHi; RPB; ViU. 56574

Jarvis, Russell, 1791-1853. Prospectus of a political newspaper opposed to Sir Van Buren to be conducted by Russell Jarvis. Philadelphia: 1839. Broadside. PPL. 56575

Jarvis, Samuel Farmer, 1786-1851. Long home of man; a sermon preached in St. Stephen's church, East Haddam, on Tuesday, January 16th, 1838, at the funeral of the Rev. Stephen Beach, late rector of that parish, by...rector of Christ church, Middletown. New York: L. Sherman, 1839. 24 p. CtMW; MBC; NNG; PHi; RPB. 56576.

Jarvis, Sarah McCurdy [Hart] The great divorce case! A full and impartial history of the trial of the petition of Mrs. Sarah M. Jarvis; for a divorce from

her husband; the Rev. Samuel F. Jarvis...before a committee of the legislature of the state of Connecticut.... New York: 1839. 60 p. CtMW; MB; MH-L; NNLI. 56577

----. Report of the proceedings on the petition of Mrs. Sarah M. Jarvis, for a divorce from her husband, Rev. Samuel F. Jarvis, D.D., LL.D. Before a committee of the legislature of Connecticut. Hartford: Review Press, 1839. 116 p. CtSoP; CtY; MB; MH-L; PPB. 56578

----. ----. 2nd edition. Hartford: Review Press, 1839. 116 p. Ct; MBD; NjR; OCLaw. 56579

Jay, John, 1817-1894. Thoughts on the duty of the Episcopal church, in relation to slavery: being a speech delivered in N. Y. A. S. convention, February 12, 1839. New York: Piercy and Reed, printers, 1839. 11 p. DLC; MH; NNUT; OClWHi; RPB. 56580

Jay, John Clarkson, 1808-1891. A catalogue of the shells, arranged according to the Lamarckian system; together with descriptions of new or rare species, contained in the collection of John C. Jay.... 3rd edition. New York and London: Wiley and Putnam, 1839. 125 [1] p. CU; DLC; IaGG; PPM; ViU. 56581

Jay, William, 1769-1853. Evening exercises for the closet: for every day in the year.... New York: Robinson and Franklin, 1839. 2 v. in 1. DLC; ICBB; TxAuPt. 56582

----. Exercises for the closet, for every day in the year. New York: Ezra Collier, 1839. 2 v. in 1. CBCDS; MB; NBLiHi. 56583

Jay, William, 1789-1858. A view of the action of the Federal government in behalf of slavery. By William Jay. New York: J. S. Taylor, 1839. 217 p. CtMW; MBC; NBuG; PHC; TxU. 56584

----. ----. 2nd edition. New York: American Anti-slavery Society, 1839. 240 p. CtY; InI; MHi; PPL-R; ScCoT. 56585

Jefferson College, Canonsburg, Pennsylvania. Catalogue of the officers and students of Jefferson College, Canonsburg, July, 1839. Washington, Pa.: printed by Thomas W. Grayson and Company [1839] 28 p. CSansS; MdHi; PWCHi; PWW. 56586

----. Franklin Literary Society. Catalogue of the

members and library of the Frankln Literary Society of Jefferson College, Canonsburg, Pa., from its formation, Nov. 14, 1797, to June 3, 1839. Pittsburgh: Alexander Jaynes, 1839. 32 p. MnSM; PPL; PPPrHi; PWW. 56587

Jefferson College, Washington, Mississippi. Address to the public [Natchez? 1839] 2 p. Ms-Ar; TxU. 56588

----. [Blank separated by 3 vertical lines for names of subscribers and sums subscribed. Natchez? 1839] Broadside. Ms-Ar. 56589

Jefferson County, Florida. Citizens. Public meeting of the citizens of Jefferson County, held at Monticello, Jefferson County, Florida, July 2, 1839. Together with a detail of the causes which led to the founding of the Dade Institute. Tallahassee: printed by S. S. Sibley, 1839. 11 p. M; TKL-Mc; TxU. 56590

Jenifer, Daniel, 1791 1855. Speech of Mr. Jenifer, of Maryland, on the resolution offered by Mr. Prentiss to expel Mr. Duncan, of Ohio. Delivered in the House of Representatives, February 21, 1839. Washington: printed by Gales and Seaton, 1839. 11 p. DLC; MdHi; PHi. 56591

Jenkins, Warren. The Ohio gazetteer, and traveller's guide; containing a description of the several towns, townships and counties, with their water course, roads, improvements, mineral productions, etc., etc.... Revised edition. Columbus: I. N. Whiting, 1839. 546 p. ICN; KyLo; MH; MWA; PHi. 56592

----. The school and township officer's manual and executor's and administrator's guide; with forms for conveyancing, official bonds, bills, accounts, notes, etc., etc., etc. Columbus: I. N. Whiting, 1839. 310 p. CoCsC; OClr; OClWHi; OCLaw. 56593

Jerram, Charles. Conversations on infant baptism by Charles Jerram.... New York: Swords, Stanford and Company, 1839. 210 p. GDecCT; InID; NBu; NcCJ; NCH. 56594

Jerrold, Douglas William, 1805-1857. Adam Buff, and other men of character. By Douglas Jerrold. Philadelphia: Lea and Blanchard, 1839. 2 v. LNH; MB; MBL; NNS; PHi. 56595

Jesuits. Rules of the Society of Jesus.

Washington: printed by Jacob Gideon, Jun., 1839. CoDR; MdW; MoSU; MWH; NBuCC. 56596

The jewel, or token of friendship. 2nd edition. New York: R. Lockwood, 1839. 246 p. MWA; NcD; RPB. 56597

Jewell, Willson, 1800-1867. The baptism; or the little inquirer. Designed for the use of Sabbath schools. By Willson Jewell, M.D. Boston: New England Sabbath School Union, 1839. 90 p. NCHS; NRAB; PCA. 56598

Jewett, Milo Parker, 1808-1882. Mode and subjects of baptism. 1st edition. Boston: John Putnam, 1839. NcCJ; NHCS; PCC; RPB. 56599

----. ----. 2nd edition. Boston: Gould, Kendall and Lincoln, 1839. 122 p. CBB; IEG; MBC; OO; PCA. 56600

Johnson, Edwin Ferry, 1803-1872. Communication from the Secretary of State, transmitting the report of a survey of a railroad from Ogdensburgh to Lake Champlain [Albany: 1839] 57 p. CSt; MB; MH- BA. 56601

----. Table of cubical quantities, for determining the amount of excavation and embankment, in the construction of railroads and canals.... New York: Railroad Journal office, 1839. 20, 13 p. CtY; DLC; MiU; NNE. 56602

Johnson, Evan Malbone, 1791-1865. Missionary fanaticism opposed to Chrisitan zeal, a discourse...with explanatory notes. New York: L. Sherman, 1839. 32 p. CtHT; MBC; MWA; NCH; RPB. 56603

----. A pastoral letter [Brooklyn: 1839] MB. 56604

Johnson, Francis. ...Celebrated Victoria Gallop.... Philadelphia: L. Meignen, 1839. NN. 56605

Johnson, J. Lecture delivered before the Williamsburgh Lyceum on the Revolutionary history of Long Island and its vicinity. Williamsburgh: 1839. 25 p. NBLIHI. 56606

Johnson, Joseph, Iron Merchant, Liverpool. Report of the iron trade in Scotland and South Wales, in May, 1839.... Philadelphia: printed by J. C. Clark, 1839. 18 p. DLC; InU; MH-Z; PHi. 56607

Johnson, Lorenzo Dow, 1805-1867. The spirit of Roger Williams, with a portrait of one of his descendants.... Boston: published for the author, by Cassady and March, 1839. 94 p. CU; ICN; MWA; NCH; RNR. 56608

[Johnson, Oliver] 1809-1889. Sectarianism renounced [Boston: 1839] 8 p. D. DLC; OO. 56609

Johnson, Ovid Frazer, 1807-1854. Address delivered before the Phrenakosmian Society of Pennsylvania College, at their 8th anniversary celebration, February 22, 1839. Gettysburgh: the society, 1839. 23 p. DLC; ICP; MdBLC; PHi; PU. 56610

Johnson, Richard Mentor, 1781-1850. Biography of Richard M. Johnson, of Kentucky. New York: Mason, 1839. O. 56611

Johnson, Robert Gibbon, 1771-1850. An historical account of the first settlement of Salem, in West Jersey, by John Fenwick, esq., chief proprietor of the same; with many of the important events that have occured, down to the present generation, embracing a period of 150 years. Philadelphia: O. Rogers, 1839. 173 p. DLC; MBAt; MWA; PPA; WHi. 56612

Johnson, Samuel, 1709-1784. Johnson's English dictionary: in which the words are deduced form their originals; explained in their different meanings; and authorized by the names of the writers who have used them and their pronunciation accurately marked. Abstracted form the folio edition, by the author, Samuel Johnson, LL.D. A new edition.... Cincinnati: V. P. James, 1839. KyLoSM; NbU. 56613

----. ----. As improved by Todd and abridged by Chalmers; with Walker's pronouncing dictionary combined; to which is added Walkers key to the classical pronounciation of Greek, Latin and Scripture proper names. Philadelphia: Kimker and Sharpless, 1839. 1156 p. CSt-L; InHuP; MdBD;NjPT; PU-L. 56614

----. The history of Rasselas, Prince of Abissinia. New edition. Boston: Weeks, Jordan and Company, 1839. 124 p. InU; NCH; NRU. 56615

Johnson, Samuel, 1723-1772. On scoffing at religion. New York: Protestant Episcopal Tract Society, 1839. CtHC; DLC; InID; 56616

Johnson, Samuel Roosevelt, 1802-1873. Cautions concerning the spirit of the age. An address delivered at the 5th anniversary of the Western Literary Society of Wabash College, July 9, 1839. Crawfordsville: Bartholomew, 1839. 16 p. In; PPPrHi. 56617

Johnson, Walter R[ogers], 1794-1852. Address deliverd on laying the corner stone of the Academy of Natural Sciences of Philadelphia, May 15th, 1839.... Philadelphia: printed by T. K. and P. G. Collins, 1839. 8 p. CtY; DLC; MH; PPAmP; PU. 56618

----. Analysis of some of the anthracites and iron ores found on the head waters of Beaver Creek, in the counties of Luzerne, Northampton and Schuylkill, Pa.... [Philadelphia: 1839] 10 p. DLC; MH; OClWHi; PPAN. 56619

---. Analysis of some of the minerals found at Karthaus and Three Runs, on the west branch of the Susquehanna River, Clearfield County, Pennsylvania; accompanied by a section of the mineral ground [Philadelphia: 1839] 8 p. DLC; PPAN. 56620

----. Examination of some of the anthracites.... [Philadelphia: 1839] 5 p. MH; MH-Z; PPAN. 56621

----. Report of an examination of the mines, iron works and other property belonging to the Clearfield Coke and Iron Company.... Philadelphia: L. R. Bailey, 1839. 64 p. MB; MH; OClWHi; PPAN; PHi. 56622

Johnson, William Cost, 1806-1860. Speech of William Cost Johnson, of Maryland, on the state of the defences of the country. Delivered in the House of Representatives, March 2, 1839. Washington: printed by Gales and Seaton, 1839. 8 p. DLC; MdHi. 56623

Johnson's pocket almanac for 1840 [Philadelphia: Willard Johnson, 1839] MWA. 56624

[Johnstone, Christian Isobel] 1781-1857. ...Lives and voyages of Drake, Cavendish and Dampier, including an introductory view of the earlier discoveries in the South Sea, and the history of the bucaniers [sic.] New York: Harper, 1839. 332 p. CU; MPeaI; NAlf; ScDuE; TxGR. 56625

Jones, George, 1800-1870. Excursions to Cairo,

Jerusalem, Damascus and Balbec from the United States ship Delaware, during her recent cruise.... New York: Van Nostrand and Dwight, 1839. 388 p. RPAt; RPB. 56626

Jones, Henry. The scripture searched; or Christ's second coming and kingdom at hand.... New York: Gould, Newman and Saxton, 1839. 240 p. CTHWatk; KPea; NBuDD; RPB. 56627

Jones, Joseph Huntington, 1797-1868. Outline of a work of grace in the Presbyterian congregation at New Brusnwick, N.J., during the year 1837 [including a description of the tornado of 1835] By Joseph H. Jones, pastor of the 6th Presbyterian church, Philadelphia: Philadelphia: Henry Perkins, 1839. 148 p. CtY; InCW; MBC; NjMD; PPPrHi. 56628

Jones, Joseph Stevens, 1811-1877. The people's lawyer; a comedy in two acts. New York: T. H. French [1839?] 24 p. OCl. 56629

Jones, Joshua. Thoughts on the literary prospects of America. An essay: by J. Jones. Baltimore: printed by John Murphy, 1839. 16 p. CtY; DLC; MdHi; ScU. 56630

Jones, Lot, d. 1865. Memoir of Mrs. Sarah Louise Taylor, or an illustration of the work of the Holy Spirit in awakening, renewing and sanctifying the heart.... New York: John S. Taylor, 1839. 324 p. DLC; GDC; NjNbS; RPB; WHi. 56631

Jones, Silas. Practical phrenology.... 2nd edition. New York: S. Colman, 1839. 336 p. CtMW; DLC; IaFair. 56632

Jones, Thomas P., 1773-1848. New conversations on chemistry, adapted to the present state of that science: by Thomas P. Jones, M.D.... Philadelphia: John Grigg, 1839. 332 p. NNNAM; OOxM; OSW; PU; ScCliP. 56633

Jone's stories related to Rollo and Lucy.... New York: Clark, Austin and Gunther, 1839. MH. 56634

Joseph, son of Jacob. The favorite son race.... Boston: 1839. 72 p. MWA. 56635

Josephus, Flavius. The genuine works of Flavius Josephus translated by WIlliam Whiston. New York: Robinson and Franklin, successors to Leavitt, Lord and Company, 1839. 6 v. GEU;

NBLiHi; NNebg; NPen; 56636

----. Die werke des Flavius Josephus, der beruhmten Judischen Geschichtschreibers...und das leben des Josephus von ihm selbst geschrieben. 7th edition. Philadelphia: herausgegeben von Kimber und Scharpletz, 1839. 903 p. OBerB; PATM; PPG; PU. 56637

----. The works of Josephus, with a life written by himself. Translated from the original Greek, including explanatory notes and observations, by William Whinston, A.M. With complete index. Stereotyped edition. Baltimore: Armstrong and Perry, 1839. 648 p. MdBP; NBuDD; ScDuE; UU. 56638

----. The works of Flavius Josephus, ...containing twenty books of the Jewish antiquities, seven books of the Jewish war, and the life of Josephus, written by himself. Translated from the original Greek according to Haver-Camp's accurate edition. Together with explanatory notes and observations. Embellished with elegant engravings. By the late William Whiston...From the last London edition of 1827.... Philadelphia: J. Grigg, 1839. 2 v. Vi; VtB. 56639

Josse, Augustin Luis. A grammar of the Spanish language, with practical exercises. Revised by F. Sales, 9th American edition. Boston: J. Munroe and Company, 1839. MB; MH; MH-AH; NjP. 56640

Journal of Christian education.... v. 1-4, Jan., 1839-Dec., 1842. New York: Union Depository [etc., etc.] 1839-1842. 4 v. in 3. CtHT; ICN; MnHi; NNG; PPL. 56641

Journal of religious education and family and Sunday school visitor. Edited by the Rev. Benjamin O. Peers, and the Rev. Benjamin I. Haight. January, 1839. Published by the General Protestant Episcopal Sunday School Union. New York: Union Depository, 1839 [-1842] V. 1. MBD. 56642

The journal, or token of friendship. New York: 1839. 246 p. MWA. 56643

The judge. New York: Protestant Episcopal Tract Society, 1839. 4 p. DLC; InID. 56644

Judson, L. Carroll. A biography of the signers of the Declaration of Independence, and of Washington and Patrick Henry. With an appendix, containing the Constitution of the United States and other documents. By L. Carroll Judson.... Philadelphia: J. Dobson, and Thomas, Cowperthwait and Company, 1839. 354 p. DLC; LN; MdBJ; NUt; PMA. 56645

Junkin, David Xavier, 1808-1888. The believer dead yet speaking; a sermon preached Sabbath, July 7th, 1839, in the 1st Presbyterian Church, Greenwich, N.J., occasioned by the death of the Rev. William B. Sloan, former pastor of said church. Easton, [Pa.] printed on the college press, 1839? 12 p. NjR. 56646

Junkin, George. A treatise on justification. Philadelphia: J. Whetham, 1839. 328 p. GDecCT; ICP; InGo; PPPrHi. 56647

The jurist: or law and equity reporter containing full reports of all the cases argued and determined in the several courts of law and equity in England. New York: 1839-40. 2 v. in 1. MiD-B; NIC-L. 56648

The juvenile forget me not, a Christmas, New Year's and birthday present.... Philadelphia: Thomas T. Ash and Henry F. Anners, 1839-1841. DLC; MWA; NjR; RPB; TxU. 56649

Juvenile poems; to be read and learned.... Providence: George Daniels, 1839. 16 p. CtY. 56650

Juvenile primmer, or first book for children, arranged on the most simple principles. Honolulu: 1839. 16 p. DLC. 56651

K

Kames, Henry Home, 1696-1782. An abridgement of elements of criticisms by the Honorable Henry Home, of Kames. Edited by John Frost, A.M. 4th edition. Philadelphia: Haswell, Barrington and Haswell, New Orleans: Alexander Towar, 1839. 300 p. DLC: InPerM; ODaU. 56652

----. Elements of criticism, by Henry Home, lord Kames...with analyses, and translations of ancient and foreign illustrations. Edited by Abraham Mills.... New edition. New York: F.J. Huntington and Company, 1839. 504 p. DLC; IaDuU; OO; ScNC; ViRut. 56653

----. ----. 3rd edition. Philadelphia: 1839. 300 p. OO. 56654

Kaskaskia River Bridge Company. Bridge builders! Notice is hereby given, that proposals are invited to build a bridge across the Kaskaskia River, at Kaskaskia...March, 1839. Alton: printed at the Telegraph office [1839] Broadside. IHi. 56655

Kaufmann, Peter. Eine Abhandlung uber Amerikanische Volks- Erziehung.... Canton, Ohio: Gedruckt bey Peter Kaufmann und Company, 1839. 52 p. NN; ViU. 56656

----. A treatise on American popular education. Canton: Kaufmann, 1839. 50 p. OCl; OClWHi; OHi; PHi; PPL. 56657

Keep, John, 1781-1870. Moral influence; a sermon preached Oct. 25, 1838, at the installation of the Rev. D. N. Merritt, as pastor of the Congregational church in Riga, Monroe County, N.Y. Rochester: Sheppard, 1839. 30 p. CSmH; MBC; NCH; PPPrHi; RPB. 56658

Keightley, Thomas, 1789-1872. The history of Greece. To which is added, a chronological table of contemporary history. By Joshua Toulmin Smith.... Boston: Hilliard, Gray and Company, 1839. 490 p. CU; GU; PPiW; RPA; TxU. 56659

----. The history of Rome.... To which is added a chronological table of contemporary history. By Joshua Toulmin Smith.... Boston: Hilliard, Gray and Company, 1839. 480 p. CtY; ICP; MBL; RPB; ScCC. 56660

----. Outlines of universal history; by Dionysius Lardner. Illustrated by 49 engravings on wood.... Philadelphia: Hogan and Thomson, 1839. 514 p. MeBa; MH; WvU. 56661

Keith, Alexander, 1791-1880. Demonstration of the truth of the Christian religion.... From the 2nd Edinburgh edition. New York: Harper and Brothers, 1839. 336 p. MBC; NCaS; PMA; TJaL; ViRU. 56662

----. ...Evidence of the truth of the Christian religion derived from the literal fulfilment of prophecy.... From the 6th Edinburgh edition. New York: Harper and Brothers, 1839. 284 p. GDecCT; MH; MWA; NbOM; TKC. 56663

Keith, Thomas, 1759-1824. Keith's arithmetic. Practical and self- explanatory.... Revised and adapted to American currency, and use in American schools. By an experienced teacher of mathematics.... Philadelphia: Thomas, Cowperthwait and Company, 1839. 290 p. DAU; NcWsS. 56664

Kellogg and Company's Alabama almanac, for the year 1839: Being the 3rd after bissextile, and until July 4th, the 63rd of American independence. Adapted to the latitude and meridian of Mobile. By David Young, Philom. Mobile: J. S. Kellogg and Company, 1839. 45 [1] p. MWA. 56665

Kelsey, David B. The family dyer, containing 30 receipts of the most approved methods of colouring small articles. By David B. Kelsey. Bangor [Me.] S. S. Smith, printer, 1839. 36 p. DLC. 56666

Kendall, Edward Augustus, 1776?-1842. Keeper's travels in search of his master. Newburyport: John G. Tilton, 1839. 2 v. MNe. 56667

Kennedy, John Pendleton, 1795-1870. Speech, on the bill making appropriations for the civil and diplomatic service for the year 1839, delivered in the House of Representatives, February 19, 1839. Washington: 1839. 38 p. MBAt; MdHi; MHi; PPL. 56668

Kenrick, Francis Patrick, 1797-1863. Theologiae dogmaticae tractatus tres, De revelatione. De ecclesia at De verbo Dei, quos concinnavit...Franciscius Patricius Kenrick.... Philadelphia: typis L. Johnson, 1839-1840. 4 v. CtY; MBAt; MdBS; NhD; OCX. 56669

Kenrick, William, 1789-1872. The American silk growers guide; or the art of raising the mulberry and silk.... Boston: Weeks, Jordan and Company, 1839. 167 p. IaAS; MWA; NN; OHi; PMA. 56670

----. ----. 2nd edition, enlarged and improved. By William Kenrick. Boston: Weeks, Jordan and Company, 1839. 167 p. CU; LN; MH; PP; ViMc. 56671

Kent, James, 1763-1847. An analytical abridgment of Kent's commentaries on American law. With a full series of questions for examination, adapted both to the analysis, and to the original commentaries. By J. Eastman Johnson.... New York: Halsted and Voorhies, 1839. 389 p. CtMW; DLC; MAnP; NRU; PPB. 56672

Kentucky. General Assembly. House. Journal of the House of Representatives of the commonwealth of Kentucky, begun and held in the town of Frankfort on Monday, the 2nd day of December, in the year of our Lord 1839, and of the commonwealth, the 48th. Frankfort, Ky.: A. G. Hodges, state printer, 1839. 656 p. InU; Ky; KyU. 56673

----. ----. Senate. Journal of the Senate of the commonwealth of Kentucky, begun and held in the town of Frankfort on Monday, the 2nd day of December, in the year of our Lord, 1839, and of the commonwealth the 48th. Frankfort, Ky.: A. G. Hodges, state printer, 1839. 483 p. Ky; KyHi; KyU. 56674

----. Laws, Statutes, etc. Acts of the General Assembly of the commonwealth of Kentucky: December session, 1838. James Clark, Governor. Published by authority. Frankfort, Ky.: A. G. Hodges, state printer, 1839. 415 p. A-SC; KyHi; MdBB; Mi-L; Nj. 56675

----. Mechanics' Institute of Louisville. Charter, constitutuion and by-laws of the Mechanics' Institute of Louisville, March, 1839. Louisville: 1839. 11 p. MBAt; MHi. 56676

THe key of Heaven; or a manuel [!] of prayer.... 22nd edition, revised...by Right Reverend J. M., Catholic bishop. 1st American stereotype edition.... New York: Patrick Kavanagh, 1839. 365 p. CSansS. 56677

Keystone agricultural almanac for 1849. Philadelphia: William W. Walker [1839] MWA. 56678

The kidnapped clergyman; or experience the best teacher.... Boston: Dow and Jackson, 1839. 123 p. CtHWatk; ICN MB; NN; PHi. 56679

Kilpin, Samuel, 1774-1830. Memoir of Rev. Samuel Kilpin...with some extracts from his correspondence.... New York: American Tract Society [1839?] 156 p. CtHT. 56680

Kimball, David T. I dwell among my own people. A sermon.... By David T. Kimball. Ipswich: Register Press, 1839. 24 p. ICMe. 56681

----. A sermon on the utility of a permanent ministry.... Ipswich: Register Press, 1839. 24 p. CtY; MHi; MiD-B; NjPT; PPPrHi. 56682

King, Alonzo. Memoir of George Dana Boardman, late missionary to Burmah.... With an introductory essay. New and improved stereotype edition. Boston: Gould, Kendall and Lincoln [1839] CtHC; GEU-T; LNB; NNMn; RPB. 56683

King, Charles, 1789-1867. The late Samuel Ward. New York: J. P. Wright, 1839? 16 p. NN. 56684

King, Thomas Butler. Address to the voters of the 1st district of Georgia [Savannah: 1839?] MBAt. 56685

Kingsley, Charles, 1819-1875. Sir Walter Raleigh and his time. Boston: 1839. MWbro. 56686

Kingsley, George, 1811-1884. The sacred choir: a collection of church music consisting of selections from the most distinguished authors...with several pieces of music by the editor, also a progressive elementary system of instruction for pupils; 3rd edition corrected. New York: Appleton and Company, 1839. 342 p. CtMW; CtY; MB; NRU. 56687

----. The social choir, designed for a class book, or the domestic circle, consisting of selections of music from the most distinguished authors, among whom are the names of Mozart, Handel, Haydn.... 8th edition. Boston: Crocker and Brewster, etc., etc., 1839. MH. 56688

Kingston, Massachusetts. School Committee. Report of the school committee...read April 1, 1839 [Plymouth] James Thurber, 1839. 8 p. DE; DHEW; MB; MH; MKi. 56689

Kinmont, Alexander, 1799-1838. Twelve lectures on the natural history of man, and the rise and progress of philosophy. With a biographical sketch of the author.... Cincinnati: U. P. James, 1839. 355 p. CoD; ICN; MB; OUr; PPWa. 56690

Kinne, Asa. The most important parts of Blackstone's commentaries, reduced to questions and answers. By Asa Kinne. 2nd edition. New York: W. E. Dean [etc.] Philadelphia: Thomas, Cowperthwait and Company, 1839. 266 p. DLC; NcD; NRAL; PPA. 56691

----. The most important parts of Kent's commentaries, reduced to questions and answers. New York: W. E. Dean, Collins, Keese and Company, Philadelphia: Thomas, Cowperthwait and Company, 1839. 127 p. MWiW; NNIA; OO; PU-L; WaU. 56692

----. Questions and answers on law alphabetically arranged with references to the most approved authors. New York: published for the author, 1839 [4] 244 p. Pr. 56693

Kippis, Andrew, 1725-1795. A narrative of the voyages round the world, performed by Captain James Cook.... Philadelphia: Haswell, Barrington and Haswell, 1839. 2 v. in 1. ViU. 56694

Kirk, Edward Norris, 1802-1874. Jesus, the great missionary. A sermon delivered in Bowdoin Street Church, Boston, on the evening of November 13, 1839, at the ordination of Samuel Wolcott, as a foreign missionary.... Boston: printed by Perkins and Marvin, 1839. 32 p. CU; MiD-B; MnHi; PPPr-Hi; WHi. 56695

Kirkham, Samuel. English grammar in familiar lectures, accompanied by a compendium embrac-

ing a new systematick order of parsing.... Last edition. Cincinnati, O.: E. Morgan and Company, 1839. 228 p. MH. 56696

----. ----. 105th edition. Baltimore: Plaskitt and Cugle, 1839. 228 p. MBAt; MH; NBHM; NBuG; PEaL. 56697

----. ----. 107th edition. New York: Collins, Keese and Company, 1839. 228 p. D. MB; OO. 56698

----. English grammar in familiar lectures: embracing a new systematic order of parsing, a new system of punctuation...to which are added, a compendium, an appendix, and a key to the exercises.... Stereotyped by William Hagar and Company, New York. 45th edition, enlarged and improved. Rochester, N.Y.: William Alling, 1839. 228 p. CoGrS; ICU; MiU-C; MWA; NRU. 56699

----. ----. 46th edition. Rochester, N.Y.: William Alling, 1839. 228 p. NRHi. 56700

----. An essay on elocution, designed for the use of schools and private learners.... New York: Robinson, Pratt and Company, 1839. 357 p. PWCHi. 56701

[Kirkland, Caroline Matilda (Stansbury)] 1801-1864. A new home-who'll follow? or glimpses of western life. By Mrs. Mary Clavers [pseud.]... New York: C. S. Francis, Boston: J. H. Francis, 1839. 317 p. IEN; MBL; OFH; RPA; TxDaM. 56702

Kirkpatrick, Joseph S. Private thoughts on theology, to the serious enquirer after truth.... Dubuque [Iowa] Russell and Reeves, printers, 1839. 28 p. IaHi. 56703

Knapp, Sameul Lorenzo, 1784-1838. Library of American history: a reprint of standard works: connected by editorial remarks, abounding with copious notes, biographical sketches and miscellaneous matter, intended to give the reader a full view of American history. Edited by Samuel L. Knapp.... 2nd edition. New York: J. C. Riker, 1839. 2 v. in 1. MB; MdBE; NbOC; PHi; TxShA. 56704

----. Tales of the garden of Kosciuszko.... 2nd edition. New York: Levison and Brother, 1839. 216 p. CSmH; OClW; RPA; ViU. 56705

Knauff, George P. Virginia reels; selected and arranged for the piano forte by G. P. Knauff. Baltimore [Md.] George Willig, Jr., 1839. 3 v. in 1. NRU. 56706

Knickerbocker almanac for 1840. By David Young. New York, N.Y.: H. and S. Raynor [1839?] MWA. 56707

----. By David Young. New York: Turner and Fisher, 1839. MWA. 56708

Knight, Elleanor [Warner] b. 1799. A narrative of the Christian experience, life and adventures, trials and labours of Elleanor Knight, written by herself. Providence: 1839. 126 p. ICN; NNU-W; RPB. 56709

Knight, Isaac. A narrative of the captivity and sufferings of Isaac Knight from Indian barbarity.... Communicated by himself, and at his request written by Hiram A. Hunter. Evansville: printed at the Journal office, 1839. 34 p. CSmH; ICN; KHayF; OCHP; PPiO. 56710

Knill, Richard, 1787-1857. The missionary's wife; or a brief account of Mrs. Loveless, of Madras.... Philadelphia: Presb., 1839. 24 p. CSansS; GDecCT; IaDuU; MnSM; PPM; TxShA. 56711

Knowles, James Davis, 1798-1838. Memoir of Mrs. Ann H. Judson, late missionary to Burmah; including a history of the American Baptist mission in the Burman Empire...24th thousand with a continuation of the history of the mission. Boston: Gould, Kendall and Lincoln, 1839. 395 p. TxU. 56712

Knowles, James Sheridan, 1784-1862. Love; a play in five acts.... New York: Samuel French [1839?] 69 p. NbU; OCl. 56713

Knowles, John Power, 1808-1887. Political contributions to newspapers, 1839 [Providence: 1839] 8 p. RPB. 56714

Knowlton, Charles. Fruits of philosophy, or the private companion of adult people. 4th editon, with additions. Philadelphia: Rogers, 1839. 128 p. MH-M; NNN. 56715

Knowlton, Miner, 1804-1870. Land belonging to the United States at West Point, New York....

West Point: 1839. 68 p. NBu; NN; NWM. 56716

Knox, James. A token of affectionate remembrance: being a farewell discourse...in Norwalk [Conn.] ... Philadelphia: 1839. 59 p. CtY; MiD-B. 56717

Knox, John, 1790-1858. The church glorious; a discourse delivered on the occasion of the opening, for divine worship.... By the Rev. John Knox, senior pastor of the Collegiate Church. New York: Robert Carter, 1839. 38 p. CSansS; MBC; MWA; NjR; PPrHi. 56718

The Knox County Mutual Insurance Company. Circular, by-laws and act of incorporation.... Mount Vernon, Ohio: published at the office of the Democratic Banner, 1839. 20 p. OClWHi. 56719

Koch, Christophe Guillaume de, 1737-1813. History of the revolutions in Europe, from the subversion of the Roman empire in the west, to the Congress of Vienna. From the French of Christopher William Koch. With a continuation to the year 1815, by M. Schoell. Revised and corrected by J. G. Cogswell. With a sketch of the late revolutions in France, Belgium, Poland and Greece. Embellished with engravings. Middletown: Hunt and Noyes, 1839. 2 v. in 1. PPFr; TJal; TNP. 56720

Kock, Charles Paul de, 1794-1871. The barber of Paris; or moral retribution. By Paul De Kock, author of "Andrew the Savoyard," "Good Fellow," etc., etc. Philadelphia: Carey and Hart, 1839. 2 v. CtY; MsN; NNS; MWA. 56721

Kramer, John Theophilus. The slave auction.... Boston: Robert F. Wallcut, 1839. DLC; ICU; MWA; NcD; PHi. 56722

Krummacher, F. A. The little dove. From the German of F. A. Krummacher. Boston: Weeks, Jordan and Company, 1839. 140 p. MB; MWbor-Hi. 56723

Kurek, Adam. Lawrence quick step, respectfully dedicated to S. Abbot Lawrence and the members of the New England Guards, composed by Kurek and arranged by Knaebel. Boston: Keith and Moore, 1839. 4 p. MB; MBNEC; MH. 56724

L

Lac Superier et avtres lieux ou sont les missions des peres de la compagnie de iesus comprises sors le nom d'Ovataovacs. Louisville: 1839. IU. 56725

The ladder of learning, to be ascended early in the morning. New Haven: S. Babcock, 1839. 24 p. DLC; MH; MiD-B. 56726

Ladies Charitable Association of Concord, New Hampashire. Constitution.... Concord: 1839. Nh. 56727

Ladies New York City Anti-slavery Society. Constitution and by- laws. New York: William Dorr, 1839. 8 p. InU; NNC. 56728

Lady Chavely; or the woman of honor. A new version of Cheverly, the man of honor.... Philadlephia: Carey and Hart, 1839. 47. CtY; KyLx; MB; NcD; PPL. 56729

Lafayette. Worster Carpenters. The book of pieces.... Lafayette: 1839. 31 p. In. 56730

Lafever, Minard. The beauties of modern architecture. Illustrated by 48 original plates, designed expressly for this work. 3rd edition. New York: D. Appleton and Company, 1839. 176 p. DLC; IaAS; KyBC; NcU; ScU. 56731

La Fontaine, Jean de, 1621-1695. La Fontaine. A present for the young. From the French. Boston: Weeks, Jordan and Company, 1839. 108 p. DLC; ICBB; MBevHi; MW. 56732

Lallemand, Francois, 1790-1853. On involuntary seminal discharges...translated from the French by William Wood.... Philadelphia: A. Waldie, 1839. 152 p. CoCsC; ICMe; MeB; NBMS; PPA. 56733

Lamb, Dana. Complete list of the Congregational ministers and churches in Addison County, Vermont, from the first settlement to the present time.... Boston: Perkins and Marvin, printers, 1839. 14 p. MiD-B; VtMidbC; WHi. 56734

Lamennais, Hugues Felicite Robert de, 1782-1854. The people's own book. Boston: Charles C. Little and James Brown, 1839. 188 p. GDecCT; MB; NN; PPL. 56735

----. ----. 144 p. DLC; MWA; PPL; PU. 56736

La Motte-Fouque, Friedrich Heinrich Karl, freiherr de, 1777-1843. Undine: a miniature romance: from the German to Baron de La Motte Fouque.... New York: S. Coleman, 1839. 211 p. DLC; MdBLC; MGS; NNS; PPL. 56737

Lamson, Alvan, 1792-1864. A history of the first church and parish in Dedham, in three discourses, delivered on occasion of the completion, November 18, 1838, of the second century since the gathering of said church. Dedham [Mass.] printed by H. Mann, 1839. 104 p. CBPac, ICMe; MnHi; MWA; RPB. 56738

Lamson, Silas. A flying roll. Massachusetts: 1839. DLC. 56739

Lancaster Academy, Lancaster, New Hampshire. A catalogue of the trustees, instructors and students, of Lancaster Academy, for the year ending November 1839. Lancaster, New Hampshire: printed by Rix and Whittemore, 1839. 11 p. MeHi. 56740

Lancaster County, Pennsylvania. Citizens. The voice of Lancaster County, on the subject of a national foundry. Lancaster: J. W. Forney, printer, 1839. 19 p. PHi; PPi; PPL. 56741

Lander, Richard Lemon, 1804-1834. Journal on expedition to explore the course and termination of the Niger...by Richard and John Lander. New York: Harper and Brothers, 1839. 2 v. MH; MnHi; OAU; ScAb; WWaN. 56742

Landis, John, b. 1805. Discourses on the depravity of the human family; particularly applied to this nation and these times. Harrisburg: printed by R. S. Elliott and Company, 1839. 177 p. DLC; MoWgT; MWiW; PHi; PU. 56743

----. Hymns and sacred pieces, never before published. By John Landis, sacred historical painter...and fifteen sermons, relative to the nation and these times. Harrisburg: printed for the author, 1839. 128 p. DLC; PRHi; RPB; PPL; PSt. 56744

----. The Messiah: a poem...by John Landis, sacred historical painter. 2nd edition. Harrisburg: 1839. 64 p. CtHT-W; MB; P. 56745

----. Jehovah! the glorious God, considered in the creation: being poetical effussions with hymns, some of which are descriptive of the judgement. Harrisburg: 1839. 24 p. RPB. 56746

----. The soul's aid. Things of importance to the converted and unconverted.... Harrisburg: R. S. Elliott and Company, printers, 1839. 91 p. PRHi; MiGr; NcD; PLF. 56747

Landis, Robert Wharton, 1809-1883. The obligation and duty of parents in respect to the claims of the 7th commandment explained and enforced. New York: 1839. 12 p. CtY. 56748

Landon, Letitia Elizabeth, 1802-1838. The poetical works of Miss Landon.... Philadlephia: E. L. Carey and A. Hart, 1839. 348 p. AMob; InCW; KyBC; PPA; WGr. 56749

----. Works. Philadelphia: E. L. Carey and A. Hart, 1839. 2 v. NT; PU. 56750

Landor, Walter Savage, 1775-1864. Pericles and Aspasia.... Philadelphia: E. L. Carey and A. Hart, 1839. 2 v. GEU; MB; MWA; RNR; ScU. 56751

Lane, Horace. The wandering boy, careless sailor, and result in inconsideration. A true narrative. Skaneateles [N. Y.] printed for the author by L. A. Pratt, 1839 224 p. DLC; NN. 56752

Langtree and O'Sullivan. Prospectus of the Madison papers to be published in the city of Washington, in July, 1839.... [Washington: Langtree and O'Sullivan, 1839?] 7 p. IU; MiU-C; PPL. 56753

The language of flowers; with illustrative poetry, to which is now first added, the calendar of flowers. Revised by the editor of "Forget me not". 5th American edition. Philadelphia: Lea and Blanchard, 1839. AU; CtY; MAnP; NN; PPL. 56754

Landwirths und Seidenbauers calender fur 1840. Lancaster, Pa.: Johann Bar [1839] MWA. 56755

Lankester, Ewin, 1814-1874. Vegetable substances used for the food of man.... New York: Harper, 1839. 271 p. DLC; MSbo; NBuCC; NRU; RKi. 56756

Lanman, James Henry, 1812-1887. History of Michigan, civil and topographical, in a compendious form; with a view of the surrounding lakes. New York: E. French, 1839. 397 p. 56757

Larrabee, Charles, 1782-1863. A report on the manner pensions have been granted and paid by the United States government. By Major Charles Larrabee, Late Major in the United States Army. Hartford: 1839. 24 p. CtHT-W; CtY; MWA. 56758

Laurel Hill Cemetery, Philadelphia, Pennsylvania. Regulations...on the River Schuylkill, near Philadelphia. Incorporated by the legislature of Pennsylvania. Philadelphia: printed by John C. Clark, 1839. 20 p. MB; NjR; PPL. 56759

----. Statues of Old Morality and his pony and of Sir Walter Scott at Laurel Hill.... Philadelphia: A. Waldie, 1839. PPL; ViU. 56760

Lavater, Johann Caspar, 1741-1801. The pocket lavater, or the science of physiognomy to which is added, an inquiry into the analogy existing between brute and human physiognomy, from the Italian of Porta. New York: Robinson and Franklin, 1839. 116 p. NN; PU. 56761

Law, John, 1796-1873. Address delivered before the Vincennes Historical and Antiquarian Society, February 22, 1839.... Louisville: Prentice and Weissinger, 1839. 48 p. CSmH; InHi; MWA; Nh-Hi; PPi. 56762

Law, William, 1686-1761. A serious call to a devout and holy life.... Boston: 1839. NN. 56763

Law Academy of Philadelphia. Charter, constitution and by-laws, argument-lists, 1853-1860, and discourse by Job R. Tyson, George Sharswood and Benjamin H. Brewster. Philadelphia: 1839-1859. PPL. 56764

Lawremce, Levin. No. 2. Series of letters to Nicholas Biddle...upon the subject of a supply of money.... Baltimore: 1839. 15 p. MB; MBAt. 56765

The laws of etiquette; or short rules and reflections for conduct in society. By a gentleman.... Philadelphia: Carey, Lea and Blanchard, 1839. 224 p. CtY; MH; MHi; NjR. 56766

Lay, George Tradescant. Notes made during the voyage of the Himmaleh in the Malayan Archepilago, etc. Voyages made in 1837. New York: E. French, 1839. 2 v. MiD; NIC; NN. 56767

Lea, Albert Miller, 1807-1890. Notes on Wisconsin Territory particularly with reference to the Iowa district or Black Hawk Purchase. Philadelphia: H. Tanner and Company, 1839. IaHA. 56768

Leavitt, Joshua, 1794-1873. The Christian Lyre; a collection of hymns and tunes adapted for social worship, prayer meetings, and revivals of religion. With a supplement. 19th edition, revised. New York: Robinson and Franklin, 1839. 2 v. AmSSchU; NNUT; WWaupu. 56769

----. Easy lessons in reading. Keene, N. H.: J. and J. W. Prentiss, 1839. ICU; MH. 56770

----. Supplement to the Christian lyre; containing more than 100 psalm tunes, such as are most used in church's of all denominations. New York: Robinson and Franklin, etc., etc., 1839. 106 p. NNUT. 56771

Leavitt, O. S. Strictures on the new school laws of Ohio and Michigan; with some general observation on the system of other states.... Cincinnati: Isaac Hefley and Company, printers, 1839. 31 p. MB; OClWHi. 56772

Le Brethon, J. J. P. Guide to the French language.... 1st American from the 7th London edition, corrected, enlarged and improved; by P. Bekeart.... New York: W. E. Dean, 1839. 338 p. CtY; DLC; GDecCT; PV; ScCMu. 56773

----. Key to the pronunciation of the French Language, extracted from the author's celebrated grammar, and forming a suitable introduction to all the most approved systems of instruction now in use. Revised and enlarged by Daniel C. Underhill. New York: Neely, 1839. 94 p. CtMW; MiOC. 56774

Lectures to sabbath school teachers, on mental cultivation; delivered at the Odeon, in Boston, September, 1838. Boston: Whipple and Damrell, 1839. 115 p. DLC; MBC; MB-HP; MH. 56775

Lectures to sunday school teachers. Boston: 1839. MB. 56776

The lecturess; or women's sphere. Boston: Whipple and Damrell, 1839. 124 p. CtY; MB; MWA; OO; RPB. 56777

Lee, Abby. Little Ellen and other pleasing poetical stories. By A. L. of Newport, R. I. Published with Rhode Island tales. New York: Mahlon Day and Company, 1839. RPB. 56778

Lee, Charles Alfred, 1801-1872. The elements of geology for popular use, containing a description of the geological formations and mineral resources of the United States. New York: Harper, 1839. 384 p. CtMW; IaU; MB; NBuCC; RKi. 56779

----. Human physiology.... 2nd edition. New York: published by the American Common School Union, 1839. 336 p. KyLxT; MBM; MHM; NNN; ViRMC. 56780

Lee, Hannah Farnham [Sawyer] 1780-1865. The life and times of Martin Luther, by the author of "Three experiments in living." Boston: Hilliard, Gray and company, 1839. 324 p. CBPac; IEG; MWA; PPLT; RP. 56781

----. Rosanna; or scenes in Boston. A story.... Cambridge: J. Owen, 1839. 134 p. DLC; MB; MnU; MWA; TxU. 56782

Lee, Henry, 1787-1837. Observations on the writings of Thomas Jefferson, with particular reference to the attack they contain on the memory of the late General Henry Lee in a series of letters.... 2nd edition, with an introduction and notes by Charles Carter Lee. Philadelphia: J. Dobson, etc., 1839. 262 p. CtY; NBu; PPA; TMeC; WHi. 56783

Lee, Jarena, b. 1783. Life and religious experience of Jarena Lee, a colored lady, giving an account of her call to preach the gospel. Revised and corrected from the original manuscript written by herself. 2nd edition. Cincinnati, printed and published for the author, 1839. 24 p. MB. 56784

Lee, John. A fourth letter on the vexatious and cruel injustice and fallacy of the rectangular system of survey practised in the United States addressed to the editor of the Boston Courier, Cambridge [Mass.] 1839. MB. MBAt. 56785

----. Letter to the president of the United States: proposing a method whereby the conflicting claims of the United States and Great Britain, on the disputed fromtier may be determined, by scientific princilples, etc. Cambridge [Mass.] Metcalf, Torry and Ballou, 1839. 22 p. CtY; DLC; InHi; MB; WHi. 56786

Lee, N. K. M. The cook's own book and housekeeper's register; comprehending all valuable receipts for cooking meet, fish and fowl.... By a Boston housekeeper; to which is added Miss Leslie's 75 receipts for pastry, cakes and sweetmeats.... Boston: Munroe and Francis, New York: C. S. Francis, etc., etc., 1839. 300, 37 p. CtY; NNT-C. 56787

Lee, Thomas, J., d. 1835. A spelling book, containing the rudiments of the English language, with appropriate reading lessons. Boston: Munroe and Francis, etc., etc., 1839. MH. 56788

Lee, Zaccheus Collins, 1805-1859. Address delivered before the Horticultural Society of Maryland, at its annual exhibition, June 6, 1839.... Baltimore: J. D. Toy, printer, 32 p. DLC; MdBP; MdHi; PPL. 56789

Leeser, Isaac, 1806-1868. Catechism for Jewish children. 3rd edition. Philadelphia: L. Johnson and Company, 5616 [1839] 134 p. LNB; OrCS; OrU. 56790

----. ----. 4th edition. Cincinnati: Block [5599, 1839] 134 p. CL; OrU. 56791

Le Fevre, Clement Fall, 1797-1882. The sunday school hymn book, designed for Universalist sunday schools, throughout the United States. New York: P. Price, Universalist Union Press, 1839. 64 p. ICN; MMeT-Hi. 56792

Legare, Hugh Swinton, 1797-1843. Speeches...on the recognition of Hayti; in favor of a southern naval depot...December 18, 1838. and January 11 and 15, 1839. Washington: 1839. 24 p. CU; KSalW; MdHi; MH. 56793

Legendre, Adrien Marie, 1752-1833. Elements of geometry and trigonometry. Translated from the French of A. M. Legendre, by David Brewster. Revised and adapted to the course of mathematical instruction in the United States, by Charles Davis.... Hartford: A. S. Barnes and Company, New York: Wiley and Putnam [etc., etc.] 1839. 297

p. MCM; MH; NHem; RPB; ViU. 56794

----. ----. Philadelphia: A. S. Barnes and Company [1839?] DLC. 56795

Leib, James Ronaldson. Thoughts on the elective franchise. Philadelphia: printed by J. C. Clark, 1839. 20 p. MH; MiD; MWA; PHi; TxU. 56796

The leisure hour book. New York: Charles S. Francis, Boston: Joseph H. Francis, 1839 334 p. MBox; NhPet. 56797

Leland, Aaron Whitney, 1783-1871. A discourse at the annual examinnation of the students in the Theological Seminary, Columbia, S. C. Columbia, S. C.: printed at Morgan's Book and Job office, 1839. 25 p. CSmH; GDecCT; NcMHi; NcD; NNUT. 56798

Lemon, Mark, 1809-1870. My sister kate; a farce, in one act. New York: H. Kimber and Company, 1839. 24 p. MB; Mh; NIC; RPB. 56799

Lemonnier, Ceran. A synopsis of natural histroy; embracing the natural history of animals, with human and general animal physiology, vegetable physiology and geology. Translated from the French by Thomas Wyatt.... Philadelphia: T. Wardle, 1839. 191 p. CU; KyLxT; MB; NjP; PPi. 56800

Lempriere, John, 1765?-1824. Bibliotheca classica: or a dictionary of all the principal names and terms relating to the geography, topography, history, literature and mythology of antiquity and of the ancients: With a chronological table. 10th American edition, greatly enlarged. New York: Collins, Keese and Company, 1839. 803 p. IGK; KHi; MNe; NNebg; ScCC. 56801

Leonard, George. A practical treatise on arithmetic, wherein every principle taught is explained in a simple and obvious manner.... Boston: George W. Light, 1839. 347 p. DAU; MBAt; MeU; OO. 56802

Leonard, Levi Washburn, 1790?-1864. The North American spelling book, conformed to Worcester's dictionary. 13th revised edition. Keene, N. H.: G. Tilden, etc., etc., 1839. MH; Nh. 56803

----. A selection of reading lessons for common schools. By the author of the literary and scientific class book. Keene, N. H.: J. and J. W. Prentiss, 1839. Nh; NhHi. 56804

Leonard, Zenas, 1809-1859. Narrative of the adventures of Zenas Leonard, a native of Clearfield County, Pa. who spent five years in trapping furs, trading with the Indians, etc., etc., of the Rocky Mountains; written by himself. Clearfield, Pa.: D. W. Moore, 1839. 87 p. CLU; CSmH; ICN; MWA; WHi. 56805

Leonhard, Karl Casar von, 1779-1862. Popular lectures on geology, treated in a very comprehensive manner. Translated by Rev. J. G. Morris and edited by Professor F. Hall.... Baltimore: N. Hickman, 1839. 397 p. CtY; DLC; NNN; PPAN; ScU. 56806

Le Sage, Alain Rene, 1668-1747. The adventures of Gil Blas of Santillane; translated from the French by Tobias Smollett, to which is prefixed a life of the author. Exeter: J. and B. Williams, 1839. 4 v. MB; OCl; NN; OrU. 56807

Leslie, Eliza, 1787-1858. Directions for cookery, in its various branches. 6th edition. Philadelphia: Carey and Hart, 1839. 466 p. OClW. 56808

----. Seventy-five receipts for pastry, cakes and sweetmeats. 11th edition. Boston: Munroe, 1839. 107 p. PP. 56809

Leslie, John, 1766-1832. Narrative of discovery and adventure in the Polar Seas and regions...By Professor Jameson, and Hugh Murray, Esq. New York: Harper and Brothers, 1839. 373 p. MB-HP; NRU; NGlc; Nh-Hi; TxGR. 56810

Lester, Charles Edwards, 1815-1890. Chains and freedom: or the life and adventures of Peter Wheeler, a colored man yet living.... New York: E. S. Arnold and Company, 1839. 260 p. MB; MH; NN; NUtHi; OC. 56811

Letcher, Montgomery E. Wonderful discovery: being an account of a recent exploration of the celebrated Mammoth cave in Edmonson County, Kentucky, by Dr. Rowan, Prof. Simmons and others...to its termination in an inhabited region in the interior of the earth.... New York: R. H. Elton, 1839. 24 p. KyBgW; Pam; PPiU; WHi. 56812

Letters to the Hon. Harrison Gray Otis, by a citizen of Massachusetts. Occasioned by the petition of himself and others for a repeal of the licence law of 1838.... Boston: Whipple and Damrell, 1839. 36 p. MBAt; MBC; MH; MiD-B; NvHi. 56813

Leuret, Francois, 1797-1851. Anatomie comparee du systeme nerveux, consideredans ses rapports avec l'intelligence, par French Leuret et P. Gratiolet. Accompagnee d'un atlasde 32 plaches dessinees d' apres nature et gravees...Paris: J. B. Bailliere et fils, New York: H. Bailliere [etc., etc.] 1839-1857. 2 v. DLC; KyU; MdUM; PPWI; WU-M. 56814

Lever, Charles James, 1806-1872. The confessions of Harry Lorrequer. New York: George Routledge and Sons, 1839. 382 p. IEN; MB; MoRH; WU. 56815

----. Harry Lorrequer with his confessions. New York: American News Company, 1839. 341 p. KyBgB; NcHy; NN; PATM; PW. 56816

Leverett, Frederick Percival, 1803-1836. A new and copious lexicon of the Latin language; compiled chiefly from the magnum totius latinitatis lexicon of Facciolati and Forcellini, and the German works of Scheller and Luenemann. Boston: J. H. Wilkins and R. B. Carter [etc.] 1839. CSt; ICN; NbOC; OO; RPA. 56817

----. The new Latin tutor; exercises in etymology, syntax and prosody.... Boston: 1839. IGK; ODW. 56818

Levi Buckingham vs. Cincinnati. Cincinnati: 1839. PPL. 56819

Levizac, Jean Pons Victor Lecoutz de. d. 1813. Theoretical and practical grammar of the French language...with numerous corrections...and the additions of a complete treatise on the genders of French nouns.... By A. bolmar. 5th edition. Philadelphia: E. L. Carey and A. Hart, 1839. 294, 173 p. CtMW; CtY. 56820

----. The theoretical and practical grammar of the French tongue; in which the present usage is displayed agreeably to the French Academy. By M. De Levizac. Revised and corrected by M. Stephen Pasquier. 15th American edition. New York: W. E. Dean, etc., 1839. 446 p. CSmH; IaCrC; NPalK; OWoC. 56821

Levy, E. The republican bank: being an essay on the present system of banking: showing its evil tendency.... By a citizen of Indiana. Madison: printed by W. H. Webb, 1839. 24 p. CSmH; DLC; In; MB. 56822

Lewin, Thomas, 1805-1877. A practical treatise on the law of trusts and trustees. Philadelphia: John S. Littell, New York: Halstead and Voorhies, 1839. 410 p. Md; LNL-L; Nj; PU-L; WU-L. 56823

Lewis, Enoch, 1776-1856. Essay on baptism; showing that the baptism of the spirit, and not with water, is the true Christian baptism. Philadelphia: Uriah Hunt, 1839. 63 p. CtY; InRchE; MBAt; MWA; NjR. 56824

Lewis, Taylor, 1802-1877. Natural religion the remains of primitive revelation. A discourse, pronounced at Burlington, before the literary societies of the University of Vermont, August 6th, 1839. New York: University Press, 1839. 52 p. CSmH; IaB; MH; NNG; OClWHi. 56825

Lexington, Massachusetts. First Baptist Church. Declaration of faith with the covenant and list of members of the church, constituted December 11, 1833. Boston: J. Howe, 1839. 25 p. M; MH. 56826

L'Homond, Charles Francois, 1727-1794. Epitome Historiae Sacrae. Auctore L'Homond. Editia nova. Adomavit Georgins ironside, editia. Viginti. Thomas S. Joy, Philadelphia: J. H. Butler and Company, 1839. 156 p. KyLoS; MdBLC; NRMA. 56827

----. Viri illustres ubis Romae a Romula ad augustin...to which is added a dictionary of all the words which occur in the book...by James Hardie. New York: George Long, 1839. 136 p. CLO; In-StmaS; MH; PU. 56828

----. Viri Romae; with introductory exercises, intended as a first book in the study of Latin with English notes. By Frederic P. Leverett and Thomas G. Bradford. Boston: Hilliard, Gray and Company, 1839. 211 p. DLC; IGK; MII; MiD-M; NNC. 56829

The liberty bell. By friends of freedom. Boston: American Anti- slavery Society, Massachusetts Anti-slavery Fair; National Anti- Slavery bazar, 1839-1858. 6 v. CtHC; MnU; PHi; TxU; WU. 56830

Library of dental science. New York: 1839. 10 v. PPWa. 56831

Lieber, Francis, 1800-1872. Legal and political hermeneutic; or principles of interpretation and construction in law and politics... Boston: C. C. Little and J. Brown, 1839. 240 p. LNH; MB: OO; PPCP; ViU. 56832

----. Letter to his excellency, Patrick Noble, governor of South Carolina, on the Penitentiary system, 1839. 62 p. A-Ar; DLC; MBAt; NcU; ScU. 56833

Life of John Knox. See McCrie, Thomas, 1772-1835.

The life of the Rev. C. F. Swartz, Missionary of Trichinopoly and Tanjore, in India. New York: 1839. IEG. 56834

Life's lessons; a narrative, by the author of "Tales that might be true." 1st American, from the 1st London edition. New York: John S. Taylor, 1839. 204 p. GDecCT; NjHo; ViRut. 56835

Liguori, Alfonso Marie de, Saint, 1696-1787. The glories of Mary, Mother of God, containing a beautiful paraphrase of the Salne Regina translated from the Italian of Saint Aophonsus Liguori, and carefully revised by a Catholic priest. With an appendix.... Philadelphia: Henry McGrath, 1839. 3 v. MoS; MWH; OClStM. 56836

----. Reflections on spiritual subjects, and on the passion of Jesus Christ. Translated from the Italian of St. Alphonsus Liguori. Approved by the right Rev. Bishop Fitzpatrick. Boston: Patrick Donahoe [1839] 331 p. MoSU. 56837

Lilly, Lambert See Hawks, Francis Lister.

The lily: a holiday present. With steel embellishments. New York [1839] 232 p. AzPrHi; MBMu; NIC. 56838

Lincoln, Robert W. Lives of the presidents of the United States. With a portrait of each of the presidents. Brattleboro, Vt.: Brattleboro Typographic Company, 1839. 522 p. ICN; MdBE; OCY; PEaL; TNP. 56839

----. ----. With biographical notices of the signers of the Declaration of Independence; sketches of the most remarkable events in the history of the country.... New York: H. Wright and Company, 1839. 522 p. CMary, MB; OCHP; VtMidSM. 56840

Lincoln Academy, Newcastle, Maine. Catalogue of the officers and students of Lincoln Academy, 1839. New Castle, Maine: printed by J. Griffin, 1839. 12 p. Me. 56841

Linley, George. Mornings ruddy beam. Song of the Alpine hunters. Written and composed by George Linley, esq. New York: Firth, Pond and Company, 1839. 5 p. KU. 56842

Linn, William, 1790-1867. The life of Thomas Jefferson. 2nd editon. Ithaca, New York: Mack. Andrus and Woodruff, 1839. 267 p. CtSoP; LNH; MB; NjMD; ViU. 56843

Linsley, James Harvey, 1787-1843. Select hymns adapted to the devotional exercises of the Baptist denomination by James Linsley and Gustavas F. Davis. 3rd edition. Hartford: Canfield and Robins, 1839. 416 p. IEG; NN. 56844

Lipscomb, Andrew Adgate. Life of the Rev. Charles W. Jacobs, minister of the Methodist Protestand Church.... Baltimore: printed by Matchett and Neilson, 1839. 196 p. MdBE; MdHi; NcD; TxU. 56845

Lisfranc, Jacques, 1790-1847. Diseases of the uterus; a series of clinical lectures delivered at the hospital La Pitie. Edited by H. Pauly, M. D. translated from the French by J. Henry Lodge, M. D. Boston: W. D. Ticknor, 1839. 401 p. CtMW; KyLxT; MB; NbU; RPM. 56846

The literary examiner and western monthly review. Edited by E. Burke Fisher. V. 1; May-Dec. 1839. Pittsburgh, Pa.: Whitney and M'Cord, 1839. 464 p. DLC; MnHi; NcU; TxU; WaSp. 56847

The literary geminae; articles in French and English. Nos. 1-12, all pub. Worcester, Mass.: 1839-1840. CtHT-W; DLC; MH; MiU; MMeT- L. 56848

Little, C. J. The social spirit oration. New Haven: 1839. MB. 56849

Little, Sophia Louisa [Robbins] b. 1799. The last days of Jesus; a poem.... Pawtucket, R. I.: printed for the author, 1839. 60 p. MBC; MWA; NcD; NNC; RNR. 56850

The little boy's question. New York: T. Mason and G. Lane, for the Sunday School Union of the Methodist Episcopal Church, 1839. 8 p. 56851

Little genius. September 25, 1839. Philadelphia: published by the proprietor, 1839. PPL-R. 56852

The little haymakers. Boston: printed by Freeman and Bolles, 1839. MH; MWA. 56853

Little Mary; or the pleasant day. A good example for good little girls. New Haven: S. Babcock, 1839. 24 p. CtY. 56854

Little Miami Railroad Company. Engineer. Report of the engineer to the president and directors of the Little Miami Railroad Company. Cincinnati: printed at the Cincinnati Gazette office, 1839. 14 p. DLC; MiU; OCHP. 56855

A little of everything or short notes about voting for the people, before they vote in October next. Baltimore: 1839? 36 p. NN. 56856

Little Rock, Arkansas. Ordinances. The revised ordinances of the city of Little Rock, together with the act of incorporation.... Little Rock: Budd, Colby and Steck, printers, 1839. 99 p. NN. 56857

Little Schuykill and Susquehanna Railroad Company. Annual report of the chief engineer. First Report. Philadelphia: 1839-1840. DLC; MH-BA; PPamP; PPL. 56858

The little soldiers; or holiday sports; dedicated to all good boys. Embellished with engravings. New Haven: S. Babcock, 1839. 24 p. CtY; PP. 56859

Litton, Samuel George. Christ and the church. A sermon preached at the opening of the 11th annual convention of the diocese of Tennessee, in St. Paul's Church on April 10, 1839, Randolph. Randolph: published by request at the Whig office, 1839. 10 p. PPiXT. 56860

Livermore, Abiel Abbot, 1811-1892. An address before the ladies Bible Association of Dublin [N. H.] August 7, 1839. Keene: J. and J. W. Prentiss, 1839. 12 p. CSmH; MH-AH. 56861

Lives and bloody exploits of the most noted pirates, their trials and executions, including correct accounts of the late piracies, committed in the West Indies and the expedition of Commodore Porter, also those committed on the brig Mexican, who were executed at Boston in 1835. Hartford: Ezra Strong, 18349. 298 p. MB; MBu; MH-L; OCLaw; OMC. 56862

The lives and exploits of the banditti and robbers of all nations. Philadelphia: R. W. Pomeroy, 1839. 2 v. PPM. 56863

Livingston, John Henry. Psalms and hymns with the catechism, confession of faith, and liturgy of the Reformed Dutch Church in North America.... Philadlephia: G. W. Mentz and Son, 1839. 592, 81 p. IEG; PPLT; PPM; PPPrHi; UPB. 56864

Livius, Titus. The history of Rome. Translated from the original, with notes and illustrations by George Baker. A new edition, carefully corrected and revised. Philadelphia: Thomas Wardle, 1839. [8] 585 [6] p. AU; GEU; KKc; NbU; ViU. 56865

----. Titi Livii Patovini historiarm; liber primus et selecta quaedam capita; curavit notulisque instruxit Carolus Folsom. Boston: Hilliard, 1839. 286 p. CSt; IEG; KyLo; MHi; NNC. 56866

Lobe, Guillermo, d. 1883. Cartas a mis hijos, durante un viaje a los Estados Unidos, Francia e Inglaterra; en los sieta ultimos meses de 1837. Nueva York: J. De La Granja, 1839. Mh; MiU; MoSM; NN. 56867

Lobstein, Johann Friedrich Daniel, 1777-1840. Dialogues between patients and the physician on the several principal diseases in this country, with the physicians advice. New York: the author, 1839. 143 p. DLC; IaU; NBMS; PPCP; ViU-M. 56868

Locke, John, 1632-1704. A treatise on the conduct of the understanding; to which is added a sketch of his life. New edition. Boston: Weeks, Jordan and Company, 1839. 132 p. PV. 56869

Locke, John, 1792-1856. An introductory lecture on chemistry and geology; delivered November 6, 1838, before the class of the medical college of Ohio. Cincinnati: 1839. 18 p. DSG; NNNAM; OClM; PPiXT; TxU. 56870

Lockhart, John Gibson, 1794-1854. The history of Napoleon Bonaparte. With copperplate engravings.... New York: Harper and Brothers, 1839. 2 v. MWA; NbOM; PPM; ScDuE; TxGR. 56871

----. The life of Napoleon Bonaparte. Philadelphia: Porter and Coates, 1839. 392 p. PReaAT. 56872

----. Memoirs of the life of Sir Walter Scott.

Philadelphia: Lea and Blanchard, 1839. 7 v. MB; MdBJ; RWe; ScSoh; TSewU. 56873

Lockport, New York. First Free Congregatioal Church. Manual. n. p.: 1839. 10 p. MBC. 56874

The locksmith of Philadelphia. Revised by the editors. New York: T. Mason and G. Lane, for the Sunday School Union of the Methodist Episcopal Church, 1839. NN. 56875

Lomax, John Tayloe, 1781-1862. Digest of the laws respecting real property, generally adopted and in use in the United States; embracing, more especially, the law of real property in Virginia. Philadelphia: J. S. Littell, 1839. 3 v. KyLxT; MdBJ; PPB; ViL; WvBe. 56876

The London dissector, or guide to anatomy, for the use of students.... From the 1st American edition. Revised and corrected by Edward J. Chaisty.... Baltimore: Murphy, etc., etc., 1839. 273 p. DLC; ICJ; MiU; OrUM; PPC. 56877

London in 1838, by an American. New York: Samuel Coleman, 1839. 216 p. MB; MWA; NRU; RPA; WHi. 56878

Long, George, 1780-1868. A treatise on the law relative to sales of personal property. 2nd American edition, with additions by Benjamin Rand.... Boston: C. C. Little and J. Brown, 1839. 506 p. KyLxT; MB; NcD; TU; WaU. 56879

Long, Stephen Harriman, 1784-1864. Specifications of a brace bridge and of a suspension bridge. Philadelphia: 1839. DLC; MH- BA. 56880

Long Island Rural cemetery. An act to incorporate the Long Island Rural Cemetery. Passed April 10, 1839. New York: E. b. Clayton, 1839. 8 p. NSmb; NSm. 56881

Long life of M. Barber. Richmond: 1839. PPL. 56882

Longfellow, Henry Wadsworth, 1807-1882. Hyperion, a romance. New York: S. Coleman, 1839. 2v. in 1. DLC; MB; MWA; NN; PPA. 56883

----. Poetical works; with bibliographical and critical notes. Riverside edition [Boston: 1839-1906] 6 v. MBAt; MBSi. 56884

Longking, Joseph. Questions on the Gospels.

New York: T. Mason and G. Lane, 1839. 4 v. NcD; ViU. 56885

Longworth's almanac New York register and city directory from the 64th year of American Independence. New York: Thomas Longworth, 1839. 752 p. RNHi. 56886

Loomis, Elias. Astronomical observations made at the observatory; with some account of the building and instruments [Philadelphia] 1839. NIC; NN. 56887

Loomis' No. 6. Pittsburgh almanac...for...1840...calculated by Sanford C. Hill, Esq., to equal, mean, or clock time for the horizon and meridian of Pittsburgh.... Pittsburgh: Luke Loomis, [1839] 30 p. MnHi; MWA; WHi. 56888

Lord, Eleazar, 1788-1871. The prophetic office of Christ, as related to the verbal inspiration of the Holy Scriptures. New York: Randolph, 1839. 154 p. CU; ICU; NjPT; NN; PPPrHI. 56889

Lord, John, 1810-1894. An address delivered before the Peace Society of Amherst College, July 4, 1839.... Amherst: J. S. and C. Adams, 1839. 31 p. CtHC; DLC; MH; NjR; TxU. 56890

Lord, John Chase, 1805-1877. The immateriality an natural immorality of the soul, an address delivered before the literary societies of Western Reserve College, August 27, 1839. Published by request of the societies. Hudson, Ohio: Charles Aikin [1839] 16 p. CSmH; MWiW; NAuT; OClWHi. 56891

----. Pride, fulness of bread, and abundance of idleness; prominent causes of the present pecuniary distress of the country: sermon. Buffalo: Thomas and Company, 1839. 20 p. CSmH; MBC; NAuT; NBu. 56892

Lord, Nathan, 1793-1870. Cause of seamen: services performed in the North Congrgational Chruch, Comcord [N. H.] October 9, 1839. on occasion of the ordination of Mr. Ezra E. Adams as chaplain to seamen. Concord: Asa McFarland, 1839. 44 p. CoD; MB; Nh-Hi; RPB. 56893

----. A sermon preached at the funeral of the Rev. David Peabody, October 20, 1839. By the president. Published by request. Hanover, N. H.: T. Mann, printer [1839] 15 p. DLC; MB; MH; Nh; RPB. 56894

Lorimore, John G. Revealed religion. New York: Hamilton: Adams Company, 1839. 572 p. IaPeC. 56895

Loring, Thomas. Speech of Thomas Loring, of Hingham, in the Houes of Representatives of Massachusetts, March 20, 1839, upon the bill, granting farther aid in the construction of the Western Railroad. Boston: printed by Ezra Lincoln, 1839. 28 p. MB; MPiB; NNE: OClWHi; WU. 56896

Louis, Pierre Charles Alexandre, 1787-1872. Anatomical, pathological, therapeutic researches on the yellow fever of Gibraltar in 1828: Translated from the manuscript by G. C. Shattuck Jr. Boston: C. C. Little and J. Brown, 1839. 374 p. MeB; PPCP; RPM; WU-M. 56897

Louisiana. Laws, Statutes, etc. An act to provide for the draining and clearing of the marshy grounds and cypress swamps, situated between the city of New Orleans, its incorporated suburbs and Lake Pontchartrain.... New Orleans: printed by Bousee and Lesseps, 1839. 31 p. LNH. 56898

----. ----. Acts passed at the first session of the 14th Legislature of the state of Louisiana, begun and held in the city of New Orleans, January 7, 1839. Published by authority. New Orleans: J. C. De St. Romes, state printer, 1839. 241 p. A-SC; Ky; LNH; MdBB; Wa-L. 56899

----. ----. Code of practice in civil cases, for the states of Louiiana; with annotations by Wheelock S. Upton, counsellor at law.... New Orleans: E. Johns and Company, 1839. AU; DLC; NcD; PHi; WaU-L. 56900

----. ----. Code of practice of the state of Louisiana, containing rules of procedure in civil actions: with an abstract of the decisions of the Supreme court...and the laws relative to justices of the peace. By M. Greiner.... New Orleans: printed by M. Greiner, 1839. 10, 1, 281 p. DLC; MdBB; MnU; PHi; TxU. 56901

----. Legislature. House. Journal of the House, during the first session of the legislature of the state of Louisiana. By order of the House. New Orleans: J. C. De St. Romes, state printer, 1839. 114 p. L. 56902

----. State University. Laws for the government of the college of Louisiana, 1839. Jackson: 1839.

21 p. MHi. 56903

----. Supreme Court. Condensed reports of cases in the Superior court of the territory of Orleans, and in the Supreme court of Louisiana; containing the decisions of those courts from the autumn term, 1809, to the March term, 1839.... Edited by J. Burton Harrison. New Orleans: E. Johns and Company, 1839-1840. 4 v. DLC; In-SC; LNT-L; PU-L; WaU-L. 56904

Louisiana Native American Association. Address...to the citizens of Louisiana and the inhabitants of the United States. New Orleans: printed by D. Felt and Company, 1839. 20 p. CSmH; LU; Nh-Hi; PPL; RPB. 56905

Louisville, Kentucky. Chamber of Commerce. Constitution, by-laws, and regulations of the Louisville Chamber of Commerce. Adopted November, 1839. Louisville, Ky.: 1839. 16 p. MHi; OCHP. 56906

----. University. Medical Department. Catalogue of the officers and students of the medical institute of the city of Louisville, January 1839. Louisville: Prentice and Weissinger, 1839. 12, 2 p. CSmH; MHi; NNNAM; OCHP. 56907

Louisville, Cincinnati and Charleston Railroad. Charter...as passed by the legislature of Kentucky, Tennesseee, North and South Carolina, with last amendments; also the charter of the Southwestern Railroad Bank... by-laws as amended. 2nd edition. Charleston: A. E. Miller, 1839. 36 p. WM. 56908

----. Claims of the road to the support of the legislature and the people of the state of Kentucky. Charleston? 1839? DLC. 56909

Lovejoy, Joseph Cammet, 1805-1871. An address delivered before the Penobscot Association of Teachers and Friends of Popular Education, at Bangor, December 26, 1838. Bangor: Samuel S. Smith, printer, 1839. 16 p. MBC; MeBa; MeHi; Nh. 56910

Lovelass, Peter, 1786-1812. The law's disposal of a person's estate who dies without will or testament; to which is added the disposal of a person's estate by will and testament, with an explanation of the mortmain act...From the 12th London edition, enlarged...by A. Barron.... Philadelphia: Littell, 1839. 322 p. KyLxT; NcS; OO; PPB; ScSC. 56911

Lovell, John Epy, 1795-1892. New school dialogues; or dramatic selections for the use of schools, academies, and families.... 3rd edition. Revised, enlarged, and greatly improved. Philadelphia: Theodore Bliss and Company [1839?] 432 p. IaDuW; MH; NcWsS; OEly. 56912

----. Rhetorical dialogues; or dramatic selections, for the use of schools, academies and families.... New Haven: Durrie and Peck, 1839. 514 p. MA; MB; MPiB; MWHi; RPB. 56913

----. United States speaker. Revised and improved edition. Charleston: S. Babcok and Company, etc., etc., 1839. MH. 56914

----. ----. A copious selection of exercises in elocution; consisting of prose, poetry, and dialogue...designed for the use of colleges and schools. New Haven: S. Babcock, 1839. 504 p. MB; MH; PLFM; RNR: ViU. 56915

Low, David. Elements of practical agriculture, conprehending the cultivation of plants, the husbandry of domestic animals and the economy of the farm with alterations and additions adapted to the climate and peculiarities of the United States, by S. Fleet. 1st American from the 2nd London edition. New York: 1839. 236, 48 p. IaCeC; MiGr; WOccR. 56916

Lowe, Peter Perlee, b. 1801. An oration delivered on the fiftieth anniversary of our national independence at Dayton, Ohio. n. p.: reprinted, 1839. 8 p. OClWHi; PHi; WHi. 56917

Lowell, Massachusetts. The charter of the city of Lowell, rules and orders. Lowell: L. Huntress, 1839. 35 p. MLow. 56818

----. Chesterfield Congregational Church. Articles of faith and covenant. Lowell: 1839. 8 p. MBC. 56919

----. School Committee. Papers relating to the building of houses for the high and grammar schools in Lowell. Lowell: Leonard Huntress, 1839. 14 p. MLow. 56920

----. ----. Rules of the school committee and regulations at the public schools of the city of Lowell adopted by the school committee, May, 1839. Lowell: L. Huntress, printer, 1839. 19 p. M; MB. 56921

Lowell directory. Directory containing the names of inhabitants, their occupations.... By Benjamin Floyd. Lowell, 1839. MBC. 56922

Luckett, Oliver A. Oration delivered before the philodemic Society of Georgetown College, on the 4th of July 1839. Georgetown: John L. Smith, 1839. 16 p. MWH. 56923

Luckey, Samuel. Wesleyan Methodists a Christian Church. A sermon preached in substance at the Greene Street Methodist Episcopal Church, New York, October 25, 1839. on occasion of the celebration of the centenary of Wesleyan Methodism [New York: 1839] 40 p. IEG; MBNMHi; WHi. 56924

Luckock, Benjamin. A sermon preached in St. Paul's Church, Fredericksted, St. Croix, April 20, 1834, on the death of William Henry Bard, of New York, in his 19th year. By Benjamin Luckock, minister of the English churches of St. John and St. Paul, in that island. New York: Protestant Episcopal Press, printer, 1839. 27 p. TChU. 56925

Lunt, George, 1803-1885. Poems by George Lunt.... New York: Gould and Newman, 1839. 160 p. ICU; MB; NBuG; RPB; WU. 56926

Luther, Martin, 1483-1546. Der kleine catechismus des seligen Dr. Martin Luthers.... Lancaster: gedruckt und zu haben bey Johann Bar, 1839. 142 p. MiU-C; PHi; PLERC-Hi; PReaHi; PSt. 56927

----. ----. Philadelphia: Herausgegeben von G. W. Mentz und Sohn, 1839. 144 p. CSmH; PPeSchw. 56928

Lyell, Charles, 1797-1875. Elements of geology. 1st American, from the 1st London edition. Philadlephia: J. Kay, Jr. and Brother, Pittsburgh: C. H. Kay and Company, 1839. 316 p. A-GS; VU; ICP; PPA; ScC. 56929

Lyman, Giles. Purity of heart. An address before the Moral Reform Society of Winchendon. Delivered February 14, 1839. Boston: Dow and Jackson, 1839. 14 p. MB; MH; MWA; NNUT. 56930

Lyman, Samuel P., 1804-1869. The speech of Samuel P. Lyman, of Utica, at the convention of delegates, held at Ithaca, July 11, 1839 on the subject of the New York and Erie Railroad. New York: Narine and Company, printers, 1839. 38 p.

CSt; DLC; NjP; WHi. 56931

Lynch, Edward A. Address delivered before the Philamathian Society of Mount St. Mary's College, Emmittsburg at the annual commencement June 27, 1839. By Edward Lynch, Esq. of Frederick City, Maryland. Frederick: Ezekiel Hughes, 1839. 36 p. CSmH; MH; OCX; PPL; TxU. 56932

Lyon, Charles Harrison. Considerations in favor of classical studies. A lecture, delivered in the Irving Institute. New York: printed by William G. Boggs, 1839. 19 p. MH; MWA; NNC; ScU; TxU. 56933

----. Oration delivered...near the ground on which Major Andre was taken, at Tarrytown, on July 4, 1839.... New York: Bryant and Boggs, 1839. 16 p. NN. 56934

Lyon, James A. A defence against certain attacks in a letter...pastor of the Presbyterian Church at Rogersville, E. T. printed at the Seninel office, Jonesborough, 1839. 4-23 p. PPPrHi; T; TkL-Mc. 56935

Lyon, Mary. Female education. See Mount Holyoke College.

Lytton, Edward Bulwer Lytton, 1803-1873. The disowned. Exeter: J. and B. Williams, 1839. 2 v. MH. 56936

----. Falkland.... Exeter: J. and B. Williams, 1839. 132 p. MeWebr; NLag. 56937

----. Paul Clifford. Exeter: J. and B. Williams, 1839. 2 v. in 1. CtHWatk: MeWebr. 56938

----. Pelham; or the adventures of a gentleman. Exeter: Williams, 1839. 2 v. MB; MH. 56939

----. The pilgrims of the Rhine. Exeter: J. and B. Williams, 1839. 234 p. OClWHi; PP; ViU. 56940

----. Richelieu; or the conspiracy. A play in five acts. Baltimore: J. Robinson [1839] 96 p. MdBJ; MWH. 56941

----. ----. New York: Harper and Brothers, 1839. CSmH; NNC; RPB; TNP; ViU. 56942

----. ----. New York: G. P. Putnam's Sons [1839] 191 p. DCU. 56943

----. ----. New York: Samuel French [1839] 96 p. MB; NNC; RPB. 56944

----. ----. New York: Turner and Fisher, Boston: J. Fisher [1839?] 96 p. MB; MH; NN. 56945

----. ----. Philadelphia: Turner and Fisher [1839] IU; MH. 56946

----. ----. Rienzi, the last of the tribunes. Exeter: J. and B. Williams, 1839. 2 v. in 1. MH. 56947

----. The sea captain; or the birthright. A drama. In five acts. New York: Harper and Brothers, 1839. 88 p. CSmH; MWA; NjP; NN; RPB. 56948

----. The student.... Exeter: J. and B. Williams, 1839. 2 v. 179 p. MeWebr; NLag. 56949

----. Cheveley; or the man of honour. By Lady Lytton Bulwer.... New York: Harper, 1839. 2 v. ICU; MoS; RBr; TNP; WGr. 56950

M

McAnally, D. R. The substance of a serman on the relative duties of parents and children, preached at a camp meeting in Pickens District, S. C. September 14, 1838.... Greenville, S. C.: O. H. Wells, printer, 1839. 27 p. MoS. 56951

NcCaffrey, John, 1806-1882. Discourse on the Right Reverend Simon Gabriel Brute. Bishop of Vincennes pronounced in Mt. St. Mary's Church.... Emmitsburg: M'Clean, Duphorn and Troxel, printers, 1839. 33 p. CtHW; IaDuC; MdHi; Phi; WHi. 56952

McCalla, John M. Address delivered at the celebration of the 50th anniversary of the Lexington Light Infantry Company. Lexington: J. C. Noble, printer, 1839. 16 p. CSmH; ICU. 56953

M'Carter's Carolina and Georgia almanac for 1839. The astronomical part by Robert Greer. Charleston, S. C.: J. J. McCarter and Company, 1839. GMWa; GSDe; PPL-R. 56954

McCarter's Carolina and Georgia almanac for 1840. Charleston, S. C.: J. J. McCarter and Company [1839] MWA; ScCMu. 56955

M'Chesney, James. A brief review of the proceedings of the annual conference of the Methodist Episcopal Church, her discipline, and administration of government.... New York: 1839. 44 p. MBAt; MBC; PPL. 56956

----. Philomath's researches. Proceedings of the New York annual conference of the Methodist Episcopal Church.... New York: 1839. 60 p. USlC. 56957

McClellan, Abraham. Circular letter to the people of the Second Congregational District in the state of Tennessee. Washington: 1839. MdBP. 56958

McClung, John Alexander, 1804-1859. Sketches of western adventure: containing an account of the most interesting incidents connected with the settlement of the west, from 1755 to 1794: with an ap-

pendix. Revised and corrected. Cincinnati: U. P. James, 1839. 315 p. IaHi; KyLxT; MH; NNC; PWW. 56959

M'Clure, William B. Address delivered before the Philological Institute, on December 8, 1838, the 11th anniversary. Pittsburgh: printed by Alexander Jaynes, 1839. 24 p. DLC; KyU; NjR; PPL. 56960

McCluskey, John. Discourse in behalf of the African race delivered at West Middletown, January 18, 1838. Washington: 1839. 32 p. PHi. 56961

M'Cook, Daniel. Trial on articles of impeachment for breach of good behavior in office [Court of Common Pleas, 1837, State of Ohio, Carroll County] reported by the prosecutor. Cincinnati: 1839. Mh-L. 56962

McCoskry, Samuel Allen, 1804-1886. The hinderances to ministerial success; an address delivered at the commencement in the General Theological Seminary of the Protestant Episcopal Church in the United States, held in Saint Peters Church. New York...on June 28, 1839. New York: Swords, Stanford and Company, 1839. 14 p. CtY; InID; MB; NCH; PPL. 56963

McCoy, C. F. Notes on the differential and integral calculus, for the use of the University of Georgia. Athens, Ga.: printed at the office of the Southern Banner, 1839. 48 p. PEaL. 56964

McCrie, Thomas, 1772-1835. Life of John Knox, the Scottish reformer, abridged from McCrie's life of Knox.... Philadelphia: Presbyterian Board of Publication, 1839. 286 p. MiU; PU; TNM; TxDaTS. 56965

McCullock, John Ramsay, 1789-1864. A dictionary, practical, theoretical and historical of commerce and commercial navigation. Philadelphia: A. Hart, 1839. 2 v. InEv. 56966

McCullough, Samuel D. Kentucky almanac for

the year of our Lord, 1839.... Lexington: Lexington Intelligencer, printer, 1839. 32 p. OC. 56967

MacDonnel, D. E. A dictionary of select and popular quotations.... 6th American edition. Philadelphia: 1839. 312 p. MHi. 56968

[McDougall, Frances Harriet (Whipple) Greene] 1805-1878. Elleanor's second book.... Providence: B. T. Albro, printer, 1839. 128 p. MB; MH; Nh-Hi; NHem; RPB. 56969

McDowell, James, 1796-1851. Address delivered before the alumni association of th College of New Jersey, September 26, 1838. 2nd edition. Princeton: R. E. Horner, 1839. 37 p. DLC; KHi; MH; NjP; TxU. 56970

McElroy, A. Philadelphia directory, 1839-1867. Philadelphia: 1839-1867. 29 v. PHi. 56971

----. Philadelphia directory...1839. 2nd edition. Philadelphia: 1839. 1 v. CtSoP; Phi. 56972

McEwen, William, 1734-1762. An illustration of the types, allegories, and prophecies of the Old Testament.... Philadelphia: William S. Martien, 1839. 272 p. GDecCT; OClW; TxBrdD. 56973

MacFarlane, Charles, 1799-1858. Lives and exploits of bandits and robbers in all parts of the world.... From the 2nd London edition. Including an account of Blackbird and Kid. Philadelphia: 1839. 2 v. CtY; DLC; OrP. 56974

McGuffey, William Holmes, 1800-1873. The eclectic fourth reader, containing elegant extracts in prose and poetry, from the best American and English writers. With copious rules for reading, and directions for avoiding commom errors. 6th edition. Cincinnati: Truman and smith, 1839. CtHWatk; DLC; IaHA; TxU-T. 56975

McIlvaine, Charles Pettit, 1799-1873. The origin and design of the Christian ministry: a sermon preached at an ordination held in the chapel of the theological seminary of the diocese of Ohio, at Gambier, October 26, 1839. Gambier, Ohio: Meyers, 1839. 22 p. CSmH; InID; MdBD; OCHP; PHi. 56976

M'Kay, Lauchlan, 1811-1895. The practical shipbuilder, containing the best mechanical and philosophical principles for the construction of different classes of vessels.... New York: Collins,

Keese, and Company, 1839. 107 p. CoU; DSI; MCM; NN; OCl. 56977

MacKay, Margaret. Family at Heatherdale; or the influence of Christian principles. New York: R. Carter, 1839. 266 p. NN; RPA. 56978

McKee, R. Lectures on botany...at the Albany Female Academy.... Albany: printed by J. Munsell, 1839. 20 p. MH; NjR. 56979

McKinney, Mordecai, 1796-1867. The Pennsylvania justice of the peace: containing the law practice and process in proceeding before justices of the peace and alderman in criminal cases.... Harrisburg: printed for the author, 1839. 2 v. in 1. ICLaw; IU; MiU-L; PPB. 56980

M'Lain, William, 1806-1873. Discourse occasioned by the death of John Coyle; preached in the First Presbyterian Church, Washington City. Washington City: Gideon, 1839. PPPrHi. 56981

M'lane, R. An examination into the cause of explosions by steam on the western waters. Louisville, Ky.: 1839. 15 p. MHi. 56982

Maclay, William Brown, 1812-1882. Oration delivered at the Democratic Republican celebration of the 63rd anniversary of the independence of the United States, in the city of New York, July 4, 1839. New York: J. W. Bell, 1839. 24 p. MdBJ; N; NIC; ScU. 56983

M'Lean, Archibald. A reply to Mr. Fuller's appendix to his book on the gospel worthy of all acceptation. Particularly to his doctrine of antecedent holiness, and the nature and object of justifying faith. New York: Scatcherd and Adams, 1839. 137 p. IU; MBC; MH; NjP; PSC-Hi. 56984

McLellan, Rufus Charles. The foundling; or yankee fidelity. A drama in two acts. Philadelphia: printed by King and Baird, 1839. 68 p. DLC; MB; RPB. 56985

McMahan, Bernard, 1775-1816. The American gardener's calender, adapted to the climates and season of the United States.... 9th edition. Philadelphia: A. McMahon, 1839. 613 p. MSaP; NcAS; PPWa; TxU; ViU. 56986

MacMaster, Erasmus Darwin, 1806-1866. Address delivered to the candidates for the degree of bachelor of arts, in Hanover College, Indiana, at the anniversary commencement, September 25, 1839. Cincinnati: printed by R. P. Brooks, 1839. 16 p. KyDC; In; MWA; NjPT; PHi. 56987

M'Michael, Morton, 1807-1879. Address before the Northern Lyceum of Philadelphia. Philadelphia: 1839. 36 p. PHi; PPL; PPM; PU. 56988

McNally, William. Evils and abuses in the naval and merchant services, exposed; with proposals for their remedy and redress. Boston: Cassady and March, 1839. 201 p. DLC; ICU; MdBP; RPA; WHi. 56989

Macnish, Robert, 1802-1837. The philosophy of sleep and the anatomy of drunkenness. New York: W. Mather, 1839. 96 p. MBC; NBMS. 56990

Macpherson, James, 1736-1796. The poems of Ossian. Translated by James Macpherson, esq. To which is prefixed a life of the translator; a preliminary discourse, or review of the controversy relative to the authenticity of the poems; and dissertations on the era and poems of Ossian. Philadelphia: Thomas, Cowperthwait and Company, 1839. 413 p. FOA; NjR; OO; ScDuE; TNP. 56991

McQueen, Hugh. An address delivered before the alumni and graduating class of the University of North Carolina, on the afternoon preceding commemcement day, in Gerard Hall, June 23, 1839. Raleigh: printed at the office of the Raleigh Register, 1839. 46. p. DLC; MH; NcAS; PPPrHi; TxU. 56992

Madden, Richard Robert. A letter to W. E. Channing, on the subject of the abuse of the flag of the United States in the Island of Cuba and the advantage taken of its protection in promoting the slave trade. Boston: William D. Ticknor, 1839. 32 p. A-Ar; MBC; MWA; PHi; TxDaM. 56993

Maffitt, John Newland, 1794-1850. Ireland: a poem. Louisville: Prentice and Weissinger, 1839. 79 p. KyHi; NN; PU; RPB; TxDaM. 56994

----. An oration delivered on St. John's day, June 25, 1838, before the royal arch chapter, the harmony, and Andrew Jackson Lodges of Free and Accepted Masons in the city of Natchez.... Rathway: printed by John Jackson, 1839. 12 p. IaCrM. 56995

----. Poem. Louisville: Prentice and Weissinger, 1839. 144 p. IEG; MB; NcAS; NcD; PHi. 56996

----. Pulpit sketches. First series. Louisville, Ky.: W. H. Johnston, 1839. 178 p. AB; IaHA; NcAS; OBerB; PPM. 56997

Magee, William, 1766-1831. Discourses and dissertations on the scriptural doctrines of atonement and sacrifice...with an appendix, containing some strictures on Mr. Belsham's account of the Unitarian scheme.... From the 5th London editon.... New York: D. Appleton and Company, 1839. 2 v. CtHC; GHi; MB; NBuDD; RPB. 56998

Magendie, Francois, 1783-1855. Lectures on the blood: and on the changes which it undergoes during disease. Delivered at the Colllege of France in 1837-1838. Philadelphia: Haswell, Barrington and Haswell, New Orleans: J. J. Haswell and Company, 1839. 276 p. CU-M; MB; NhD; OCLM; PPA. 56999

Mahan, Asa, 1800-1889. Scripture doctrine of Christian perfection; with other kindred subjects. Boston: D. S. King, 1839. 237 p. CtHC; ICU; MB; OClW; ViRu. 57000

----. ----. 2nd edition. Boston: D. S. King, 1839. 193 p. CBPSR; NbOM; OO; OSW. 57001

Mahan, Jason M. Private instructor; or mathematics simplified; comprising everything necessary in arithmetic, book-keeping, conveying.... Harrisburg: printed for the author, 1839. 304 p. PPT; PWeT. 57002

The maid of Florence: or a woman's vengeance. A pseudo-historical tragedy, in five acts. Charleston: printed by S. S. Miller, 1839. 92 p. DLC; MB; MH; PU; RPB. 57003

Maine. Adjutant General of the Militia. Report...December 31, 1839. Augusta: Smith and Robinson, printers, 1839. 24 [16] p. MeB; MeHi; MeLR; MeU; WHi. 57004

----. Governor, 1838-1839 [Edward Kent] Message of Governor Kent to the legislature of Maine, January 2, 1839, with the report of the commissioners appointed to survey the boundary line n. p.: 1839] 23 p. DLC; MdHi; PU. 57005

----. ----. Message of Edward Kent, Governor, January 1839 and 22 documents relating to the North Eastern Boundary [n. p.: 1839] 113 p. DLC;

MeHi; MHi; MMal; Nh-Hi. 57006

----. ----. To the Senate and House: in compliance with the request of the Governor of the state of Georgia...Daniel Philbrook and Edward Kelleran...January 2, 1839 [Augusta, Me.: 1839] MB; MBAt; NIC; NN. 57007

----.Governor, 1839-1841 [John Fairfield] Message...to both branches of the legislature of the state of Maine, January, 1839. Augusta: Smith and Robinson, printers, 1839. 23 p. MeHi; Me-LR; MiU-C. 57008

----. Laws, Statutes, etc. Private and special acts of the state of Maine, passed by the legislature at its session held in January, 1839. Published agreeably to the resolve of June 28, 1820. Protland: 1839 [3] 608-685 p. Ia; MeLR. 57009

----. ----. ----. 77 p. IaU-L; Me-LR; Mo; R. 57010

----. ----. Public acts of the state of Maine, passed by the 19th legislature, January session, 1839. Published agreeably to the resolve of June 28, 1820. Augusta: Smith and Robinson, printers to the state, 1839. 68 p. Ia; MeLR; R; TxU-L. 57011

----. ----. Resolves of the 19th legislature of the state of Maine, 1839, paseed at the session.... Augusta: Smith and Robinson, 1839. 171 p. CU-Law; Me-LR; Nj; TxU-L; Wa-L. 57012

----. Legislature. House. Documents relating to trespassers on the public lands.... Augusta: Smith and Robinson, 1839. 47 p. IaHi; MdBP; MiU-C; NNC; WHi. 57013

----. ----. ----. Rules and orders of the House of Representatives of the state of Maine. Augusta: Smith and Robinson, 1839. 83 p. MeHi; Me-LR. 57014

----. ----. Joint Special Committee on Slavery. Report [n. p.] Smith and Robinson [1839] 12 p. NIC. 57015

----. ----. Senate. Rules and orders to be observed in the Senate of the state of Maine...1839. Augusta: Smith and Robinson, printers, 1839. 84 p. MeBa; MeHi. 57016

----. Secretary of State. Abstract from the returns of the directors of the several incorporated banks of Maine, as they existed on the Saturday preceding the first Monday of June, 1839.... By Asaph R. Nichols, Secretary of State. Augusta: Smith and Robinson, 1839. 11 p. MeHi; Me-LR. 57017

----. ----. List of stockholders, in the banks of Maine.... Augusta: Smith and Robinson, printers to the state, 1839. 98 p. MeHi; Me-LR. 57018

Maine farmer's almanack. By Daniel Robinson. Augusta: R. D. Rice, 1839. MWA. 57019

----. Gardiner: W. Palmer, 1839. MWA. 57020

Maine farmer's almanack. By Robert Thomas. Portland: Colman and Chisholm, 1839. MWA. 57021

Maine farmers' almanack for 1840. By Daniel Robinson. Hallowell, Me.: Glazier, Masters and Smith [1839] MWA; PTU. 57022

----. Hallowell, Me.: Glazier, Masters and Smith, Portland: William Hyde [1839] MWA; WHi. 57023

Maine Wesleyan Seminary and Female College. Catalogue of the officers and students...1839-1840. Augusta: Severance and Dorr, printers, 1839 [6] 10 p. Me; MeHi [24 p.] 57024

Mair, John, 1802 or 3-1769. Introduction to Latin Syntaz...From Edinburgh stereotype edition. New York: W.E. Dean, etc., 1839. DLC; ODW; MH; NjNbS. 57025

Malcolmson, John Grant. Clinical remarks os some cases of liver abscess presenting externally. Philadelphia: Haswell, Barrington and Haswell, 1839. 43 p. CSt; KyLxT; PPA; RNR; ViU. 57026

Malcom, Howard, 1799-1879. Travels in Southeastern Asia. Embracing Hidustan, Malaya, Siam and China. Boston: Gould, Kendall and Lincoln, 1839. 2 v. IaDm; GAU; MWA; PPA; ScSoh. 57027

----. ----. 2nd edition. Boston: Gould, Kendall and Lincoln, 1839. 2 v. in 1. CSt; KyHi; MPiB; MWiW; ViRU. 57028

----. ----. 3rd edition. Boston: Gould, Kendall and Lincoln, 1839. CSansS; GHi; ICU; NBu; RPA. 57029

Maltby, John, 1795-1860. "Wo to that man by whom the offence cometh"; a discourse delivered in Bangor and Brewer at the request of temperance associations. Bangor: E. F. Duren, 1839. 28 p. CBPSR; IaGG; MBC; MH; RPB. 57030

Mamma's lessons for her little boys and girls. In two parts. With numerous copperplate engravings.... 4th American Edition. Salem: W. and S. B. Ives, 1839. 72 [5]-96 p. MHaHi; NcD; NHem. 57031

Manesca, John, 1774-1834. An oral system of teaching living languages; illustrated by a practical course of lessons in French, through the medium of the English. 3rd edition. New York: Van Norden, 1839. 2 v. CtMW; DLC; MH; TxU-T; Vi. 57032

Manley, James R. 1781-1851. Introductory address to the students in medicine of the College of Physicians and Surgeons.... New York: published by the students, 1839. 28 p. DNLM, DSG; NNNAM. 57033

Mann, Cyrus, 1785-1859. Astronomy; or the perfections of God displayed in his works. Written for the Massachusetts Sabbath School Society, and revised by the committee of publication. 2nd edition. Boston: Massachusetts Sabbath School Society, 1839. 210 p. InCW; NbOM; OO; OSW. 57034

----. Epitome of the evidence of Christianity...for families, sabbath schools and Bible classes. 3rd edition. Boston: Massachusetts Sabbath School Society, 1839. 144 p. InCW; NcCJ; OO. 57035

Mannering, E. Christian consistency or the connection between experimental and practical religion, designed for young Christians. Philadelphia: Presbyterian Board of Publication of tracts and sabbath school books. 1839. ICP; NbOP; OWoC; PPWe; ViRut. 57036

Mansel, George Barclay. A treatise on the law and practice of demurrer to pleadings and evidence...in personal actions. With an introduction to the nature and forms of pleadings. To which is added a selection of precedents. Philadelphia: John S. Littell, Halstead and Voorhies, 1839. 298 p. IaU-L MdUL; NNIA; PP; Sc-SC. 57037

Mansfield, Edward Deering, 1801-1880. The political grammar of the United States; or a complete view of the theory and practice of the general and state governments, with the relations between them.... Cincinnati: Truman and smith, 1839. 336 p. DLC; InNd; MiD-U. OC; PNt. 57038

Mansfield, Massachusetts. Orthodox Congregational Church. Confession of faith and covenant. Boston: 1839. 18 p. MBC. 57039

Mantell, Gideon Algernon, 1790-1852. The wonders of geology; or a familiar exposition of gelological phenomena; being the substance of a course of lectures delivered at Brighton. 1st American edition from the 3rd London edition. New Haven: Maltby, 1839. 2 v. GU; ICJ; NNC; OOxM; ScU. 57040

Manufactures and Mechanics Bank of Northern Liberties. Act to incorporate the Manufactures and Mechanics Bank of the Northern Liberties in the county of Philadelphia. Philadelphia: Geddes, 1839. 62 p. PPL; PU. 57041

Manvill, P. D. Lucinda; or the mountain mourner; being recent facts in a series of letters from Mrs Manvill, of the state of New York to her sister in Pennsylvania. To which is added the stranger; a tale, founded on fact. 6th edition. Ithaca: Mack, Andrus and Woodruff, 1839. CtY; OU; TU; WHi. 57042

Map of Pennsylvania, New Jersey and Delaware.... Philadelphia: Mitchell, 1839. OCel; PPL; PU. 57043

Marblehead, Massachusetts. By-laws of the town of Marblehead. Salem: Salem Gazette Press [1839] 8 p. MMh. 57044

Marcet, Jane [Haldimand] 1769-1858. Conversations on chemistry; in which the elements of that science are familiarly explained and illustrated by experiments and engravings. 15th American edition. Hartford: Belknap, 1839. 356 p. CtMW; GU-M; NcHPC; ScK. 57045

----. Conversations on natural philosophy, in which the elements of that science are familiarly explained, and adapted to the comprehension of young pupils. Boston: Gould, Kendall and Lincoln, 1839. 276 p. MWHi; MoS; NPV; TxU-T. 57046

----. Willy's rambles for young children. New York: 1839. 143 p. MWA. 57047

----. Willy's stories for young children. New York: S. Coleman, 1839. 144 p. DLC. 57048

Marietta College, Marietta, Ohio. Annual circular of Marietta College, with the inaugural address of the president, delivered July 25, 1838. Cincinnati: Isaac Hefley and Company, printers, 1839. 14 p. MiD-B; MWA; OClWHi; TNL. 57049

Marietta Female Seminary, Marietta, Ohio. Catalogue...for the year ending March, 1839. Together with a plan of the contemplated primary school. Marietta: Gazette office, I. Maxon, printer, 1839. 12 p. MH; OMC. 57050

Markham, Gervase, 1568?-1637. The citizen and countryman's experienced farrier. To all Which is added a valuable and fine collection of the surest and best receipts in the known world for the cure of all maladies and distempers that are incident to horses.... Chambersburg, Pa.: Wright, 1839. 332 p. CtY; NcSC; NCRA; P. Vi. 57051

Marriot, John, 1762-1797. Mialma, a tale by John Marriot, a member of the Society of Friends, in England. Philadelphia: Merrihew and Thompson, 1839. MWA; PHi; PSC-Hi. 57052

Marryat, Frederick, 1792-1848. The complete works of Captain E. Marryat. Sanbornton, N. H.: Clarles Lane, 1839. 2 v. MdU; MWelC. 57053

----. A diary in America, with remarks on its institutions. New York: D. Appleton and Company, 1839. 263 p. CtHT; In; OAU; PU. 57054

----. ----. New York: Wm. H. Colyer, 1839. 263 p. IaU; MWA; OC; PU; VtB. 57055

----. ----. Philadelphia: Carey and Hart, 1839. 2 v. CtMW; NBuU; OCl; PPA; WGr. 57056

----. ----. 263 p. AU; MWA; OC. 57057

----. Frank Mildmay; or the naval officer. Sanbornton, N. H.: Charles Lane, 1839. 2 v. MnSS; PLFM. 57058

----. Japhet in search of his father. Sandbornton, N. H.: Charles Lane, 1839. 2 v. CtY; MsJMC. 57059

----. The king's own. Sandbornton, N. H.: Charles Lane, 1839. 2 v. MdBLC; MnSS; MsJMC. 57060

----. The phantom ship, a tale of the sea. Boston: Weeks, Jordan and Company, 1839. 133 p. CtY. 57061

----. ----. New York: W. H. Colyer, 1839. 237 p. CtHT; MNF; NbOM; PLFM. 57062

----. ----. Philadelphia: E. L. Carey and A. Hart, 1839. 2 v. DLC; MB; MBBCHS; MCli; OAU. 57063

----. ----. Sandbornton, N. H.: Charles Lane, 1839. 2 v. NCanHi; NhD; Nh-Hi; NNU; PHi. 57064

Marsh, Abram, 1802-1877. The importance of the sanctuary. A sermon, preached at the dedication of the new congregational church, in Tolland, Connecticut, October 25, 1838.... Hartford: J. L. Boswell, 1839. 20 p. Ct; CtHC; ICN; MBC. 57065

Marsh, Christopher Columbus, 1806-1884. The art of single entry book-keeping improved by the introduction of the proof of balance... 3rd edition. New York: J. E. Riker, 1839. 126 p. MB. 57066

----. The science of double-entry book keeping, simplified by the introduction of an infallible rule for Dr. and Cr. calculated to insure a complete knowledge of the theory and practice of accounts. Philadelphia: Hogan and Thompson, 1839. 16, 199 p. MH; NNC; P; PMA. 57067

Marsh, Edwards. An address, delivered at York, before the Livinston County Total Abstinence Temperance Society, February 5, 1839. Geeseo [N. Y.] printed by S. P. Allen, 1839. 16 p. CSmH; MB. 57068

Marsh, John, 1788-1868. An epitome of general ecclesiastical history, from the earliest history to the present time.... 5th edition. New York: J. Tilden and Company, 1839. 462 p. MH; MoKDT; NSherb. 57069

Marsh, William, fl. 1839. England, and other poems. New York: the author, 1839. 112 p. DLC; MH; MWA; NIC; NSmb; RPB. 57070

Marshall, Christopher, 1709-1797. Passages from the diary of Christopher Marshall, kept in Philadelphia and Lancaster during the American revolution. Edited by Wm. Duane. Philadelphia: Hazard and Mitchell, 1839-1849. 2 v. DeWi; IU; MeHI; PPA; WaU. 57071

----. Passages from the remembrances of Christopher Marshall. Edited by William Duane.... Philadelphia: printed by J. Crissy, 1839. 124 p. GHi; MH; NbCrD; PPi; RPA. 57072

Marshall, Elihu F. Marshall's spelling book of the English language; or the teacher's assistant in which the orthography and pronunciation are in accordance with the principles of Walker. 1st revised edition. Concord, N. H.: Boyd and White, 1839. MH. 57073

Marshall, John, 1755-1835. The life of George Washington, commander...the American forces.... Written for the use of schools. 2nd edition, revised and corrected by the author. Philadelphia: J. Crissy and Thomas, Cowperthwait and Company, 1839. 2 v. LNT; MB; MiU; NcW; PU. 57074

----. ----. 3rd edition. Philadelphia: James Crissy, 1839. 379 p. MHarw; ViU. 57075

----. 4th edition. Philadelphia: printed by J. Crissy, 1939. 379 p. MH; MiD-B; NcD; NLam; PHi. 57076

----. ----. 5th edition. Philadelphia: James Crissy, Thomas, Cowperthwait and Company, 1839. 379 p. OMC; TNP; Vi. 57077

----. ----. 6th edition. Philadelphia: James Crissy, Thomas, Cowperthwait and Company, 1839. 379 p. MB; MNan; TNP. 57078

----. ----. 9th edition. Philadelphia: J. Crissy, 1839. 379 p. DLC; MeLewB; MiD-B; OaU; PHi. 57079

----. ----. 10th edition. Philadelphia: J. Crissy, etc., 1839. 379 p. NAmS; OCl; ViW. 57080

----. The writings of John Marshall, late chief justice of the United States, upon the federal constitution.... Boston: James Munroe and Company [1839] 728 p. LU; MBBC; NGH; PWW; TMeC. 57081

Marshall, Thomas Alexander, 1794-1871. An introductory address, delivered before the law class of Transylvania University, on November 9, 1839. Lexington: Finnell and Virden, printers, 1839. 16 p. DLC; MoSHi. 57082

Marshall College, Mercersburg, Pennsylvania. Catalogue of the officers and students in Marshall College, Mercersburg, Pennsylvania, 1838-1839. Chambersburg, Pa.: printed by Henry Ruby, 1839. 23 p. PHi; PLERC-Hi. 57083

[Martin, Morgan Lewis] 1805-1887. To the public. I have lately been informed that rumors have been industriously circulated through the territory, charging me with the frauds committed by the Bank of Wisconsin.... Green Bay: 1839. Broadside. WHi. 57084

Martineau, Hrriet, 1802-1876. Deerbrook.... New York: Harper and Brothers, 1839. 2 v. LN; MBAt; PU; RPB; VtU. 57085

----. The martyr age of the United States. Boston: Weeks, Jordan and Company [etc.] New York: J. S.Taylor, 1839. 84 p. CBPac; IaU; MPiB; OO; PU. 57086

----. ----. New York: S. W. Benedict, 1839. 36 p. InHi; KyLx; NN; OO; RP. 57087

----. Retrospect of western travel. New York: Harper and Brothers, 1839. 2 v. MeBa. 57088

----. Traditions of Palestine. Edited by H. Martineau. Boston: William Crosby and Company, 1839. 138 p. GEU; MH; MoSpD; VtU. 57089

Mary Inglis, the beloved domestic. Boston: Massachusetts Sabbath School Scoiety, 1839. 90 p. MdBMP. 57090

Maryland. Committee on Judicial Procedures. Report of a minority of the committee on judicial proceedings, in favor of this state, and diminish the expenses thereof. Annapolis: William M'Neir, printer, 1839. 10 p. MdHi. 57091

----. Constitution. The declaration of rights, constitution and form of government of the state of Maryland, together with its amendements to April, 1839. Frederick: printed by E. Hughes, 1839. 31 p. ICN; MdBE; MdBP; MdHi; NN. 57092

----. Court of Appeals. Opinion of the Court of Appeals of Maryland in the case of the University of Maryland, delivered by Ch. J. Buchanan. Baltimore: printed by Lucas and Deaver, 1839. 42 p. DLC; MdBLC; MdBM; PPAmP; PHi. 57093

----. Genral Assembly. Approximate estimate of that portion of the "Brookville Route" of the Maryland canal, surveyed during the summer of

1838 [n. p.] 1839. 52 p. NjP; ViU. 57094

----. ----. Committee on Elections. Report of the minority of the committee on elections, in relation to the election of senators for Carroll County. Annapolis: William M'Neir, printer, 1839. 6 p. MdHi. 57095

----. ----. House of Delegates. Journal...December session 1838. Annapolis: printed by Jeremiah Hughes, 1838 [i. e. 1839] 954 p. MdBB; MdHi. 57096

----. ----. ----. Report.... Baltimore: 1839. 11 p. DSG. 57097

----. ----. ----. Committee on Internal Improvements. Communication from the chairman of the committee, in reply to a communication of the C. and O. Canal Company [Annapolis?] 1839. 7 p. ViU. 57098

----. ----. ----. ----. Report in obedience to an order of the House in reference to what amount of money has been borrowed, on a pledge of the certificates of stock of the state of Maryland, issued last year, and what portion remains unexpended [Annapolis] 1839. 8 p. ViU. 57099

----. ----. ----. Select Committee on the Charters of the Pennsylvania, Delaware and Maryland Railroad Company and the New Castle an Frenchtown Turnpike and Railroad Company. Report of the minority of the select committee appointed by the order of the House, February 11 1839.... [Annapolis?] 1839. 12 p. MdBE; MdHi. 57100

----. ----. ----. Select Committee to inquire into the affairs of the Eastern Shore Road Company. Testimony taken by the select committee.... Annapolis: William M'Neir, printer, 1839. 28, 29- 191 p. MdBP; MdHI. 57101

----. ----. Joint Committee on the Memorial of the Regents of the University of Maryland. One of the reports of the.... Annapolis: William M'Neir, printer, 1839. 15 p. MdBP; MdHi; WHi. 57102

----. ----. ----. Report.... Annapolis: William M'Neir, printer, 1839. 10 p. MdBP; MdHi. 57103

----. ----. Senate. Journal of proceedings of the Seante of Maryland, at the December session, 1838. Annapolis: William M'Neir, printer, 1839.

DLC; MdHi; MdBB; MdBP. 57104

----. ----. ----. Committee on Colored Population. Report on the colored population [Annapolis? 1839] 7 p. DLC. 57105

----. ----. ----. Committee on Judicial proceedings. Report of a majority of the committee agianst the bill to reform the judiciary of this state and diminish the expenses thereof. Annapolis: William M'Neir, printer, 1839. 9 p. MdHi; WHi. 57106

----. ----. ----. ----. Report of the majority of the committee to which was referred the bill for the relief of the University of Mayland [Annapolis: 1839] 5 p. WHi. 57107

----. ----. ----. Select Committee on the Communication and Resolutions of the Council and General Assembly. Report of the select committee on the communication and resolutions of the council and General Assembly of New Jersey. Annapolis: William M'Neir, printer, 1839. 8 p. MdHi; PHi; WHi. 57108

----. Governor. Annual message from the governor to the legisalture of Maryland, December session, 1838. Annapolis: Jeremiah Hughes, printer, 1839. 14 p. MBAt; MdHi; MiD-B; WHi. 57109

----. Laws, Statutes, etc. Acts of incorporation and the supplemnets thereto [of the Susquehanna and Tide Water Canal Companies...] Baltimore: Hall and Tuttle, 1839. 71 p. DBRE; DLC; MdHi; PHi. 57110

----. ----. Acts relating to the Chesapeake and Ohio Canal Company, passed by the General Assembly at Maryland, at December session, 1838 [n. p.: 1839] 6 p. DLC; NN; ViU. 57111

----. ----. Laws made and passed by the Genral Assembly of the State of Maryland, at a session begun and held at Annapolis, on December 30, 1838 and ended April 6, 1839. Published by authority. Annapolis: Jeremiah Hughes [1839] 613 p. IaU-L; MdBB; MdHi; NNLI; R. 57112

Maryland. University. School of Medicine. Annual Circulars for the sessions of 1839 -1840 to 1841-1842. Baltimore: 1839-1912. DLC; DSG. 57113

----. ----. ----. Prospectus of the faculty of physic.... Baltimore: J. Murphy, 1839. 7 p. DLC;

MH. 57114

Maryland and New York Iron and Coal Company. Charter and by-laws. Incorporated by an act of the General Assembly of the state of Maryland. New York: Statioers' Hall Press, 1839. 20 p. NN. 57115

Maryland Mining Company. Loan of the Maryland Minig Company [Baltimore] Darling and Son, printer [1839] 46 p. MH-Ba; NN. 57116

The Maryland Pocket manual for the year of our Lord, 1839. Annapolis: Jeremiah Hughes [1839] 223 p. MdBS; MdBP; MdHi; MWA; PHi. 57117

Mason, Catharinge George [Ward] b. 1787. The mysterious marriage; or the will of my father. New York: J. C. Riker, 1839. 477 p. LNMus. 57118

Mason, Henry M. Relation between religion and science; address before the Delta Phi and Athensean Societies of Newark College, Delaware: E. G. Dorsey, 1839. 23 p. CtHT; MdBLC; MH; OClWHi; RPB. 57119

Mason, Lowell, 1792-1872. The Boston anthem book; being a collection of Anthems, collects, motetts, and other set pieces. Boston: J. H. Wilkins and R. B. Carter, and Jenks and Palmer [etc., etc.] 1839. 296 p. ICU; MBC; MdBP; NNUT; PPL. 57120

----. ----. 2nd edition. Boston: 1839. CtHWatk; MB. 57121

----. The Boston glee book, consisting of an extensive collection of glees, madrigals, and rounds.... Boston: J. H. Wilkins and R. B. Carter, and G. W. Palmer and Company, 1839. 264 p. CtHWatk; MBNEC; MiU; MLanc. 57122

----. The choir.... 9th edition. Boston: J. H. Wilkins and R. B. Carter, 1839. 357 p. ICN. 57123

----. Church psalmody: a collection of psalms and hymnss, adapted to public worship. Selected from Dr. Watts and other authors. Boston: Perkins and Marvin [etc., etc.] 1839. 598 p. CoCsC; DLC; MB; MnU; NmStM. 57124

----. Juvenile music, originally published in the sabbath school visitor; furnished by Lowell Mason...No. 1. Revised by the committee of publication. Boston: Massachusetts Sabbath School Society, 1839. 36 p. CtHWatk; CtSoP; NNUT. 57125

----. The juvenile singing school. By Lowell Mason and G. J. Webb. Boston: J. H. Wilkins and R. B. Carter, 1839. MBC; MDeeP; MH; NUtHi; WaU. 57126

----. Manual of Christian psalmody: a collection of Psalms and hymns for public worship. Hartford: Canfield and Robbins, 1839. 58 p. MBU-T. 57127

----. Manual of the Boston Academy of Music, for instruction in the elements of vocal music on the system of Pestalozzi. 5th edition. Boston: Wilkins, 1839. 252 p. MB; MiU; NN; OCX; ViRU. 57128

----. The modern psalmist; a collection of church music, psalm and hymn tunes and occasional pieces in general use. Boston: J. H. Wilkins and R. B. Carter, 1839. 352 p. ICN; MB: OO; PPL; Vi. 57129

----. The sabbath school harp: bieing a collection of tunes and hymns adapted to the wants of sabbath schools, families and social meetings. 3rd edition. Boston: Massachusetts Sabbath School Society, 1839. 96 p. DLC; MB; RPB. 57130

Mason, M. M. The southern first class book; or exercise in reading and declamation selected principally from American authors, and designed for the use of schools and academies in the southern and western states. Macon: B. F. Griffin and John M. Cooper, Augusta: J. W. and T. S. Stoy and T. H. Plant; etc., etc., etc., 1839. 336 p. DLC; G. 57131

Mason, Timothy Battelle, 1801-1861. Mason's young minstrel; a new collection of juvenile songs, with appropriate music. Revised, enlarged and stereotyped. 4th edition. Boston: Crocker and Brewster [etc.] 1839. MoK; NBuG; OClWHi; RPB. 57132

Massachusetts. Public documents of Massachusetts. Boston: state printers [1839]-1906. ICJ; ICU. 57133

----. Ancient and Honorable Artillery Company. Rules and regulations...with the charter. Boston: J. Howe, 1839. MB-FA. 57134

----. Attorney Genral's Office. Report and

opinion of the attorney general on the subject of the expenses of criminal justice made to the Senate, under an order passed on January 15, 1839. n. p.: 1839. 52 p. MH. 57135

----. Board of Education. Communication from the Secretary [Boston: 1839] 12 p. DHEW; DLC; MBC. 57136

----. Commissioners for Survey of Boston Harbor. Report...for fixing the line of private property in Boston Harbor [Boston: 1839] MBAt. 57137

----. Commissioners on Criminal Law. Preliminary report [Boston: 1839] 59 p. DLC; MBAt; MBC; MH; OCLaw. 57138

----. Comptroller's Office. Report and bill establishing a comptroller's office, 1839. 12 p. MBC. 57139

----. General Court. Acts and resolves...Genral Court...1839- 1876.... Boston: 1839- [1876] Ky; MCon; MQ; Nb; WaU. 57140

----. ----. Papers relating to the north eastern boundary [Boston: 1839] 44 p. M; MH; PLFM. 57141

----. ----. Report and resolves on the subject of the foreign slave trade [Boston: 1839] MB; MH; MnHi. 57142

----. ----. Resolves in relation to Boston harbor [Boston: 1839] 2 p. DLC. 57143

----. ----. Statement of evidence before the committee of the legislature, at the session of 1839, on the petition of the city of Boston, for the introduction of pure water. Boston: John H. Eastburn, printer, 1839. 62 p. DLC; MBAt; MHi; NjR; NN. 57144

----. ----. Committee on Capital Punishment. Report and bill to provide for the punishment of highway robbery and burglary [by the committee to consider the expediency of abolishing punishment by death] Boston: 1839. 12 p. CtY; MBAt; MBC. 57145

----. ----. Committee on Railways and Canals. Report and bill concerning the Seakonk Branch Railroad Company, and the Boston and Providence Railroad Corporation [Boston? 1839] 13 p. CSt; CtY; M. 57146

----. ----. ----. Report and bill regulating the use of railroads [Boston? 1839] 20 p. CSt; CtY; PPL. 57147

----. ----. Committee on the Petition of Manning Leonard and Others. Report...inhabitants of Sturbridge [to be set off from Sturbridge, and annexed to Southbridge] Boston: 1839. 11 p. M; OClWHi. 57148

----. ----. House. An act in addition to an act to regulate the sale of spiritous liquors. Boston: 1839. 7 p. VtU. 57149

----. ----. ----. Reports, resolves, etc., relating to the Marshpee Indians [Boston] 1839. ICN. 57150

----. ----. ----. Committee on Capital Punishment. Report and bill.... [Boston: 1839] 12 p. CtY. 57151

----. ----. ----. Committee on petition S. P. Sanford and Others. Report...concerning distinctions of color [Boston: 1839] 34 p. DLC; ICN; MB; MBC; NNC. 57152

----. ----. ----. Committee on Removal of Seat of Government. Report [Boston: 1839] 16 p. MBC; DLC. 57153

----. ----. ----. Committee on the Judiary. Report on sundry petitions respecting distinctions of color [Boston: 1839] ICN; MB: MH; NIC. 57154

----. ----. ----. Speicial Committee on Public Archives. Report and resolve relating to the public archives [Boston: 1839] 15 p. DLC; MBC; MH; MHi. 57155

----. ----. Joint Committee on Deliverance of Citizens Liable to be Sold as Slaves. Report [Boston: 1839] 36 p. DLC; MB; MBC; OClWHi; TNF. 57156

----. ----. Joint Committee on Investigation of the Fifteen Gallon Laws of Massachusetts. Investigation into the fifteen gallon law of Massachusetts, before a joint committee of the legislature...February 20, 1839, upon the memorial of Harrison Gray Otis and others for the repeal of the law.... Boston: printed by J. H., Buckingham, 1839. 111 p. ICN; MB: MdBP; PU-L; WHi. 57157

----. ----. Joint Select Committee on the Western Railroad. Report on the construction of the western railroad [Boston? 1839] 27 p. CSt; IU;

MiU. 57158

----. ----. Joint Special Committee on Banks and Banking. Report and bill concerning the City Bank, at Lowell [Boston?] 1839. 7 p. IU; MBC. 57159

----. ----. Joint Special Committee on Northeastern Boundary. Resolves concerning the northeastern boundary [Boston: 1839] 4 p. NN. 57160

----. ----. Joint Special Committee on Petition of Jairus Lincoln and Others. Report on the subject of domestic slavery [Boston: 1839] 11 p. MB; MH; NIC. 57161

----. ----. Joint Special Committee on Public Lands. Report and resolves concerning the public lands of the United States. n. p. [1839] 22 p. TxU. 57162

----. ----. Joint Speical Committee on Sale of Spiritous Liquors. Reports and bills relating to the sale of spiritous liquors [Boston: 1839] 46 p. DLC; MBC. 57163

----. ----. Joint Special Committee on the Eastern Railroad Company. Report and bill to aid in the construction of the Eastern Railroad [Boston: 1839] 16 p. CSt. 57164

----. ----. Joint Special Committee on the Farmers and Merchants Bank. Report and bill concerning the Farmers and Merchants Bank, at South Adams [Boston] 1839. 12 p. MBC. 57165

----. ----. Joint Standing Committee on Roads and Bridges. Report and bill relating to Charles River and Warren Brdges [Boston? 1839] 30 p. DLC; MH. 57166

----. ----. Library. Catalogue of the library of the General Court. Boston: Dutton and Wentworth, 1839. ICU; IU; MB. 57167

----. ----. Senate. Committee on Charitable Institutions. Report concerning public charitable institutions [Boston: 1839] 19 p. WHi. 57168

----. ----. Special Joint Committee of the Senate and House. Report and bill relating to the coal mines of the state [Boston: 1839] 45 p. DGS; DIGS; PPL; MWHi. 57169

----. Governor, 1836-1839 [Edward Everett] Address to the two branches of the legislature on the organization of the governomet for the political year commencing January 2, 1839. Boston: Dutton and Wentworth, 1839. DLC; OCHP; MHi; PU; WHi. 57170

----. Laws, Statutes, etc. An act concerning the sinking fund of the railroad [Boston: 1839?] 7 p. WU. 57171

----. ----. An act to establish regulations concerning the harbor of Boston [Boston: 1839] 4 p. DLC. 57172

----. ----. An act to provide for supplying the city of Boston with soft water [Boston: 1839] 11 p. DLC; Mh-AH. 57173

----. ----. Acts and resolves passed by the legislature of Massachusetts, in the year 1839. Boston: Dutton and Wentworth, printers to the state, 1839. 175 p. IaU-L; MoU; OrSC; TxU-L; Wa- L. 57174

----. ----. Laws of the commonwealth for the government of the Massachusetts State Prison, with the rules and regulations of the board of inspectors, and details of the police and discipline adopted by the warden, 1839. Boston: printed by E. Lincoln, 1839. 88 p. MB; MdBB; MH; RPB; WHi. 57175

----. Secretary of the Commonwealth. Statement...of the books, manuscripts, and documents belonging to the public archives [Boston: 1839] 12 p. MBC; MHi. 57176

----. State Library. Catalogue. Boston: 1839. MBAt. 57177

----. Registers. Statistical tables relating to Massachusetts, accompanied by a map of the state. Worcester: Dorr, Howland and Company, 1839. 32 p. CSt. 57178

----. Zoological and Botanical Survey. Reports on the fishes, reptiles and birds of Massachusetts. Published agreeably to an order of the legislature, by the commissioners on the zoological and botanical survey of the state. Boston: Dutton and Wentworth, state printers, 1839. 426 p. IU; Nh-Hi; OClW; ScCC; WHi. 57179

Massachusetts Abolition Society. Formation of the Massachusetts Abolition Society [Boston?

1839?] 36 p. DLC; MBC; TNF; WHi. 57180

Massachusetts Charitable Mechanic Association. The second exhibition...at Quincy Hall in the city of Boston, September 23, 1839. Boston: Isaac R. Butts, for the association, 1839. 136, 36 p. NbHi; RP. 57181

Massachusetts Horticultural Society. Report of the transactions of the Massachusetts Horticultural Society, for the year 1837- 1838, with preliminary observations. By John Lewis Russell.... Boston: Tuttle, Dennett and Chisholm, 1839. 116 p. DLC; MWA; NN; Or; WaS. 57182

Massachusetts Hospital Life Insurance Company, Boston. Proposals of the Massachusetts Hospital Life Insurance Company.... Boston: printed by Perkins and Marvin, 1839. 56 p. MB; MBC; MHi; MWA. 57183

Massachusetts Medical Society. Report on the constitution and by- laws of the society. n. p. [1839] 8 p. DNLM; MBAt. 57184

Massachusetts register and business directory [The Massachusetts register and United States claendar, for 1840] containing the tariff, the insolvent law, city officers in Boston, and other useful informantion. Boston: James Loring [1839] 250 p. MHa; MoSpD. 57185

Massachusetts Sabbath School Society. Bad Billy. Boston: 1839. CMadC. 57186

----. The sheep and lambs.... Boston: 1839. 8 p. MHi. 57187

----. Third annual descriptive catalogue of the publications.... Boston: Massachusetts Sabbath School Society, 1839. 40 p. IaGG; NNUT. 57188

Massachusetts Universalist Sunday School Association. Annual Report. Boston: Tompkins, 1839-1854. 5 v. in 1. MB. 57189

Mather, William Williams, 1804-1859. Report on the geoloical reconnoissance of Kentucky, made in 1838. By W. W. Mather, geologist and mining engineer [Frankfort, Ky.: 1839] 40 p. DLC; ICJ; KyHi; MHi; PPL. 57190

Mathews, Anne [Jackson] 1782?-1869. Continuation of the memoirs of Charles Mathews...including his correspondence.... Philadelphia: Lea

and Blanchard, 1839. 2 v. CtU; InGrD; MPiB; NbU; ScCC. 57191

----. Memoirs of Charles Mathews, comedian. Philadelphia: Lea and Blanchard, 1839. 2 v. LU; MB; NjP; OClWHi; PPA. 57192

----. Memoirs of Charles Mathews, comedian; with a continuation, including his correspondence and an account of his residence in the United States. Philadelphia: 1839. 4 v. MCli; MdBP. 57193

[Mathews, Cornelius] 1817-1889. Behemoth: a legend of the mound builders. New York: J. and H. G. Langley, Boston: Weeks, Jordan and Company, 1839. 192 p. DLC; IaK; MB; MWA; WU. 57194

----. The true aims of life: an address delivered before the alumni of the New York University...July 16, 1839. New York: Wiley and Putnam, 1839. 41 p. NcD; NN. 57195

Matthews, John T. A key to the Old and New Testaments, exhibited by the initials of the white stone. New York: 1839. 15 p. MH. 57196

Mattison, Seth. Substance od discourse delivered June 15, 1838, at the opening of the church at Yatesville, New York. Seneca Falls: Fuller and Bloomer, printers, 1839. 24 p. N. 57197

Maturin, Edward. Sejanus, and other roman tales...[anon.] New York: F. Saunders, 1839. 220 p. CSmH; NN; RPB. 57198

Maxson, William B. An inquiry into the prophetic character, of the Messiah [in Hebrew] By William Maxson, of the seventh Day Baptist Church. New York: 1839. 43 p. PCA. 57199

May, Henry, 1816-1863. The future exposure of James P. Heath and John H. Sothoron... [Washington: 1839] 18 p. DLC. 57200

May, John Frederick. An introductory lecture, delivered at the opening of the medical department of the Columbian College, November 4, 1839. Washington: printed by P. Force, 1839. 24 p. DLC; ICJ; MdBM; MHi; NHC-S. 57201

Mayo, Elizabeth, 1793-1865. Lessons on objects; their origin, nature, and uses. 3rd edition. Pennsylvania: Haswell, Barrington and Haswell, 1839. 204

p. NN. 57202

Mayo, H. B. An address delivered before the citizens of Oxford on July 4, 1839.... Oxford, Ohio: printed by W. W. Bishop, 1839. 16 p. NN; OUr; PPiXT. 57203

Mayo, Herbert, 1796-1852. Outlines on human pathology. Philadlephia: A. Waldie, 1839. 436 p. GU-M; MB; NhD; PPA; WMAM. 57204

Mayo, Robert, 1784-1864. Political sketches of eight years in Washington; in four parts, with annotations to each. Also a general appendix; an alphabetical index; and a series of charts.... Baltimore: F. Lucas, Jr., New York: G. and C. Carvill and Company [etc., etc.] 1839. 216 p. CSt; KU; LNH; MWA; PPA. 57205

[Mayo, Sarah Carter Edgarton] 1819-1848. Ellen Clifford; or the genius of reform. Boston: A. Tompkins and B. B. Mussey, 1839. 142 p. CtY; MMeT-Hi; MShi; NNC; ViU. 57206

Mayo, Thomas, 1790-1871. Elements of the pathology of the human mind. Philadelphia: A. Waldie, 1839. 73 p. CSt-L; ICJ; MdBM; OO; PU. 57207

Meadows, F. C. A new French and English pronouncing dictionary, on the basis of Nugent's with many new words in general use...To which are prefixed, principles of French pronunciation, and an abridged grammar.... 4th American edition, corrected and improved... New York: Blake, 1839. 352, 376 p. AU; CL; PPF. 57208

Meade, William, 1789-1862. The candidate for confirmation re- examined: with questions and addresses to ministers, parents, sponsors, and others. Philadlephia: William Stavely and Company, 1839. 30 p. CSmH; LNB; MdBD; NjP; NNC. 57209

----. Sermon of the assistant bishop of Virginia, to the students of the Theological Seminary.... Washington: 1839. 16 p. ICP; MdBD; MH-AH; NcU; PHi. 57210

Mechanics' Banking Association. Articles of Association. New York: printed by James Van Norden, 1839. 11 p. MH-BA. 57211

Medford, Massachusetts. City documents. Boston, Medford, Massachusetts: 1839-1939. 101 v.

M. 57212

----. Second Congregational Church. A manual of the Second Congregational Church in Medford. Andover: Gould, Newman and Saxton, 1839. 24 p. MBD. 57213

Medical Convention of Ohio. Journal of the proceedings...at its third session, held in Cleveland, May 14 and 15th, 1839. Cleveland: Penniman and Bemis, 1839. 84 p. CSmH; IEN-M; NNNAM. 57214

Medical Society of New Jersey. Law incorporating medical societies, and the by-laws, rules and regulations, with the table of fees and rates for charging of the Medical Society of New Jersey. Newark, N. J.: Olds, 1839. 72 p. CSmH; DLC; PPCP; MH; NNN. 57215

Medical Society of the County of New York. Statutes regulating the practice of physic and surgery in the state of New York; and the by-laws...adopted July, 1839. New York: printed by John Windt, 1839. 20 p. DLC; NNC-M; MiU; NjR; NNNAM. 57216

Medical Society of the County of Wastenaw, Ann Arbor, Michigan. Report on the miasmal fevers of the west, to the Medical Society.... Ann Arbor: 1839. 71 p. CSmH; DNLM; MiDW-M; MiU. 57217

Medical Society of the District of Columbia. Constitution and by- laws, with the act of incorporation. Washington: Moore [etc.] 1839. DNLM. 57218

----. Constitution...to which is prefixed the act of incorporation. Washington: A. B. Claxton and Company, printers, 1839. 11 p. DLC; DNLM; OC. 57219

Medical Society of the State of New York. By-laws...with the rules of order.... Albany: printed by J. Munsell, 1839. 23 p. CtY; DLC; MHi; NjR. 57220

Medway, Massachusetts. Village Church. Confession of faith and covenant of the Village Church, Medway, organized September 7, 1838. Boston: printed by D. Clapp, 1839. 10 p. MiD-B. 57221

Meigs, Charles Delucena, 1792-1869. The

Augustan age. A lecture at the Athenian Institute, February, 1839. Philadelphia: A. Waldie, 1839. 52 p. NjPT; OCHP; PHi; PPAmP; PPL. 57222

Mellen, Grenville, 1799-1841. A book of the United States. Exhibiting its geography, divisions, constitution, and government.... Hartford: H. F. Sumner and Company, 1839. 824 p. TChMcS. 57223

----. ----. New York: G. C. Smith and Company, 1839. 824 p. DLC; MH; MWA; NNC; PU. 57224

----. ----. New York: H. T. Sumner and Company, 1839. 804 p. CtHT; IaCrM; MoS; NbU; OClW. 57225

----. ----. New York: N. Watson and Company, 1839. 804 p. MWA; NIC. 57226

----. Poem, pronounced at New Haven, before the society of the Beta Kappa, August 20, 1839. New Haven: printed by B. L. Hamlin, 1839. 52 p. MBC; MH; NNUT: RPB. 57227

----. Poem, pronounced before the literary societies in Amherst College, August 27, 1839. Amherst: J. S. and C. Adams, 1839. 35 p. IaPec; MB; MH; NNC; PPM; 57228

Melvill, Henry, 1798-1871. Sermons. 1st American edition. New York: Sword, Stanford and Company, 1839. 266 p. CtMW; NRCR; WM. 57229

----. ----. 2nd American edition. New York: Swords, Stanford and Company, 1839. 2 v. GDecCT; KyBC; NcU; ScDuE; ViU. 57230

Memes, John Smythe. Memoirs of the Empress Josephine. New York: Harper and Brothers, 1839. 396 p. MB-HP; Me; MPeaI; NcMfC; TxGR. 57231

Memminger, Christopher Gustavus, 1803-1888. Speech...before the legislature of Kentucky, upon the proposition to co-operate in making a railroad from Charleston to the Ohio River. Frankfort, Ky.: A. G. Hodges, state printer, 1839. 28 p. IU; KyU; MB; MH; PPAmP. 57232

Memoir of Andrew Jackson, late Major General and commander in chief of the southern division of the army of the United States. Compiled by a citizen of Massachusetts. Philadelphia: 1839. 334 p. NIl. 57233

Memoir of Martin Van Buren, comprising an account of the intrigues by which he sought and acquired to the nomination and election to the office of chief magistrate; together with develpments of his political character, by a citizen of New York. 2nd edition. New York: Roberts, 1839. 137 p. ICN; NCH. 57234

Memoir of Mary King; who died in Rochester, Massachusetts, March 3, 1839...Written for the American Sunday School Union and revised by the committee of publication. Philadelphia: American Sunday School Union [1839] 34 p. CtHC; DLC; MB. 57235

Memoir of Rev. Samuel Davies, formerly predideint of the College of New Jersey...reivised by the committee of publication. 2nd edition. Boston: Massachusetts Sabbath School Society, 1839. 138 p. MBC; MBNEH. 57236

Memoir of the Hon. Caleb Strong, governor of Massachusetts [Boston: 1839] 12 p. ICN. 57237

Memorial and remonstrance relating to Massachusetts Medical Society. n. p.: 1839. OO. 57238

Memoir of the life and writings of Mrs. Hemans, See Owen, Harriet Mary [Browne] d. 1858.

Mendelssohn, Bartholdy Felix, 1809-1847. The conversion of St. Paul. Grand oratorio...as performed by the Baltimore Musical Association, May 13, 1839. Baltimore: John Murphy, printer, 1839. 14 p. MdBP; MdHi. 57239

Der Mensch, nach den Forderungen der vernunft und des Herzens. Erste Amerikanische Ausgabe. New York: M. Birk, 1839. 2 v. in 1. NN; OCU; PPG. 57240

Mercantile Library Association, Boston. Constitution and by- laws...together with a catalogue of books and names of members. Boston: 1839. 77 p. MHi. 57241

The merchants' and planters' almanac for 1840. by Thomas Spofford. New Orleans: D. Felt and Company [1839] MWA. 57242

Merchant's magazine and commercial review. New York: 1839 -1870. 63 v. CoU; MH; PU; ScU; WaS. 57243

Merle, d'Aubigne, Jean Henri, 1794-1872. History of the Great Reformation of 16th century in Germany, Switzerland. New York: American Tract Society, 1839? 3 v. IaDuU-Sen. 57244

[Merriam, George, 1803-1880] The child's guide: comprising familiar lessons, designed to aid in correct reading, spelling, defining, thinking and acting. Stereotype edition. Springfield: G. and C. Merriam, 1839. 152 p. CoGrS; Ct; MH; NLock. 57245

----. Easy primer, containing children, first lessons.... Springfield: Merriam, 1839. 70 p. PU. 57246

----. The intelligent reader: designed as a sequel to The child's guide. Springfield: G. and C. Merriam, 1839. MH; MNF; NRHi; OClW. 57247

Merrick, John M. Discourse on Sandwich [Massachusetts] February 17, 1839. Yarmouth [Mass.] Manning and Fisher, 1839. 15 p. MBC; RPB. 57248

Merrill, Thomas, 1814-1849. The catastrophe; or a tale of a new Englander. A poem.... Newburyport: printed by J. Gelman, 1839. 12 p. DLC; RPB. 57249

Messia, Alfonso S. J., 1665-1732. The devotion of the three hours agony in honor of our Lord Jesus Christ, on the cross.... New York: John Doyle, 1839. 52 p. InNd; MiD-M; MoSU. 57250

Messler, Abraham. Paul's gratitude for friendship of Onesiphorus; a sermon. New York: D. Fanshaw, printer, 1839. 24 p. NjPT; NjR; OClWHi; PPPrHi. 57251

Methodist almanac for 1840. Calculated to the horizon and meridian of Boston: By David Young, Philom. New York: J. Collord, 1839. IEG; MWA; NjR. 57252

----. By David Young. New York: T. Mason and G. Lane [1839] IEG; KBB; MiGr; MWA; NNMHi. 57253

Methodist Episcopal Church. A collection of hymns, for the use of the Methodist Episcopal Church principally from the collection of the Rev. John Wesley...revised and corrected with a supplement. New York: T. Mason and G. Lane, 1839. 623 p. IEG; MB; MiU; PPL; ViRC. 57254

----. The doctrines and discipline of the Methodist Episcopal Church. New York: T. Mason and G. Lane, 1839. 192 p. IEG; MBC; MdBAHi; TNS. 57255

----. Sammlung von geistlichen liedem fur kirhchlichen and hauslichen gottes dienst mit beifugung deutshcer and englishcher melodien. Cincinnati: J. F. Wright, 1839. 480 p. CtMW; DLC. 57256

----. Conferences. Minutes of the annual conference...for the year 1838-1839. New York: T. Mason and G. Lane, 1839. 98 p. CoDI; NNMHi; TU. 57257

Methodist Protestant Church. Constitution and discipline of the Methodist Protestant Church. 3rd edition. Baltimore: 1839. 178 p. NN; OClWHi; TxU. 57258

The metropolitan Catholic almanac and laity's directory, for the year of our Lord, 1840. Baltimore: Fielding Lucas, Jr., 1839. 174 p. MdHi; MoKCC; MWA; WStfSF. 57259

Miami University, Oxford, Ohio. Catalogue...of the University, July, 1839. Oxford: W. W. Bishop, 1839. 16 p. ICHi; PPiXT. 57260

Michigan. Laws, Statutes, etc. Acts of the legislature of the state of Michigan, passed at the annual session of 1839. With an appendix containing the treasurer's annual report.... Detroit: John S. Bagg, state printer, 1839. 382 p. Ar-SC; MHi; Wa-L. 57261

Middlebrook's almanac for 1840. By Elijah Middlebrook. Bridgeport, Conn.: Josiah B. Baldwin [1839] MWA. 57262

----. New Haven, Conn.: Durrie and Peck [1839] MHi; MWA. 57263

----. Westport, Conn.: J. W. Taylor [1840] MWA. 57264

Middlebury College, Middlebury, Vermont. Address delivered at the inauguration of the Professors of Middlebury College, March 18, 1839. Middlebury: office of the People's Press, 1839. 56 p. MBC; MiD-B; NCH; OCHP; RPB. 57265

----. The laws of Middlebury College. Middlebury: printed at the office of the People's Press,

1839. 24 p. DLC; MBC; N; VtMiS. 57266

Milam Guards. Constitution and by-laws of the Milam Guards.... Houston: Telegraph Power Press, 1839. 11 p. TxU. 57267

The military magazine: and record of the volunteers of the city and county of Philadlephia. Comprising authentic data of their institution,...Edited by William M. Huddy. Philadelphia: W. M. Huddy, 1839. DLC; NNC. 57268

----. v. 1-3; March 1839-June 1842. Philadelphia: 1839-1842. 3 v. IaAS; ICRL; LU; MoU. 57269

Miles, Henry Adolphus, 1809-1895. A sermon delivered at the South Cnogrgational church in Lowell, on the sabbath following the funeral of the Hon. Luther Lawrence, who died April 17, 1839. Lowell: L. Huntress, printer, 1839. 14 p. InID; MBC; MH; MoS; WHi. 57270

Millard, David, 1794-1873. Hymns and spiritual songs, original and selected for the use of Christians. 7th edition. Union Mills, New York: Christian General Book Association, 1839. 386 p. N; RPB. 57271

Miller, J. R. The history of Great Britain, from the death of George II, to the coronation of George IV, designed as a continuation of Hume and Smollett. Philadelphia: M'Carty and Davis, 1839. 724 p. MdBJ; MNonsA; NNF; ViRU. 57272

Miller, James P. Biographical sketches and sermons, of some of the first ministers of the Associate Church in America.... Albany: printed by Hoffman and White [1839] 512 p. CSansC; ICP; MPiB; PPPrHI; ViRut. 57273

Miller, S. G. Catechismus fur kleine kinder. New Berlin, Pa.: Carl Hammer, 1839. 32 p. PReaAT. 57274

----. Die geschichte des kleinen Georgs und Seines pfennigs. New Berlin, Pa.: C. Hammer, 1839. 21 p. PReaAT. 57275

----. Von der Stern-Kunde.... New Berlin, Pa.: Carl Hammer, 1839. 14 p. PReaAT. 57276

Miller, Samuel, 1769-1850. Letters of a grandfather, to the surviving children of Mrs. Margaret Breckinridge. Philadelphia: Martien, 1839. 103 p. DLC; PPPrHi. 57277

----. Lives of Jonathan Edwards, and David Brainerd. New York: Harper, 1839. 373 p. NICLA; NNC: ScCliP. 57278

----. Presbyterianism; the truley primitive and apostolical constitution of the Church of Christ. Philadelphia: Presbyterian Board of Publication, 1839. 98 p. NHuntL; ViRut. 57279

----. The utility and importance of creeds and confessions: addressed particularly to candidates for the ministry. Philadelphia: William S. Martien, 1839. 119 p. CSansS; GDecCT; IaMp; PPLT; ViRut. 57280

Miller, Thomas, 1807-1874. Fair Rosamond; or the days of King Henry II. An historical romance. Philadelphia: Carey and Hart, 1839. 2 v. CtY. 57281

Miller, William Hallows, 1801-1880. A treatise on crystallography. Cambridge: for J. and J. J. Deighton [etc., etc.] 1839. 139 p. CSt; MB; MdBJ; MH; ScCC. 57282

The miller's wife. Northampton [John Metcalf] 1839. 18 p. CtY. 57283

Millington, John, 1779-1868. Elements of civil engineering: being an attempt to consolidate the principles of the various operations of the civil engineer into one point of view.... PHiladelphia: J. Dobson, Richmond, Va.: Smith and Palmer, 1839. 725 p. IaAS; LU; NNE; PPM; ViU. 57284

Milman, Henry Hart, 1791-1869. The history of the Jews. From the earliest period to the present time. With maps and engravings. New York: Harper and Brothers, 1839. 2 v. Gu-M; MH-AH; OC; OkGu; TWcW. 57285

Milton, John, 1608-1674. Paradise lost, a poem in 12 books...with explanatory notes and a life of the author by the Rev. H. Stebbing. Philadelphia: James Kay, Junior and Brother, Pittsburgh: D. H. Kay and Company, 1839. 294 p. MH; OCl; PU; RPB; TNT. 57286

----. The poetical works of John Milton. With notes and life of the author. A new edition. Boston: Hilliard, Gray and Company, 1839. 2 v. CoPu; GEU; MH; OCY; ViU. 57287

Miner, Thomas, 1777-1841. The annual address to the candidates for degrees and licenses, in the medical institution of Yale College, February 26, 1839. New Haven: printed by B. L. Hamlem, 1839. 20 p. CtMW; IEN-M; MdBM; NCH; PHI. 57288

Miners' Free Press, Mineral Point, Wisconsin. Carriers address of the Miners' Free Press. January 1, 1840. Mineral Point, Wisconsin: 1839. Broadside. WHi. 57289

A minute and circumstantial narrative of the loss of the steam- packet Pulaski which burst her boiler, and sunk on the coast of North Crolina, June 14, 1838.... Providence: H. H. Brown, 1839. 24 p. DLC; MiD-B; McD; NcU; NSmb. 57290

Miscellanies on homoeopathy, edited by an association of homoeopathic physicians. Philadelphia: W. L. J. Kiderlen and Company, 1839. 1 v. MBM; NNNAM; NT; OCGHM; PPCP. 57291

Missionary advocate and intelligencer. Philadelphia: Alexander, 1839 . v. 1 . PPPrHi. 57292

Mississippi. Bank Commissioners. Report of the Bank commissioners, to the legislature of the state of Mississippi, delivered January 8, 1839. Printed by order of the House. Jackson: printed by B. D. Howard, 1839. 96 p. Ms-Ar; NcD; MsWJ. 57293

----. Governor, 1838-1842 [A. G. McNutt] Circular. Executive department, City of Jackson, December 16, 1839. To the presidents of the several colleges. and male and female academies in the state of Mississippi [Jackson: 1839] 4 p. Ms-Ar. 57294

----. ----. Message of the Governor to the legislature of the state of Mississippi. Delivered January 8, 1839. Printed by order of the House. Jackson: B. D. Howard, 1839. 28 p. MB; Ms-Ar; NNC. 57295

----. High Court of Errors and Appeals. Reports of cases, argued and determined in the High Court of Errors and Appeals, of the State of Mississippi. By Volney E. Howard.... Philadelphia: T. K. and P. G. Collins, 1839-1844. 7 v. DLC; LNB; OrSC; PU-L; WvW-L. 57296

----. Laws, Statutes, etc. A digest of the laws of Mississippi, comprising all the laws of a general nature, including the acts of the session of 1839. By T. J. Fox Alden, and J. A. Van Hoesen. New York: A. S. Gould, printer, 1839. 1009 p. IU; OClW; TxU; RPL; WaU. 57297

----. ----. Laws of the state of Mississippi; passed at an adjourned session of the legislature, held in the city of Jackson, from January 7, to February 16, 1839. Jackson: E. D. Howard, 1839. 491 p. ArSC; InSC; MH-L; NNLI; RPL. 57298

----. Legislature. House. Journal of the House of Representatives of the state of Mississippi, at an adjourned session thereof, held in the city of Jackson. Printed by order of the House. Jackson: printed by B. D. Howard, 1839. 382 p. DLC; NN; TxU. 57299

----. ----. Joint Committee on the Mississippi Union Bank. Report of the majority of the Joint Select Committee to examine the Mississippi Union Bank: Delivered to the Senate January 25, and to the House of Representatives, January 26, 1839. Printed by order of the Senate and House. Jackson: printed by B. D. Howard, 1839. 23 p. Ms-Ar. 57300

----. ----. ----. Report of the minority...submitted to the House, January 31, 1839. Br General H. S. Foote. Jackson: printed by B. D. Howard, 1839. 32 p. Ms-Ar. 57301

----. ----. Senate. Journal...at an adjourned session thereof, Held in the cith of Jackson. Printed by order of the Senate. Jackson: printed by B. D. Howard, 1839. 365 p. Ms; Ms-Ar. 57302

----. Miitia. Military notice. The citizens of Vicksburg subject to military duty, are informed that the colonel commandant has arranged and numbered the several beats of this city in the following order.... Vicksburg: 1839. Broadside. Ms-Ar; MsJS. 57303

----. State Library, Jackson. A catalogue...arranged alphabetically, under different heads, with the number, size and cost of the volume of each work specified. To which are prefixed the rules and regulations provided for its government. Jackson: printed by B. D. Howard, 1839. 27 p. DLC. 57304

Mississippi Free Trader. Extra. Natchez, September 17, 1839. Vindication, of Robert J. Walker from the charges of S. S. Prentiss, to the people of the state of Mississippi [Natchez: 1839] 8 p. CSmH. 57305

Mississippi Free Trader and Natchez Gazette. Weekly free trader, extra...October 10, 1839.

Natchez: 1839. 1 p. NcU. 57306

Mississippi Importing Company. Charter.... An act to incorporate the subscribers to the Grand Gulf and Port Gibson Shipping Company, and for other purposes.... Approved February, 1839 [Jackson: 1839] Broadside. Ms-Ar. 57307

----. Jackson, March 20, 1839. Sir...respectfully, your obedient servant, T. B. J. Hadley [Jackson: 1839] Broadside. Ms-Ar. 57308

Mississippi Typographical Association. Constitution and by- laws...revised and adopted July 4, 1838. To which is appended a scale of prices. Jackson: printed by B. D. Howard, 1839. 24 p. Ms-Ar. 57309

Mississippi Union Bank. Argument of Caswell R. Clifton, against the right of the bank commissioners to examine the bank under the authority of the act of the legislature of May 12, 1837. Prepared at the request of the Directors of said bank. Jackson: printed by B. D. Howard, 1839. 24 p. Ms-Ar. 57310

Mitchell, Chauncey L. A synoptical table ot thoracic percussion and auscultation. New York: 1839. MBCo. 57311

Mitchell, D. M. A discourse on Christian baptism.... Preached in Waldsboro, on the Lord's day, May 12, 1839. Waldsboro: printed by T. W. and E. W. Nichol, 1839. 36 p. MBC; MBNEB; MeHi; RPB. 57312

Mitchell, John Kearsley, 1798-1858. Indecision, a tale of the far west; and other poems. Philadelphia: E. L. Carey and A. Hart, 1839. 212 p. ICN; NcAs; PP; RPM; ViU. 57313

Mitchell, Samuel Augustus, 1792-1868. An accompaniment to Mitchell's map of the world, on Mercator's projection; containing
an index to the various countries, citites, towns, islands, etc., represented on the map.... Philadelphia: R. S. Barnes, 1839. 572 p. ArBaA; GEU; LU; MB; RPA. 57314

----. An accompaniment to Mitchell's reference and distance map of the United States containing an index of all the counties, districts, townships, towns.... Philadelphia: R. L. Barns, 1839. 344 p. DLC; MWA; OCHP; OMC; ScU. 57315

----. Mitchell's American system of standard school geography in a series: adapted to the progressive development capacities and increasing acquirements of youth. Philadelphia: Thomas, Cowperthwait and Company [1839?] 69 p. NcWsM. 57316

----. Mitchell's atlas of outline maps, intended to be filled up by pupils studying Mitchell's school geography and atlas. Philadelphia: Thomas, Cowperthwait and Company, 1839. CtHWatk; MH; NcWsS; NPV. 57317

----. Map of Illinois. Philadelphia: 1839. PPL. 57318

----. Map of Kentucky and Tennessee. Philadelphia: 1839. MWA. 57319

----. Map of Louisiana, Alabama and Mississippi. Philadelphia: 1839. NjR. 57320

----. Map of North Carolina, South Carolina and Georgia. Philadelphia: 1839. 1 p. PHi. 57321

----. Map of the southern states. N. p.: 1839. AU. 57322

----. Map of the state of New York, compiled from the latest authorities. Philadelphia: 1839. NIC. 57323

----. Map of the states of Ohio, Indiana and Illinois, with the settled part of Michigan. Philadelphia: Mitchell, 1839. IU; O. 57324

----. Mitchell's map of the United States; showing the principal traveling, turnpike and common roads. Philadelphia: S. Mitchell, 1839. ArU. 57325

----. Mitchell's school atlas. Philadelphia: Thomas, Cowperthwait and Company, 1839. 44 p. KU; MB: NcU; TxU-T; WaU. 57326

----. Mitchell's school geography. A system of modern geography comprising a description of the present state of the world.... Philadelphia: Thomas, Cowperthwait and Company, 1839. 336 p. CtHWatk; DLC; MH; PPeSchw; PPiHi. 57327

----. The tourist's pocket map of Michigan, exhibiting its internal improvements. Road distances by J. H. Young. Philadlephi: Mitchell, 1839. IGK. 57328

----. Tourist pocket map of the state of Ohio, exhibiting its internal improvements, roads, distances, by J. H. Young. Philadelphia: Mitchell, 1839. IGK. 57329

----. Mitchell's travellers's guide through the United States...stage, steamboat, canal, and railroad routes.... Philadelphia: Thomas, Cowperthwait and Company, 1839. 78 p. Ct; IJI; KHi; MnHi; PHi. 57330

Mitchell, Thomas Duche, 1791-1865. Annual address to the College of Physicians and Surgeons of Lexington; in which the principals and practice of medical ethics are illustrated...delivered in the medical hall, January 1, 1839. Lexington: Noble and Dunlop, 1839. 32 p. DNLM; KyU; NNNAM. 57331

----. The pains and pleasures of a medical life; being an introductory to a course of lectures on materia medica and therapeutics. Lexington, Ky.: the medical class, James Virden, printer, 1839. 23 p. CSmH; DLC; KyLxT; KyU; OC. 57332

Moffat, William B. The medical manual; containing information concerning the most prevalent diseases and most approved remedies. New York: 1839. 64 p. DLC; MBAt; NcU. 57333

Mogridge, George, 1787-1854. The juvenile moralists. New York: C. Wells, 1839. 80 p. MH; MHi. 57334

Mohawk and Hudson Railroad Company. Report of the superintendent to the president and directors of the Mohawk and Hudson Railroad Company.... Albany: printed by Packard, Van Benthuysen and Company, 1839. 17 p. NNE. 57335

Money and banking, or their nature and effects considered. See Beck, William.

Monfort, David. Reply to the views of A. R. Hinkley of sermons on Christian Baptism, Indianapolis, 1830. Two sermons on Christian baptism, Cincinnati: 1839. OCHP. 57336

----. Two sermons on Christian baptism, delivered in Franklin, Indiana, July 1838. Cincinnati: 1839. 48 p. OC; OCHP. 57337

Monkland, Mrs. Elvira, the nabor's wife. By Mrs Monkland. Philadelphia: Lea and Blanchard,

1839. 2 v. MBAt; NN; PReaAT. 57338

Monson Academy, Monson, Massachusetts. Catalogue of the trustees, instructors, and students of Monson Academy, for the year ending August 6, 1839. Springfield: Merriam, Wood and Company, printers, 1839. 12 p. MB; MH; MMons-A. 57339

Montgomery, George Washington, 1804-1841. Narrative of a journey to Guatemala, in Central America, in 1838. New York: Wiley and Putnam, 1839. 195 p. CLU; MdBP; PPA; RPB; TxU. 57340

Montgomery, George Washington, 1810-1898. An essay on the law of kindness. Utica: printed by Grosh and Hutchinson, 1839. 27 p. MMeT. 57341

Montgomery, James, 1771-1854. Lectures on general literature, poetry, etc., delivered at the royal Institution in 1830 and 1831. New York: Harper and Brothers, 1839. 321 p. AMoJ; IEG; MoSpD; OAU; RNR. 57342

Montgomery, William Fetherston, 1797-1859. An exposition of the signs and symptoms of pregnancy, the period of human gestation and the signs of delivery. Philadelphia: A. Waldie, 1839. 220 p. CoCsE; KyU; MB; PU; ViU. 57343

The monthly chronicle of interesting and useful knowledge, embracing education, internal improvements, and the arts. With notices of general literature and passing events. Edited by Edward D. Mansfield. Cincinnati: A. Pugh, 1839. 568 p. MiD-W; DLC; FMU; KyU; OClWHi. 57344

The monthly law reporter. Boston: Weeks, Jordan and Company, 1839-[1866] 27 v. Ar-SC; CU; MB; NjP; OClW. 57345

The monthly miscellany of religion and letters. Boston: W. Crosby and Company, 1839-1843. 9 v. DLC; IU; MB; NIC; OOxM. 57346

Moore, Ely, 1798-1861. Remarks in the House, February 4, 1839, on presenting a remonstrance from citizens of the District of Columbia agianst the reception of abolition petitions, etc. [Washington: 1839] 16 p. MdHi; NjR; OClWHi; TNF; WHi. 57347

Moore, Jacob Bailey, 1797-1853. Biographical notice of John Farmer, late corresponding secretary of the New Hampshire Historical

Society [Boston: Perkins, Marvin, 1839] 13 p. MH. 57348

Moore, THomas. Araby's daughter and the meeting of the waters. Boston: Oliver Ditson; 1839. 4 p. KU. 57349

Moore, Thoams, 1779-1852. Lalla Rockh, an oriental romance. From the 19th edition. Illustrated with engravings from the drawings by eminent artists under the superintendence of Mr. Charles Heath. Philadelphia: Lea and Blanchard, 1839. 397 p. DeWi; GSAJS; KyBC; MPiB; NcAs. 57350

----. The poetical works, including his melodies, ballads.... Phialdelphia: J. Crissy, 1839. 419 p. InCW; NNS; OWoC; PU; ViRU. 57351

----. ----. Philadelphia: Crissy and Markley and Thomas, Cowperthwait [1839?] 431 p. WU. 57352

Moorman, John J. A directory for the use of the white sulphur waters.... Philadelphia: printed by T. K. and P. G. Collins, 1839. 35 p. MB; MHi; NN; NNN. 57353

Moral almanac for 1840. Philadelphia: Tract Association of Friends [1839] MWA. 57354

The moral teacher: Designed as a class book for the common schools in the United States of America. By a clergyman. New York: Robinson and Franklin, 1839. 196 p. ICBB; KMK; MB; MH; NNT-C. 57355

More, Hannah, 1745-1833. The book of private devotion. New York: Robinson and Franklin, Boston: Crocker and Brewster, 1839. 256 p. CtHWatk; CtY; IU; MMC-T; PPWa. 57356

----. The works of Hannah More. 1st complete American edition. New York: Harper and Brothers, 1839. 2 v. LNL; MBBC; MoMe; OUrC; Wv. 57357

Morgan, Gilbert. Address before the Bible Society of Saratoga County.... Ballston Spa: printed by James Comstock, 1839. 12 p. NjR. 57358

Morrison, John Hopkins, 1808-1896. An address delivered at the centennial celebration in Peterborough, N. H. Boston: printed by Isaac R. Butts, 1839. 99 p. CtHT; MBC; NhD; PPL; RPB. 57359

----. An address before the Golden Branch Society of Phillips Exeter Academy, August 22, 1839. Boston: I. R. Butts, 1839. 23 p.MBAU; MdBJ; MH; NCH; PHi. 57360

Morley, Charles. A practical guide to composition, with progressive exercises in prose and poetry; embellished with cuts. Hartford: R. White, New York: Robinson, Pratt and Company, 1839. 96 p. InCW; MBAt; NNT-C; RPB. 57361

The Morning Sun, February 25, 1839. v. 1. no. 1. Geneva, N. Y.: 1839-. MBAt. 57362

Morris, George Pope, 1802-1864. The little Frenchman and his water lots, with other sketches of the times. Philadelphia: Lea and Blanchard, 1839. 155 p. CtHT; ICU; MdBE; MWA; RPA. 57363

Morris, Thomas, 1776-1844. Speech...in reply to the speech of the Hon. Henry Clay. In Senate, February 9, 1839. New York: American Anti-slavery Society, 1839. 40 p. CtHC; MdBJ; MH; OCHP; PHC. 57364

Morris, William E. Report to Judge Burnside and others, of the survey for a railroad by the valley of the Bald Eagle...also, the letter of Thomas Brunside to Nicholas Biddle upon the importance of the proposed Communication. Philadelphia: Clark, 1839. 8 p. MH-BA; OCHP; PHi; PPAmP. 57365

Morton, Daniel Oliver, 1788-1852. A sermon, Winchemdon, February 19, 1839, funeral of Colonel Jacob B. Woodbury, and a brief account of his life. Andover: Gould, Newman and Saxton, 1839. 23 p. MiD-B; MB; NjR; PPPrHi; RPB. 57366

Morton, John Maddison, 1811-1891. My husband's ghost, a comic interlude in one act.... Boston: 1839. 14 p. PHC. 57367

Morton, Samuel George, 1799-1851. Crania Americana; or a comparative view of the skulls of North and South America.... Philadelphia: J. Dobson, 1839. 296 p. MB; MdBP; NcU; PPL. 57368

----. Essays on the geology and organic remains of a part of the Atlantic Frontier of the United States.... Philadlephia: 1839. PPAN. 57369

Moseley, Henry, 1801-1872. Illustrations of

mechanics.... Revised by James Renwick.... New York: Harper and Brothers, 1839. 332 p. MoSpD; NBuCC; OCl; OrP; RJa. 57370

Mosheim, Johann Lorenz von, 1674-1755. Institutes of ecclesiastical history, ancient and modern, in four books, much corrected, enlarged and improved from the primary authorities.... A new and literal translation from the original Latin.... 2nd edition, revised and enlarged. New York: Harper and Brothers, 1839. 3 v. CBB; LyLo; MBC; ScDuE. WBeloC. 57371

[Motley, John Lothrop] 1814-1877. Morton's Hope or the memoirs of a provincial.... [1st edition] New York: Harper and Brothers, 1839. 2 v. CSmH; DLC; MH; NN; OCU. 57372

Mott, Abigail [Field] 1766-1851. Biographical sketches and interesting anecdotes of persons of color. To which is added a selection of pieces in poetry. 2nd edition, much enlarged. New York: M. Day, 1839. 408 p. KWiF; MH-AH; NcD; PHi; TxHR. 57373

Motte, Mellish Irving. The religion of a happy child. A sermon delivered before the South Congrational Society, August 4, 1839. Printed for the sunday school at their request. Boston: Tuttle, Dennett and Chisholm, printers, 1839. 19 p. ICMe; MB; NNC; RPB; TxU. 57374

Moultrie, James Jr. Introductory address, of the medical college of South Carolina, on the restitution to the faculty, by the medical society, of their former edifice. Charleston: Burges and James, 1839. 24 p. NBMS; NNNAM; ScCC. 57375

Mount Aubrn Cemetery, Cambridge, Massachusetts. [Announcement of the issue on new tickets to the cemetery. Boston] 1839. Broadside. MB. 57376

----. Catalogue of lots laid out in the cemetery of Mount Auburn, with the terms of subscription, regulations concerning visitors and interments, and a directory to the avenues and paths. Boston: N. Dearborn, 1839. 23 p. CSmH; MB; MH; MnHi; MWA. 57377

Mount Auburn guide. Boston: 1839. MB. 57378

Mount Holyoke College. Female education. Tendencies of the principles embraced, and the system adopted in the Mount Holyoke Female Seminary [South Hadley, Mass.: 1839] 26 p. CtHWatk; ICU; MBC; MH; MiD-B. 57379

Moyamensing, Pennsylvania. All Saint's Church. Constitution and by-laws of All Saint's Church, in the township of Moyamensing and County of Philadelphia. Adopted March 15, 1838. Philadelphia: printed by William Stavely and Company, 1839. 14 p. MB. 57380

Mudie, Robert, 1777-1842. A popular guide to the observation of nature; or hints of inducement to the study of natural productions and appearances, in their connections and relations. New York: Harper and Brothers, 1839. 343 p. GEU; IU; Me; NCH; ScSp. 57381

Muenscher, Joseph, 1798-1884. The church choir; a collection of sacred music, comprising a great variety of psalm and hymn tunes, anthems and chants, arranged for the organ of pianoforte and adapted particularly to the worship of the Protestand Episcopal Church in the United States.... Boston: Oliver Ditson and Company [1839] 2 pts. in 1. LU; MHi; OC; OC; OO. 57382

----. ----. New York: Stanford and Swords, Columbus, Ohio; Isaac Whiting, 1839. 295, 136 p. CtHT; MdBP; NBuDD; NNUT; PPL. 57383

Mutter, Thomas Dent, 1811-1859. A lecture on loxarthrus, or club foot. Philadelphia: Hooker and claxton, 1839. 104 p. ICJ; LNT-M; MdBJ-W; NBuU-M; ViU. 57384

Munsell, Joel, 1808-1880. Outline of the history of printing, and sketches of the early printers. Albany: printed by J. Munsell, 1839. 32 p. IaU; MB; MHi; MWA; NN. 57385

Murchison, R. To the voters of the thirteenth congressional district of North Carolina; comprising Ashe, Iredell, Surry and Wilkes County. Jefferson, N. C.: 1839. 2 p. NcU. 57386

Murray, Charles Augustus, 1806-1895. Travels in North America during the years 1834, 1835, and 1836, including a summer residence with the Pawnee Tribe of Inidans in the remote prairies of Missouri and a visit to Cuba and the Azore islands. New York: Harper, 1839. 2 v. GAuY; MNe; PPA; RPA; TJoT. 57387

Murray, Hugh, 1779-1846. The encyclopedia of geography, comprising a complete description of the earth, physical, statistical, civil and political. Philadelphia: Lea and Blanchard, 1839. 3 v. FU; LNB; MnHi; NjR; PPAN. 57388

----. Historical and descriptive account of British India from the most remote period to the present time. New York: Harper and Brothers, 1839. 3 v. CSfMA; KyLxT; MB-HP; MPeaI; NUt. 57389

Murray, John A. Child's book of devotion. New York: Taylor and D., 1839. 108 p. MB. 57390

Murray, Lindley, 1745-1826. Abridgement of Murray's English grammar, with an appendix, containing exercises in orthography parsing, in syntax and in punctuation, designed for the younger classes of learners....Adapted to the use of the English exercise. By Israel Alger. Boston: R. S. Davis, etc., 1839. MH. 57391

----. An abridgement of English grammar: Comprehending the principles and rules of the language. With exercises in orthography, in parsing, in syntax, and in punctuation. Designed for the younger classes of learners. Concord, N. H.: Marsh, Capen and Lyon, 1839. 100 p. MH; NNC; NRivHi; PatM. 57392

----. English exercises, adapted to Murray's English grammar, consisting of exercises in parsing, instances of false orthography, violations of the rules of syntax, defects in punctuation.... New York: Dean, 1839. 180 p. PU. 57393

----. English grammar, adapted to the different classes of learners. New London: W. and J. Bolles, 1839. 232 p. OrPD. 57394

----. ----. New York: 1839. CtHWatk. 57395

----. ----. From the last English edition. Newark, N. J.: J. B. Olds, 1839. CU; MH; NjP. 57396

----. The English reader; or pieces in prose and poetry. Selected from the best writers, etc. Bridgeport, Conn.: Josiah B. Baldwin, 1839. 262 p. ICU; MH: NBuG; NN. 57397

----. ----. New London: W. and J. Bolles, etc., etc., 1839. MH; PPeSchw. 57398

----. The English reader; or pieces in prose and verse, from the best writers; designed to assist young persons to read with propriety and effect.... Canandaigua, N. Y.: C. Morse, 1839. 252 p. CSmH. 57399

----. ----. Newark, N. J.: Olds, 1839. 252 p. CSmH; MH; NcD; OO; OU. 57400

----. ----. Philadelphia: R. W. Desilver, 1839. 252 p. DLC; NcD; PSC-Hi. 57401

----. Introduction to the English reader, or a selection of pieces in prose and poetry. Cincinnati: Ely and Strong, 1839. 156 p. IaDaP; ICN. 57402

----. ----. Philadelphia: H. Probasco, 1839. 167 p. DLC; PPL; PSC-Hi. 57403

----. Sequel to the English reader: or elegant selections in prose and poetry.... New York: John S. Taylor, 1839. 358 p. CtHWatk; MH; NbHi; WaPS. 57404

----. Murray's system of English grammar, improved and adapted to the present mode of instruction in this branch of science. 10th edition. Worcester: Dorr, Howland and Company, 1839. MH. 57405

Museum der Deutschen klassiker. New York: Radde, 1839. 3 v. PPG. 57406

Musical magazine; or repository of musical science, literature and intelligence. Bi-weekly. Boston: Otis, Broaders and Company, 1839-1842. 3 v. IaU; ICN; MBAt; MCon; PPi. 57407

Musical review, and record of musical science, literature and intelligence. Edited under the supervisional direction of an association of gentlemen, by E. Ives, jr., New York: W. Osburn, 1839. 422 p. MB; NN; NRU; NT. 57408

Musselman, Henry Kobler. The trial of Henry Kobler Musselman and Lewis Willman for the murder of the unfortunate Lazarus Zellerbach.... Lancaster: Forney, printer, 1839. 56, 15 p. MH-L; MoU; NIC; NN; PP. 57409

Mussey, Reuben Dimond, 1780-1866. An essay on the influence of tobacco upon the life and health. 2nd edition. Boston: Perkins and Marvin, 1839. 48 p. DLC; MH. 57410

----. ----. 3rd edition. Cincinnati: George L. Weed, at the Bible and Tract Depository, 1839. 48 p. DLC; IEN-M; MNBedf; OCHP. 57411

Mute's almanac for the year 1840...calculated for the meridian of Albany, by Levi S. Blackus.... Canajoharie, N. Y.: printed by L. S. Blackus [1839] 36 p. MWA; NjR. 57412

Muzzey, Artemas Bowers] 1802-1892. The moral teacher... See under title.

My niece, or the stranger's grave. New York: E. Walker, 1839. MH. 57413

My son's book. New York: F. W. Bradley and Company, 1839. 192 p. MB. 57414

Myers, Peter D. The Zion songster: A collection of hymns and spiritual songs, generally sung at camp and prayer meetings, and in revivals of religion. Compiled by Peter Myers. Revised and corrected by the compiler. New York: Collins, Reese and Company, 1839. 319 p. WyHi. 57415

N

Nack, James, 1809-1879. Earl Rupert, and other tales and poems. With a memoir of the author, by P. M. Wetmore, New York: G. Adlard, 1839. 220 p. CtMW; InCW; MB; NNS; TxU. 57416

Narrative of a mission of inquiry to the Jews from the church of Scotland. See Bonar, Andrew Alexander, 1810-1892.

Nash, Frederick. An address delivered before the members of Eagle Lodge, no. 71 on the anniversary of St. John the evangelist, December 27, 1838. Hillsborough: Dennis Heartt, 1839. 17 p. NcU. 57417

National almanac, and pocket calendar for 1840. By J. W. Herschell. New York [1839] MWA. 57418

The national magazine and republican review.... Washington: Fulton and Smith, 1839. 1 v. ICN; LU; MiD; NTaHi; OOxM. 57419

National reformer...v. 1. no. 1. February, 1839 [Philadelphia] Board of manages of the A. N. R. Soceity, 1839. 1 v. MB; OClWHi; 57420

Nature: on freedom of mind; and other poems. Boston: Dutton and Wentworth, 1839. 36 p. CtMW; MB; MH; NNC; TxU. 57421

The nautical almanac and astronomical ephemeris for the year 1840. Published by order of the Lords Commissioners of the Admiralty, London. New York: republished by Alexander Megarey at his navigation warehouse, 1839. 123 p. MNanMMA. 57422

The nautical almanac and astronomical ephemeris, for the year 1842. New York: E. and G. W. Blunt, 1839. 268 p. MsWJ; MWA. 57423

Neal, Joseph Clay, 1807-1847. Charcoal sketches; or scenes in a metropolis. With illustrations by David C. Johnston, Philadelphia: E. L. Carey and A. Hart, 1839. 222 p. DLC; GU; InU; MB; PU. 57424

----. ----. 3rd edition. Philadelphia: printed by T. K. and P. G. Collins, E. L. Carey and A. Hart, 1839. 222 p. KTW; MNe; MoSW. 57425

----. ----. 4th edition. Philadelphia: E. L. Carey and A. Hart, 1839. 222 p. CSmH; KTW; MiD-W; MnU; NNC. 57426

----. ----. 181 p. ICN; NcU: NNC; PP. 57427

Neilson, William, 1760?-1821. Exercise on the syntax of the Greek language. To which are subjoined, exercises in metaphrasis, etc.... New York: Swords, Stanford and Company, Philadelphia: Thomas, Cowperthwait and Company, 1839. 211 p. NbOC; PPWa. 57428

Nepos, Cornelius. De vita excellentium imperatorum: ex editione quarta J. H. Bremi. Accedunt notae anglicae, atque index historicus et geograhicus. Editio seunda. Bostoniae: Hilliard, Gray et soc., 1839. 192 p. CoD; MB; MBBC; NCH; WBeloC. 57429

Neue Americanische Landwirthschafts calender, 1840. Von Carl Friedrich Egelmann. Reading, Pa.: Johann Ritter und Company [1839] MWA. 57430

Neuer calender fur die bauern und handwerker, 1840. Von Carl F. Egelmann. Philadelphia: George W. Mentz [1839] MWA. 57431

Neuer calender fur Nord Amerika, 1840. Von Carl F. Egelmann. Philadelphia: George W. Mentz und Sohn [1839] MWA. 57432

Neuer gemeinnutziger Pennsylvanischer calender, 1840. Lancaster, Pa.: printed by John Bar, 1839. 35 p. MWA; PReaHi. 57433

Neuman, Henry. Dictionary of the Spanish and English languages...A great variety of terms, relating to the arts, sciences, navigation.... Boston: Hilliard, Gray and Company, 1839. 2 v. InLPU; LNBA; MH; NjR; PPC. 57434

----. A pocket dictionary of the Spanish and English languages. Compiled from the last improved editions of Newman and Baretti. In Two Parts.... Philadelphia: Lea and Blanchard, 1839. 714 p. MeLewB; PU. 57435

New American comic all-my-nack. New York: Elton, 1839. V. 1. No. 1. MWA. 57436

The new American primer; containing short and easy lessons for little children. Cincinnati, E. Morgan, 1839. ICU; IU; MH; OC. 57437

New Bedford. North Congregational Church. Official papers. Rev. Sylvester Holmes and the North Congregational Church [New Bedford: 1839-1843] 8 p. MNBedf. 57438

New Bedford directory. New Bedford, Massachusetts directory...to which is added a list of vessels employed in the whale fishery, belonging to the United States. By Henry H. Crapo. New Bedford: printed by Benjamin Lindsey, 1839. 168 p. CtHT-W; MB; MBC; MH; MNBedf. 57439

New Bedford Social Library. Catalogue of books belonging to the New Bedford Social Library. New Bedford: Benjamin Lindsey, 1839. 48 p. MiD-B; MNBedf. 57440

New England almanack, for 1840. Dudley Leavitt. Concord, N. H.: Marsh, Capen, Lyon and Wells [1839] MiD-B; MWA; Nh-Hi; NjR; WHi. 57441

----. By Nathan Daboll. New London, Conn.: E. Williams [1839] CSmH; ICMcHi; MWA; WHi. 57442

New England farmer, and horticultural register. Containing essays...relating to agriculture and domestic economy, with the prices of country produce, by Henry Colman. Boston: Breck and Company, 1839. 416 p. MNBedf; NNNBG; PPFrankI. 57443

New England farmer's almanac 1840. Truman W. Abell. Claremont, N. H.: Claremont Bookstore [1839] MWA; NhHi. 57444

New England farmer's and mechanic's almanac...1839. By Anson Allen Philom. Hartford: 1839. WHi. 57445

New England farmer's and scholar's almanac...by Dudley Leavitt, 1839. Concord, N. H.: Marsh, Capen and Lyons [1839] 38 [10] p. MeHi. 57446

New England Guards. Constitution of the New England Guards, revised, January, 1839. 5th edition. Boston: printed at the Daily Times offfice, 1839. 14 p. DLC; MB; MH. 57447

New England Non-resistance Society. National organization. Prepared for the New England Non-resistance Society. Published by the executive committee. Boston: I. Knaff, 1839. 32 p. MiD-B; NN. 57448

----. Principles of the Non-resistance Society. Boston: New England Non-resistance Society, 1839. 15 p. CtHWatk; MH; NN. 57449

The New England primer, or an easy and pleasant guide to the art of reading. Adorned with cuts. To which is added the catechism. Boston: Massachusetts Sabbath School Society, 1839. 64 p. DLC; MB; NNC; PPPrHi; WHi. 57450

New England Sabbath School Union. The New England sabbath school question book. Written for the New England Sabbath School Union and revised by the committee of publication. 6th edition. Boston: New England Sabbath School Union, 1839. 143 p. CaNSWA; WyHi. 57451

A new English-German and German-English dictionary; containing all the words in general use, designating the various parts of speech in both languages with the genders and plurals of the German nouns. Compiled for the dictionaries of Lloyd, Nohden.... Philadelphia: G. W. Mentz and Son, 1839. 2 v. DLC; IaG; MA; NFri; TxAuPT. 57452

The New Hampshire annual register, and United States calendar, for the year 1840. By Jacob B. Moore.... Concord: Marsh, Capen, Lyon and Webb, 1839. 141 p. MHa; MiD-B; MnHi; MWA. 57453

New establishment. Jease Bradshaw wholesale and retail confectioner. Having taken the new store, just erected on site of the Boston store. Boston: 1839. Broadside. MHi. 57454

New Hampshire. General Court. Rules and orders of the Senate and House of Representatives of the state of New Hampshire, with the joint rules of both houses, etc. Concord: 1839. MH. 57455

----. Laws, Statutes, etc. Laws of the state of New Hampshire; passed June session, 1839. Published by authority. Concord: Cyrus Barton, state printer, 1839. 125 p. Ar-SC; IaU-L; MdBB; Nh-Hi; W. 57456

The New Hampshire monthly review of employment and unemployment. No. 1-. October, 1839-. Concord: 1839-. CU; DLC; NN. 57457

New Hampshire Mutual Fire Insurance Company. Extracts from the records, relative to the memorial of Lyman B. Walker, 1839. 24 p. MBC. 57458

New Harmony, Indiana. Working Men's Institute. The charter, constitution and by-laws of the New Harmony Working Men's Institute.... New Harmony, Indiana: 1839. 7 p. InNHW. 57459

New Haven. Citizens. Report and resolutions in favor of a loan of credit by the city in aid of the [New Haven and Northampton] canal. New Haven: 1839. 8 p. CtY; MB; NNC. 57460

----. New Burying Ground. Report of the committee, appointed to inquire into the condition of the New Haven burying ground, and to propose a plan for its improvemnt. New Haven: printed by B. L. Hamlen, 1839. 28 p. MB; MH; NNUT; PPAmP; WHi. 57461

New Haven County Agricultural Society. To the farmers of New Haven County [New Haven: Babcock and Galpin, printers, 1839] 8 p. Ct; CtY. 57462

New Jersey. Laws, Statutes, etc. An act to incorporate the New Jersey Steam Navigation Company. Passed February 28, 1839. Newark, New Jersey: Benjamin Olds, 1839. 11 p. RPJCB. 57463

----. ----. An act to regulate elections [Princeton: R. E. Horner, printer, 1839] 32 p. NjR. 57464

----. ----. Acts of the 63rd General Assembly of the state of New Jersey. At a sessin begun at Trenton, on October 23, 1838. Being the second sitting. Camden [N. J.] printed by P. J. Gray, 1839. 272 p. In-SC; MdBB; NjR; ODaL. 57465

----. Legislature. General Assembly. Rules for the government of the General Assembly of the

state of New Jersey. Adopted to their proceedings on business of legislature. Trenton: 1839. 10 p. CSmH; NjR. 57466

----. ----. ----. Votes and proceedings othe the 63 General Assembly of the state of New Jersey, at a session begun at Trenton...being the first sitting. Newark: M. S. Harrison and Company, 1839. 638 p. Nj. 57467

----. ----. ----. Committee on Agriculture. Report.... Trenton: James T. Sherman, printer, 1839. 6, 29, 3 p. Nj. 57468

----. ----. ----. ----. Report. Trenton: Phillips and Boswell, printers, 1839. 8 p. Nj. 57469

----. ----. ----. ----. Report...of the House of Assembly of New Jersey, by William P. Forman. Trenton: James T. Sherman, printer, 1839. 7 p. Nj. 57470

----. ----. Joint Committee on the Public Lands. Report...January 23, 1839. Trenton: James T. Sherman, 1839. 8 p. Nj; NjR; PP. 57471

----. ----. Joint Committee on the State Prison Accounts. Report...November 5, 1839. Trenton: printed by Phillips and Boswell. 1839. 56 p. CU; Nj; PP. 57472

----. ----. Legislative Council. Journal of th proceedings...the first sitting of the 63rd session. Somerville, New Jersey: S. L. B. Baldwin, printer, 1839. 372, 72 p. NN. 57473

----. ----. ----. Rules for the government of the legislative council of the state of New Jersey, adapted to their proceedings on business of legislation. Adopted October 25, 1839. Trenton: Phillips and Boswell, 1839. 8 p. CSmH; NjR. 57474

----. ----. Senate. Select Committee on the Subject of a State Lunatic Asylum. Report...February, 1839. Tenton: Phillips and Boswell, 1839. 8 p. Nj; NjP; NjR. 57475

----. Trustees of the School Fund. Annual report...Trenton: Phillips and Boswell, 1839. 23 p. Nj; NjR; PPM. 57476

New mechanical power. The application of electro-magnetism as a motive power to machinery; containing a synopsis of the most important facts and discoveries, in electricity, magnetism and electro-magnetism; with a sketch of recent inventions and opinions of scientific men. New York: Wiley and Putnam, etc., 1839. 42 p. DLC. 57477

New Orleans. Comite des Finances. Rapport du comite des finances, de la seconde municipalite sur trois messages du Maire: avec la decision do juge Buchanan, sur les droits et pouvoirs relatifs du Maire et du conseil. Nouvelle Orleans: imprime par Benjamin Levy, 1839. 62 p. BWK. 57478

----. Finance Committee. Report of the finance committee of the second municipality, on three messages of the mayor.... New Orleans: Levy, 1839. 56 p. CtHT-W. 57479

----. Mayor, 1838-1840 [Charles Genois] Address of the mayor...being a refutation of a pamphlet entitled "Report of the finance committee on three messages of the mayor".... New Orleans: printed at the office of the Louisianian, 1839. 14 p. LNH; NcD. 57480

New universal atlas in 81 sheets and forming a series of 145 maps. Philadelphia: 1839. PPL-R. 57481

The new universal letter-writer; or complete art of polite correspondence.... Philadelphia: Hogan and Thompson, 1839. 216 p. CtY; IU; MBC; OCIW. 57482

The new world. V. 1- [no. 1-] October 26, 1839-. New York: J. Winchester, 1839-. DLC; M; MWiW; TxU; ViU. 57483

New year's address.... [Office of the Newport Mercury, January 1, 1839] Broadside. RNHi. 57484

The new year's day; and story reading by the same author. Boston: 1839. 52 p. RHi. 57485

New York [City] Board of Alderman. Report of the special committee to whom was referred the resolution to inquire into, and report the causes existing, and which have tended to increase the city expenditures, remedy, etc. [New York: 1839] 90. MH. 57486

----. ----. Committee on Streets. Report...in relation to the rails of the Harlaem Railroad in the Bowery, South of Broome Street [New York: 1839] 13 p. NN. 57487

----. Braodway Tabernacle Church. Proceedings of the session of Broadway Tabernacle, against Lewis Tappan, with the action of the Presbytery and General Assembly. New York: 1839. 64 p. MBC; MeBat; MH-AH; OO; NNUT. 57488

----. College of Physicians and Surgeons. Catalogue for 1838- 1839. New York: 1839. 12 p. MHi. 57489

----. Common Council. By-laws and ordinances. Revised 1838-1839. New York: 1839-1845. 2 v. NIC. 57490

----. Community Church. Act of incorporation and by-laws of the Second Congregational Unitarian Church, worshipping in the church of the Messiah. New York: Stationers Hall Press, 1839. 27 p. DLC. 57491

----. Comptroller's Office. Annual reports on the receipts and expenditures of the city government and receipts and investments of the commissioners of the sinking fund. 1838. New York: 1839-1884. 22 v. NBLiHi; WHi. 57492

----. Democratic Republican General Committee. Address of the Democratic Republican General Committee of the city of New York to the electors of the state of New York. New York: J. W. Bell, 1839. 8 p. MBC; MoSHi; PHi. 57493

----. Evangelical Union Anti-slavery Society. Address to the churches of Jesus Christ; with the constitution, names of officers, board of managers, and executive committee, April, 1839. New York: 1839. 52 p. CtSoP. 57494

----. Fire Department. The constitution and by-laws of the fire department of the city of New York. To which are added, the act of incorporation and the laws of the state relating to fires, firemen, the fire department, etc. New York: printed by J. W. Bell, 1839. 60 p. DLC. 57495

----. Greenwood Cemetery. Exposition of the plans and objects. New York: 1839. 28 p. MBC; OCHP. 57496

----. Mayor, 1837-1839 [Aaron Clark] Communication from the honor the mayor, in relation to the precautionary measures adopted by him to secure the public peace at the recent election. etc. New York: 1839. 64 p. MBC. 57497

----. ----. ----. with documents.... New York: order of the common council, 1839. 186 p. OClWHi. 57498

----. Mercantile Library Association. Constitution, rules, regulations.... New York: James Van Norden, 1839. CSmH. 57499

----. ----. Outlines of chemistry, inorganic bodies. Used as a text-book in the chemical class of the Mercantile Library Association of New York. New York: W. Jackson, 1839. 128 p. NN. 57500

----. Murray Street. Presbyterian Church. Annual Report of the Murray Street Church Sabbath School Missionary Society, auxilary to the American Home Missionary Society. New York: Mercein, 1839. PPPrHi. 57501

----. National Academy of Design. Constitution and by-laws.... New York: Clayton, 1839. 18 p. NhD; NNC; PPPM. 57502

----. North Baptist Church. Declaration of the faith and practice with the church covenant and list of members. New York: 1839. 16 p. NHC-S. 57503

----. Ordinances. By-laws and ordinances of the mayor, aldermen and commonalty of the city of New York. revised, 1838-1839. Published by authority of the Common Council. New York: printed by W. B. Townsend, 1839. 394 p. DLC; IU; MH-L; MBuG; NNC. 57504

----. St. George's Church. Report of the board of directors of the association of St. George's Church, New York, for the promotion of Christianity. New York: printed by George F. Bunce, 1839. 14 p. NNG. 57505

----. St. Paul's Congregation. Remarks of the committee of St. Paul's congregation, upon the report of the committee of the vestry of Trinity Parish, and upon the decision of the vestry on the memorial of the pewholders and worshippers...praying that the said Chapel may be set apart as a separate church. New York: 1839. 12 p. CtHT; MB; MdBD; PHi. 57506

----. Trinity Church. At a meeting of the corporation of Trinity Church, on March 11, 1839. The special committee on the memorial of various pew-holders and worshippers in St. Pauls chapel, praying that the congregation of the chapel may

be set off as a separate parish [New York: 1839] 9 p. MH; NNC. 57507

----. ----. Documents concerning recent measures of the vestry of Trinity Church, in the city of New York [New York: 1839] 8 p. NN. 57508

----. ----. [Proceedings at a meeting of the Corporation of Trinity Church, on the 11th of March, 1839. New York: 1839] 8 p. DLC. 57509

----. Union Theological Seminary. Catalogue of the officers and students of the New York Theological Seminary, January, 1839. New York: printed by William Osborn, 1839. 12 p. MdBD. 57510

----. ----. Constitution and by-laws...founded on the 18th of January...1836. New York: printed by William Osborn, 1839. 18 p. MBC; NNUT; PPPr-Hi; PPWe; PU. 57511

----. Third Universalist Society. The annual exercises, of the sunday school attached to the Third Universalist Society in New York: New York: Universalist Union Press, 1839. 46 p. MMeT-Hi. 57512

New York [State] Canal Commissioners. Report...on a resolution of the asseembly, of the 20th February [relative to work of the Erie Canal] Albany: 1839. 32 p. WHi. 57513

----. ----. Report...in answer to a resolution of the 21st of February...[on the Genesee Valley an Black River canals. Albany? 1839?] 9 p. MH-BA. 57514

----. ----. Report in answer to a resolution of the Assembly on the 27th of March [Albany: 1839] 3 p. NN. 57515

----. Comptroller's Office. Report...in relation to the bank fund [Albany: 1839?] MH-BA. 57516

----. Court of Chancery. Rules and orders of the Court of Chancery. Albany: 1839. NN. 57517

----. ----. Reports of cases...by Samuel M. Hopkins...Albany: Wm. and A. Gould and Company. New York: A. S. Gould, printer, 1839- 1848. 617 p. CU; MH-L; MiD-B; PPB; Tx-SC. 57518

----. Department of Public Instruction. Circular...containing an act...passed May 3, 1839....

Albany: Alfred Southwick, printer, 1839. NN. 57519

----. ----. Circular...to county treasirers...issued February 26, 1839.... Albany: printed by Croswell Van Benthuysen and Bury, 1839. NN. 57520

----. ----. Circular...containing "an act respecting school district libraries," passed April 15, 1839.... Albany: Hoff, 1839. 24 . CtHT-W; CtHWatk; DHEW; WHi. 57521

----. Engineer and Surveyor. Report of the Surveyor General in relation to land owned by the state in the counties of Hamilton, Essex, Clinton, Franklin and St. Lawrence [Albany: 1839] 9 p. WHi. 57522

----. Governor, 1838-1843. Communication from the governor relative to the geographical survey of the state. Albany: 1839. 351 p. CtHC; CtY; IU; WHi. 57523

----. Kappa Lambda Club. A history of the Kappa Lambda conspiracy. New York: William Stewart, 1839. 32 P MHI 57524

----. Laws, Statutes, etc. An act of the legislature...entitled "An act to perfect an amendment of the constitution providing for the election of mayors by the people". Albany: printed by E. Croswell, printer to the state, 1839. NN. 57525

----. ----. An act respecting convictions in criminal Courts...passed April 29, 1839. Albany: 1839. 14 p. MHi. 57526

----. ----. An act to amend an act to reduce several laws relative to New York city, into one act [New York: 1839?] MB. 57527

----. ----. An act to incorporate the Palladium Fire Insurance Company in the city of New York. Passed May 2, 1839. New York: E.B. Clayton, 1839. 10 p. DLC. 57528

----. ----. An act to provide for the construction of a railroad from Lake Erie to the Hudson River [Albany: 1939] 5 p. CSt; MB. 57529

----. ----. Circular of the superintendent of common schools to supervisors, county treasurers, etc.... Passed May 3, 1839; with instructions for its execution, and regulations concerning appeals. Issued May 15, 1839. Albany: A. Southwick, 1839.

30 p. CSmH; CoD; DHEW; MdBJ; WHi. 57530

----. ----. Laws of the state of New York passed at the 62nd session of the legislature begun and held at the city of Albany.... Albany: printed by E. Croswell, 1839. 433 p. Ar-SC; IaU-L Jy; OClWHi; Wa-L. 57531

----. ----. Statutes relating to elections, other than for militia and town officers, passed by the legislature of the state of New York. New York: J. W. Bell, 1839. 80 p. MH. 57532

----. Legislature. Assembly. Journal...62nd session begun and held at the capitol, in the city of Albany.... Albany: printed by E. Croswell, 1839 1476 p. NNLI. 57533

----. ----. ----. Committee on Canals and Internal Improvements. Report...on petitions for, and remonstrances against the extension of the Chemung Canal Feeder [Albany: 1839] 9 p, NRU. 57534

----. ----. ----. ----. Report...on the petition of the proprietors of the canal Basin at Rochester, known as "Child's Slip." [Albany: 1839] 10 p. NRU. 57535

----. ----. ----. Committee on Harlem River. Report of the select Committee on several petitions relative to the navigation of the Harlem River [Albany] 1839 15 p. WHi. 57536

----. ----. ----. Committee on Prisons. Report of the committee on state prisons in relation to the Mount Pleasant Prison. In Assembly, March 30, 1839. Albany: 1839. 64 p. WHi. 57537

----. ----. ----. Committee on Railroads. Memorial, statistics and correspondence in relation to a railroad from Ogdensburgh to Lake Champlain...submitted to the legislature of New York: 1839. 53 p. NN; NNC; R; RPB. 57538

----. ----. ----. ----. Mr Seoles' report in relation to the New York and Albany Railroad [Albany? 1839] 28 p. CtY; MB; MWA; NN; ViU. 57539

----. ----. ----. ----. Report...in relation to a survey of the Mohawk and St. Lawrence Railroad. In Assembly, February 28, 1839. Albany: 1839. 17 p. WHi. 57540

----. ----. ----. ----. Report of the majority of the

committee on the petitions of the New York and Albany Railroad Company and others [Albany: 1839] 39 p. NRU. 57541

----. ----. ----. ----. Report...on the memorial of the president, directors and company of the New York and Erie Railroad Company, and the memorials and petitions of citizens of sundry counties [Albany: 1839] 22 p. CSmH; CSt; MnHi; OClWHi. 57542

----. ----. ---. ----. Report...on the petition of inhabitants of the county of St. Lawrence, Franklin, Clinton and Essex, in relation to the Ogdensburgh and Lake Champlain Railroad. In Assembly, February 20, 1839 [Albany: 1839] 15 p. WHi. 57543

----. ----. ----. ----. Report...on the petition of the president and directors of the Schenectady and Troy Railroad Company [Albany: 1839] 8 p. NRU. 57544

----. ----. ----. ----. Report on the petition of the president, directors and company of the Canajoharie and Catskill Railroad Company, and others [Albany: 1839] 5 p. NRU. 57545

----. ----. ----. ----. Report...on the petitions of the Saratoga and Washington Railroad Company, and others. Albany: 1839. 10 p. WHi. 57546

----. ----. ----. Committee on Taxing. Report of the select committee of citizens of New York, relative to taxing seamen. Albany: 1839. 8 p. WHi. 57547

----. ----. ----. Committee on the Judiciary. Report on the petitions for abolishment of capital punishment. April 16, 1839 [Albany: 1839] 12 p. NN; WHi. 57548

----. ----. ----. Committee on Ways and Means. Report...on a resolution of the 11th April inst. [relative to the amount of money spent for railroads and canals] In Assembly, April 23, 1839. Albany: 1839. 13 p. WHi. 57549

----. ----. ----. ----. Report..on the state of the treasury and expenditures of government, made to the House of Representatives, January 24, 1839. New York: William G. Boggs, 1839. 28 p. MdHi. 57550

----. ----. ----. ----. Report upon the finances and internal improvements of the state of New York.

1838. Boston: reprinted by Dutton and Wentworth [1839] 65, 6 p. DLC; MH; NNC; PPL; WHi. 57551

----. ----. ----. Select Committee on Appointment of a United States Senator. Report...on a resolution from the Senate, relative to the appointment of an United States senator [Albany: 1839] 9 p. DLC; WHi. 57552

----. ----. ----. Select Committee on the Petition of Washington Irving and Others, to preserve Washington's Headquarters in Newburgh. Report.... [Albany: 1839] 5 p. DLC; WHi. 57553

----. ----. ----. Select Committee on the Resolutions of the State of Connecticut, Relating to the Disposition of Public Lands. Report.... n. p. [1839] 16 p. NjR; OClWHi. 57554

----. ----. Senate. General orders of the Senate to the 22d of April, 1839. New York: 1839. 10 p. NjR. 57555

----. ----. ----. Journal of the Senate of the state of New York, at the 62nd session, begun and held at the capitol, in the city of Albany, on the first day of January, 1839. Albany: printed by E. Croswell, printer to the state, 1839. 578 p. NNLI. 57556

----. ----. ----. Committee of the Whole. Speech when in the Committee of the Whole, in the Senate of New York, on the several bills and resolutions for the amendment of the law and the reform of the judiciary system. Albany: 1839. 31 p. WHi. 57557

----. ----. ----. Committee on Banks and Insurance Companies. Report...relative to the Delaware and Hudson Canal Company. In Senate February 25, 1839. Albany: 1839. 14 p. WHi. 57558

----. ----. ----. Committee on Canals. Report...on the bill to authorize the United States to construct the Niagara Ship Canal. In Senate, January 30, 1839. Albany: 1839. 14 p. WHi. 57559

----. ----. ----. Committee on Finance. Report of Mr. Verplanck, from the Committe on Finance, in relation to the revenue, debt and financial policy of the state [New York: 1839?] 19 p. MH; WHi. 57560

----. ----. ----. ----. Report of Mr. Young, Chairman of the Committee.... [Albany: 1839] 42 p.

DLC; WHi. 57561

----. ----. ----. ----. Report...on a resolution of the Senate March 13. New York: 1839. 13 p. NjR; WHi. 57562

----. ----. ----. Committee on Railroads. Report...on sundry petitions for the immediate construction of the New York and Erie Railroad by the state [Albany: 1839] 15 p. CSt; MB; MnHi. 57563

----. ----. ----. Select Committee on the Concurrent of the Assembly in Relation to the Right of Petition. Report.... [Albany? 1839] 27 p. PU; TxU; WHi. 57564

----. Natural History Survey. Message from the governor, transmitting several reports in relation to the geological survey of the state...May 5, 1839 [Albany: 1839] 21 p. NN. 57565

----. Secretary of State. Communication from the Secretary of State transmitting the report to survey a railroad from Ogdensburgh to Lake Champlain. In Assembly, January 30, 1839. Albany: 1839. 57 p. WHi. 57566

----. University. Instructions from the regents of the University to the academies subject to their visitation. Prescribing a minimum in value for the libraries and philosophical apparatus of academies....Albany: printed by E. Croswell, 1839. 24 p. NjR; NLew. 57567

New York and Albany Railroad Compnay. Report of E. F. Johnson, esq., chief engineer. Janaury, 1839. New York: printed at the railroad journal office, 1839. 24 p. CSt; MB; NjP; PPL. 57568

New York and Boston Illinois Land Company. Articles of Association, with amendments, etc. Philadelphia: L. Ashmead and Company, 1839. 27 p. DLC; ICHi; IGK; MiU-C; PHi. 57569

New York and Erie Railroad Company. Report...giving a list of the stockholders. New York: 25th February, 1839 [Albany: 1839] 16 p. CSmH. 57570

----. Resolutions passed by the board of directors.... [Albany: 1839] 4 p. CSmH. 57571

New York book of poetry. New York: Dearborn, 1839. 253 p. PP. 57572

New York Historical Society. The charter and by-laws...with amendments and a list of resident members. New York: 1839-1840. CtY. 57573

----. The constitution and by-laws.... New York: W. B. and T. Smith, printers, 1839. 23 p. DLC; MH; NN; PPAmP; WHi. 57574

New York Life Insurance and Trust Company. In chancery. Before the chancellor. In the matter of the New York Life Insurance and Trust Company. Answer and report. 1838. New York: J. Van Norden, printer, 1839. 71 p. DLC; InHi; MB; NN. 57575

The New York literary gazette. No. 1-24; February 2-July 13, 1839. New York: 1839. FU; MoU; OClWHi; PSt. 57576

Newcomb, Harvey, 1803-1863. The Benjamite king; or the history of Saul, the first king of Israel. Boston: Massachusetts Sabbath School Society, 1839. 198 p. DLC. 57577

----. Infant school question book. Written for the Massachusetts Sabbath School Society, and revised by the committee of publication. Boston; Massachusetts Sabbath School Society, 1839. 107 p. CtHC; MBC; NNUT; OMC. 57578

----. A practical directory for young Christian females. Boston: 1839. InCW. 57579

----. The protestants, being a continuation of the reformation in Germany, from 1525, to 1532, including the confession of Augsburg. Boston: Massachusetts Sabbath School Society, 1839. 198 p. DLC; MBC; NN; OO. 57580

----. Sabbath school teacher's aid: a collection of anecdotes. Boston: Massachusetts Sabbath School Society, 1839. MBC. 57581

----. The tract distributor. Boston: Massachusetts Sabbath School Society, 1839. MBC. 57582

----. The Wea mission, a conversation between a mother and her children, giving an account of the missions among the Wea Indians. Boston: Massachusetts Sabbath School Society, 1839. 72 p. CSmH; NN. 57583

----. The Wyandot chief; or the history of barnet, a converted indian, and his two sons; written for the Massachusetts Sabbath School Society, and revised by the committee of publication. 2nd edition. Boston: 1839. 81 p. CtHWatk; MBC; WHi. 57584

----. The young ladies guide to the harmonious development of Christian character. Boston: James B. Dow, 1839. InLogCM. 57585

Newell, Harriet [Atwood] 1793-1812. A sermon preached at Haverhill [Mass.] in rememberance of Mrs. Harriet Newell, wife of Rev.Samuel Newell, missionary to India...by Leonaryd Woods.... 9th edition. n. p.: published for A. Brown, 1839. CSmH; DLC; MB. 57586

Newland, W. A. Nothing else to do. Comic song [Accomp. for pianoforte] Boston: Reed, 1839. 2 p. MB. 57587

Newman, Samuel Phillips, 1797-1842. A practical system of rhetoric; or the principles and rules of style, inferred from examples of writing to which is added a historical dissertation on English style. 5th edition. Andover and New York: Gould and Newman, 1839. 311 p. CSt. 57588

----. ----. 7th edition. Andover: Gould and Newman, 1839. 311 p. CtHT; MH; NjR; PU; ViRut. 57589

Newton, Calvin P. A discourse on Christian baptism; preached in the Baptist meeting house, Waldoborough, August 11, 1839. Waldoboro': G. W. and F. W. Nichols, printers, 1839. 47 p. MeHi; MNtcA; PCA. 57590

Newton, John, 1725-1807. The pleasures of personal religion. Illustrated in 41 familiar letters, originally published under the signature of Omicrom and Virgil. Boston: Loring, 1839. 328 p. IaCec; MeBat; MH; OCl; PPLT. 57591

----. The works of the Rev. John Newton...containing an authentic narrative, etc. Letters on religious subjects.... To which are prefixed, memoirs of his life, etc., by the Rev. John Cecil.... Philadelphia: Hunt, 1839. 2 v. InRch; MB; NNC; PWW; ScDuE. 57592

Newton Theological Institution, Newton Center, Massachusetts. Laws. Boston: press of John Putnam, 1839. 12 p. MH. 57593

Nicholas, Robert Carter. Letter to the governor of Louisiana on the resolutions of the General Assembly. Washington: Blair and Rives, 1839. DLC; NNC; PPL. 57594

Nichols, Thomas Low, 1815-1901. Address delivered at Niagara Falls, on the evening of December 29, 1838, the anniversary of the burning of the Caroline. Buffalo: printed by Charles Faxon, 1839. 14 p. MHi; NBu; NBuHi. 57595

----. Vindication of the so-called "clique." Published by order of the executive committee. Buffalo: 1839. 24 p. NBuHi. 57596

Nicollet, Joseph Nicolas, 1786-1843. Essay on meteorological observations...Printed by order of the war department [Washington] J. Gideon, jr., printer, 1839. 45 p. LNH; MdHi; NhD; PPL; WaU. 57597

Niles, John Milton, 1787-1856. Connecticut civil officer, in three parts...together with numerous legal forms of common use and general convenience. 3rd edition. Hartford: Huntington, 1839. 371 p. Ct; CtHT; CtHWatk; TJoT. 57598

----. History of South America and Mexico; comprising their discovery, geography, politics, commerce and revolutions. Hartford: H. Huntington, Jun., 1839. 2 v. in 1. ICU; GCuA; LNH; NcU; TxDa. 57599

----. Speech of Mr. Niles, of Connecticut [In Senate, January 5, 1839. In reply to the remarks of Mr. Rives on...Transactions between the government and the bank of the United States.... n. p.: 1839?] 16 p. CSmH; DLC; MB; MiU-C; TxU. 57600

Noble, Samuel, 1779-1853. The plenary inspiration of the Scriptures asserted, and the principles of their composition investigated. Cincinnati: Book Committee of the western Convention, 1839. GMM; ICU; MB; MoS; OUrC. 57601

Nolcini, Charles. The grasshopper waltz, composed by Nolcini. Boston: Henry Prentiss, 1839. 4 p. MB; MChiA; MHi; MNF. 57602

The non-resistant. Boston: New England Non-resistant Society, 1839-1845. 5 v. MBC; MH; NcD; PPL; WaPS. 57603

None but suitable persons. Rhode Island

temperance tale, by a rum-seller. Founded on fact [anon.] Providence: B. T. Alboro, printer, 1839. 64 p. MH; MWA. 57604

Nordheimer, Isaac, 1809-1842. A critical grammar of the Hebrew language. New York: Wiley and Putnam, 1839. 2 v. CtY; FTaSU; NjR; ODaB. 57605

Norris, William H. Certificates of the cures of cancers and cancerous affections, performed by...on citizens of the United States, chiefly resident in Philadelphia. Philadelphia: Bakestraw, 1839. 31 p. PPCP; PPL. 57606

North, N. Greene. Doings of the Mississippi Legislature for the suppression and prevention of tippling. Natchez: published for the author, 1839. 16 p. NN. 57607

North, Simeon, 1802-1884. The college system of education; a discourse, delivered before the trustees of Hamilton College, May 8, 1839 on the occasion of his inauguration as president of the college. Utica: Bennett and Bright, 1839. 20 p. CtSoP; ICP; MH; NCH; RP. 57608

North American calendar...Wilmington: R. Porter, 1839. MWA. 57609

The north American tourist. New York: A. T. Goodrich, 1839. 506 p. ABBS; ICN; KyU; MB; NcU. 57610

North Branch Coal and Iron Company. Charter. Philadlephia: 1839. 10 p. Phi. 57611

North Carolina. General Assembly. Journal of the Senate and House of Commons at the session in 1838-1839. Raleigh: Thomas Lemay, 1839. 551 p. NcW. 57612

----. Laws, Statutes, etc. Acts of assembly in relation to the Fayetteville and Western Railroad, passed at the session of 1838- 1839. 7 p. NcU. 57613

----. ----. Laws of the state of North Carolina, passed by the General Assembly, at the session of 1838-1839. Raleigh: printed by J. Gales and Son, 1839. 220 p. Ar-SC; IaU-L; MdBB; Nj; R. 57614

North Star. [Boston] published for the Nassachusetts Anti-slavery Fair. October 29, 1839. 1 v. MB. 57615

Northern Liberties, Pennsylvania. Ordinances. Digest of acts of assembly and ordinances of the Northern Liberties. Philadelphia: 1839. 220 p. PHi; PPL. 57616

Northern Pacific Railroad Company. Rules for railway location and construction by E. H. McHenry. New York: Eng. news publishing Company, 1839. 74 p. PU. 57617

Norton, Andrews, 1786-1853. Additional notices of Mr. Buckminster [B.: 1839] [12] p. MH. 57618

----. A discourse on the latest form of infidelity; delivered at the request of the Association of the alumni of the Cambridge Theological School, on July 19, 1839. With notes. Cambridge: J. Owens, 1839. 64 p. CBPac; ICP; MeBa; PCA; RPaw. 57619

----. Remarks no a pamphlet entitled "The latest form of infidelity examined." Cambridge: John Owen, 1839. 72 p. CBPac; ICMe; MeBa; NNUT; PPL. 57620

Norton, William Augustus, 1810-1883. An elementary treatise on astronomy, designed for use in text book in schools and colleges.... New York: Wiley and Putnam, etc., etc., etc., 1839. 373, 112 p. GU; MH; PU; ScCC; ViU. 57621

Norvell, John, 1790-1850. Speech...of Michigan, on the bill of Mr. Crittenden to prevent the interference of certain federal officers in elections. Delivered in the Senate of the United States, February, 1839. Washington: printed by Blair and Rives, 1839. 13 p. CtY; MiD-B; MiU-C; NNC; WHi. 57622

Norwich, Massachusetts. Sabbath school celebration, July 4, 1839 [Norwich: 1839] MB. 57623

Norwich and Worcester Railroad. Act of incorporation. New York: Coolidge and Lambert, 1839. 22 p. DBRE. 57624

Nott, Samuel, 1788-1869. The "preaching and procedure" of Rev. Samuel Nott, Jr. for distribution among the people at Wareham, Massachusetts. Boston: Crocker and Brewster, 1839. 24 p. Ct; MBC; MH-AH; OMC. 57625

Nourse, James. Views of colonization. 2nd edition. New York: the American Anti-slavery

Society, 1839. 60 p. MB; NB; OO; RP; TxU. 57626

Noyes, George Rapall, 1798-1868. Jesus Christ, the church corner stone. Boston: James Munroe and Company for the American Unitarian Association, 1839. 16 p. CBPac; ICMe; KyHi; MB; MeB. 57627

Noyes, John. Discourse in Nor[th]field, May 29, 1836, at the close of the 50th year of ministry. New Haven: Hitchcock and Stafford, 1839. 20 p. CtHT; IaB; MBC; PPAmP; RPB. 57628

Nurseries for heaven [New York Protestant

Episcopal Tract Society, 1839] 4 p. DLC; InID. 57629

Nuttall, Thomas, 1786-1859. Manual of ornithology of United States and Canada. Boston: 1839. MWhB. 57630

Nye, Arius. Fragment of the early history of the state of Ohio. Address at Marietta on 48th anniversary of the first settlement of the state. In historical and philosophical society of Ohio transactions. Cincinnati: 1839. OCLaw; OMC. 57631

O

Oakeley, Frederick, 1802-1880. Order and ceremonial of the most holy and adorable sacrifice of the Mass.... New York: Catholic Publishing Society [1839] 144 p. P. 57632

Oberlin College. Catalogue of the officers and students...1839- 1840, 1840-1841. Oberlin [O.] printed by James Steele, 1839-1840. CSmH; MBC. 57633

----. Circular [informing the friends of the Oberlin Collegiate Institute that the American Education Society refuses any longer to aid students at Oberlin] Oberlin: 1839. 1 p. folder. D. In portfolio. OO. 57634

The Oberlin evangelist. A semi-monthly periodical devoted to the promotion of religion.... Oberlin, O.: J. M. Fitch, 1839-1862. 24 v. in 22. DLC; IEG; MiD-B; PPC; TxH. 57635

O'Brien's Philadelphia wholesale business directory and southern and western merchant pocket directory, to the principal mercantile houses in the city of Philadelphia, for the year 1839. Philadelphia: John G. O'Brien, 1839. 66 p. PAtM. 57636

The observer and record of agriculture, science and art. Edited by D. Pierce. Philadelphia: Merrihew and Thompson, printers, 1839. 192 p. CU; MsN; MU; NIC-A. 57637

Odd Fellows, Independent order of. Ohio. Columbus lodge, no. 9. Constitution and by-laws...adopted July 4th, 1839. Lancaster: C. H. Brough [1839?] 24 p. OClWHi. 57638

----. Patriarchs Militant. The charges and regulations necessary to be observed, in constituting an encampment of patriarchs. Baltimore: Matchett and Neilson, 1839. 23 p. Ct. 57639

[Odwin, Thomas] A voice in the city; to water drinkers. A recitative poem. By Bostonius. Boston: 1839. CtHWatk; MBAt. 57640

Oelschlager, J. C. Remarks on the system of teaching modern languages and arithmetic; with a prospectus of an academy of modern languages and commercial institute. Philadelphia: Stollmeyer, 1839. 15 p. PPAmP. 57641

Ogden, Benjamin, 1797-1853. Address, delivered before the Philomathean Society of the White Pigeon branch of the University of Michigan. White Pigeon: Munger, 1839. 15 p. NjP. 57642

Ogden, David Longworth, d. 1863. Review of a pamphlet entitled "Reply of the Congregational church in Whitesboro to a question of the Oneida Presbytery." Utica: Northway, 1839. 16 p. CtHT-W; MWA; PPPrHi. 57643

Ohio. Auditor of State. Report...in answer to a resolution of the House as to the amount of moneys drawn for and paid by each bank, insurance and bridge company, January 21, 1839 [Columbus: 1839] 10 p. WHi. 57644

----. ----. Report...in reply to a resolution of the House relative to the three percent fund, January 11, 1839 [Columbus: 1839] 2 p. WHi. 57645

----. ----. Report...in reply to a resolution relative to a surrender by the banks of Ohio of the right to issue small bills, under the act of 1836. January 16, 1839 [Columbus: 1839] 16 p. WHi. 57646

----. ----. Report...in reply to certain resolutions of the last session, relative to the tax upon bank dividends, etc. [Columbus: 1839] 7 p. WHi. 57647

----. ----. Report...on the expenses of the militia system...January 18, 1839 [Columbus: 1839] 1 p. WHi. 57648

----. ----. Special report...in reply to a resolution of the House calling for information relative to the expenditures on the public works of the state, December 20, 1839 [Columbus: 1839] 10 p. WHi. 57649

----. ----. Special report...transmitting statement of the organization of the financial department of the state of Pennsylvania, December 19, 1839 [Columbus: 1839] 6 p. WHi. 57650

----. ----. Special report...under a resolution of the House calling for an exhibit of the liabilities of the state. January 4, 1839 [Columbus: 1839] 7 p. WHi. 57651

----. ----. Tabular view of the condition of the several banks of Ohio, which institutions have replied to the resolutions of the Legislature of the session of 1839-7...Auditor of State [Columbus: 1839] Broadside. WHi. 57652

----. Board of Bank Commissioners. Annual report. 1st. Columbus: 1839. DLC; ICU; MH-BA; PU. 57653

----. Board of Canal Commissioners. Special report...in answer to a resolution of the House of Representatives, in relation to the employment of the state engineers and assistants by private companies. February 4, 1839 [Columbus: 1839] 4 p. WHi. 57654

----. ----. Special report...in relation to the southern termination of the Ohio canal. February 4, 1839 [Columbus: 1839] 46 p. OClWHi; WHi. 57655

----. ----. Special report...in relation to the surveys, plans and estimates of cost of the Vernon and Mohican Canals. February 4, 1839 [Columbus: 1839] 34 p. OClWHi; WHi. 57656

----. ----. Special report...in reply to a resolution of the General Assembly, calling for a certain report and estimate from Andrew Young, former resident engineer, on the extension of the Miami Canal. February 14th, 1839 [Columbus: 1839] 6 p. WHi. 57657

----. ----. Special report...in reply to a resolution of the House asking for information in relation to the transportation and sale of specie by certain banks therein named, December 28, 1839 [Columbus: 1839] 5 p. WHi. 57658

----. ----. Special report...in reply to a resolution of the House in relation to alterations in the general turnpike law, February 6, 1839 [Columbus: 1839] 6 p. WHi. 57659

----. ----. Special report...in reply to a resolution of the House, in relation to the amount due to the Zanesvlle Canal and Manufacturing Company, and other matters. February 19, 1839 [Columbus: 1839] 4 p. OClWHi; WHi. 57660

----. ----. Special report...in reply to a resolution of the House, relative to a branch canal from the Mad River Feeder to Urbana. February 16, 1839 [Columbus: 1839] 4 p. WHi. 57661

----. ----. Special report...in reply to a resolution of the House relative to John M'Carthy. February 19, 1839 [Columbus: 1839] 3 p. WHi. 57662

----. ----. Special report...in reply to a resolution of the House relative to the original and present estimates of cost of certain state improvements. February 6, 1839 [Columbus: 1839] 10 p. WHi. 57663

----. ----. Special report...in reply to a resolution of the Senate relative to the claim of Abner Enoch. February 12, 1839 [Columbus: 1839] 11 p. OClWHi; WHi. 57664

----. ----. Special report...in reply to a resolution of the Senate relative to the claim of Caleb Imlay. February 15, 1839 [Columbus: 1839] 5 p. WHi. 57665

----. ----. Special report...in reply to a resolution of the Senate relative to the claim of Morris Seely, February 19, 1839 [Columbus: 1839?] 8 p. OClWHi; OU; WHi. 57666

----. ----. Special report...in reply to certain interrogatories in relating to the navigable feeder of the Miami Canal extended. January 24, 1839 [Columbus: 1839] 6 p. WHi. 57667

----. ----. Special report...on the examination of Raccoon Creek. January 19, 1839 [Columbus: 1839] 1 p. WHi. 57668

----. ----. Special report...on the extension of the Mad River Navigable Feeder to West Liberty, January 19, 1839 [Columbus: 1839] 3 p. WHi. 57669

----. ----. Special report...on the surveys and estimates of the Woodsfield and Sisterville, and of the Marietta, Bridgeport and Wellsville Turnpikes, January 21, 1839 [Columbus: 1839] 9 p. WHi. 57670

----. ----. Special report...on the survey and estimates of the Wooster, Chippeway and Clinton Canal, January 19, 1839 [Columbus: 1839] 7 p. WHi. 57671

----. Board of Public Works. Acts for the protection of the canals, and other public works of Ohio, and for regulating the navigation and collection of tolls on the same; together with the orders.... Columbus: S. Medary and Brothers, 1839. 35 p. DLC. 57672

----. ----. Report...in relation to the rate of tolls charged on the national road. Columbus: 1839. 2 p. WHi. 57673

----. ----. Special report...to the General Assembly, transmitting the report of the agent appointed to examine into the affairs of turnpike, canal and slackwater navigation companies. December 14, 1839 [Columbus: 1839] 62 p. WHi. 57674

----. ----. Special report...transmitting the report of the superintendent of the national road, December 30, 1839 [Columbus: 1839] 12 p. WHi. 57675

----. Canal Fund Commissioners. Special report...[in answer to interrogatories contained in a resolution adopted January 25th, 1839, relative to the fund] January 29, 1839 [Columbus: 1839] 2 p. OClWHi; WHi. 57676

----. General Assembly. Court of Impeachment. Trial of Daniel M'Cook, Esq., clerk of the Court of Common Pleas of Carroll County, on articles of impeachment for breach of good behaviour in office. Reported by the prosecutor. Cincinnati: Hefley, Hubbell and Company, printers, 1839. 72 p. In-SC; MH-L; OCHP; OCLaw. 57677

----. ----. House. Committee on the Judiciary. Report of the majority of the Committee on the Judiciary, on the resolution of the House touching the official conduct of the Hon. Peter Hitchcock, one of the judges of the Supreme Court. February 14, 1839. n.p. [1839] 37 p. KyU; OCLaw; OClWHi; PPL. 57678

----. ----. ----. Committee on the Penitentiary. Testimony taken by the Committee on the Penitentiary in House, February 19, 1839 [Columbus: 1839?] 34 p. OO. 57679

----. Governor [Joseph Vance] Special message from the Governor [Joseph Vance], transmitting communications from the Governors of other states...Dec. 7, 1838 [Columbus: 1839] 21 p. WHi. 57680

----. Governor, 1838-1840 [Wilson Shannon] Communication from the Governor [Wilson Shannon] in relation to the location of lands granted by Congress to the state of Ohio. March 5, 1839 [Columbus: 1839] 13 p. WHi. 57681

----. ----. Jaehrliche botschaft des Gouverneurs W. Shannon an die gesetzgebende versammlung von Ohio. Lancaster, Ohio: Gedruckt bey V. Kastner, 1839. 30 p. CSmH; MB. 57682

----. ----. Special message of the Governor [of Ohio, Wilson Shannon] transmitting a communication [concerning fugitive slaves] from Messrs. Morehead and Smith, commissioners from Kentucky [Columbus: 1839] 11 p. OClWHi; WHi. 57683

----. Laws, Statutes, etc. Acts of a general nature, passed by the 37th General Assembly of Ohio, at its first session held in the city of Columbus, and commencing December 3, 1838, in the 37th year of said state. Columbus: Samuel Medary, printer to the state, 1839. 431 p. 17, 8 p. IaU-L; In-SC; MdBB; Nb; TxU-L. 57684

----. ----. Deutsches gesezbuch: enthaltend, nebst der unabhangigkeitserklarung und verfassung der Vereinigten Staaten; die verfassung und allgemeinen gesege des staates Ohio; gesammelt und ubers. von Georg Walker. Germantown, O.: 1839. 312 p. IU. 57685

----. Secretary of State. Special report...in relation to weights and measures [Columbus: 1839] 8 p. WHi. 57686

----. State Hospital, Columbus. Annual report of the directors and superintendent of the Ohio lunatic asylum.... [1st] 1839. Columbus: S. Medary, printer [etc.] 1839. CSmH; DLC; MiU-C; OFH; PPCP. 57687

----. ----. Special report of the directors of the Ohio Lunatic Asylum. January 24, 1839 [Columbus?: 1839?] 4 p. CSmH; NN; WHi. 57688

----. State printer. Reply to the state printer to a resolution of the House. February 19, 1839 [Columbus: 1839] 8 p. WHi. 57689

----. State School for the Blind, Worthington. Special report of the trustees of the Ohio institution for the blind in answer to a certain resolution of the House of Representatives [in relation to the expenses incurred in and connected with the erection of the buildings] [Columbus: 1839] 4 p. WHi. 57690

----. Superintendent of Common Schools. Report...on state institutions for teachers and others, in answer to sundry resolutions [of the General Assembly] passed March 19, 1838 [February 16, 1839] Columbus?: 1839. 20 p. DHEW; NN; OHi; WHi. 57691

----. ----. Reports...in answer to a joint resolution calling for a statement of the expenses of his department, January 24, 1839 [Columbus: 1839] 7 p. OC; WHi. 57692

----. Superintendent of the National Road. Report...December 24, 1838 [Columbus: 1839] 17 p. WHi. 57693

Ohio Anti-slavery Society. Condition of the people of color in the state of Ohio. With interesting anecdotes. Boston: I. Knapp, 1839. 48 p. DLC; MH; PPL. 57694

----. The declaration of sentiments and constitution of the Ohio State Anti-slavery Society. Cincinnati: Ohio Anti-slavery Society, 1839. 12 p. OCHP; OClWHi. 57695

----. Report of the 4th anniversary of the Ohio Anti-slavery Society...1839. Cincinnati: Ohio Anti-slavery Society, 1839. 1 v. CSmH; OMC; TxH. 57696

Ohio Mechanics Institute, Cincinnati. Proceedings of the 2nd annual fair of the Ohio Mechanics Institute, held during the 3rd week in June, in the city of Cincinnati. Cincinnati: printed by R. F. Brooks, 1839. 32 p. OC. 57697

The Ohio state bulletin. V. 1, no. 4, 6, 15, May 22, June 12, Aug. 14, 1839. Columbus: 1839. 1 v. OU. 57698

Olaneta, Jose Antonio de. Juicio de residencia del escelentisimo senor don Miguel Tacon, vizconde del Bayamo, marquez de la Union de Cuba...gobernador y capitan general que fue de la isla de Cuba. ...Filadelfia: Impr. de A. Walker, 1839. 201 p. CtY; DLC; LU; MB; NcD. 57699

The old American almanac for 1840. New series. Whole number X. Number XX. Boston: S. N. Dickinson [1839] [34] p. MsJS. 57700

The old American comic almanac 1840. Boston: S. N. Dickinson [1839] MBC; MHi; MWA; WaSp; WHi. 57701

Olds, Chauncey Newell. A valedictory address to the graduates of the Union Literary Society of Miami University, delivered August 7th, 1839.... Oxford, Ohio: printed by W. W. Bishop, 1839. 21 p. CSmH; MH; OCHP; OHi; OUr. 57702

Olmsted, Denison, 1791-1859. The atmosphere and its phenomena. New York: 1839. PPL-R. 57703

----. A compendium of astronomy; containing the elements of the science...By Denison Olmsted, A.M.... New York: Collins, Brothers and Company, 1839. 276 p. ArU; CtY; MH; MiU; NcAS. 57704

----. A compendium of natural philosophy: adapted to the use of the general reader, and of schools and academies.... 4th edition with numerous improvements. New Haven: S. Babcock, 1839. 360 p. CtY; ICRL; MH; Nh; PPF. 57705

----. An introduction to astronomy designed as a textbook for the students of Yale College.... New York: Collins, Keese and Company, 1839. 276 p. ANA; CU; KyLxT; PPM; TJaU. 57706

----. Outlines of lectures on the atmosphere and its phenomena.... New York: printed at the Xylographic Press, 1839. 12 p. MWA; NNC; NNS; PPL-R. 57707

Olney, Jesse, 1798-1872. Easy reader: or introduction to the national preceptor: consisting of familiar and progressive lessons designed to aid in thinking, spelling, defining and correct reading. New Haven: 1839. 144 p. Ct; CtHWatk. 57708

----. The family book of history: comprising a concise view of the most interesting and important events in the history of all civilized nations of the earth.... By J. Olney, and John W. Barber. Philadelphia: G. N. Loomis, 1839. 720 p. GAuY; NcMHi; NjR; OMC; TNP. 57709

----. A history of the United States on a new plan,

adapted to the capacity of youth, to which is added the Declaration of Independence and the Constitution of the United States, by J. Olney, A.M. New Haven: Durrie and Peck, 1839. 288 p. Ct; MH; WOshT. 57710

----. An improved system of arithmetic for the use of families, schools and academies. Hartford: Canfield and Robin, 1839. 312 p. Ct; CtMW; NAnge; NNC; RLa. 57711

----. The national preceptor; or selections in prose and poetry; consisting of narrative, descriptive, argumentative, didactic, pathetic and humorous pieces; together with dialogues, addresses, orations, speeches, etc.... 6th edtion. New York: Robinson, Pratt and Company, 1839. InBra; MHad; MWHi. 57712

----. A practical system of modern geography, or a view of the present state of the world. 30th edition. New York: Robinson, Pratt and Company, 1839. 288 p. A-Ar; CtY; MH. 57713

----. ----. 31st edition. New York: Robinson, Pratt and Company, 1839. 288 p. PPsCh. 57714

----. ----. 32nd edition. New York: Robinson, Pratt and Company, 1839. 288 p. CtHT; MnHi; NRivHi; OClWHi; PPM. 57715

Olshausen, Hermann, 1796-1839. The last days of the Saviour, or history of the Lord's passion.... Boston: J. Munroe and Company, 1839. 248 p. FSa; IEG; MH-AH; RPB; WHi. 57716

----. Proof of the genuineness of the writings of the New Testament: for intelligent readers of all classes. Translated from the German, with notes by David Fosdick, Jr. Andover: Gould and Newman, 1839. 216 p. CBPSR. 57717

On remembering our creator in the days of our youth [New York: Protestant Episcopal Tract Society, 1839] 8 p. DLC; InID. 57718

On the condition of the free people of color in the United States. New York: American Anti-slavery Society, 1839. 23 p. CU; ICN; MiU; OClWHi; PHi. 57719

On the evil tendency and injurious effects of theatrical exhibitions; and their inconsistency with Christianity.... Philadelphia: L. R. Bailey, 1839. 15 p. MnU. 57720

Onderdonk, Benjamin Tredwell, 1791-1861. THe Christian ministry; a sermon, preached in St. Paul's Church, Baltimore, at the ordination for the vacant diocese of Maryland, of a deacon and a priest. On the 23rd Sunday after Trinity, November 3, 1839. Baltimore: J. D. Toy, 1839. 14 p. MdBD; PHi; TSewU. 57721

----. The edifying of the church. A sermon.... By Benjamin T. Onderdonk.... Published by request of the convention. New York: Swords, Stanford and Company, 1839. 18 p. CtHT; MdBD; MWA; NBuDD; PHi. 57722

----. The Episcopal office. A sermon, preached in St. Peter's Church, Auburn, Cayuga County, N.Y., May 9th, 1839; on occasion of the consecration of the Rt. Rev. William Heathcote De Lancey, D.D., bishop of the diocese of western New York.... Utica: Hobart Press, 1839. 20 p. CtHT: MBD; MdBD; NBuDD; PPiXT. 57723

----. Pastoral letter to the clergy and laity of the diocese of New York, on the duty of aiding in education for the holy ministry, and in the missionary operations of the diocese [New York: J. Van Norden, 1839] 8 p. MH. 57724

Onderdonk, Henry Ustick, 1789-1858. The father of lights; a sermon, Auburn [N.Y.] May 8, 1839. Utica: printed by Hobart Press, 1839. 14 p. MdBD; NjR; PHi; RPB; WHi. 57725

Oneida almanac for the year of our Lord 1839: 3rd after bissextile or Leap Year...and, till July 4th, the 63rd of American independence. Utica, N.Y.: Gardiner Tracy, 1839 [24] p. NUtHi. 57726

Onomastikou Trigolotto "Ovowatlkov. Tply-Awttov; or trilingual nomenclature; an English, Latin and Greek vocabulary, combined from Howard and Greenwood. Philadelphia: J. Whetham, 1839. 154 p. MH; NN; PHi. 57727

Ontario and Livingston Mutual Insurance Company. A circular, by-laws and act of incorporation, of the Ontario and Livingston Mutual Insurance Company. Canandaigua: printed by C. Morse, 1839. 18 p. N. 57728

Ontario Female Seminary. Catalogue and circular of the Ontario Female Seminary, Canandaigua: for the year ending June, 1839. [Canandaigua] printed by C. Morse, 1839. 8 p. NCanHi; NGH. 57729

Opie, Amelia Alderoon. A cure for scandal; or detraction displayed, as exhibited by gossips.... Boston: James Loring, 1839. 208 p. KyBC; MBC; MBedf; OMC; RPA. 57730

----. Illustrations of lying, in all its branches. By Amelia Opie. From the 2nd London edition. New York: Robinson and Franklin, 1839. 283 p. IEG; GOgU; NbOM; NFred; PCC. 57731

Oregon. Citizens....Memorial of a number of citizens of the Oregon Territory, praying Congress to take possession of, and extend their jurisdiction over, the said territory.... n.p.: 1839. 3 p. MdBJ. 57732

The origin, history and influence of Roman legislation. From the New York Review, for Oct., 1839. New York: 1839. 64 p. DLC; MH. 57733

Original charades.... Cambridge: Folsom, Wells and Thurston, printers, 1839. 88, 4 p. ICU; MBL; MH; RNR. 57734

The orphan stranger, a tale for the lyceum fair. Cambridge, [Mass.] Metcalf, Torrey and Ballou, 1839 [3] 94 p. CtY; MB; MH. 57735

Orwig, Wilhelm, 1810-1889. Aufange-buch, oder Ein eingang zu grossern schulbuchern. Zion gebraugh fur Kleine Kinder. Verfasst von Wilhelm W. Orwig. Neu-Berlin, Pa.: Verlegt von C. Hammer fur die Evangelische gemeinschaft, 1839. 31 p. DLC. 57736

----. Eine Berufung auf Thatsachen und Gesunden Menschenverstand oder eine vernunftige Beweisung des verderbten und verlorenen Standes der Menschen.... New Berlin, Pa.: Herausgegeben von W. W. Orwig, J. Seybert und J. Rank fur die Evnagelische Gemeinschaft, S.G. Miller Drucker....1839. 246 p. PReaHi. 57737

Osage Mining and Smelting Company. A plan of operation.... Baltimore: John W. Woods, printer, 1839. 11 p. MH- BA. 57738

Osgood, Samuel, 1812-1880. Truths joined by God not to be sundered by man.... Boston: James Munroe and Company, 1839. 18 p. CBPac; ICMe; MB; MPeeP; RHi. 57739

Otheman, Edward. An address delivered at the Sabbath school celebration in Marblehead on the 4th of July, 1839.... Marblehead: S. Avery, 1839. 32

p. MiD-B; OO. 57740

Ottley, Dewey. The life of John Hunter. Philadelphia: Haswell, Barrington and Haswell, 1839. 139 p. CSt; LNOP; MdBJ; NjR; PPA. 57741

Our answer to them that do examine us. Reply of the Congregational Church in Whitesboro, to a question of the Oneida Presbytery. Whitesboro: the Oneida Institute, 1839. 11 p. NUtHi. 57742

Our Saviour's days; a Jewish tale. 2nd American edition. Boston: James B. Dow, 1839. 142 p. MH; MH-AH. 57743

Ovidius Naso, Publius. Excerpta ex scriptis Publii Ovidii Nasonis Accedunt notulae Anglicae et questions. In usum scholae Bostoniensis. Editio stereotypa. Bostoniae: Hilliard, Gray, et. Soc., 1839. 287 p. ArL; IEG; NbOC; PV. 57744

Owen, B. Review of the speech of Hon. Henry Clay, on abolition. Conneaut, O.: 1839. 20 p. MBC. 57745

Owen, Harriet Mary [Browne] d. 1858. Memoir of the life and writings of Mrs. Hemans. By her sister. Philadelphia: Lea and Blanchard, 1839. 317 p. DeWi; MWA; NjP; PPA; TxDa. 57746

Owen, John, 1616-1683. The glorious mystery of the person of Christ, God and man. To which are subjoined, meditations and discourses on the glory of Christ.... With an introductory notice, by John Hendricks. New York: Robert Carter, 1839. 612 p. CoD; ICU; NjR; PPWe; RPB. 57747

Owen, Robert Dale, 1801-1877. Pocahantas, a historical drama. New York: 1839. MB. 57748

----. Speech of internal improvement, by Robert Dale Owen [1839?] Broadside. MNBedf; NN. 57749

Oxenford, John, 1812-1877. Doctor Dilworth; a farce, in one act.... New York [etc.] Samuel French and Son [1839?] 18 p. OCl. 57750

Ozanne, P. M. Tarif des draits de douane des Etats-nis d' Amerique contenant les draits jusqu'a 1842, et les changements qui aurant lieu a celte ejcoque....Par P. M. Ozanne, calculateur et L. Deltra, dejunti controleur de la douane de la Nouvelle- Orleans. Nouvelle-Orleans: G. F. Duclere, 1839 [8]-132 p. DLC. 57751

P

Pabodie, William Jewett, 1813-1870. Calidore; a legendary poem.... Boston: Marsh, Capen, Lyon and Webb, 1839. 48 p. MB; MBAt; NbU; OC; TxU. 57752

Packard, Frederick Adolphus, 1794-1867. The teacher taught, an humble attempt to make the path of the Sunday school teacher straight and plain.... Philadelphia: American Sunday School Union [1839] 396 p. CtHC; FTU; IaHi; OClW; TJaL. 57753

----. The union Bible dictionary, prepared for the American Sunday School Union and revised by the Committee of Publication. Philadelphia: American Sunday School Union, 1839. 522 p. IU; MeB; NbOP; OWoC; PPA. 57754

----. A vindication of the separate system of prison discipline from the misrepresentations of the North American Review, July, 1839. Philadelphia: J. Dobson, 1839. 56 p. A-Ar; IEG; MB; NjR; PPL. 57755

Packard, George, b. 1868. An address delivered before the Female Temperance Society of Saco and Biddeford, June 17, 1839. Saco: printed by S. and C. Webster, 1839. 14 p. MeB. 57756

Packard, Levi, 1793-1857. A sermon preached at the dedication of the meeting-house in Spencer, Mass. Nov. 14, 1838. By Levi Packard, pastor of the church in Spencer. Brookfield: E. and L. Merriam, 1839. 24 p. CSmH; MB; MBAt; MBC. 57757

Page, D. C. The only true criterion of Christianity, a discourse, delivered by request, at Oakland College, Miss., April 3rd, 1839, it being the day preceding the annual commencement. Natchez: printed at the office of the Natchez Daily Courier, 1839. 16 p. Ms-Ar. 57758

Paine, David. Portland Sacred Music Society's collection of church music.... Portland: William Hyde, and Colman and Chisholm, 1839. 340 p. MB; MeHi. 57759

Paine, Elijah, 1757-1842. A collection of facts in regard to Liberia, to which is added the correspondence to the Rev. B. Tappan...and F. S. K., etc. Woodstock [Vt.] A. Palmer, 1839. CtY; CtHT; DLC; MWA. 57760

Paine, Emerson, 1786-1851. A sermon, preached at Halifax, Lord's Day, January 31, 1839, occasioned by the death of Mr. Samuel S. Sturtevant.... Plymouth: printed by James Thurber, 1839. 16 p. CSmH; MBC. 57761

Paine, Phebe. Address before the young ladies of the Spartanburgh Female Seminary, on the 14th of August, 1839. Greenville, S.C.: O. H. Wells, printer, 1839. 12 p. MnHi. 57762

Paine, Thomas, 1737-1809. The crisis; a work written while with the army of the revolution, with a view of stimulating that patriotic band to persevere in their glorious struggle for the rights of men. Nos. 1-16, Dec. 23, 1776-Dec. 9, 1783. Middletown, N.J.: Evans, 1839. 71 p. Ia; ICN; KyU; LNH; PU. 57763

----. The political writings of Thomas Paine, secretary to the committee of foreign affairs in the American Revolution.... Granville, Middletown, N.J.: George H. Evans, 1839. 2 v. CoGrS; KyDC; MWH; RPaw; WHi. 57764

Paley, William, 1743-1805. Natural theology; or evidences of the existence and attributes of the Deity...with additional notes, original and selected for this edition.... Boston: Gould, Kendall and Lincoln, 1839. 344 p. NPSC; OClW. 57765

----. ----. Boston: Marsh, Capen, Lyon and Webb, 1839. 2 v. AAP; InCW; MBBC; NjMD; PP; WaPS. 57766

----. ----. New York: Harper, 1839. 2 v. in 1. MeU; NBuCC; NCH; OrP; PPGi. 57767

----. The principles of moral and political philosophy. By William Paley, D.D. New York:

Collins, Keese and Company, 1839. 2 v. in 1. CtHT; LNT; OWoC; PWW; ScDuE. 57768

Palfrey, John Gorham, 1796-1881. Address at Barnstable on the anniversary of the settlement of Cape Cod. Boston: 1839. PPL. 57769

----. The theory and uses of natural religion: being the Dudleian lecture.... Boston: Ferdinand Andrews, 1839. 76 p. IEG; MB; MiD- B; RPB; WHi. 57770

Palmer, David. Anniversary address to the class of graduates of the Vermont Medical College, in Woodstock, delivered June 12th, 1839. Woodstock: Augustus Palmer, 1839. DSG; IEN-M; MH-M; OCGHM; WHi. 57771

Palmer, Edward. An address on the origin and evil influences of money. By Edward Palmer: who has nothing to do with money; being convinced that it is an engine of oppression, and an anti-Christian institution. Boston: 1839. 45 p. CoFcS; IU; MB; MH-BA; WHi. 57772

Palmer, Ray, 1808-1887. A doctrinal textbook, designed to aid Bible classes, families and churches in the systematic study of the cardinal doctrines of Christianity. Part I...Revised by the Committee of Publication.... Boston: Massachusetts Sabbath School Union, 1839. 72 p. CtSOP; IaB; MB; MBC; NNUT. 57773

----. How to live: or the Christian daughter's model. A memoir of Mrs. Catherine W. Watson. Boston: Whipple and Damrell, 1839. 244 p. CtHC; MB; MiD-B; MoSpD. 57774

----. Spiritual improvement: or aid to growth in grace. A companion for the Christian's closet. Boston: Perkins and Marvin, 1839. 239 p. CtHC; IEG; InCW; MeBa; PPM. 57775

----. The study of history commended to the active classes of society: a lecture delivered before the Bath Mechanic Association, December 4th, 1838. Bath: printed by E. Clarke, 1839. 16 p. MBC; MeBat; MeHi; MH-AH. 57776

A panacea; or an investigation of the superstitions of the age in which we live.... Louisville, Ky.: 1839. 8 p. ICMe. 57777

Pancoast, Joseph. Art of prolonging life briefly considered...a lecture. Jan., 1839.... Philadelphia:

Waldie, 1839. 40 p. MBAt; PPCP; PPDrop; PPM. 57778

----. A lecture introductory to the course of surgery, in the Jefferson Medical College, of Philadephia, for the session of 1839-1840. Published by the members of the class. Philadelphia: printed by William F. Geddes, 1839. IEN-M; JeffMedC; MB; PPM. 57779

Papineau, Louis Joseph, 1786-1871. Histoire de linsurrection du Canada. par L. J. Papineau.... En refutation du rapport de Lord Durham, Premiere parlie; Extratie de La Revue du Progress, journal public a Paris [Burlington, Vt.: Duvernay] 1839. 35 p. CaBVaU; DLC; IaU; MH. 57780

Pardoe [Julia] The romance of the harem. By Miss Pardoe, author of "the city of the sultan," etc. Philadelphia: E. L. Carey and A. Hart, 1839. 2 v. MB; MNan; PPL-R; ScSch; TNP. 57781

The parenological journal. V. I. Volumes land 2 pub. in Philadelphia only. Philadelphia: A. Waldie, 1839. PPeSchw. 57782

Park, Edwards Amasa, 1808-1900. Duties of a theologian. An anniversary address, delivered before the Theological Society of Dartmouth College, July 24, 1839. New York: American Biblical Repository, 1839. 35 p. MH-AH; NNC; PAnL; RHi; VtU. 57783

Parker, James W., b. 1797. Defence of James W. Parker, against slanderous accusations preferred against him. Houston: 1839. 7 p. DLC; TxU. 57784

Parker, Langston, 1803-1871.... The stomach in its morbid states; being a practical inquiry into the nature and treatment of diseases of that organ.... Philadelphia: A. Waldie, 1839. 194 p. CSt-L; MeB; PPA; ViU; WMAN. 57785

Parker, Richard Green, 1798-1869. The Boston school compendium of natural and experimental philosophy, embracing the elementary principles of mechanics, pneumatis, hydraulics. 2nd edition. Boston: Marsh, Capen and Lyon, 1839. 213 p. CSt; MB; MH; NjP; NN. 57786

----. ----. 4th edition, stereotyped. Boston: Marsh, Capen, Lyon and Webb, 1839. MH; MNBedf; PU. 57787

----. ----. 5th edition. Boston: Marsh, Capen,

Lyon and Webb, 1839. 237 p. C; MH; MHans; MWHi; NNC. 57788

----. Progressive exercises in English composition. 25th stereotype edition. Boston: Robert S. Davis, New York: Robinson, Pratt and Company, 1839. 107 p. MH; NjR; NmStM. 57789

----. Progressive exercises in English grammar. Part I. By R. G. Parker and C. Fox. 7th edition. Boston: Crocker and Brewster, 1839. CtHWatk; MH; WU. 57790

----. ----. Part II. 4th edition. Boston: Crocker and Brewster, etc., etc., 1839. CtHWatk; MH; WU. 57791

Parkman, Francis, 1788-1852. Enquiring of the fathers, or wisdom from the past. Discourses preached in the new North Church...December 9th, on the completion of the 124th year from the establishment of the church.... Boston: S. W. Dickinson, 1839. 40 p. CtSoP; ICMe; NNUT; OClWHi; WHi. 57792

Parley's book of books. Consisting of extracts from Parley's magazine and other sources. 2nd edition. Illustrated. New York: press of Mahlon Day and Company, James Eybert, printer, 1839. 383 p. 57793

The parlour book. New York: Charles S. Francis, Boston: Joseph H. Francis, 1839. 334 p. MBox; NjR. 57794

Parmelee, Ashbel. The origin, coruptions and destruction of popery: exhibited in a sermon [on 1 Tim. iv. 1-3] preached...August 26, 1838, etc. New York: Malone, 1839. 20 p. CtY. 57795

Parr, S. S. One baptism: a sermon, preached in the First Baptist Church, Ithaca, February 24, 1839. Ithaca: Mack, Andrus and Woodruff, printers, 1839. 24 p. CSmH; NjR; NRAB; PCA. 57796

Parry, Thomas, 1806-1862. The lucky horse shoe; or woman's trials; a domestic drama in three acts. London and New York: Samuel French [1839] 32 p. InU; NN; OCl. 57797

Parsons, Isaac, 1790-1868. Memoir of the life and character of Rev. Joseph Vaill, late pastor of the Church of Christ in Hadlyme. New York: 1839. 236 p. Ct; MBC; MH-AH; PCC; RWe. 57798

A parting gift to a Christian friend.... Hartford: Brown and Parsons, 1839. InU. 57799

Partridge, Francis M. Nunneries as they are. New York: 1839. RPB. 57800

Patrick, Joseph Homer. The tears of Jesus an example for mourners; a sermon preached...at the funeral of Miss Sarah Ann Frances Powers. Worcester, Mass.: Massachusetts Spy, 1839. PPPrHi; RPB. 57801

Pauling, James Kirke, 1778-1860. A life of Washington. New York: Harper and Brothers, 1839. 2 v. IU; MdBJ; OClWHi; ScDuE; TxGR. 57802

----. The merry tales of the three wise men of Gotham. By the author of "the Dutchman's fireside," "westward ho!" ...New York: Harper and Brothers, 1839. 236 p. ICU; LNH; MH; TxDa; WU. 57803

Paxton, John D., 1784-1868. Letters on Palestine and Egypt, written during a two years residence. Lexington, Ky.: A. T. Skillman, 1839. 320 p. CSans-S; GDecCT; ICP; KyRE; PPA. 57804

Payne, John Howard. Therese, the orphan of Geneva; a drama in three acts. Philadelphia: etc., Turner and Fisher [1839?] 47 p. ICU; MB; MH; NcU; PHi. 57805

Peabody, Andrew Preston, 1811-1893. Sermon delivered at the ordination of W. H. Lord over the First church and parish, Southborough, Mass. Oct. 31, 1838. Boston: 1839. 16 p. CBPac; MH-AH; MW; RPB. 57806

Peabody, Ephraim, 1807-1856. An address delivered at the centennial celebration in Wilton, N.H., Sept. 25, 1839.... With an appendix. Boston: B. H. Greene, 1839. 102 p. CtSoP; MBAt; NhD; RHi; WHi. 57807

----. On mystery, reason and faith. By E. Peabody. Printed for the American Unitarian Association. Boston: James Munroe and Company, 1839. 16 p. CBPac; ICMe; MBC; MDeeP; Nh-Hi. 57808

----. ----. 2nd edition. Printed for the American Unitarian Association. Boston: J. Munroe and Company, 1839. 16 p. MH; MH- AH. 57809

Peale, Rembrandt, 1778-1860. Portfolio of an artist. Philadelphia: H. Perkins, Boston: Perkins and Marvin, 1839. 263 p. CtSoP; IU; OO; PPi; ScC. 57810

The pearl; or affections gift. For 1840. A Christmas and New Year's present. Philadelphia: Henry F. Anners [1839] 222 p. GMWa; LNH; NbCrD; NcD. 57811

Peck, John Mason, 1789-1858. A new guide for emigrants to the west. Boston: Gould, 1839. WLacT. 57812

----. The principles and tendencies of democracy: an address, made in Belleville, St. Clair County, Illinois, July 4th, 1839. By J. M. Peck, of Rockspring, Illinois. Belleville, Illinois: J. R. Cannon, printer, 1839. 11. MH; MoSM; NlC; RPB. 57813

----. The traveler's directory for Illinois; containing accurate sketches of the state, a particular description of each county, etc.... New York: J. H. Colton, 1839. 219 p. IGK; MBC; MHi; MoSW; WHi. 57814

A peep into the state prison at Auburn, N.Y., with an appendix. By one who knows [Auburn] printed and published for the author, 1839. 75, 63 p. DLC; NAuHi; NB. 57815

Peirce, Oliver Beale. The grammar of the English language. New York: Robinson and Franklin, 1839. 384 p. CtHC; MBAt; MH; NNC; OO. 57816

Pembroke Academy. Pembroke, New Hampshire. Catalogue of officers, instructors and students, Nov. 21, 1839. Concord: 1839. 12 p. CtSoP; MH. 57817

Pencil, Mark [pseud.] White sulphur papers; or life at the springs of western Virginia. New York: S. Colman, 1839. 166 p. GDecCT; MdBJ; NjP; PU; WvU. 57818

Pendleton, John Strother, 1802-1868. Speech of Mr. Pendleton of Rappahannock on the election of a U. S. Senator, delivered in House of Delegates, Feb. 15, 1839. Richmond: Bailie and Gallaher, 1839. 23 p. MdBP; PHi. 57819

Penitent Females' Refuge and Bethesda Society, Boston. Appeal to the public in behalf of the Penitent Females' refuge in the city of Boston. Boston: Perkins and Marvin, 1839. 14 p. Ct; MB; MHi; MWA. 57820

Pennington, William, 1796-1862. Message from the governor of New Jersey to both houses of the 64th legislature.... Trenton: Sherman and Harron, printers, 1839. 18 p. Nj. 57821

----. Opinion of Governor Pennington, of New Jersey; argument of Mr. Armstrong, member of the legislative council; and letter of Mr. Maxwell...in relation to the powers and duty of the Governor and privy council, in canvassing the votes for representatives in Congress. Washington: [1839?] 12 p. IU; MiU-C. 57822

Pennock, Caspar Wistar, 1799?-1867. Report of experiments on the action of the heart, by C. W. Pennock, M.D.... and E. M. Moore, M.D.... Philadelphia: printed by Merrihew and Thompson, 1839. 18 p. DLC; MHi; NNNAM; OO; PHi. 57823

Pennsylvania. Constitutions of Pennsylvania, of 1790 and 1838. Printed by order of the House of Representatives. Harrisburg: printed by Boas and Coplan, 1839. 28 p. MiD-B; P; PHi; PP; PWCHi. 57824

----. Constitution of Pennsylvania, 1837-1838. Chambersburg, Pa.: 1839. 23 p. PHi. 57825

----. Board of Canal Commissioners. Communication, accompanied with documents relative to the connexion of the improvements of the state of N.Y. with the North Branch Canal. Harrisburg: 1839. 24 p. PHi. 57826

----. ----. Communication from the Canal Commissioners, exhibiting the condition of the canals and railroads. Read in the House, March 11, 1839. Harrisburg: Boas and Coplan, 1839. 78 p. ICJ; OSW; PBL; WHi. 57827

----. ----. ----. Read in Senate, March 11, 1839. Harrisburg: printed by E. Guyer, 1839, 84 p. DLC; MH-BA; PPAmP; PPF; ViU. 57828

----. ----. Communication from the secretary of the commonwealth, accompanied with a report of James D. Harris, engineer, to avoid the Schuykill inclined plane. Read in the House of Representatives, February 21, 1839. Harrisburg: Boas and Coplan, 1839. 33 p. DLC; NNE; PEaL; ViU. 57829

----. ----. Message from the governor, accompanied with a report. Read in the House, December 27, 1838. Harrisburg: Boas and Coplan, 1839. 146 p. ViU. 57830

----. ----. Report...relative to the abandonment of the contracts on the North and West branches...Harrisburg: Boas and Coplan, 1839. 7 p. DLC. 57831

----. ----. Report relative to the survey of a railroad from Chambersburg to Pittsburg, and the survey of the Roystown branch of the Juniata River, with estimates of the cost of the works. And a report of a survey and estimate of the cost of constructing a m'adamized or block road from Laughlinstown to Chambersburg. Harrisburg: E. Guyer, 1839. 122 p. DBRE; DLC; MH-BA; MiU-T; NNE. 57832

----. Courts. Rules and orders for regulating the practice in the several courts in the 16th district composed of the counties of Franklin, Bedford and Somerset. Chambersburg, Pa.: Thomas J. Wright, printer, 1839. 50 p. MH-L. 57833

----. ----. Rules for the regulation of the practice in the several courts within the 6th judicial district of Pennsylvania. Meadville, Pa.: 1839. 32 p. MH-L. 57834

----. Department of Public Instruction. By-laws for the first section of the first school districts...also, rules for the government of the primary schools: adopted.... Feb. 5, 1839. Philadelphia: A. Waldie, 1839. 16 p. ScC. 57835

----. ----. Jahrlicher bercht.... Harrisburg: 1839. PPAmP. 57836

----. ----. Report of the superintendent of common schools, accompanied with bills relating to the common school system. Read in the House of Representatives, Jan. 15, 1839. Harrisburg: Boas and Coplan, printers, 1839. 61 p. MnHi. 57837

----. General Assembly. Report of the minority of the committee appointed to investigate the conduct of the late Board of Canal Commissioners. Harrisburg: 1839. 47 p. PHi. 57838

----. ----. Report to the Legislature of Pennsylvania containing the description of the Bear Valley Coal basin, situated on the counties of Dauphin and Schuykill, illustrated with a map and diagram. Harrisburg: printed by Packer, Barrett and Parke, 1839. 12 p. P; PPF; PPi; PPL. 57839

----. ----. Testimony taken before the Select Committee appointed to examine into the return of James Hanna, as a Senator from the 2nd Senatorial District. Mr. C. Frailey, Chairman. Read in Senate. Jan. 26, 1829. Harrisburg: printed by E. Guyer, 1839. 51 p. P; PHi; PRHi. 57840

----. ----. House. A further report of the survey of a railroad from Chambersburg to Pittsburg, with an estimate of the cost of the work; also, a further report of the survey of the Raystown branch of the Juniata River, with an estimate of the cost of the work, by Hother Hage and the report of Charles De Hass...read...Jan. 28, 1839. Harrisburg: Boas, 1838. 114 p. PPAmP; PEaL; PHi; PPL. 57841

----. ----. ----. Report in relation to an asylum for the insane poor. Mr. Konigmacher, chairman. Read in the House of Representatives, March 22, 1839. Harrisburg: Boas and Coplan, printers, 1839. 24 p. CtY-M; DLC; MiD-B; PP; PPAmP. 57842

----. ----. ----. Report of the committee of accounts relative to the payment of the assistant sergeant's-at-arms. Mr. Park, Chairman. Read in the House of Representatives, March 5, 1839. Harrisburg: Boas and Company, 1839. 8 p. MH. 57843

----. ----. ----. Report to the Legislature of Pennsylvania, containing a description of the Swatara Mining District, illustrated by diagrams. Henry K. Strong, Chairman. Presented by Mr. M'Elwee, and printed by order of the House of Representatives. Harrisburg: printed by Boas and Coplan, 1839. 61 p. MB. 57844

---. ----. ----. Committee of Ways and Means. Report of the committee...upon the finances of the commonwealth. Mr. Flenniken, Chairman. Harrisburg: Boas and Coplan, printers, 1839. 12 p. MnHi; OSW; P. 57845

----. ----. ----. Committee on disturbances of seat of government. Report of the committee appointed to enquire into the causes of the disturbances at the seat of government, in December, 1838. Mr. Snowden, Chairman. Read in the House of Representatives, June 18, 1839. Harrisburg: Boas and Coplan, printers, 1839. 163 p. CSmH; DeU; DLC; MeU; NIC. 57846

----. ----. ----. ----. ----. Mr. Zeilin, Chairman. Read in the House of Representatives, June 24, 1839. Harrisburg: Boas and Coplan, printers, 1839. 247 p. CSmH; DLC; PP. 57847

----. ----. ----. Committee on Sunbury and Erie Railroad. Report upon the construction of the Sunbury and Erie Railroad: Mr. Walts, Chairman. Read, March 22, 1839. Harrisburg: Boas and Coplan, 1839. 10 p. DBRE; PHi. 57848

----. ----. ----. Committee on Revenue Bills. Report of the committee on revenue bills, relative to the state loan, authorized by the act of Jan. 26, 1839. To which is added, a message from the governor.... Harrisburg: printed by E. Guyer, 1839. 13 p. MnHi; OSW; PHi. 57849

----. ----. ----. Committee on the Judiciary. Report...relative to the abolition of slavery in the District of Columbia and in relation to the colored population of this country. Mr. Smith, of Franklin, Chairman. Read June 24, 1839. Harrisburg: Boas and Coplan, 1839. 14 p. MdBP; MoU; NIC. 57850

----. ----. ----. Committee on the Militia System. Report of the committee on the militia system, in relation to the payment of the troops of the 1st and 11th divisions, Pennsylvania Militia, who were ordered into service by the late governor. Mr. Hegins, Chairman. Read in the House of Representatives, Feb. 25, 1839. Harrisburg: Boas and Coplan, printers, 1839. 7 p. DLC; P; PHi. 57851

----. ----. ----. Committee Relative to the Gettysburg Railroad. Report...accompanied with testimony. Mr. McElwee, Chairman. Read in the House June 15, 1839. Harrisburg: Boas and Coplan, 1839. 80 p. CtY; DLC; MiU; NNC; PPAmP. 57852

----. ----. ----. Select committee. Report of the select committee, relative to the Philadelphia Loan Company, accompanied with testimony, opinion of counsel and bill. Read in the House of Representatives, Feb. 2, 1839, Harrisburg: Boas and Coplan, printers, 1839. 14 p. OSW; PHi. 57853

----. ----. Senate. Statement of the names of the associate judges, with the dates of their commissions; also a statement showing how the country offices are held. Read in Senate, Jan. 25, 1839. Harrisburg: printed by E. Guyer, 1839. 8 p. P. 57854

----. ----. ----. Committee Appointed to Examine into the Return of Thomas S. Bell. Report.... Harrisburg: printed by E. Guyer, 1839. 48 p. MnHi; NN; PPi. 57855

----. ----. ----. Committee on Roads, Bridges and Inland Investigation. Report...relative to canals and railroads of the commonwealth. Harrisburg: 1839. 29 p. DLC; IU; PPAmP. 57856

----. ----. ----. Committee on Vice and Immorality. Report...relative to the appointment of a moral instructor in the eastern penitentiary. Mr. Fullerton, Chairman. Read in Senate, May 27, 1839. Harrisburg: printed by E. Guyer, 1839. 5 p. P. 57857

----. ----. ----. ----. ----. 7 p. MH-L. 57858

---. ----. ----. Select Committee Appointed to Visit and Examine the Western Penitentiary. Report...together with the annual report of that institution. Feb. 3, 1839. Harrisburg: E. Guyer, 1839. 16 p. P; ScC. 57859

----. ----. ----. Select Committee on Armed Force at the Capitol. Report of the select committee appointed to inquire into the cause of an armed force, being brought to the capitol of Pennsylvania...on the 4th December, 1838, etc.; together with the report of the minority of the committee, and the testimony taken thereon. Mr. Barclay, Chairman. Read in Senate, June 24, 1839. Harrisburg: 1839. 247 p. MB; MiD-B; MnU; OCl; PHi; PP. 57860

----. ----. ----. Select Committee on the Public Works of New York and Pennsylvania. Report of the select committee appointed to confer with the authorities of the state of New York relative to a connection of the public works of New York and Pennsylvania. Read May 15, 1839. Harrisburg: E. Guyer, 1839. 15 p. DLC; IU; ViU. 57861

----. ----. ----. Select Committee to Inquire into the Authorship of a Speech Delivered by Thomas C. Miller. Report of the select committee appointed to inquire into the authorship of a speech, purporting to have been delivered on the floor of the Senate by Thomas C. Miller, a Senator from Adams county; together with the report of the minority of the committee, and the testimony taken theron. Mr. Ewing, Chairman. Read in Senate, June 3, 1839. Harrisburg: E. Guyer, 1839. 31 p. PMA. 57862

----. Governor [David R. Porter] Inaugural address of David R. Porter, Governor of Pennsylvania, delivered in the hall of the House of Representatives, Jan. 15, 1839. Harrisburg: E. Guyer, 1839. 10 p. P. 57863

----. ----. Message accompanied with a report of the canal commissioners and accompanying documents read in the House of Representatives, Dec. 27, 1838. Harrisburg: Boas, printer, 1839. 146 p. NNE; P. 57864

----. ----. Message from the Governor. Finances of the commonwealth. Read in the House of Representatives, Jan. 26, 1839. Harrisburg: printed by Boas and Coplan, 1839. 12 p. P. 57865

----. ----. ----. ----. Message from the governor of the commonwewalth relative to the condition of the Treasury. Read in the Senate, Jan. 26, 1839. Harrisburg: E. Guyer, 1839. 14 p. DLC; PHi; PPM. 57866

----. ----. Message of the governor...vetoing the local appropriation bill.... Read May 9, 1839. Harrisburg: 1839. 11 p. PHi. 57867

----. Laws, Statutes, etc. Abstract of the general election law; to which is appended the law for the election of prothonotaries, registers, etc.,and the law for the election of aldermen and justices of the peace.... [Philadelphia] T. B. Town, printer, 1839. 16 p. NNC. 57868

----. ----. Act for the regulation of the militia of the commonwealth of Pennsylvania...together with the several supplements thereto. Harrisburg: Holbrook, printer, 1839. 99 p. P; PHi; PPL. 57869

----. ----. The act of 13th June, 1836, consolidating the several acts for establishing a general system of education by common schools.... Harrisburg: Boas and Coplan, printer, 1839. 32 p. NjR. 57870

----. ----. A digest of county laws; containing the acts of assembly relating to counties and townships throughout the state and local laws relating to the county of Philadelphia. Philadelphia: Crissy, 1839. 531 p. PP; PU. 57871

----. ----. Draft of a revised common school law, and of a law relative to the preparation of common school teachers; with explanatory remarks, and a set of district regulations. Read in the Senate, Jan.

15, 1838. Harrisburg: E. Guyer, 1839. 61 p. DLC; MB; MnU; PP; PU. 57872

----. ----. Election law of Pa. 1833-1839. Philadelphia: 1839. 52 p. PHi. 57873

----. ----. Laws of the General Assembly of the commonwealth of Pennsylvania, passed at the session of 1838-1839, in the 63rd year of independence. Published by authority. Harrisburg: printed by Packer, Barrett and Parke, 1839. CU-Law; IaHi; MdBB; TxU-L; Wa-L. 57874

----. Memorial. Memorial of a convention of citizens of the commonwealth for aid to enlarge the Union Canal, read in Senate, Jan. 17, 1839. Harrisburg: E. Guyer, 1839. 14 p. MH-BA; PPAmP. 57875

----. Secretary of the commonwealth. Report relative to the county prisons of the state, read in Senate, Jan. 14, 1839.... Harrisburg: E. Guyer, 1839. 28 p. PPAmP. 57876

----. State library, Harrisburg. Catalogue of the Pennsylvania State Library; to which is annexed, a copious index. Published by order of the joint library committee. Harrisburg: printed by E. Guyer, 1839. 168 p. DLC; IChoy; MnU; P; PPAmP. 57877

----. University. School of Medicine. Catalogue of the medical graduates of the University of Pennsylvania; with an historical sketch of the origin, progress and present state of the medical department. Published by direction of the medical faculty of the University. 2nd edition. Philadelphia: Lydia R. Bailey, 1839. DLC; MH; NcD; PU; ViRA. 57878

Pennsylvania almanac for 1840. Calculated by John Ward. Philadelphia: M'Carty and Davis [1839] KHi; MWA; NjR. 57879

Pennsylvania and New Jersey almanac for 1840. Philadelphia: Thomas L. Bonsal [1839] MWA; PHi. 57880

The Pennsylvania hermit; a narrative of the extraordinary life of Amos Wilson who expired in a cave in the neighborhood of Harrisburg, after having lived in solitary retirement for a space of 19 years. Philadelphia: 1839. 24 p. ICN; KHi; MB; PHi; OO. 57881

Pennsylvania Horticultural Society. Premiums for culinary vegetables, fruits and flowers, 1839. Philadelphia: 1839. PPAmP. 57882

----. Transactions of the Pennsylvania Horticultural Society. Philadelphia: William Stavely and Company, printer, 1839-1896. 228 p. NjR; PHi; PP; PPAmP; PPL. 57883

Pennsylvania Silk Society. Proceedings of the...convention held at Harrisburg on the 22nd and 23rd...of February, 1839.... Harrisburg: E. Guyer, 1839. 36 p. DeU; ICU; PHi; PPAmP. 57884

----. Proceeding of the state silk convention, of Pennsylvania, held at Lancaster: J. W. Forney, 1839. 10 p. DLC. 57885

Penrose, Charles Bingham, 1798-1857. Address of the Hon. Charles B. Penrose, speaker of the Senate; and the speeches of Messrs. Fraley [city] Williams, Pearson and Penrose, delivered in the Senate of Pennsylvania, on the subject of the insurrection at Harrisburg ["Buckshot war"] in Dec., 1838. Harrisburg: E. Guyer, 1839. 207 p. CU; DLC; MB; NN; PU. 57886

The people's almanac, containing five sets of calculations, embracing the whole United States and the Canadas, 1840.... Boston: S. N. Dickinson [1839] 32 p. MiD-B; MsJS; MWA; NjR. 57887

The people's almanac, of useful and entertaining knowledge. Vol. I, no. 5 [1838] Vol. II., no. 1 [1839] New York: Sold by D. Felt and Company [1839] NBuG. 57888

Perceval, Arthur Philip, 1799-1853. An apology for the doctrine of apostolical succession. With an appendix on the English orders. By the Hon. and Rev. A. P. Perceval.... New York: Protestant Episcopal Tract Society [1839?] 144 p. CU; LNB; MH-AH; NcD; WNaE. 57889

Percy anecdotes; revised edition to which is added a valuable collection of American anecdotes, original and select. Illustrated with 14 fine portraits. New York: Harper and Brothers, 1839. 2 v. in 1. NN; NTaM. 57890

Perennes, P. Guatimozin, ou Le Dernier jour de L'empire Mexicain, tragedie en cinq actes. Par P. Perennes. Nouvelle Orelans: Par J. L. Sollee, 1839. 33 p. 57891

Perils of the sea; being authentic narratives of remarkable and affecting disasters upon the deep, with illustrations of the power and goodness of God, in wonderful preservations. New York: Harper and Brothers, 1839. 205 p. CtY; MB; MWA; NBuG; OO. 57892

Perkins, James Handasyd. A discourse delivered before the Ohio Historical Society. Cincinnati: Bradbury, 1839. OMC. 57893

Perkins, Jonas. A sermon preached on Lord's Day in the meeting house of the Union Religious Society of Weymouth and Braintree. December 9, 1838. Published by request. Quincy: John A. Green, printer, 1839. 16 p. ICN; MH-AH; MWey; MWeyHi. 57894

Perkins, Josephine Amelia. The female prisoner; a narrative of the life and singular adventures of Josephing Amelia Perkins.... Annexed is a well-written address to parents and children. New York: C. Harrison, and others, 1839. MB; MdHi; NIC-L; RPB. 57895

Perkins, Samuel, 1767-1850. The world as it is: containing a view of the present condition of its principal nations, as to their forms of government, military and naval strength, revenues.... 4th edition. Philadelphia: Thomas Belknap, 1839. 462 p. MH; MNowdHi. 57896

----. ----. 5th edition [Connecticut] Thomas Belknap, 1839. 462 p. CLSU; ICN; MBevHi; MH; MWA. 57897

Permanent Bridge Company. Address of the directors to the public, February, 1839. Philadelphia: 1839. 6 p. PHi. 57898

Perrin, Jean Baptiste, fl. 1786. The elements of French and English conversation. Revised and corrected by C. Pruedhomme. Philadelphia: R. W. Pomeroy, 1839. MH. 57899

----. Fables, amusantes, avec une table generals et particuliere des mots de leur signification en anglais, selon l'ordre des fables. Ed. revue et corrigee par un maitre de langue francaise. Philadelphia: R. W. Pomeroy, 1839. MH. 57900

----. A selection of 100 of Perrin's fables, accompanied with a key; containing the text, a literal and free translation.... the whole preceded by a short treatise on the sounds of the French language, compared with those of the English..... a new edition. Philadelphia: Lea and Blanchard, 1839. 181 p. IaDmU; MH; NjR; PP; ViU. 57901

Perry, John. Heavenly home; a sermon...in reference to the death of Susan de Benneville Keim. Philadelphia: 1839. 15 p. PU. 57902

Peter Parley's tales [Philadelphia: Thomas, Cowperthwait and Company, 1839-] 1 v. DLC; 57903

Phelps, Almira Hart Lincoln, 1793-1884. Botany for beginners: an introduction to Mrs. Lincoln's lectures on botany. For the use of common schools and the younger pupils of higher schools and academies. 5th edition. New York: Huntington, 1839. 216 p. CtHT; NcHiC; NIC. 57904

----. Caroline Westerley: or the young traveller from Ohio: containing the letters of a young lady of seventeen written to her sister. New York: Harper, 1839. NICLA; OCo; PReaAT. 57905

----. Chemistry for beginners: designed for common schools, and the younger pupils of higher schools and academies.... New York: F. J. Huntington and Company, 1839. 216 p. NRMA; OO; TWoW; ViRMC. 57906

----. Essay on female education, and prospectus of the Rahway Institute by Mrs. Lincoln Phelps. Newark: printed by A. Guest, 1839. 8 p. MdBP; MH. 57907

----. Familiar lectures on botany...With an appendix...for the use of seminaries and private students. 8th edition, revised and enlarged.... New York: F. J. Huntington and Company, 1839. 246, 186 p. CU-S; CoU; IaDu; MSaP; NcU; NNBG. 57908

----. ----. 9th edition. New York: F. J. Huntington and Company, 1839. 246, 186 p. CoFcS; KBB; MiU; NNN. 57909

----. Natural philosophy for beginners: designed for common schools and families. New York: F. J. Huntington and Company, 1839. 218 p. S. MH; WHi. 57910

Phelps and Ensign's traveller's guide through the United States: containing stage, steamboat, canal and railroad routes, with the distances from place to place.... New York: Phelps and Ensign, 1839. 4-

53 p. CtY; InU; MH; NN; OOxM. 57911

Philadelphia. Proceedings relative to the formation of an anti- slavery church in...Philadelphia. Philadelphia: 1839. 10 p. KyDC. 57912

----. Church of Jesus Christ of Latter Day Saints. Minutes of the Church of Jesus Christ of Latter Day Saints in Philadelphia: 1839 [-1854] 101 p. MoInRC. 57913

----. Citizens. The opera house [Philadelphia? 1839] 15 p. MH; NN; WHi. 57914

----. Committee on Transatlantic Steam Navigation. Report of the Philadelphia committee on the subject of transatlantic steam navigation, Feb. 7, 1839. Philadelphia: Clark, 1839. 16 p. DLC; PHi; PPAmP; ScC. 57915

----. Friends' Library. A catalogue of books in Friends' Library.... Philadelphia: printed by J. Richards, 1839. 64 p. MiD-B. 57916

----. Library association of Friends. Catalogue of books in Friends' Library. Cherry St. Philadelphia: 1839. 64 p. PHi. 57917

----. Monument Cemetery. Act of incorporation, by-laws, rules, names of officers and members and annual reports, 2, 3, 4. Philadelphia: 1839-42. 24, 24, 34 p. Mh; PHi. 57918

----. Presbyterian Church. Report...By a member of the Philadelphia Bar. No. 2, April 8, 1839. Philadelphia: 72 p. PHi. 57919

----. Protestant Episcopal Church. St. James' Church. Philadelphia, May 15, 1839. Sir, You are requested to attend a meeting of the friends of the Episcopal Church, to be held in St. James' Church, on Saturday evening, 18th May, at 8 o'clock, to take into consideration the propriety of establishing at "Kemper College," near St.Louis, in Missouri, a "Bishop White Professorship." [Philadelphia: 1839?] WHi. Broadside. 57920

----. School of Painting and Design. Catalogues of the second exhibition, and of the School of Painting and Design, April, 1839. Philadelphia: W. F. Rackliff, 1839. 12 p. PHi. 57921

----. Western Presbyterian Church. Constiution and by-laws. Philadelphia: Sharp, 1839. PPPrHi. 57922

Philadelphia and Erie Railroad Company. Report of the chief engineer of the Sunbury and Erie Railroad.... Philadelphia: 1839- 1854. ICJ. 57923

Philadelphia and Reading Railroad. Report of the engineers of the Philadelphia and Reading Railroad Company, with accompanying documents. Printed by order of the managers, December, 1839. Philadelphia: printed by John C. Clark, 1839. 14 p. DLC; MdHi; NN. 57924

Philadelphia Association of Friends for the Instruction of Poor Children. The origin and proceedings of the Philadelphia Association of Friends, for the Instruction of Poor Children, together with the constitution, by-laws, etc. Philadelphia: printed by Joseph and William Kite, 1839. 19 p. DLC; MH; PHC; PHi. 57925

Philadelphia County. Ordinances. Digest of the Philadelphia County laws containing acts of assembly and local laws. Philadelphia: 1839. 531 p. PHi. 57926

Philadelphia Gas Works. Terms upon which the public will be supplied with gas by the trustees.... Philadelphia: J. Crissy, printer, 1839. 6 p. MH-BA; PPAmP. 57927

----. ----. 2nd edition. Philadelphia: 1839. 8 p. PHi. 57928

Philadelphia Museum of Art. A descriptive catalogue of the Chinese collection, in Philadelphia. With miscellaneous remarks upon the manners, customs, trade and government of the celestial empire. Philadelphia [1839] 120 p. MWA; OU; PSC. 57929

Philadelphia School District. By-laws...for the first section of the first school district of...Pennsylvania. Also rules for the government of the primary schools, adopted...Feb. 5, 1839. Philadelphia: Waldie, 1839. 16 p. PPAmP. 57930

Philadelphia, Wilmington and Baltimore Railroad Company. The first annual report of the Philadelphia, Wilmington and Baltimore Railroad Company, since the union of the original companies. 1st -. 1838. Philadelphia: 1839. v. 1-. ICU; MB; P; PHi; PP; PPAmP. 57931

A philanthropist the guardian genius of the federal union or human slavery being the first part of the beauties of philanthropy. New York: published for the author, 1839. 288 p. ViHaI. 57932

Philip, Robert, 1791-1858. The life, times and characteristics of John Bunyan, New York: Appleton Publishing Company, 1839. 498 p. CSansS; ICMe; MH-AH; PPF; RPA. 57933

----. The Marys, or the beauty of female holiness. 10th edition. New York: D. Appleton and Company, 1839. MH; PPM. 57934

Philleo, Calvin. "The literati of the land are respectfully requested to let this little stranger pass through their dominions, unmolested, into the houses and hands of the common people, who have neither time nor disposition to read larger and more learned productions." Pawtucket: H. H. Brown, printer, 1839. 12 p. NHC-S. 57935

Phillipps, Samuel March, 1780-1862. Law of evidence. To which is added the theory of presumptive proof. 5th American from 7th and 8th London editions. Assisted by Nicholas Hill, Jr. New York: 1839. 2 v. MH-L. 57936

----. A treatise on the law of evidence; 4th American from the 7th London edition. With notes to the first volume by Esek Cowen assisted by Nicholas Hill. New York: Gould, Banks, Albany: Gould, 1839. 2 v. LNB; MnU; PPB; ScAb; TU. 57937

----. ----. 5th American from the 8th London edition, with considerable additions. With notes and references to American cases. New York: Halsted and Voorhies, 1839. 2 v. MiDU-L; MoU; PPB; RPB; WaU. 57938

Phillips, Richard, 1767-1840. A million of facts, connected with the studies, pursuits and interests of mankind serving as a commonplace book of useful reference on all subjects of research and curiosity; collected from the most respectable modern authorities. 4th edition, revised, corrected and improved with additions. New York: Collins, Keese and Company, 1839. 3 v. in 1. WMMD. 57939

Phillips Exeter Academy. Catalogue of the officers and students of Phillips Exeter Academy. Exeter: 1839. 12 p. MHi. 57940

----. Correspondence between the trustees of the

Phillips Exeter Academy and the Rev. Mr. Hurd. Exeter: 1839. 12 p. Nh-Hi. 57941

[Philpot, Francis.] Facts for white Americans, with a plain hint for dupes and a bone to pick for white nigger demagogues, and amalgamation abolitionists, including the parentage, brief career and execution of amalgamation abolitionism, whose funeral sermon was preached at Washington on the 7th of February, 1839.... Philadelphia: the author, 1839. 62 p. DLC; NcAS; OOxM. 57942

Phinney's calendar, or western almanack for 1840. By George R. Perkins. Cooperstown, N.Y.: H. and E. Phinney [1839] DLC MWA; NUtHi; WHi. 57943

Phrenological almanac for 1840. By L. N. Fowler. Boston: George Oscar Bartlett [1839] MHi; MWA. 57944

----. New York: O. S. and L. N. Fowler [1839-1844] DLC; MWA; PSt; RP; WHi. 57945

Pickering, Ellen, d. 1843. Nan Darrell; or the gipsy mother. By the author of "the heiress,".... Philadelphia: Carey and Hart, 1839. 2 v. PHi; ViU. 57946

----. The prince and the pedler [sic.] or the seige of Bristol. By the author of "the heiress," "the merchant's daughter," etc. [Ellen Pickering].... New York: Harper and Brothers, 1839. 2 v. KyHi; MBAt; NjR; RJa; VtU. 57947

Pickering, John, 1777-1846. Review of Du Ponceau's dissertation on the nature and character of the Chinese system of writing. Cambridge [Mass.] Folsom, Wells and Thurston, 1839. 42 p. DLC; PPAmP. 57948

Picket, Albert, 1771-1850. Introduction to Picket's exposition; containing exercises in English etymology: definition and reading being the sequel to the author's spelling book; and part I.... Cincinnati: U. P. James, 1839. 216 p. OC. 57949

----. Picket's juvenile spelling book, or analogical pronouncer of the English language.... New York: 1839. 214 p. CtSoP. 57950

Pictures and stories, for children. Boston: 1839. MB. 57951

The picturesque pocket companion, and visitor's guide, through Mount Auburn.... Boston: Otis, Broaders and Company, 1839. 252 p. CU; MeHi; OO; RPA; WHi. 57952

Pierce, George Foster, 1811-1884. An address on female education delivered in the chapel of the Georgia Female College, on Thursday, the last day of the examination. Macon: printed at the office of Southern Post, 1839. 20 p. CSmH; MBNMHi; MH. 57953

Pierce, Isaac Bliss. A discourse preached at Newport, Herkimer County, New York, at the funeral of Mrs. Sarah Willoughby.... Albany: printed by Hoffman and White, 1839. 20 p. MBAt; MBAU; MBNEH; NjR. 57954

Pierce, Maris Bryant, 1811-1874. Address on the present condition and prospects of the aboriginal inhabitants of North America, with particular reference to the Seneca nation.... Philadelphia: J. Richards, printer, 1839. 24 p. CSt; ICN; MBC; PHC; WHi. 57955

Pierpont, John, 1785-1866. The American first class book: or exercises in reading and recitation: 25th edition. Boston: David H. Williams, 1839. 480 p. MAbD; MH; MoSpD; NN; PU. 57956

----. Introduction to the national reader a selection of easy lessons, compilations of Guy, Mylius and Pinnock, in those of Great Britain. Boston: David H. Williams, 1839. 168 p. MBAt; MBU- E; MH; MLexHi. 57957

----. The little learner or rudiments of learning. New York: Cooledge, 1839. MNS. 57958

----. Moral rule on political action. A discourse delivered in Hollis Street Church, Sunday, January 27, 1839. Boston: James Munroe and Company, 1839. 24 p. DLC; ICMe; MBC; MH-AH; MWA; NjR. 57959

----. The national reader; a selection of exercises in reading and speaking.... 28th edition. Boston: David H. Williams, 1839. 276 p. MB; MH; MWHi; NNC; RPB. 57960

----. Ode. Air. -"when the trump fo fame." [Boston?: 1839?] Broadside. Mh. 57961

----. Ode. Air. -"ye mariners of England." [Boston?: 1839?] MH. 57962

----. Proceedings of a meeting of friends of Rev. John Pierpont, and his reply to the charges of the committee of Hollis street society. October 26th, 1839. Boston: S. N. Dickinson, 1839. 48 p. CBPac; MH-AH; MHi; MiD-B; MWiW; TNP. 57963

----. ----. With proceedings in the controversey between the proprietors and their pastor. Boston: S. N. Dickinson [1839] 60 p. CtY; DLC; MB; MH; MnU. 57964

----. The young reader.... 15th edition.... Boston: David H. Williams, American Common School Union, New York: Thomas, Cowperthwait and Company, 1839. 162 p. CSt; MH; MWHi; NNC; OOxM. 57965

Pike, Albert, 1809-1891. Address, delivered before the Arkansas Bar Association...in the supreme court room, at the city of Little Rock, on the 13th of July, 1839. Little Rock: printed by Edward Cole, printer to the state, 1839. 19 p. CtY. 57966

Pike, John, 1813-1899. A discourse occasioned by the loss at sea of Capt. Ward Eldred, and Mr. William Eldred, delivered in the Congregational Church, North Falmouth, July 14, 1839. Boston: Whipple and Damrell, 1839. 22 p. CtSoP; MBC; Me; MeBat; MNe. 57967

Pike, John Gregory, 1784-1854. Persuasives to early piety. New York: American Tract Society [1839] 359 p. NHC-S; NPalK. 57968

Pike, Stephen. The teacher's assistant, or a system of practical arithmetic wherein several rules of that useful science are illustrated by a variety of examples a large proportion of which are in federal money, the whole designed to abridge the labours of teachers and to. ...compiled by Stephen Pike.... Philadelphia: 1839. 6, 176 p. ViRVal; ViU. 57969

Pilkington, James, fl. 1841. The artist's and mechanic's repository and workingman's informant.... 2nd edition. Philadelphia: J. M. Brown, 1839. 378, 108 p. MoSpD; OClW; RPB; WOccR. 57970

Pinckney, Henry Laurens, 1794-1863. Remarks addressed to the citizens of Charleston, on the subject of interments, and the policy of establishing a public cemetery, beyond the precincts of the city. By H. L. Pinckney, Mayor, Charleston:

printed by W. Riley, 1839. 32 p. DLC; MH; ScU; WHi. 57971

Pinkham, Tobias. A sermon on baptism, Worthen Street Baptist Meeting House, Lowell, Mass. June 7, 1839. Lowell: B. F. Watson, 1839. 16 p. NHCS; RPB. 57972

Pinkney, Ninian, 1811-1877. The nervous system of the human body; embracing a dissertation delivered to the medical profession of Philadelphia, and students of the two universities, on the subject of the nerves, brain and organs of sense. By Ninian Pinkney, U. S. Navy. Philadelphia: printed by William F. Geddes, 1839. 32 p. DLC; DNLM; MdHi. 57973

The pious minstrel and Christian's companion. A collection of sacred poetry. Boston: Whipple and Damrell, 1839 [15]-329 p. CSansS; CtHC; MB; NNUT. 57974

Pipe, J. S. Conversations of sanctificaton for the use of those who are seeking full salvation, by Rev. J. S. Pipe. Philadelphia: James Harmstead, 1839. 144 p. CoDI; MsBrW. 57975

Pittsburgh. Ladies' Association. Constitution and by-laws. Pittsburgh: printed by E. Burke Fisher and Company, 1839. 13 p. PHi. 57976

Planche, James Robinson, 1796-1880.... Faint heart never won fair lady; a comedy in one act.... New York and London: Samuel French, [1839?] 31 p. OCl. 57977

Planters' and Merchants' almanac. ...1840. ...calculated by David Young.... 2nd edition. Charleston, S.C.: A. E. Miller [1839] [48] p. MWA; WHi. 57978

Playfair, John, 1748-1819. Elements of geometry containing the first six books of Euclid, with a supplement on the quadrature of the circle, and the geometry of solids; to which is added elements of plane and spherical trigonometry. Dean's stereotyped edition, from the last London edition, enlarged. New York: W.E. Dean, 1839. 317 p. CtHT; DeU; NjR; NN; PPF. 57979

----. ----. Philadelphpia: Walker, 1839. 333 p. CtY; ICP; ICU; PPFrankI. 57980

Plea for the heathen: or heathenism ancient and modern. 2nd edition. Boston: 1839. IEG. 57981

A plea for the Western Theological Seminary, at Allegheny; addressed to the members of the Presbyterian Church.... Pittsburgh: William B. Stewart, 1839. 15 p. PPPrHi; PSt. 57982

Plutarchus. Plutarch's lives of the most select and illustrious characters of antiquity. Translated from the original Greek; with notes, historical and critical, by John Langhorne, M.D. and William Langhorne, A.M. and others. By William Mayor, L.L.D. Ithaca: Mack, Andrus and Woodruff, 1839. 432 p. CSansS; MoU; NFri; NIC; PRosC. 57983

----. ----. A new edition carefully revised and corrected. New York: Harper and Brothers, 1839. 748 p. PMA; RKi; RPB; Vi; WMMt. 57984

----. ----. New York: Harper and Brothers, 1839. 4 v. MAm; MDeeP; NGlf; NRU. 57985

Plymouth, Massachusetts. Church of Pilgrimage. The articles of faith and form of covenant, of the Third Congregational Church in Plymouth, with scripture proofs and illustrations.... Plymouth: James Thurber, 1839. 11 p. ICN. 57986

Plymouth, New Hampshire. Teacher's Seminary. Catalogue.... 1839. Concord: 1839. 22 p. MHi. 57987

Pocket almanac. By Thomas Spofford. New York: David Felt and Company, 1839. MWA. 57988

The pocket letter writer; consisting of letters on every occcurence in life, with complimentary cards, etc. 3rd edition. Providence: B. Cranston and Company, 1839. MWA; NNC. 57989

Poe, Edgar Allan, 1809-1849. The conchologist's first book: or a system of testaceous malacology, arranged expressly for the use of schools.... Philadelphia: published for the author, by Haswell, Barrington and Haswell, 1839. 156 p. CSt; LU; NjP; OCX; ViU. 57990

The poems of Ossian. See Macpherson, James, 1736-1796.

Poetic stories. Northampton: J. Metcalf, 1839. ICBB; NN; RPB. 57991

The poetic wreath; consisting of select passages

from the works of English poets, from Chaucer to Wadsworth, alphabetically arranged. Philadelphia: Lea and Blanchard, successors to Carey and Company, 1839. 370 p. ICU; LU; MoSpD; NIC-L; PPWa. 57992

The poetical works of Coleridge, Shelley and Keats. Philadelphia: Thomas, Cowperthwait and Company, 1839. 575 p. NPlva. 57993

The poetical works of Milton, Young, Gray, Beattie and Collins. Complete in one volume. Philadelphia: J. Grigg, 1839. IU; MoU; NCaS. 57994

The poetical works of Rogers, Campbell, J. Montgomery, Lamb and Kirke White. Philadelphia: J. Grigg, 1839. MH; NAlf; NcC; PU; ScCC. 57995

Polk, James Knox. Address of James K. Polk, to the people of Tennessee. April 3, 1839. Columbia, Tenn.: T. H. Thompson, printer, 1839. 28, 8 p. DLC; T; TKL-Mc; TxU. 57996

Pollok, Robert. The course of time. A poem. Revised edition. Boston: Benjamin B. Mussey, 1839. 286 p. GHi; IaDa; MBAt; MH; NbCrD. 57997

----. ----. New York: C. Welles, 1839. 248 p. KU. 57998

----. ----. Philadelphia: James Kay, jun. and Brother, 1839. 256 p. CLSU; IaScW; MiRic; NNC; WGr. 58999

----. ----. Portland: Oliver L. Sanbora, 1839. 276 p. RPB. 58000

Pond, Enoch, 1791-1882. Memoir of Count Zinzendorf: comprising a succinct history of the Church of the United Brethren from its renewal at Herrnhut to the death of its illustrious patron....Boston: Massachuseetts Sabbath School Society, 1839 [9]-195 p. InCW; MnHi; MnU. 58001

Pond, Samuel William, 1808-1891. The history of Joseph, in the language of the Dakota or Sioux Indians. translated from Genesis, by Samuel W. and Gideon H. Pond.... Cincinnati: Kendall and Henry, printers, 1839. 56 p. DLC; MBAt; MHi; MnHi; NN. 58002

Poole, John, 1786-1872. Little Pedlington and the Pedlingtonians.... New York: Henry Colburn, 1839. 2 v. MHa. 58003

Poor heathen children. Boston: Massachusetts Sabbath School Society, 1839. 8 p. illus. MHolli-Hi. 58004

Poor Richard's new farmer's almanack. Concord: Roby, Kimball and Merrill, 1839. MWA. 58005

Poor Will's almanac, for the year 1840.... Philadelphia: Joseph M'Dowell [1839] [34] p. MWA; NjR; WHi. 58006

Pope, Alexander, 1688-1744. An essay on man, in four epistles to H. St. John, to which are added the universal prayer, and other pieces, by Alexander Pope, Esq. Ithaca: Mack, Andrus and Woodruff, 1839. 70 p. CtMW; MdBC; MH; MiPon; NIC. 58007

----. ----. Portland: W. Hyde, 1839. 72 p. MH; MWA; MWborHi; RPB. 58008

----. ----. Worcester: Charles A. Mirick, 1839. CtY; MH; MWA; NN; RPB. 58009

----. The poetical works of Alexander Pope. To which is prefixed a life of the author. Exeter: J. and B. Williams, 1839. 2 v. FP; MWA; OkU; TNT; ViU. 58010

----. ----. New edition. Philadelphia: J. J. Woodward, 1839. 484 p. ICHi; KyBgW; MH; PPL; ScU. 58011

Pope, John, 1770-1845. Speech delivered in the House of Representatives of the United States, on Friday, Feb. 15th, 1839, in committee of the whole on the bill making appropriations for the civil and diplomatic expenses of government for the year 1839. Washington [1839] 14 p. DLC; WHi. 58012

The popular magazine; or the 1,000 nights' entertainments; containing a choice collection of interesting tales, wit and sentiment.... Philadelphia: Alexander, 1839. 5 v. ICN; NjR; PHi. 58013

Porter, Ebenezer, 1772-1834. Analysis of the principles of rhetorical delivery as applied in reading and speaking. 8th edition. Andover: Gould, Newman and Saxton, 1839. 388 p. KAS; MdAS; O. 58014

----. The rhetorical reader; consisting of instructions for regulating the voice with a rhetorical notation.... 49th edition. Andover, Mass.: Gould and Newman, 1839. 304 p. OU. 58015

----. ----. [50th edition?] with an appendix. Andover: Gould and Newman, New York: Leavitt, Lord and Company, 1839. 304 p. NNC. 58016

----. ----. 51st edition. By Ebenezer Porter. Andover: printed by Gould and Newman, 1839. MH; MNF. 58017

----. ----. 52nd edition with an appendix. Andover: Gould and Newman, New York: Leavitt, Lord and Company, 1839. 304 p. CtHWatk; MPeHi; NbO; NNC; RNR. 58018

----. ----. 53rd edition, etc. Andover: Gould and Newman, etc., etc., 1839. MeHi; MH. 58019

Porter, Jane, 1776-1850. Thaddeus of Warsaw.... Exeter: J. and B. Williams, 1839. 2 v. MB; MeLewB; MH. 58020

Porter, Lemuel. Sermon on the license law of 1838. Preached in the Worthen Street Baptist Meeting House, in Lowell, June 23, 1839. Lowell: F. F. Watson, 1839. 15 p. CSmH; Nh. 58021

Porteus, Bielby. Lectures on the gospel of St. Mathew...by the Right Reverend Bielby Porteus, D.D. New York: Robert Carter, 1839. 334 p. MLow; OrPD; PPM; ViRu. 58022

Portland, Maine. Athenaeum. Catalogue of the library; with the by-laws and regulations of the institution. Portland: 1839. 88 p. LNh; MeHi; MH. 58023

----. Fire Department. Engine Company No. 5. Constitution and by-laws. Portland: Gerrish and Edwards, city printers, 1839. 18 p. MeHi; NN. 58024

----. High Street Church. Covenant and rules of High Street Church with catalgoue of its members, April, 1839. Portland: A. Shirley, printer, 1839. 6-34 p. MB; MBC; MWo. 58025

----. Overseers of the poor. Annual report...1838-1839. Portland: 1839. CSmH; DLC; MB; MeHi; MHi. 58026

----. School Committee. Memorial of the school

committee of Portland, on the subject of a board of education [Augusta] Smith and Robinson [1839] 24 p. IaU; MH. 58027

Portland Boat Club. The constitution...Portland Boat Club. Portland: Gerrish and Edward, printers, 1839. 18 p. MeHi. 58028

Portsmouth register and directory. Edmonds' town directory; containing the names of the inhabitants, their occupations, places of business and residence, with lists of the streets, lanes and wharves, the town officers, public offices, and banks, and other useful informaton. Portsmouth, N.H.: Joseph M. Edmonds, 1839. 1 v. CSmH; MHi; OHi. 58029

Potheir, Robert Joseph, 1699-1772. Treatise on the contract of sale. Translated from the French by L. S. Cushing. Boston: Charles C. Little and James Brown, 1839. 406 p. C; LNL L; MdBB; Me; Tx-SC. 58030

----. A treatise on the law of obligations, or contracts. By M. Pothier. Translated from the French, with an introduction, appendix, and notes, illustrative of the English law on the subject. By William David Evans.... 2nd American edition. Philadelphia: R. H. Small, 1839. 2 v. CU; IaU-L; KyU-L; PU-L; ViU. 58031

Potter, Nathaniel, 1770-1843. Notes on the locusta Septentrionalis Americanae decem septima.... Baltimore: 1839. 27 p. MdHi; MH; NNC; NNN; PPL-R. 58032

Poughkeepsie Lyceum of Literature, Science and Mechanic Arts. Charter, together with the rules, regulations and by-laws of the society. Poughkeepsie: Jackson and Schram, 1839. 16 p. CSmH; N; NP. 58033

Powers, Grant, 1784-1841. An address delivered to the people of Goshen, Conn., at their 1st centennial celebration, Sept. 28, 1838. Hartford: printed by Elihu Geer, 1839. 68 p. Ct; IaHA; MB; OClWHi; RHi. 58034

Pratt, Daniel Darwin, 1813-1877. Address at the celebration of the anniversary of St. John.... Logansport, Ind.: Herald office, 1839. 22 p. ICN; In; InU. 58035

Pratt, Parley Parker, 1807-1857. History of the late persecution inflicted by the state of Missouri upon the Mormons...written during 8 months imprisonment in that state. Detroit: Dawson and Bates, 1839. 84 p. CtY; NjP. 58036

----. A voice of warning, and instruction to all people, or an introduction to the faith and doctrine of the Church of Jesus Christ of Latter Day Saints. 2nd edition, revised. New York: J. W. Harrison, 1839. 216 p. ICHi; MH; OClWHi; PCC; WaSp. 58037

Pray, Edmund. A discourse on the 2nd death. "and death and hell----the 2nd death." Rev. XX 14 by Edmund Pray. Boston: press of J. H. and F. F. Farwell, 1839. 202 p. KyBgW; MeBaT; MH; MMeT- Hi; NCaS. 58038

Pray, Isaac Clark, 1813-1869. Julietta Gordini, the miser's daughter. A play in five acts. Written for Miss Sarah Hildreth. New York: 1839. 40 p. ICU; MH; MiU; MoSM; RPB. 58039

Pray, Lewis Glover, 1793-1882. The Boston Sunday school hymn book. By a superintendent. Boston: Benjamin H. Greene, 1839. 121 p. MB; MH-AH; RPB. 58040

The prayers of the church; a connected series of reflections on the liturgy. 1st American edition, adapted to the liturgy of the Protestant Episcopal church in the United States.... By Joseph Walker. Philadelphia: William Stavely and Company, New York: Swords, Stanford and Company [etc., etc.] 1839. 215 p. GHi; MBD; NNG; OrPD; ViAl. 58041

The preacher: a collection of sermons, from various authors, doctrinal and practical. New York: P. Price [etc.] 1839. 285 p. ICP; IEG; NCaS; NNUT; TxDaM. 58042

Prentiss, Seargent Smith, 1808-1850. Speech of Mr. Prentiss of Mississippi on the defalcations of the government. Delivered in the House of Representatives, December 28, 1838. Washington: Gales and Seaton, 1839. 28 p. GEU; KHi; MsJS; OClWHi; TxU. 58043

Presbyterian Church in the U. S. A. The constitution of the Presbyterian church in the United States of America; containing the confession of faith. By Presbyterian board. Pittsburgh: published by Presbyterian Board of Publication. 1839. 547 p. PWaybu. 58044

----. ----. The catechisms, and the directory for the worship of God; together with the plan of government and discipline as...amended in 1833. Philadelphia: Presbyterian Board of Publication, [1839?] 9-547 p. CSaT; KyU; MH-AH; OClWHi; PU. 58045

----. Constitution der Presbyterianischen kirche in den Vereinigten Staaten von Amerika.... Bestaetigt wurde Durch die General versammlung in ihren sitzungen im Mai 1821 und verbessert im jahre 1833.... Philadelphia: Presbyterianische Board fuer Veroessentlichung religioeser Schriften [1839?] 468 p. IaDuU; ODaB. 58046

----. General Assembly. Minutes of the General Assembly of the Presbyterian church in the United States of America. With an appendix. New York: printed by W. Molineux, 1839. 119 p. CSans-S; OCHP; TU; WHi. 58047

----. ----. A statement of the difficulties of the Presbyterian church in their leanings on the southern churches, with an appendix relating to the Charleston Union Presbytery. Charleston: Hussey, 1839. 32 p. MH; NcU. 58048

----. Synods. Cincinnati. Extracts from the minutes of the Synod of Cincinnati, at its late meeting in Oxford, Ohio, published by order of the synod, Cincinnati: F. P. Brooks, 1839. 12 p. ICP; ICU; MiD-B; OClWHi. 58049

----. ----. Green Bay, Wisconsin [territory] Summary confession of faith and covenant with proof texts and references, adopted by the Presbyterian church of Green Bay, Wisconsin [Green Bay: 1839] 12 p. OO. 58050

----. ----. Indiana. Circular letter to the churches of Indiana in connection with the constitutional General Assembly, charging them on the subject of doctrine. Indianapolis: printed by Douglass, 1839. 7 p. NNUT; PPPrHi. 58051

Prescott, William H[ickling] History of the reign of Ferdinand and Isabella the Catholic.... Boston: Charles C. Little and James Brown, 1839. 3 v. GU; NNebg; PNt; ScNC. 58052

----. ----. 5th edition. Boston: C. C. Little and J. Brown, 1839. 3 v. CSansS; GU; LNB; MH; Vi. 58053

----. ----. 6th edition. Boston: C. C. Little and J.

Brown, 1839. 3 v. NHerm; OAk; OClW; PPiW; ViAlt. 58054

Pressly, John Taylor. An address to the students of the Theological Seminary of the First Associate Reformed Synod of the West at the opening of the session December 2, 1839. Pittsburgh: printed by D. N. White, 1839. 15 p. CSmH; ICHi; NcMHi; OClWHi; PPPrHi. 58055

Preston, D. R. Funeral sermon on the death of Gen. Francis Preston. Delivered at Abingdon, Virginia, September 25, A.D. 1838. Philadelphia: Haswell, Barrington and Haswell, 1839. 20 p. PPL; ViU. 58056

Preston, Lyman, d. 1795. Preston's complete time table showing number of days from any date in any given month to any date in any other month, embracing upwards of 130,000 combinations of dates...[Abridged edition] New York: Huntington, 1839. 24 p. NcU; NN; NNC. 58057

----. Stories for the whole family, ...by Lyman Preston. New York: published by a family friend, 1839. 210 p. MeBaT. 58058

----. Tables of interest, computed at 6 percent.... New York: Collins, Keese and Company, 1839. 107 p. MB. 58059

----. Preston's tables of interest computed at 7 percent...together with calculations of rebate or discount.... New York: Huntington, 18329. NcD; NN; NNC; PPM. 58060

Priest, Josiah, 1788-1851. The anti-universalist; or history of the fallen angels of the Scriptures: proofs of the being of Satan and of wil spirits, and many other curious matters connected therewith.... Albany: printed by J. Munsell, 1839, 420 p. ICU; KyLoP; OClWHi; PPL; ViU. 58061

----. The low Dutch boy, a prisoner among the Indians; being an account of the capture of Frederick Schermerhorn, when a lad of 17 years old, by a party of Mohawks in the time of the revolution.... Also the story of the hermit of Virginia. New London, Conn.: E. Williams, printer, 1839. 32 p. CtY; ICN; NN; Vi. 58062

----. Low Dutch prisoner, being an account of the capture of Frederick Schernerhorn by mohawks, also story of the hermit of the Allegany mountains. ...Albany: 1839. 32 p. CtHWatk; DLC; ICN; VtU;

WHi. 58063

----. The robber; or the narrative of Pye and the highwayman. Being a detailed and particular account of an attempted robbery of the inn of John Pye, between the cities of Albany and Troy, in 1808.... Together with a history of the old men of the mountain, the gold hunters of Joes Hills.... 2nd edition. Albany: printed by Hoffman and White, 1839. 32 p. MWA; NjP; NN; PHi; ViU. 58064

----. A view of the expected Christian millenium.... Albany: published for subscribers, Loomis Press, 1839. 408 p. N. 58065

Prince, Joseph H. An address delivered before the Columbian Society, of Marblehead, on the 8th of January, 1839, by Joseph H. Prince.... Salem: printed at the Gazette office, 1839. 44 p. ICU; MH; MiD-B; NNC; OClWHi. 58066

Prince, firm, nurseryman, Flushing. Annual catalogue of fruit and ornamental trees and plants cultivated at the Linnaean botanical garden and nurseries. William Prince and son.... 31st edition. New York: G. P. Scott [1839?] 88 p. MiU-C. 58067

Princeton University. Catalogus Collegii neo-Caesariensis, Rerum publicarum Faederatarum Americae Summae Potestatis, Anno LXIV. Princetoniae: Robert E. Homor, 1839. 53 p. CSmH; MH; NN; OCHP; WM. 58068

----. Laws of the college of New Jersey; revised, amended and adopted by the board of trustees, July, 1839. Princeton, N.J.: R. E. Hornor, 1839. 24 [2] p. DLC; MdHi; MH. 58069

Prindle's almanac for 1840. By Charles Prindle. New Haven, Conn.: A. H. Maltby and Company [1839] CtMW; MWA; WHi. 58070

Prison discipline; the Auburn and Pennsylvania systems compared. New York: A. V. Blake, 1839. 20 p. A-Ar; CU; NN; PHi; PPAmP. 58071

Pritts, Joseph. Abentheuerliche Ereignisse aus dem Leben der ersten Ansiedler an den Grenzen der mittleren und westlichen Staaten. Ubers. von Benjamin S. Schneck. Chambersburg, Pa.: H. Ruby, 1839. 537 p. DLC; ICN; MH; OrP; PPM. 58072

----. Incidents of border life, illustrative of the times and condition of the first settlements in parts of the middle and western states.... With an appendix and a review.... Compiled from authentic sources. Chambersburg, Pa.: J. Pritts, 1839. 511 p. ICN; OFH; PHi; PPA. WHi. 58073

Proceedings of meetings on the 9th November, and 4th December, and report of the committee of 12 concerning the plans of the proposed operatic and dramatic house, the interest and security of the investment, etc. Philadelphia: T. Thompson, printer, 1839. PHi; PPAmP. 58074

Protestant Episcopal Church in the U. S. A. A catechism of the Protestant Episcopal Church: With an explanation; to which are added, a catechism on confirmaton, and a catechism on church government, and a liturgy for Sunday schools. Baltimore: Armstrong and Berry, 1839. 48 p. MdBD. 58075

----. Alabama (Diocese) Journal of the proceedings of the 8th annual convention of the Protestant Episcopal Church in the diocese of Alabama, held in the town of Selma, on Friday, May 3rd, and Saturday, May 4th, A.D. 1839. Mobile: printed at the Chronicle office, 1839. 27 p. MBD; N; NN. 58076

----. Board of Missions. Proceedings of the Board of Missions of the Protestant Episcopal Church in the United States of America. New York: printed by William Osborne, 1839. 88 p. DLC; MBD; NBuDD. 58077

----. Book of Common Prayer. The book of common prayer, and administration of the sacraments, and other rites and ceremonies of the church, according to the use of the Protestant Episcopal Church in the United States of America: together with the Psalter, or Psalms of David. Buffalo: William B. Hayden, 1839. 370, 24 p. NN. 58078

----. ----. ----. 7p. 6l. 21-570 p. NN. 58079

----. ----. ----. New York: H. and S. Raynor, 1839. GMM; MCET; NNS. 58080

----. ----. ----. Philadelphia: E. L. Carey and A. Hart, 1839. 520, 144 p. ArL; IEG; MBD; PLERC-Hi. 58081

----. ----. ----. Philadelphia: Female Protestant Prayer Book Society of Pennsylvania, 1839. 248 p. WGrNM. 58082

----. ----. ----. 531 p. MdBD. 58083

----. ----. ----. 779 p. WKenHi. 58084

----. ----. ----. Philadelphia: Henry F. Anners, 1839. 399 p. MBC; MBD; NN; TxU. 58085

----. ----. ----. Philadelphia: T. T. Ash and H. F. Anners, 1839. 376, 127, 118 p. NjR. 58086

----. ----. ----. Philadelphia: Thomas, Cowperthwait and Company, 1839 [3] 3234 p. ViFre. 58087

----. ----. ----. 531 p. MBD; NN. 58088

----. ----. ----. 531, 248 p. MBD; ViU. 58089

----. Delaware (Diocese) Journal of the proceedings of the 49th annual convention of the Protestant Episcopal church, of the diocese of Delaware.... Wilmington, Delaware: printed by Porter and Naff, 1839. 18 p. MoWgT. 58090

----. ----. A review of facts relative to the late ecclesiastical proceedings, in a presentment, and an inquiry in the diocese of Delware [Philadelphia: 1839] 20 p. MnHi. 58091

----. Florida (Diocese) Journal of the 2nd annual convention...in St. John's Church, Tallahassee, in January, 1839. Tallahassee: Knowles and Hutchins, printers, 1839. 28 p. MB; MiD-B; NBuDD; NN. 58092

----. Georgia (Diocese) Journal of the proceedings of the 17th annual convention, of the Protestant Episcopal Church, in the diocese of Georgia, held in St. Paul's Church, Augusta, on the 15th and 16th April, 1839. Columbus: printed at the Georgia Argus office, 1839. 27 p. NBuDD; NN. 58093

----. Hymnal. Hymns of the Protestant Episcopal Church.... New York: Robinson and Franklin, 1839. 124 p. NNG. 58094

----. ----. Philadelphia: E. L. Carey and A. Hart, 1839 [63]-144 p. NNG. 58095

----. ----. Philadelphia: Thomas, Cowperthwait and Company, 1839 [111]-248 p. NNG. 58096

----. Illinois (Diocese) A journal of the 5th annual convention, of the Protestant Episcopal Church, of the diocese of Illinois.... Chicago:

printed at the office of the Chicago American, 1839. 21 p. ICN; MBD; MiD-MCh; NN. 58097

----. Kentucky (Diocese) Journal of the proceedings of the 11th convention...in Calvary Church, Smithland...June, 1839. Princeton, Ky.: Princeton Examiner, printer, 1839. 24 p. MBD; MiD-B; NBuDD; NN. 58098

----. Louisiana (Diocese) Journal of the proceedings of the 1st convention...in Christ Church, in the city of New Orleans, on Wednesday, the 16th of January, 1839. New Orleans: 1839. 9 p. CtHT; LU; MiD-MCh; NN. 58099

----. Maryland (Diocese) Journal of a convention of the Protestant Episcopal Church of Maryland, held in St. Paul's Church, Baltimore, Wednesday, May 29th, Thursday, 30th, Friday, 31st, and Saturday, June 1st, 1839. Baltimore: Jas. Lucas and E. K. Deaver, 1839. 66 p. MBD; MdBD; NBuDD. 58100

----. ----. Journal of a special convention of the Protestant Episcopal Church of Maryland, held at St. Paul's Church, Baltimore, on Thursday, November 28th. Baltimore: Lucas and Deaver, 1839. 27 p. MBD; MdBE; MdHi; NBuDD; NNUT. 58101

----. Massachusetts (Diocese) Journal of the proceedings of the annual convention...Newton Lower Falls, September 25, 1839.... Boston: James B. Dow, 1839. 18 p. MiD-B. 58102

----. ----. Journal of the proceedings of the 49th annual convention of the Protestant Episcopal Church in the commonwealth of Massachusetts...with an appendix. Boston: James B. Dow, 1839. 67 p. MBD; MW. 58103

----. Mississippi (Diocese) Journal of the proceedings of the 14th annual convention of the Protestant Episcopal Church in the diocese of Mississippi, held in St. Paul's Church, Woodville, Wednesday, May 1, 1839. Natchez: printed at the Daily Courier office, 1839. 24 p. Ms-Ar; MsJPED; NBuDD; NN. 58104

----. New Hampshire (Diocese) Journal of the proceedings of the 39th convention...Claremont...June 26, 1839. Concord: printed by Asa McFarland, 1839. 12 p. MBD; MiD-B. 58105

----. New Jersey (Diocese) Jouranl of the 56th annual convention of the Protestant Episcopal Church. ...state of New Jersey. ...St. Mary's Church, Burlington. Burlington: Missionary press, 1839. (37), 36 p. NBuDD; NjR. 58106

----. New York (Diocese) Journal of the proceedings of the 55th convention of the diocese of New York. ...Also a list of the clergy of the diocese. New York: 1839. 120 p. MBD; NBuDD; NGH; NjR. 58107

----. North Carolina (Diocese) ...of the proceedings of the 23rd annual convention of the Protestant Episcopal Church in North Carolina. Fayetteville: printed by Edward J. Hale, 1839. 43 p. MBD; NBuDD; NcHiC. 58108

----. Ohio (Diocese) Journal of the 22nd annual convention...in St. Paul's Church, Steubenville, on Thursday the 12th, Friday the 13th, and Saturday the 14th days of September, 1839. Gambier, O.. G. W. Meyers [1839] 80 p. MBD; MiD-B; NN; OCoC. 58109

----. Pennsylvania (Diocese) Journal of the proceedings of the 55th convention of the Protestant Episcopal Church in the state of Pennsylvania.... Philadelphia: published by order of the convention, Jesper Harding, printer, 1839. 54 p. MBD; NBuDD. 58110

----. ----. ----. 88 p. MiD-MCh; NBuDD; TxU. 58111

----. Rhode Island (Diocese) Journal of the proceedings of the 49th annual convention of the Protestant Episcopal Church of the state of Rhode Island, held in St. John's Church, Providence, on Tuesday, June 11, and Wednesday, June 12, A.D. 1839. Providence: printed by H. H. Brown, 1839. 36 p. MBD; NBuDD. 58112

----. South Carolina (Diocese) Journal of the proceedings of the 50th annual convention of the Protestant Episcopal Church in South Carolina, held in St. Michael's Church, Charleston, on the 6th, 7th and 8th of February, 1839. Charleston: printed by A. E. Miller, 1839. 51 p. MBD; NBuDD; NN. 58113

----. Tennessee (Diocese) Journal of the proceedings of the 11th annual convention of the clergy and laity of the Protestant Episcopal Church, in the diocese of Tennessee. Held at St.

Paul's Church, Randolph, on the 10th, 11th, 12th and 13th of April, 1839. Nashville: S. Nye and Company, 1839. 36 p. CtHT; MBD; MnHi; NN; T. 58114

----. Vermont (Diocese) Journal of the proceedings of the 49th annual convention of the Protestant Episcopal Church in the diocese of Vermont, etc. Burlington: C. Goodrich, 1839. 48 p. MBD; MH; MiD-B; NBuDD; WNaE. 58115

----. Virginia (Diocese) Journal of the convention of the Protestant Episcopal Church in the diocese of Virginia.... Richmond: printed by B. R. Wren, 1839. 40 p. IEG; MBD; NBuDD. 58116

----. Western New York (Diocese) Journal of the proceedings of the 2nd annual convention of the Protestant Episcopal Church in the diocese of Western New York, Utica: press of Griffith and Bush [1839] 91 p. MBD; MWA; NN; PPiXT. 58117

----. ----. Journal of the proceedings of a special convention...Auburn...May 8th and 9th, 1839. Utica: press of Eli Maynard, 1839. 38 p. CBCDS; MiD-B; NBuDD; NNC; NUt. 58118

Proud and penitent; or how to repent. Written for the Massachusetts Sabbath School Society, and revised by the Committee of Publication. 2nd edition. Boston: Massachusetts Sabbath School Society, 1839. 87 p. ScCliTO. 58119

Providence. A list of persons assessed in the city tax of 55,000 dollars, ordered by the city council, June, 1839. With the amount of valuation and tax of each. Providence: H. H. Brown, 1839. 56 p. RHi. 58120

----. African Methodist Episcopal Church. The act of incorporation and by-laws of the African Methodist Episcopal Church in Providence. Providence: 1839. 8 p. RHi. 58121

----. Arkwright and Fiskville Baptist Church. A brief history of the organization of the Arkwright and Fiskville Baptist Church. Providence: H. H. Brown, printer, 1839. 8 p. RHi. 58122

----. Athenaeum. First supplementary catalogue of the Athenaeum Library.... Providence: Knowles and Vose, 1839. 107 p. MBC; MH- AH; MH-L; NNS; RP. 58123

----. First Congregational Church, Juvenile Library. Catalogue. Providence: 1839. 14 p. RP. 58124

----. School committee. By-laws...and regulations of the public schools.... Providence: printed by Knowles and Vose, 1839. 26 [3]- 26 p. RPB. 58125

Public buildings and statuary of the government: the public buildings and architectural ornaments of the capitol of the United States, at the city of Washington. Washington: P. Haas [1839] 3, 44 p. CSfCW; DLC. 58126

Publius, pseud. A letter to William H. Seward, on the new banking law. New York: 1839. 11 p MH-BA. 58127

Putnam, John Milton, 1794-1871. A sermon on the nature of Christian courage, and its importance at the present day. Preached at Dunbarton, N.H. December 5, 1839. Concord: printed by Asa McFarland, 1839. 15 p. MA; Nh-Hi. 58128

Pusey, Edward Bouverie. A letter to the Right Rev. Father in God; Richard Lord Bishop of Oxford, on the tendency to Romanism, imputed to doctrines held of old, as now, in the English church. From the 2nd Oxford edition. New York: Charles Henry, 1839. 160, 24 p. IaDa; LNB; MB; NNUT; RPB. 58129

Pym, William W. Word of warning in the last days. By the Rev. William W. Pym, A.M.... Philadelphia: J. Dobson and J. Whetham, 1839. 129 p. ICBB; MNtCA; MoInRC. 58130

Q - R

Questions adopted to Paleys moral and political philosophy by a citizen of Massachusetts. New York: Collins, Keese and Company, 1839. 42 p. OWoC; OMC. TJaLam. 58131

Questions on the monthly subjects for scripture proofs. Sixth series. New York: 1839. IEG; T. 58132

Quinby, George Washington, 1810-1884. Reply to the "substance of a discourse, : originally delivered at the Universalist church, in West Livermore, by elder Ferdinand Ellis, of the First Baptist Church, Livermore. Portland: 1839. 40 p. DLC; Nh-Hi; NNG; PHi. 58133

Quinby, Hosea, 1804-1878. A short examination of the scriptural subjects, art and design of Christian Baptism.... Dover: Trustees of the Freewill Baptist Connections, 1839. 48 p. DLC; IEG; MeLewB; Nh; TxU. 58134

Quincy, Edmund, 1808-1877. Introductory lecture delivered before the Adelphic Union, November 19, 1838. Boston: Isaac Knapp, 1839. 22 p. DLC; ICJ; MB; MiD-B; PHi. 58135

The Quincy House Company, Quincy, Illinois. An act to incorporate the Quincy House Company, passed March 1, 1839. New York: W. E. Dean, 1839. DLC. 58136

Rachel Ford. A gift to the children of the sunday and sewing schools at the Pitts Street Chapel, from a teacher. Boston: S. G. Simpkins, 1839. 18 p. MB; WHi. 58137

Raciborski, Adam, 1809-1871. An elementary treatise on auscultation and percussion; or the application of acoustics to the diagonsis of diseases.... Translated by Minnturn Post, M. D. New York: Collins, Keese and Company, 1839. 216 p. CU-M; ICJ; MeB; PPiU; TNV. 58138

Rafinesque, Constantine Samuel, 1783-1840. American manual of the mulberry trees. Their history, cultivation, properties...with hints on the production of silk. Philadelphia: 1839. 96 p. ICJ; LNH; OMC; PPL; WHi. 58139

----. Improvements of universities, colleges and other seats of learning or elocution, in North America. Philadelphia: printed for the eleutherium of knowledge, 1839. 18 p. DLC. 58140

Raguet, Condy, 1784-1842. A treatise on currency and banking.... Philadelphia: Grigg and Elliott, 1839. 264 p. IaU; MiD; NNF; PU; WU. 58141

Raikes, Thomas, 1777-1848. The city of the Czar; or a visit to St. Petersburg in the winter of 1822-1830. Philadelphia: Lea and Blanchard. 1839. 2 v. GHi; MBAt; PPA; RPB; WGr. 58142

Ramadge, Francis Hopkins. Consumption curable: and the manner in which nature as well as remedial art operates in effecting a healing process in cases of consumption.... 1st American from the 3rd London edition. New York: J. M. Howe, Wiley and Putnam, 1839. 160 p. ArL; IaGG; KMK; LNOP; PPL. 58143

Ramshorn, Johann Gottlob Ludwig, 1768-1837. Dictionary of Latin synonymes, for the use of schools and private students, with a complete index. From the German, by F. Lieber. Boston: C. C. Little and J. Brown, 1839. 475 p. CU; GU; MjR; PAtM; RPB. 58144

----. ----. Philadelphia: E. H. Butter and Company, 1839. 475 p. CU; OWorP. 58145

Randanne, J. A comprehensive grammar of the Latin language for the use of St. Mary's College, Baltimore.... Baltimore: J. Robinson, 1839. 375 p. MdBS. 58146

Randolph, Jacob, 1796-1848. A memoir on the life and character of Philip Syng Physick, M. D.... Philadelphia: printed by T. K. and P. G. Collins, 1839. 114 p. CSt; ICU; MB; P; WHi. 58147

Randolph, Joseph Fitz, 1803-1873. Speech...on the attempt to organize the House of Representatives by excluding five of the New Jersey members, December 6, 1839. Washington: 1839. 8 p. MiD-B; P. 58148

Randolph, Mary, 1762-1828. The Virginia housewife, or methodical cook. Baltimore: Plaskitt and Cugle, 1839. 180 p. RNR; ViU. 58149

Rankin, Joseph K. A brief refutation of the Bible doctrine of slavery; or a reply to a letter of Rev. H. B. of middle Tennessee, addressed to some individuals living in Decatur County, Iowa. Rushville: Davis and Wallace, 1839. 16 p. In. 58150

Raper, William H. 1793-1852. A discourse on Universalism.... Cincinnati: R. P. Thompson, printer, 1839. 36 p. DLC; MiD-B. 58151

Ray, Joseph. Ray's eclectic arithmetic on the inductive and analytic methods of instruction. Designed for common schools and academies.... 10th edition, revised, corrected and stereotyped. Cincinnati: Truman and Smith, 1839. 239 p. OCHP. 58152

Raymond, James, 1796-1858. Digested chancery cases, contained in the reports of the Court of Appeals of Maryland.... Baltimore: Cushing and Brother, 1839. 480 p. Ar-SC; DLC; MdBP; NIC-L; PU. 58153

Rayner, Kenneth, 1808-1884. Speech...of North Carolina, on the proposition to refuse the oath to five members returned from the state of New Jersey: delivered before the representatives of the 26th congress, December 18, 1839. Washington: Gales and Seaton, 1839. 11 p. Ct; DLC; NcD; NRU. 58154

Rayner, Menzies, 1770-1850. The Universalist manual; or book of prayers and other religious exercises: adapted to the use both of public and private devotion in churches, sunday schools and families.... New York: P. Price, Boston: A. Tomkins, 1839. 191, 95 p. MSa; MBuGG; MH; NCaS; WHi. 58155

Read, Daniel, 1805-1878. Address of Professor D. Read, to the students of the Ohio University, delivered...May, 1839. Athens, Ohio: published by the students of the unniversity, 1839. 15 p. CSmH; MB; OClWHi; OWervO. 58156

[Reade, Thomas Shaw Bancroft] Christian retirement: or spiritual exercises of the heart....

New York: John I. Taylor, 1839. 476 p. CtY; KyU; NjNbS. 58157

The Reading Railroad; its advantages for the cheap transportation of coal as compared with the Schuylkill Navigation and Lehigh Canal. By X. Philadelphia: Haswell, Barrington and Haswell, 1839. 43 p. DBRE; MB; PHi; PU; WU. 58158

Real Estate Bank of Baltimore. Notification to the public that the subscription book for increasing the capital of the bank will be opened on Monday next, April 15 [1839] at the banking house of Messrs. J. I. Cohen, Jr. and Brothers.... [Baltimore] K. Robinson, printer [1839] 11 p. MdHi. 58159

Realities of life; sketches designed for improvement of the head and heart. By a Philanthropist. New Haven: S. Babcock, 1839. 197 p. CU; DLC; LNH; MH; ScCoB. 58160

Rebecca Wilson. The Cumberland girl. Boston: Joseph Dowe, 1839. 68 p. MB; MVh. 58161

Redfield, William Charles, 1789-1857. The courses of hurricanes [New Haven: 1839] MB. 58162

----. Genealogical list of the descendants in the male line of Theophilus Redfield, of Killingworth, Connecticut. New York: 1839. 10 p. MWA. 58163

----. Geonealogy of the Redfield family in the United States [New York] J. S. Redfield, 1839. 13 p. MB; NN; OClWHi. 58164

----. Letter to the Secretary of the Treasury on the history and causes of steamboat explosions and the means of prevention. Revised edition. New York: Osborn, 1839. 39 p. CtHWatk; DLC; MdBP; MiU; PPAmP. 58165

----. Remarks on Mr. Eshy's theory of centripetal storms. Including a refutation of his positions relative to the storm of September 3, 1821.... From the Journal of the Franklin Institute [New York: 1839] 32 p. NN. 58166

----. ----. [Philadelphia: 1839] 32 p. DLC; NN. 58167

----. Whirlwinds excited by fire, with further notices of the tyfoons [sic.] of the China Sea.... [New Haven: 1839] 14 p. DLC; NN. 58168

Reed, Anna C. Vie de George Washington. Pris de panglais, et dedie a la, jeunesse americaine, par A. N. Girault.... 9th edition. Philadelphie: H. Perkins, Boston: Perkins and Marvin, 1839. 321 p. CLSU; MBC; MWA; NGH; PWW. 58169

Reed, Fitch, 1794-1871. Methodism; evangelical in its means and influence, substance of a sermon preached at the Methodist Episcopal Church in Sand Street, Brooklyn, October 25, 1839. Brooklyn, New York: 1839. 28 p. IEG; NcD; NNC; RPB. 58170

Reed, Sampson, 1800-1880. Correspondences for children of the New Church. Published by direction od the committee of the convention on moral and religious instruction. Boston: Otis Clapp, 1839. 71 p. MCNC; PBa; OUrC. 58171

Reed, Silas, b. 1807. Letters on the subject of a line of railroads, from Boston to the Mississippi. Boston: printed at the Morning Post Office, 1839. 12 p. CSmH; MBAt; MWA; Nh; WU. 58172

Reed, Thomas C. Christian consolation. A sermon occasioned by the death of Mrs. Sarah Maria Potter, preached, on Sunday, March 24, 1839. Schenectady: printed by S. S. Riggs, 1839. 23 p. MB; MH-AH; NCH; RPB. 58173

Reed, William Bradford, 1806-1876. The infancy of the union. A discourse delivered before the New York Historical Society, 1839. Philadelphia: J. Crissey, 1839. 50 p. MWA; PPHa; PPM. 58174

----. A lecture on the romance of American history. Delivered at the Athenian Institute, February 19, 1839. Philadlephia: printed by A. Waldie, 1839. 46 p. CtY; MiU; NN; NNC; PHi. 58175

Rees, James, 1802-1885. The battle of Saratoga: a poem, with historical and explanatory notes. New York: 1839. 20 p. MB; NN; RPB; WHi. 58176

----. The dwarf, a dramatic poem.... New York: F. Saunders, 1839. 8, 62 p. ICU; MH; RPB. 58177

Reese, David Meredith, 1800-1861. Introductory lecture delivered at the opening of the Albany Medical College, in the Anatomical theatre, January 2, 1839. Albany: printed by Hoffman and White, 1839. 44 p. DLC; IEN-M; MdUM; NjR; PPL. 58178

----. Lectures to the children of a sabbath school, on the subject of temperance. New York: T. Mason, and G. Lane, 1839. 63 p. OkentU. 58179

[Reeve, Clara] 1829-1807. The old English baron. A gothic story. Philadelphia: Charles Bell, 1839. 317 p. MB; MWA. 58180

Reformed Church in America. The psalms and hymns with the catechism, confession of faith, and liturgy of the Dutch Reformed Church in North America...selected at the request of the general synod by John H. Livingston.... Philadelphia: G. W. Mentz and Son, 1839. 592, 81 p. IaU; MBU-T; NN; NNUT. 58181

Reformed Church in the United States. Acts and proceedings of a general convention of the General Reformed Church, in the United States, convened in Philadelphia, September 28, 1839. Gettysburg: printed by H. C. Nienstadt, 1839. 93 p. MdBLC; MoWgT; NcMIIi, PLT. 58182

----. Proceedings of the synod of the German Reformed Church in the United States, convened at Lancaster, Pa., September 29, to October 6, 1838. Gettysburg, Pa., printed by H. C. Neinstedt, 1839. 70 p. MdBLC; MoWgt; NcMHi; PLT: PPLT. 58183

----. Verhandlungen einer allgemeinen synode der hochdeutschen reformirten kirche in den vereingten staaten. Gehalten zu Philadelphia, vom 28sten September bis zum 7ten Oktober, 1839. Gettysburg: Gedruckt bey Heinrich C. Neinstedt, 1839. 92 p. MdBSHG; MoWgT; PLERCHi. 58184

Reformed Dissenting Presbyterian Church in North America. A narrative of the introduction and progress of Christianity in Scotland before the Reformation: And of the Reformation and the progress of religion, since in Scotland and America, especially among Presbyterians. West Union, Ohio: Smith, 1839. 127 p. OClWHi; PPPr-Hi. 58185

Rehoboth, Massachusetts. Congregational Church. Articles of faith and covenant. Taunton: 1839. 7 p. Nh-Hi; RHi. 58186

Reid, John R., d. 1841. An address delivered on the anniversary of St. John the Baptist, before the Society of Ancient York Mansion. Houston, Texas: Houston Telegraph Press, 1839. 16 p. CtY;

PPFM; TNJ-S; TxH. 58187

Reid, William Hamilton, d. 1826. Memoirs of the public and private life of Napoleon Banaparte. Translated from the French of M. V. Arnault.... Boston: C. Littlefield, 1839. 2 v. CSfP; MnHi; PPM; WBeloC. 58188

The religious keepsake for holiday presents; edited by Mrs. L. H. Sigourney. Hartford: Andrus [1839?] 288 p. CSmH; MiD; MWA; OO; RPB. 58189

Remarks on Allston's paintings. Boston: William D. Ticknor, 1839. 28 p. ICU; MH; MiD-B; NjR; RPB. 58190

Remarks upon slavery and the slave trade, addressed to the Hon. Henry Clay, 1839. 23 p. DLC; MdBP; MH; NIC. 58191

Remarks upon the speech of Hon. Ingersoll, on being conducted to the chair, at the late democratic convention, held at Hartford. New Haven: 1839. 16 p. OClWHi. 58192

Rencher, Abraham. Circular of Abraham Rencher, to the freemen of the tenth congressional district of North Carolina. March 9, 1839. 13 p. MdHi; NcD. 58193

Rennie, James, 1787-1867. The natural history of insects. New York: Harper and Brothers, 1839, 38. 2 v. CU; DLC; LN; NWM; ViU. 58194

----. ----. Illustrated by engravings. First series. New York: Harper and Brothers, 1839. 292 p. IaCrM; NGlc; PPL; ScDuE; TxGR. 58195

Renouard, Augustin Charles. Theory of the rights of authors [in literature, sciences and the fine arts] Translated from the French by L. S. C. [Luther Stearns Cushing] Boston: 1839. 56 p. MBAt; MH. 58196

Renwick, James, 1790-1863. Familiar illustrations of natural philosophy. Selected principally from Daniell's chymical philosophy.... New York: Harper and Brothers, 1839. 403 p. CtMW; DLC; NGlc; OOC; NRU-W. 58197

----. Treatise on the steam engine. 2nd edition, revised and enlarged. New York: Carvill and Company, 1839. 327 p. ICJ; MiD; NNC; PPCP; Vi. 58198

Report on the origin and cause of the late epidemic, in Augusta, Ga.... Augusta, Georgia: Browne, Cushney and McCafferty, printers, 1839. 30 p. OC. 58199

Resolutions of Maine, Connecticut and Georgia [Boston: 1839] 29 p. MB. 58200

Reston, W. L. The fairy waltz. Composed by W. L. Reston. Albany: R. Nealham, 1839. 4 p. KU. 58201

Retroprogression; an account of a short residence in the celebrated town of Jumbleborough. Boston: 1839. 83 p. CtW; MH. 58202

A review of Elder S. S. Parr's sermon on baptism. Ithaca: printed by Mack, Andrus and Woodrufff, 1839. 15 p. MBC; NAuT. 58203

Review of Parker and Fox's grammar; Part 1. Published by several friends of real improvement. Boston: Samuel Harris, printer, 1839. v. 1-. 38 p. MB; NNC; P; PPL. 58204

Review of W. J. Green's sermon on apostolic teaching. By a Baptist. Augusta, Ga.: Browne, Cushney and McCafferty, 1839. 16 p. KyLoS. 58205

The reviewer of Mrs. Emma Willard Reviewed. Philadelphia: C. Sherman and Company, 1839. 29 p. N; PHi; VtBrt. 58206

Reynolds, George William MacArthur, 1814-1879. Alfred de Rosann; or the adventures of a French gentleman.... Philadlephia: Carey and Hart, 1839. 2 v. CoU; DLC; IaK; IaU; NcU. 58207

----. Pickwick abroad. A companion to the "Pickwick Papers" [by Boz] Philadelphia: T. B. Peterson and Brothers, 1839. 207 [7] p. NvHi. 58208

Reynolds, John. Recollections of Windsor prison.... 3rd edition. Boston: A. Wright, 1839. DLC; ICJ; MBAt; MiD; OClW. 58209

Rhett, Robert Barnwell, 1800-1876. Speech of...of South Carolina on the report of the Committee of Ways and means delivered in the House, February 1. 1839. Washington: 1839. 15 p. DLC; NcD; WHi. 58210

----. Speech...to his constituents, on the Salt

Kitchner River, at a dinner given on July 4, 1839. Charleston: printed by Burges and James, 1839. 19 p. NcD; PPL; ScU. 58211

Rhode Island. Democratic Republican and farmers' prox. For governor, Nathaniel Bullock...For lieutenant governor, Benjamin B. Thurston. Providence [1839] Broadside. CtY. 58212

----. Democratic Republican ticket. For representatives the the 26th congress of the United States. Benjamin B. Thurston...Thomas W. Dorr.... [Providence? 1839] Broadside. CtY. 58213

----. Political frauds exposed by Aristides. Philadelphia: 1839. PPL. 58214

----. General Assembly. Committee Relative to Petitions for the Abolition of Slavery. Report and resolutions concerning slavery with dissent by John Whipple, submitted to the Rhode Island legislature, January session, 1839 [n. p.: 1839] 30 p. CLU. 68215

----. ----. House. Select Commmittee to Whom Were Referred the Resolutions of Mr. Wells on Slavery. Report to the Rhode Island legislature. Mr. Whipple's report and Mr. Otis's letter. Boston: printed by Cassady and March, 1839. 30 p. IaHi; MB; MHi; PHi; RP. 58216

----. ----. ----. ----. Report......touching certain resolutions of the House of the United States relating to petitions of sundry citizens of this state, relative to the rights of petition [Providence? printed order of the House] 1839. 8 p. DLC; NIC; RP. 58217

----. Laws, Statutes, etc. Acts relating to public school, published by order of the General Assembly, January session, 1839 [Providence? 1839] 34 p. DLC; MH; RP; RPA. 58218

Rhode Island almanac for the year 1840...By Isaac Bickerstaff. Providence: H. H. Brown, 1839. 24 p. MWA; RNHi. 58219

Rhode Island and Providence Plantations. Laws, Statutes, etc. [Public laws...passed since the sessions of 1831-1839. Newport: 1839?] 749-1083 p. Mi-L. 58220

Rhymes for my children. By a mother. 2nd edition. New York: S. Coleman, etc., etc., 1839. 71 p. MH. 58221

Richardson, Charles, 1775-1865. A new dictionary of the English language.... London: W. Pickering, New York: W. Jackson, 1839. 2 v. GEU-T; ICU; MdBS; NhD; RPB. 58222

Richardson, Jacob D. A collection of hymns for the use of the African Methodist Episcopal Church in America. New York: J. C. Beaman, 1839. DLC; OOC. 58223

Richardson, John, 1647-1896. The necessity of a well experienced souldiery, or a Christian commonwealth ought to be well instructed and experienced military art, delivered in a sermon upon an artillery election, June 10, 1675.... Cambridge: Samuel Green, 1679, Boston: reprinted by Company vote, 1839. 16 p. KWiU; MHi; NiD-B; NN; OClWHi. 58224

Richardson, William M. Life of Wiliam M. Richardson. Concord: 1839. OCLaw. 58225

Richmond, Hiram Lawton, 1810-1885. Oration delivered at Saegerstown on July 4, 1839. Meadville [Pa.] J. C. Hays, printer, 1839. 18 p. DLC; PMA. 58226

Richmond, Legh, 1772-1827. Memoir of Hannah Sinclair, to which is prefixed Miss Sinclair's letter on the principles of the Christian faith. 2nd American from the 19th London edition. New York: 1839. 117 p. PPiW; WHi. 58227

Richmond, Virginia. First Independent Christian Church. Constitution...adopted July 31, 1839. Richmond: 1839. 11 p. Vi. 58228

----. Mercantile Library Association. Catalogue of books, November 15, 1839. Richmond: Shepard and Colin, 1839. 20 p. CSmH; ViU. 58229

Richmond Lyceum, Richmond, Virginia. Constitution and by- laws...adopted March, 1837. Amended March 1839. Richmond: P. D. Bernard, 1839. CSmH. 58230

Ricord, Elizabeth [Stryker] 1788-1866. Elements of the philosophy of mind, applied to the development of thought and feeling.... Geneva, New York: J. N. Bogert, 1839. 408 p. InNd. 58231

Riddle, David Hunter, 1805-1888. An address

delivered in the Third Presbyterian Church on the sabbath evening of February 17, 1839, to the young men of the city of Pittsburgh. Pittsburgh: printed by E. B. Fisher and Company, 1839. 24 p. CSans-S; ICP; MBC; OClWHi; PPPrHi. 58232

The ride on the sled: or the punishment of disobedience. Boston New England Sabbath School Union [1839] 64 p. MB; NRAB. 58233

Riggs, Stephen Return, 1812-1883. The Dakota first reading book...printed for the American Board of Commissioners for Foreign Missions. Cincinnati: Kendall and Henry, printers, 1839. 39 p. DLC; MHi; MnHi; NN. 58234

Riley, James, 1777-1840. An authentic narrative of the loss of the American brig Commerce, wrecked on the western coast of Africa, in the month of August 1815, with an account of the suffering of the surviving officers and crew. Revised, January, 1828. New York: Robinson and Franklin, 1839. 271 p. MnU; NUt; OClW; PHi; WM. 58235

Rilliet, Frederic, 1814-1861. A treatise on the pneumonia of children. Translated from the French, by S. Parkman.... Philadelphia: A. Waldie, 1839. 100 p. CSt-L; MeB; NcD; PP; ViU. 58236

Ripley, Charles, 1816-1866. An oration, on the colonization of New England, delivered December 22, 1838, before the Pilgrim Society of Louisville. Louisville, Kentucky, 1839. 44 p. KyLoF; MH-AH; MWA; RPB; WHi. 58237

[Ripley, George] 1802-1880. "The latest form of infidelity" examined; a letter to Mr. Andrews Norton, occasioned by his discourse before the Association of the alumni of the Cambridge Theological School...July 19, 1839. Boston: James Munroe and Company, 1839. 160 p. DLC; ICMe; MBC; MeBa; WHi. 58238

Rippon, John, 1751-1836. A selection of hymns, from the best authors, including a great number of originals: intended to be an appendix to Dr. Watt's psalms and hymns. 8th American from the 18th London edition, with the enlargements. Philadelphia: David Clark, 1839. 410 p. NNC. 58239

Riverview Academy, Poughkeepsie. Biennial catalogue of the trustees and pupils of the Poughkeepsie Collegiate School for 1837-1839. Poughkeepsie: Jackson and Schram, 1839. 6 p. NP. 58240

Rives, William Cabell, 1793-1868. Address of W. C. Rives, to the people of Virginia.... Charlottesville: printed by James Alexander, 1839. 16 p. CtY; MH; NjR; NNC; ViU. 58241

----. Speech...at a public dinner given him at Louisa C. H., Va. on the 7th September, 1839. Charlottesville: Alexander, 1839. 24 p. CSmH; MB; MBAt; RPB; Vi. 58242

----. Speech...in vindication of the freedom of elections against the interference of federal executive officers. Delivered in the Senate of the United States, February 12, 1839. Washington: printed by Gales and Seaton, 1839. 23 p. DLC; MdHi; MWA; Vi; ViU. 58243

----. Speech...on his resolutions calling upon the treasury department for information respecting its fiscal arrangements with the Bank of the United States. Washington: 1839. 16 p. MdHi; MiD-B; NcD; PHi; RNR. 58244

---. Substance of the speech on his second call for information respecting the fiscal arrangements with the Bank of the United States. Delivered, January 14, 1839. Washington: 1839. 16 p. PHi; Vi. 58245

Rivington, J. G. F. Remains of Late Rev. R. H. Froud. Derby: 1839. 2 v. in 4. MB. 58246

Roane, W. H. Speech...in the United States Senate, February 15, 1839, on the bill to prevent the interference of certain federal officers with elections. Portsmouth, Va.: Old Dominion Power Press, 1839. 16 p. Ct; DLC; MBC; N; OCHP. 58247

Robbins, Asher, 1757-1845. Proposals to publish a treatise on the eloquence of the ancients. Newport: 1839. PPL. 58248

----. Speech on the subject on an institution to be founded on the Smithsonian legacy; delivered in the Senate...January 10, 1839. Washington: 1839. MeB; MiGr; NN; PHi; TxU. 58249

[Robbins, Eliza] 1786-1853. American popular lessons, chiefly selected from the writings of Mrs. Barbauld, Miss Edgeworth, and other approved writers. Revised and improved by the author.... New York: R. Lockwood, at his school book depository [1839] 240 p. MB; MH; MPiB; NNC; PPeSchw. 58250

----. English history: adapted to the use of schools, and young persons. Illustrated by a map and engravings.... 3rd edition. New York: W. E. Dean, 1839. 386 p. MB; MH; NGlf. 58251

----. The school friend, or lessons in prose and verse. New York: Robinson and Franklin, 1839. MB; MH. 58252

----. Tales from American history. In three volumes. Each volume comprising a distinct subject and complete in itself...for the use of young persons and schools. New York: Harper and Brothers, 1839. 3 v. MH; OClWHi; ScDuE. 58253

Robbins, Royal, 1787-1861. Outlines of ancient and modern history.... 8th edition revised. Hartford: Belknap and Hammersley, 1839. 2 v. in 1. CU; DLC; MNF; OCl; TNP. 58254

Robert Merry's annual. For all season. New York; James P. Giffing, 1839. 200 p. MPiB; WU. 58255

Roberts, Edward P. A manual containing directions for sowing, transplanting and raising the mulberry tree, together with proper instructions for propogating the same by cutings, layers etc., and also directions for the culture of silk. 4th edition with improvements and additions. Baltimore: S. Sands, 1839. MdBP; MH; NIC; OCHP; PPi. 58256

Roberts, William, Civil Engineer. A specification and treatise on monumental surveying. To which is annexed a series of observations taken on the annual and diurnal variations of the needle. Troy: Tuttle, 1839. 56 p. NTRPI. 58257

Roberts, William, 1709-1849. Memoirs of the life and correspondence of Mrs. Hannah More. New York: Harper and Brothers, 1839. 2 v. IEG; LNB; MdBD; MWA: NN. 58258

Robertson, John, 1787-1873. Speech...on the amendment proposed by him to the report of the select committee on the public lands; delivered in the House during the morning hour of February, 1839. Washington: Gales and Seaton, 1839. 22 p. Ct; MBAt; MWA; NNC; Vi. 58259

Robertson, John Parish, 1792-1843. Francia's reign of terror, being a sequel to letters on Paraquay. By J. P. and W. P. Robertson. Philadelphia: E. L. Carey and A. Hart, 1839. 2 v. LNH; MoSU; PPA; WGr. 58260

----. Solomon Seesaw.... Philadelphia: Lea and Blanchard, 1839. 2 v. IaBo; LNH; LU; TJoT. 58261

Robertson, William, 1721-1793. Historical disquistion concerning the knowledge which the ancients had in India. New York: Harper and Brothers, 1839. 146 p. NP; NLock; NN; OCl. 58262

----. The history of Scotland during the reigns of Queen Mary and King James VI. Till his accesseion to the crown of England. With a review of the Scottish history previous to that period.... 11th edition. New YOrk: Harper and Brothers, 1839. 460 p. NGoS; NN; NP; OCIW. 58263

----. The history of the discovery and settlement of America...with an account of his life and writings.... New York: Harper and Brothers, 1839. 570 p. CLO, ICU; MiD; ODa; PSal 58264

----. The history of the reign of the Emperor Charles V., with a view of the progress of society in Europe from the subversion of the Roman Empire to the beginning of the 16th century. New York: Harper and Brothers, 1839. 643 p. LNL; MH; NGos; NUtHi; TxU. 58265

Robins, Gordon. Practical hints on the culture of the mulberry tree; together with the art of raising silk worms in the best manner, with the cheapest and most simple furniture and fixtures...by a citizen of Mansfield, Connecticut. Hartford: G. Robins, jr., 1839. 82 p. Ct; CtHWatk; MB; Mi; NjR. 58266

Robinson, James Watts, 1827-1918. The farmers and traders guide showig at one view, the wholesale or retail value of any commodity from one quarter of a cent to 15 dollars in Dollars and cents; with a variety of useful tables. Pumpkintown: E. Tenn.: printed by Johnston and Edwards; 1839. 136 p. NcD; T. 58267

Robinson, firm, printer and stationer, Baltimore. Catalogue of Robinson's Circulating Library. Baltimore: In three parts. Baltimore: 1839. MdBP. 58268

Roche, Regina Maria. The children of the abbey: a tale. Exeter: J. and B. Williams, 1839. 3 v. FSar; IU; KyHi. 58269

Rochester. Young Men's Association. Proceedings...at the first annual meeting, November 26, 1838. Embracing a report of the condition of that institution.... Rochester: printed by Luther Tucker, 1839. 8, 6 p. NN; NRHi. 58270

Rochester Female Association for the Relief of Orphan and Destitute Children. History...together with its organization, by- laws, etc. Rochester: Shepard and Strong, 1839. 19 p. NRHi. 58271

Rochester Institute of Technology. Library. Catalogue of the Rochester city library, April, 1839 with a notice of the city reading rooms, etc. under the care of the Young Men's Association. Rochester: Shepard, Strong and Dawson, 1839. 26, 6 p. DLC; NN; NR; NRHi. 58272

Rockwell, S. An address delivered before Constantine Chapter and Macon Lodge in the Presbyterian Church, Macon, at the installation of the officers. Macon [GA.] S. Rose, printer, 1839. 24 p. CSmH. 58273

Rodgers, F. A. Commentary upon the Holy Bible. New York: Religious Tract Society, 1839. 648 p. IaPeC. 58274

Rogers, George, fl. 1838. Pro and con of universalism both as to its doctrines and moral bearings; in a series of original articles. Cincinnati: Brooks, 1839. 384 p. IaDmD; IEG; NCaS; PPL. 58275

----. ----. 351 p. NcD; PP. 58276

Rogers, Henry Darwin, 1808-1866. Geologischen untersuchung. Harrisburg: Joseph Ehrenfried, 1839. PPeSchw. 58277

Rogers, Molton Cropper, d. 1865. James Todd et al vs. Asshbel Green et al. Charge to the Jury, March 26, 1839 [Philadelphia?1839] 34 p. PHi. 58278

Rogers, William A. Address delivered before the Springfield High School, at the close of the summer session, October 1839. Springfield: published by the board of trustees, 1839. 14 p. OCHP. 58279

Roget, Peter Mark, 1779-1869. Animal and vegetable physiology, considered with reference to natural theology. 2nd American from last London edition. Philadelphia: Lea and Blanchard,

1839. 2 v. CSansS; NNN; OU; PMA; ViW. 58280

----. Outlines of physiology: with an appendix on phrenology. 1st American edition, revised, with numerous notes. Philadelphia: Lea and Blanchard, 1839. 516 p. GU; IaGG; MB; PPA; RPM. 58281

Rollin, Charles, 1661-1741. The ancient history of the Egyptians, Carthaginians, Assyrians.... 1st complete American edition. New York: Harper and Brothers, 1839. 2 v. GAU; IGK; MH; PPiW; WvU. 58282

----. ----. from the 15th London edition, revised and corrected. New York: Robinson and Franklin, 1839. 8 v. GHi; NN; OO; ScDuE, TNT. 58283

Romagnesi, Henri, 1781-1850. The little beggar girl [Song, A. or Bar. Accomp.] arranged for the guitar by A. Schmitz. Philadelphia: Fiot, 1839. 3 p. DLC; MB. 58284

Romaine, Benjamin. Review. The tomb of the martyrs, adjoining the United States navy yard, Brooklyn City, in Jackson Street; who died in dungeons and pestilential prison ships, in and about the city of New York, during the seven years of our revolutionary war. New York: C. C. and E. Childs, 1839. 7 p. MB; MdBJ; MH; MiU- C; WHi. 58285

Romaine, William, 1714-1795. Treatises upon the life, walk and triumph of faith. New York: Robinson and Franklin, 1839. 339 p. 58286

Rooker, John, b. 1755. An essay on the sovereignty of God, dedicated to and a legacy for the Baptist Church of Christ, on Sugar Creek. Charlestown: printed by W. Riley, 1839. 16 p. KyLoS. 58287

Root, David, 1791-1873. A bi-centennial sermon: or the two hundredth anniversary of the formation of the First Congregational Church in Dover, N. H. Delivered Thanksgiving day, November 29, 1838. Dover, N. H.: printed by G. Wadleigh, 1839. 31 p. DLC; MB; NhD; RPB; WHi. 58288

----. A farewell discourse to the young men of Dover. Dover, N. H.: G. and E. Wadleigh, 1839. 11 p. CtSoP; MBNEH; MeBat; Nh; RPB. 58289

----. Modern expediency considered: in a discourse delivered in Dr. Heron's Church, Pittsburgh, April 14, 1839. Dover, N. H.: published by request [1839?] 23 p. MB. 58290

----. ----. [Pittsburgh? 1839] 23 p. MH. 58291

Ropes, A. Oration on the 20th anniversary, of the Independent order of Odd Fellows. Baltimore: 1839. PPL. 58292

The rose. Boston: Massachusetts Sabbath School Society, 1839. 8 p. Nn. 58293

Rose and her lamb and other tales. Boston: 1839. 24 p. MWA. 58294

Rose of the valley, a flower of the west that blooms to enrich the mind; devoted to literature, instruction, amusement and interesting biography. Cincinnati: 1839-1840. 2 v. CSt; ICRL; MiU, OCY, PSt. 58295

Rosina; or the virtuous country maid: memoirs of the Marchioness of Leminton. New York: Riker, 1839. 542 p. FOA. 58296

Rossini. Cinderella, an opera in three acts, music by Rossini.... Baltimore: Jos. Robinson, 1839. 23 p. PU. 58297

Rowbotham, John, 1793-1846. A practical grammar of the French language, with alterations and additions. 3rd edition. Boston: Hilliard, Gray and Company, 1839. 324 p. ICartC; MB; MH; OCir; TxU-T. 58298

Rowson, Susanna [Haswell] 1762-1824. Charlotte Temple, a tale of truth.... Hartford: Andrus, Judd and Franklin, 1839. 138 p. CtHT; ICBB; MWA; NRU. 58299

Royce, Andrew. Universalism: a modern invention, and not according to godliness. 2nd edition, with an examination of certain reviews. Windsor [Vt.] printed at the Chronicle Press, 1839. 207 p. CBPSR; IEG; MBC; MMeT-Hi; MPiB. 58300

Rudd, John C. Education and the gospel combined; an address, delivered before the trustees, instructors, and students of the institute of Hobart Hall, Holland Patent, Oneida County, N. Y. September 21, 1839. Utica: Hobart Press, 1839. 14 p. NGH; NNG; NUt. 58301

Rule of the new creature. 2nd edition. Clear

Water: 1839. NN. 58302

Rumsey, Edward, 1796-1868. Speech of Edward Rumsey, in the House...February 9, 1839 [n. p.: 1839?] 8 p. DLC; MiU-C; NNC. 58303

Runnells [E. B.] A journal of facts, descriptive of scenes and incidents in Maryland, Pennsylvania and New Jersey.... Philadelphia: 1839. 40 p. N; PHi. 58304

Rush, Benjamin. An inquiry into the influence of physical causes upon the moral faculty. Philadelphia: Haswell, Barrington and Haswell, 1839. 4, 28 p. MB; NjP; RPB, Vi; WMAN. 58305

Rush, Samuel. A discourse on the moral influence of sounds, delivered before the Chester County Cabinet of natural science, January 18, 1839. Philadelphia: 1839. 32 p. DLC; MiD-B; MWiW; PU; VtBrt. 58306

Rushville, Illinois. Ordinaces. An ordinance to amend into one of the several ordinances heretofore adopted by the president and trustees of the town of Rushville. Rushville: printed by J. B. Fulks, 1839. 28 p. NN. 58307

Russell, Archibald, 1811-1871. Principles of statistical inquiry; as illustrated in proposals for uniting an examination into the resources of the United States with the census to be taken in 1840. New York: D. Appleton and Company, 1839. 263 p. CU; ICJ; MWal; PU; WHi. 58308

Russell, Henry, 1812-1900. The old bell or for full five hundred years I've swung. Song [A. or B. pianforte accomp.] New York: Huvitt and Jafees, 1839. 7 p. MB. 58309

Russell, John. Ancient history of Greece and Rome. With introductory sketches of the history of the Jews, Egyptians, Carthaginians and othe ancient nations. With questions for examination. Philadelphia: Hogan and Thompson, 1839. 266 p. IaDuCM; NcWsS; PPiW; RPB; TNP. 58310

----. History of England, with separate historical sketches of Scotland, Wales and Ireland; from the invasion of Julius Casesar until the accession of Queen Victoria. Philadelphia: Hogan and Thompson, 1839. 244 p. DLC; NBu; NNC. 58311

----. History of France, from the earliest times to the present day. Philadelphia: Hogan and

Thompson, 1839. 234 p. IEG; LNH; MoSp;; PPWa; RPB. 58312

-----. A history of the United States of America, from the period of discovery to the present time, arranged for the use of schools, with questions for the examination of students. Philadelphia: Hogan and Thompson, 1839. 256 p. IHI; LN; NNC; PLFM. 58313

Russell, Michael, 1781-1848. History and present condition of the Barbary States.... New York: Harper and Brothers, 1839. 339 p. MB-HP. 58314

----. Life of Oliver Cromwell. New York: Harper and Brothers, 1839. 2 v. MH; Nh-Hi; OAU: ScDuE; TxGR. 58315

----. Palestine or the Holy land. From the earliest period to the present time. New York: Harper and Brothers, 1839. 330 p. InCW; KBB; MH; NCaS; TWcW. 58316

----. View of ancient and modern Egypt; with an outline of its natural history. New York: Hays and Brothers, 1839. 348 p. GMM; IEG; MPiB; OClWHi; PU; TxGR. 58317

Russell, William, 1741-1793. The history of modern Europe: with a view of the progress of society from the rise of modern kingdoms to the peace of Paris, in 1763...and a continuation of the history to the present time, by William Jones. With annotations by an American. New York: Harper and Brothers, 1839. MBC; NjP; OClW; PWW; RPaw. 58318

Russel's Spring, Tennessee. Baptist Church of Christ. An extract of the proceedings of the Baptist Church of Christ, at Russel's Spring; held at their meeting house on the first Lord's day of December, 1839. Brownsville, Tennessee: Ephraim C. Lambert, 1839. 19 p. CSmH. 58319

Rutgers Female College, New York City. Annual catalogue and circular. 1st. [New York] 1839-. MB; MH. 58320

----. Circular.... New York: printed by William Osborn, 1839. 8 p. MH. 58321

Ryan, James. An elementary treatise on algebra, theoretical and practical, adapted to the instruction of youth in schools and colleges. 4th edition. New York: J. and H. G. Langley, Collins, Keese and Company,...1839. 391 p. KWiU; LNP; NCH. 58322

----. The new American grammar of the elements of astronomy on an improved plan. In three books.... New York: W. E. Dean, 1839. 342 p. CtY; DN-Ob; IaMp. 58323

Ryland, Robert. A sermon delivered at the 16th annual meeting of the General Association of Virginia, June 1, 1839. Richmond: printed by Wm. Sands, 1839. 11 p. DLC; OOC; ViRU; WHi. 58324

S

Sabbath School Contributor, and general review.... Lyon, Massachusetts: E. N. Harris, 1839-. v. 1. DLC. 58325

Sabbath school monitor. New York: Finch and Parker, 1839-1846. NNC. 58326

St. John, James Augustus, 1801-1875. The lives of celebrated travellers.... New York: Harper and Brothers, 1839. 3 v. Me; NNUT; OAU; ScAb; TxGR. 58327

St. John's Orphan Asylum. Report of the board of managers, 1839. Philadelphia: T. Creny, 1839. MdW. 58328

St. Joseph's Ladies Society of Christian Doctrine. Origin, constitution, and the by-laws, of the St. Joseph's Ladies Society of the Christian Doctrine; with an appendix for the teachers, 1839. MdBLC. 58329

St. Mary's College, Marion County, Kentucky. Third annual announcement of St. Mary's College, for 1838-1839. Louisville: printed by Marton and Griswold [1839] 16 p. N. 58330

St. Paul's College, New York. Catalogue of the professors and students. v. 1. 1838. New York: 12839. PU. 58331

Saintine, Joseph Xavier Boniface. Picciola. The prisoner of Fenestrella; or captivity captive. 2nd edition. Philadelphia: Lea and Blanchard, 1839. 251 p. MBBC; MH; MNe; PMA. 58332

Salem. Alms House. Act of incorporation. Salem: 1839. 12 p. PHi. 58333

Salem, New York. School Library. Rules and regulations of the school library of the village of Salem. n. p. [1839] 4 p. MH. 58334

Sallustius Crispus, C. Sallust's Jugurthine war and conspiracy of Catiline, with an English commentary and geographical and historical indexes. By Charles Anthon. 9th edition, corrected and en-

larged. New York: Harper and Brothers, 1839. 332 p. CBPSR; MDeeP; OSW; TxU-T. 58335

Saltonstall, Leverett, 1783-1845. Speech of the New Jersey Case; House of Representatives, December 13 [Washington: 1839] 7 p. DLC; MBAt. 58336

Salzmann, Christian Gotthilf, 1744-1811. Der Himmel auf Erden, oder weg zur gluckseligkeit. Dargestellt von Christian Gotthilf Salzmann. Bearbeitet von Conrad Friedrich Stollmeyer. 1st Amerikanische Aufl. Philadelphia: gedruckt von C. F. Stollmeyer, 1839. ICN; MH; PReaHl; OMC, PU. 58337

Sam Slick's comic all-my-nack for 1840. New York [Elton's, 1839] MWA. 58338

Sanders, Charles Walton, 1805-1889. Sander's spelling book; containing a minute and comprehensive system on introductory orthography...designed to teach a system of orthography and orthoepy in accordance with that of Dr. Webster. For the use of Schools. Andover, New York: Gould, Newman and Saxton, 1839. 166 p. InU; MB; NjR; OO; TxU-T. 58339

Sanderson, John, 1783-1844. The American in Paris. Philadelphia: Carey and Hart, 1839. 2 v. ICU; MWal; PPA, ViU; WGr. 58340

Sandusky, Toledo and Michigan City Railroad Company. Copy of the acts incorporating the Sandusky, Toledo and Michigan City Railroad Company, with the report of the survey of the road.... Toledo: Fairbanks, 1839. 28 p. CSmH; NjP; OClWHi; PPAmP. 58341

Sanford, Elizabeth [Poole] d. 1853. Woman in her social and domestic character. 5th American edition. Boston: William Crosby and Company, 1839. 175 p. MBC; MWHi; PFal. 58342

Sandy and Baver Canal Company. Report of the stockholders...by Edward Miller. Philadelphia: Joseph and William Kite, 1839. 16 p. MH-BA;

NNE. 58343

Santangelo, Orazio Donato Gideon de Attelio. An address delivered by O. de A. Santangelo, at a public meeting held in New Orleans, on February 2, 1839, by the citizens of that place, having claims against Mexico. John Baldwin, president. Samuel Ellis, esq., secretary. New Orleans: B. Levy, 1839? 45 p. CU-B; MdHi; PU; TxWFM. 58344

----. A lesson to Mr. Jasper Harding, editor of the Pennsylvania Inquirer and daily courier. Philadelphia, from the school master. O. de A. Santangelo. New Orleans: Benjamin Levy, 1839. 54 p. CU- B; DLC. 58345

Sarah Wolston or an extract from the note of a sunday school visitor. New York: General Protestant Sunday School Union, 1839. 44 p. DLC. 58346

Sargent, Epes, 1813-1880. Valasco; a tragedy in five acts. New York: Harper and Brothers, 1839. 110 p. ICU; MPiB; NNC; PU; TxU. 58347

Sargent, John Turner, 1808-1877. A discourse on the death of Hon. William Sullivan, delivered in King's Chapel, Boston, September 15, 1839. Boston: printed by James B. Dow, 1839. 23 p. CBPac; ICMe; MMal; NNC; PPAmP. 58348

Sargent, Lucius Manlius] 1787-1867. An Irish heart. Founded on fact. Boston: Whipple and Damrell, 1839. 158 p. KU. 58349

----. As a mdeicine. Founded on fact.... Boston: Whipple and Damrell, 1839. 155 p. DLC; MH; OClWHi; OU. 58350

----. Fritz Hazell. Founded on fact. Boston: Whipple and Damrell, 1839. 98 p. CtY; NN. 58351

----. Groggy Harbor, or a smooth stone from a brook and a sheppard's sling. Boston: Whipple and Damrell, New York: Scofield and Voorhies, 1839. 76 p. CtY. 58352

----. I an afraid there is a God! Founded on fact. Boston: Whipple and Damrell, 1839. 47 p. CLU; CtY. 58353

----. The life preserver. Founded on fact. Boston and New York: 1839. 51 p. CtY; ICN; MH. 58354

----. Margaret's bridal. Founded of fact. Boston: Whipple and Damrell, New York: Scofield and

Voorhies, 1839. 86 p. CtY; CU; DLC; MB. 58355

----. My mother's gold ring. Founded on fact. Boston: Whipple and Damrell, New York: Scofield and Voorhies, 1839. 24 p. MShM. 58356

----. The prophets! Where are they? Founded on fact. Boston: Whipple and Damrell, New York: Scofield and Voorhies, etc., etc., 1839. 36 p. CtY; ICN. 58357

----. Right opposite. Founded of fact. Boston: Whipple and Damrell [etc.] 1839. 64 p. CtY. 58358

----. A sectarian thing. Boston: Whipple and Damrell, New York: Scofield and Voorhies, 1839. 48 p. 58359

----. Seed time and harvest. Founded on fact. Boston: Whipple and Damrell, New York: Scofield and Voorhies, 1839. 24 p. CtY. 58360

----. The stage coach. Boston: Whipple and Damrell, New York: Scofield and Voorhies, 1839. 288 p. CU; NjP. 58361

----. What a curse! or Johny Hodges, the blacksmith. Founded on fact. Boston: Whipple and Damrell, 1839. 32 p. CtY; CU; MH. 58362

----. Wild Dick and good little robin. Boston: Whipple and Damrell, etc., 1839. 41 p. CtY. 58363

Saunders, Frederick] 1807-1902. The author's printing and publishing assistant: including interesting details respecting the mechanism of books. New York: F. Saunders, 1839. 43 p. DLC; ICN; MB; MH; NNS. 58364

Savannah Library Society. A catalogue of the books belonging to the savannah Library Society: instituted in the year 1809, and re-organized in the year 1838, with its charter and by-laws; to which is added a brief account on the origin and process of the society, from its commencement to 1839. Savannah: T. Purse, 1839. 69 p. GHi; NcP. 58365

Sawyer, Leicester Ambrose, 1807-1898. A critical exposition of mental philosophy; or the first principles of metaphysics.... New Haven: Durrie and Peck, 1839. 316 p. DLC; MBC; MPiB; NNUT; OO. 58366

Sawyer, Lemuel, 1777-1852. Printz Hall: a record on New Sweden.... PhiladelpHia: Carey and Hart, 1839. 2 v. DeWi; DLC; MiToC; PU. 58367

----.----. Philadelphia: Carey and Hart [etc.] New York: C. and G. Carvill [etc.] 1839. 2 v. DLC; ICN; MH; NNC; ViU. 58368

Sawyer, Thomas Jefferson. Letters to the Rev. Stephen Remington, in review of his lectures on Universalism.... New York: P. Price, 1839. 160 p. MB; MH; MMeT-Hi; NNUT; PPL-R. 58369

----. Penalty of sin, a sermon by the pastor of the Orchard Street Church.... New York: Universalis Union Press, 1839. 24 p. MB; MBUGG; MeBat; MH; MMeT-Hi. 58370

Sayers, Edward. The American flower garden companion adapted to the northern and middle states. 2nd edition, revised and corrected with additions. Boston: Weeks, Jordan and Company, 1839. MB; NNC; MSaP; OWoC; RPA. 58371

----. The American fruit garden companion, being a practical treatise on the propogation and culture of fruit, adapted to the northern and middle states. Boston: Weeks, Jordan and Company, 1839. 174 p. CU; MB; OClW; PPL-R; WU-A. 58372

----.----. 2nd edition. Boston: Weeks, Jordan and Company, 1839. 174 p. MNoboro; NIC; NNNBG; TBriK. 58373

----. A treatise on the culture of the dahlia and cactas. Boston: Weeks, Jordan and Company, 1839. DLC; IU; MB; MeU; NNC. 58374

Scales, Jacob. Sermon on the principles, means and blessings of union and peace; preached at Henniker, February 24, 1839. Concord: 1839. 23 p. CtWatk; MiD-B; MWA; Nh-Hi; OO. 58375

Schabalie, Jan Philipsen, 1585?-1656. Die Wandlende Seele. Philadelphia: Herausgegeben von G. W. Mentz und Sohn, 1839. 442 p. InGop PPeSchw. 58376

Scheppard, Thomas. Weitl. predigers in London, schmaler weg zum leben. Oder die wahre bekehrung dirch Christum zu gott.... Harrisbur, Pa.: Gedruckt und zu haben bei G. S. Peters, 1839. 355 p. IaDUU; P; PHi; PPeSchw. 58377

Schiller, Johann Christoph Friedrich von, 1759-1805. Capuciner. New York: Verlag de buchhandlung von W. Radde, 1839. 23 p. MH; MNe; PU; TNJU. 58378

----. Schillers sammtliche werke in zwolk banden. Baltimore: Schwartz, 1839-1841. 12 v. CtY; NbLU; OClW; PLFM; ScC. 58379

Schlusstein Landwirthschafts Calender, 1840. Von Carl F. Egelmann. Philaldephia: Wm. W. Walker [1839] MWA. 58380

Schmid, Christoph von, 1768-1854. The basket of flowers; or piety and truth triumphant...translated from the French...by G. T. Bedell. 8th edition. Philadelphia: Henry Perkins, Boston: Perkins and Marvin, 1839. 144 p. NGos; NKings. 58381

Schmidt, Henry Immanuel, 1806-1889. Discourse delivered before the Union Sabbath School Society of Gettysburg, Pa., December 15, 1839. Gettysburg: 1839. ICN; O 58382

Schmucker, Samuel Simon, 1799-1873. Address on the anniversary of Washington's birthday, delivered before the Gettysburg guards, February 22, 1839, at Gettysburg, Pa. Gettysburg: H. C. Neinstedt, 1839. 24 p. CSmH; MiU-C; OSW; ScCoT; PU. 58383

----. Fraternal appeal to the American churches, plan for Catholic union on apostolic principles.... 2nd edition, enlarged. New York: Gould and Newman; Philadelphia: H. Perkins, 1839. 149 p. MiU; NCH; OO; PPLT. 58384

----.----. 2nd edition enlarged. New York: Taylor and Dodd, 1839. 149 p. ICU; MBC; OO; RPA; ScCoT. 58385

----. The happy adaptation of the sabbath school system to the peculiar wants of our age and country. A sermon.... Philadelphia: American Sunday School Union, 1839. 22 p. MBC; MWA; NjPT. OSW; PPLT. 58386

----. Memorial...relative to binding out minor colored children. Read in the House, March 7, 1839. Harrisburg: Boas and Coplan, printers, 1839. 7 p. DLC; OClWHi; PHi. 58387

Schomann, Georg Friedrich, 1793-1879. A dissertation on the assemblies of the Athenians.... Cambridge [Mass.] W. P. Grant, 1839. 361 p. MB; OCY; PU. 58388

The school library. Published under the sanction of the board of education of the state of Massachusetts.... Boston: March, Capen, Lyon and Webb, 1839. 3 v. DLC; KyBC; MWA; RPB; Vi. 58389

Schoolcraft, Henry Rowe, 1793-1864. Algic researches, comprising inquiries respecting the mental characteristics of the North American Indians. First series. Indian tales and legends.... New York: Harper and Brothers, 1839. 2 v. CtMW; IHi; MWA; NhD; PPA. 58390

Schroeder, John Frederick, 1800-1857. Documents concerning recent measures of the vestry of Trinity Church in the city of New York. Hanford: 1839. 8 p. CtHT; MdBD; NjP; NNC; PHi. 58391

----. Letter to the members of the congregations of the parish of Trinity Church, with an apx. New York: Scatcherd and Adams, 1839. 24 p. CtHT; MH; MnHi; NNUT; PHi. 58392

Schultes, Henry. An essay on aquatic rights; intended as an illustration of the law relative to fishing and to the property, ground or soil produced by alluvion and dereliction in the sea and rivers. Philadelphia: John S. Littell, 1839. 56 p. Ct; In-SC; NcD; PPB; Sc-SC. 58393

Schuylkill Permanet Bridge Company, Philadelphia. Address of the directors on the Permanent Bridge Company, at Market Street, to the public. Showing the nature and situation of their bridge, its site and their adjacent lots, February, 1839 [Philadelphia: 1839] 6 p. N. 58394

Scott, Elihu. Address delivered before Ladies' Moral Reform Association of Great Falls, Fast day, 1838. Pastor, Methodist Episcopal Church. Dover: Star office, 1839. 21 p. MBNMHi; Nh-Hi. 58395

Scott, James. Questions on the doctrine of the New Jerusalem respecting the sacred scripture...Published under the direction of the committee of moral and religious instruction. Boston: Otis Clapp, 1839. 52 p. MCNC; PBa. 58396

Scott, Walter, 1771-1832. The abbot; being a sequel to the monastery. Parker's edition revised and corrected. Boston: Samuel H. Parker, 1839. [v. 19. Waverly Novels] MDeeP; MEr; NCaS; RPE. 58397

----. Anne of Geierstein; or the maiden of the mist. Parker's edition, revised and corrected.... Boston: Samuel Parker, Philadelphia: Thomas, Cowperthwait and Company, New York: C. S. Francis, Baltimore, Cushing and Sons, 1839. [v. 43-44. Waverly Novels] 2 v. MEr; MDeeP. 58398

----. The antiquary. Parker's edition revised and corrected. Boston: Samuel Parker, 1839. 2 v. [v. 5-6. Waverly Novels] MDeeP; MEr; MeSaco. 58399

----. The betrothed. Boston: 1839. [V. 35. Waverly Novels] MDeeP. 58400

----. Black dwarf; old marality. Parker's edition revised and corrected, with a general preface, an introduction to each novel and notes, historical and illustrative by the author. Boston: Samuel H. Parker, 1839. 2 v. NN; TxU. 58401

----. The bride of the Lammermoor. Chicago, New York and San Francisco: Belford, Clarke and Company, 1839. 2 v. [v. 13-14. Waverly Novels] MEr; MDeeP. 58402

----. Castle dangerous. Parker's edition revised. Boston: Samuel Parker, 1839. 283 p. MB; NN. 58403

----. Chronicles of the Canongate. First series, Parker's edition revised and corrected, with a general preface...and notes, historical and illustrative by the author. Boston: Sameul Parker, Philadephia: Thomas, Cowperthwait and Company, etc., 1839. MWm; NCaS; RPE. 58404

----. ----. Chicago, New York and San Francisco: Belford, Clarke and Company, 1839. MEr. 58405

----. A collection of psalms, hymns and spiritual songs with the music of Mason's sacred harp and missouri harmony adapted by Sir Walter Scott. Carthage, Hamilton County Ohio. Cincinnati: 1839. NNUT. 58406

----. Count Robert of Paris. Boston: 1839. [v. 45-46. Waverly Novels] MDeeP. 58407

----. Description of the regatia of Scotland. New York: J. C. Wood, 1839. 24 p. DLC. 58408

----. The fortunes of Nigel. Knifegrinder story? ...Parker's edition, revised and corrected...Boston: Samuel H. Parker, Philadelphia: Thomas, Cowperthwait and Company, Baltimore: Cushing and Sons, 1839. 2 v. MDeeP; MEr; NCaS. 58409

----. Guy Mannering; or the astrologer. Boston: Samuel H. Parker, 1839. 494 p. FSaFDB; MB-FA. 58410

----. ----. Chicago, New York and San Francisco: Belford, Clarke and Company, 1839. 397 p. MEr. 58411

----. The heart of Mid-Lothian. Boston: Samuel Parker, 1839 2 v. in 1. [v. 11-12. Waverly Novels] MDeeP; NNC. 58412

----. The highland widow , in chronicles of the canongate. Boston: 1839. [V. 39. Waverly Novels] MDeeP. 58413

----.. Ivanhoe. Boston: 1839. 2 v. [v. 15-16. Waverly Novels] MD; MDeeP; MEr; ViW. 58414

----. Ivanhoe, a romance. Chicago, New York and San Francisco: Belford, Clarke and company, 1839. 447 p. MEr. 58415

----. Kenilworth. Parker's edition, revised and corrected. Boston: Samuel Parker, 1839. 2 v. in 1. [v. 21-22. Wavely Novels] FSaDDB 58416

----. Letters on demonology and withcraft addressed to J. G. Lockhart, Esq. New York: Harper and Brothers, 1839. InCW; MdW; MoS; OCl; TxGR. 58417

----. Life of Napoleon Buonaparte, Emperor of the French, with a preliminary view of the French Revolution. Exeter: J. and B. Williams, 1839. 2 v. InU; MsU; PSC; PWmpDS; USlW. 58418

----. ----. New London: W. and J. Bolles, New York: Collins, Keese and Company, 1839 3 v. in 1. DLC; KRu; PSt. 58419

----. ----. Philadelphia: E. L. Carey and A. Hart, 1839. 3 v. in 1. 702 p. MH; MWHi; NvU. 58420

----. The monastery; a romance. Parker's edition revised and corrected. Boston: Samuel H. Parker. 2 v. in 1. [v. 17-18. Waverly novels] FSaFDB. 58421

----. ----. Chicago, New York and San Francisco: Belford, Clarke and Company, 1839. 431 p. MEr. 58422

----. Peril of the peak. Chicago, New York and

San Francisco: Belford, Clarke and Company, 1839. 582 p. [v.27-28. Waverly Novels] MDeeP; MEr; NCaS. 58423

----. The pirate. Chicago, New York and San Francisco: Belford, Clarke and Company, 1839. 464 p. MEr. 58424

----. ----. Parker's edition revised and corrected. Boston: Samuel Parker, 1839. 2 v. in 1. [v. 23-24. Waverly Novels] MDeeP. 58425

----. The poetical works...with a sketch of his life by J. W. Lake. Philadelphia: J. Crissy, 1839. 443 p. IJI; NjP; NN; PU. 58426

----. ----. Philadelphia: E. L. Carey and A. Hart, 1839. 699 p. N; ViSwc. 58427

----. ----. 2 v. MWH. 58428

----. ----. Philadelphia: Lea and Blanchard, 1839. 6 v. CtMW; KyBC; PP; RPB; VtU. 58429

----. His poetical works, with a memoir. New and complete edition. Philadelphia: Porter and Coates [1839?] 859 p. IaCrest. 58430

----. Redgauntlet. Boston: B. Parker, 1839. 2 v. [v. 33. Waverly Novels] CtWatk; MB; MDeeP. 58431

----. Rob Roy. Parker's edition, revised and corrected...Boston: Samuel H. Parker, etc., etc., etc., 1839. 79, 234 p. [v. 7. Waverly Novels] FSaFDE; MDeeP; MEr; MWborHi. 58432

----. St. Roman's well. Parker's edition, revised and corrected. Boston: Samuel H. Parker, 1839. 245, 260 p. 2 v. [v. 31-32. Waverly Novels] MDeeP; NCaS. 58433

----. Saint Valentine's Day or the fair maid of Perth, in chronicles of the canongate. Second series. Boston: 1839. 2 v. [v. 41-42. Waverly Novels] MDeeP. 58434

----. The surgeon's daughter, in Chronicles of the canongate. Boston: 1839. [v. 40. Waverly Novels] MDeeP. 58435

----. Tales of a grandfather; being stories taken from Scottish history. First series. Parker's edition, published in connection with the series of Waverly Novel, which were revised, corrected and illustrated by the author. Boston: S. H. Parker, 1839. 380 p. NN. 58436

----. ----. Exeter, N. H.: J. and B. Williams, 1839. 2 v. KyHi; MDeeP; PV. 58437

----. ----. Second series. Boston: Samuel H. Parker, 1839. 2 v. [v. 49-52. Waverly Tales] LNUrs; MDeeP; MdHi; MEr; NCaS. 58438

----. ----. Third series. Parker's edition. Boston: Samuel H. Parker, 1839. 2 v. MdHi; MEr; RPaw. 58439

----. ----. Exeter, N. H.: J. and B. Williams, 1839. 2 v. in 1. MDeeP. 58440

----. ----. Fourth series. Parker's edition. Boston: Samuel Parker, etc., etc., etc., 1839. 2 v. MdHi; MEr; NCaS; ViRut. 58441

----. ----. Exeter, N. H.: 1839.. MiEM; NIC. 58442

----. ----. Humbly inscribed to Hugh Little John... Exeter, N. H.: J. and B. Williams, 1839. 8 v. PPiPT. 58443

----. Tales of my landlord. First series. Revised and corrected. Boston: Samuel H. Parker, 1839. 2 v. in 1. FSaFDB; NjPCL; ScFl. 58444

----. ----. Second series. Boston: Samuel H. Parker, 1839. 2 v. in 1. FSaFDB; PPA. 58445

----. ----. Third series. Revised and corrected. Boston: Samuel H. Parker, 1839. 2 v. in 1. FSaFDB; KyHop; NjPLC. 58446

----. ----. Fourth and last series. Boston: Samuel H. Parker, 1839. 3 v. NjPLC. 58447

----. Tales of the crusaders. Parker's edition, revised and corrected.... Boston: Samuel H. Parker, 1839. 2 v. in 1. MEr; MWA; TxHU. 58448

----. The tailsman. Parker's edition, revised and corrected.... Boston: Parker, 1839. MD-FA; MDeeP. 58449

----. The tapestried chamber or the lady in the sacque. Boston: 1839. [v. 40. Waverly Novels] MDeeP. 58450

----. Waverly novels. Parker's edition revised and corrected, with an introduction to each novel and

notes historical and illustrative by the author. Boston: Samuel H. Parker, Philadelphia: Thomas, Cowperthwait and Company, etc., etc., 1839. 18 v. in 14. DLC; MsCliM. 58451

----. ----. with the author's last corrections and additions, complete in 5 volumes. Philadelphia: E. L. Carey and A. Hart, 1839. 5 v. CLSM; IaCr; MsCliM, PHi. 58452

Scougal, Henry, 1650-1678. The works of Rev. Henry Scougal. The life of God in the soul of man...together with his funeral sermon, by the Rev. Dr. Gairden, and an account of his life and writings. New York: R. Carter, 1839. 272 p. CBPSR; GDecCT; ICU; MeBat; ViRut. 58453

The scrap book; a selection of humourous stories, interesting fables and authentic anecdotes. New York: published for the booksellers [1839] WU. 58454

Scripture sketches; a present for youth. New Haven: S. Babcock, 1839. 24 p. NN. 58455

Seabury, Samuel, 1729-1796. An earnest Persuasive to the frequent receiving of the Holy Communion. Utica: Hobart Press, 1839. 31 p. NGH; NUt. 58456

Seamen's Orphan and Childrens Friend Society, Salem, Massachusetts. Circular and constitution. Salem: Register office, 1839. 8 p. DLC. 58457

Searle, John. New and improved mode of constructing bee houses and bee hives. Concord: Asa MacFarland, 1839. 22 p. Ct; MAA; NCH; Nh-Hi. 58458

The seasons. Northampton: John Metcalf, 1839. NPV. 58459

Secker, Thomas, 1693-1768. Lectures on the catechism of the Protestant Episcopal Church; with a discourse on confirmation. Published from the original manuscripts. 2nd American, from the 14th London edition. Columbus: Isacc N. Whiting, 1839. NNUT; WHi. 58460

[Sedgwick, Catharinge Maria] 1789-1867. Home.... 15th edition. Boston: J. Munroe and Company, 1839. CtY; InU; MH; MH-AH. 58461

----. Live and let live; or domestic service illustrated. New York: Harper and Brothers, 1839.

216 p. NhLac; ScDuE. 58462

----. A love token for children. New York: Harper, 1839. 142 p. CSmH; DLC; MB; NNC; TxU. 58463

----. Means and ends; or selftraining. Boston: Marsh, Capen, Lyon and Webb, 1839. 278 p. CtY; ICN; NNC; OrHi; RPB. 58464

----. ----. 3rd edition. Boston: Marsh, Capen, Lyon and Webb, 1839. MBAt; MeBa; MH; OO. 58465

----. The poor rich man and the rich poor man.... New York: Harper and Brothers, 1839. 186 p. CtY; MWA; NPotN; RPA; ScDuE. 58466

Seidenstucker, Johann Heirich Philipp, 1763-1817. An elementry practlcal book for learning to speak the French language.... New York: Collins, Keese and Company, 1839. 130 p. ICU; MH. 58467

Selden, Richard Ely, 1797-1868. The newest keep-sake, for 1839; containing the speeches, circumstances, and doings of a recent benevolent convention.... Boston: 1839. 121 p. MB; MBC; MH; MWA; NNC. 58468

Selection of hymns...for the use of the Lutheran and German Reformed Sunday School of the borough of Reading. Reading: Albright, 1839. 127 p. PPLT. 58469

Selma and Tennessee Railroad Company. Petition of the president and the directors and other citizens of Alabama, that said company be allowed to enter a tract of land, at the minimum price.... Washington: Blair and Rives, 1839. 8 p. CtY; DBRE; IU; MWA; NjP. 58470

----. Petition of the president and directors, and other citizens of Florida, praying that said company, be permitted to enter a quantity of public land at minimum price... [Washington: Blair and Rives, 1839] 3 p. CtY; IU; MB; MH-AH; MiD. 58471

----. Second annual report...April 1, 1839. Selma: T. J. Frow, 1839. 7 p. ViU; WU. 58472

Selwyn, William, 1775-1855. An abridgment of the law of nisi prius. With notes by Hery Wheaton and Thomas Wharton. 5th American edition from the 9th London edition. Philadelphia: E. F. Bakus, 1839. 2 v. FTU; LNB; MsU; NcD; WaU. 58473

Seneca, Lucius Annaeus. Morals. By way of abstract. To which is added a discourse, under the title of an after-thought, by Roger L'Estrage, Knt. 6th American edition. Philadelphia: Grigg and Elliot, 1839. 359 p. InStmaS; TxGR. 58474

Sergeant, Henry Jonathan. Treatise on the lien on mechanics and material men in Pennsylvania: with the acts of assembly relating thereto; and various forms of claims. Philadelphia: James Kay and Brother, 1839. 132 p. DLC; NNLI; OCLaw; PPB; WU-En. 58475

Sergeant, John, 1779-1852. Lecture before the Mercantile Library Company of Philadelphia: H. Perkins, 1839. 36 p. DLC; MH; NBuU-M; NjP; PHi. 58476

The sermon on the occasion of the consecration of St. Phillip's Church in Charleston, South Carolina. By the rector. Charleston: printed by A. E. Miller, 1839. 21 p. NcU. 58477

Service book for sunday schools. Boston: 1839. MB. 58478

Services performed in the North Congregational Church, Concord [N. H.] on occasion of the ordination of Mr. Ezra E. Adams, as Chaplain to seamen. Concord: 1839. 44 p. Nh-Hi. 58479

Severance, Moses. The American manual, or new English reader; consisting of exercises in reading and speaking, both in prose and poetry; selected from the best writers. Bath, New York: R. L. Underhill and Company, 1839. 300 p. NBuG; NRMA. 58480

----. ----. Cazenovia: J. S. Redfield, 1839. CSmH; MH; NFred; PU; RAp. 58481

----. ----. New York: Henry Baker and Wright, 1839. 300 p. IaHA; TxElp. 58482

Sewall, Thomas, 1786-1845. An examination of phrenology in two lectures, delivered to the students of the Columbian College, District of Columbia, February, 1837. 2nd edition. Boston: D. S. King, 1839. 110 p. CtMW; MH-AH; OO; RPM; VtU. 58483

Sewell, Henry Devereux. A collection of psalms

and hymns for social and private worship. 3rd edition. Boston: 1839. 422 p. DLC; IU; MW; MWA. 58484

Sforzosi, Luigi. A compendious history of Italy. Translated from the original Italian by Nathaniel Greene. New York: Harper and Brothers, 1839. 319 p. MdBC; MH; NUt; OCX; WM. 58485

Shakespeare, William, 1564-1616. The beauties of Shakespeare, regularly selected from each play. With a general index, digesting them under proper heads. By the late William Dodd. Boston: Weeks, Jordan and Company, 1839. 345 p. NdFM. NSyU. 58486

----. The dramatic works and poems of William Shakespeare, with notes.... New York: Harper and Brothers, 1839. 6 v. CtWatk; ILM; LNB; ScCF. 58487

----. The dramatic works of William Shakespeare, a life of the poet and notes. Boston: Hilliard, Gray and Company, 1839. 7 v. CtMW; KyBC; MMel; PPA. 58488

----. The dramatic works of William Shakespeare accurately printed from the text of the corrected copy left by the late George Stevens, Esq. With a glossery and notes, and a sketch of the life of Shakespeare. New York: Robinson and Franklin, 1839. 2 v. PBlv; ScCliTO. 58489

----. The wisdom and genius of Shalespeare; comprising moral philosophy-delineations of character paintings of nature and the passions. Philadelphia: E. L. Carey and A. Hart, 1839. 460 p. CtHT; ICMe; KyU; PPA; WHi. 58490

Shaw, Joseph L. New Hampshire state prison cruelty exposed; or the sufferings of Joseph L. Shaw, in that institution in 1837, while John M. Daniel was warden. Exeter: for the author, 1839. 31 p. ICN; MiD-B; Nh-Hi. 58491

Shaw, Lemuel. Remarks of Chief Justice Shaw, when passing sentence of death upon Nathan Smith, for the crime of murder, June 7, 1839. Lowell: Leonard Huntress, printer, 1839. 7. MB; MH- L. 58492

Shaw, William A. The Presbyterian church vindicated from misrepresentation. Nashville, Tenn.: B. R. M'Kennie, Whig and Steam Press, 1839. 65 p. T; ViRut. 58493

Shea, John H. Bood keeping by single and double entry; simplified and arranged according to the present practice of well regulated counting houses in the United States. Baltimore: Shea, 1839. 160 p. MdBLC; MdHi; MdW; PU. 58494

Shedd, Jemima. Reasons for rejecting the doctrine of endless damnation, in a series of discourses founded on the scriptures.... Newport, N. H.: H. E. and S. C. Baldwin, printers, 1839. 234 p. IaMp; MBC; Nh-Hi. 58495

Shelley, Percy Bysshe, 1792-1822. Poetical works of Percy Bysshe Shelley by Edward Dowden. New York: James Miller [1839?] 705 p. GU; NNC; OCU. 58496

----. ----. New York: Merrill and Baker, 1839? 3 v. CSt; TxFTC. 58497

----. ----. New York: Thomas Y. Crowell and Company, 1839. 682 p. CoOrd; GCed; IaOskJF; NBuDC. 58498

----. ----. Philadelphia: Porter and Coates, 1839. 391 p. OkU; PHC; TxMck; WU. 58499

Shepard, James Biddle. Address delivered before the citizens, mechanics and guards of the city of Raleigh, July 4, 1839. Raleigh: Loring, 1839. 25 p. NcU. 58500

Sherburne, George Ann Humphreys. Imogene; or the pirate's treasure, and the demon's cave. Washington: Fischer, 1839. 180 p. IaU; ICN; Nh-Hi; PPL. 58501

Sherwood, Henry Hall. Memorial on terrestrial magnetism. Washington: 1839. 30 p. VtU. 58502

Sherwood, Mary Martha [Butt] 1775-1851. The drooping lily. New York: John S. Taylor, 1839. 69 p. CtY; NGos. 58503

----. Mary Anne: by the author of "Little Henry and his beaver." New York: Mason and G. Lane, 1839. 45 p. MoKCM. 58504

----. Shanty, the blacksmith; a tale of other times. New York: Taylor, 1839. 198 p. CLU; OClW. 58505

----. The violet leaf, and other tales. New York: Taylor and Dodd, 1839. 93 p. N. 58506

Sherwood, Reuben, 1789-1856. Both sides. A letter from the Rev. William Cruikshank, to the churchman with a few remarks thereon. Poughkeepsie: 1839. 24 p. ICN; N. 58507

Shields, Joseph D. An oration delivered before the Jefferson Society of the University of Virginia: April 13, 1839. Charlotteville: James Alexander, 1839. 19 p. LU; MsJS; TxU. 58508

Shimeall, Richard Cunningham, 1803-1874. Gems from the mount, being original pictorial illustrations of the Lord's prayer.... New York: Sherman and Trevett, 1839. 87 p. NNG. 58509

Shinn, William M. Inaugural address delivered before Philological Institute, January 12, 1839. Pittsburgh: Daily Advocate, printer, 1839. 29 p. KyU; NjR; PHi; PPiHi. 58510

The shipwreck; or the desert island. A moral take. Philadelphia: James Kay, Jun. and Brother, Pittsburgh: C. H. Kay and Company, 1839. 172 p. DLC; MHi. 58511

The shorter Catechsim.... Salem: 1839. 32 p. MWA. 58512

Shrewsbury, School Committee. Report...offered in town meeting, April 1, 1839. Worcester: printed by Spooner and Howland, 1839. 16 p. MB; MBC; MH; MHi. 58513

Sibbald, Charles Fraser. Report of the solicitor and comptrollers of the treasury, upon the case of Charles F. Sibbald, of Philadelphia.... Philadelphia: 1839. 8. DLC; OO; RPB. 58514

Siegfried, Samuel. Deutsches Rechenbuch fur volksschulen. Bath, Pa.: Gedruckt und zu haben bei dem verfasser, 1839. 108 p. PHi; PPG. 58515

Sigourney, Lydia Howard [Huntley] 1791-1865. The boy's reading book; in prose and poetry, for schools. New York: J. Orville Taylor, 1839. 307 p. CtHT; MH; NNC; OO; TxU. 58516

----. The girl's reading book in prose and poetry. For schools. 7th edition. New York: Orville Taylor, 1839. 243 p. CtHWatk; VtMidSM. 58517

----. ----. 9th edition. New York: J. Orville taylor, 1839. 274 p. CSmH; Ct; MB; MH; TxU. 58518

----. Letters to mothers. 2nd edition. New York:

Harper and Brothers, 1839. 297 p. CtSoP; IEG; KyLxT; TxDaM; WM. 58519

----. Letters to young ladies. 5th edition. New York: Harper and Brothers, 1839. 259 p. ICP; KU; MoSpD; PPC; TxDaM. 58520

----. The pastor's return [New York: 1839] Broadside, MB. 58521

----. The religious keepsake for holiday presents. See under title.

----. Sketches. Amherst: J. S. and C. Adams, 1839. 216 p. DLC; KTW; OO; RPB; WU. 58522

[Sigsby,] Life and adventures of Timothy Murphy, the benefactor of schoharie, including his history from the commencement of the revolution...Schoharie C. H., New York: printed by W. H. Gallup, 1839. CsmH; MWA; NN. 58523

The silk grower, and farmer's manual, edited by Ward Cheney and Brothers. v. 1. nos. 1-10, 12. July 1838-. Philadlephia: C. Alexander, 1839. MB; OC; PPFrankI. 58524

Silliman, Benjamin, 1799-1864. Remarks introductory to the first American edition of Dr. Mantell's wonders of geology. New Haven: Hitchcock and Stafford, printers, 1839. 31 p. MH; NjR; NNUT; WU. 58525

----. Suggestions relative to the philosophy of geology, as deduced from the facts and to the consistency of both the facts and theory of this science with sacred history. New Haven: printed by B. L. Hamlem, 1839. 119 p. MB; MBC; MMeT; OMC; WMAM. 58526

Simmons, George Frederick, 1814-1855. Who was Jesus Christ? Printed for the American Unitarian Association. Boston: James Munroe and Company, 1839. 54 p. ICMe; MBAU; MDeeP; MH-AH, NN. 58527

[Simms, William Gilmore] 1806-1870. The damsel of Darien.... Philadelphia: Lea and Blanchard, 1839. 2 v. CSt; Ia; MWA; NcD;PPA. 58528

----. Southern passages and pictures.... New York: G. Adlard, 1839. 228 p. CtMW; InU; PP; RPB; ScCoB. 58529

Simons, Thomas Young, 1798-1857. A report on

the history and causes of the stranges or yellow fever of Charleston. Charleston: printed by W. Riley, 1839. 23 p. CSt-L; DNLM; ScCC. 58530

Sinclair, Catharine, 1800-1864. Holiday house; a series of tales dedicated to Lady Diana Boyle. New York: Robert Carter, 1839. 252 p. CtHT-W. 58531

Sinclair, John. Dissertation on liturgies. Gambier, Ohio: G. W. Myers Western Church Press, 1839. 47 p. MWA; NNG; NNUT; OClWHi. 58532

The singer's own book, a well selected collection of the most popular sentimental , patriotic, naval and comic songs.... Philadelphia: Thomas, Cowperthwait and Company, 1839. 320 p. DLC; MB; MH. 58533

Sitgreaves, Charles. Report on the Bellvidere Railroad Company. Resolution.... Eaton, Pa.: Charles Priest, College Press, 1839. 15 p. MH-BA. 58534

Six weeks in Fauquier. Being the substance of a series of familiar letters, illustrating the scenery, localities, medicinal virtues...of the White Sulphur Springs, at Warrenton, Fauquier County, Virginia; written in 1838, to a gentleman in New England; by a visitor. New York: Samuel Colman, 1839. 67 p. ICJ; MH; NcD; MWA; PPCP. 58535

Sketches of United States senators of the session of 1837-1838. "By a looker on here in Verona." Washington: W. M. Morrison, 1839. 67 p. ICU; LU; MB; NhD; TxU. 58536

Skinner, Otis Ainsworth, 1807-1861. The claims of the militia. A discourse preached before the Ancient and Honorable Aritillery Company, June 3, 1839, being their 201st anniversary. Boston: Mudge and Evans, printers, 1839. 23 p. MBAt; MH; MB-FA; MWA; NCH. 58537

----. A discourse before the fifth Universalisth Society, at the dedication of their church, January 1839. Boston: Abel Tompkins, 1839. 16 p. RPB. 58538

----. Two discourses delivered before the Fifth Universalist Society in Boston: the first dedication of their church, January 30, 1839. The second on the Abbath following, February 3. Boston: Abel Tompkins, 1839. 27 p. ICU; MB; MiD-B; MMeT-Hi; Vt. 58539

----. Universalism illustrated and defended; being a system of doctrinal and practical divinity deducted from the reason and revolation. Boston: Tompkins, 1839. 356 p. CtHT; MMeT-Hi; NCaS; OHi; ScNC. 58540

Skinner, Thomas Harvey, 1791-1871. Aids to preaching and hearing. New York: John S. Taylor, 1839. 301 p. ICT; MBC; ODaB; PPP. 58541

----. Religion of the Bible in select discourses. New York: G. F. Hopkins, 1839. 222 p. GDecCT; KyLo; MBC; OO; WBeloC. 58542

Slade, William, 1786-1869. Speech of Mr. Slade, of Vermont, in the case of the New Jersey election [1838]] delivered in the House, December 10, 1839. Washington: 1839. 8 p. WHi. 58543

Slavery vindicated; or the beauty and glory of the patriarchal system illustrated.... New York: Galvanic double roary press, 1839. 12 p. MiD-B. 58544

Slatersville. Congregational Church. See Smithfield, Rhode Island. Slattersville.

Sleeman Willian Henry, 1788-1856. The thugs; or Phansigars of India: comprising a history of the rise and progress of that extraordinary fraturnity of assassins.... Philadelphia: Carey and Hart, 1839. 2 v. FSa; IU; OCLaw; OMC; PPM. 58545

Smedley, Edward, 1788-1836. Sketches from Venetian history. New York: Harper and Brothers, 1839. 2 v. FTa; Me; ScCliP; TxGR. 58546

Smellie, William, 1740-1795. The philosophy of natural history...with an introduction and various additions and alterations, intended to adopt it to the present state of knowledge. By John Ware, M. D. Boston: Hilliard, Gray and Company, 1839. 327 p. CtHT; IaGG; MBC; NNC; ViU. 58547

Smiley, Thomas Tucker, d. 1879. Smiley's atlas for the use of school and families. A new atlas, intended to illustrate the encyclopedia of geography.... Exhibiting the natural and political divisions of the fifferent countries on the globe.... Cincinnati: Ely and Strong, 1839. OO. 58548

----. Smiley's atlas. A new atlas intended to illustrate the encyclopedia of geography. Hartford: Gurdon Robins, etc., etc., 1839. CtY; MH. 58549

----. ----. Philadelphia: Hogan and Thompson, 1839. Ct; MH. 58550

----. Encyclopedia of geography, conprising a description of the earth, exhibiting its relation to the heavenly bodies, its physical structure, natural history of each country, industry of all nations.... Cincinnati: Ely and Strong, 1839. 264 p. KyU; OC; OO; TCU. 58551

----. ----. Hartford: Robins, 1839. 264 p. CtHWatk; MH; OCHP; PHi; PPM. 58552

----. ----. Hartford: Gurdon Robins, Jr., Philadelphia: Grigg and Elliot, 1839. 264 p. CaBVaU; MoK; MtHi; PLFM. 58553

----. ----. Philadelphia: Hogan and Thomson, 1839. 264 p. MH; NN; PHi; PPM. 58554

Smith, Albert, 1804-1863. An inaugural address delivered at Mercersberg, Pa., at the annual commencement of Marshall College, September 26, 1838. 2nd edition. Gettysburg, Pa.: republished by the students, printed by H. C. Neinstedt, 1839. 36 p. DLC; IaHA; MBC; PPL; ViRuT. 58555

Smith, Ashbel, 1805-1886. An account of th yellow fever which appeared in the city of Galveston, Republic of Texas, in 1839. Galveston: Stuart, [etc., etc., etc.] 1839. 78 p. CtHWatk; MBM; NBMS; NNN; TxU. 58556

Smith, Daniel, 1806-1852. Buy a book. New York: T. Mason and G. Lane, for the Sunday School Union of the Methodist Episcopal Church, 1839. 8 p. MiD-B. 58557

----. The life of Elijah. New York: T. Mason and G. Lane, 1839. 174 p. DLC. 58558

----. Life of Elisha. New York: T. Mason and G. Lane, 1839. 88 p. DLC; UU. 58559

----. Life of Moses. New York: Carlton and Lanahan, Sunday School Union, 1839. 224 p. DLC; NcD; NN. 58560

----. The life of St. Paul. New York: T. Mason and G. Lane, 1839. 174 p. DLC. 58561

----. Love to the Saviour. New York: T. Mason and G. Lane, 1839. 115 p. NNMHi. 58562

----. The most useful birds. New York: T. Mason and g. Lane, 1839. 15 p. NN. 58563

Smith, E. G. The Mentor and fireside review. By the Rev. E. G. Smith. New York: John S. Taylor, 1839. 2 v. GDecCT; MBAt; MBC; NbCrD. 58564

Smith, Elizabeth Oakes [Prince] 1806-1893. Riches without wings; or the Cleveland family. By Mrs. Seba Smith.... 3rd edition. Boston: George W. Light, 1839. 160 p. MH. 58565

Smith, Ethan, 1762-1849. Prophetic catechism, to lead to the study of the prophetic scriptures.... Boston: Crocker and Brewster, 1839. 46 p. ICBB; MBC; Nh; Nh-Hi. 58566

Smith, Gerrit, 1797-1874. A letter addressed to John Tappan, esq., on missions, May 24, 1838. Cazenovia: office of the Union Herald, 1839. 13 p. DHU; MH; N; NIC. 58567

----. Letter...to Hon. Henry Clay. New York American Anti-slavery Society, 1839. 54 p. ArU; MB; MH-AH; PPL; WHi. 58568

----. Letter on "internal improvements" To the gentlemen of the county of Madison, who shall be chosen to seats in the Legislature, at the approaching election. Peterboro: American News Company, 1839. 3 p. NN. 58569

Smith, Henry. The vocalist's pocket companion, being a collection of the most popular songs, arranged with solos, duets, and trios, by H. Smith and H. Ruby. Chambersburg; Pa.: Henry Ruby, printer, 1839. 108 p. OClWHi; PHi; PReaHi. 58570

Smith, Horatio, 1779-1849. Festivals, games and amusements. Ancient and modern. With additions by Samuel Woodworth, esq. of New York. New York: Harper and Brothers, 1839. 355 p. FTa; MB-HP; ScSp; TxGR. 58571

Smith, John Jay, 1798-1881. Celebrated trials of all countries, and remarkable cases of criminal jusrisprudence. Selected by a member of the Philadelphia Bar.... Philadelphia: E. L. Carey and A. Hart, 1839. 596 p. Ct; MH-L; NNC. 58572

Smith, John Sidney, 1804-1871. A treatise on the practice of the court of chancery. With an appendix of forms and precedents of costs, adapted to the last new orders. Ist American, from the 2nd revise and enlarged edition.... Philadelphia: P. H.

Nicklin and T. Johnson [etc.] 1839. 2 v. CU; Ia; LNB; NhD; PP. 58573.

Smith, Joshua Toulmin, 1816-1869. Childhood's hope, a poem written expressly for the fair held at Youle Cottage, Roxbury, June 20, 1839. Boston: Hall, 1839. 24 p. MH; NCH; RPB. 58574

----. Comparative view of ancient history...to which are added, observations on chronological eras.... Boston: Hilliard, Gray and Company, 1839. 122 p. IaGG; MBevHi; MH-AH; NWM; OUrC. 58575

----. The northmen in New England; or America in the tenth century. Boston: Hilliard, Gray and Company, 1839. 364 p. MBBC; Nh; PHi; RPB; WHi. 58576

Smith, Levi Ward. A poem pronounced before the senior class in Yale College, July 3, 1839. New Haven: printed by B. L. Hamlen, 1839. 183 p. CtHC; MH; MWiW; PHi; NBuU; RPA. 58577

Smith, Richard Penn, 1799-1854. Col. Crockett's exploits and adventures in Texas; wherein is contained, a full account of his journey from Tennessee to the Red River and Natchitoches and thence across Texas to San Antonio.... Cincinnati: U. P. James, 1839. Ar; CtY; MdBE; PHi. 58578

Smith, Roswell Chamberlain, 1797-1875. Smith's atlas containing: map and chart of the world, world on a polar projection, central Europe, eastern states.... Hartford: Spalding and Storrs [1839] Ct; MBAt; NGrn; TxU-T; WKenHi. 58579

----. Smith's atlas designed to accompany the geography by R. C. Smith.... New York: Paine and Burgess, 1839. 18 p. Ct; IU; MBAt; MH; TxU-T. 58580

----. English grammar on the productive system: A method of instruction recently adopted in Germany and Switzerland. Designed for schools and academies. Hartford: Spalding and Storrs, 1839. 192 p. CoGrS; CtSoP; MH; MWhor. 58581

----. ----. Philadelphia: William Marshall and Company, 1839. 192 p. MAshlHi. 58582.

----. ----. 2nd edition. Hartford: 1839. CtHWatk. 58583

----. ----. 143rd edition. Philadelphia: 1839. 192 p. CtSoP. 58584

----. Geography on the productive system; for schools, academies, and families; revised and improved. Accompanied by a large and valuable atlas. Hartford: Daniel Burgess and Company and Spalding and Storrs, 1839. 274 p. DeU; MAm; NcD; NjR; PLFM. 58585

----. Practical and mental arithmetic, on a new plan to which is added a practical system of book keeping. 51st edition. Hartford: Daniel Burgess and Company, 1839. 284 p. MH; NjR; VtMidS. 58586

[Smith, Seba] 1792-1868. Smith's letter with pictures to match. Containing reasons why John Smith should not change his name.... New York: Samuel Colman, 1839. 139 p. ICU; MeBa; MWA; PPL; TxU. 58587

Smith, Stephen Rensselaer, 1788-1850. Address delivered at the annual examination and exhibition of Clinton Liberal Institute, in Clinton, Oneida County, New York, August 28, 1839.... Albany: printed by Packard, Van Benthuysen and Company, 1839. 29 p. CsSoP; MiD-B; NBu; NCH; RPB. 58588

----. The causes of infidelity removed. Utica: Grosh and Hutchinson, 1839. 352 p. DLC; ICMe; MB; MH; NNUT. 58589

Smith, William, 1762-1840. Address of William Smith of Huntsville, Alabama. Huntsville: 1839. 14 p. A-Ar; DLC; NcD; TxU. 58590

----. Speech...in the House...in support of the resolutions which he had introduced, against the recharter of the Bank of the United States, and in support of an independent treasury system. Huntsville, Alabama: P. Woodwon, Jr., 1839. 16 p. NcD; TxU. 58591

Smith, Whiteford. A discourse on the occasion of the death of the Hon. Augustin S. Clayton.... Athens, Georgia: 1839. 16 p. CSmH; DLC; ScCC. 58592

Smithfield, Rhode Island. Slatersville Congregational Church. The doctrinal articles and covenant of the Slatersville Congrgational Church, Smithfield, Rhode Isalnd. Providence: H. H. Brown, printer, 1839. 28 p. MBC; RHi; RPB. 58593

Smollett, Tobias George, 1721-1771. The history of England, from the revolution in 1688, to the death of George the Second. Designed as a continuation of Hume. Philadelphia: M'Carty and Davis, 1839. 967 p. GMilvC; MdBJ; MMonsA. 58594

Sneider, M. Reflections at the tomb of J. R. Friedlander. Philadelphia: printed at the Pennslylvania Institution for the Instruction of the Blind, 1839. 4 p. PPPIB. 58595

Snethen, Nicholas, 1769-1845. The Indenterfur of the minister and members of the Methodist Protestant Church. 1st edition. Philadelphia: Book Committee of the Methodist Protestant Church, 1839. 107 p. IEG; MdBMP; NjMD; OSW; TxU. 58596

Snyder, William H. The disease of the moral and religious intellect set forth in a sermon delivered in Castile, January 15, 1839. Perry, New York: Mitchell, 1839. 24 p. OO. 58597

Social amusements, or holidays at Aunt Adela's cottage. Translated with some alterations, from the French "Les jeudis dans le chateau de ma tante." Boston: W. Crosby and Company, 1839. 218 p. CtHT-W; ICBB; MH; MoSpD; OO. 58598

Society for Improving the Condition and Elevating the Character of Industrious Females. To whom it may concern. Philadelphia: 1839. 8 p. PPAmP. 58599

Society of St. Vincent de Paul. Boston. Constitution...instituted in the city of Boston, 1838. Boston: printed by Patrick Donahue, 1839. 21 p. MiD-B. 58600

Society of the New York Hospital. Supplementary and analytical catalogue of the New York Hospital library.... New York: press of Mahlon Day and Company, 1839. 50 p. NNN; NNNAM. 58601

Society of the Pennsylvania Synod for the Propogation of the Gospel. Verhandlungen der Missionsgesellschaft. Easton [Pa.] A. H. Senseman, 1839. MnMNL. 58602

Society of the Sons of St. George, Philadelphia. The original painting of Queen Victoria, painted by Mr. Thomas Sully, expressly for the Society of the Sons of St. George. Philadelphia: 1839. 8 p.

DLC; MB; MiD-B; PPAmP. 58603

Soilcki, Isadore Alfonse. Map showing the connection of the Baltimore and Susquehanna Railroad. With the works of internal improvements of New York, Pennsylvania, Ohio, Virginia and North Carolina. Baltimore: E. Weber and Company [1839?] MdBE. 58604

Somerset County, Maryland. Citizens. Memorial of a committee of the citizens of Somerset County, asking a bounty on the domestic production of silk. Annapolis: William M'Neir, printer, 1839. 7 p. MdBP; MdHi; NUC. 58605

Song...for 2d cent. celebration at Barnstable. Boston [1839] MB. 58606

The songster being a choice collection of new and popular partriotic, comic, sentimental and descriptive songs. Wells River, Vt.: press of Ira White, 1839. 112 p. NTi. 58607

Sophocles, Evangelinus Apostolides, 1807-1883. First lessons in Greek. Hartford: H. Huntington, New York: F. H. Huntington, 1839. 180 p. CtY; KAS; MB; MH; OO. 58608

Sorrow improved. Abstract of a sermon. Cincinnati: 1839. 10 p. N; OCHP. 58609

Soupetard. The dish of frogs; a dramatic sketch. New York: published for the trade, 1839. 28 p. MH. 58610

South Carolina. Attourney General's Office. Report to the legislature of South Carolina upon the resolutions of December 1838, in relation to district officers and their offices. Charleston: W. Riley, 1839. 36 p. ScCC; ScU. 58611

----. Court of Appeals. Chancery cases determined in the Court of Appeals of South Carolina, April term, 1836, and February term, 1837. Charleston: W. Riley, 1839. 300 p. ICU; LNL-L; MdBB; NcD; W. 58612

----. ----. Report of law cases, determined in the Court of Appeals of South Carolina, January term, 1836, To April term, 1836, and February term. 1837. Charleston: W. Riley, 1839. 327 p. ICU; MdB; NNLI; TxDaM-L. 58613

----. ----. Reports of cases at law, argued and determined in the Court of Appeals and Court of

Errors of South Carolina, from December, 1838, to May, 1839, both inclusive. By William Rice, State reporter. Charleston: printed by Burges and James, 1839. v. 1. 535 p. ICU; OClW; ScCC; TxDaM-L; ViU-L. 58614

----. ----. Reports of cases in chancery argued and determined in the Court of Appeals and Court of Errors of South Carolina [1838- 1839] by William Rice. Charleston: Burges, 1839. 435 p. DLC; NcD; NIC-L; OClW. 58615

----. Courts. Reports of judicial decisions in the state of South Carolina, from 1793-1815. By the late Honorable Joseph Brevard, one of the associate judges.... Charleston: W. Riley, 1839- [1840] 3 v. CU; DLC; MdBB; NcD; Sc-SC. 58616

----. General Assembly. Journal of the proceedings of the Senate and House...at its regular session of 1839. Columbia: A. H. Pemberton, 1839. 171 p. Ia; In-SC; Nj; PU-L; T. 58617

----. ----. House. The rules of the House.... Various acts and resolutions containing standing orders of the House and relating to its business. The constitution of the state and the United States with indexes.... Columbia: Pemberton, 1839. 198 p. CtHT-W; M; NcD; NN; ScSp. 58618

----. Governor, 1838-1840 [Patric Noble] Governor's message and miscellaneous documents, 1839 [Charleston: 1839] ICU; MB; TxU. 58619

----. Laws, Statutes, etc. Acts and resolutions of the General Assembly of the state of South Carloina, passed in December, 1838. Columbia: A. H. and W. F. Pemberton, 1839. 168 p. ICU; MdBB; Mi-L; PU-L; Sc. 58620

----. ----. Digest of the laws relating to tax collectors, and the collection of taxes in...South Carolina. Charleston: A. E. Miller, 1839. 26 p. ScCC. 58621

----. ----. Report of the circuit sollcitors in relation to district offices and district police, as special commissioners.... Columbia, S. C.: printed by A. S. Johnston, 1839. 146 p. ScCC; ScU. 58622

----. University. Catalogues. Columbia: 1839-1854. ScC. 58623

South Carolina National Bank. Proceedings of the stockholders of the bank of Charlseton, South Carolina, held at their banking house, July 2, 1839. Charleston: printed by A. E. Miller, 1839. 8 p. NcD; ScC; ScHi. 58624

South Carolina Temperance Advocate Weekly. Columbia, S. C.: 1839- 1847. v. 1- 9. ScNC. 58625

Southern almanac...by Robert Grier. Americus, Georgia: T. P. Ashmore [1839] 58626

Southern banner [Holly Springs?] 1839-1840. MsSM. 58627

The southern primer, or child's first lessons in spelling and reading.... Improved edition.... Charleston: W. R. Babcock [1839] DLC. 58628

Southey, Robert, 1774-1843. The life of Nelson. New York: Harper and Brothers, 1839. 309 p. FTa; MS; ScCliP. 58629

----. The life of William Cowper, esq.... Boston: Otis, Broaders and Company, 1839. 2 v. CoU; GHi; NjMD; ODa; PPL-R. 58630

----. The poetical works of Robert Southey, collected by himself. New York: D. Appleton and Company, 1839. 10 v. in 1. ArL; IEG; MBBC; NcAS; PHi. 58631

A southron, a monthly magazine and review. Tuscaloosa: R. A. Eaton, 1839. 452 p. NcD; PP; TxU. 58632

Southwick, Edward. Life and memoirs, together with his views of religion and politics; written by himself. Geneva: 1839. 36 p. NAuT; NBLIHI. 58633

Southwick, Solomon, 1773-1839. An oration, delivered by appointment of the committee of the corporation, and the several civic and military societies of the city of Albany, at the Methodist Episcopal church, July 4, 1839. Albany: printed by A. Southwick, 1839. 35 p. MiD-B; MWA; NjR; OClWHi; PPL. 58634

Sowers, Eliza. The life of Eliza Sowers... See Chauncey, Henry, defendant.

Spalding, Henry Harmon, 1803-1874. Nez-Perces first book: designed for children and new beginners. Clear Water [Or. Ter.] Mission Press, 1839. 8 p. CSmH; DLC; ICN; MHI. 58635

----. ----. 20 p. CSmH; DLC; ICN; NN; WaU. 58636

Sparks, Jared, 1789-1866. The library of American biography. Conducted by Jared Sparks. New York: Harper and Brothers, 1839- 1948. 25 v. NjN. 58637

----. Life and treason of Benedict Arnold.... Boston: Hilliard, Gray and Company, 1839. 335 p. CSfP; MLow; NbCrD; OClW; PLFM. 58638

----. The life of George Washington.... Boston: F. Andrews, 1839. 562 p. CU; MWiW; PHi; RPB, Vi. 58639

----. Lives of eminent individuals, celebrated in American History.... Boston, Marsh, Capen, Lyon and Webb, 1839, 3 v. DLC; MeB; NhD; PPL; TxDaM. 58640

----. Lives of Sir William Phips, Israel Putnam, Lucretia Maria Davidson and David Rittenhouse. New York: Harper and Brothers, 1839. 398 p. NNC; NNebg; PMA. 58641

Sparrow, Patrick Jones. The duty of the educated young men of this country; an address delivered before the Eumenean and Philanthropic Society of Davidson College, North Carolina, July 31, 1839. Raleigh: Turner, 1839. 32 p. GDecCT; MH; NcU; PPPrHi; WHi. 58642

Spaulding, Ephraim. Reasons for baptising my infant child: A sermon preached at Ludlow, Vt., August 25, 1839. By E. Spaulding, late missionary to the Sandwich Islands. Windsor: printed at the Chronicle Press, 1839. 20 p. MBC; MiD-B; MWA; PPM; RPB. 58643

Specimen books, types, United States. Specimen of modern printing types, cast in the foundry of John T. White [son of Elihu White] New York: 1839. NNC. 58644

Spectator, in minature: being the principal religious, moral, humourous, satirical and critical essays. Exeter: 1839. 2 v. MB; Nh-Hi. 58645

Spencer, E. M. Answer to a letter from F. H. Ellmore, of South Carolina. Augusta, Ga.: Browne, Cushney and McCafferty, 1839. 16 p. MH; NjR. 58646

Spencer, John C. Circular by the Superintendent of Common School...preservation of the libraries.... Albany: printed by Hoffman and White, 1839. NN. 58647

Spenser, Edmund, 1552?-1599. The poetical works of Edmund Spenser. 1st American edition, with introductory observations on the Faerie queene, and notes, by the editor. Boston: C. C. Little and J. Brown, 1839. 5 v. CtMW; KyBC; MBBC; PWW; ViU. 58648

Spiritual mirror, or looking-glass; exhibiting the human heart as being either the temple of God, or habitation of devils; exemplified by ten engravings.... 5th edition. Newburyport: Charles Whipple, 1839. 80 p. CtSoP; IaCrM; RPB. 58649

Spofford's political register and United States farmers almanac.... An astronomical diary for 1839. For the middle states. By Thomas Spofford.... New York· D, Felt and Company [1839] NjR. 58650

Spofford's politcal register and Unite States farmers almanac. An astronomical diary for 1840. The farmers almanac...By Thomas Spofford.... New York [1839] NjR. 58651

Spohr, Louis, 1784-1859. Grand violin school altered and corrected from the last English edition, to correspond with Spohr's original school of violin playing by his pupil U. C. Hill. New York: Firth and Hall [1839?] CtY; MH. 58652

Spooner, Shearjashub, 1809-1859. Guide to sound teeth; or a popular treatise on the teeth.... 2nd edition. New York; Collins, Keese and Company, 1839. 15-207 p. NBMS; PU-D. 58653

Sporle, Nathan James, 1812-1853. In the days when we went gypsying. A song, the melody by N. N. Sporle. The symphonies and accompaniments newly arranged by Joseph Philip Knight. New York: Davis and Horn, 1839. 6 p. MB. 68654

Sprague, Peleg, 1793-1880. The argument of Peleg Sprague, esq. before the committee of the legislature upon the memorial of Harrison G. Otis and others, February 1839. Boston: Whipple and Damrell, 1839. 22 p. CBPac; MeB; MWA; OCLaw; VtU. 58655

----. Remarks...at Faneuil Hall...upon the character and services of General William Henry Harrison, of Ohio.... Boston: Whig Republican

Association of Boston, 1839. 16 p. ICU; MB: MWA; NcD. 58656

----. ----. 20 p. CtSoP; ICN; MWA; NNC; OO. 58657

Sprague, William Buel, 1795-1876. Letters on practical subjects to a daughter. New York: D. Appleton and Company, 1839. 281, 6 p. NIC. 58658

----. Memoir of Mrs. John V. L. Pruyn. Albany: 1839. 29 p. MBC. 58659

----. Memoir of the Rev. Edward D. Griffin...compiled chiefly from his own writings. New York: Taylor and Dodd, 1839. 270 p. Ct; MBC; PPlW; RPB; WHi. 58660

----. Religion and rank. A sermon addressed to the Second Presbyterian Convention in Albany, February 3, 1839.... Albany: printed by Packard, Van Benthuysen and Company, 1839. 33 p. ICU; MB; MHi; NCH; PPA. 58661

----. A sermon delivered December 19, 1838, at the ordination of the Rev. A. Augustus Wood, as pastor of the First Congregational Church, West Springfield. Albany, Packard, 1839. 31 p. MDeeP; MWA; NCH; PHi; RPB. 58662

Spring, Gardiner, 1785-1873. Fragments from the study of a pastor. New York: John S. Taylor, 1839. 160 p. MLow; ScDuE; TChU. 58663

----. Obligations of the world to the Bible; a series of lectures to young men. New York: Taylor, 1839. 404 p. LNH; MH-AH; NCH; OrP; PPPrHi. 58664

Spurzheim, Johann Gaspar, 1776-1832. Philosophical catechism of the natural laws of man. 5th edition improved. Boston: March, Capen, Lyon and Webb, 1839. 171 p. OHi; RPB. 58665

The spy.... Volume 1, Number 8. [Boston] Mechanics Club, printed by Kidder and Wright [1839] 4 p. MWA. 58666

Stanly, Edward, 1810-1872. Speech...in reply to Dr. Duncan, of Ohio; the defender of the administration...in which the anti- slavery letter of Dr. Duncan can be examined. Delivered in the House [Washington: 1839?] 8 p. CtY; DLC; ICN; PHi. 58667

Stanton, Henry B. Circular letter in reqard to the impending election for a representative to congress from the 4th district. Cambridgeport: 1839. 2 p. MHi. 58668

State Bank of Illinois. Letter from the predident and directors.... Springfield: Wm. Walters, 1839. 8 p. MH-BA; NN. 58669

A statement of facts, respecting the division of the Presbyterian Congregation of Rogersville. Jonesborough: L. and F. Gifford, printers, 1839. 30 p. DLC. 58670

A statement of the difficulties in the General Assembly of the Presbyterian Church in their bearing on the southern churches: with an appendix, relating to the Charleston Union Presbytery. Charleston: B. B. Mussey, 1839. 32 p. NjPT; ScC. 58671

Statler, J. P. Certain evidences of a practical religion. Sandy Spring: 1839. MB. 58672

Staunton, William, 1803-1889. Dictionary of the church...an exposition of terms, phrases and subjects connected with the external order, sacraments...of the Protestant Episcopal Church.... New York: Sherman and Trevett, 1839. 473 p. ICMe; KyBC; MnHi; NjP; PPM. 58673

----. ----. 2nd edition. New York: Louis Sherman, 1839. 473 p. CtHT; LNB; MdBD; MoS; OC. 58674

Stearns, William Augustus, 1805-1876. The life and character of Rev. Samuel H. Stearns. Boston: J. A. Stearns, 1839. 252 p. MB; MBC; MiD; MMe; TNV. 58675

----. ----. 2nd edition. Boston: J. A. Stearns, 1839. 252 p. CtHC; MB; MnHi; NNUT; PPA. 58676

Stebbins, Eli M. Boigraphical sketch of Eli M. Stebbins, who died August 11, 1839. Brattleboro: 1839. 16 p. MWA; PHi. 58677

Steele's Albany almanack for 1840. Albany: Packard, Van Benthuysen and Company [1839] MWA. 58678

Steele's western guide book, and emigrant's directory; containing different routes through New York, Ohio, Indiana, Illinois.... With descriptions of climate, soil, productions, prospects, etc. 11th edition., improved and enlarged. Buffalo:

Steele and Peck, 1839. 108 p. ICU; MH; MiD-B; OClWHi; WHi. 58679

Stephen, George, 1794-1879. Adventures of an attorney in search of practice. By the author of the adventures of a gentleman in search of a horse.... Philadelphia: Lea and Blanchard, 1839. LU; PP; ScCh; WM. 58680

[Stephens, John Lloyd] 1805-1852. Incidents of travel in Egypt, Arabia, Petraea, and the Holy Land. By an American... 10th edition with additions. New York: Harper and Brothers, 1839. 2 v. CtHT; KHi; MB; PU; ScDuE. 58681

----. Incidents of travel in Greece, Turkey, Russia and Poland. With a map and engravings.... 7th edition. New York: Harper and Brothers, 1839. 2 v. GA; KyLoP; NcU; RKi; Vi. 58682

Sterne, Laurence, 1713-1768. The works of Laurence Sterne...with a life of the author, written by himself. Philadelphia: Grigg and Elliot, 1839. 416 p. DLC; NFred; OCU; PV; VtPu. 58683

Stevens, Enos, 1816-1877. Rudiments of mental philosophy, and phrenological chart... Lampeter [Pa.] printed by H. Miller, Jr., 1839. 16 p. DLC; ICN; MH; VtU. 58684

Stevens, William Bacon, 1815-1887. An oration delivered before the Union Society of Savannah, Georgia, April 23, 1839. Savannah: T. Purse, 1839. 16 p. MH. 58685

Stewart, Charles Samuel, 1795-1870. A residence in the Sandwich Islands. Including an introduction and notes by Rev. William Ellis, from the last London editon, 5th edition enlarged. Boston: Weeks, Jordan and Company, 1839. 348 p. C-S; ICU; MB; MH-AH; RPA. 58686

Stickney, Robert. An address delivered before the Equitable Union, Union College, July 9, 1839. Schenectady: Isaac Riggs, 1839. 24 p. MNBedf; NN; PPM; WHi. 58687

Stille, Charles Janeway, 1819-1899. The social spirit; a valedictory oration pronounced at the departure of the senior class from the Society of Brothers in Unity, Yale College, June 28, 1839. New Haven: printed by B. L. Hamlen, 1839. 31 p. CtHC; IEG; MBuU; MH; PPL. 58688

Stillson, J. B. An oration delivered at the Pres-

byterian Church in the village of Scottsville, on the morning of July 4, 1839. Rochester: printed by Shepard, Strong and Dawson, 1839. 28 p. NN. 58689

Stirling, Edward, 1807-1894. The little back parlour; a farce in one act.... New York: Samuel French [1839] 18 p. OCl. 58690

Stock, John Shapland, 1804 or 5-1867. A practical treatise on the law of non compotes mentis, or persons of unsound mind. Philadelphia: J. S. Littell, New York: Halstead and Voorhies, 1839. 167 p. CU-Law; In-SC; KyLxT; OO; PP. 58691

Stockton, Joseph, 1779-1832. The western calculator; or a new system of practical arithmetic: containing the elementary principles and rules of calculation in whole, mixed and decimal numbers...In eight parts. Pittsburgh: Johnsotown and Stockton, 1839. 203 p. DLC; ICHi; MiU; OU; PPi. 58692

Stokes, George, 1789-1847. The manners and customs of the Jews, and other nations mentioned in the Bible. Illustrated by 120 engravings. 2nd American stereotype edition. Henry Benton, 1839. MBBC; OCo; VtWood; WGrNM. 58693

Stokes, William, 1804-1878. A treatise on the diagnosis and treatment of diseases of the chest; diseases of the lung and windpipe. Philadelphia: Haswell, Barrington, and Haswell, 1839. 360 p. ArCH; kyU; NNNAM; PPCP; ViNcM. 58694

Stone, Eli. The steam boat clerk. A complete...manual of accounts, for the use of steam boats.... Cincinnati: E. Lucas and Company, 1839. 22 p. DLC; MB; MnHi. 58695

Stone, John Seely, 1795-1882. The bearings of modern commerce on the progress of modern missions: the annual sermon...delivered in Trinity Church, New Haven, June 19, 1839. New York: printed by William Osborn, 1839. 44 p. ICBB; InID; MdBD; NGH; PHi. 58696

Stone, Timothy Dwight Porter, 1811-1887. Stories to teach me to think. By T. Stone, principal of the Abbott Seminary for Female Teachers. Andover, Massachusetts. Boston: Josiah A. Stearns, 1839. 180 p. MAnHi. 58697

Storer, David Humphreys, 1804-1891. Reports on the ichthyology and herpetology of Massachusetts. Boston: 1839. ICF; MBC; MdBP; OCN. 58698

----. Reptiles of Massachusetts. In reports of the fishes, reptiles and birds of Massachusetts.... Boston: 1839. CtHWatk; MDeeP; PPAN. 58699

Stories of voyages. Being authentic narratives of the most celebrated voyages from Columbus to Parry, with accounts of remarkable shipwrecks and naval adventures. Designed to interest the young in the study of geography. Boston: J. A. Noble, 1839. 288 p. CtHWatk; NN; OO; PLFM. 58700

Stories worth reading. Providence: George P. Daniels, 1839. 16 p. NUt; RPB. 58701

Storrs, John, 1801-1854. A sermon delivered in Holliston, February 19, 1839, at the funeral of Mrs. Margarett Dickinson, relict of Rev. Timothy Dickinson. By John Storrs, pastor of the Congregational Church in Holliston, Massachusetts. Boston: printed by Perkins and Nare, 1839. 19 p. CBPSR; MBC; MeBat; MoSpD; RPB. 58702

Story, Joseph, 1779-1845. Commentaries on equity jusrisprudence, as administered in England and America. 2nd edition, revised, corrected and enlarged. Boston: C. C. Little and J. Brown, 1839. 2 v. CU; NCU; PU-L; TU; VtU. 58703

----. Commentaries on the law of agency, as a branch of commercial and maritime jurisprudence, with occasional illustrations and th civil and foreign law. Boston: Little and Brown, 1839. 544 p. IaU-L; NcD; PPB; ViL; WU-L. 58704

----. Selections from the works of Joseph Story. Boston: James Burns, 1839. 219 p. ICU; MB; MBBC; MHi; MiU-C. 58705

Stoughton, J. C. Articles of faith and practice designed for such churches of the Baptist denomination as may solicit and adopt them, to which is added a brief essay on communion. Rochester: Marshall and Welles, 1839. 19 p. OClWHi. 58706

Stow, Baron, 1801-1869. A brief narrative of the Danish mission on the coast of Caromandel. 2nd edition. Boston: New England Sabbath School Union, 1839. 126 p. ViRU; WSheHi. 58707

Stowe, Calvin Ellis, 1802-1886. Common schools and teacher's seminaries. Boston: Marsh, Capen, Lyon and Webb, 1839. 100 p. Ia; MB; MiU; PU; WHi. 58708

----. Report on elementary public instruction in Europe, made to the 36th General Assembly of the state of Ohio, December 19, 1837 [Raleigh: T. J. Lemay, 1839] 68 p. ViW. 58709

Stradling, William. A description of the priority of Chilton- super-polden, and its contents. To Which is added a miscellaneous appendix, containing several ancient documents not before published. Bridgewater: G. Awbrey, etc., etc., 1839. MdBP; MH. 58710

Strain, Alexander. Paul's adieu to the elders of Ephesus: a sermon, preached September 29, 1839. Albany: printed by Alfred Southwick, 1839. 16 p. CSansS; MBC; MPiB; NjR; PPPrHi. 58711

Strange, Robert, 1796-1854. Eoneguski; or the Cherokee chief. A tale of past wars. By an American.... Washington: Frank Taylor, 1839. 2 v. INC; MB; NcAS; TxU; WHi. 58712

[Stratton, Samuel] Report of the Holden slave case, tried at the January term of the Court of Common Pleas, for the County of Worcester, 1839. Worcester: Board of directors of the Holden Anti-slavery Society, 1839. 32 p. MiD-B; MH; OClWHi; PU; RPB. 58713

Stretch, L. M. The beauties of history or examples of the opposite effects of virtue and vice. Drawn from real life for the use of families and schools with questions for examinations of students. Philadelphia: Grigg and Elliot, 1839. MLow; NhPet; OCY. 58714

Streeter, Sebastian, 1763-1867. The new hymn book designed for Universalist Societies. Compiled from approved authors with variations and additions. 23rd edition. Boston: Thomas Whittemore, 1839. 410 p. DLC; MH-AH; WOsh. 58715

----. ----. 24th edition. Boston: Thomas Whittemore, New York: P. Price, Woodstock, Vt.: Haskell and Palmer, 1839. 416 p. 58716

Streeter, Sebastian Ferris, 1810-1864. Prospectus of Mr. and Mrs. S. F. Streeter's Boarding and Day School for Young Ladies [Baltimore] J. Murphy, 1839. 12 p. NcD. 58717

Strickland, Jane. Moral lessons and stories, from the Proverbs of Solomon. New York: John S. Taylor, 1839. 189 p. GHi; ODaU. 58718

Strict Congregational Churches of Long Island. A brief history...from its organization in 1791, to the present time. New York: Piercy and Reed, printers, 1839. 36 p. N; NBHi; NBLiHi. 58719

Stuart, Moses, 1780-1852. What is the appropriate age for entering on the active duties of the Sacred Office? To the Rev. Dr. Cogswell, Secretary of the American Education Society. Andover: April 4, 1839. 15 p. CBPSR; ICJ; MBC. 58720

The student and ladies literary repository. v. 1, no. 10. March 23, 1839. New York: L. Williams and Company, 1839?-. MH. 58721

Sturges, Joseph. An address delivered before the citizens of Becket, Massachusetts, January 18, 1839. Upon the subject of slavery. Lee [Mass.] printed by E. J. Bull, 1839. 24 p. DLC; OOxM. 58722

Sturtevant, Peleg. The Harrisburg directory, and strangers guide; with a sketch of the first settlement of Harrisburg. Harrisburg: printed by the author, 1839. 48 p. DLC; MWA; NN; P. 58723

----. The buck-shot war; or the last kick of anti-masonry. A burlesque medly: poetic, prosaic, humerous, satirical.... Harrisburg: 1839. 32 p. DLC; IaCrM; N; PHi; PPFM. 58724

Stuyvesant, Peter G. Remarks by Peter G. Stuyvesant on the personal habits and character of George Washington when resident in New York. New York: 1839. PPL. 58725

Suddards, William, b. 1805. The British pupit; consisting of discourses by the most eminent divines in England, Scotland, and Ireland: accompanied with pulpit sketches: to which are added, Scriptural illustrations; and selections on the office duties and responsibilities of the Christian ministry. 3rd edition. Philadelphia: Grigg and Elliot, 1839. 2 v. KyLoS; NcD. 58726

----. ----. 4th edition. Philadelphia: Grigg and Elliot, 1839. CtHC; IaMp; IEG; ViRut; VtU. 58727

Sullivan, George, 1771-1838. Popular explanation of the system of circulating medium recently published in the form of an act of congress, shewing the destructive action of the Banks of England upon the welfare of the United States, and the means of self protection against it. New York: Samuel Colman, 1839. 15 p. DLC; ICU; MH; NHi; PHi. 58728

----. System of circulating medium and of safe keeping of the public moneys of the United States. New York: Samuel Colman, 1839. 15 p. DLC; MB; MHi; MWA; NN. 58729

Sullivan, John L. Homoeopathia, the science of specific remedies; the substance of a dissertaion read October 2, 1839. before the New Haven County Medical Society.... New Haven: Babcock and Galpin, printers, 1839. 60 p. CtY; NNNAM. 58730

Sullivan, William, 1774-1839. The political class book; intended to instruct the higher classes in schools in the origin, nature and use of political power. New edition. Boston: Charles J. Hendee and Jenks and Palmer, 1839. 193 p. MB; MeBat; MeHi; NhD. 58731

Summers, Thomas Osmund, 1812-1882. God's love to the people called Methodists: a sermon preached at the celebration of the centenary of Methodism, in friendship, Anne Arundel County, Maryland: 1839 22 p. CBPac; MBNMHi. 58732

Sunbury and Erie Railroad Company. Report of Edward Miller, engineer in chief of the Sunbury and Erie Railroad, to the managers, 1st-2d; 1838-1839. Philadelphia: printed by J. C. Clark, 1839-1840. 2 v. in 1. CSt; IU; MdBS; NBuG; PPAmP. 58733

Sunday readings; or the child's sabbath pleasantly and profitably employed. Prepared for the American Sunday School Union, and revised by the committee of publication. Philadelphia: 1839. 24 p. CtNwchA. 58734

Sunderland, La Roy, 1802-1885. Anti-slavery manual, containing a collection of facts and arguments on American slavery, 3rd edition. New York: printed by S. W. Benedict, 1839. GAU; ICN; KyBC; MB; OCY. 58735

----. The testimony of God agianst slavery. With notes. 3rd edition. New York: American Anti-slavery Society, 1839. 126 p. ICP; MH; NNUT; PU; TxU. 58736

Susan Pike; or a few years of domestic service. A tale by a lady. New York: C. S. Francis, 1839. 66 p. 58737

Susquehanna and Tide Water Canal Company. Annual report of the president and managers submitted to the stockholders...at their annual meeting held at Philadelphiam May 13, 1839. Baltimore: printe by Bull and Tuttle, 1839. 12 p. Md; MdHi; P; MHi; ViU. 58738

Sutcliffe, Joseph, 1762-1856. An introduction to Christianity; designed to preserve young people from irreligion and vice. New York: T. Mason and G. Lane, 1839. 282 p. GAU; NNMHi; OSW. 58739

Sutherland, Joel Barlow, 1791-1861. A congressional manual; or outline of the order of business in the House of Representatives.... Philadelphia: Peter Hay and Company, printers, 1839. 156, 208 p. ICU; MoSpD; NcU; PHi; WGr. 58740

Sutherland, Thomas Jefferson. Loose leaves from the portfolio of a late patriot prisoner in Canada. New York: Sackett and Sargent, 1839. 216 p. CU; NN; NNC; RPB; WHi. 58741

Swain, Benjamin. The North Carolina justice containing a summary statement of statutes and common law of this state. Raleigh: printed by Gales and Son, 1839. 540 p. MeLewB; NcU; NcD; NcWs-H. 58742

Swan, Joseph Rockwell, 1802-1884. A treatise on the laws relating to the powers and duties of justices of the peace and constables in the state of Ohio, with practical forms. 2nd edition, revised and corrected. Columbus: Isaac N. Whiting, 1839. 598 p. CtY; Ia DmD; OAkU; OClW; PU-L. 58743

Swan, William Draper, 1809-1864. Questions adapted to Emerson's North American Arithmetic, part 3d. Boston: G. W. Palmer and Company, 1839. CtWatk; MH. 58744

Swartwout, Samuel, 1783-1856. Reports on the defalcations of.... Washington: 1839. PPL. 58745

Swayze, William. Narrative of William Swayze, minister of the gospel. Written by himself.... Cincinnati: R. F. Thompson, printer, 1839. 216 p. ICU; IEG; MH; OClWHi; TxDaM. 58746

Swedenborg, Emanuel, 1688-1772. Arcana coelestia: the heavenly arcana contained in the Holy Scripture, or word of the Lord unfolded...translated from the latin of Emanuel Swedenborg, thoroughly revised and edited by the Rev. John Faulkner. Boston: Clapp, 1839-1853. 12 v. NB. 58747

----. A brief exposition of the doctrine on the New Church which is meant by the New Jerusalem in the Apocalypse; translated from the Latin of Emanuel Swedenborg.... Boston: Otis Clapp, 1839. 92 p. CtMW; IEG; MH; NjR; OU. 58748

----. Concerning the earths in our solar system which are called planets, and concerning the earths in the starry heavens.... Boston: Clapp, 1839. 113 p. CtHT; MH; MiU; NjP; OO. 58749

----. The doctrines of the New Jerusalem concerning: the Lord, the Sacred Scriptures, the white horse, faith, life also the Heavenly doctrines. Boston: Otis Clapp, 1839. 290 p. MB; MWelC; NPla; OO. 58750

Sweet, Samuel Niles, b. 1805. Practical elocution: containing illustrations of the principles of reading and public speaking. Also a selection of the best pieces from ancient and modern authors.... Rochester, N. Y.: William Alling, 1839. 300 p. DLC; FTaSU; NCH; PPC; TJo. 58751

Sweetser, Benjamin. Comberland collection of church music, being a selection of the best psalm and hymn tunes, anthems, fancy pieces...from European and American authors. Designed for the use of schools and musical societies. Portland: William Hyde, 1839. 304 p. MeHi; NBuG; NNUT; RPB. 58752

Sweigs, Charles D. Ago the...lectures at the athenian institute. February, 1839. Phialdelphia: 1839. 8 p. OCHP. 58753

Swett, Simon. Dr. Swett's genuine vegetable medicine.... Exeter, N. H.: A. R. Brown, printer, 1839. 8 p. NNNAM. 58754

Swift, Mary A. First lessons on natural philosophy for children. Hartford: Belknap and Hammersley, 1839-1845. 2 v. DLC; MH; NN. 58755

----. ----. Part II. 3rd edition. Hartford: Belknap and Hammersley, 1839. MH; MiD-B; NN. 58756

Swift, Elisha Pope, 1792-1865. Semi-contennial

retrospect. A sermon, preached in the First Presbyterian Church, Allegheny, Pa., on December 8, 1839.... Pittsburgh: Alexander Jaynes, 1839. 20 p. DLC; IaHA; NjR; PPi; RPB. 58757

Swords' pocket almanack for 1840. New York: Swords, Stanford and Company [1839] MWA; WHi. 58758

Syme, James, 1799-1870. Case of osteo-sarcoma of the lower jaw; as operated upon Robert Penman... from Coldstream. Philadelphia: printed by T. K. and P. G. Collins, 1839. 12 p. NNNAM. 58759

----. On diseases of the rectum. Philadelphia: Waldie, 1839. 42 p. DLC; MBM; OClW; PU.

58760

Symington, William, 1795-1862. Messiah the prince, or the mediatorial dominion of Jesus Christ. New York: Robert Carter, 1839. 261 p. IaMP; ICP; KyLoP; MPiB; OWoC. 58761

----. On the atonement and intercession of Jesus Christ. 2nd edition. New York: Robert Carter, 1839. 286 p. CtMW; KyLoS; MBC; ScCC; ViRut. 58762

A synoposis of some of the most important facts and discoveries in electro magnetism with opinions of scientific men, showing its applicability as a moving power to machinery. New York: C. J. Folsom, 1839. NN. 58763

T

T. D. James Academy, Philadelphia. The monthly record of lessons and conduct, of the pupils of T. D. James's Academy.... Philadelphia: 1839. 160 p. NjR. 58764

Tacitus, Cornelius. The historical annals of Cornelius Tacitus with supplements. Philadelphia: D. Neall, 1839. 3 v. OCX. 58765

Tackett, I. H. A sermon on the centenary of Methodism, preached on the 25th of October, in Ohio City, by I. H. Tackett.... Ohio City: printed by T. H. Smead, 1839. 31 p. MoS; WHi. 58766

Tailfer, Patrick. A true and historical narrative of the colony of Georgia 1741; transactions of the American Historical Society, by H. Anderson, P. Tailfer and D. Douglas. Washington: 1839. NjMD. 58767

Tales for little girls and boys. Industry, and the lost child. By a lady. Portland: S. H. Colesworthy, 1839. 79 p. MeBa. 58768

Tales of the revolution; being rare and remarkable passages of the history of the war of 1775. New York: Harper and Brothers, 1839. CtMW; ICU; MB; Nh-Hi; ScDuE. 58769

Tallmadge, Nathaniel Pitcher, 1795-1864. Speech...on the finances of the government, delivered at Masonic Hall, March 8, 1839, with the introductory remarks of James Brooks, Esq.; Speech of W. C. Rives, of Virginia, in vindication of the freedom of elections against the interferance of federal executive officers, delivered in the Senate of the United States, February 12, 1839. New York: N. T. Eldridge, 1839. 21 p. NcD; Vi; ViU. 58770

Tanner, Henry Schenck. The American traveller; or guide through the United States. Containing brief notices of the several states, cities, principal towns, canals and railroads, etc.... 4th edition. Philadelphia: the author, 1839. 144 p. InThT; LNStM; MHi; NjP; PHi. 58771

----. ----. 5th edition. Philadelphia: the author, 1839. 144 p. FTaB; MiU; PHi; PPM. 58772

----. Kentucky and Tennessee. Philadelphia: 1839. ViU. 58773

----. Map of North and South Carolina. Philadelphia: 1839. NcU. 58774

----. Map of the canals and railroads of Pennsylvania and New Jersey and the adjoining states. Philadelphia: Tanner, 1839. PHi; PPL; PPLT. 58775

----. A map of the seat of war in Texas, consisting of a general map of Mexico, with a supplementary map of Texas, showing the counties, towns, forts, etc., etc. [New York: H. S. Tanner, 1839?] TxU. 58776

----. New American atlas, containing maps of the several states of the North American Union and of Mexico and of Asia. Philadelphia: 1839. DLC; OCHP. 58777

----. A new map of Louisiana, with its canals, roads and distances from place to place, along the stage and steamboat routes. Philadelphia: Carey and Hart, 1839. LU; NcU; PHi. 58778

----. A new universal atlas containing maps of the various empires, kingdoms, states and republics of the world. With a special map of each of the United States, plans of cities, etc. Comprehended in 70 sheets and forming a series of 117 maps, plans and sections.... Philadelphia: the author, 1839. 68 p. IHi; InU; NRU; PHi. 58779

----. United States of America. Philadelphia: 1839. DLC; IU. 58780

Tappan, Henry Philip, 1805-1881. A review of Edward's "inquiry into the freedom of the will."... New York: J. S. Taylor, 1839. 300 p. InGrD; KyBC; NbOM; OU; PPA. 58781

Tappan, Lewis, 1788-1873. The African captives. Trial of the prisoners of the Amistad on the writ of Habeas Corpus, before the Circuit Court of the United States, for the District of Connecticut, at Hartford, Judges Thompson and Judson. Sept. term, 1839. New York: 1839. 47 p. NIC. 58782

----. Proceedings of the session of Broadway Tabernacle, against Lewis Tappan, with the action of the Presbytery and General Assembly. New York: 1839. 64 p. CtSoP; MH; NIC; OO; PPrHi. 58783

Tarascon [Louis Anastasius] b. 1759. Raisonie ou Douce Demeure, Sweet Home de la Raison: etablissement le permier de son genre a etre forme sur un beau champ agricole a portee aisce des grandes villes Philadelphie et New York.... New York: imprimerie de J. F. Curcy, 1839. 42 p. CtY; DLC; NN. 58784

Tarbell, John P. An oration delivered before the Democratic citizens of the north part of Middlesex county at Groton, July 4th, 1839. Lowell: A. Watson, 1839. 33 p. CSmH; ICU; MB; NjR; PHi. 58785

Taylor, A. D. An honest exposure of the honest manner in which certain honest officials conduct the public business in the British Colonies. Burlington, Vt.: 1839. 28 p. NN. 58786

Taylor, Benjamin Cook, 1801-1881. The school of the prophets. A sermon...by the Rev. Benjamin C. Taylor.... New York: Robert Carter, 1839. 38 p. ICN; MBAt; MWA; NjR; PPPrHi. 58787

Taylor, C. B. Allgemeine Geschichte der Vereinigten Staaten von Amerika. Enthaltend den ganzen Zeitraum seit den ersetn Entdeckungen bis zu der jetzigen Zeit. Mit einer Beschreibung der westlichen Staaten, ihres Bodens, ihrer Ansiedlungen, Zunahme an Bevolkerung. In drei Theilen. Von C. B. Taylor. Aus dem Englishen ubersetzt von Wilhelm Beschke. New York: Erza Strong, 1839. 612 p. MdBSHC; MoSHi; PPL-R. 58788

----. A universal history of the United States of America, embracing the whole period, from the earliest discoveries, down to the present time. Giving a description of the western country, its soil, settlements, increase of population, etc. In three parts. New York: Ezra Strong, 1839. 606 p. MoFayC; NN; OFH; TNP. 58789

Taylor, Emily, 1795-1872. Sabbath recreations; or select poetry of a religious kind, chiefly taken from the works of modern poets; with original pieces never before published. By Miss Emily Taylor. 1st American revised edition, in which many pieces have been withdrawn from the English and others substituted. Boston: Otis, Broaders and Company, 1839. 288 p. IEG; KyBC; MH; MWA; NhPet. 58790

Taylor, F. A sketch of the military bounty tract of Illinois: descriptive of its unequalled fertility of soil, superior inducements for an emigrant's location, agricultural productions, climate, facilities of education, travelling route and expenses and suggestions to emigrants. Philadelphia: printed by I. Ashmead and Company, 1839. 12 p. DLC; ICJ; MBAt; OFH; PPM. 58791

Taylor, George, agent of the British college of health. An enquiry into the origin of disease, and an attempt to establish certainty in medicine, by an interpretation of nature. New York: published for the author [1839] 48 p. DLC. 58792

Taylor, Jane, 1783-1824. Physiology for children. New York: American Common School Society, 1839. 91 p. CtHWatk; MB; MNF. 58793

----. Original poems for infant minds.... Boston: Munroe and Francis, 1839. 208 p. NjN. 58794

----. The pleasures of taste, and other stories; selected from the writing of Miss Jane Taylor: with a sketch of her life, by Mrs. Sarah J. Hale.... Boston: Marsh, Capen, Lyon and Webb, 1839. 388 p. DLC; MB; MWA; PU; WHi. 58795

----. Primary lessons in physiology for children. New York: George F. Cooledge and Brothers, 1839. 130 p. LStBA; MH; MNf. 58796

----. Rhymes for the nursery. By the authors of "original poems." New York: James Egbert, printer, 1839. 114 p. RPB. 58797

Taylor, J[oash] Rice. Ode, written for the celebration of the national anniversary, at Kenyon College, July 4, 1839.... Gambier: G. W. Myers [1839] 8 p. NN. 58798

Taylor, John. The pocket lacon; comprising nearly 1,000 extracts from the best authors, selected by John Taylor. Philadelphia: Griggs and Company, 1839. 2 v. GDecCT; LNH; MH; PPL;

TNP. 58799

Taylor, John, 1808-1887. A short account of the murders, robberies, burnings, thefts and other outrages committed by the mob and milita of the state of Missouri.... [Springfield? Ill: 1839] 8 p. CSmH; NN. 58800

Taylor, John Orville, 1807-1890. The farmers' school book. Prepared and written by Prof. J. Orville Taylor, author of the "district school," and editor of the "common school assistant." Ithaca: Mack, Andrus and Woodruff, 1839. 236 p. NIDHi; NNU-W. 58801

----. Satirical hits on the people's education. New York: American Common School Union, 1839. 98 p. CSt; CtMW: MH; NcU. 58802

Taylor, Oliver Alden, 1801-1851. Brief views of the Saviour, with reflections on his doctrines, parables, etc., designed chiefly for the young. Andover: Gould, Newman and Saxton, etc., 1839. 264 p. PPM. 58803

Taylor, Richard B. The postillion waltz, arranged by R. B. Taylor. Providence: 1839. 3 p. MB; RHi. 58804

----. The second fairy dance, composed.... Providence: 1839. 2 p. F. RHi. 58805

Taylor, Richard Cowling, 1789-1851. Extracts from R. C. Taylor's report, on the surveys undertaken with a view to the establishment of a railroad from the coal and iron mines near Blossburg, or Peter's Camp, Pennsylvania, to the termination of the west branch of the Chemung Canal, at Corning, Steuben County, New York; a mineralogical report on the coal region in the environs of Blossburg. Albany: 1839. 16 p. NN; PPL; WHi. 58806

Taylor, William. Remarks, on the resolution of New York, on the resolution to appoint a committee to investigate the Swartwout defalcation. Washington: 1839. 7 p. DLC. 58807

Taylor, William Cooke, 1800-1849. History of Ireland, from the Anglo-Norman invasion till the union of the country with Great Britain. By W. C. Taylor. With additions by William Sampson. New York: Harper and Brothers, 1839. 2 v. IEG; LNh; Me; MnHi; TxGR. 58808

The teacher's gift. Portland: 1839. 16 p. MB. 58809

Teacher's Seminary and Classical Institution, Plymouth, New Hampshire. Circular. n.p. [1839?] MH. 58810

Tefft, Benjamin Franklin, 1813-1885. True greatness as illustrated by the character of Wesley, being a discourse, delivered before the Methodist society and citizens of Bangor, on the evening of the 15th of October, 1839, on occasion of the celebration of the centenary of Methodism. By Rev. Benjamin F. Tefft.... Published by request. Bangor: printed by S. S. Smith, 1839. 24 p. CtMW; MnHi; RPB. 58811

The temperance almanac for the year 1840.... Boston: Whipple and Damrell [1839] [32] p. MNS; MWA; NjR; WHi. 58812

----. Calculations by G. R. Perkins. 2nd edition. Albany, N.Y.: Packard and Van Benthuysen and Company [1839] MWA; NN. 58813

Temperance convention, Pittsburgh, 1839. Proceedings of the Temperance convention, which met in Philo Hall, Pittsburgh, Nov. 6, 1839. Pittsburgh: Alexander Jaynes, 1839. 18, 48, 16 p. CSmH; MnSM. 58814

Ten Eyck, Anthony. Report...on the claims of creditors for debts and depredations committed by the Saginaw tribe.... Detroit: Bagg, 1839. 101 p. CtHT-W. 58815

Tennessee. Comptroller of the Treasury. Report of the Comptroller of the Treasury of the state of Tennessee, October 9th, 1839. Nashville: J. M. Smith, printer to the Senate, 1839. 8 [1] p. T. 58816

----. Dept. of Public Instruction. Report of the superintendent of Public Instruction, to the General Assembly of Tennessese, October 8, 1839. Nashville: J. George Harris, printer to the Senate, 1839. 88 p. T. 58817

----. General Assembly. Preamble and resolutions adopted by the legislature of the state of Tennessee, November 14, 1839, and the reply and resignation of Ephraim H. Foster, a Senator from said state in the Congress of the United States; delivered November 15, 1839. Nashville, Tenn.: printed by B. R. M'Kennis, Whig and Steam Press, 1839. 36 p. NcD; NHi; NNC; TNV; TxU. 58818

----. ----. House of Representatives. Journal of the House of Representatives of the state of Tennessee, at the 23rd General Assembly, held at Nashville. Lawson Gifford, printer to the state. Knoxville: printed at the Argus and Herald office, by Gifford and Eastman, 1839. 844 p. NN; T; TMeC; TU; WHi. 58819

----. ----. Joint Select Committee on Common School Monies. Report...Nashville: J. George Harris, public printer, 1839. 15, 19-22 p. DE; DHEW; DLC; T; TNP. 58820

----. ----. Senate. Rules and orders for conducting business in the Senate of the General Assembly of the state of Tennessee. Being the 1st session of the 25th General Assembly of said state. Nasvhille: J. M. Smith, printer, 1839. 11 p. T. 58821

----. Governor, 1839 1841 [James K. Polk] Governor Polk's inaugural address, delivered at Nashville on the 14th of October, 1839, in presence of two houses of the General Assembly and a large concourse of his fellow citizens.... [Nashville: 1839] Broadside. T. 58822

----. ----. Message of Governor Polk to the two houses of the legislature of Tennessee, on the 22nd of October, 1839 [Nashville: Union office, 1839?] 16 p. MiU-C; T; THi. 58823

----. ----. Message, with accompanying statements of the South Western Railroad Bank, Charleston, S.C., and its branch at Knoxville. Nashville: J. George Harris, public printer, 1839. 8 p. T. 58824

----. Laws, Statutes, etc. An act to establish a system of common schools, in the state of Tennessee, passed, January 24th, 1838, with an appendix, containing a synopsis of the duties of constables, commissioners, county court clerks and county trustees under the school act, forms of reports.... Nashville: B. R. M'Kennie, 1839. 28 p. ICP; MB; MdHi; T; WHi. 58825

Terentius Afer, Publius. Pub Terentii Afri Andria Adelphique, Ex Editione Westerhoviana. Accidunt notae Anglicae. Cura C. K. Dillaway, A.M. Bostoniae: Perkins ey Marvin, Philadelphiae: H. Perkins, 1839. 186 p. ICU; MeB; OkU; RPB; ScCC. 58826

Terry, Daniel. Guy Mannering, or the gipsy's prophecy; a musical play, in three acts. Baltimore:

J. Robinson, 1839. MH; MWA. 58827

Texas [Provisional Government] Journal of the proceedings of the General Council of the Republic of Texas, held at San Felipe de Austin, November 14th, 1835 [-March 11th, 1836] Houston: National Intelligencer office, 1839. 363 p. DLC; IU; NN; Tx; TxDaN. 58828

----. Army. Report of the Major General Sam Houston, to his Excellency, Henry Smith, Governor, January 30th, 1836. Houston [Telegraph Power press, 1839] 13 p. TxU. 58829

Texas [Republic] Rules and articles for the government of the armies of the Republic of Texas. Houston: 1839. 20 p. CU; DLC. 58830

----. Adjutant General's Office. Report. November, 1839. Austin [Whiting's, printer] 1839. 3 p. TxU; TxWFM. 58831

----. Army. Uniform of the Army of the Republic of Texas prescribed and published by order of the president. Houston: S. Whiting, 1839. 12 p. CtY; TxU. 58832

----. Congress. House of Representatives. Committee on Foreign Relations. By order of House of Representatives [Austin: Whiting's press, 1839] 4-45 p. DLC. 58833

----. ----. ----. Committee on Public Lands. Report of the committee on public lands [Austin: Austin City Gazette, printer, 1839] 7 p. TxU. 58834

----. ----. ----. Committee on the state of the Republic. Report. Austin: Austin Gazette, printer [1839] 4 p. TxU; TxWFM. 58835

----. ----. Senate. Journal of the Senate, of the Republic of Texas: 1st session of the 3rd Congress...1838. By order of the secretary of state, Houston: National Intelligencer office [S. Whiting, printer] 1839. 132 p. DLC; NN; TxU. 58836

----. ----. ----. Reprimand delivered by the president of the Senate, to Hon. Robert Wilson. By order of the Senate. January 13, 1839. Houston: Telegraph Power Press, 1839. 8 p. MH; TxWFM. 58837

----. ----. ----. Rules for conducting business in the Senate [3rd Congress 1838-39. Houston?: 1839] 8 p. Tx; TxU. 58838

----. ----. ----. Committee on finance. Report [Austin: Whiting's press, 1839?] 4 p. TxU. 58839

----. ----. ----. Committee on Public Lands. Report of the committee on public lands on land bill. Printed by order of the Senate [Hosuton: Whiting's press, 1839] 7 p. DLC. 58840

----. ----. ----. Special Committee on Tariff. Report of the special committee to whom was referred that portion of the president's message relating to the tariff. Houston: 1839. 14 p. CtY; DLC; RPB; TxU. 58841

----. Laws, Statutes, etc. Alphabetical index to the laws of Texas arranged by a member of the bar [Houston?] 1839. CtY; DLC; Ia; MH-L; TxU. 58842

----. ----. Laws of the Republic of Texas, passed at the 1st session of the 3rd Congress. In one volume. Houston: Telegraph Power Press, 1839 [2] 145 p. CSmH; CU-Law; MdBB; Tx; TxU; TxU-L. 58843

----. Post Office Department. Report of the post office master general of the condition of his department, October, 1839 [Austin: Austin City gazette, 1839] Broadside. CtY; Tx. 58844

----. President, 1838-1841 [Mirabeau B. Lamar] Letter...to Bowles and others [Houston] Whiting's printer, [1839?] 7 p. CtY; RPB; TxGR; TxH. 58845

----. ----. Proclamation, by the pressdient of the Republic of Texas.... Houston: 1839. CU-BANC; Tx. 58846

----. Secretary of Navy. Annual report of the secretary of the navy. November, 1839. Printed by order of Congress [Austin: Whiting's, printer, . 1839] 56 p. DLC; PHi; RPB; TxU; TxWFM. 58847

----. Secretary of the Treasury Department. Special report of the secretary of the treasury. November, 1839. Printed by order of Congress [Austin: Whiting's, printer] 12 p. DLC; PHi; RPB; TxU; TxWFM. 58848

----. War Department. Annual report, November, 1839 [Houston] Whiting's, printer, 1839. 52 p. ICN; NcD; RPB; TxU. 58849

----. ----. Government of the army of the Republic of Texas. Printed in accordance with a joint resolution of Congress, approved January 23rd, 1838, by order of the Secretary of War. Houston: Intelligencer office, 1839. 187 p. CtY; DNW; ICN; TxGR; TxH. 58850

Texas San Saba Company.... Constitution, May 9th, 1839. Houston: Telegraph Power press, 1839. 13 p. CtY; CU; MH; TxU. 58851

Thatcher, Benjamin Bussey, 1809-1840. Indian biography: or an historical account of those individuals who have been distinguished among the North American natives as orators, warriors, statesmen and other remarkable characters. New York: Harper and Brothers, 1839. 2 v. GNM; Me; MU; OWoC; WaS. 58852

----. Indian traits: being sketches of the manners, customs and character of the North American natives.... New York: Harper and Brothers, 1839. 2 v. DLC; MBAt; NUT; OClWHi; ScDuE. 58853

Third book of history being a compendium of Jewish history.... By a student of history.... New York: Carlton and Porter, Sunday School Union [1839] 158 p. DLC; KHi; KU; NN; TNT. 58854

Thomas, Abel Charles, 1807-1880. Hymns of Zion, with appropriate music designed as an aid to devotion in families, social circles and meetings for public worship. By an evangelist. Philadelphia: Thomas, Cowperthwait and Company, 1839. 216 p. CtY; IGK; MB; NNUT; PPPrHi. 58855

Thomas, R. Interesting and authentic narratives of the most remarkable shipwrecks, fires, famines, calamities, providential deliverances and lamentable disasters on the seas, in most parts of the world.... Hartford: E. Strong, 1839. 324 p. DLC; MWA; OCl; OrPD; TMeC. 58856

Thomas, Seth James. An address delivered before the Democratic citizens of Plymouth County, Massachusetts, at East Abington, July 4, 1839. By Seth J. Thomas. Boston: printed by Beals and Greene, 1839. 52 p. ICN; MB; MWA; PHi; RBB. 58857

Thomason, D. R. The church the bride of Christ: a sermon, in which the claims of episcopacy to the title of the only true church, are examined. Delivered at Randolph, Tenn., on Lord's Day, May 5, 1839, by Rev. D. R. Thomason. Published by request [Randolph?] McPherson and Rankin, printers, 1839. 21 p. MnHi; TSewU. 58858

----. The examiner examined: a review of a sermon, published at Randolph and purporting to be an examination of the claims of episcopacy. Memphis, Tenn.: printed at the Western World office, 1839. 30 p. CSmH; TSewU. 58859

Thomaston Theological Institution, Maine. Catalogue of the officers and students of the Thomaston Theological Institution, 1838-9. Thomaston: H. P. Coombs, 1839 [8] p. CBPSR; MeBa; MH. 58860

Thome, James Armstrong, d. 1873. Emancipation in the West Indies. A six months tour in Antigua, Barbados and Jamaica, in the year 1837. By James A. Thome, and J. Horace Kimball. 2nd edition. New York: The American Anti-slavery Society, 1839 [21]-412 p. DLC; FMU; MdBP; NCH; OO. 58861

Thompson, Benjamin Franklin, 1784-1849. History of Long Island; containing an account of the discovery and settlement; with other important and interesting matters to the present time. By Benjamin F. Thompson. New York: E. French, 1839. 536 p. FOA; IaHi; NhD; PU; VtU. 58862

Thompson, Daniel Pierce, 1795-1868. The green mountain boys. By Judge D. P. Thompson.... Boston: Lothrop, Lee and Shepard Company [1839] [6] 366 p. COroB; KyRE; MH; PU; WaU. 58863

----. The green mountain boys, a historical tale of the early settlement of Vermont.... 1st edition. By Carlos B. Buel, Montpelier: W. P. Walton and Sons, 1839. 2 v. CtMW; MB; MWA; NjP; VtHi. 58864

Thompson, Henry. Oration...on the 2nd of March, 1839. Anniversary of the independence of Texas. Houston: National Intelligencer office, 1839. 12 p. TxWFM. 58865

----. Texas. Sketches of character; moral and political conditions of the republic; the judiciary, etc. By Milam [pseud.]... Philadelphia: Brown, Bicking and Guilbert, printers, 1839. 95 p. CU-B; DLC; Phi; TxU; TxWB. 58866

Thompson, Loyal B. Arithmetical demonstration, or an authenticated system of practical arithmetic, wherein the several rules of that useful science are illustrated by a variety of examples alternately proving each other, and adapted to the currency of the United States. Compiled by Loyal

B. Thompson. Knoxville, Tenn.: printed by Ramsey and Craighead, 1839. 226 p. MoS. 58867

Thompson, Oliver Dana. Trial for murder. A report of the trial of Oliver Dana Thompson, for the murder of his wife, in Cornwall, Vt., February 16, 1837. Before the Addison Co. Court, June term, 1838. Middlebury, Vt.: office of the Green Mountain, 1839. 24 p. VtHi; VtMidSM; VtMiM. 58868

Thompson, P. Quiot Club Carols, or Noctes Gymnasii. Published by order of the Washington Social Gymnasium. Washington: 1839. 39 p. MWA. 58869

Thompson, Sally. Trial and defence of Mrs. Sally Thompson, on complaint of insubordination to the rules of the Methodist Episcopal Church. Lowell: B. F. Hildreth, 1839. 24 p. Nh-Hi; NHi. 58870

Thompson, Samuel. Trial for libel against Paine D. Badger. Boston: printed by Henry P. Lewis, 1839. 52 p. Ia; MH-L; NPV. 58871

Thompson, Waddy, 1798-1868. Remarks of the Hon. Waddy Thompson, on the proposition to recognise the Republic of Hayti; on the motion to print certain documents relating to defalcations; and on certain appropriations for navy yards. Delivered in the House of Representatives, Dec. 22 and 28, 1838, and Jan. 10, 1839. Washington: printed by Gales and Seaton, 1839. 11 p. A-Ar; DLC. 58872

----. Speech of Waddy Thompson, of South Carolina, in the House of Representatives of the United States, being in committee of the whole on the state of the Union. Delivered February 5, 1839. Washington: printed at the Madisonian office, 1839. 14 p. A-Ar; ICU; MdHi; MWA; NcD. 58873

Thompson, William. Memoirs of the Rev. Samuel Munson, and the Rev. Henry Lyman, late missionaries to the Indian Archipelago, with the journal of their exploring tour. New York: D. Appleton and Company, 1839. 196 p. CtB; CtHC; GAGTh; NNMr; PPl; WHi. 58874

Thompson, Connecticut. Congregational Church. Catalogue of books belonging to the First Congregational Sabbath School Library, in Thompson, March 9, 1839.... Providence: H. H. Brown [1839] 12 p. Ct. 58875

Thompson's Island, Boston. Farm and Trade School. Statement, acts, by-laws and rules and regulations. Boston: Isaac R. Butts, [1839] 32 p. MB; MH; MiD-B. 58876

Thomson, Edward. An oration delivered at the court house in Norwalk, July 4th, 1839, at the celebration of the 63rd anniversary of American independence. By E. Thomson, principal of the Norwalk seminary. Norwalk, Ohio: S. and C. A. Preston, printers, 1839. 14 p. NNMHi; OClWHi. 58877

Thomson, J. Edgar. Map of the Georgia Railroad and the several lines connecting with it. Philadelphia: 1839. MBAt. 58878

Thomson, James, 1700-1748. The seasons. By James Thomson. A new edition. Boston: Weeks, Jordan and Company, 1839. 154 p. CtY; NLan. 58879

----. ----. To which is prefixed the life of the author, by P. Murdoch.... New York: Robinson and Franklin, 1839. 190 p. IEG; MLaw; NRU; OHi; WaSp. 58880

Thomson, Samuel, 1769-1843. The law of libel. Report of the trial of Dr. Samuel Thomson, the founder of the Thomsonian practice, for an alleged libel in warning the public against the impositions of Paine D. Badger.... Municipal Court of Boston, April term, 1839. Boston: printed by Henry P. Lewis, 1839. 52 p. DLC; MoU; MWA; NHi; WaU-L. 58881

The Thomsonian almanac for 1839. The 3rd after bissextile, or leap year; containing, in addition to the almanac, fact, philosophy and science, as delivered in the writings and sayings of medical men and others.... Poughkeepsie, N.Y.: office of the Thomsonian, 1839. 36 p. NUtHi. 58882

Thomsonian almanac for 1840. Boston: Dr. Samuel Thomson [1839] MB; MWA; NbHM. 58883

[Thorn, John Van Epe] d. 1854. A review of facts relative to the late ecclesiastical proceedings in a presentment...in the diocese of Delaware [Philadelphia? 1839?] 20 p. DLC; MHi. 58884

Thornton, Henry. Family prayers; to which is added, a family commentary upon the Sermon on the Mount, by the late Henry Thornton.... 5th American edition. Edited by the Rev. Mauton Eastburn.... New York: Swords, Stanford and Company, 1839. 168, 160 p. LU; MB. 58885

Thucydides. History of the Peloponnesian war, translated from the Greek of Thucydides, by William Smith, A.M.... A new edition, corrected and revised in two volumes. New York: Harper and Brothers, 1839. 2 v. C; ICU; MoSU; OCX; PMy. 58886

Ticknor, Caleb Bingham, 1804-1840. A guide for mothers and nurses in the management of young children. New York: Taylor and Dodd, 1839. 244 p. DLC; FTa; IaGG; OClM; TJaU. 58887

----. The philosophy of living; or the way to enjoy life and its comforts.... New York: Harper and Brothers, 1839. 36 p. FTa; MPeaI; NBMS; PSal; TxGR. 58888

----. A popular treatise on medical philosophy, or an exposition on quackery and imposture in medicine. Read before the Phi Beta Kappa Society of Union College, at its anniversary meeting and, in conformity with a resolution published as a part of its transactions. 2nd edition. New York: Gould and Newman, 1839. 283 p. CtY-M. 58889

Tidyman, Philip. On the abuse of the pardoning power. By P. Tidyman and Samuel R. Wood. Philadelphia: John C. Clark, 1839. 13 p. MdHi; PHi; PPAmP. 58890

Tieck, Johann Ludwig, 1773-1853. Pietro von Abano; oder, Petrus Apone: zaubergeschichte. New York: Radde, 1839. 70 p. CtMW: MH; NN; TNJU. 58891

----. Das zauberschloss novelle vonLudwig Tieck. New York: Verlag der Buchhandlung von W. Radde, 1839. 84 p. CtMW; MH; NN; PU; TNJU. 58892

Timbs, John, 1801-1875. Laconics; or the best words of the best authors. Philadelphia: Carey, 1839. 3 v. PP. 58893

Tippecanoe Club. Pennsylvania. Constitution and by-laws of the Tippecanoe Club, No. 1, of the state of Pennsylvania. n.p.: 1839. 8 p. PHi. 58894

Tired soldier; or mustered in and out of service. Dedicated to the volunteer troops at Harrisburg,

December, 1838.... Philadelphia: printed for the publisher, 1839. 12 p. DLC; PHi. 58895

To a resolution of the committee of arrangements, and of the common council, of the city of Albany. Albany: printed by Alfred Southwick, 1839. 800 p. CtY; DLC; MBAt; MWA; NHi. 58896

To the cotton planters, merchants, factors and presidents and directors of the several banks of the southern states. Circular [New York: 1839?] 16 p. GEU. 58897

To the voters of the 10th Congressional district [n.p.: 1839?] Broadside. NcU. 58898

Tobey, William. Address delivered before the Honesdale Colonization Society...1839. Honesdale, Pa.: Kingsbury, 1839. PPPrHi. 58899

Tocqueville, Alexis Charles Henri Maurice Clerel de, 1805-1859. Democracy in America. By Alexis de Tocqueville...Translated by Henry Reeve, esq. With an original preface and notes by John C. Spencer.... 3rd American edition, revised and corrected. New York: G. Adlard, 1839. 2 v. OO; PV; RPA; Tx; ViU. 58900

Todd, Charles Stewart, 1791-1871. Annual address before the Kentucky State Agricultural Society, delivered at the capitol in Frankfort, January 14, 1839, on the dignity of the profession of agriculture, and the propriety of legislation for its improvement, by Col. C. S. Todd, of Shelby, vice-president of the 8th district. Frankfort, Ky.: printed by F. D. Pettit, at the Franklin Farmer office, 1839. 15 p. DLC; DSG; KyDC; MWA; PPL. 58901

Todd, Isaac. The Scripture mode of baptism.... The divine authority of affusion and sprinkling. By the Rev. Isaac Todd.... New York: R. Carter, 1839. 67 p. NjR; NRAB; NRCR. 58902

Todd, John, 1800-1873. Index rerum; or index of subjects, intended as a manual to aid the student and the professional man in preparing himself for usefulness.... 4th edition. Northampton: Butler, 1839. 272 p. NjP; NNC. 58903

----. The student's manual; designed by specific directions to aid in forming and strengthening the intellectual and moral character and habits of the student. By Rev. John Todd.... 9th edition. Northampton: J. H. Butler, 1839. 392 p. IaGG; KyU;

MH; NjR; ViU. 58904

----. Truth made simple: being the first volume of a system of theology for children. Character of God. By Rev. John Todd, pastor of the First Congregational Church of Philadelphia.... Northampton: J. H. Butler, 1839. 18-424 p. CoCs; DLC; KyLoP; PP; VtVe. 58905

----. ----. 2nd edition. Northampton: J. H. Butler, 1839. 424 p. ICBB; LNB; MPiB; PCA. 58906

Togno, Joseph. An account of a solar and gas speculum and of an obstinate disease of the ear successfully treated. Philadelphia: Haswell, 1839. 12 p. PPAmP. 58907

The token and Atlantic souvenir; a Christmas and New Year's present. Edited by S. G. Goodrich. Boston: Otis, Broaders and Company, 1839. 294 p. KU; MWHi; NjP; ScUn; ViU. 58908

The token: or affections gift, a Christmas and New Year's present. Edited by S. G. Goodrich. New York: A and C. B. Edwards, 1839? 312 p. IU; MoSW. 58909

Tom Thumb. Philadelphia: sold by William N. Stevens, 1839. 8 p. MH. 58910

Tomlinson, J. S. An address on the duties, difficulties and rewards of educated young men; delivered before the Chamberlain and Deinologian Societies of Centre College, September 26, 1839. Frankfort, Ky.: A. G. Hodges, 1839. 23 p. KyLx; MH. 58911

Torrey, Henry Warren, 1814-1893. An English Latin lexicon, prepared to accompany Leveretts' Latin-English lexicon. Boston: J. H. Wilkins and R. B. Carter, and Charles C. Little and Company, 1839. 318 p. CoDR; ICP; MWelC; NbCrD. 58912

Torrey, Jesse, fl. 1787-1834. The moral instructor and guide to virtue being a compendium of moral philosophy in eight parts.... 25th edition. Philadelphia: John Grigg, 1839. OWoC. 58913

----. A pleasing companion for little girls and boys. Blending instruction with amusement. Philadlephia: Grigg, 1839. InNea. 58914

Town, Ithiel, 1784-1844. A description of Ithiel Town's improvement in the principle construction and practical execution of bridges, for roads, railroads and aqueducts. Also critical remarks on other modes of construction with practical and scientific remarks on the strength, etc., of materials, etc. New York: published by the author, 1839. 16 p. CtY; MB; MH; NN; PPAmP. 58915

Town, Salem. Town's spelling and defining book being an introduction to Town's analysis. New York: American Common School Society, 1839? 160 p. NRU; OrU. 58916

----. ----. Rochester: Fisher and Company [1839?] 167 p. NR; NRHi. 58917

----. ----. 83rd edition. Critically revised and corrected. New York: American Common School Society, 1839. 160 p. CtSoP; DLC; ICBB; OO; WMMD. 58918

Town and country almanac. New York: Turner and Fisher, 1839. MWA. 58919

Towndraw, Thomas, 1810-1898. Complete series of ornamental copies, comprising elegent specimens of German text, old English, Italian Church text marking letters, etc., etc. Salem: Ives and Jewett, 1839 [16] p. MiD-B; NhD. 58920

----. Guide to caligraphy; being a new and complete series of fine-hand copies. Part (IV). Salem: Ives and Jewett, etc., etc., etc., 1839. NNC. 58921

----. ----. Part I. Salem: Ives and Jewett, 1839. NN. 58922

----. New and complete system of penmanship.... Salem: Ives and Jewett, 1839. CtHWatk; NN. 58923

----. New and improved writing books, to be used in connection with his "guide to caligraphy." Part I-[IV] Salem: J. P. Jewett, etc., etc., 1839. NNC. 58924

----. New series of easy lessons in chirography.... Salem: Ives and Jewett, etc., etc., 1839. MH. 58925

Townsend, John Kirk, 1809-1851. Narrative of a journey across the Rocky Mountains, to the Columbia River, and a visit to the Sandwich Islands, Chile.... Philadelphia: H. Perkins, Boston: Perkins and Marvin, 1839. 352 p. CoD; LNH; MnHi; PPA; WaU. 58926

----. Ornithology of the United States of America; or, descriptions of the birds inhabiting the states and territories of the Union, with an accurate figure of each, drawn and coloured from nature. Philadelphia: 1839. 12 p. MH-A; NHi; PHi; PPAN. 58927

Townsend, Robert. An inquiry into the cause of social evil; with its remedy. An inaugural address, delivered July 8, 1839. New York: published by the society, 1839. ICJ; NHi; NNUT. 58928

Townsend, Thompson. The bell ringer of St. Paul's; or the huntsman and the spy; a melodrama, in three acts. London and New York: Samuel French [1839] 30 p. OCl. 58929

Townsend, William W. Dairyman's manual containing some of the most important processes from the best sources for making butter and cheese; with an essay on mechanical powers, as applied to domestic uses. Illustrated with wood engravings. Vergennes, Vt.: Rufus W. Griswold, 1839. ICU; NNC; VtVe. 58930

Tracts for the times. By members of the University of Oxford. Vol. I. New York: Louis Sherman, Protestant Episcopal Press, 1839. 611 p. CtHt; InID; MH-AH; MdBS; PPLT; VtU. 58931

----. 2nd edition. New York: Richard C. Valentine, 1839-1840. GDecCT; ICP; NNG; RBr; TChU; WM. 58932

Tracy, Joseph, 1794-1874. An address before the Society for Religious Inquiry in the University of Vermont, August 6, 1839. Boston: Crocker and Brewster, 1839. 28 p. IU; MBC; MiD-B; MnHi; NNG. 58933

----. The three last things: the resurrection of the body, the day of judgement and final retribution. Boston: Crocker and Brewster, 1839. 104 p. MH; MMeT-Hi; NjP; NNUT. 58934

A tragedy in five acts. By a South Carolinian. Charleston, S.C.: B. E. Hussey, 1839. 71 p. PU; ScC. 58935

Trail, William. A guide to Christian communicants in the exercises of self-examination.... Philadelphia: Presbyterian Board of Publication [1839] 112 p. DLC; IEG; NPalk; ViRut. 58936

Transylvania University. Medical Department. Lexington. Annual announcement of the Medical

Department of Transylvania University...published by the medical faculty. Lexington, Ky.: Lexington Intelligencer, printer, 1839. 16 p. KyU; NNN; PPCP. 58937

Trautwine, John C. Some remarks on the internal improvement system of the South. Philadelphia: 1839. 15 p. InHi; MdBP; PHi; PPAN; PPL. 58938

The treasury of knowledge and library of reference. 7th edition. New York: Collins, Keese and Company, 1839. GMar; NcDaD; NNebg; WMMD. 58939

Treatises on prayer, doctrinal and practical; intended for the use of the juvenile members of the Protestant Episcopal church.... New York: General Protestant Episcopal Sabbath School Union, 1839. 122 p. InID; NNG. 58940

Tremont Theatre. Blotter [1839-1841] Boston: 1839-1841. MB. 58941

----. Copy of report of directors...1839. Boston: 1839. MB. 58942

Trial of Marsaud and Raymond, at Brest, for the murder of the captain and six men on board the French ship Alexandre. Including the confessions of Marsaud and Raymond. Translated from the French report...for Rhode Island Republican. With editorial remarks annexed. Newport: 1839. RNR. 58943

Trifles in verse. Philadelphia: Thomas B. Town, 1839. 72 p. CtY; MWH; PU; RPB; ViU. 58944

Trilingual nomenclature; an English, Latin and Greek vocabulary, being a combination of Howard's Greek and Greenwood's Latin vocabularies, with many additional notes on science and classical literature. Philadelphia: Whetham, 1839. 160 p. NNC; NNiaU. 58945

Trist, Nicholas Philip, 1800-1874. Commander Babbit and Consul Trist, at Havana [Washington: 1839] CSmH; MB; NN; PPL; ViU. 58946

----. Condition of American seamen at the port of Havana; with illustrations of the nature of consular duties. Printed by order House [Washington: 1839?] 90 p. CSmH; DLC; MBAt; NN; PPL. 58947

Trollope, Francis [Milton] 1780-1863. Domestic manners of the Americans.... With an introduction by Michael Sadleir.... 5th edition. New York: Dodd, 1839. 398 p. KyBgW; OBogSC. 58948

The troublesome garden, or employment for all. New York: Protestant Episcopal Tract Society, 1839. DLC; InID. 58949

Trousseau, Armand, 1801-1867. A practical treatise on earyngeal phthisis, chronic laryngitis and diseases of the voice, by A. Trousseau...and H. Belloc...Translated by J. A. Warder.... Philadelphia: A. Waldie, 1839. 186 p. CSt-L; GEU-M; NBuU-M; NhD; PPA. 58950

Troy almanac for 1840. Troy, N.Y.: Elias Gates [1839] MWA; PHi. 58951

----. Troy, N.Y.: Robert Wasson [1839] CSmH; MWA; NjR; NT. 58952

The Troy directory...1839-1840. Troy: Kellogg and Cook, 1839. NN. 58953

The truant boy; prepared for the Massachusetts Sabbath School Society and revised by the committee of publication. Boston: Massachusetts Sabbath School Society, 1839. MNS. 58954

True history of the African chief Jingua and his comrades. Hartford: 1839. 32 p. MW. 58955

True Reformed Dutch Church in the United States of America. The acts and proceedings of the general synod...at New York, June 4, 1838. New York: printed by G. A. C. Van Beuren, 1839. 12 p. IaDuU-Sem. 58956

Trumbull, Henry. Life and adventures of Robert the hermit of Massachusetts. Providence: 1839. MB; NcD. 58957

Trunbull, John, 1750-1831. M'Fingal: a modern epic poem. By John Trumbull, Esq. [A Whig of 1776] With explanatory notes. Philadelphia: C. P. Fessenden, 1839. 120 p. CtHT; LNH; MH; Nb: PHi. 58958

Tucker, George, 1775-1861. The theory of money and banks investigated. Boston: C. C. Little and J. Brown, 1839. 412 p. IU; NcU; PU; ScU; TxDaM. 58959

Tucker, Ephraim W. Five months in Labrador

and Newfoundland, during the summer of 1838. Concord: I. S. Boyd and W. White, 1839. 156 p. IaDuC; MdBE; MH; PP; WHi. 58960

Tucker, Luther, 1802-1873. The monthly Genesee farmer and horticulturalist, devoted to the improvement of agriculture, horticulture and floriculture, and to rural and domestic economy. By Luther Tucker, assisted by Willis Gaylord and others. Volume IV. Rochester: Luther Tucker, 1839. NBatHL; NBuU. 58961

Tucker, Mark, 1795-1875. A sermon preached in the Beneficent Congregational Church, Providence, September 29, 1839, occasioned by the death of James Wilson. Providence: B.T. Albro, 1839. 35 p. CtHC; DLC; MH-AH; MoSpD; RPB. 58962

Tucker, Nathaniel Beverley, 1784-1851. A discourse on the genius of the federative system of the United States. Prepared by Prof. Beverley Tucker and read before the Young Men's Society of Lynchburg, Aug., 26, 1838. Richmond: printed by T. W. White, 1839. 24 p. CSmH; MBAt; MH; MHi; PHi. 58963

[Tuckerman, Henry Theodore] 1813-1871. Isabel; or Sicily [a pilgrimage.... By Henry T. Tuckerman.... Philadelphia: Lea and Blanchard, 1839] 230 p. KyLo; MB; PPL; RPB; WvU. 58964

Tuckerman, Samuel Parkman. Long time ago. A glee arranged for four voices.... Boston: Prentiss, 1839. 3 p. MB. 58965

Turley, Edward Astbury. First lines of education...four lectures delivered to the literary and scientific institution, Worcester...1839. Worcester: 1839. 6, 84 p. CtY; DNLM; NNC. 58966

Turnbull, Robert, 1809-1877. THe theatre in its influence upon literature, morals and religion. By Robert Turnbull.... 2nd edition. Boston: Gould, Kendall and Lincoln, 1839. 110 p. IaGG; MH; MWA; NjR; RPB. 58967

Turner, Elizabeth, d. 1846. The daisy, or cautionary stories in verse, adapted to the ideas of children, from four to eight years old. From the 15th London edition. 2nd New York edition, enlarged. New York: Maholon Day, 1839. 80 p. MnU; NUt. 58968

Turner, Francois. Lists of French adjectives and verbs that require different prepositions after them in English. New Haven: Hitchcock and Stafford, 1839. 36 p. DLC; MB. 58969

Turner, Sharon, 1768-1847. Sacred history of the world, attempted to be philosophically considered, in a series of letters to a son.... New York: Harper and Brothers, 1839. 3 v. KyLxT; MH; NbOC; PP; TWcW. 58970

Turner's comick almanack for 1840. New York: Turner and Fisher [1839] MWA; PHi. 58971

Tussaud, Marie [Gresholtz] 1760-1850. Memoirs and reminiscences of the French revolution. By Mme. Marie Tussaud. Philadelphia: Lea and Blanchard, 1839. 2 v. GHi; PU; ScDuE; TMeC; WvF. 58972

Tuthill, Louisa Carolina [Huggins] 1799-1879. The young lady's home. By Mrs. Louisa C. Tuthill. New Haven: S. Babcock, 1839. 369 p. CoPu; GAuY; ICN; NUT; TWcW. 58973

----. The young lady's reader; arranged for examples in rhetoric for the higher classes in seminaries. New Haven: Babcock, 1839. 458 p. CtHT; ICU; KyBC; NGos; PU. 58974

Tuttle, Henry. An historical catechism...11th edition, with additions. Newark, N.J.: Henry Tuttle, 1839. 36 p. DLC; NNC. 58975

Tuttle, Sarah. Anna Elmore, or trials of infancy [Anon.] 3rd edition. Boston: Massachusetts Sabbath School Society, 1839. 105 p. MB. 58976

----. History of the American mission to the Pawnee Indians. By the author of conversations on the Indian missions.... 2nd edition.... Boston: Massachusetts Sabbath School Society, 1839. 72 p. ICN; IEN-M; OkT. 58977

----. Letters on the mission to the Ojibwa Indians.... Boston: Massachusetts Sabbath School Society, 1839. 90 p. MH-AH; MnHi; NjR; NN. 58978

Two articles on the projected ship canal to connect the Atlantic and Pacific oceans. Washington: 1839. 22, 12 p. DLC; PPL. 58979

The two yellow-birds. Embellished with cuts. Providence: Daniels, 1839. 23 p. MB; RHi. 58980

Tyler, Edward Royall, 1800-1848. Slaveholding a malum in se, or invariably sinful. By E. R. Tyler. 2nd edition. Hartford: printed by Case, Tiffany and Company, 1839. 48 p. CU; ICN; MidHi; PHi; TNF. 58981

Tyler, Robert, 1816-1877. Poems: comprising the lost man, the elements of the beautiful; and death. By Robert Tyler. Philadelphia: Henry Perkins, 1839. 101 p. DLC; MdBP; RPB; ViW. 58982

Tyng, Stephen Higginson, 1800-1885. Lessons on the acts of the apostles, designed for more advanced Bible classes. 2nd edition, revised. Philadelphia: R. S. H. George, 1839. 101 p. MdBD; NjP; NjPT. 58983

----. Sermons preached in the church of the Epiphany, Philadelphia. By Stephen H. Tyng, D.D., rector. Philadelphia: printed by William Stavely, 1839. 307 p. CoAl; InID; MnHi; OrPD; PPP. 58984

----. The trial of American principles. An oration, delivered July 4, 1839, in the salon of the Philadelphia museum. By Stephen H. Tyng, D.D. Philadelphia: T. K. and P. G. Collins, 1839. 47 p. IU; MdBD; NNC; PHi; PPPrHi. 58985

Tyson, Job Roberts, 1803-1858. Discourse on the integrity of the legal character, delivered before the law academy of Philadelphia. By Job R. Tyson, Esq., one of the vice-provosts. Published by order of the law academy. Philadelphia: printed by John C. Clark, 1839. 36 p. MBAt; NIC; OCLaw; PPB; W. 58986

Tytler, Patrick Fraser, 1791-1849. Historical view of the process of discovery on the more northern coasts of America.... By Patrick Fraser Tytler, Esq., R. S. and F. S. A.... New York: Harper and Brothers, 1839. 360 p. CLCM; InRch; MLy; NCH; NUT. 58987

U

Uncle Sam's large almanack for 1840. Philadelphia: William W. Walker [1839] 35 p. MWA; NCH; PPeSchw; WHi. 58988

Underwood, Joseph R. The late defalcations of public officers...speech. Jan. 16, 1839. Washington: 1839. DLC. 58989

Union Academy [Old Concord, Campbell, Virginia] Catalogue. Lynchburg: 1839. MBC. 58990

Union Canal Convention, Harrisburg, Pennsylvania, 1838. Proceedings of the Union Canal Convention, assembled at Harrisburg, December 4, 1838. Harrisburg: printed by Boas and Coplan, 1839. 19 p. DLC; MB; MH; MH-BA; OCHP. 58991

Union College, Schnectady. Catalogue of the officers and students...1839-40. Schnectady: Riggs and Norris, printers, 1839. 23 p. DLC; MB; MWA; NN. 58992

Union Congregational Anti-slavery Society, Providence, Rhode Island. Constitution. Providence: 1839. 19 p. MBC. 58993

Union Village Academy. Catalogue, 1838-1839. Troy: 1839. 12 p. OCHP. 58994

United States almanac for 1840. New York: Collins, Keese and Company [1839] MWA. 58995

----. Calculations by Charles Frederick Egelmann. Philadelphia: George W. Mentz [1839] MWA. 58996

United States almanack, for the year 1840. Carefully calculated for the latitutde and meridian of Philadelphia by Charles Frederick Egelmann.... Philadelphia: George W. Mentz and Son [1839] 34 p. NjR. 58997

United States comic almanac for 1840. Boston [1839] MWA. 58998

The United States commercial and statistical register; edited by Samuel Hazard. Philadelphia: n. pub., printed by William F. Geddes, 1839 [-1841] 4 v. NjR; OCLaw. 58999

United States Land Company. Annual report of the trustees...at a meeting of the shareholders. Boston: press of John Putnam, 1839. 11 p. DLC; MH-BA. 59000

United States Military Academy [West Point] Regulations established for the organization and government...by order of the President of the United States; with an appendix...Revised and amended to 1839. New York: Wiley and Putnam, 1839. 137 p. Ct; MoSpD; NNG; TxU. 59001

United States school primer. Designed for schools and families, carefully compiled for the instruction and improvement of the infant mind and heart. New York: G. F. Cooledge [1839] 48 p. MB; MH; NBuG; RPB. 59002

United States spelling book with appropriate reading lessons; being an easy standard for spelling, reading and pronouncing the English language according to the rules established by John Walker, in his critical and pronouncing dictionary. By sundry experienced teachers.... Pittsburgh: Johnston and Stockton, 1839. 156 p. MNC; PPi. 59003

United States Thomsonian almanac for 1840. Poughkeepsie, N.Y.: Lapham and Platt [1839] MWA. 59004

The United States Trust and Banking Company. Articles of association, and by-laws of the United States Trust and Banking Company: also, the General Banking Law, passed by the legislature of the state of New York, April 18, 1838, under which the company is organized. New York: printed by J. M. Elliott, 1839. 7 p. NN. 59005

A universal history of Christian persecutions and martyrdom, an authentic account of the most horrid cruelties and lectures inflicted upon early Christians [illustraded] numerous engravings by

R. Thomas Hartford.... Stereotyped by Thomas Moore. Boston: 1839. 4, 324 p. 59006

Universalist register and almanac; containing the statistics of the denomination, for 1840. Utica: Grosh and Hutchinson, New York: A. Tompkins [1839] 36 p. MeB; MH; MMeT-Hi; MWA; NCan-Hi. 59007

The Universalist Union, embracing the New York Christian Messenger and Philadelphia Universalist, Inquirer and Anchor, and Southern Pioneer. Editorial contributors: T. J. Sawyer, C. F. Lefevre, A. C. Thomas, I. D. Williamson, R. O.Williams, A. Moore. New York: P. Price, 1838. 3 v. 412 p. MChiA. 59008

Ein Unpartheyisches Gesang-Buch, zum allgemeinen Gebrauch des Wahren Gottesdienstes. Mit einem doppelten Register. Canton, Ohio: Gedruckt bey Peter Kaufmann und Company, 1839. 320 p. InGo; KNM. 59009

Upham, Thomas Cogswell, 1799-1872. Elements of mental philosophy, embracing the two departments of the intellect and the sensibilities.... 3rd edition. Portland: W. Hyde, 1839. 2 v. DLC; IU; MiOC; NGH; TxShA. 59010

Upper Alton Ladies School. Ladies' School. Miss Whitehead [lately from London] takes this opportunity of informing the inhabitants of Upper Alton and its vicinity, that she will commence the 2nd session on Tuesday, March 5th, at the brick school room...February 25, 1839. Upper Alton: Telegraph office, 1839. Broadside. ICHi. 59011

Urcullu, D. Jose De. Gramatica Englesa, and reducida a veinte Y Dos Lecciones. Por D. Jose De Urcullu. Quinta Edicion. Nueva York: Imprenta De Don Juan De La Granja, 1839. 340 p. CtMW. 59012

Urquhart, David, 1805-1877. The spirit of the east, illustrated in a journal of travels through Roumeli during an eventful period.... Philadelphia: E. L. Carey and A. Hart, 1839. 2 v. LNP; OCY; PPA; RPA; WM. 59013

The Ursuline manual; or a collection of prayers, spiritual exercises, etc., interspersed with the various instructions necessary for forming youth to the practice of solid piety. Originally arranged for the young ladies educated at the Ursuline Convent, Cork. Revised by the Very Rev. John Power, and approved by the Rt. Rev. Bishop Hughes.... New York: Edward Dunigan, 1839. 518 p. FTa; MoSU; NNerC; PRosC. 59014

Utica, New York, Female Academy. Catalogue of the officers and members of the Utica Female Academy during the year ending August 3, 1839. Utica: Bennett and Bright, 1839. 22 p. OCHP; OClWHi; NUt. 59015

The Utica directory and city advertiser. Compiled by A. P. Vates. Utica, N.Y.: printed by R. Northway, Jr., 1839. 94 p. MWA; NUt. 59016

V

Vale, Gilbert, 1788-1866. Life of Thomas Paine...With observations on his writings. New York: Citizen of the World office [1839?] 192 p. MnHi. 59017

Valpy, Richard, 1754-1836. Delectus sententiarum graecarum, ad usum tironum accommodatus; cum notulis et lexico. Ed. Americana 5, prioribus emendatior. Bostoniae: Hillard, 1839. 102 p. DeWi; MCNC; MiD-B; NjP. 59018

----. The elements of Greek grammar. By Richard Valpy, D.D. F.A.S. With additions by C. Anthon Jay, professor of languages in Columbia College, New York. 12th edition. New York: W. E. Dean, 1839. 301 p. TU. 59019

Van Court, J. Van Court's counterfeit detector and bank note list. Philadelphia: 1839-1858. 21 v. in 9. PPL. 59020

Van Rensselaer, Stephen. Discourse, Albany, April 23, 1839, on life, services and character of...with historical sketch of colony, etc., maner of Ransselaerwyck...by Daniel D. Barnard. Albany: 1839. OCHP. 59021

Van Wagenen, John Hardenbergh, 1802-1844. A discourse, in behalf of disabled ministers, and of the widows and children of ministers of the Reformed Dutch Church.... By J. H. Van Wagenen. Hudson: Ashbel Stoddard, printer, 1839. 22 p. MBC; MH; NjR; OClWHi; PPPrHi. 59022

Vandewater, Robert J. The tourist, or pocket manual for travellers on the Hudson River, the western and northern canals and railroads.... 6th edition. New York: Harper and Brothers, 1839. 108 p. MB; MH; MWA; NjP. 59023

[Varle, Charles] Moral encyclopedia, or self-instructor, in literature, duties of life and rules of good breeding. Interspersed with popular quotations, mottos, maxims and adages, in Latin and other languages. Also with the French words generally met with in newspapers, and works of taste and fancy. Faithfully translated.... New York: E. Wilbur, printer, 1839. 301 p. MtBiP; MWA; PU; TNP. 59024

Vattel, Emmerich de, 1714-1767. The law of nations; or principles of the law of nature, applied to the conduct and affairs of nations, and sovereigns.... 5th American edition, from a new edition by Joseph Chitty.... Philadelphia: T. and J. W. Johnson, 1839. 500 p. MoS; NcD; OO; ViU; WaU. 59025

Venegas, Miguel, 1680-1764? Manualito de parrocos, para los autos del ministerio mas precison, y auuxiliar and los enformos. tomado del de el P. Juan Francisco Lopez. huevo Mexico, Imprenta del Presbitero Antonio Jose Martinez a cargo de J. M. Baca, 1839. 52 p. DLC; ICN; NmHi. 59026

Vergilius Maro, Publius. Bucolilca, Georgica, et Aeneis. Accedunt clavis metrica, notulae englicab, et questioes. Cura B. A. Gould. Bostoniae, sumptibus Hilliard, Gray et soc., 1839. 491 p. MiU-C. 59027

----. Opera; or the works of Virgil.... Compiled from the best commentators, with many that are new.... To which is added, a table of reference. By the Rev. J. G. Cooper, A.M. 9th stereotype edition. New York: Robinson, Pratt and Company, 1839. 615 p. ICU; OBerB; PPCCH. 59028

----. Virgil, the Eclogues translated by Wrangham, the Georgics by Sotheby, and the Aeneid by Dryden, in two volumes. New York: Harper and Brothers, 1839. 2 v. LNP; NNF; PMy; TxH; ViU. 59029

Vermilye, Thomas Edward, 1803-1893. A funeral discourse, occasioned by the death of the Hon. Stephen Van Rensselaer, delivered in the North Dutch Church, Albany, on Sabbath evening, Feb. 3, 1839. By Thomas E. Vermilye.... By request. Albany: printed by J. Munsell, 1839. 43 p. CtHT; ICMe; NjR; PHi; WHi. 59030

Vermont. General Assembly. House. Journal of

the House of Representatives of the state of Vermont, Oct. session, 1838. Published by authority. Montpelier: E. P. Walton and Sons, 1839. 234 p. ICU; MH; Mi; MnU; NhD; WHi. 59031

----. ----. Senate. Journal of the Senate of the state of Vermont, Oct. session, 1838. Published by authority. Montpelier: E. P. Walton and Sons, 1839. 102 p. M; MH; Mi; MNU; VtMidSM; WHi. 59032

----. Governor, 1835-1841 [Jenison] Governor's message. In House of Representatives, October 12, 1839 [Montpelier, Vt.: 1839] 16 p. ICJ; ICN; MB; Nh; VtU. 59033

----. Laws, Statutes, etc. Acts and resolves passed by the legislature of the state of Vermont, at their October session, 1839. Published by authority. Montpelier [Vt.] E.P. Walton and Sons, printers, 1839. 102 p. IaU-L; MdBB; NBuG; R; TxU-L. 59034

Verplanck, Gulian Crommelin, 1786-1870. Speech when in committee of the whole, in the Senate of New York, on the several bills and resolutions for the amendment of the law and the reform of the judiciary system. Albany: Hoffman and White, 1839. 31 p. CtY; MH; N; NN; RNR. 59035

Very, Jones, 1813-1880. Essays and poems.... Boston: C. C. Little and J. Brown, 1839. 175 p. CtMW; IaU; KyBC; MB; TxU. 59036

Viele, John J. Address delivered before the New York State Agricultural Society, by John J. Viele. Albany: Packard, Van Benthuysen and Company, 1839. KyDC; MB; MWA; NN. 59037

Viereck, John Conrad. La perle, Grand galop brillant sur le postillon de Mme. ablon, musique de clapisson arrange' dans un style facile et brillant pour le piano forte et dedie a Mademoiselle M. E. McCord a loccasion de son jour de naissance par J. C. Viereck. Opus 19.... Philadelphia: J. C. Viereck [1839?] 7 p. ViU. 59038

Vigilant Fire Engine Company. Constitution and by-laws, Sept. 24, 1839. Philadelphia: printed by D. Schneek, 1839. 21 p. PHi. 59039

The village pastor: or the origin and progress of the American Bible Society. By the author of conversations and letters on the Sandwich Islands and Bombay missions, etc. Written for the Massachusetts Sabbath School Scoiety, and revised by the committee of publication. 2nd edition, enlarged. Boston: Massachusetts Sabbath School Society, 1839. 177 p. ICBB; InCW; InPerM; MWA; PPL. 59040

A vindication of the separate system of prison discipline...See Packard, Frederick Adolphus.

The violet: a Christmas and New Year's present. 1840. Edited by Miss Leslie. Philadelphia: Carey and Hart [1839] ICU; KU; MWA; PP; TxAu. 59041

Virginia. General Assembly. House of Delegates. Journal of the House of Delegates of the commonwealth of Virginia.... Richmond: printed by Thomas Ritchie, 1839. 42 p. NBu; Vi. 59042

----. Grand Council. Proceedings of the Grand Council of the state of Virginia. Richmond: printed by John Warrock, 1839. 3 p. NNFM. 59043

----. Laws, statutes, etc. Acts of assembly relating to the city of Richmond, and ordinances of the common council, subsequent to January, 1831. Collected and printed by order of the common council. Richmond: J. Warrock, 1839. 80 p. Vi. 59044

----. ----. Acts of the General Assembly of Virginia, passed at the session commencing 7th January, and ending 10th April, 1839, in the 63rd year of the commonwealth. Richmond [Va.] Samuel Shepherd, printer to the commonwealth, 1839. 287 p. IaU-L; Ky; MdHi; Tx; WvW. 59045

----. ----. A collection of the acts of Virginia and Kentucky relative to the Louisville and Portland with the charter of the city of Louisville and the amendments thereto. Louisville: Prentice, 1839. 211 p. ICU; KyLo; MiD-B; OFH; TxU. 59046

----. School for the Deaf and the Blind. A list of the officers, a copy of the act of the legislature establishing and of the by-laws of the...institution.... Richmond: Bernard, 1839. 13 p. MHi; PPAmP; PPL; WHi. 59047

----. University. Catalogue of the officers and students of the University of Virginia. Session of 1838-39. Richmond: Shepherd and Colin, printers, 1839 [5]-23 p. In; LNB; ScU. 59048

Virginia and North Carolina almanack for 1840. By David Richardson. Richmond, Va.: John Warrock [1839] MWA. 59049

The Virginia lyceum. Published by an association of gentlemen. V. 1, no. 1-April, 1839...L. R. Streeter, editor.... Richmond: P. D. Bernard, printer, 1839. 1 v. CSmH; CtY; NcD; Vi. 59050

Virginia Military Instutite, Lexington, Virginia. Regulations of the Virginia Military Institute at Lexington. Richmond: Shepherd and Colin, printer, 1839. 36 p. MH. 59051

A visti to Nahant, being a sequel to the wonders of the deep. By a lady. New York: Protestant Episcopal Sunday School Union, 1839. 196 p. DLC; FMU; NUtHi; RPB. 59052

A visit to the country; a tale. By the author of "letters to a mother," "Ellen," "happy valley," etc. Boston: W. Crosby and Company, 1839. MH. 59053

The visiter. Vol. 1, no. 24, Saturday, September 14, 1839. Newark, N.J.: 1839. OClWHi. 59054

Volksfreund und Hagerstauner calendar, 1840. Hagerstown, Md.: Johan Gruber [1839] MWA. 59055

Voltaire, Francois Marie Arouet de, 1694-1778. The history of Charles the 12th, king of Sweden. By M. De Voltaire. A new translation from the last Paris edition. Hartford: Andrus, Judd and Franklin, 1839. 276 p. MFALM. 59056

----. ----. New York: Robinson and Franklin, 1839. 276 p. NSherb; OSW; ScCliP. 59057

W

Waage, Friedrich. Weise verens Waage: oder Richt aus dem dunklen eck.... Philadelphia: gedruckt bei C. F. Stollmeyer, 1839. 69 p. N. 59058

----. Weiser versus Waage; oder, Licht aus dem dunklen Eck. Philadelphia: C. F. Stollmeyer, 1839. PPG; PPeSchw. 59059

Wadsworth, James, 1768-1844. Copy of a letter addressed to...Daniel Webster, on the colonization of the Indians. New York: Piercy and Reed, printers, 1838. 8 p. MB; MH. 59060

Wake Forest College, Wake Forest, North Carolina. The charter and laws of the Wake Forest College, North Carolina; enacted by the corporation, December, 1838. Raleigh: printed at the Recorder office, 1839. 15 p. DE; DLC; MH; NcU. 59061

Walker, Alexander. Intermarriage: or the mode in which, and the causes why, beauty, health and intellect, result from certain unions, and deformity, disease and insanity, from others.... By Alexander Walker. New York: J. and H. G. Langley, 1839. 384 p. IEN-M; LU; MWA; NcD; PPA. 59062

----. Woman, physiologically considered as to mind, morals, marriage, etc. New York: J. and H. G. Langley, 1839. 432 p. IEdS; MiOC; NN. 59063

Walker, George, 1803-1879. Chess made easy, being a new introduction to the rudiments of that scientific and popular game. Baltimore: J. Neal, 1839. 124 p. MdBE; NjP; OCl; PP; WU. 59064

Walker, James, 1794-1874. A discourse delivered in Harvard church, Charlestown, July 14, 1839, on taking leave of society.... Cambridge: Metcalf, Torry and Ballou, 1839. 40 p. ICMe; MH-AH; OClWHi; RPB; WHi. 59065

----. A farewell discourse to the children in his society, delivered in Harvard church, Charlestown, June 23, 1839. Cambridge: Metcalf, Torry and Ballou, 1839. 24 p. ICMe; MBAU; MH- AH;

PHi; RPB. 59066

----. Unitarianism vindicated against the charge of skeptical tendencies.... Boston: James Munroe and Company, 1893. 27 p. CBPac; ICMe; MBC; MDeeP; MeBat. 59067

Walker, John, 1732-1807. Walker's critical pronouncing dictionary, and exposition of the English language. To which is annexed...Walker's key to the pronunciation of Greek, Latin and Scripture proper names. Boston school edition, abridged. Boston: Robert S. Davis, 1839. 468 p. IEG; MBilHi; MH; NjP. 59068

----. ----. New London: W. and J. Bolles, 1839. 609 p. NjP; NN. 59069

----.----. New York: Collins, Keese and Company, 1839. 710 p. NPlva. 59070

Walker, Joseph R. The prayers of the church. See under title.

Walker, Robert James, 1801-1869. Vindication, of Robert J. Walker from the charges of S. S. Prentiss. To the people of the state of Mississippi [Natchez: 1839] 8 p. CSmH; NcD. 59071

Wall, William, 1647-1728. A conference between two men that had doubts about infant baptism, by the Rev. W. Wall. New York: Protestant Episcopal Society, 1839. 38 p. InID; Nh; NHC-S. 59072

Wallace, William Clay. A treatise on the eye: containing discoveries of the causes of near and far sightedness, and of the affections of the retina, with remarks on the use of medicines, for the use of spectacles. Clay Wallace, oculist. 2nd edition. New York: S. Coleman, 1839. 68 p. CSt-L; KWiU; MdBM; PPCP; RPM. 59073

Walley, Samuel Hurd, 1805-1877. Address delivered at the 22nd anniversary of the Mason Street Sabbath School. Boston: Perkins and Marvin, 1839. MB. 59074

Walter, W[illiam] Joseph, d. 1846. Sir Thomas More. His life and times, illustrated from his own writings, and from contemporary documents.... Philadelphia: E. L. Carey and A. Hart [etc., etc.] 1839. 382 p. InNd; MH; NNF; OCX; PU. 59075

Waltham, Massachusetts. Independent Congregational Society. By- laws and plan of pews, together with an account of the sale of pews in the Society [Meeting House] of the Independent Congregational Meeting House [Society] in Waltham. Boston: D. H. Ela, 1839. 8 p. MH. 59076

Walton, Augustus Q. A history of the detection, conviction, life and designs of John A. Mural, the great western land pirate, together with his system of villany, and plan of exciting negro rebellion, also a catalogue of the names of 455 of his mystic clan fellows and followers, and a statement of their efforts for the destruction of Virgil A. Stewart, who detected him. By A. Q. Walton. New York: G. Cunningham, 1839. 40 p. NcAS; NIC; NRAB. 59077

Wanastrocht, N. A grammar of the French language with practical exercises.... Philadelphia: Hermon Hooker, 1839. MsCLiM. 59078

Warburg, Daniel, 1789-1860? Buy a lottery ticket; or a chance to get rid of money.... New Orleans: printed by E. Johns and Company, 1839. 8 p. 59079

----. "The goddess Eve." Two tables, constructed to demonstrate by numbers the true mode of extracting the square root out of all entire numbers above 100, and the cubic root out of all entire numbers above 1000. Besides: multiplication and the rule of three with entire numbers... .New Orleans: printed by E. Johns and Company, 1839. 11 p. DLC. 59080

Ward, James Wilson, 1803-1873. Slavery a sin that concerns non- slaveholding states: a sermon...on the day of the annual fast...March 28, 1839. Boston: Knapp, 1839. 32 p. MB; MBC; NHi; NNC. 59081

Ward, Samuel, 1786-1839. Battle of Long Island: a lecture, delivered before the New York Historical Society, February 7, 1839. New York: printed by W. Osborn, 1839. 22 p. DLC: MH; NIC; WHi. 59082

Wardwell, Stephen S. The village of Hermonia, a temperance poem; delivered...Nov. 8, 1839....

Providence: Knowles and Vose, 1839. 32 p. ICN; MBC; NN; RP; RPB. 59083

Ware, Henry, Jr., 1794-1843. How to spend a day; thoughts for the new year on the duty of improvement. Boston: 1839. 22 p. CBPac IaPeC; MBAt; MeBat; RP. 59084

----. On the formation of the Christian character. Addressed to those who are seeking to lead a religious life. By Henry Ware, Jr., professor of pulpit eloquence and the Pastoral Cave in Harvard University. 11th edition. Boston: James Munroe and Company, 1839. 176 p. LNB; MH; MWA; PPRETS. 59085

Ware, Thomas, 1758-1842. Sketches of the life and travels of Rev. Thomas Ware, who has been an itinerant Methodist preacher for more than 50 years. Written by himself, revised by the editors. New York: Mason and Lane, 1839. 264 p. CtMW: ICU; MB; PHi; TxDaM. 59086

Ware, Thomas E. Medical adviser; and book of directions and receipts, with directions for the use of the cold and hot bath. And his mode of administering Thomsonian and botanical remedies. Salem, N.J. [S. Prior] 1839. 94 p. DeU. 59087

Ware, William, 1797-1852. Letters of Lucius M. Piso [pseud.] from Palmyra to his friend Marcus Curtius at Rome.... New York: C. S. Francis, 1839. 2 v. MWA. 59088

----. Zenolia, or the fall of Palmyra. New York: C. S. Francis, 1839. 288 p. MBAt; MeBa; NGH; NLook. 59089

Warner, Aaron, 1794-1876. A sermon preached at Wolfborough, Nov. 1, 1838, at the ordination of Jeremiah Blake. Gilmanton, N.H.: A. Prescott, 1839. 15 p. CtSoP; MBC; MH; Nh-Hi; RPB. 59090

Warner, Joseph A. Phrenology in the family; or, the utility of phrenology in early domestic education. Dedicated to mothers. Philadelphia: George W. Donohue, 1839. KyLxT; MB; OAlM; PPL; ScDuE. 59091

Warren, John Bliss, 1794-1844. A discourse on domestic missions, delivered at Vicksburgh, Oct. 24, 1838.... [Baton Rouge, La.] Baton Rouge Gazette, printer, 1839. 17 p. CSmH. 59092

Warren, John Collins, 1778-1856. A comparative

view of the sensorial and nervous systems in men and animals. Boston: Ingraham, 1839. 159 p. MH-M. 59093

----. Surgical observations on tumours with cases and operations. By John C. Warren.... Boston: Crocker and Brewster, London: J. Churchill, 1839. 607 p. CtMW; ICU; MB; MdBJ; PPC. 59094

Warren, Samuel, 1807-1877. Passages from the diary of a late physician. By Samuel Warren, F.R.S. From the 5th London edition. New York: Harper and Brothers, 1839. 3 v. ICN; MB; MiU; NBuU-M; PPWI. 59095

Warren Ladies' Seminary. Catalogue of the officers and pupils of the Warren Ladies' Seminary, for the year ending December, 1839. Providence: printed by Knowles and Vose, 1839. 11 p. RHi. 59096

Warrington, Joseph. The nurse's guide, containing a series of instructions to families who wish to engage in the important business of nursing mother and child in the lying-in chamber. Philadelphia: Thomas, 1839. 131 p. MdBM; MTop; PP; PPCP; ViRA. 59097

The wars of America: or a general history of all the important tragic events that have occured in the United States of North America, since the discovery of the western continent by Christopher Columbus. By a Revolutionary soldier. Baltimore: Hazard and Bloomer, 1839. 464 p. ICN; MiD; PPL; RPB; WHi. 59098

Washburn, Emory, 1800-1877. Address at the 27th annual meeting of the Massachusetts Temperance Society. Boston: 1839. 27 p. MBC; MWHi; PPAmP; PPL. 59099

----. Anniversary of the Massachusetts Temperance Society. Annual address. Boston: Cassady and March, Temperance Press, 1839. 46 p. ICP; MeB; MWA; PPM; TxH. 59100

Washington, George, 1732-1799. Washington's abschieds addresse. Harrisburg: Joseph Ehrenfried, 1839. 22 p. PHi; PPeSchw. 59101

----. Facsimilies of letters from his excellency George Washington, President of the United States to Sir John Sinclair, Bart., M.P. Philadelphia: T. K. and P. G. Collins, printers, 1839. 57 p. MB; MBBC; NjR; OC; TNL. 59102

----. Farewell address. Harrisburg: 1839. 22 p. PHi. 59103

----. Washington's valedictory address to the people of the United States, published in September, A.D. 1796: together with the Declaration of Independence. Harrisburg: Boas and Coplan, printers, 1839. 22 p. ICN; MB; MiD-B; NCH; PHi. 59104

----. The writings of George Washington; being his correspondence, addresses, messages, and other papers, official and private, selected and published from the original manuscripts; with a life of the author, notes and illustrations. By Jared Sparks. Boston: Ferdenand Andrews, 1839. 12 v. ABBS; ILM; MNe; ODaU; WaSp. 59105

----. ----. Boston: F. Andrews, Charleston, S.C.: A. Mygatt, 1839-1840. 12 v. DN; LNB; OkU. 59106

Washington College, Washington, Pennsylvania. Catalogue of the officers and students of Washington College. Washington, Pa.: printed by George W. Brice, 1839. 16 p. PHi; PPPrHi; PWW. 59107

Washington Medical College of Baltimore. First annual report to the General Assembly of Maryland, of the president and board of visitors of the Washington Medical College of Baltimore. Jan., 1839. Baltimore: printed by John D. Toy, 1839. 8 p. Md; NNN. 59108

The watchman. Boston. Christian watchman, a weekly religious newspaper. 2 weekly copies January to December inclusive, 1839. Boston: William Nichols [1839] 4 p. MNtCA. 59109

Waters, Francis, 1792-1868. Salvation and prosperity: a sermon, delivered in St. John's Church, Baltimore...on the 3rd April, 1839. By Francis Waters, D.D.... Baltimore John D. Toy, printer, 1839. 21 p. MBAt; MdBMP; PPLT; PPM; PPPrHi. 59110

Waterston, Robert Cassie, 1812-1893. Arthur Lee and Tom Palmer: or the sailor reclaimed. 2nd edition. Boston: James Munroe and Company, 1839. 78 p. DLC; NNU; TxU. 59111

----. Thoughts on prison discipline. Boston: J. Munroe and Company, 1839. 26 p. CtY; DLC; MH; NN; WHi. 59112

Waterworth, James, 1806-1876. Six historical lectures on the original progress in England, of the change in religion, called reformation. Newark: W. M. Watson, 1839. MdW. 59113

----. The substance of six historical lectures, on the origin and progress in this country on the change of religion, called the reformation, delivered in the Catholic church of the Holy Trinity.... Newark: W. M. Watson, 1839. 468 p. ArLSJ; P; PV. 59114

Watson, Richard, 1781-1833. Conversations for the young; designed to promote the profitable reading of the Holy Scriptures, by Richard Watson.... New York: T. Mason and G. Lane, for the Methodist Episcopal Church, at the conference office, 1839. 300 p. MsV; NjNbS. 59115

----. The life of the Rev. John Wesley, A.M. By Richard Watson. 1st American official edition, with translations and notes, by John Emory. New York: T. Mason and G. Lane, 1839. 323 p. CBPSR; IaU; InEvC; IU; KyDW; MoK. 59116

Watts, Isaac, 1674-1748. The Psalms and hymns of Dr. Watts, arranged by Dr. Rippon: with Dr. Rippon's selection. Corrected and improved, by Rev. C. G. Sommers, pastor of South Baptist Church, N.Y.; and Rev. John L. Dagg, president of the Alabama Female Atheneum. Philadelphia: David Clark, 1839. AAP; DWT; NRAB. 59117

----. The Psalms, hymns and spiritual songs of the Rev. Isaac Watts, D.D., to which are added select hymns from other authors and directions for musical expression by Samuel Worcester, D.D.... New edition, enlarged and index greatly improved by Samuel W. Worcester, A.M.... Boston: Crocker and Brewster, 1839. 776 p. IEG; MBC; OCl; NbOP; PPWe. 59118

The way of salvation familiarly explained in a conversation between a father and his children. Philadelphia: William S. Martien, 1839. 49 p. DLC; KyHi; NjP; NjPT; ViRut. 59119

"The way of the transgresor is hard;" illustrated in the history of Madam Tiquet, who was beheaded in France, for the attempted murder of her husband, of John Van Alstine, convicted of the murder of William Huddlestone; and of James Hackman, a professed minister of the gospel, who was executed for the murder of Miss Reay. New York: S. W. Barnes, 1839. 24 p. MH. 59120

Wwayland, Francis, 1796-1865. Elements of moral science: By Francis Wayland, D.D.... Abridged and adapted to the use of schools and academies, by the author. Boston: Gould, Kendall and Lincoln, 1839. 239, 11 p. MH; NNC. 59121

----. ----. 8th edition. Revised and stereotyped. Boston: Gould, Kendall and Lincoln, 1839. 398 p. ICBB; NN; OMC; OO. 59122

----. ----. 9th edition. Revised and stereotyped. Boston: Gould, Kendall and Lincoln, 1839. 398 p. DLC; OO. 59123

----. ----. 10th edition. Revised and stereotyped. Boston: Gould, Kendall and Lincoln, 1839. 398 p. CtHT; LNT; MiU; MWo; NRU. 59124

----. ----. 11th edition. Revised and stereotyped. Boston: Gould, Kendall and Lincoln, 1839. 398 p. KTW. 59125

Webb, George James, 1803-1887. The odeon; a collection of secular melodies, arranged and harmonized for four voices, designed for adult singing schools, and for social music parties, by G. J. Webb and Lowell Mason.... 3rd edition. Boston: J. H. Wilkins and R. B. Carter, 1839. 304 p. IG; MH-AH; NBu; OWoC; WHi. 59126

Webbe, Cornelius. The man about town, by Cornelius Webbe, author of "glances at life". Philadelphia: 1839. 2 v. MCli; PV; ScDuE; WU. 59127

Webber, George. Discourse delivered in Portland, at the celebration of the centenary of Wesleyan Methodism, by George Webber, pastor, Oct. 25, 1839. Portland: Day, Lyons and Company, 1839. 24 p. MBNMHi; RPB. 59128

Webster, Daniel, 1782-1852. The beauties of the Hon. Daniel Webster: selected and arranged...By James Rees. New York: J. and H. G. Langley, 1839. 95 p. InCW; MeHi; MWA; NhD; WHi. 59129

----. ----. 2nd edition. New York: Edward Walker, 1839. 196 p. GU; MdBP; MiD; PU-L; ViU. 59130

----. ----. 3rd edition, with a portrait, and considerable additions. New York: Edward Walker, etc., 1839. 196 p. NIC-LA. 59131

----. Speeches and forensic arguments.... Boston:

Perkins and Marvin, Philadelphia: Henry Perkins, 1839. 2 v. MMe; NUT; PP; RPB; TMeB. 59132

----. ----. Boston: Perkins and Marvin, 1839-1846. 3 v. MHi; MoSM; OClW; ScCC. 59133

Webster, John White, 1793-1850. A manual of chemistry; containing the principal facts of the science, in the order in which they are discussed and illustrated in the lectures of Harvard University, N.E. and several other medical schools in the U.S.... Boston: Marsh, Capen, Lyon and Webb, 1839. 556 p. ICJ; KY; MB; TNB; WaU. 59134

----. ----. 3rd edition. Boston: Marsh, Capen, Lyon and Webb, 1839. 556 p. CSt; IaGG; KyLxT; MH; PP. 59135

Webster, Noah, 1758-1848. An American dictionary of the English language; exhibiting the origin, orthography, pronunciation and definitions of words.... New York: White and Sheffield, 1839. 1011 p. AzU; CoU; MB; MiU; WHi. 59136

----. The American spelling book, containing the rudiments of the English language, for the use of schools in the United States. By Noah Webster, esq. New York: Collins, Keese and Company, 1839. 156 p. MBilHi; PEaL. 59137

----. ----. Philadelphia: 1839. 168 p. NcD. 59138

----. A dictionary for primary schools. New York: F. J. Huntington and Company, 1839. 341 p. CtY; MB; MNF; NN; ViU. 59139

----. A dictionary of the English language; abridged from the American dictionary, for the use of primary schools and the counting house; 19th edition. New York: Huntington, 1839. 536 p. NjP. 59140

----. The elementary spelling book; being an improvement on the American spelling book.... Cleveland: Sanford and Lott, 1839. 168 p. NN. 59141

----. ----. Montpelier: 1839. CtHT-W; CtHWatk. 59142

----. ----. Portland, Me.: O. L. Sanborn, 1839.168 p. MH; MWHi; NFred; RPB. 59143

----. ----. Watertown, N.Y.: Knowlton and Rice, 1839. 166 p. MNHi; NBatHL. 59144

----. History of the United States, to which is prefixed a brief historical account of our [English] ancestors, from the dispersion at Babel to their migration to America and of the conquest of South America by the Spaniards. New Haven: Sidney Babcock [1839] 358 p. NN. 59145

----. Improved grammar of the English language. New Haven: Sidney Babcock, 1839. 192 p. CtMW; KWiU; MdBS; MH; OO. 59146

----. A manual of useful studies for the instruction of young persons of both sexes, in families and schools. New Haven: Babcock, 1839. 248 p. CtMW; MB; NNC; OOxM; PPM. 59147

----. Observations on language, and on the errors of class-books; addressed to the members of the New York lyceum. Also observations on commerce addressed to the Mercantile Library Association, in New York. New Haven: printed by S. Babcock, 1839. 39 p. MBC; MH-AH; MPiB; NDu; NjR. 59148

----. The prompter; a commentary on common sayings which are full of common sense, the best sense in the world. New Haven: S. Babcock, 1839. 94 p. Ct; NN; NP. 59149

Webster's almanac for the year of 1839. Lockport, N.Y.: N. Leonard, 1839. NHor. 59150

Webster's calendar, or the Albany almanack for 1840. 2nd edition. By Edwin E. Prentiss. Albany, N.Y.: E. W. and C. Skinner [1839] MWA; NN; WHi. 59151

Weeks, John Moseley, 1786-1858. A manual, or an easy method of managing bees in the most profitable manner to their owner, with infallible rules to prevent their destruction by the moth. 4th edition. Brandon, Vt.: 1839. 96 p. NIC; OO; PPM; VtHi. 59152

Weeks, William Raymond, 1783-1848. The doctrine of the universal decrees and agency of God, asserted and vindicated; nine sermons.... 3rd editon. Newark, N.J.: Ecclesiastical Board of Trustees for Propagation of the Gospel, 1839. 203 p. PPPrHi. 59153

----. Nine sermons on the decrees and agency of God.... 3rd edition. Newark, N.J.: Ecclesiastical Board of Trustees for the Propagation of the Gospel, John R. Weeks, printer, 1839. 170 p. MB;

MH-AH; MoSpD; NbCrD; OO. 59154

Weems, Mason Locke, 1759-1825. The life of Gen. Francis Marion, a celebrated partisan officer in the Revolutionary war...By Brig. Gen. P. Horry, of Marion's brigade, and M. L. Weems.... Stereotyped by L. Johnson. Philadelphia: Joseph Allen, 1839. 252 p. GS; MoS; PLFM; ScU; TxU. 59155

The well bred boy; or new school of good manners. Boston: William Crosby and Company, 1839. 94 p. ICU; MHi; MNS. 59156

Wells, George W. Two discourses preached to the first parish in Kennebunk, October 21, 1838. Kennebunk: James K. Remich, printer, 1839. 19 p. MB; MeHi; RPB. 59157

Wells, William A. Miscellanies in verse. Boston: 1839. 15 p. MB; Mh. 59158

Welsh, Joseph S. Harp of the west: a volume of poems.... Cincinnati: printed by Dawson and Fisher, 1839. 204 p. CSmH; InCW; M; NcU; OFH. 59159

Wesley, John, 1703-1791. Select letters, chiefly on personal religion. By the Rev. John Wesley, A.M. with a sketch of his character by Rev. Samuel Bradburn. New York: T. Mason and G. Lane for the Methodist Episcopal Church, 1839. 240 p. OrSaW. 59160

----. Sermons on several occasions.... New York: T. Mason and G. Lane, 1839. 2 v. CoD; FJC; MeLewB; ODaB; TJaU. 59161

----. Thoughts on slavery. Written in 1774. New York: American Anti-slavery Society, 1839. 96 p. MBNMHi; MiU. 59162

----. The works of the Reverend John Wesley, A.M. 1st American complete and standard edition, from the latest London edition, with the last corrections of the author: comprehending also numerous translations, notes and an original preface. New York: T. Mason, 1839-40. 7 v. ArCC; MeB; MH; NN; OrU; WaS. 59163

Wesley's family physician, revised and Ware's medical adviser. A book of receipts, with directions for the use of Dr. Samuel Thomson's medicine and bath. For the benefit of families, clergymen, philanthropists, and reformers. 27th edition of the primitive physic. Salem, N.J.: S. Prior, jr., 1839. 96, 94 p. MCHiA; NjR; OCLloyd; WjMD. 59164

West, George Montgomery. The true principles of American greatness: address before Kensington Institute, Washington Assembly and Jefferson Literary Association, March 8, 1839. With addenda. Philadelphia; J. Perry, 1839. 94 p. CtY; DLC; PHi. 59165

West, Nathaniel. The importance of correct principle, etc. An address delivered before the literary society of Allegheny College, Meadville, September 12, 1839. Pittsburgh: White, 1839. 16 p. PHi; PPPrHi. 59166

Westcott, James Diament, 1802-1880. Masonic address...funeral of Col. Abraham Bellamy, at Monticello, Jefferson County, Florida, September 23rd, A.L. 5839...Tallahassee: Samuel S. Sibley, printer, 1839. 20 p. DLC. 59167

Western almanac. By R. Falley. Columbus; E. Glover, 1839. MWA. 59168

The western almanac, for the year 1840.... By David Young.... New York: Collins, Keese and Company [1839] 35 p. MWA; NjR; NRHi. 59169

...Western almanack.... 1840.... Latitude and longitude of Washington city. Ithaca, N.Y.: Mack, Andrus and Woodruff [1839] MWA; NIC; NRU; WHi. 59170

Western almanack for the year of our Lord 1840.... Rochester: William Alling, successor to Marshall and Dean [1839] 18 p. NRHi. 59171

Western and Atlantic Railroad Company. Report on routes surveyed for the Western and Atlantic Railroad, between Cross Plains and Tennessee River, rendered to the board of commissioners. Milledgeville [Ga.] Grieve and Orme [1839] 31 p. GU. 59172

The western farmers' almanac for 1840: being the 64th-65th year of American independence. Calculated for the western part of New York, and will serve for the western part of Pennsylvania, and northern part of Ohio, Michigan, Upper Canada, etc. Auburn: Oliphant and Skinner [1839] [24] p. ICHi; MWA; N; NCH; NiDHi; WHi. 59173

----. Medina, Ohio: Joseph W. White [1839]

MWA. 59174

Western Methodist Historical Society in the Mississippi Valley. Proceedings of the board of managers of the Western Methodist Historical Society...containing an account of the origin of the society.... Cincinnati: Methodist Book Room, 1839. 16 p. IHi; KyLx; OClWHi; PU; WHi. 59175

The western patriot and Canton almanack, for the year of our Lord 1839, being the 3rd after bisextile, or leap year...by Charles F. Egelmann [calculator of the Hagerstown almanack] 23rd edition. Canton, Stark County, Ohio [1839] 32 p. InU. 59176

The western peace-maker and monthly religious journal. Conducted by R. H. Bishop, C. E. Stowe and J. W. Scott. Vol. 1, no. 1. Oxford: V. W. Bishop, 1839-. MB; NN; OClWIIi. 59177

Western Railroad Corporation. A brief statement of facts in relation to the Western Railroad, February, 1839 [Boston? 1839] 7 p. CSt; IU. 59178

----. Reports of the engineers of the Western Railroad Corporation...1837-8. Springfield: printed by Merriam, Wood and Company, 1839. 64 p. MeHi; NNC; PPAmP; TxU. 59179

Western Reserve University. Catalogue of the officers and students of the Western Reserve College: Hudson, Ohio, November, 1839. Cleveland: Penniman and Aikin, printers, 1839 [2]-18 p. WBeloC. 59180

----. Catalogus senatus academici...in Collegio Reservationis Occiduae, Hudsoni, in republica Ohioensi. Cleveland: Typis Penniman et Aikin, 1839 [3]-6 p. WBeloC. 59181

----. Adelbert College. Scheme of examination of Western Reserve College, August 20th-24th. n.p.: 1839. Broadside. OClWHi. 59182

Westminster. Congregational Church. The confession of faith, and covenant of the Congregational Church in Westminster East Parrish with a catalogue of members, May, 1839. Bellows Falls: John W. Moore, printer, 1839. 24 p. CSmH; MBC; MWHi. 59183

Westminster Assembly of Divines. The explanatory catechism; being the shorter catechism of the Westminster Assembly. Philadelphia: Pres-

byterian Board of Publication of Tracts and Sabbath School Books, 1839. 59 p. PLT. 59184

----. The larger catechism, agreed upon by the Assembly of Divines at Westminster with the assistance of commissioners from the church of Scotland.... Philadelphia: W. S. Young, 1839. CBPac. 59185

Westminster East Parish Congregational Church [Vermont] The confession of faith, and covenant of the Congregational Church in...with a catalogue of members, May, 1839. Bellows Falls: 1839. 24 p. MBC. 59186

A wet sheet and a flowing sea [Song] Composed...by Thomas Walton. (Words by Allan Cunningham.) Arranged for the Spanish guitar by F. Weiland. Philadelphia: Hewitt and Company, 1839. 2 p. MB. 59187

Wetmore, William Jarvis, b. 1809. Away to the hills; a ballad. The poetry written and the music composed and respectfully dedicated to F. W. Cleveland by William J. Wetmore. New York: Millets Music Saloon, 1839. 5 p. NcD. 59188

The whale, and the dangers of whaling. With beautiful and appropriate engravings. New Haven: S. Babcock, 1839. 24 p. MH; NN. 59189

Whatley, Richard, 1787-1863. Elements of logic, comprising the substance of the article in the encyclopaedia metropolitana: with additions, etc. By Richard Whatley.... From the last London edition. New York: William Jackson, 1839. 359 p. MB; MiD; OWoC; RPB; TNT. 59190

----. Elements of rhetoric. Comprising the substance of the article in the encyclopaedia metropolitana with additions and etc. By Richard Whately. ...Boston: James Munroe and Company, 1839. 347 p. InNd; LNB; MoS; OBerB; PU. 59191

Wheaton, Henry, 1785-1848. Lives of William Pinkney, William Ellery and Cotton Mather, by Jared Sparks. Boston: Hilliard, Gray and Company, 1839. 350 p. InCW; MBNEH; PMA; ViU. 59192

Whedon, Daniel Denison, 1808-1885. Baccalaureate sermon, delivered in the chapel of the Wesleyan University, at the close of the collegiate year, 1838-9. to the candidates for the bachelor's degree.... Middletown: C. H. Pelton, 1839. 31 p.

CtHC; IU; MB; Nh; RPB. 59193

----. A tribute to the memory of President Fisk; delivered before the Young Men's Missionary and Bible Societies at the John Street Methodist Episcopal Church, New York, May 17, 1839. New York: T. Mason and G. Lane, 1839. 23 p. Ct; IEG; MBC; MH; PPM. 59194

Wheeler, Charles Stearns, 1816-1843. Biographical notices of Mr. Charles Hayward, Jr. and Mr. Samuel T. Hildreth. Reprinted with additions from the Christian Examiner for September, 1839. Cambridge: Metcalf, Torry and Ballou [1839] 36 p. MoSpD; MWA; Nh-Hi; PHi; RPB. 59195

Wheeler, John E. Speech of Mr. Wheeler of the Senate, upon the instructing resolutions. Nashville: printed at the Union press, 1839. 16 p. T. 59196

Whelpley, Samuel, 1766-1817. A compend of history, from the earliest times: comprehending a general view of the present state of the world. 11th edition. New York: Collins, Keese and Company, 1839. MH; NcDaD; NIC; OClWHi. 59197

Whewell, William, 1794-1866. On the foundations of morals: four sermons preached before the University of Cambridge, Nov., 1837.... With additional discourses and essays by C. S. Henry. Andover: Gould, 1839. 239 p. CtMW; InCW; MH; NNUT; PPM. 59198

Whig party. Alabama. Convention. 1839. Proceedings of the Whig convention of the state of Alabama, held at Tuscaloosa, on the 7th, 8th, 9th and 10th of January, 1839, with an address to the people of Alabama. Tuscaloosa: M. D. J. Slade, 1839. 16 p. AB. 59199

----. Indiana. Congressional Convention, 1839. The address of the Whig district convention to the voters of the 3rd congressional district of Indiana. Printed by order of the convention. n.p. [1839] 32 p. In; MiD-B. 59200

----. National Convention, Harrisburg, 1839. Proceedings of the Democratic Whig National Convention which assembled at Harrisburg on the 4th Dec., 1839, for the purpose of nominating candidates for president and vice president of the United States. Harrisburg: R. S. Elliott, 1839. 42 p. DLC; ICJ; NjP; TU; WHi. 59201

----. Pennsylvania Convention, 1839. Proceedings of the Democratic Whig state convention held in Chambersburg, Pa., on the 13th and 14th of June, 1839. Chambersburg, Pa.: printed by Harper and Catlin, 1839. 32 p. DLC; ICJ; ICT; OClWHi. 59202

Whig Young Men of Massachusetts. Proceedings of the state convention of the Whig Young Men of Massachusetts.... September 11th, 1839. Boston: printed by Samuel N. Dickinson, 1839. 32 p. CtY; ICN; MB; MH; PPL. 59203

[Whipple, Charles King] 1808-1900. Evils of the revolutionary war. Boston: New England Nonresistance Society, 1839. 16 p. ICN; MH; MHi; Nh-Hi; WHi. 59204

White, Charles Ignatius, 1807-1877. Discourse delivered at the funeral service of the late John Nenninger, which took place in the Cathedral of Baltimore, March 14, 1839; on which occasion, the members of the choir performed the celebrated Requiem of Mozart.... Baltimore: John Murphy, printer, 1839. 20 p. MdBLC; MdHi. 59205

----. The secular's office; or appropriate exercises for every day in the week, arranged in a form similar to that of the Roman Breviary.... Baltimore: Murphy, 1839. 416 p. MdBS; MdW. 59206

White, Joseph M., 1781-1839. A new collection of laws, charters and local ordinances of the governments of Great Britain, France and Spain.... Philadelphia: T. and J. W. Johnson, 1839. 2 v. Λ- Ar; CU; LNH; MoS; PPB; TxDaM. 59207

White, P. Frederick. Oh! tell me not. New York [1839] MB. 59208

Whitesboro, New York: Congregational Church. Our answer to them that do examine us; reply of the Congregational in Whitesboro to a question of the Oneida Presbytery.... Whitesboro: press of the Oneida Institute, 1839. 11 p. CtY; NjPT; OClWHi; RP; WHi. 59209

Whitman, Jason, 1799-1848. Helps for young Christians, with introductory remarks. Portland: S. H. Colesworthy, 1839. 192 p. DLC; NBuG. 59210

----. The young lady's aid to usefulness and happiness. Portland: 1839. MBAt; ICBB. 59211

----. ----. 2nd edition, improved and enlarged. Portland: Colesworthy, 1839. 288 p. MBAt; MeHi; MH; NdU. 59212

Whitmarsh, Samuel. Eight years experience and observation in the culture of the mulberry tree, and in the care of the silk worm.... Northampton: J. H. Butler, 1839. 156 p. Ct; ICN; MiU; RPA; WU-A. 59213

Whittemore, Thomas, 1800-1861. Songs of Zion; or the Cambridge collection of sacred music.... Boston: printed by William A. Hall and Company, 1839. 356 p. MH; MHi; MPiB; RPE. 59214

Whittlesey, Thomas T. Letter [on the independent treasury bill and its effect upon our manufactures] Washington: 1839? 16 p. Ct; IU; OCIWHi. 59215

Wickliffe, Robert, Jr., 1755-1859. An address delivered on the occasion of laying the corner stone of the new medical hall of Transylvania University, July, 1839. Lexington: Noble and Dunlop, printers, 1839. 29 p. KyDC; KyU; MH; OCHP; PPL. 59216

----. Southern Bank of Kentucky. Debate...[Frankfort, Ky.: A. G.Hodges, 1839] 16 p. MH-BA. 59217

----. Speech of Robert Wickliffe...on the bill to confer banking privileges on the South-Western Railroad Bank. Lexington, Ky.: printed at the Observer and Reporter office, 1839. 56 p. MH-BA; PPL-R. 59218

Wightman, Joseph Milner, 1812-1885. A companion to the air pump, with a description of Claxton's improved single cylinder lever air pumps and a descriptive explanation of a great variety of apparatus and experiments, many of which are original. Boston: G. W. Light, 1839. 44 p. MHi; NN. 59219

Wilber, Lewis. Confession...executed at Morrisville, N.Y., October 3, 1839, for the murder of Robert Barber...printed for the benefit of the publisher, Rochester: 1839. 16 p. DLC; NHi; NIC-L. 59220

----. The trial of Lewis Wilber for murder of Robert Barber, Madison Co., over and terminer, Mar. 17, 18, 19, 1839. Cazenovia: printed by Republican Moniter, 1839. 48 p. MH-L; NIC-L.
59221

Wilberforce, Robert Isaac, 1822-1857. The life of William Wilberforce; by his sons, Robert Isaac Wilberforce, M.A...and Samuel Wilberforce, M.A.... Abridged from the London edition by Caspar Morris, M.D. Philadelphia: Henry Perkins, Boston: Perkins and Marvin, 1839. 544 p. CBPac; KyLoP; MBC; PPA; ViU. 59222

Wilbur, Hervey, 1787-1852. Elements of astronomy, descriptive and physical.... New edition, improved by the addition of problems in practical astronomy by Rev. E. Davis. New York: Scofield and Voorhies, 1839. 144 p. MB; MBC; MH; PPM. 59223

Wilkeson, Samuel, 1781-1848. A concise history of the commencement, progress and present condition of the Amercian colonies in Liberia.... Washington: printed at the Madisonian office, 1839. 88 p. MBC; MnU; OC; PPM; TxH. 59224

Wilkey, Major Walter [pseud.] Western emigration. Narrative of a tour to, and one years' residence in "Edensburgh," [Illinois] by Major Walter Wilkey, an honest yeoman of Mooseboro', state of Maine.... New York: G. Claiborne, and others, 1839. 24 p. DLC; ICN; MiD-B; NjP; NN. 59225

Wilkinson, Edward C. Trial of Judge Wilkinson, Dr. Wilkinson and Mr. Murdaugh on indictments for the murder of John Rothwell and Alexander H. Meeks, in an affray which occured at the Galt House, Louisville, Ky., on the 15th of December, 1838. Reported by T. Egerton Browne. Louisville: Daily Reporter office, 1839. MH; MoSM; NN; OCLaw; PPL-R. 59226

Wilkinson, Eliza [Yonge] Letters of Eliza Wilkinson, during the invasion and possession of Charleston, S.C., by the British in the revolutionary war. Arranged from the original manuscripts, by Caroline Gilman, New York: S. Coleman, 1839 [9]-108 p. CSt; MdBP; PPA; RPA; ScC. 59227

Willard, Emma [Hart] 1787-1870. Atlas to accompany a system of universal history. By Emma Yates. New York: F. J. Huntington and Company, 1839. CtHWatk; MH. 59228

----. History of the United Staes, or republic of America. Continued to the close of the Mexican war. New York: A. S. Barnes and Company, 1839.

496 p. NNF. 59229

----. A system of universal history in perspective. Accompanied by an atlas, exhibiting chronology in a picture of nations and...a series of maps. 2nd editon, revised and corrected. New York: F. J. Huntington and Company, 1839. 459 p. IaHa; MH; NcWsS; NNiaU; OO. 59230

Willard, Joseph, 1798-1865. Memoir of Rev. Samuel Willard. Boston: printed by Perkins and Marvin, 1839. 11 p. DLC; MHi; MWA; RNR; RPB. 59231

[Willard, Samuel] 1776-1859. Franklin primer. Greenfield: 1839. MDeeP. 59232

----. The popular reader, or complete scholar; intended as a reading book for the higher classes in academies and other schools in the United States. By the author of "the Franklin primer".... 5th edition. Greenfield: Phelps and Ingersoll, Boston: Crocker and Brewster, 1839. 336 p. CoGrS; CtY. 59233

----. Secondary lessons, or the improved reader; intended as a sequel to the Franklin primer.... 33rd edition. Greenfield, Mass.: Phelps and Ingersoll, Boston: Crocker and Brewster, New York: Mahlon Day, 1839. 186 p. MH; NNC. 59234

----. ----. 35th edition. Greenfield, Mass.: Phelps and Ingersol [etc.] 1839. 186 p. ICU; NhD; NNC. 59235

Willet, W. N. Charles Vincent; or the two clerks. A tale of commercial life...[anon.] New York: Harper and Brothers, 1839. 2 v. CSmH; DLC; MB; MnU; OkU. 59236

Willett, William Marinus, 1803-1895. An account of the Wyandot mission: abridged from "a history of the missions under the care of the missionary society of the Methodist Episcopal Church," by the Rev. W. M. Willett. New York: T. Mason and G. Lane, 1839. 40 p. MiD-B; OClWHi. 59237

William Bell; or the advantages of Sabbath school instruction. Written for the Massachusetts Sabbath School Society, and revised by the committee of publication. Boston: Massachusetts Sabbath School Society, 1839. 83 p. DLC. 59238

William Kendrick Nursery. Abridged catalogue

nos. 1 and 11...1838 and 1839. Nursery of William Kendrick...of fruit and hardy ornamental trees, shrubs, herbaceous plants, etc....with an appendix on the culture of silk. Boston: John H. Eastburn, printer, 1839. 30 p. NjR. 59239

Williams, Catherine R. [Arnold] 1790-1872. Biography of revolutionary heroes; containing the life of Brigadier Gen. William Barton, and also, of Captain Stephen Olney. By Mrs. Williams. Providence: the author, New York: Wiley and Putnam, [etc., etc.] 1839. 312 p. CtHT; ICHi; PPi; TJoV; WvU. 59240

Williams, Charles James Blasius, 1805-1889. Lectures on the physiology and diseases of the chest.... By Charles James Blasius Williams. Philadelphia: Haswell, Barrington and Haswell, 1839. 347 p. IU; MB; NhD; PPA; ScCMe. 59241

Williams, David. Address, Winchester Mechanics' Institute. Winchester: 1839. CtHT. 59242

Williams, George. A critical pronouncing spelling book, or youth's first literary guide.... By George Williams. Revised edition. Stereotyped by G. J. Loomis, Albany. Hamilton, N.Y.: Williams and Maynard, 1839. 163 p. NNC. 59243

Williams, John. Dr. John Williams' last legacy, or the useful family herb bill, 1827. Wooster: reprinted for the publisher, 1839. 22 p. Mi. 59244

Williams, John. The life and actions of Alexander the Great. By the Rev. J. Williams, A.M., vicar of Lampeter. New York: Harper and Brothers, 1839. 351 p. CLCM; LNB; OAU; P; ScDuE. 59245

Williams, John Lee. The territory of Florida, or sketches of the topography of the country, climate and Indian tribes, from the first discovery to the present time.... New York: A. T. Goodrich, 1839. 304 p. CLU; FDeS; MoKU; OC; WHi. 59246

[Williams, Robert Folkestone] 1805 [ca.]-1872. Shakespeare and his friends; or the golden age, of Merry England.... Philadelphia: Lea and Blanchard, 1839. 3 v. CtMW; IaK; MB; PPA; ViU. 59247

Williams, Thomas, 1779-1876. The domestic chaplain. Hartford: Spalding and Storrs, 1839. CSPSR; ICBB; MBAt; MBC; RPB. 59248

Williams, William, 1717-1791. Caniadau Sion; sef casgliad o hymnau a salmau. Yr hymnau gan mwyaf o waith y Parch. William Williams, gynt o Bant y Celyn; a Dr. Isaac Watts. A'r Salmau, gan Edmund Prys, gynt Arch-Diacon Meirionydd. Utica: R. W. Roberts, 1839. 362 p. MH; NUt; ViRU. 59249

Williams, William, 1763-1824. Journal of the life, travels and gospel labours of William Williams, a minister of the Society of Friends, late of White Water, Indiana. Cincinnati: 1839. 195 p. ICN; OCIWHi; PHC; PSC-Hi; TxCM. 59250

Williams College. Catalogue of the corporation, officers and students of Williams College, 1839-40. Troy, N.Y.: N. Tuttle, printer, 1839. 20 p. IaGG. 59251

----. Catalogue of the social fraternity, Williams College, October, 1839. n.p.: 1839. 12 p. IaGG. 59252

----. Williamstown, Massachusetts. Catalogue of the officers and students of Williams College, and of the Berkshire Medical Institution connected with it, Oct., 1839. Albany: printed by Packard, Van Benthuysen and Company, 1839. 10 p. NNNAM. 59253

Williamsburgh Bank, Williamsburgh, New York. Articles of association and by-laws of the Williamsburgh Bank. Williamsburgh, [N.Y.] printed by L. Darbee, at the Gazette office, 1839. 18 p. NBLIHI; NN. 59254

Williamson, Isaac David. An argument for the truth of Christianity, in a series of discourses. By I. D. Williamson, Albany, N.Y. Stereotyped by Redfield and Lindsay. New York: P. Price, 1839. 252 p. IEG; MB; MBUPH; MeBaT; MVh. 59255

----. Reconciliation to God. A sermon delivered in the First Independent Christian Church, Richmond, Va. On the 30th of June, 1839, by Rev. I. D. Williamson, of Baltimore. Published by the Berean Institute. Richmond: printed by Baile and Gallaher, 1839. 12 p. MMeT; Vi. 59256

Williamson, William Durkee, 1779-1846. History of the state of Maine, from its first discovery, A.D. 1602, to the separation A.D. 1820, inclusive, with an appendix and general index. Hallowell: Glazier, 1839. 2 v. CU; MeAu; NhD; OCY; PPGi. 59257

Williamsport and Elmira Railroad Company. Connexion of Philadlephia with Lake Erie and Lake Ontario. Philadelphia: 1839. 1 p. PHi. 59258

Williamsport and Philadelphia Lumber Company. Articles of association, report of the committee, and schedule of property of the Williamsport and Philadelphia Lumber Company. Philadelphia: 1839. 15 p. PHi; PPL. 59259

Willis, Nathaniel Parker, 1806-1867. A l'abri, or the tent pitched. New York: S. Coleman, 1839. 172 p. CSmH; ICU; MB; Nh-Hi; PU. 59260

----. Bianca Visconti; or the heart overtasked. New York: Samuel Coleman, 1839. 108 p. IU; MeB; NcU; PU; TxU. 59261

----. A patri, or the tent pitch'd. New York: S. Coleman, 1839. 172 p. IaU; MdBJ; MH; NcD; ViU. 59262

----. The tent pitch'd. New York: 1839. MBAt; OClStM. 59263

----. Tortesa the usurer: a play.... New York: Samuel Coleman [Scatcherd and Adams] 1839. 149 p. MH; MnU; NjR; OWoC; TxU. 59264

----. Two ways of "dying for a husband." Shown in two dramas of Bianca Visconti and Tortesa the usurer. New York: Morris and Willis, pub. office of the New Mirror, 1839. 31 p. PU. 59265

Willis, Robert, 1799-1878. Urinary diseass, and their treatment. Philadelphia: Haswell, Barrington and Haswell, 1839. 232 p. GU-M; ICJ; KyLxT; Nh; PPA. 59266

Willison, John. The young communicants catechism, with questions and counsel for young converts. New York: E. Collier, 1839. 70 p. MBAt; PPPrHi. 59267

Williston, Payson, 1763-1856. The resolution of an aged minister to refresh the minds of his people with the truths he has preached to them.... A half-century sermon.... Northampton: 1839. 24 p. MB; MHi; MWF; OO; RPB. 59268

Willson, Marcius. A treatise on civil polity and political economy with an appendix containing an account of the powers, duties and salaries of national, state, county and town officers. New York: American Common School Union, 1839. 299 p.

MH; MiU; NPV; OClW; OO. 59269

Wilmsen, Friedrich Philipp, 1770-1831. F. P. Wilmsen's Deutscher Kinderfreund fur Schule und Haus. Nach der 146 sten Original Ausgabe...Nebst einem Anhaug enthaltend eine Geographie von Amerika.... Philadelphia: I. G.Wesselhoeft, 1839. 300 p. DLC; PHi; PPG; PPM; PU. 59270

Wilson, Alexander, 1766-1813. Wilson's American ornithology, with notes by Jardine: to which is added a synopsis of American birds, including those described by Bonaparte, Audubon, Nuttall and Richardson; New York: C. L. Cornish, 1839. 746 p. ICJ; MiD; OFB; PHatU. 59271

Wilson, Amos. The Pennsylvania hermit See under title.

Wilson, Bird, 1777-1859. Memoir of the life of the Right Reverend William White, D.D.... Philadelphia: J. Kay, jun. and Brother, Pittsburgh: C. H. Kay and Company, 1839. 430 p. CtMW; ICU; Nh-Hi; PPA; WHi. 59272

Wilson, Caroline [Fry] Christ our example. By Caroline Fry, author of "the listener," "Christ our law," "Scriptures reader's guide," etc. To which is prefixed an autobiography of the author. New York: American Tract Society, 1839. KyBvU; NcSaIL; ViLxW. 59273

Wilson, George S. Oration delivered on the 63rd anniversary of American independence. Sackets Harbor, N.Y., July 4, 1839. Sackets Harbor: Edmund M. Luff, 1839. 17 p. NUt. 59274

Wilson, John, 1785-1854. Lights and shadows of Scottish life. New York: 1839. MB. 59275

Wilson, John Grover, 1810-1885. The lyre of my youth. Being a collection of original poems, by John G. Wilson. Philadlephia; J. G. Wilson, 1839. 143 p. CSmH; MdBMP; RPB; TxU. 59276

Wilson, Joshua Lacy, 1774-1846. Relations and duties of servants and masters; by J. L. Wilson.... Cincinnati: Isaac Hefley and Company, printers, 1839. 34 p. ICP; MB; MH-AH; OCHP; PPPrHi. 59277

Wilson, Samuel Farmer, 1805-1870. History of the American Revolution with a preliminary view of the character and principles of the colonists....

With additions...to the Rev. J. L. Blake, D.D. Baltimore; N. Hick, 1839. 372 p. MdBLC; MdBS; MdHi; OClWHi; PPM. 59278

Wilson, William Dexter, 1816-1900. A discourse on slavery: delivered before the anti-slavery society in Littleton, N.H., February 22, 1839.... Concord: Asa McFarland, 1839. 51 p. MB; NhD; OClWhi; PHi; TxU. 59279

Winchell, Horace. A plea for reform...the cause of the innocent and the injured.... Lee, Mass.: printed for the author, by E. J. Bull, 1839. 36 p. CtY; NBu. 59280

Winchester, Samuel Gover, 1805-1841. The importance of doctrinal and instructive preaching, by the Rev. S. G. Winchester. Philadelphia: Presbyterian Board of Publication, William S. Martien, 1839. 36 p. ICP; MiU; NjR. 59281

Wines, Enoch Calib, 1806-1879. How shall I govern my school? Addressed to young teachers; and also adapted to assist parents in family government. 2nd edition. Philadelphia: J. Whiteham, 1839. 309 p. CU; GDecCT; MiD; PU; WHi. 59282

----. Letters to school children. By E. C. Wines. Boston: Marsh, Capen and Lyon, 1839. 135 p. DLC; MLow; MVh; NcD. 59283

----. A peep at China, in Mr. Dunn's Chinese collection; with miscellaneous notices relating to the institutions and customs of the Chinese and our commercial intercourse with them. Philadelphia: printed for N. Dunn, 1839. 103 p. CU; KHi; MWA; NjR; PPA. 59284

Winslow, Hubbard, 1799-1864. The importance of sustaining the law. A discourse deliverd in Bowdoin Street Church, on Sunday morning, June 16, 1839.... Boston: Crocker and Brewster, 1839. 31 p. ICN; MB; NN. 59285

----. Woman as she should be. The appropriate sphere of woman. The influence of Christianity of woman. The Christian education of woman. 4th edition. Boston: Whipple and Damrell, 1839. 81 p. MoSM; PU. 59286

----. The young man's aid to knowledge, virtue and happiness by Rev. Hubbard Winslow. 2nd edition. Boston: Crocker and Brewster, 1839. 330 p. InLW; MAnHi; MH-AH; OSW. 59287

----. ----. 3rd edition. Boston: Crocker and Brewster, 1839. 330 p. OO; T. 59288

Winsor, Henry. Pebblebrook and the Harding family [anon.] Boston: Benjamin H. Greene, 1839. 207 p. CSmH; DLC; MH; MiD-B; NN; RPB. 59289

Winsted High School, Winsted, Connecticut. Catalogue...1838-1839. Hartford? Hurlbut, 1839. 8 p. CtHWatk. 59290

Winter in the West Indies and Florida: containing general observations upon modes of travelling, manners and customs...By an invalid. New York: Wiley and Putnam, 1839. CtMW; KyHi; MWA; PPA; WHi. 59291

Wirt, William, 1772-1834. Sketches of the life and character of Patrick Henry.... Revised edition with headings to each chapter, and such an arrangement of the notes contained in the former editions as to render the work suitable for a class book in academies and schools. Ithaca, N.Y.: Andrus and Gauntlett, 1839. 306 p. OT; OU; RPB; ViU; WHi. 59292

----. ----. Philadelphia: Thomas, Cowperthwaite and Company, 1839. 306 p. ArAO; IaMpI; MdW; MnM; PPB. 59293

----. ----. 9th edition, corrected by the author. Philadelphia: Thomas, Cowperthwaite and Company, 1839. 468 p. CoCs; PU; ScDuE; USI; WaPS. 59294

Wisconsin [Territory] Report on the petition of the inhabitants of the Wisconsin mining district. [n.p.?] 1839. PPL. 59295

----. Adjutant General's office. Report of the adjutant general of Wisconsin Territory, made November 25, 1839. Madison: Josiah A. Noonan, printer, 1839. 6 p. WHi. 59296

----. Attorney General. Report of the attorney general of the territory, relating to the Bank of Wisconsin [Green Bay] to the...House of Representatives...[Dec. 31, 1839. Madison: 1839] 3 p. WHi; WM. 59297

----. Governor. Annual message of the governor of Wisconsin [Henry Dodge] transmitted to the legislative assembly, Dec. 3rd, 1839. Madison: 1839. 11 p. WHi; WM. 59298

----. Laws, Statutes, etc. Local acts of the legislature of Wisconsin, passed at Madison, during the session of 1838 and 1839. Published by authority. Milwaukee, W.T.: printed by Daniel H. Richards, 1839. 154, 34 p. IaU-L; In-SC; NNLI; WHi. 59299

----. ----. Statutes of the territory of Wisconsin, passed by the legislative assembly thereof, at a session commencing in November, 1838, and at an adjourned session commencing in January, 1839, published by authority of the legislative assembly. Albany, N.Y.: printed by Packard, Van Benthuysen and Company, 1839. 457 p. Ct; MdBB; OCHP; TxHuT; WHi. 59300

----. Legislative Assembly. Bank report [by] the committee appointed by a joint resolution of the council and House of Representatives, at its last session, to examine into and investigate the state of Wisconsin bank...[Jan. 9th, 1839. Madison: 1839] 12 p. WHi; WM. 59301

----. ----. Memorial of the legislative assembly of the territory of Wisconsin, praying the alteration of the boundary of said territory, January 28, 1839. n.p.: 1839. WHi. 59302

----. ----. Council. Journal. First session. Green Bay: 1839. MH. 59303

----. ----. ----. Journal of the council, second session of the second legislative assembly of Wisconsin, begun and held at Madison, on Monday, the 21st day of January, in the year of our Lord 1839. Green Bay, W.T.: Charles C. Sholes, 1839. 281 p. DLC; IaU-L; MH; W; WBeloC; WHi. 59304

----. ----. House. Journal of the house, of the second Legislative Assembly of Wisconsin... on January 23, 1839. Mineral Point, W.T.: Welsh and Plowman, 1839. 376 p. DLC; IaU-L; ICU; MH; WBeloC. 59305

----. ----. ----. Report of Moses M. Strong, late fiscal agent of the territory, Dec. 20, 1839. To the Honorable...[Madison: Josiah A. Noonan, 1839] 4 p. WHi; WM. 59306

----. ----. ----. Report of the select committee, to whom was referred the petition and remonstrance of the citizens of Brown county, in relation to the removal of the seat of justice of said county [from De Pere to Green Bay, Dec., 1839. Madison: 1839] Broadside. 1 p. WHi. 59307

----. ----. ----. Rules for the government of the House of Representatives, Wisconsin Territory. 3rd session of 2nd Legislative Assembly, commenced Dec. 2nd, 1839. Madison: Josiah A. Noonan, printer, 1839. 8 p. WHi; WM. 59308

Wisconsin statistics in Dutch. Milwaukee: 1839. 32 p. PHi. 59309

Wise, Henry Alexander, 1806-1876. Speech at Louisa C. H., November 16, 1839. Richmond: J. S. Gallaher, printer, 1839. 15 p. MH; NcD; Vi. 59310

Wisner, William, 1782-1871. Covenant of grace and its seal; a sermon, preached in the First Presbyterian church, at Ithaca, Feb. 24th, 1839. Ithaca: Mack, 1839. 16 p. NCh; PPPrHi. 59311

Wistar, Caspar, 1761-1818. A system of anatomy for the use of students of medicine by Caspar Wistar, late professor of anatomy in the University of Pennsylvania. With notes and additions by William E. Horner, M.D. 7th edition. Illustrated. In two volumes. Philadelphia: Thomas, Cowperthwaite and Company, 1839. 2 v. CoCsE; InVi; MdBM; NNN; PU. 59312

Withington, Leonard. An address before the Essex Agricultural Society at Topsfield, September 27, 1838, at their 3rd annual cattle show, by Leonard Withington. Salem: printed at the Gazette office, 1839. 24 p. MeBaT. 59313

Woburn Agricultural and Mechanic Association. Charter and by-laws of the Woburn Agricultural and Mechanic Association. Boston: press of J. Howe, 1839. 12 p. MWo. 59314

Woman's Mission. First American edition. New York: Wiley and Putnam, 1839. 149 p. LU; MBC; NcWsS; NjR; RKi; ScCMu. 59315

The wonders of the universe, or curiosities of nature and art; including memoirs and anecdotes of wonderful and eccentric characters of every age and nation from the earliest period to the present time. The whole collected from the most original and authentic sources of information. Exeter: J. and B. Williams, 1839. 439 p. MAm; MH; NbOM; PP; ViU. 59316

Wood, George Bacon, 1797-1879. The dispensatory of the United States of America. By George B. Wood...and Franklin Bache.... 4th edition. Philadelphia: Grigg and Elliot, 1839. 1249 p. IaU; MH; PPCP; TNV. 59317

Wood, Samuel R. Defendent. Important case of alleged fraud upon the revenue. District Court of the United States for the southern district of New York term. Before Judge Betts: the United States vs. Samuel R. Wood, June 6th, 7th, 8th, 10th and 12th, 1839. New York: 1839. 16 p. MB; MBC; MHi; WHi. 59318

Woodhouselee, Alexander Fraser, 1747-1813. Elements of general history, ancient and modern by Alexander Fraser Tytler, Lord Woodhouselee, F.R.S.E. ...with a continuation terminating at the demise of King George III, 1820, by Rev. Edward Nares, D.D.... to which are added a succinct history of the United States with additions and alterations by an American gentleman...75th edition. Concord, N.H.: John F. Brown, 1839. 527, 40 p. ICN; KyNiW; PWcHi; ViU. 59319

----. Universal history, from the creation of the world to the beginning of the 18th century. By the late Hon. Alexander Fraser Tytler, Lord Woodhouselee.... Boston: Hilliard, Gray and Company, 1839. 2 v. GU; IaGG; MBC; OClW; PU. 59320

----. ----. New York: Harper and Brothers, 1839. 6 v. CtHT; NRU; RKi. 59321

Woods, Leonard, 1774-1854. The minister wholly in his work. A sermon delivered at the ordination of the Rev. Daniel Bates Woods, as pastor of the Presbyterian church in Springwater, Livingston Co., New York. Andover: printed by Gould, Newman and Saxton, 1839. 16 p. MBC; MH; MoSpD; N; NjR; RPB. 59322

Woodward College. Cincinnati. Annual circular and catalogue of the Woodward College, and of the high school with an address by the president, How shall our country be educated? Cincinnati: 1839. 29 p. ICP; MiU-C; MWA; OCHP. 59323

Woodworth, Samuel, 1785-1842. Sunday morning reflections. New York: S. Colman, 1839. 14-78 p. MBC; MCNC; MH. 59324

Wooldridge, A. D. Sermon on the trinity. Jackson: 1839. 59325

Woolman, John, 1720-1772. Considerations on the keeping of negroes. Recommended to the professors of Christianity of every denomination. Philadelphia: T. E. Chapman, 1839. 109 p. ICBB;

PHC. 59326

Worcester, Joseph Emerson, 1784-1865. Worcester's ancient classical and scripture atlas. Boston: D. H. Williams, 1839. 10 maps. MH. 59327

----. A comprehensive pronouncing and explanatory dictionary of the English language. ...by J. E. Worcester. Carefully revised and enlarged. Boston: Jenks and Palmer, Philadelphia: Thomas, Cowperthwaite and Company, 1839. 624 p. ODW. 59328

----. Elementary dictionary for common schools; with pronouncing vocabularies of classical, scripture and modern geographical names. Boston: Jenks, 1839. 324 p. MH; OO. 59329

----. Elements of ancient classical and scripture geography; with an atlas. By J. E. Worcester. Boston: Phillips and Sampson, 1839. 74 p. MB; MdW; MeBa; MH; NNC. 59330

----. Elements of geography; ancient and modern; with an atlas. New edition. Boston: D. H. Williams, 1839. DLC; MCE. 59331

----. ----. Improved edition. Boston: David H. Williams, 1839. 257, 74 p. DLC; MB; NcWsM. 59332

----. Elements of history, ancient and modern: with a chart and tables of history, included within the volume.... Boston: Hilliard, Gray and Company, 1839. 403 p. MH; PPA. 59333

----. Elements of modern geography, with an atlas. Improved editon. Boston: David H. Williams, 1839. 248 p. MBAMC. 59334

----. A geography for common schools; with an atlas. By J. E. Worcester. Boston: Hilliard, Gray and Company, 1839. 176 p. MH; NNC; PP. 59335

Worcester, Leonard, 1767-1846. A memorial of what God hath wrought. A discourse delivered at Peacham [Vermont] March 31, 1839.... Montpelier: E. P. Walton and Sons, 1839. 116 p. CSmH; MWA; Nh-Hi; OO; VtMidbC. 59336

Worcester, Samuel. A fourth book of lessons for reading; with rules and instructions. By Samuel Worcester...stereotyped edition. Boston: Charles J. Hendee and Jenks and Palmer, 1839. 408 p. CLCM; KyLo; MH; NBuG; NNC. 59337

----. ----. Louisville: Kellog, 1839. KyLo. 59338

----. A second book for reading and spelling. New edition. Boston: C. J.Hendee, etc., 1839. MH; Nh. 59339

----. A third book for reading and spelling. By Samuel Worcester. 20th edition. Boston: Charles J. Hendee, and Jenks and Palmer, 1839. 240 p. ICU; MMidb. 59340

Worcester, Samuel Melanchthon, 1801-1866. Hymns selected from various authors; with a key of musical expression.... New edition. 270 hymns and occasional pieces added, with indexes.... Boston: Crocker, 1839. 16 [505]-776 p. ICN; MBC; MeBat; MH; RPB. 59341

Worcester, Massachusetts. Selectmen. Report of the selectmen of Worcester. February, 1839. Worcester: printed by Colton and Howland, 1839. 15 p. MiD-B; MWHi; OClWIIi. 59342

Wordsworth, William, 1770-1850. The complete poetical works of William Wordsworth together with a description of the country of the lakes in the north of England, now first published with his works.... Philadelphia: James Kay, Jun. and Brother, Boston: James Munroe and Company, Pittsburgh: C. H. Kay and Company, 1839. 361 p. CoBru; InU; OOxM; PBa; ViU. 59343

Wright, Albert D. Elements of the English language; or an analyltical orthography, etc. New York: J. O. Taylor, 1839. 82 p. DLC. 59344

Wright, David. Memoir of Alvan Stone of Goshen, Mass. Boston: 1839. MDeeP. 59345

Wright, H. N. Oration, delivered at the invitation of the students of the Oneida Conference Seminary...at Cazenovia, 4th of July, 1839. Cazenovia: 1839. 32 p. N; RPB. 59346

Wright, Robert Emmet, 1810-1886. The Pennsylvania justice; a practical digest of the statute and common law of Pennsylvania, on the rights, duties, authority and jurisdiction of the alderman and justice of the peace.... By R. E. Wright, attorney at law. Philadlephia: Robert H. Small, 1839. 400, 88 p. MH-L; NNLI; PP; PPeSchw; ViU. 59347

Wright, Silas, 1795-1847. Address; delivered 4th of July, 1839, at Canton, N.Y., by Silas Wright, jr.

[Canton? 1839?] 28 p. DLC; NAUT; NN; PPL; TxU. 59348

----. ----. Ogdensburgh: J. M. Tillotson [1839] 28 p. MWA. 59349

----. Speech of Mr. Wright, of New York, on the report of the secretary of the treasury, on the 27th of December, 1838, and the message of the president of the 11th of January last...Delivered in the Senate of the United States, January 25, 1839. Washington: Blair and Rives, printers, 1839. 16 p. N; PPL; TxDaM. 59350

Wyatt. Unfading beauties; or illustrations of flowers and fruit; principally from nature. By Wyatt and Ackerman.... Hartford: D. W. Kellog and Company, 1839. 52 p. NcAS. 59351

Wyatt, Thomas. A synopsis of natural history... See Lemonnier, Ceran.

Wyatt, William Edward. A scriptural exposition of the church catechism.... Newly arranged and enlarged by William E. Wyatt.... Baltimore: P. E. Female Tract Society, 1839. 4, 140 p. MDBD; MdHi; NNG; OCMtSM. 59352

Wylie, Andrew, 1789-1851. Baccalaureate address delivered to the senior class of Indiana University, at the annual commencement, September 25, 1839. Bloomington: 1839. 21 p. InU; NN; PU. 59353

----. Perfect man; a sermon occasioned by the death of Jonathan Nichols.... Bloomington: printed at the office of the Equator, 1839. 22 p. In; NN; PPPrHi. 59354

Wyoming, Pennsylvania. Revolutionary war. Wyoming sufferers. Petition of the sufferers of Wyoming, Pa., by depredations committed by the Indians in the Revolutionary war. February 18, 1839.... [Washington] Thomas Allen, printer [1839] 40 p. NN. 59355

X - Y - Z

Xenophon. The anabasis, translated by Edward Spelman, esq. New York: Harper and Brothers, 1839. 2 v. CSansS; MeBaT; MoSU; NN; WStfSF. 59356

----. The cyropaedia. Translated by the Hon. Maurice Ashly Cooper. In two volumes. New York: Harper and Brothers, 1839. 2 v. OClJC; TJaU. 59357

----. Xenophon's expedition of Cyrus, with English notes, prepared for the use of colleges and schools with a life of the author, by Charles Dexter Cleveland. Boston: Hilliard, Gray and Company, 1839. CtY; DLC; MH; OO; PPL. 59358

----. Memorabilia of Socrates, with English notes, by Alpheus S. Packard.... Andover, N.Y.: Gould, Newman and Saxton, 1839. 264 p. CtMW; ICU; MeHi; OWoC; ViU. 59359

Yale University. Annual report on the case of indigent pious students in Yale College. 9th edition. 1839 [New Haven] 1839. 7 p. CtY; NIC. 59360

----. Catalogue of the officers and students in Yale College, 1838-1839 [New Haven?] printed by B. L. Hamlen [1839] 35 p. Ct; KWiU; MNBedf; TxHU. 59361

----. Calliopean Society. Catalugue of the Calliopean Society, Yale College. New Haven: 1839. 32 p. Ct; ICN; MHi; NNN; PPL. 59362

----. Class of 1836. Proceedings of the class of 1836, at their first general meeting [New Haven: New Haven Palladium press, 1839] 16 p. CtY. 59363

Yankee miscellany. Boston: 1839. V. 1, no. 1-12. DLC; IU; MB: NcD; OU. 59364

The Yankee; or farmer's almanac for the year...1840. By Thomas Spoffard. Boston: Thomas Groom [1839] 35 p. MHi; MWA. 59365

Yates, John A. "Righteousness exalteth a na-

tion," a discourse delivered in the First Protestant Reformed Dutch church of Albany, Nov. 28, 1839. Schenectady: Riggs and Norris, 1839. 28 p. MB; MH; MH-AH; NjR; PPPrHi. 59366

The year book, or manual of every day reference; arranged in such a manner that the memorable events of each day in the year may be at once ascertained. From the London edition, with numerous additions. Edited by B. B. Edwards. Several engravings. Philadelphia: Herman Hooker, 1839. 498 p. ICBB. 59367

Yes! and No! From the English edition, revised by the committee of publication. Boston: New England Sabbath School Union, 1839. 32 p. MHi. 59368

Young, Andrew White, 1802-1877. Introduction to the science of government, and compend of the constitutional and civil jurisprudence of the United States; with a brief treatise on political economy. Designed for the use of families and schools. 3rd edition. Albany: W. C. Little, 1839. 332 p. DeU; GU; NBu; RPB; WU. 59369

Young, Edward, 1683-1765. The complaint and consolation of night thoughts of life, death and immortality, to which is added the force of religion. A new edition. Boston: Weeks, Jordan and Company, 1839. 288 p. CoCsUP; MoSpD; ScCoB. 59370

----. ----. New York: Robinson and Franklin, successors to Leavitt, Lord and Company, 1839. 4, 324, 2 p. CoMo; MDeeP. 59371

----. ----. Portland: Oliver L. Sanborn, 1839. 288 p. CtY; MH; MPlyA; PHi; RPB. 59372

----. ----. New York: A. S. Barnes and Company [1839] 516 p. ICLoy. 59373

----. ----. Philadelphia: James Kay, Jun. and Brother, 1839. 301 p. IaHA; MiMus; NcAS; PPM; ViSwc. 59374

Young, James Hamilton, b. 1793. Map of North America, engraved to illustrate Mitchell's school and family geography. J. H. Young, engineer [Philadlephia] S. Augustus Mitchell, 1839. WaU. 59375

----. The tourist's pocket map of Michigan. Philadelphia: 1839. 1 p. MiD; PHi. 59376

----. The tourist's pocket map of the state of Georgia, exhibiting its internal improvements, roads, distances, etc. Philadelphia: S. A. Mitchell, 1839. ICN; NN; ViU. 59377

----. The tourist's map of the state of Illinois, exhibiting its internal improvements, roads, distances, etc. Philadelphia: S. A. Mitchell, 1839. IHi; NN. 59378

----. The tourist's pocket map of the state of Indiana, exhibiting its internal improvements, roads, distances, etc. Philadelphia: S. A. Mitchell, 1839. In. 59379

----. The tourist's pocket map of the state of Ohio, exhibiting its internal improvements, roads, distances, etc. Philadelphia: S. A. Mitchell, 1839. MWA. 59380

----. The tourist's pocket map of the state of Pennsylvania, exhibiting its internal improvements, roads, distances, etc. Philadelphia: S. A. Mitchell, 1839. NN. 59381

----. The tourist's pocket map of Virginia: roads, etc. Philadelphia: 1839. 1 p. PHi. 59382

Young, John Radford, 1799-1885. An elementary treatise on algebra, theoretical and practical, with attempts to simplify some of the more difficult parts of the science.... Philadelphia: Hogan and Thompson, 1839. MH. 59383

----. The elements of analytical geometry; comprehending the doctrine of the conic sections.... By J. R. Young.... Revised and corrected by John D. Williams.... Philadelphia: Hogan and Thompson, 1839. 288 p. CoCsC; CStclU; Ia; Lu; NcU; NjP. 59384

----. Elements of geometry, with notes, revised and corrected with additions.... New edition. Philadelphia: Hogan, 1839. PU. 59385

----. The elements of mechanics, comprehending statics and dynamics. With a copious collection of mechanical problems. ...By J. R. Young.... Revised and corrected by John D. Williams.... Philadelphia: Hogan and Thompson, 1839. 258 p. CSt; IaK; KU; MdBP; PP. 59386

----. Elements of plane and spherical trigonometry, with its applications to the principles of navigation and nautical astronomy. With the logarithmic and trigonometical tables.... A new edition. Philadelphia: Hogan and Thompson, 1839. 148 p. IaHoL; MdBS; NjR; ViU. 59387

----. The elements of the differential calculus: comprehending the general theory of curve surfaces.... Philadelphia: Hogan and Thompson, 1839. 255 p. CSt; DLC; GAuY; NjP; PLFM. 59388

----. The elements of the integral calculus with its applications to geometry and to the summation of infinite series.... Philadelphia: Hogan and Thompson, 1839. 292 p. AB; ILM; LNT; MdBP; NNC. 59389

----. Mathematical tables; comprehending the logarithms of all numbers from 1 to 36,000; also the natural and logarithmic sines and tangents...with several other tables.... Revised and corrected by J. D. Willliams. Philadelphia: Hogan and Thompson, 1839. 200 p. CtY; IaHoL; ViU. 59390

Young, N. D. A rejoinder or series of letters addressed to the Rev. C. Henkel on the reformation.... Somerset, O.: S. H. McAfee, printer, 1839. 52 p. OClWHi. 59391

Young, Richard. Remarks of Richard M. Young, of Illinois, on the bill to graduate and reduce the price of the public lands.... Washington: printed by Blair and Rives, 1839. 8 p. MdHi; NjR; WHi. 59392

Young botanist; or, a sketch of the life Linnaew. Boston [1839] RPB. 59393

Young Catholics Friend Society. Constitution and by-laws and names of the members...to which is added the regulations of St. Aloysius Sunday School, instituted April, 1835. Boston: Donahoe, 1839. DLC; MB. 59394

The young child's first reader; or dialogues in short sentences [Brattleboro, Vt.] Brattleboro Bookstore, 1839. MH. 59395

The young husband's book; a manual of the duties, moral, religious and domestic, imposed by the relations of married life. By the author of "the young wife's book." Philadelphia: Lea and Blanchard, 1839. MB; MH; NNC; PU. 59396

Young ladies' book of romantic tales. By Thomas Moore, Mrs. S. C. Hall...T. Crofton Crocker...and others. Boston: E. Littlefield, 1839. 2 p. 1., 284 p. MdBJ. 59397

The young lady's equestrian manual. Philadelphia: Haswell, Barrington and Haswell, New Orleans: Alexander Towar, 1839 [4] 102 p. DLC; DSI; PReaHi. 59398

Young lady's own book, manual of intellectual improvement and moral deportment.... Philadelphia: Thomas, 1839. 320 p. NhD; PU. 59399

The young man's book of classical letters, consisting of epistolary selections...with introductory rules and observations on epistolary composition. By the author of the young man's own book. Philadelphia: Thomas, Cowperthwait and Company, 1839. 320 p. MdBLC; MoSMa; PP. 59400

The young man's manual. Portland: S. M. Colesworthy, 1839. 15 p. MH. 59401

The young man's own book. A manual of politeness, intellectual improvement and moral deportment, calculated to form the character on a solid basis, and to insure respectability and success in life.... Philadelphia: Thomas, Cowperthwaite and Company, 1839. 320 p. LNH; MdBLC; OClWHi. 59402

The young man's Sunday book; a practical exhibition of doctrines, duties and principles. Philadelphia: Thomas, Cowperthwaite and Company, 1839. 320 p. MdBLC. 59403

Young Men's Association, Albany. The annual report of the president of the Young Men's Association for mutual improvement, in the city of Albany.... Albany: printed by Alfred Southwick, 1839. 15 p. NjR; NN; WHi. 59404

Young Men's Charitable Association of Charlestown, Massachusetts. Constitution [Charlestown: 1839] MB. 59405

Young scholar's reference book...being a collection of useful tables together with such abbreviations and phrases as frequently occur in writings of the present day. By a teacher. Andover: Gould, Newman and Saxton, 1839. MH. 59406

The youth's book of puzzles: or fireside amusements.... New Haven: S. Babcock, 1839. 24 p. MB; WHi. 59407

The youth's friend. Revised by the committee of publication. Philadelphia: American Sunday School Union, 1839. 192 p. DLC; NRCR; PHi. 59408

The youth's sketch book. Boston: T. H. Carter, 1839. 224 p. NNS. 59409

Youth's temperance advocate. New York: American Temperance Union, 1839. MB; MnU; PPL. 59410

Zeuner, Charles, 1795-1857. The American harp: being a collection of new and original church music...arranged and composed by Charles Zeuner.... Boston: Hilliard, Gray and Company, 1839. 392 p. MHaHi; MMe. 59411

----. The ancient lyre; a collection of old, new and original church music.... 10th edition, revised and improved. Boston: Crocker and Brewster, 1839. 363 p. ICN; MB; MWbor; PPPrHi. 59412

Zollikofer, Johannes, 1633-1692. A newly opened treasury of heaven by incense; 6th edition.... By Rev. John Zollikofer. New York: Martin Lambert and Company, 1839. 612 p. DLC; ICMe; NjN; TxH. 59413

Zschokke, Heinrich, 1771-1848. Der todte gast. Erzaehlung von Heinrich Zschokke. New York: Verlag der Buchhandlung von W. Radde, 1839. 76 p. CtMW; MH; NN; PU; TNJU. 59414

Zula: a tragedy in four acts. By a Kentuckian. Philadelphia: 1839. 48 p. CtY; MB; MH; PU; RPB. 59415